Fundamentals of
Biological Anthropology

Reviewers

Fundamentals of
Biological Anthropology

Kenneth A. Bennett
University of Wisconsin, Madison

Wm. C. Brown Company Publishers
Dubuque, Iowa

wcb **Wm. C. Brown,** Chairman of the Board
Larry W. Brown, President, WCB Group

Book Team

Wm. J. Fitzgerald, Editor
Marilyn A. Phelps, Designer
Ruth Richard, Production Editor
Mary Ellen Landwehr, Assistant
Production Editor

Wm. C. Brown Company Publishers, College Division

Lawrence E. Cremer, President
Raymond C. Deveaux, Executive Director of
Product Development
David Wm. Smith, National Sales Manager
David A. Corona, Director of Production
Development and Design
Marilyn A. Phelps, Manager of Design

To Helen, Letitia, and Cheri
    for their profound influences on my life

and to Theodosius Dobzhansky, Ernst Mayr, and George Gaylord Simpson
    whose works have shaped my view of nature

Contents

Preface

I have maintained several basic and long-standing convictions while writing this book. One is that biological anthropology is a natural science which probably has fewer formal boundaries than any other scientific discipline. Another is that its practitioners must be as rigorous and as analytically objective as those in any other area of scientific inquiry. Yet another is that the teaching of biological anthropology must also be rigorous and demanding if it is to satisfactorily transmit the exceedingly complex hypotheses, methods, and principles relevant to interpreting the evolutionary history and contemporary variation of the human species. And finally, I have always been convinced that the majority of undergraduate students, like the majority of those in any other artificially constructed class, are both intelligent and receptive to new information. Indeed, I have never had any reason to doubt that the needs and interests of anthropology students in an introductory course in general biological anthropology are best served by a comprehensive and detailed approach to the subject.

Theme

The overriding theme in this book centers around human evolution. It strives to be comprehensive in explaining the genetic mechanisms involved with small evolutionary changes, presents the fossil evidence for human evolution through time, and concludes with discussions of the evolutionary meaning of the differences among modern human populations. Theoretical contributions are emphasized throughout the book, and special attention is given to appropriate methodological procedures. The rationale for the latter is that an understanding of general processes and principles is especially enhanced when the student is given the opportunity to learn how such findings are derived.

Organization

Fundamentals of Biological Anthropology consists of 19 chapters divided into three main sections. The first is "The Genetic Background." This section provides basic information about Mendelian genetics, human inheritance patterns, principles of population genetics, and the ways in which populations undergo genetic change through generations. A transitional chapter in which the principles of species formation and the rules of taxonomy are discussed follows.

The second section, "The Origin and Evolution of the Human Species," begins with a general survey of primate biology and behavior and proceeds to a fairly detailed chapter in which the student may acquire the anatomical information necessary for interpreting the paleontological evidence for the evolution of nonhuman primates and of other genera and species both within and close to the lineage to which modern *Homo sapiens* belongs. This evidence is given in the four succeeding chapters and followed by a second transitional chapter in the third section, "Topics on Modern Human Biology." Chapter 16 begins by outlining several hypotheses that relate to the origin of modern populations and concludes with a rather theoretical discussion of the meaning and utility of classifying modern human groups. The book closes with discussions of modern human variation. Rather than simply describing the extent to which modern populations vary, Chapters 17 and 18 place special emphasis upon how such variation arose and the known and hypothesized mechanisms responsible for its present maintenance.

Some Special Features

The usefulness of this book, both for the instructor and the student, is enhanced by the inclusion of several pedagogical aids. Chapters begin with a brief introduction and conclude with a summary that abstracts the chapter contents. Terms that are important, in addition to those that may be unfamiliar to the student, are included in the Glossary. Of particular importance, given the methodological emphases, is the presence of the general introduction to statistics in Appendix I. This was felt necessary for the interpretation of much of the experimental data in the first section of the book. It is realized that more about statistics appears than can be covered in a one-semester course in general biological anthropology, but this addition should be of special value for more inquisitive students and for instructors who offer formal laboratory training in conjunction with their lecture courses.

Acknowledgments

I owe a substantial debt to my colleagues and graduate students in the Biological Anthropology Program at the University of Wisconsin-Madison. In particular, Richard H. Osborne has endured a "question-and-answer" session of nearly four years duration; Walter Leutenegger read and criticized the chapters on primates and human paleontology; and Sheelah Dooley and James Kelly read and commented on nearly all of the chapters on genetics. I am also grateful to Roberta L. Hall, of Oregon State University, and to Howard S. Barden, of the University of Illinois-Chicago Circle, for reading and criticizing several chapters. Howard Barden also contributed the chapter on "Human Growth," for which I am deeply grateful. I very much appreciate the high tolerance levels exhibited by our graduate students, and I offer a special acknowledgment to a host of anonymous reviewers who pointed out a rather distressing number of overt blunders and misinterpretations. Needless to say, none of these individuals bears any responsibility for the material contained herein.

I am indebted to Bob Nash, editor at Wm. C. Brown Company Publishers, who started the project and saw it through in spite of my occasional obstinance. Thanks also go to Merlin Williams for his photographic skill and to Ellen Dudley for some of the finest original art work to be found.

My deepest appreciation goes to my wife, Helen. Not only did she perform many menial tasks related to researching the literature, but she also provided the encouragement and stimulation necessary for the completion of this book.

Kenneth A. Bennett

1 Introduction

Introduction

"Owing to this struggle for life, any variation, however slight and from whatever cause proceeding, if it be in any degree profitable to an individual or any species, in its infinitely complex relations to other organic beings and to external nature, will tend to the preservation of that individual, and will generally be inherited by its offspring. The offspring, also, will thus have a better chance of surviving, for, of the many individuals of any species which are periodically born, but a small number can survive. I have called this principle . . . Natural Selection" (Charles R. Darwin 1859).

There is a good reason for beginning an introductory textbook in biological anthropology with this seemingly straightforward quotation, because it represents Darwin's classic work that led to the theory of evolution by natural selection. This theory and that of Gregor Mendel in 1865 (Mendel 1866)—that parents transmit sets of particles (now called genes) to their offspring—are without doubt the two most momentous occurrences in the history of biological science.

Dobzhansky has observed that "in discovering the genes, Mendel . . . furnished the keystone of the arch which Darwin was building" (1965:211), and this relationship between these two discoveries will become more evident in the next several chapters. For the moment it may be stated that Darwin's theory, independently formulated by A. R. Wallace (Darwin and Wallace 1859), and Mendel's principles, independently rediscovered in 1900 by three botanists (de Vries 1900; Correns 1900; Von Tschermak 1900), laid the basic groundwork for modern biological anthropology. Likewise, other scientific disciplines whose historical development has either been based upon or is inextricably linked with genetic and evolutionary theory might scarcely have progressed beyond their positions at the turn of the century. These disciplines, among others, include biology, geology, zoology, taxonomy, paleontology, agriculture, ecology, and immunology.

In spite of the formidable practical and theoretical accomplishments of scientists in these disciplines, the concept of evolution by natural selection has always been attacked by those who, for reasons peculiar to themselves, consider evolution as a repugnant threat to their own belief systems. Worse still, some consider evolution a belief system in itself. With perhaps the exception of those who adhere to the belief that the world is flat, nothing could be more irrational. Evolution is no more a faith than chemistry, physics, or mathematics. Whether one likes it or not, all populations of living organisms on this planet evolve. Human populations are not excluded. Furthermore, most of the basic processes that govern the evolution of plant and animal species apply to humans as well. There is, of course, a fundamental difference between our species and all others. For thousands of generations, human populations have been able to transmit learned patterns of behavior (culture) from one generation to the next and from one society to another in a social rather than genetic fashion. Thus, we have altered our effective environment to an extent unrivaled by any other species, and in so doing have also altered our own evolution.

The scientific study of our biological basis and how this interacts with culture—what we are and how we came to be this way—is the overriding concern of biological anthropology. In this book I have tried to introduce the fundamental framework of the discipline, but I make no rash claims as to total coverage. Perhaps the only area of agreement among professionals is that the field is staggeringly diverse and complex. To understand in depth only one or two subareas usually requires years of concentrated study, and to fully comprehend the entire discipline is, for most of us, impossible. In few areas of science are there as many unanswered questions, and this makes biological anthropology a stimulating field for the inquisitive mind.

It is an unfortunate fact that an introductory textbook to such a broadly based discipline must make a number of compromises in coverage. In attempting to outline the basic framework of biological anthropology, one of these necessary compromises is the conspicuous omission of the historical development of evolutionary and genetic thought. This has traditionally been the province of biologists, who have contributed a number of excellent historical reconstructions of the ideas of biology and the individuals associated with them (e.g., Mayr 1959a; Glass et al. 1959; Eiseley 1961; de Beer 1963; Sturtevant 1965; articles in *Proc. Am. Phil. Soc.,* vol. 109, 1965; Medvedev 1969; Ghiselin 1969). Historians of science (Irvine 1955; Greene 1959; Coleman 1971) and philosophers (Lovejoy 1936) have also provided excellent historical accounts. Those of you interested in the history of evolutionary thought will find the above references both enjoyable reading and perceptive analyses of major historical figures and periods.

Biological Anthropology Defined

In 1972, nine professional anthropologists published brief descriptions of their conceptions of the nature of the field. All nine were different. The range of opinion was considerable and may be illustrated by the following excerpts:

1. W. W. Howells, Harvard University: "Physical anthropology is the understanding of human evolution and of individual and population variation. It is not a straight biological study with man as the subject . . . physical anthropologists are anthropologists, not biologists . . . " (1972:141).

2. E. Hunt, Pennsylvania State University: "Professional physical anthropologists are biologists in exile. . . . Physical anthropology is a branch of natural history" (1972:142).

3. T. W. McKern, Simon Fraser University: " . . . physical anthropology . . . (is) . . . a dynamic field of inquiry that embraces the entire realm of biological interest, encompassing the development, present nature, and future evolution of man . . . (and) . . . a science deeply involved in man's cultural nature.

The relegation of physical anthropology to the too-often proposed area of human biology is a refutation of an historically prescribed responsibility" (1972:144).

4. G. W. Lasker, Wayne State University: " . . . physical anthropology has two chief subjects: (1) the unique evolutionary history of man and (2) general biological processes in man such as the mechanisms of variation in time and space" (1972:146–147).

5. A. T. Steegmann, Jr., State University of New York at Buffalo: "Our richest discipline . . . is the positioning of man in the three-dimensional matrix of biological and cultural evolution. Our true strength derives from anthropology" (1972:154).

6. K. A. R. Kennedy, Cornell University: "The place of . . . physical anthropology . . . is defined as that science that forms a bridge between the social and biological fields because it has something significant to say about both and, more important, about the interactions of the social and biological realms, as they apply to questions about human evolution" (1972:156).

Although these opinions are obviously somewhat diverse, several implied or expressed areas of agreement are held in common. First, nearly all physical anthropologists today recognize the overwhelming importance of biological principles at the field's foundation. This became obvious upon receipt of 125 completed questionnaires distributed to individuals who either by training or profession classed themselves as physical anthropologists (Osborne et al. 1971). These respondents felt that the most important seven areas encompassed by physical anthropologists for future years (in descending order of importance) were anatomy, genetics, physiology, zoology, mathematics, paleontology, and ecology. With the sole exception of mathematics, all of these fields are either heavily influenced by or are branches of biology. Furthermore, the same individuals felt that their graduate training was most deficient in the areas of mathematics, chemistry, genetics, biology, and anatomy (in that order).

Second, almost all physical anthropologists would agree that culture is equal in importance to biology as the force which has shaped and maintained the human species. In recent years, there has emerged an intense interest in biocultural interactions and in the relationships among biology, culture, and ecology. If nothing else, this indicates an acceptance and awareness of the fact that elements of biology and culture have always interacted in determining the human condition.

Third, most physical anthropologists clearly recognize the interdisciplinary nature of the field. Professional physical anthropologists often receive most of their graduate training outside anthropology departments. They utilize research methods and techniques from other fields. They often hold major appointments and teach primarily in other disciplines, including orthodontics, anatomy, physiology, and genetics. And they publish their research reports in a wide variety of non-anthropological journals and periodicals.

In light of the diverse interests of physical anthropologists, it is remarkable that they do possess a strong sense of unity. This is due, no doubt, not only to a common basic anthropological orientation, but mostly to the fact that they are generally interested in human evolution from both anthropological and biological viewpoints. For all of these reasons, and because anthropology is too often taken to mean only cultural anthropology, many of us today prefer to label ourselves as "biological anthropologists." This is the title that will be used in all succeeding chapters.

The central theme in this book revolves around the evolution of past and present human populations. More precisely, the foci are upon (1) the factors associated with or responsible for the evolution of natural populations, (2) the observed evidence for evolutionary changes in human populations through time, and (3) the biology of modern populations. These broad subject areas form the core of the discipline in the sense that past and present research in biological anthropology is nearly always related to one of these three areas. Thus in the chapters that follow, every attempt has been made to provide a general background to biological anthropology that emphasizes the fundamentals of evolutionary biology and genetics.

Biological Anthropology Today: The Diffuse Nature of a Unified Discipline

Like all other scientific disciplines, the number of subdivisions one wishes to recognize in biological anthropology is purely a matter of individual choice. Many biological anthropologists are engaged in highly specialized studies that may seem only indirectly related to the field. This has led to numerous labels given to and adopted by many individual researchers, including "paleoanthropologists," "anthropological geneticists," "biobehavioral anthropologists," "human biologists," "paleoprimatologists," "human ecologists," and many others. This is not to disparage in any way either the contributions or legitimate standing of these fields of inquiry, because all of these approaches increase our understanding of ourselves. As a matter of fact, the term "biological anthropology" is a relatively new term most synonymous with human biology as envisioned by Harrison et al. (1964).

To the extent that scientists working in these diverse areas regard themselves as biological anthropologists, however, most would agree that their efforts are ultimately related to a primary focus of the discipline. This focus is on the explanation of the evolution and maintenance of our species through the integrated action of all relevant natural and cultural processes. To many, the words evolution and maintenance imply past and present respectively, although these two concepts have no clear demarcation. It is only for the purpose of convenience, therefore, that the following discussion of trends and developments in biological anthropology is divided into living versus past populations.

Trends and Developments in the Study of Living Populations
Studies of living human populations up to the middle 1950s seemed to serve two main purposes. First, literally hundreds of reports described basic survey information from the world's populations. These surveys included frequencies of various genetic traits (such as the ABO blood groups), demographic statistics, and measurements and observations of a wide variety of physical characteristics. Much of this information was used to revise existing racial classifications, but more importantly, it led to serious analysis and considerable controversy over the questions of (1) the biological meaning

of differences within and between human populations and (2) the existence or nonexistence of human races (e.g., Coon 1962; Newman 1963; Livingstone 1964a). By no means have anthropologists yet settled this controversy.

This survey information also indicated that human populations were remarkably genetically diverse, which led to the second purpose of many early studies. These were attempts to clarify and demonstrate the roles played by various evolutionary processes in the differentiation of small human groups. A number of significant papers (e.g., Glass, et al. 1952; Glass and Li 1953; Glass 1954; Neel 1958) showed how small evolutionary changes altered human populations. These studies led rather quickly to the broad multidisciplinary approaches that are beginning to characterize field research today.

In the middle 1960s there was a shift in emphasis from the elucidation of evolutionary mechanisms toward an effort to understand the relationships between the demographic, genetic, social, and ecological variables that affect the structure of human populations. These studies have necessarily required changes in the composition of field research personnel. Whereas information was once gathered by only one or two scientists, perhaps trained in anthropology, genetics, or medicine, modern field research is being carried out by integrated teams of biological anthropologists, geneticists, linguists, demographers, clinicians, cultural anthropologists, and in some cases, physiologists.

The broadened scope of these endeavors has been prompted by recognition of two factors: (1) the structure of human populations is determined by complex sets of social, biological, and ecological factors, and a full understanding of the interrelationships between these sets is necessary for reaching meaningful conclusions (Bennett et al. 1975) and (2) if small, semi-isolated, or the so-called "primitive" populations are to be studied, then there is a very real urgency to do so now, because the genetic integrity of most of these groups is being altered rapidly and permanently by technologically advanced societies. The results of integrated efforts on such isolated groups began to appear in the middle 1960s and are occupying an increasingly prominent position in the literature that stresses human genetics and population biology (e.g., Neel et al. 1964; Steinberg et al. 1967; Martin et al. 1973; Neel et al. 1972). It is anticipated that many unanswered questions about the genetics and structure of small human populations will be resolved by the team approach.

The central role of demography in the solution of similar problems is becoming increasingly evident with recognition of the fact that the structure and dynamics of populations can be fully understood only in terms of the effects that fertility, mortality, emigration, and immigration have on age and sex composition. Many important problems in this area are being given serious attention. Some of these may be phrased roughly as follows:

1. To what extent have fertility, mortality, migration, and physical geography affected the present distribution of human populations?

2. What are the interrelationships between certain social factors and fertility patterns?

3. What are the interrelationships between social mobility and the genetic structure of human populations?

4. What is the effect on mate selection of the demographic forces that

influence population size and mobility? What social factors might affect the determination of secondary sex ratios which, in turn, may exert an influence on demographic structure?

5. What are the primary ecological factors, such as disease patterns, climate, and agricultural practices, that influence both demographic and genetic structures of human populations?

These are a few typical questions that can be answered most adequately by (1) the collection of information through the combined efforts of research teams on small, semi-isolated populations and (2) the development and application of statistical and genetic models to the data. This is an area of intense interest in biological anthropology, and several collections of original research reports (Crawford and Workman 1973; Dyke and MacCluer 1974; Harrison and Boyce 1972; Morton 1973) illustrate some important new directions for the analysis of human population structure.

That the primary strength of biological anthropology derives from a multidisciplinary framework is also indicated by the methods used for the study of living populations. There are many new and important advances in analytical procedures for the interpretation of population data, most of which have been developed in other disciplines for other purposes.

From demography have come mathematical models and computer simulation studies (e.g., Keyfitz and Flieger 1971; U. N. Population Studies 1968) based on stable, semi-stable and quasi-stable population theory. From statistics have come the diverse techniques of multivariate analysis (Cooley and Lohnes 1971; Morrison 1967) that characterize nearly all research areas in modern biological anthropology. Biochemical genetics and molecular biology have produced within just a few years a virtual treasure of new ideas and methods for the analysis of amino acid sequences in various proteins, evolutionary change in DNA (Smith 1972; Kohne et al. 1972), and other aspects of genetics and evolution. These are being quickly adopted and applied to anthropological problems. From ecology have come mathematical models (MacArthur 1972; Emlen 1973; Pianka, 1974) and ideas relating to environmental structures, species morphology and behavior, and the dynamics of population change (Levins 1968). And from the medical sciences are new epidemiological advances that can aid in our understanding of the relationships between disease patterns, mortality profiles, population densities and movements, and population genetics. Even orthodox Darwinian theory has received a strong challenge (Kimura 1968) that has been supported in the influential paper by King and Jukes (1969), and recently discussed in depth in a symposium (LeCam et al. 1972).

From about 1960, fundamental concepts and methods within the field of environmental physiology have been employed by biological anthropologists in attempting to understand how human populations respond to environmental stress. Having led to insights into the patterns of intrapopulation variability as it may be affected by age, sex, and morbidity, these studies hold considerable promise for the establishment of baseline information needed to cope with the effects that changing life styles, occupations, and environmental alterations have upon the morbidity and general health of people in both developed and underdeveloped countries.

In the past, much of the research in environmental physiology was conducted within the realms of preventive medicine and physical education where, by necessity, it was directed toward applied rather than theoretical objectives. The broader integrative orientation of biological anthropology, however, has provided a framework in which questions of evolutionary biology can be given attention. One of the more relevant questions in this regard involves the genetic contribution to measurable physiological variation. Little is known about the heritable components affecting the observed variation in physiological characteristics, although some indications (Klissouras 1971) suggest that genetic factors are quite important.

Comparisons of individuals from different populations living in harsh environments also suggest that part of the observed differences are genetic (Baker 1969; Little et al. 1971), and, further, that the ability to acclimatize—to compensate functionally over a period of days or weeks in response to a set of environmental factors—is partially genetic. In addition, general constitutional factors and the effects of conditioning have been shown to contribute to physiological variability both between and within populations (Balke 1960). These studies all imply that there is a strong genetic component for physiological variation, and one of the most challenging areas in biological anthropology today concerns the search for these genetic factors.

During the early development of biological anthropology it was often assumed that an understanding of the variation between and evolution of human populations could be enhanced by racial classifications. Before 1950 most classifications relied heavily upon easily observed external characteristics, including skin color, hair color, facial features, and other morphological characteristics. Thus, most definitions of race were similar to that given by Coon, Garn, and Birdsell as "a population which differs phenotypically from all others with which it has been compared" (1950:112). The application of population genetics principles to human populations (Dobzhansky 1950) led to the influential book by Boyd (1950) which contained not only a new racial classification but also an important new concept of race. Boyd defined a human race as "a population which differs significantly from other human populations in regard to the frequency of one or more of the genes it possesses" (1950:207).

This definition, which stresses gene frequency differences between populations, has subsequently received acceptance by many who are involved in studies on human races and their classifications. Coon changed his earlier definition of race to "a general term referring to genetically distinct divisions of a species" (1962:720). Goldsby states that "a race is a breeding population characterized by frequencies of a collection of inherited traits that differ from those of other populations of the same species" (1971:21). Others have deviated even farther and claim that the term "race" is either defunct (Birdsell 1975:505) or synonymous with the subspecies (e.g., Garn 1971; Baker 1974; Birdsell 1975). The subspecies is the only infraspecific category recognized in the taxonomic hierarchy of living organisms (Mayr 1969).

In any case, racial studies in biological anthropology have diminished drastically in recent years, and studies designed specifically either to establish new or support old racial typologies have almost been totally abandoned. One cannot disagree with Ernst Mayr that the typological concept of racists is thoroughly odious; that from the biological standpoint how many races one wishes to recognize is entirely arbitrary; and that

> the essential point is to recognize the genetic and biological continuity of all these gene pools, localized in space and time, and to recognize the biological meaning of their adaptations and specializations (1963:644).

One of the more active research areas in modern biological anthropology concerns aspects of human growth and development. Anthropologists became involved in this area after the advent of the outstanding contributions of Franz Boas shortly before the turn of the century (Boas 1892) and for several decades thereafter (Boas 1932, 1935). The early influential work by G. T. Bowles (1932) on growth of Americans attending Harvard University probably also stimulated biological anthropologists' involvement with growth studies. Much of the work before 1960 dealt with descriptions of normal growth patterns and sexual differences in growth in different geographical and ecological settings and in different social strata. In recent years, however, the approach has become more analytical, with the strongest emphasis being placed on nutritional aspects of growth and development. In these studies, parents have often been used as models for the examination of both growth progress and behavioral development of their offspring.

The description and measurement of growth and maturation rely heavily on techniques that are traditionally anthropological, including assessments of body composition, constitutional typologies, and anthropometric measurements. As might be expected, therefore, biological anthropologists have played central roles in this area and have acquired considerable sophistication in the analysis and interpretation of growth data.

Studies of Past Populations

The study of skeletons from past populations has been a primary center of activity from the early developmental years of biological anthropology until the present time. A casual glance through various regional journals reveals that many who are now considered specialists in other areas, such as human genetics, primate biology, and so forth, began their professional careers by measuring and describing human skeletons. For the most part, the purposes of most of the early studies (as well as of some today) were solely for description and classification. A number of major attempts were made to classify early American Indian populations into regional "varieties" or "physical types" (Neumann 1952; Hooton 1930). Single and often fragmentary crania were measured, observed, and classed as belonging to or being reminiscent of a certain physical type. Aside from the inadequacy of statistical methods, the assumption of genetic discontinuity between assumed types indicated either a distressing reversion to typological thinking or a fundamental ignorance of population thinking (see Chapter 5).

During the last decade or so there has been a sharp decline in studies designed for classifying populations into regional varieties. This has probably been due to recognition of the fact that typological methods are inadequate for determining inter- and intrapopulation relationships. For these purposes, the conceptual and methodological advantages of newer statistical techniques have been outlined in several significant papers (Bronowski and Long 1951; Giles and Elliot 1963; Howells 1969a), all of which are based on earlier contributions by mathematical statisticians. These and other papers led to an abrupt switch in statistical methodology in biological anthropology, which represents one of the most important recent trends that crosscuts every area within the discipline. Predictably, there has been a considerable increase in the number of skeletal studies that have been designed for and purport to show genetic relationships between early populations.

Other areas related to the study of skeletal populations are receiving long-overdue attention. W. W. Howells (1969b, 1973a) has questioned the anatomical relevance of many traditional skeletal dimensions. And Björk's (1963, 1964) on craniofacial growth, Solow's (1966) on craniofacial associations, and numerous papers in Moyers and Krogman (1971) have also provided important contributions in this area. Biological anthropologists trained in pathology, microbiology, radiology, and other related medical subjects are currently studying the geographical distribution of diseases in early populations (Brothwell and Sandison 1967; Cockburn 1971). Such paleopathological studies hold promise for documentation of ancient disease patterns and their effects on population distributions and mortality profiles. However, rapid progress in this area has been difficult to achieve. The relationship between the cause of a disease (the etiology) and the disease process itself is never on a precise, one-to-one basis. As Johnson (1966) notes, the etiological nonspecificity coupled with the nonspecificity of diagnostic osteological features make it very difficult to diagnose certain diseases solely on the basis of skeletal evidence.

To many who are unacquainted with the varied research interests discussed so far, biological anthropology is equated with human paleontology, the study of the fossil evidence for human evolution. "Fossil man" studies have always been predominant in the field, and they constitute one of the primary reasons why individuals choose biological anthropology as a career. Perhaps in no other area in the field is the literature as voluminous and the controversies as intense as in fossil studies. This is completely understandable because humans are usually far more interested in their own origins than in those of other organisms.

Most of the controversies stem from differences in evolutionary interpretations of the fossil evidence and the classification of the fossils. Certainly this has been the case for the different classifications of fossils ancestral to *Homo sapiens* (hominids), as George Gaylord Simpson has clearly stated:

> Many fossil hominids have been described and named by workers with no other experience in taxonomy. They have inevitably lacked the sense of balance and the interpretive skill of zoologists who have worked extensively on larger groups of animals. It must, however, be sadly noted that even broadly equipped zoologists often seem to lose their judgment if they work on hominids. Here factors of prestige, of personal involvement, of emotional investment rarely fail to affect the fully human scientist, although they hardly trouble the workers on, say, angleworms or dung beetles. (1963:6–7).

The difficulties in classifying fossils, often consisting of little more than a handful of fragments, are of course inherently greater than for a group of easily obtained organisms like dung beetles. Simpson was admonishing anthropologists for not using the proper rules of zoological nomenclature in their pre-1960 taxonomic studies. These rules have since been followed by Simons and Pilbeam (1965), Robinson (1967), Campbell (1973), and Tattersall and Schwartz (1974) in recent examples of taxonomic studies of particular primate forms.

Modern paleoanthropologists utilize methods from a variety of other scientific disciplines for inferences about human evolution. Thus principles of anatomy and engineering mechanics are being used with advanced statistical methods to study the function and structure of anatomical complexes (Oxnard 1969, 1972) and the meaning of anatomical changes through time. Also, the methods of biochemistry and molecular biology are providing new and exciting insights into the evolutionary change of protein molecules, times of divergence between various primate species, and the genetic similarities between humans and other primates (e.g., Goodman, Barnabas, and Moore 1973).

Current interest in the biology and behavior of primates has reached such proportions that primatology, the study of primates, has almost become a separate discipline. For many years it was assumed that inferences about human evolution could be drawn from comparative anatomical studies of our closest primate relatives. The anatomical dissection of nonhuman primates for inferences to humans is a very old practice indeed, dating to a time before the Greek medical schools. For example, the famous physician Galen, born in A.D. 130, relied heavily on the dissection of apes for understanding human anatomy (Lambert et al. 1952).

Until the 1950s, however, research in nonhuman primate anatomy remained largely comparative in this classical descriptive sense. These studies served as the basis from which evolutionary relationships between primate species, including ourselves, were inferred (Le Gros Clark 1959). In the early 1960s the emphasis shifted toward attempts to understand the function of anatomical features in certain environmental settings (Erikson 1963; Napier 1963). Of special interest were analyses of the evolutionary changes in anatomical systems and the ecological components associated with these changes. The continuation of this trend is clearly reflected in various papers in Tuttle (1972).

Biological anthropologists have adopted and modified many analytical techniques from diverse scientific disciplines in attempting to clarify the functional adaptations of anatomical systems in primates. For about 20 years, for example, a profusion of experimental and theoretical methods has led to a more adequate interpretation of the functional and evolutionary aspects of primate locomotion. Experimental studies on locomotion through the use of electromyography (Tuttle et al. 1972) and cineradiography (Jenkins 1971) are two examples of advances in this area.

A major subdivision of primatology concerns the behavioral patterns of both wild and captive primates. Field studies began in the late 1920s and early 1930s with the notable publications of Zuckerman (1932), Carpenter (1934), and others. The number of field studies increased slowly for the next three decades, but in the early 1960s, studies of all aspects of primate social behavior increased almost explosively. Of particular interest today are the observations of behavioral patterns in primates over extended periods of time (longitudinal studies), such as Sade's (1972) on a colony of rhesus monkeys. Sade demonstrates convincingly that longitudinal studies may lead to conclusions quite different from those based solely on investigations of limited duration.

Where Are We?

The preceding discussion of the varied interests of biological anthropologists should underscore an earlier comment about the field's remarkable diversity. By no means, however, do these subject areas represent the totality of professional interests. Rather, they indicate only some of the major foci of concentration. Other research areas of great importance for our overall comprehension of our species include dental anthropology, medical anthropology, and others too numerous to mention. In short, biological anthropology serves as the bridge between the social and natural sciences. In the search for answers about the evolution and maintenance of our species, we bring to bear the fullest possible range of appropriate techniques, information, and theories from other disciplines.

Compared to other disciplines in the natural and physical sciences, such as biology and physics respectively, biological anthropology is still in its infancy. Some have referred to Johann Friedrich Blumenbach (1752–1840) as the father of physical anthropology, mainly for his racial classification in *De Generis Humani Varietate Nativa (On the Natural Variety of Mankind),* published in 1775. Biological anthropology in the United States is of much more recent origin, however, and owes much, if not most, of its development to two men. One was Ales Hrdlicka (1869–1943) who, with Fay Cooper Cole, Charles H. Davenport, George A. Dorsey, William K. Gregory, Earnest A. Hooton, and Robert J. Terry, founded the *American Association of Physical Anthropologists* in 1928 (Comas 1969). Hrdlicka also served as the first president of this association. The other was E. A. Hooton (1887–1954) who was directly responsible for the training of a large percentage of the most respected biological anthropologists in this country.

Kaplan (1964) has noted perceptively that the historical progress of science is marked by the dissolution of old partnerships such as natural philosophy (biology-philosophy), and the formation of new ones such as social psychology (sociology-psychology) or biophysics (biology-physics). At the present time, most if not all scientific fields are witnessing a proliferation of interdisciplinary approaches. This expresses the realization that such unions offer the promise of greater understanding of the interrelationships between social, physical, and biological phenomena. All sciences, in other words, can interbreed and produce offspring more capable than themselves of extending the search for knowledge. Biological anthropology is a particularly good example of such an amalgamation. It derives its strength not only from biology or anthropology, but from a multitude of disciplines.

1

The Genetic Background

2 Cells and Chromosomes

Introduction

People and all other living organisms are composed of cells, which are small structures that multiply themselves during the development and life of the individual. Of how many cells does a mature adult consist? The number is far too high for most of us to appreciate. Bonner (1962) estimates conservatively over a trillion, Dobzhansky (1970) about 10 trillion, and Levitan and Montagu (1971) about 100 quadrillion.

It is fruitless to generalize about the size of a "typical" cell because the dimensions of individual cells differ from each other and from one body tissue to the next. However, cells are usually measured in microns (one micron = 1/1000th of a millimeter), and many cells are only a few microns in diameter.

It is astounding to realize that each of us begins as a single cell—the zygote, or fertilized egg—and that all of the genetic material inherited from our parents is contained within this cell. This is indeed a small beginning, the miniscule dimensions of which might be appreciated by some very rough calculations. The weight of a single human ovum is estimated at about one-millionth of a gram. Assuming that about four billion people are living today, the total weight of all ova necessary for production of the present world's population is about 3.6 kg. Spermatozoa are much smaller—about 5 billion to the gram. The total weight of all sperm necessary for fertilization of these ova is about 0.8 g. The actual hereditary material (DNA) contained in these ova and sperm, however, is only a tiny fraction of their masses. Assuming the weight of the DNA in a fertilized egg as approximately 6.5 trillionths (6.5×10^{-12}) of a gram, the total weight of DNA required to specify the hereditary makeup of four billion people is less than 3/100 g.

To adequately survey present knowledge of cell biology and DNA would require several textbooks as large or larger than this, aside from the fact that the study of these topics properly belongs to other disciplines. A basic understanding of both, however, is a prerequisite for the modern study of human inheritance.

Biology of the Cell

In 1940, Szent-Gyorgyi commented:

> If I look upon the cell as a mechanism and upon the molecule as a wheel of this mechanism, then by saying that I take my vitamins from the plant, I say that there are two mechanisms, the plant cell and my cells, whose parts, the single

wheels, are interchangeable. Two mechanisms, whose parts are interchangeable, cannot be very different. This is the first scientific evidence for the great, fundamental chemical unity of living Nature. There is no real difference between cabbages and kings, we are all recent leaves on the old tree of life. (1940:160)

To be accurate, there are a great many different types of cells (Table 2.1), occurring in a myriad of sizes (Table 2.2), but most cells possess certain similarities in their intracellular organization.

Most cells contain the features seen in Figure 2.1, a composite diagram of a "typical" animal cell. The cell consists of a **nucleus** surrounded by the nuclear membrane, and a **cytoplasm** bounded by the plasma membrane. In the cytoplasm are a number of small structures called **organelles.** These serve specific functions within the cell. The organelles and their functions are as follows:

1. **Plasma membrane.** As observed with the electron microscope, the width of this membrane is about 75 Å (Picken 1960). An angstrom (Å) is a unit of length equal to one 10-thousandth of a micron, or 100-millionth of a centimeter. The plasma membrane encloses the cellular contents and allows selective passage of certain elements into and out of the cell.

Table 2.1 Examples of Different Types of Human Cells, Descriptions of Their Shapes, and Their Locations in the Individual (After Giese 1962.)

Type of Cell	Typical Shape	Location
Epithelial	Cuboidal, brick-shaped	Skin (epidermis, glandular lining)
Muscular	Spindle	Smooth and striated muscle
Nervous	Cell body with long fibers	Sensory neuron, motor neuron
Connective tissue	Spheroidal	Cartilage, bone, tendon
Blood	Disc-shaped	Red blood cells
Ova	Spherical	Ovaries
Sperm	Flagellated	Testes

Table 2.2 Approximate Mass of Cells in Different Organisms (After Giese 1962.)

Organism	Mean Mass of Cell in Grams
Ostrich egg, dinosaur egg	10^3 to 10^2
Frog eggs	10^{-2} to 10^{-3}
Human striated muscle	10^{-4}
Human ovum	10^{-5}
Human smooth muscle, liver cell	10^{-7}
Human sperm, malarial parasite	10^{-9}
Anthrax bacillus	10^{-11}
Tubercle bacteria	10^{-12}
Smallest bacteria	10^{-14}
Filter passing viruses	10^{-15}

Figure 2.1 A graphic diagram of a typical animal cell. (From J. Brachet, The Living Cell, *Scientific American,* September 1961; and A. L. Lehninger, *Biochemistry.* 2nd Ed., 1975. Worth Publishers: New York

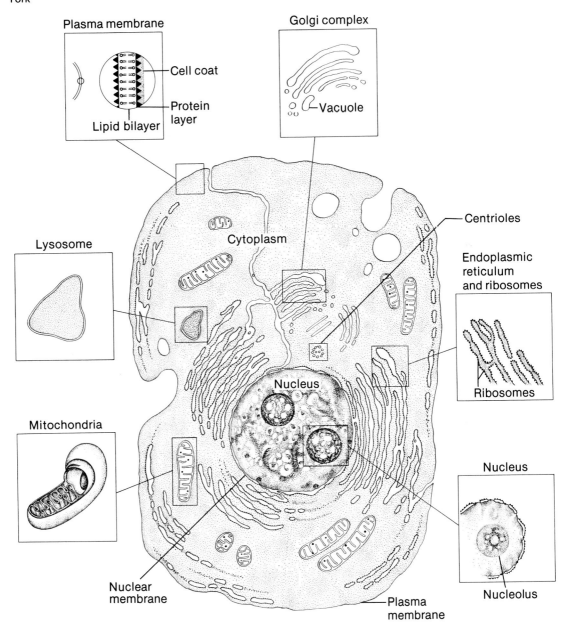

Plasma membrane

Cell coat

Protein layer

Lipid bilayer

Golgi complex

Vacuole

Lysosome

Cytoplasm

Centrioles

Endoplasmic reticulum and ribosomes

Ribosomes

Mitochondria

Nucleus

Nucleus

Nucleolus

Nuclear membrane

Plasma membrane

2. **Endoplasmic reticulum.** This is a network comprised of membrane-bound tubules with osmotic properties, and is continuous with both the golgi apparatus and the outer layer of the nuclear membrane. It may control entry or exit of elements into the nucleus. The **enzymes** within the endoplasmic reticulum are probably involved in cholesterol and triglyceride synthesis, and it is also thought that this structure is the site of lipid metabolism. Lipids are substances comprised of higher fatty acids and their naturally occurring compounds, and other substances chemically associated with them (Cantarow and Schepartz 1954). The primary role of these substances is for energy storage.

3. **Ribosomes.** These are small granular structures consisting of **RNA** and protein. They function as sites of protein synthesis (Watson 1976).

4. **Mitochondria.** These small organelles (0.5 to 1.0 microns in diameter and usually less than 7 microns long) are filamentous or granular structures that may be rod-shaped or globular in form. The production of energy is their primary function, i.e., they are quite literally the powerhouses of the cell. Mitochondria are highly motile, making contact at different intervals with other parts of the cell. They supply energy for protein synthesis and in so doing make contact with the ribosomes on the endoplasmic reticulum.

5. **Golgi apparatus.** The golgi apparatus is a membranous structure that stores and may form secretory products. It may also be involved in lysosome formation, and it has been hypothesized (Grundmann 1966) that it comprises part of the intracellular water transfer system.

6. **Lysosomes.** These are small, spherical structures involved in the breakdown of complex molecules in an injured or dying cell. They probably rupture spontaneously, releasing certain enzymes that digest the old and dead cells.

7. **Centrioles.** These are small (about 0.2 microns in diameter) cylindrical structures located near the nucleus. They are paired, the two invariably oriented at right angles to each other. Centrioles are involved in cell division and originate from a common body called the centrosome.

The nucleus is located approximately at the center of the cell. It is separated from the cytoplasm by the nuclear membrane, which consists of two separate layers. The thickness of the two layers and the space between is approximately 300–350 Å. Communication between the nucleus and the cytoplasm is through a system of pores which, depending upon the specific cell, may range between 400–700 Å in diameter in the outer layer.

For descriptive purposes, it is convenient to divide the cell into the nucleus and the cytoplasm. However, a finely balanced relationship exists between the two components and neither can survive or multiply on its own. Upon removal from the cytoplasm, the nucleus dies within a few hours even if kept in physiological balance. Chemical activity in the cytoplasm may continue for a time, but it too will eventually die. Experiments on amoeba have shown that both are dependent upon each other—the nucleus takes up and uses nutrients from the cytoplasm, and the activities of the cytoplasm are initiated and regulated by the nucleus.

The nucleus contains the primary genetic information—the nucleic acids—in addition to proteins that make up the chromatic network. During cell division the threads in the network form into the **chromosomes,** which are located within the nucleus. A more thorough discussion of chromosomes appears later in this chapter.

Eggs, Sperm, and Fertilization

A general characteristic of all vertebrates is bisexual reproduction, the initial phase being **gametogenesis,** the production of germ cells (gametes). The second phase is fertilization, the fusion between the male spermatozoon and the female ovum to form the fertilized egg (**zygote**).

Gametogenesis includes two distinct processes: **spermatogenesis** and **oogenesis,** both of which are discussed in more detail below under "Meiosis." Spermatogenesis, or the production of **sperm,** usually begins just after puberty and in some individuals continues throughout life. This is apparently a noncyclical process which takes place in the cellular walls of the **seminiferous tubules** (Fig. 2.2), the testicular structural units. The seminiferous tubules are continuous with a network of channels called the rete testis, which opens into the efferent ductules. These in turn are

Figure 2.2 A schematic cross section of the human testis, illustrating the relationships between tubules and ducts.

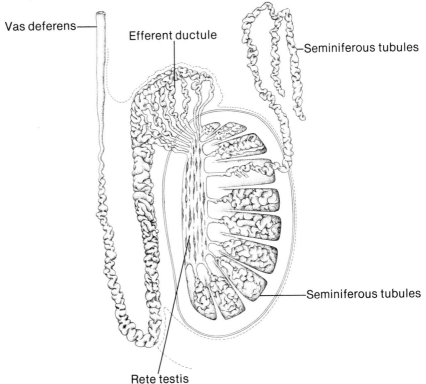

Vas deferens

Efferent ductule

Seminiferous tubules

Seminiferous tubules

Rete testis

Figure 2.3 A graphic cross section of the male reproductive organs, showing the route that sperm take from the seminiferous tubules to the prostatic urethra.

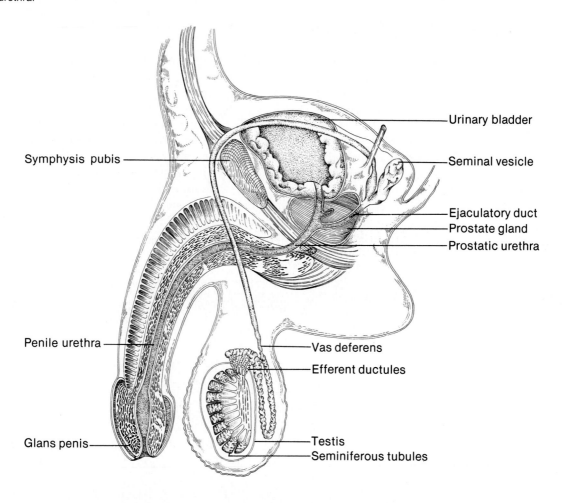

continuous with a thick-walled duct called the vas deferens which, through the ejaculatory duct, opens into the prostatic urethra (Fig. 2.3).

The mature human spermatozoon consists of a head, neck, middlepiece, and tail (Fig. 2.4). Approximately 60 microns long and less than 5 microns in diameter at the head, over half of its length is contributed by the tail. Spermatozoa are combined with secretions from accessory glands and expelled during ejaculation as seminal fluid, or semen. The estimated number of sperm in the typical ejaculation varies considerably from one investigation to the next. Allan (1969) estimates about 350 million, while Wolfers and Wolfers (1974) suggest that as many as a billion may be released. Nearly everyone agrees that sperm mortality is very high, but the estimates of minimum sperm count necessary for fertilization are also quite diverse. A

Figure 2.4 Schematic cross section of a human sperm. (Redrawn from J. Schultz-Larsen, *The Morphology of the Human Sperm,* 1958. Munksgaard, Copenhagen.)

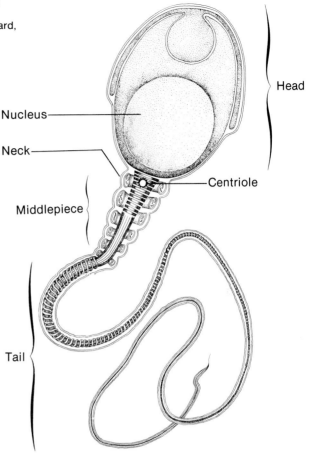

Nucleus

Neck

Middlepiece

Tail

Head

Centriole

frequently quoted criterion for male infertility is 60 million sperm or less per ejaculation, but cases have been recorded where conception was achieved by men with average sperm counts of less than 500,000 per cubic centimeter.

Compared to a sperm cell, the human **ovum** is quite large. It is spherical, measures about 140 microns in diameter—a point somewhat less than half the diameter of the dot over an "i" on this page—and at times can be seen with the naked eye. The ova are produced in the primary sex organs of the female, the two ovaries (Fig. 2.5). In the adult female, each ovary weighs approximately 5 grams—although this is quite variable—and is shaped roughly like a very large bean (Hamilton et al. 1964).

Oogenesis, the production of ova, begins in fetal life, becomes latent until puberty, and continues thereafter until menopause. It involves, and is dependent upon, cells of the ovarian cortex called ovarian follicles. These are cellular clusters that surround each ovum. When stimulated with follicle stimulating hormone (FSH) from the **pituitary gland,** the follicle and its enclosed ovum begin to enlarge. Concurrently,

Figure 2.5 The human ovary in cross section, showing the developmental sequence of events from the origin of the ovarian follicle to the rupture of the follicle and subsequent release of the ovum.

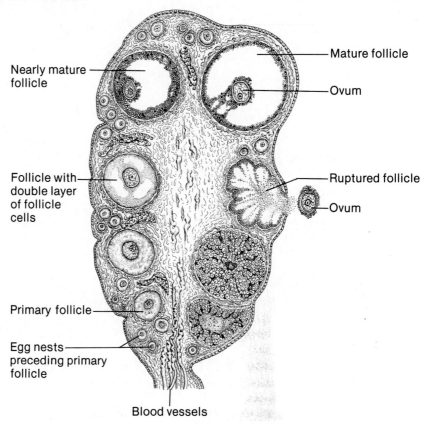

Nearly mature follicle

Mature follicle

Ovum

Follicle with double layer of follicle cells

Ruptured follicle

Ovum

Primary follicle

Egg nests preceding primary follicle

Blood vessels

the follicular wall becomes multilayered as the follicular cells multiply. Shortly thereafter, a membrane called the **zona pellucida** surrounds the developing ovum, and a cavity is formed that separates the follicular cell layers on one side of the ovum. The cavity expands, fills with fluid containing estrogenic hormones, and eventually a mature ovarian follicle is formed. At this time the ovum is displaced from its central position and approaches the surface where it will be expelled during **ovulation.** Ovulation, or release of the ovum, normally occurs once approximately every 28 days. When the ovum is discharged, it enters the oviduct and is carried into the uterus. If unfertilized at this time, it will die and undergo either resorption or expulsion during menstruation. When fertilization does occur, usually in the upper third of the oviduct, the zygote is carried into the uterus. Here it will implant into the outer layer of the uterine wall where it develops into the fetus during the prenatal period—usually lasting approximately nine months.

Fertilization occurs when the spermatozoon penetrates the zona pellucida of the ovum and the nuclei of the two cells fuse together. Almost immediately a "block to polyspermy," a mechanism not fully understood, renders the zona pellucida impervious to entry by additional sperm. At least three major events occur with fertilization: (1) the full (**diploid**) number of chromosomes is restored, half from the father's and half from the mother's gametes; (2) the sex of the zygote is determined—an X-chromosome in the sperm cell results in a female zygote and a Y-sex chromosome produces a male zygote; and (3) **cleavage** begins. This latter process is a rapid succession of mitotic cell divisions that results in the large zygote being reduced to smaller cells.

Cell Division and Chromosome Duplication

Mitosis

The body (**somatic**) **cells** in an individual multiply from the original zygote to thousands of billions in the adult by a process called **mitosis.** It is a continuous process, because cells in body tissues are constantly being lost and must be replenished. Mitosis ensures that each cell will be supplied with a copy of the chromosomes of the original zygote. The duplication of **DNA** in the cell is accomplished prior to mitosis, which is merely the mechanism responsible for equal distribution of genetic information to the two daughter cell nuclei.

By convention, the mitotic process is divided into five separate stages, on the basis of characteristic chromosomal movements and rearrangements during the process. In reality, mitosis is a continuous process that is best appreciated via motion pictures. The process of mitotic cell division has been known for many years and is described in nearly every textbook on biology and genetics, but a number of questions still remain. What mechanism initiates cell division? Why do some tissue cells (skin, blood, connective tissue) divide continuously throughout life, while other cells (heart muscle and nerve tissue) seemingly lose their capacity to divide once mature? What initiates and maintains the abnormal cell division commonly observed in cancers and tumors? These questions belong to a branch of biology called cytology, the study of the cell.

The five stages of mitosis include (1) interphase, (2) prophase, (3), metaphase, (4) anaphase, and (5) telophase. The entire process is illustrated diagrammatically in Figure 2.6 and is described as follows:

1. Interphase. Early in cytological research it was thought that interphase was a "resting stage" because no visible cellular activity was discernible. However, it is now known that this is a period of intense metabolic activity within the cell. The chromosomes are quite long, very slender, and usually cannot be seen with a light microscope. The nucleus has a reticulated appearance and may contain one or more small bodies called **nucleoli.** These bodies are sites where a nucleic acid called rRNA and the ribosomes are synthesized.

Interphase itself is divisible into three stages denoted as G_1 (the G stands for gap), S (for synthesis) and G_2. At the beginning of interphase, each cell

Figure 2.6 A diagrammatic drawing of the sequences of mitotic cell division (see text for explanation).

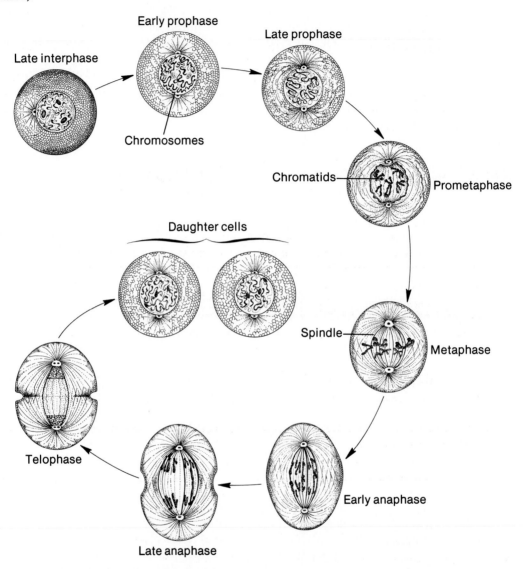

Late interphase

Early prophase

Late prophase

Chromosomes

Chromatids — Prometaphase

Daughter cells

Spindle — Metaphase

Telophase

Early anaphase

Late anaphase

enters the G_1 phase. At this time RNA and proteins are synthesized. This is followed by the S phase, when the synthesis of RNA and proteins continues and DNA replication occurs. During the next (G_2) stage, DNA replication is stopped and protein synthesis reduced as the cell prepares to enter prophase. In late interphase, the centrosome on the surface of the nuclear membrane becomes apparent.

2. Prophase. The onset of prophase is usually indicated when the chromosomes become clearly visible. They become shorter, thicker, and more tightly

coiled as prophase proceeds, and each chromosome appears to be two closely associated filaments termed **chromatids.** The two sister chromatids are attached to each other at a point called the **centromere.** The location of the centromere commonly marks a noticeable constriction of the chromosome. In early prophase the nucleoli begin to disperse and usually cannot be seen in late prophase. In the meantime, the centrosome divides into the two daughter centrioles which migrate to opposite poles of the nucleus. Radiating outward from the centrioles are astral rays. Between the two centrioles are the spindle fibers which are tubular fibrils composed of cytoplasmic molecules and a small amount of RNA. The combination of astral rays, centrioles, and spindle fibers is termed collectively the **spindle.** In late prophase, the nuclear membrane begins to disintegrate. The chromosomes, now at their maximum thickness and minimum length, begin to approach the equator of the spindle. The equator is the plane equidistant from the two spindle poles.

3. Metaphase. The onset of metaphase is marked by spindle formation and alignment of the centromeres along the spindle equator. Although the arms of the chromosomes may extend in various directions, the spindle keeps the centromeres at the equator.

4. Anaphase. Each centromere divides, resulting in two daughter chromatids (now termed chromosomes) that begin to move toward the opposite poles. To each centromere is attached a spindle fiber, and by a process called karyokinesis, these fibers appear to pull the chromosomes toward the poles. In late anaphase, as the chromosomes near the poles, the cell begins to pinch inward.

5. Telophase. The chromosomes, having reached their respective poles, begin to reaggregate. In the meantime, the cytoplasm is dividing into two parts by invagination of the cell membrane from opposite sides of the equator. The spindle degenerates, nuclear membranes begin to reform around the coalesced chromosomes, and nucleoli once again appear in each thusly formed daughter cell. The chromosomes in each cell become indiscernible, and the two daughter cells, each a copy of the parent cell, return to interphase.

The duration of the mitotic process in humans varies somewhat between different cell types and depends upon whether the division is normal or abnormal. Probably about 90% of the time, however, the cells are in interphase. Examples of the duration of the various stages in mitosis in highly specific cells from various species, excluding humans, may be found in Grundmann (1966) and Strickberger (1976).

Meiosis

In contrast to mitosis, which occurs in all cells, meiotic cell division occurs only in the sex cells and reduces the chromosome number from the diploid to the **haploid** state. Like mitosis, **meiosis** is an unbroken process (Fig. 2.7) that may conveniently be described in successive stages. Meiosis, however, involves two divisions instead of one.

The formation of eggs and sperm are quite similar in their chromosomal stages. The two gametogenic processes are different in some aspects, however, and thus receive separate discussions below. The four distinct stages in the cellular development of spermatozoa may be described in terms of four cell types, including **spermatogonia,** primary **spermatocytes,** secondary spermatocytes, and **spermatids:**

1. Spermatogonia. These are testicular cells, each containing the diploid (46) number of chromosomes. Spermatogonia are constantly generated after puberty by mitotic division, one of the daughter cells usually remaining as a spermatogonial cell and the other developing into a primary spermatocyte.

2. Primary spermatocyte. These cells also possess the full number of chromosomes. During this stage, the nuclear membrane breaks down and synapsis takes place. This is a process occurring at the onset of mid-prophase when the chromosomes pair. They may also twist around each other and exchange genetic material (see Chapter 4). Shortly thereafter, two chromatids are produced from each dividing chromosome. The sister chromatids remain attached, because the centromere does not divide. The four closely associated chromatids from the pair of chromosomes, called a tetrad, become aligned at metaphase with their centromeres at the cell equator. Each chromosome in the tetrad then separates from its homologue and moves toward an opposite pole in the same fashion as chromosomes moved in mitosis. This is followed by nuclear membrane formation and cytoplasmic division, resulting in two daughter cells called secondary spermatocytes. This completes the first meiotic division.

3. Secondary spermatocyte. Each secondary spermatocyte has only half (23) the number of chromosomes, and each consists of two chromatids held together by a centromere. The second meiotic division now occurs, with the sister chromatids aligning once again at the equator, dividing, and moving toward opposite poles. Because the centromeres divide during this division, however, four cells rather than two are produced. Each of these is haploid, containing 23 chromosomes, and is called a spermatid.

4. Spermatid. No further division takes place, and any one of these cells represents the beginning of the functional male gamete. After a period of cellular differentiation, the spermatids become highly motile spermatozoa.

The meiotic process in oogenesis (Fig. 2.8) differs little from that in spermatogenesis and need not be repeated in detail. However, there is considerable difference in cell cleavage and subsequent cytoplasmic distribution. Like spermatogenesis, the stages may be described in the context of **oogonia,** primary **oocytes,** secondary oocytes, and ootids.

1. Oogonia. An oogonium is a diploid cell which by mitotic division produces daughter cells that may become surrounded by ovarian follicles. After a period of growth, an oogonium becomes a primary oocyte.

2. Primary oocyte. Similar to primary spermatocytes, synapsis occurs, tetrads are formed, and the cell undergoes the first meiotic division. There is unequal cleavage, however, giving rise to one large and one small cell. The large cell, containing most of the cytoplasm, becomes the secondary oocyte. The small cell is called the first polar body.

3. Secondary oocyte. During the second meiotic division the same unequal cleavage occurs. As before with secondary spermatocytes, these are haploid cells. Since the first polar body may also divide, the final products of meiosis in oogenesis are three polar bodies and one cell that receives most of the cytoplasm. The latter is the ootid, which need not undergo any further change to be a functional ovum. The three polar bodies are usually resorbed.

Figure 2.7 Schematic drawing of meiosis in a male, showing two pairs of chromosomes in a diploid nucleus as they undergo a reduction to four haploid gametes (see text for explanation).

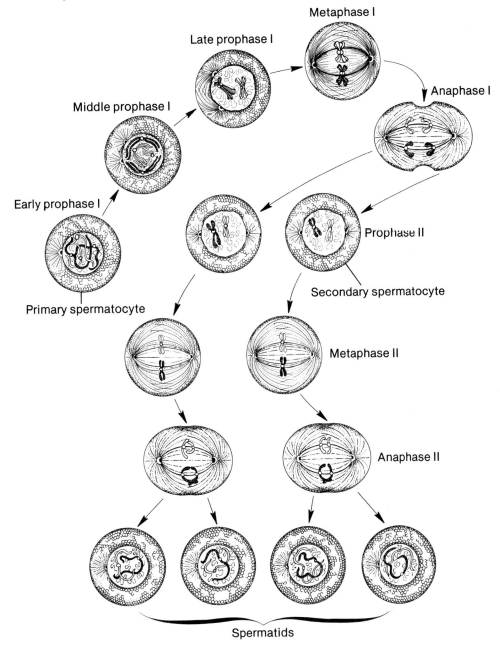

Metaphase I

Late prophase I

Anaphase I

Middle prophase I

Prophase II

Early prophase I

Secondary spermatocyte

Primary spermatocyte

Metaphase II

Anaphase II

Spermatids

Figure 2.8 Oogenesis (meiotic cell division in a female).

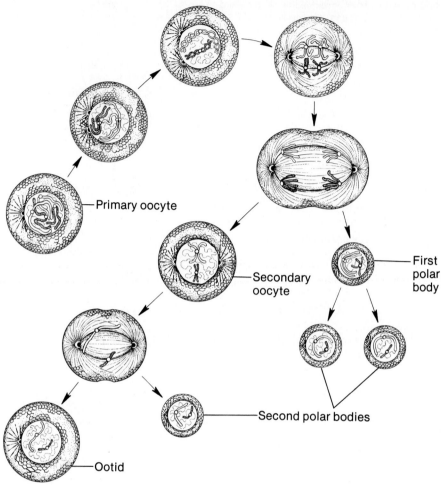

Primary oocyte

Secondary oocyte

First polar body

Second polar bodies

Ootid

Chromosomes

We have referred a number of times to the actions of chromosomes without any explicit clarification of their nature, structure, or function. That chromosomes are the vehicle of inheritance has been known for many years. The word chromosome itself, introduced by Waldeyer in 1888, is derived from the Greek words *chromos* (color)—because chromosomes have specific staining properties—and *soma* (body).

Chromosome Structure

When viewed with a light microscope, the basic element of most chromosomes, the chromonema (plural = chromonemata), resembles a fine thread. Upon examination with an electron microscope, the chromonema appears as a bundle of even finer threads, or perhaps a single coiled or supercoiled fibril. The chemical constituents of chromosomes include deoxyribonucleic acid (DNA), a class of proteins called histones, **ribonucleic acid (RNA),** and water. The surrounding of the DNA double helices by histones results in chemical complexes sometimes called nucleoproteins.

Studies on human metaphase chromosomes indicate the presence of a spiral structure in which each chromatid is composed of two chromonemata. A popular hypothesis holds that the chromonemata are further divided into two secondary subunits (e.g., Bartalos and Baramki 1967). The subunits, in turn, are each composed of four tertiary subunits, each being composed of histone and RNA attached to double-stranded helical DNA. DuPraw (1972), however, casts some doubt on this interpretation and emphasizes that neither secondary nor tertiary substructures can be seen in the great majority of metaphase chromosomes.

Chromosome Numbers

The number of chromosomes in different animal species varies widely, from 2 pairs in some scale insects and flatworms to well over 100 pairs in a species of crab (White 1973). Every species, however, has a characteristic number. An indication of the variation in chromosome number in primates may be found in Table 2.3. The diploid chromosome number in humans has been accurately known for only a short time (Tjio and Levan 1956) and consists of 22 pairs of **autosomes** and two sex chromosomes. In the male, the sex chromosomes are designated XY and in the female, XX. By convention, the human chromosome complement has been divided into seven groups

Table 2.3 The Normal Diploid Chromosome Number in Selected Primate Species (After Napier and Napier 1967.)

Taxonomic Name	Vernacular Name	Chromosome Number
Ateles paniscus	Black Spider Monkey	34
Galago senegalensis	Lesser Bushbaby	38
Papio cynocephalus	Yellow Baboon	42
Macaca mulatta	Rhesus Monkey	42
Saimiri sciureus	Squirrel Monkey	44
Hylobates lar	White-Handed Gibbon	44
Lemur variegatus	Ruffed Lemur	46
Homo sapiens	Man, Woman	46
Callithrix jacchus	Common Marmoset	46
Pongo pygmaeus	Orang-Utan	48
Pan troglodytes	Chimpanzee	48
Gorilla gorilla gorilla	Western Lowland Gorilla	48
Nycticebus coucang	Slow Loris	50
Symphalangus syndactylus	Siamang	50
Erythrocebus patas	Patas Monkey	54
Cercopithecus diana	Diana Monkey	58
Cercopithecus aethiops	Vervet	60
Galago crassicaudatus	Greater Bushbaby	62
Cheirogaleus major	Greater Dwarf Lemur	66
Cercopithecus mitis	Blue Monkey	72
Tarsius bancanus	Horsfield's Tarsier	80

Figure 2.9 The chromosomes of a human male, arranged as a karyotype according to the chromosome sizes and relative lengths of their arms. (Courtesy of Dr. Margery W. Shaw.)

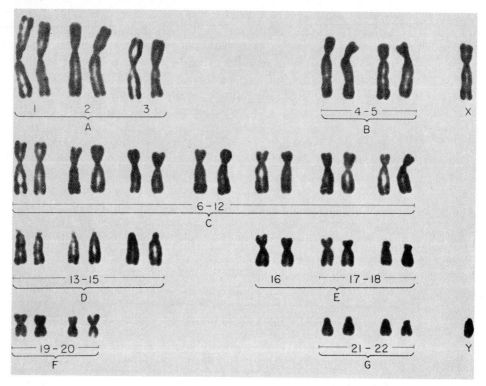

according to (1) their relative lengths and (2) the position of the centromere in those chromosomes of approximately the same size (Fig. 2.9). The representation of chromosomes by these groups is called a **karyotype.**

Chromosome Mutations

A **chromosome mutation** is a heritable change in the structure or number of chromosomes. Although cell division is a remarkably accurate process, chromosomes in daughter cells are not always identical copies of those in the parent cell. For a variety of reasons things sometimes go wrong. Chromosome mutations may occur spontaneously, which is a nice way of stating our ignorance of the underlying cause, or they may be induced artificially by exposure to a number of known mutagenic agents (Table 2.4). For the most part, mutagenic capability of these agents has been demonstrated in experimental organisms, such as bacteria, viruses, and insects. Their mutagenicity to human chromosomes, however, remains largely unknown.

The question of the frequency of human chromosome mutations has no satisfactory answer at present, although recent evidence (Carr 1969; Sergovich et al. 1969) suggests that earlier estimates of chromosomal mutation rates were far too low.

Table 2.4 A Classification of Some Known Mutagenic Agents (After Levitan and Montagu 1971.)

I. Radiations
  A. Ionizing radiation, including X rays, alpha and beta particles, gamma rays, and neutrons

  B. Nonionizing radiation, including light and near-visible light of specific wavelengths

II. Temperature changes, including thermal shocks

III. Chemicals
  A. Compounds related to DNA or RNA bases
    1. Purines, including caffeine
    2. Purine analogues, including 2-amino purine, 2,6-diamino purine, theobromide
    3. Pyrimidine analogue, including 5-bromouracil
    4. Substances that react with purines and pyrimidines, including formaldehyde and nitrous oxide
    5. Deoxyribonuclease (DNA metabolic enzyme)
  B. Alkylating agents, including nitrogen and sulphur mustards, and other compounds related to mustard gases
  C. Acridine dyes, including acridine orange, acriflavine, proflavine
  D. Carcinogens, including methyl cholanthene, benzpyrene, and others
  E. Inorganic salts, including copper sulphate, ferrous chloride, and manganous chloride
  F. Organic and inorganic acids, including acetic acid, carbolic acid, formic acid, lactic acid, and boric acid
  G. Miscellaneous compounds, including ammonia, hydrogen peroxide, and many others

The main difficulty in determining these rates in humans stems from the undetected chromosome mutations in resorbed fetuses and the large number of spontaneous abortions that are not available for chromosome analysis. Nevertheless, it has been estimated that gross chromosomal abnormalities occur in about 3.5% of all recovered spontaneous abortions. If this is an accurate figure, it represents at best a very minimum estimate.

　　　An individual with a chromosome mutation will possess either an abnormal number of chromosomes or a structural alteration in one or more chromosomes in the set. This, in turn, means that the individual will suffer a loss, rearrangement, or multiplication of genes in the affected chromosomes. The ultimate result is often serious mental or physical defects or both. A recent summary of the physical effects from several well-known chromosomal abnormalities may be found in Pfeiffer (1967).

　　　For convenience, chromosome mutations may be described by classifying the various types of changes. Although most classifications differ slightly, many are similar to Dobzhansky's (1970) basic scheme:

I. Structural chromosomal changes that affect the chromosomes in terms of a loss, gain, or rearrangement of genes.
  A. Changes involving a loss or duplication of genes.
    1. **Deficiency.** This is the loss of a gene or block of genes from a chromosome.

Assume a chromosome carries a sequence of genes denoted as ABCDEFG. If a break occurs between D and E, the deficient chromosome may contain only ABCD. The phenotypic severity of a deficiency will obviously depend upon the particular genes that are lost. In general, the loss of genes involved with physiological or developmental processes is detrimental and sometimes fatal to the individual.

2. **Duplication.** The presence of an additional segment in a chromosome is called a duplication. The extra segment may be attached to one of the pair of **homologous** chromosomes; it may be independent, and if so is soon lost; it may attach to a **nonhomologous** chromosome. The chromosomal segment DE in the normal sequence ABCDE-FGHI (the hyphen representing the centromere) might duplicate and appear in tandem (ABCDEDE-FGHI); in reverse tandem (ABCDEED-FGHI); it may be displaced on the same arm (ABDECDE-FGHI); or to a nonhomologous chromosome at any point (JKDEL-MNOP).

B. Changes involving a linear rearrangement of genes.

1. **Translocation.** One section of a chromosome may transfer to a nonhomologous chromosome. The most common form is a reciprocal translocation which occurs when two nonhomologous chromosomes break and exchange the broken sections. For example, chromosomes with the sequences ABC-DEF and GHI-JKL may break between BC and HI, exchange segments, and give rise to chromosomes with the sequences ABI-JKL and GHC-DEF. Translocations may have profound consequences, again depending upon the sections exchanged, because they disrupt the linkage relationships between genes (see Chapter 4).

2. **Inversion.** This is a rearrangement of the gene order within a single chromosome, and also may disrupt linkage relationships. Two main types of inversions are usually recognized: those that include the centromere within the inverted region (pericentric) and those that do not (paracentric). In a chromosome with the gene order ABCDE-FGHI, a pericentric inversion could result in the order ABCF-EDGHI, and a paracentric inversion in the order ADCBE-FGHI.

3. **Transpositions.** Sometimes these changes are called shifts and are basically similar to translocations, except that the same chromosome breaks in three places instead of two. If the chromosome with the gene order ABCDEFG-HIJ breaks between A and B, C and D, and E and F, the sections could translocate to form the order ADEBCFG-HIJ.

II. Changes in chromosome number.

A. **Euploidy.** A chromosomal change resulting in variation of the entire set of chromosomes is called euploidy. The general term **polyploidy** refers to a situation in which the number of chromosome sets is greater than that in the diploid ($2n$) state. More specifically, a polyploid with three sets ($3n$) of chromosomes is called a triploid, with four sets ($4n$) a tetraploid, with eight sets ($8n$) an octoploid, and so forth. Polyploidy may occur in either some or all cells of the individual. In aborted human fetuses, triploids ($3n = 69$) and tetraploids ($4n = 92$) have been found, and cancer cells are often found to contain multiples of the diploid number. Although polyploidy is common and sometimes advantageous in plant species, it is usually highly detrimental in humans and other mammals.

B. **Aneuploidy.** This involves the lack or multiplication of one or more chromosomes in the normal set. For example, consider a diploid individual with homologous chromosomes containing the alleles AABBCC. Aneuploids derived from this could take the following forms:

Type	Chromosome Set	Loci
nullosomic	$2n - 2$	*AABB*
monosomic	$2n - 1$	*AABBC*
disomic (normal)	$2n$	*AABBCC*
trisomic	$2n + 1$	*AABBCCC*
double trisomic	$2n + 1 + 1$	*AABBBCCC*
tetrasomic	$2n + 2$	*AABBCCCC*
etc.		

Changes in chromosome number occur most often during late metaphase or anaphase and usually involve the failure of the chromosomes to disjoin or to move normally to the opposite poles. This process is called **nondisjunction.** It may occur in cells with the normal chromosome set (primary nondisjunction) or in cells that already possess an abnormal number of chromosomes because of a previous failure (secondary nondisjunction). Furthermore, nondisjunction can be either mitotic or meiotic and can occur in either or both meiotic divisions.

Fertilization of gametes that have undergone nondisjunction can result in a wide variety of sex chromosome constitutions, as indicated in Table 2.5. In most of these cases the affected individual suffers from numerous physical and mental abnormalities, some of the clinical symptoms appearing below.

Sex Chromosomes	**Clinical Symptoms or Characteristics**
1. YO, OO, and YY (O = absence of chromosome)	Lethal
2. XO (Turner's Syndrome, Gonadal Dysgenesis)	Highly lethal, with an estimated 97% dying *in utero*. Those who survive are usually sterile. The exact incidence of this condition is unknown but high, with about 2% of spontaneous abortuses having the 45, XO karyotype (Hecht and Macfarlane 1969). Physical characteristics include short stature, webbed neck, widely spaced nipples and underdeveloped breasts, small uterus and fibrous streaks instead of normal ovaries (Goldberg et al. 1968), occasional nerve deafness (Lemli and Smith 1963), but normal mentality.
3. XXXX (X-Tetrasomy)	These are apparently fertile females of unknown incidence. They appear to be mentally retarded, with I.Q.s ranging from 30 to 80 (Carr et al. 1961; DiCagno and

Franceschini 1968). Observed hip dislocations and minor abnormalities of the face and hands may or may not be associated with this syndrome.

4. XXY (Klinefelter's Syndrome)

These individuals are infertile males with enlargement of the breasts, reduction in size of the testes (Laron and Hochman 1971), increased stature, occasional obesity, elevated urinary gonadotropins, and apparently normal intelligence. However, the frequency of XXY patients in mental hospitals is three times as high as is suspected for the general population.

5. XXXXX (X-Penta-somy)

This is a rare condition, having been described in only three young children and one teenage female. Caution must be exercised in associating phenotypic characteristics with the syndrome. All were mentally retarded, two had short necks (Brody et al. 1967; Yamada and Neriishi 1971), and the older female had underdeveloped secondary sex characteristics (Sergovich et al. 1971).

6. XYY (XYY Syndrome)

A great deal of work is presently under way on males with the XYY condition because of their alleged predisposition toward aggressive and criminal behavior (Benezech 1973). That their behavior is related directly to the presence of the extra Y-chromosome, however, has yet to be convincingly demonstrated (Hook 1973). The physical differences between these individuals and normal males are often slight, which has complicated attempts to compare the relatively high frequency of XYY males in penal institutions to that in the general population. There seems to be a tendency for XYY males to be tall, slightly subnormal mentally, and sometimes obese. Reports suggesting a higher frequency of developmental anomalies of the internal and external genitalia have yet to be adequately verified.

There is little reason to go into more specific detail on the other conditions listed in Table 2.5. It should be understood, however, that some of the other sex chromosome abnormalities (including XXYY, XXXY, and XXXXY) represent syndromes with at least two striking similarities to those just discussed. These are varying degrees of mental retardation and maldevelopment of the sex characteristics. The reason for these similar effects will remain unknown until additional information is available on the relationship between sex hormones and brain development. This will also depend upon two factors: (1) an adequate definition of mental retardation, and how it differs between individuals and (2) what genetic material is carried on the sex chromosomes, and how it interacts with other genes during development.

A condition called Down's syndrome was the first autosomal abnormality discovered and, perhaps, is the best studied. It is the most common autosomal

Table 2.5 Possible Zygotic Combinations of Sex Chromosomes Resulting from Meiotic Non-disjunction in Male and Female Gametes (Adapted from Levitan and Montagu 1971.)

		Male Gametes								
		Normal Meiosis		Primary Meiosis I Nondisjunction		Primary Meiosis II Nondisjunction		Secondary Meiosis II Nondisjunction		
	Gamete	X	Y	O	XY	XX	YY	XXY	XYY	XXYY
Normal Meiosis	X	XX	XY	XO	XXY	XXX	XYY	XXXY	XXYY	XXXYY
Normal Meiosis	O	XO	YO	OO	XY	XX	YY	XXY	XYY	XXYY
Primary Nondisjunction	XX	XXX	XXY	XX	XXY	XXXX	XXYY	XXXXY	XXXYY	XXXXYY
Secondary Meiosis II Nondisjunction	XXX	XXXX	XXXY	XXX	XXXXY	XXXXX	XXXYY	XXXXXY	XXXXYY	XXXXXYY
Secondary Meiosis II Nondisjunction	XXXX	XXXXX	XXXXY	XXXX	XXXXXY	XXXXXX	XXXXYY	XXXXXXY	XXXXXYY	XXXXXXYY

(Left margin label: Female Gametes)

abnormality known, occurring in approximately 1 of every 700 live births. Down's syndrome is sometimes called "mongolism," because of the presence of an epicanthic eyefold which is similar to that found in East Asian populations, and is caused by the presence of an extra G-group chromosome. The 21st and 22nd chromosomes which comprise the G-group are quite similar in size and in their staining properties, and it has been difficult to determine which one appears in triplicate. General agreement was reached some time ago that the 21st chromosome was the trisomic—hence the now familiar synonym "Trisomy-21." However, Caspersson et al. (1970) and O'Riordan et al. (1971) found by new methods that the 22nd chromosome was the trisomic. In any case, the condition results from a G-group trisomy, and most of the individuals with Down's syndrome have a very poor expectation of life span. About half die within the first five years of life, the average life expectancy being just over 16 years (Penrose and Smith 1966). Particularly frequent causes of death include a high susceptibility to upper respiratory infections and congenital heart disease.

Some of the typical clinical manifestations in G-trisomy include brachycephaly (round head); a round, flat face; epicanthic eyefolds; eye anomalies; dental abnormalities; and minor malformations of the hands, feet, and digits. Mental retardation is mild to severe, with I.Q.s ranging from less than 25 to about 75. Of particular interest in the etiology of G-trisomy is the influence of maternal age on the frequency of births of these individuals. Fabia (1969) reported that the incidence of G-trisomy increases from 1 : 1600 for mothers under 20 years of age to 1 : 75 for mothers over 40 years of age. The reasons for this association are still obscure, but a number of possible explanations have been reviewed by Yamamoto et al. (1973) and Mikkelsen and Stene (1972).

Down's syndrome is only one of a number of autosomal abnormalities. Other conditions, such as Trisomy-E18 (the Edwards syndrome) and Trisomy-13 (the D_1-Trisomy syndrome), are even more detrimental. These typically result in multiple congenital defects, at times affecting nearly all organ systems, and usually are fatal. To the extent that chromosomal mutations affect the visible phenotype, they are generally harmful to the individual. By affecting normal developmental systems, they impose a selective disadvantage upon the individual. This, in turn, has profound implications for certain aspects of evolutionary genetics which will be examined in Chapter 6.

Mendelian Inheritance

Abnormal characteristics such as those just discussed clearly have a genetic basis, as do our blood group **antigens,** enzyme systems, stature, skin pigmentation, and all other physical traits that comprise the biology of the individual. The development of the elementary principles involved in the hereditary transmission of such biological characteristics requires a basic vocabulary, and some very useful definitions are given below before proceeding further.

1. **Gene.** A segment of DNA recognized by its specific function. A much older, but still useful definition, is simply "a unit of inheritance."

2. **Allele.** An alternate expression of a gene. The ABO blood group gene, for example, may occur in the allelic forms I^A, I^B, or I^O (the meaning of the capital letter I is discussed in Chapter 4).

3. **Locus.** The position of a given gene on a chromosome.

4. **Genotype.** All of the genetic factors responsible for the genetic constitution of an individual. Generally, we speak of an individual's genotype in specific terms, such as the ABO blood group genotype.

5. **Heterozygous.** This denotes the presence of unlike alleles at homologous loci on a pair of chromosomes. A person is heterozygous, for example, if he or she has an I^A allele on one member of a pair of homologous chromosomes and an I^O allele on the other. The noun heterozygote is used to denote this individual.

6. **Homozygous.** This denotes the presence of like alleles on a pair of homologous chromosomes. A person homozygous for blood group B, for example, has the I^B allele at each locus on both chromosomes and would be referred to as a homozygote.

7. **Dominance.** This is a state—a physiological or functional effect—in which an allele is phenotypically expressed in both the homozygote and the heterozygote. Such an allele in heterozygous form masks its recessive counterpart. An $I^A I^O$ heterozygote will test out as type A, since A is dominant over O.

8. **Recessiveness.** This is the alternative to dominance—the failure of an allele to express itself phenotypically when in the heterozygous state.

9. **Phenotype.** The appearance of an individual: all of the characteristics produced as a result of the interaction between the genotype and the environment.

Phenotypes, like genotypes, are often spoken of with reference to a single characteristic, such as red, black, blond, or brown hair color.

We concentrate in this short section only on segregation and independent assortment, the two Mendelian "laws" generally credited as the fundamental principles upon which the field of genetics is based. Mendel's findings have been shown to have universal validity for all diploid species, including ourselves.

Segregation

It is often assumed that the genetic characteristics of a child represent a fusion, or blending, of equal parts of the mother's and father's blood. This notion was proven false decades ago. Mendel's work led eventually to the demonstration that traits were transmitted from parent to offspring by particulate bodies that many years later were named genes, and also that these discrete units did not blend with each other in the offspring. That only one of a pair of genes is transmitted from a parent to the offspring is the fundamental concept known as the law of **segregation.**

It was shown earlier that fusion between the haploid male and female gametes results in a diploid zygote. In this manner an individual receives equal amounts of genetic material from both the father and mother. The genetic material in the offspring follows the same process when he or she produces his or her own gametes.

For clarification, consider the postulated mating between a normal female and an albino male in Figure 2.10. For convenience, the dominant allele is designated by the capital A and the recessive allele by the small a. Since albinism is a recessive disorder, the male genotype is aa. Although the female is phenotypically normal in the heterozygous Aa state, assume in this example that she is homozygous AA. Clearly, the female can produce only A gametes and the male only a gametes. Thus the first generation (F_1) offspring will all be normal Aa heterozygotes.

The F_1 heterozygotes, however, produce in equal numbers gametes containing either A or a, and a mating between two heterozygous individuals will, on the average, result in individuals with the genotypes given in the box in Figure 2.10. Approximately one-fourth of the offspring will be homozygous dominant and normal, two-fourths will be heterozygous and normal, and one-fourth will be homozygous recessive and albino. The genotypic ratio, then, is $1AA : 2Aa : 1aa$, and the phenotypic ratio, since A is dominant to a, is 3 unaffected to 1 affected. Obviously, mating between homozygous dominant individuals will produce only AA children, and matings between two albinos will produce only albino children.

Independent Assortment

Mendel's second law, the principle of **independent assortment,** is little more than an extension of the law of segregation. Instead of a single pair of genes in one homologous pair of chromosomes, the segregation of two or more genes on two or more chromosomes is involved.

For simplicity, the principle of independent assortment may be illustrated by adding the taster gene to the gene for albinism in the mother and father in Figure 2.10. More will be said about the taster gene in a later chapter, but for now suffice it to say that some people can taste a bitter substance called phenylthiourea (PTC) and others cannot. Nontasters are homozygous recessive (tt) and tasters are

Figure 2.10 Mendel's principle of segregation.
Cross between a homozygous dominant normal female
and a homozygous recessive albino male.

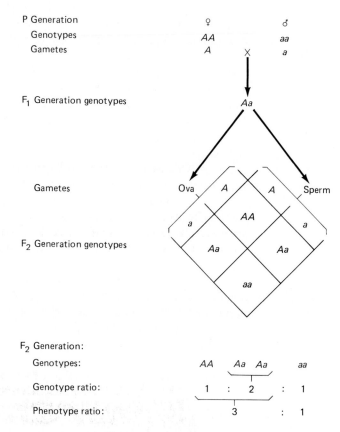

P Generation		♀	♂
Genotypes		AA	aa
Gametes		A ✕	a

F_1 Generation genotypes — Aa

Gametes — Ova A A Sperm

F_2 Generation genotypes

a AA a
Aa Aa
aa

F_2 Generation:

Genotypes:	AA	Aa Aa	aa
Genotype ratio:	1 :	2	: 1
Phenotype ratio:		3	: 1

either heterozygous (*Tt*) or homozygous dominant (*TT*). In Figure 2.11, the mother is represented as a homozygous taster and the father as a nontaster.

In the same manner already described for segregation, the gametes produced by the mother and father will be *AT* and *at* respectively, and all offspring from this mating will be heterozygous individuals with normal skin pigmentation who can taste PTC. These offspring produce in equal proportions four different kinds of gametes, including *AT, At, aT,* and *at.* When gametes with these alleles unite at random to form F_2 zygotes, we expect the proportions of F_2 genotypes as given in the box in Figure 2.11.

When combined into phenotypes, the ratio becomes 9 (double dominants) : 3 (one allele dominant and one recessive) : 3 (the other allele dominant and one recessive) : 1 (double recessive). In this manner, genes on nonhomologous chromosome pairs are passed from parent to offspring independently of each other. However, genes on the same chromosomes generally do not follow the rule of independent assortment. The reasons for this follow in Chapter 4.

Figure 2.11 Mendel's principle of independent assortment. Cross between a double homozygous dominant female and a double homozygous recessive male.

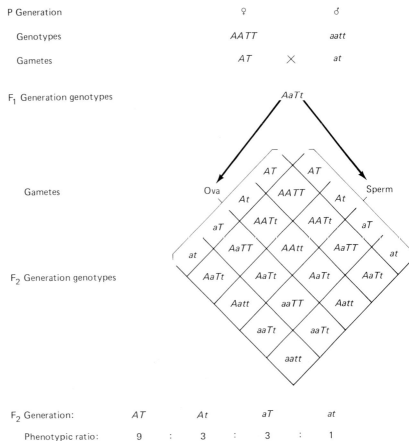

P Generation ♀ ♂

Genotypes *AATT* *aatt*

Gametes *AT* × *at*

F₁ Generation genotypes *AaTt*

Gametes Ova Sperm

F₂ Generation genotypes

F₂ Generation:	*AT*	*At*	*aT*	*at*
Phenotypic ratio:	9 :	3 :	3 :	1

Summary

All living organisms consist of cells, which vary immensely in size and shape according to their specific functions in the particular tissues that they comprise. Such variation notwithstanding, nearly all cells of higher organisms consist of two major structures, the nucleus and cytoplasm, both of which contain a number of smaller components. The nucleus, which is separated from the cytoplasm by the nuclear membrane, contains the nucleic acids and chromosomes responsible for inheritance. The cytoplasm, in turn, is bounded by the semipermeable plasma membrane and contains several organelles that serve specific and necessary functions related to protein synthesis, cell division, and the maintenance of cellular life.

The bisexual mode of reproduction characteristic of vertebrates initially involves the formation of male and female gametes (the sperm and ova respectively) by the distinct but related processes of spermatogenesis and oogenesis. Fertilization takes place when these two germ cells fuse. The full chromosome complement is restored in the zygote thus formed. In addition, the sex is determined and the relatively large zygote is reduced into smaller cells by a process called cleavage.

There are two different processes of cell division. One is called mitosis, which occurs in somatic cells and is responsible for cellular proliferation from the original zygote to the billions of cells in the mature adult. Mitosis also ensures the existence of the identical chromosome set in every normal cell of the body, in addition to being responsible for the replenishment of dead cells. The other process is meiosis, which occurs only in the sex cells and leads to gametes with only half the full chromosome complement.

Chromosomes are small structures that appear to be elongated bundles of very fine threads or fibrils when examined with the electron microscope. Their constituents include DNA, RNA, proteins, and water. Barring abnormalities, the number of chromosomes is characteristic of all individuals of any particular species and, in humans, the set includes 22 autosomes and two sex chromosomes. It has been shown in nonhuman experimental organisms that various external agents can cause chromosomal mutations, and it can be inferred with some confidence that these are also capable of inducing alterations in the structure or number of chromosomes in humans. When such changes occur, the results are often fatal and perhaps always detrimental.

The segments of DNA that are usually called genes are integral parts of chromosomes. Based upon Mendel's principles of segregation and independent asssortment, both of which were formulated over 100 years ago, it is now known that (1) each parent transmits only one of each pair of genes to the offspring and (2) genes on different chromosomes segregate independently of each other.

3 Genes and the Molecular Basis of Inheritance

Introduction

Few other achievements of modern science are as important and far-reaching as that which clarified the chemical nature of the gene. This discovery led rapidly to the conclusion that the transmission of a trait from a parent to an offspring is dependent upon DNA, a giant molecule that contains within its molecular structure a blueprint coded specifically for the trait.

The units of inheritance, called genes, may be defined as segments of DNA. They are recognizable by their specific function (Cavalli-Sforza and Bodmer 1971), and they are carried by the chromosomes. Thus, as the basic chemical of both the gene and the chromosome, DNA is the nucleic acid that plays the direct hereditary role. RNA, which is located in the nucleolus and the cytoplasm, serves as the intermediary between DNA and protein synthesis.

Organization and Replication of DNA

DNA, RNA, and proteins are polymeric molecules, that is, they are composed of smaller subunits. In DNA and RNA these subunits are called **nucleotides,** each of which consists of three components. These components include (1) a 5-carbon (pentose) sugar molecule, called ribose or deoxyribose when lacking one oxygen atom, (2) phosphoric acid, and (3) the nucleotide base. There are four kinds of nucleotide bases in DNA, including **adenine** (A), **guanine** (G), **thymine** (T), and **cytosine** (C). Adenine and guanine belong to a class of chemical compounds called purines, and thymine and cytosine to another class called pyrimidines. In its chemical structure, RNA is differentiated from DNA by the replacement of thymine by **uracil** (U), and in the replacement of deoxyribose by ribose.

DNA is composed of four different deoxyribonucleotides, each of which has a different base. These include the following:

1. phosphate-deoxyribose-adenine: deoxyadenylic acid
2. phosphate-deoxyribose-cytosine: deoxycytidylic acid
3. phosphate-deoxyribose-guanine: deoxyguanylic acid
4. phosphate-deoxyribose-thymine: deoxythymidylic acid

The DNA molecule is a long polynucleotide chain consisting of hundreds or thousands of these four deoxyribonucleotides, often called simply nucleotides, in different arrangements. The number and kinds of nucleotides in the chain are important for the genetic "message," but the linear sequence of the nucleotides is of primary significance. In other words, the specific arrangement of nucleotides in the DNA chains constitutes a genetic message that conveys highly specific information for the eventual synthesis of protein molecules.

DNA occurs as a double rather than a single polynucleotide chain. It consists of two complementary or paired strands that run parallel to each other, and which are coiled to form the well-known "double-helix" first described by Watson and Crick (1953). By analogy, the two chains might be said to resemble a spiral staircase with a handrail on both sides and a series of equidistant steps extending from one rail to the other (Fig. 3.1). The handrails, representing the sugar-phosphate linkages, repeat without change and run continuously for the length of the molecule. The steps represent the bases on either strand, each of which is connected to its partner by hydrogen bonds. These base pairs are bonded to each other in very specific ways and are therefore called complementary bases. Adenine on one chain bonds to thymine on the other (and vice versa) by means of two hydrogen bonds, and guanine to cytosine (and vice versa) by means of three hydrogen bonds (Fig. 3.2).

The DNA molecule begins duplication by uncoiling itself. The paired strands begin to separate at one end by breaking the relatively weak hydrogen bonds between base pairs. Each strand becomes a template to which unattached nucleotides, already present in the nucleus, are attracted. These nucleotides then join with their complements on the parent strand (Fig. 3.3). Identical replications of the original DNA molecule are insured by the specific hydrogen bonds mentioned above: adenine pairs only with thymine, and cytosine with guanine. Hence, the same molecular structure as in the original DNA molecule is passed on to all cell division products in the individual.

The Genetic Code

Upon initial consideration, one might assume that a macromolecule made up of only four different nucleotides in various sequences could not possibly be so variable as to supply all the genetic messages that must exist. However, consider the fact that the four different bases (A, C, G, and T) provide four alternative nucleotides at each position on the chain. For example, if a certain sequence existed in which G specified a message different from those of the other three bases, then four possible messages could be coded at that position—one each for A, G, T, and C. If two positions on the chain are considered in sequence, then the total number of possible arrangements would be 16, or 4^2 (AA, AC, AG, AT, CA, CC, CG, CT, GA, GC, GG, GT, TA, TC, TG, and TT). The total number of possible arrangements, and thus the genetic messages, increases exponentially as nucleotides are added to the sequence. The number of messages possible in a sequence of five nucleotides is 4^5 (1024), of ten nucleotides 4^{10} (1,048,576), and so forth.

Of how many nucleotides is a chain of human DNA composed? This is unknown, although several investigators have made crude estimates. Ohno (1972), for example, suggests that the mammalian genome contains roughly 3.0×10^9 base pairs. If this is close to the number of base pairs in humans, then the total number of possible

Figure 3.1 Diagrammatic representation of the Watson and Crick model for the DNA molecule showing the double helix arrangement.

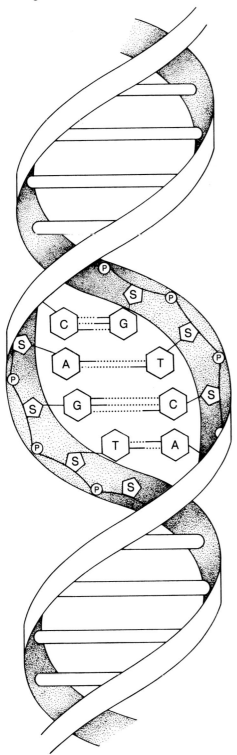

Figure 3.2 A schematic diagram of a section of DNA, showing the hydrogen bonds between thymine and adenine (2) and guanine and cytosine (3).

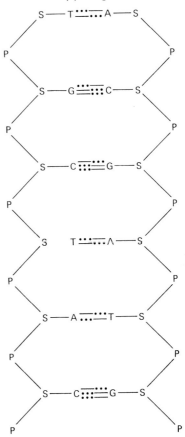

C: Cytosine
G: Guanine
A: Adenine
T: Thymine
S: Sugar molecule
P: Phosphoric acid

Figure 3.3 Diagram of DNA replication, showing the parent strand as it separates and subsequently develops into two identical copies.

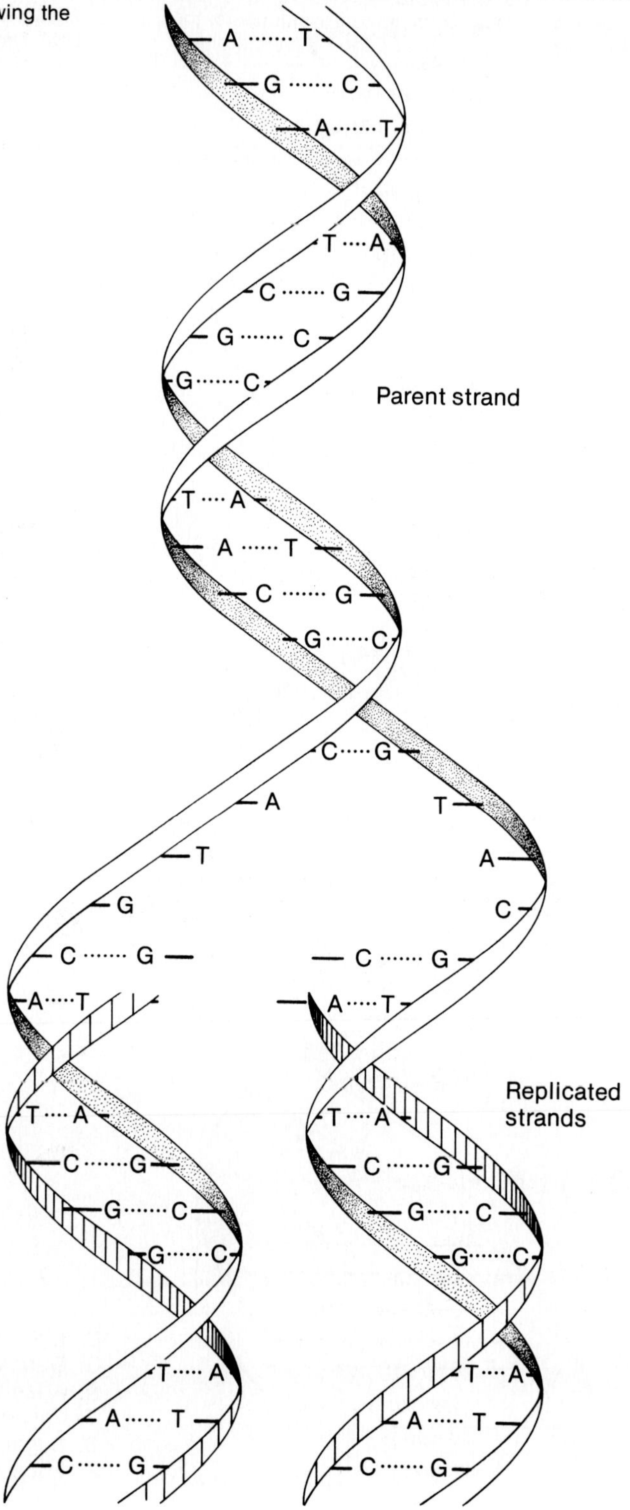

Parent strand

Replicated strands

combinations is unimaginably great. Even if it takes several hundred thousand nucleotides to code for a single complex protein molecule, there is little doubt that we possess far more DNA than necessary. There is considerable difference of opinion on how many of our DNA base sequences are utilized as genes, one estimate (Kimura and Ohta 1971) being about 6 percent.

DNA is often considered the universal hereditary language, and it is a good deal simpler to learn than English. It may be described as consisting of a four-letter alphabet (the bases A, T, G, and C) that forms only three-letter words called triplets, or **codons.** Obviously, the vocabulary of DNA is far smaller than for other languages. The four bases can be arranged to form only 64 (4^3) different codons, the meaning of each being known.

A codon specifies one of 20 different amino acids, which in turn serve as the building blocks of proteins. The amino acids and their abbreviations are given below:

ALA	Alanine	GLY	Glycine	PRO	Proline
ARG	Arginine	HIS	Histidine	SER	Serine
ASN	Asparagine	ILE	Isoleucine	THR	Threonine
ASP	Aspartic acid	LEU	Leucine	TRP	Tryptophan
CYS	Cysteine	LYS	Lysine	TYR	Tyrosine
GLN	Glutamine	MET	Methionine	VAL	Valine
GLU	Glutamic acid	PHE	Phenylalanine		

As the language of DNA is simple, so is the dictionary. In Figure 3.4 are the definitions, that is, the amino acids which are specified by each of the 64 codons. Also included in Figure 3.4 is the code for RNA which, you will recall, substitutes uracil for thymine. The DNA codon AAA, for example, specifies phenylalanine through its RNA codon UUU; the DNA codon GGG specifies proline through its RNA codon CCC, and so forth. For all but five codons there is a degeneracy in the code when several different codons specify the same amino acid. Thus, SER, LEU, and ARG are each specified by six codons, others by four, three, and two, and MET and TRP by only one. The RNA codons UAA, UAG, and UGA are "terminators," and call a halt to protein synthesis. Those of you with a knowledge or interest in molecular biology will find many interesting topics dealing with the genetic code in Vol. 31 of the *Cold Spring Harbor Symposia on Quantitative Biology* (1966).

RNA and Proteins

DNA directs protein synthesis indirectly by synthesizing complementary strands of one form of RNA, messenger RNA (mRNA), in a fashion similar to the DNA replication process. Messenger RNA differs from DNA not only in the replacement of uracil for thymine and ribose for deoxyribose, but also because it occurs as a single rather than a double strand. The synthesis of mRNA takes place in the cell nucleus by a process called **transcription.** DNA splits again at each hydrogen bond, and one strand is transcribed into mRNA by the attachment of mRNA nucleotides in the same way as DNA nucleotides are attracted in DNA duplication. Each RNA codon is, thus,

Figure 3.4 The genetic code.

Second nucleotide

First nucleotide	A or U DNA	A or U RNA	A or U AA	G or C DNA	G or C RNA	G or C AA	T or A DNA	T or A RNA	T or A AA	C or G DNA	C or G RNA	C or G AA	Third nucleotide
A or U	AAA	UUU	} PHE	AGA	UCU		ATA	UAU	} TYR	ACA	UGU	} CYS	A or U
	AAG	UUC	} PHE	AGG	UCC	} SER	ATG	UAC	} TYR	ACG	UGC	} CYS	G or C
	AAT	UUA	} LEU	AGT	UCA	} SER	ATT	UAA	} STOP	ACT	UGA	STOP	T or A
	AAC	UUG	} LEU	AGC	UCG		ATC	UAG	} STOP	ACC	UGG	TRP	C or G
G or C	GAA	CUU		GGA	CCU		GTA	CAU	} HIS	GCA	CGU		A or U
	GAG	CUC	} LEU	GGG	CCC	} PRO	GTG	CAC	} HIS	GCG	CGC	} ARG	G or C
	GAT	CUA	} LEU	GGT	CCA	} PRO	GTT	CAA	} GLN	GCT	CGA	} ARG	T or A
	GAC	CUG		GGC	CCG		GTC	CAG	} GLN	GCC	CGG		C or G
T or A	TAA	AUU		TGA	ACU		TTA	AAU	} ASN	TCA	AGU		A or U
	TAG	AUC	} ILE	TGG	ACC	} THR	TTG	AAC	} ASN	TCG	AGC	} SER	G or C
	TAT	AUA		TGT	ACA	} THR	TTT	AAA	} LYS	TCT	AGA		T or A
	TAC	AUG	MET	TGC	ACG		TTC	AAG	} LYS	TCC	AGG	} ARG	C or G
C or G	CAA	GUU		CGA	GCU		CTA	GAU	} ASP	CCA	GGU		A or U
	CAG	GUC	} VAL	CGG	GCC	} ALA	CTG	GAC	} ASP	CCG	GGC	} GLY	G or C
	CAT	GUA	} VAL	CGT	GCA	} ALA	CTT	GAA	} GLU	CCT	GGA	} GLY	T or A
	CAC	GUG		CGC	GCG		CTC	GAG	} GLU	CCC	GGG		C or G

a complement of its DNA codon. The sequence of DNA codons AAC - CCG - TTG - TTA, for example, gives rise to the mRNA codons UUG - GGC - AAC - AAU.

From the nucleus, mRNA enters the cytoplasm of the cell where it attaches to the surface of a ribosome containing ribosomal RNA (rRNA). At this stage the coded message from the original nuclear DNA is deciphered. This requires yet another form of RNA called transfer RNA (tRNA). There are more than 20 different kinds of tRNA, each of which has an attachment site specific for one of the 20 different amino acids. In this way, tRNA is responsible for transporting free amino acids to the ribosomes. Also, each tRNA possesses an anticodon that may bond temporarily to a complementary mRNA codon. As the ribosome moves along the mRNA chain, each codon is read in succession and attracts the appropriate tRNA carrying its amino acid. The amino acids are fitted together into the sequence as predetermined by the original DNA strand. As the amino acids move into position, they are joined together by peptide bonds that are formed by cellular enzymes.

This simplified summary of protein synthesis is illustrated diagrammatically in Figure 3.5. Additional information on protein synthesis and the genetic code

Figure 3.5 A graphic outline of the relationships between the nucleic acids in protein synthesis.

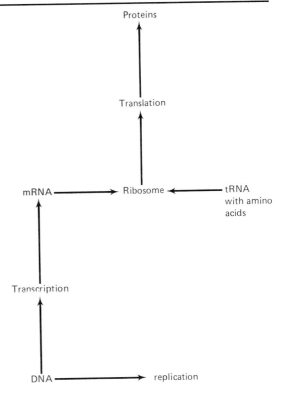

may be found in the highly readable accounts by Crick (1962, 1966), Nirenberg (1963), and Yanofsky (1967).

We have seen that combinations of the 20 amino acids are formed by peptide linkages. These combinations form long chains called **polypeptides,** or proteins, and it is difficult to overemphasize the importance of such proteins in living organisms. They serve not only as enzymes—which act as organic catalysts that play indispensable roles in nearly all of the chemical reactions that maintain life itself (e.g., temperature regulation)—but also as structural elements in the various body tissues. The organic matrix of bone and the other connective tissues, the contractile muscle fibers, the skin, hair, and nails, and other tissues are composed largely of proteins.

When the linear sequence of amino acids in a protein is altered, the protein may also be altered. As will be shown shortly, a change in a single amino acid in a polypeptide can result in a considerably different protein, sometimes with harmful results to the individual. We do not know how many different proteins comprise complex animals like ourselves—perhaps thousands or hundreds of thousands—but we do know that certain well-analyzed proteins have chemical structures that allow them to perform specific functions. The wide variation in protein function is beyond the scope of this book, but some indication can be given by a few selected examples:

1. Hemoglobin. The primary function is to transport oxygen from the lungs to the tissues, but it also binds iron.

2. Haptoglobin. Prevents hemoglobin loss and thus iron loss in urination (Allison 1958).

3. Transferrin. Binds and transports iron to the cells (Holmberg and Laurell 1945; Schade and Caroline 1946).

4. Ceruloplasmin. Stores and transports copper (Bearn 1972).

5. Carbonic anhydrase. An enzyme that increases the reaction rate between carbon dioxide (CO_2) and water. This allows blood to react with large amounts of CO_2, thus insuring an efficient transport of CO_2 from the tissues to the lungs.

6. Erythropoietin. Increases the rate of red blood cell production in the bone marrow (Guyton 1976a).

7. Fibrinogen. Reacts with yet another enzyme, thrombin, to form blood clots.

Proteins are often large and complex molecules, with molecular weights ranging from 10,000 or so into the millions. For purposes of comparison, the molecular weight of water (H_2O) is 18.015—two hydrogen atoms, each with an atomic weight of 1.00797, and one oxygen atom with an atomic weight of 15.9994. This may be contrasted with hemoglobin ($C_{3032}H_{4816}O_{872}N_{780}S_8Fe_4$) which when compared to most other proteins is a simple molecule, but whose molecular weight is approximately 66,629. The molecular weight of collagen (with over 20 times as many amino acids as hemoglobin), the principal structural protein in all vertebrates, is 300,000 or greater (Clark and Veis 1972).

We have discussed proteins as if they were long, drawn-out polypeptides because this provides an easily conceptualized model. In reality, most proteins are coiled or twisted into what is called an alpha helix. The helix is, furthermore, folded and bent so that the configuration is more spherical then spiral. These structures are brought about and maintained by hydrogen bonds that bond amino acids in different parts of the chain together.

Protein molecules are often studied, then, from the standpoint of three levels of organization. The first level is called the primary structure, the linear sequence of amino acids in the polypeptides. For some proteins the primary structure has been well defined, such as the alpha and beta chains of human hemoglobin (Fig. 3.6). In the last few years, comparisons of amino acid sequences between different species have led to new theoretical insights on molecular evolution, a subject discussed later in the book.

The next level of organization is called the secondary structure, the configuration of the protein that results from the hydrogen bonds. Most often the configuration takes the form of an alpha (a) helix, but some proteins assume a beta (β) helix and others occur as a triple helix. The β configuration occurs when adjacent polypeptides are held together by hydrogen bonds. A good example of a triple helix is bone collagen, which in its final form is a rodlike structure composed of bundles of collagen molecules. These, in turn, consist of three polypeptides interconnected by hydrogen bonds and several other chemically distinct covalent and noncovalent intrachain links (Glimcher and Katz 1965). These chains are arranged in the form of a left-handed helix (Ramachandran 1967), a number of helices joining together to form the long collagen fibril (Miller 1973).

Figure 3.6 Amino acid sequence in the normal α and β chains of human hemoglobin. The positions of amino acids are numbered sequentially from the N-terminal, and those amino acids enclosed by solid lines occupy the same relative positions in both chains. (Reprinted with permission of Macmillan Publishing Co., Inc., from *Genetics*. Copyright © 1968, 1976 by Monroe W. Strickberger.)

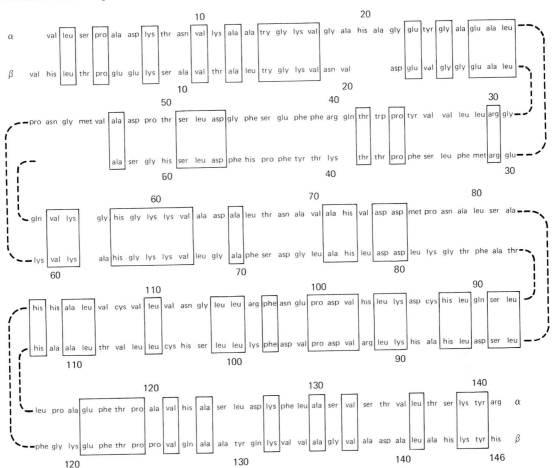

The third level of organization of proteins is the tertiary structure, the bending and folding of the helix. Most of the biologically active proteins, such as hormones and enzymes, are globular and display complex convolutions (Fig. 3.7). These bends and folds occur as a result of ionic bonds, disulfide bonds, van der Waals forces, and other interactions between closely adjacent atoms. Tertiary structures of proteins are often studied by breaking these bonds by means of artificial stimuli, such as treatment with heat, acids, or other chemicals. This effectively denatures or unfolds the polypeptides and results in a loss of the specific biological activity of the protein.

Figure 3.7 A model of the tertiary structure of human hemoglobin. (From M. F. Perutz, *The Hemoglobin Molecule.* Copyright © 1964 by Scientific American, Inc. All Rights reserved.)

Top view

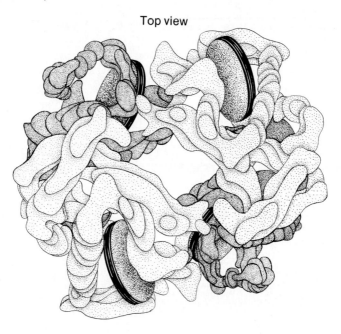

Side view

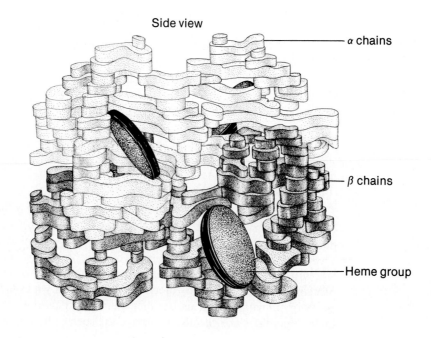

α chains

β chains

Heme group

Gene Mutations

We defined a gene previously as a segment of DNA recognizable by its specific function. Now that we have had an opportunity to discuss certain aspects of DNA, the genetic code, RNA, and proteins, are we in a better position to reevaluate this definition? If a gene is defined as a DNA segment, how much DNA is required? Is it one, two, three, or more nucleotide pairs? Is a gene a single unit that possesses the capability to serve a specific function, to recombine with other genes, to change or mutate? For human genes, we have little direct evidence helping to answer these questions. For bacterial viruses, however, Benzer (1962) has indicated that the gene as a **recombination** unit (a recon) and as a mutation unit (muton) is very small—on the order of a single nucleotide. Genes as functional units, or **cistrons** in Benzer's terminology, are much larger and may consist of hundreds of nucleotides. In other words, mutation and recombination can occur within the linear units that comprise the traditional concept of the gene. For most of the purposes in this book, the gene should be considered as a unit playing a part in the expression of some characteristic. The definition given above is quite acceptable as long as one remains at a level of integration above that of genetic fine structure.

DNA replicates itself faithfully for the most part, but mistakes do occur. The heritable changes in the sequential order of base pairs in the DNA molecule are called **gene mutations** and, as mentioned above, they may take place within a single cistron. Although nearly everything we know about gene mutations has been gained from experimental organisms rather than humans, there is no reason to believe that gene mutations in the latter behave differently than those in the former. The usual methods for detection of mutations in the fruit fly *Drosophila,* for example, cannot be used for humans because of our long generation time and reluctance to undergo breeding experiments. The detection of mutations in humans, then, is accomplished mainly through pedigree analysis (see Chapter 4). Aside from the fact that human **pedigrees** may often be suspect, due to illegitimacy, adoptions, etc., there are other problems. When a gene mutation is autosomal and recessive, it is very difficult to detect because the mutation is expressed only in the homozygous recessive state. One is never quite sure whether the homozygote was produced as a result of matings between two heterozygous parents or because of a new mutation in one of the parents.

Most of our information on human mutations has been gained from observing the sudden appearance of dominant genes. In pedigrees that have never shown a certain trait, the appearance of a new trait in an individual born to two homozygous parents without the trait may be indicative of a new mutation. This may sound like a relatively foolproof way of detecting a new dominant mutation, but there are other aspects to be considered. For the trait to be due unequivocally to a dominant mutation, it must be fully penetrant. This means that everyone with the gene will have the trait. It is a fact, however, that dominant genes do not always produce their expected phenotypic expression. When this happens, those genes are said to be imcompletely penetrant (see Chapter 4 for a discussion of **penetrance** and other aspects of gene action). A parent might therefore have a dominant gene that is not expressed and pass it on to the offspring who expresses the trait. In these cases a seemingly new dominant mutation turns out not to be a mutation at all.

The definition of a gene mutation as a change in the DNA base sequence implies that a number of different kinds of mistakes can occur. Bases may simply be deleted; a wrong base may take the place of the correct one; an additional different base may be inserted in the sequence. In any case, the genetic message is altered and, since the sequence of amino acids specified by DNA is all-important, the polypeptide resulting from a gene mutation may be altered and have different biological activity or no activity at all. As we shall see shortly, such changes have profound effects upon the normal development and health of the individual.

To illustrate a few types of mutations that may occur we may arbitrarily select the amino acid residues at positions 568 through 573 from the primary structure of the α1 chain of calf skin collagen (Hulmes et al. 1973). We have no idea of the mRNA codons involved due to degeneracy in the code and, therefore, arbitrarily assign alternative codons from Figure 3.4 to the amino acids.

Normal Sequence

DNA codons	CCC	CTG	CGA	CCT	GGT	TTT
mRNA codons	GGG	GAC	GCU	GGA	CCA	AAA
Amino acids	Gly	Asp	Ala	Gly	Pro	Lys

What would be the result if a gene mutation changed one base in the DNA codon CCC, to either CCA, CCT, or CCG? Nothing, because all four of these codons specify glycine, and the mutation would be utterly impossible to detect. But suppose that the third nucleotide in the DNA codon CTG mutated to CTT in the following manner.

Missense Substitution

DNA codons	CCC	*CTT*	CGA	CCT	GGT	TTT
mRNA codons	GGG	*GAA*	GCU	GGA	CCA	AAA
Amino acids	Gly	*Glu*	Ala	Gly	Pro	Lys

In this case, glutamic acid is specified instead of aspartic acid. The entire collagen molecule resulting from this **missense substitution** could have a significantly altered biological activity. Suppose, instead, that a change occurs in the first nucleotide of the fourth codon—from CCT to ACT—specifying a termination to protein synthesis.

Nonsense Substitution

DNA codons	CCC	CTG	CGA	*ACT*	GGT	TTT
mRNA codons	GGG	GAC	GCU	*Stop*	CCA	AAA
Amino acids	Gly	Asp	Ala	–––	–––	–––

What happens in this instance? The "Stop" codon prevents the protein from being completed. If the protein were an enzyme indispensable to a vital chemical reaction, for example, the result could be highly detrimental or even fatal.

In general, the effect of a **nonsense substitution** depends upon the position at which the mutation takes place. If the mutation occurs at the beginning of the polypeptide and prevents the synthesis of the protein, the results are likely to be more severe than if it occurs toward the end of the sequence. A mutation close to the end is more likely to produce a polypeptide which imparts a modified biological activity to the protein. It follows that the detection of nonsense substitutions, especially those at the beginning or in the middle of a genetic message, is usually a relatively simple matter owing to the incompleteness of the polypeptide released from the ribosome. This is particularly true for proteins that perform a vital function. The detection of missense substitutions, however, is more difficult because the biological activity of the completed protein may be only slightly altered.

Two other types of gene mutations involve insertions or deletions of one or two nucleotides into the sequence, thus altering all codons that follow. These mutations result in a shift of the reading frame, and are therefore called **frameshift mutations.** Recall that the normal sequence of DNA codons at the start of this discussion was

CCC   CTG   CGA   CCT   GGT   TTT.

Suppose that an extra nucleotide, G, was inserted at a point between CTG and CGA.

Frameshift Missense Insertion

DNA codons	CCC	CTG	*G*CG	ACC	TGG	TTT	T--
mRNA codons	GGG	GAC	CGC	UGG	ACC	AAA	A--
Amino acids	Gly	Asp	Arg	Trp	Thr	Lys	---

Assume, instead, that the nucleotide G in the second codon in the original sequence was deleted.

Frameshift Missense Deletion

DNA codons	CCC	CTC	GAC	CTG	GTT	TT-
mRNA codons	GGG	GAG	CUG	GAC	CAA	AA-
Amino acids	Gly	Glu	Leu	Asp	Gly	---

In the two cases above, all of the codons that follow the insertion or deletion are changed, resulting in a modified polypeptide that may have no biological activity. In a similar manner, frameshift mutations may result in nonsense insertions or deletions.

In light of the fact that the preceding types of gene mutations have been discovered by experimental studies on nonhuman organisms, it is interesting that one of the clearest demonstrations of a missense substitution occurs in humans. This involves polypeptide variations in the globin part of the hemoglobin molecule. With exception of the human blood groups, we have more information about the blood protein hemoglobin and its abnormal forms than any other genetically controlled characteristic. Over 175 different hemoglobin variants have been described, most being listed in the recent summary by Livingstone (1973).

The veritable explosion in our knowledge of the genetics of hemoglobin and other human proteins has been made possible by two biochemical techniques, **electrophoresis** and **fingerprinting.** Since these two methods are of great importance for studies in human genetics and evolution, it is desirable to outline their operation. As will become evident, one may consider electrophoresis as the method which demonstrates the existence of genetic differences in proteins, and fingerprinting as the method showing the underlying cause for the difference.

Zone electrophoresis may be defined as the movement of charged particles, suspended in a medium, under the influence of an applied electrical field (Overbeek and Lijklema 1959). Most of you may know that negatively charged particles of any kind will be attracted to a positive pole and vice versa. Proteins not only vary widely in their size and shape, but also in their net electrical charges. In addition, proteins are amphoteric. This means that they will act either as acids or bases, depending upon the pH of the medium in which they are placed. Thus the pH of the surrounding medium determines whether the net charge on a protein will be positive, negative, or zero. This may be illustrated roughly as follows. Suppose you have a protein of the type $NH_3^+ - R - COO^-$ (the symbol R represents the rest of the molecule, which need not be given here). This protein will have no net charge, because the positive charge on NH_3^+ cancels the negative charge on COO^-. If you place this protein in an alkaline, or basic medium, it will assume a net negative charge since the negative hydroxyl ions (OH^-) predominate over the positive ions.

$$NH_3^+ - R - COO^- \text{ added to } OH^- \longrightarrow NH_2 - R - COO^- + H_2O.$$

If the same protein is placed in an acidic medium, one in which there is an excess of hydrogen ions (H^+), the hydrogen ions will combine with the protein and thus impart a net positive charge.

$$NH_3^+ - R - COO^- \text{ added to } H^+ \longrightarrow NH_3^+ - R - COOH.$$

It should be evident, then, that the pH of the buffer solution, the solution added to the medium for the purpose of "carrying" the protein as it migrates, is of critical importance. Without going into detail, it has been found that buffers with pH 8.6, or slightly alkaline, are admirably suited for electrophoresis of human serum proteins.

The medium can be any of a number of substances, including cellulose acetate, starch gel, paper strips, agar gel, porous glass, and so forth. The primary function of the medium is to serve as a matrix of known density and pore size which, when mixed with the buffer, allows the proteins to migrate toward one pole or the other. It also is a structure to which the protein becomes attached upon removal of the electric field. The medium can thus be regarded as a trap in which the migrating protein can be fixed, stained, and examined after the electric current is withdrawn.

To describe this process, assume that you wish to analyze a protein by means of agar-gel electrophoresis. Agar gel may be conceptualized as a sponge with a very fine meshwork whose pores are large compared to the size of the protein. Only four basic components are needed: the medium, the buffer, a power source, and the protein or proteins to be examined (Fig. 3.8).

When proteins are placed in the buffered medium and the electric current applied, several things occur simultaneously. First, any protein with a negative charge will tend to move toward the positive pole (anode), and those with a positive charge will begin to move toward the negative pole (cathode). The agar gel also has a charge, usually negative, and there is a tendency for it also to move toward the anode. The gel is fixed, however, and cannot move. To the extent that the tendency for the reaction exists, there must be an equal and opposite reaction, according to Sir Isaac Newton's third law of motion: "To every action there is always opposed an equal reaction." The opposite reaction is provided by the buffer in the gel, a phenomenon called electroosmosis.

Since most agar gels are negatively charged, the force of the buffer is toward the cathode. If electroosmosis is minimal and the protein negatively charged, it will migrate toward the anode to a greater extent than if the force of the buffer had

Figure 3.8 The basic components used in electrophoresis.

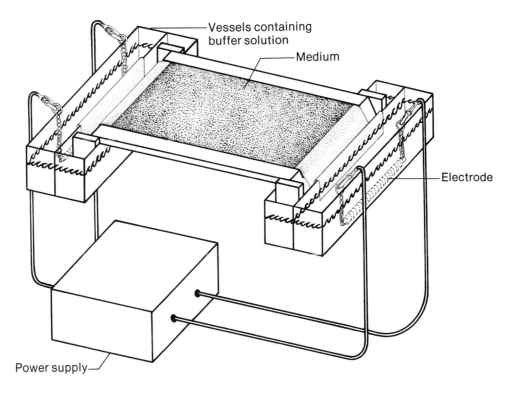

been stronger. The **electrophoretic mobility** of proteins, or the distance that they will migrate under a given set of conditions, therefore, depends upon the difference between the charge on the protein and the resistance due to electroosmosis. This is an important point because it explains why two different proteins, both with net negative charges, appear to migrate in opposite directions from a common point of origin. Suppose you have two negatively charged proteins, A and B, the former with a stronger charge than the latter. Both will be attracted to the positive pole, but if the electroosmotic force is greater than the charge on protein B, this protein will actually be carried toward the negative pole and thus appear to have migrated in a direction opposite that of protein A.

Most proteins have characteristic charges and thus characteristic electrophoretic mobilities. However, if due to a mutation an amino acid with a different charge replaces the normal amino acid in a polypeptide, the net charge of the protein and hence its mobility will also change. Likewise, if the tertiary structure of the protein is altered so that different charged groups are either hidden or exposed, the mobility may be different from the normal. Herein lies the value of electrophoresis for the study of protein differences, for these abnormal variants can be detected regardless of whether they impart any visible physical abnormalities.

Suppose now that the protein under consideration is human hemoglobin, and that you wish to determine if there is any difference between the

Figure 3.9 Red blood cells from normal, **a,** and sickle-cell, **b,** homozygotes. (Courtesy of Dr. C. L. Conley.)

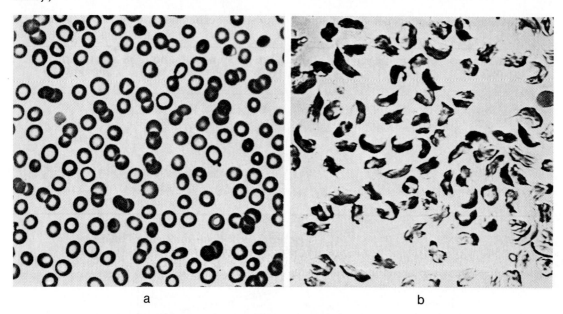

a   b

electrophoretic mobility in hemoglobin taken from normal individuals and from individuals suffering from sickle-cell anemia. In performing this experiment, you are essentially duplicating the efforts of Pauling, Itano, Singer, and Wells (1949), who demonstrated the correctness of the independently formulated hypotheses of Neel (1949) and Beet (1949).

Some individuals have red blood cells that undergo a peculiar change in shape when subjected to reduced oxygen tension. Under oxygenated conditions their red blood cells are like those of normal individuals, round and biconcave (Fig. 3.9*a*). When deoxygenated, however, they assume an elongated and irregular sickle-shaped form (Fig. 3.9*b*). These people are said to have the sickle-cell trait, and under ordinary conditions show no ill effects.

In other people, sickling of the red blood cells leads to rapid cellular destruction, called sickle-cell anemia, and to a number of other severely debilitating effects. These include circulatory disturbances, leading in turn to heart failure, brain damage, and subsequent paralysis; damage in other organs that leads to pneumonia, rheumatism, kidney failure, and poor development; and degeneration of the spleen. The sickle-cell trait and sickle-cell anemia are found primarily in populations in central Africa and in black populations elsewhere that trace their ancestry to Africa, and the frequency of sickle-cell anemia is high enough for it to be considered a significant world health problem.

Both Beet and Neel formulated the hypothesis that a mutant gene on one of the autosomes was responsible for sickling and that individuals with the trait were heterozygous for the gene. Those with sickle-cell anemia, furthermore, were homozygous for the gene. This was confirmed by Pauling and his colleagues, who

Figure 3.10 An illustration of the electrophoretic differences between normal hemoglobin, sickle-cell anemia hemoglobin, and sickle-cell trait hemoglobin. In each case, the arrow indicates the point of sample application.

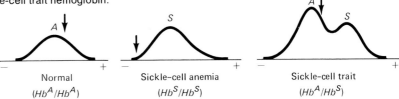

showed that the electrophoretic mobility of hemoglobin in the red blood cells differed between normal and sickle-cell anemic individuals (Fig. 3.10). In addition, they found that people with the trait possessed both the normal and abnormal hemoglobins. These were termed types A and S respectively, and the alleles (the alternative expressions of the gene) were given the designations Hb^A and Hb^S. Thus a person with the trait is genotypically Hb^A/Hb^S, and the individual with sickle-cell anemia has the Hb^S/Hb^S genotype. The following year, Itano and Neel (1950) discovered another abnormal hemoglobin, called Hb^C, an allele at the same locus as Hb^A and Hb^S. Like the sickle-cell trait, people who are heterozygous Hb^A/Hb^C have the hemoglobin C trait, and those homozygous for Hb^C are said to have the hemoglobin C disease. Fortunately, hemoglobin C in the homozygous state causes a less severe anemia than sickle-cell anemia.

Each type of hemoglobin possesses a slightly different electrophoretic mobility, indicating that each molecule has its own characteristic charge. This implies that each molecule has a structural difference, either in terms of one or more amino acid differences on one of the polypeptides or in the tertiary structure of the molecule. As seen in Figure 3.6, four polypeptides make up the hemoglobin molecule. By convention, two are called alpha (α) and the other two beta (β) chains. The two α chains are identical in their primary structure, as are the two β chains. Furthermore, each α and β chain contains 141 and 146 amino acids respectively.

Since there are many abnormal hemoglobin variants, precision in nomenclature is particularly important. Thus, human hemoglobin is designated as $\alpha_2\beta_2$, the subscripts indicating identity between the two different chains. When both contain the normal sequence of amino acids, the capital letter A is used as a superscript, and the resultant designation for normal human hemoglobin becomes $\alpha_2^A\beta_2^A$. The same notational system is used to indicate, for example, human hemoglobin in individuals with sickle-cell anemia ($\alpha_2^A\beta_2^S$), and for other abnormal variants such as hemoglobin C.

The underlying cause for the difference between the electrophoretic mobility of normal versus abnormal hemoglobin variants was discovered by Ingram (1957, 1959), who found that the difference between Hb^A and Hb^S alleles was due to a single amino acid substitution in the β-polypeptide. By the technique called fingerprinting, it was shown that Hb^S differed from Hb^A by the substitution of the amino acid valine for glutamic acid at the sixth position in one of the peptides (No. 4) of the β chain.

When a protein is analyzed by fingerprinting, it is subjected to digestion by an enzyme such as trypsin. Trypsin is secreted by the pancreas as an inactive

Figure 3.11 Chromatographic comparison of peptides produced by trypsin digestion of normal (*Hb^A*) and sickle-cell (*Hb^S*) hemoglobins, showing shift in the position of peptide 4. (Reprinted with permission of Macmillan Publishing Co., Inc., from *Genetics*. Copyright © 1968, 1976 by Monroe W. Strickberger.)

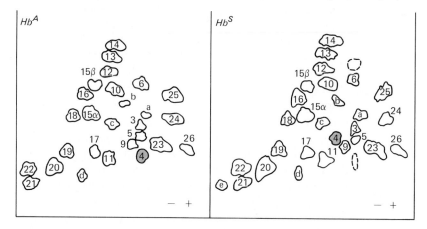

proenzyme, trypsinogen, and converted in the intestine to the active enzyme, trypsin, by another enzyme called enterokinase. The function of trypsin in the body is to attack and digest nearly all types of proteins. Trypsin digestion breaks the polypeptide at a number of separate points to produce shorter peptides. These peptides are then separated from each other in a two-dimensional manner by electrophoresis and chromatography, producing the peptide "spots" seen in Figure 3.11.

Upon examination of Figure 3.11, it should be evident that *Hb^A* and *Hb^S* are nearly identical, the most noticeable exception being in the relative position of peptide four. This is part of the β chain. When the fourth peptide, referred to as $\beta T_p I$ (Ingram 1959), was isolated in both the normal and abnormal hemoglobins and its primary structure determined, it was found that it contained eight amino acids. Furthermore, the amino acid sequence in this peptide in both types of hemoglobin was identical except for the sixth position. It was found later by the same method that the electrophoretic mobility of hemoglobin C differed from the other two because of the substitution of lysine at the same position in the β chain.

	1	2	3	4	5	6	7	8
Hb^A	val	his	leu	thr	pro	*glu*	glu	lys
Hb^S	val	his	leu	thr	pro	*val*	glu	lys
Hb^C	val	his	leu	thr	pro	*lys*	glu	lys

The differences in electrophoretic mobility are due to the charge differentials between glutamic acid (negative charge), valine (neutral), and lysine (positive charge). To return to the discussion of gene mutations, and specifically to the missense substitution, it has become abundantly clear that a change in the coding for a single amino acid in the DNA molecule is the smallest mutable unit and, thus, the smallest inheritable unit. However, it should be understood that there is nothing extraordinary about the sixth position in the β chain. Nearly all of the 175-plus abnormal hemoglobins differ in a similar fashion by a single amino acid substitution, but at other positions on both the α and β chains.

Inborn Errors of Metabolism

Gene mutations are also responsible for protein changes leading to inborn errors of metabolism. **Metabolism** is defined as "the sum of all the physical and chemical processes by which living organized substance is produced and maintained and also that transformation by which energy is made available for the uses of the organism" (*Dorland's Illustrated Medical Dictionary*, 1965). A gene mutation that causes a defect in a protein (usually an enzyme) or that alters the mechanism regulating protein synthesis will likely disrupt physical and chemical processes and result in an inherited metabolic defect. Most metabolic defects are, in turn, caused by some form of metabolic block, the loss in the ability to catalyze a reaction vital to specific developmental or physiological process.

One of the long-standing tenets of genetics is that every protein synthesized in an organism either has or has had a certain function. If this is true, then a mutation affecting the function of an enzyme will result in a loss or alteration of the specific reaction in which the enzyme plays a mediating role. The consequences of a metabolic block, of course, vary from those without any clinical significance to those that are quickly fatal.

A highly simplified but easily conceptualized model of a metabolic block may be outlined as follows:

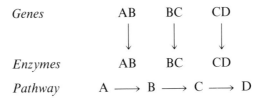

This represents three hypothetical genes that produce three enzymes, each of which is necessary for the reaction sequence from A to D. Suppose a mutation occurs in gene BC, thus deactivating enzyme BC. The result would be a blocked sequence:

$$A \longrightarrow B \not\longrightarrow C \longrightarrow D$$

A number of different results can occur from a block of this sort. For example, products C and D may be absent, and if the sequence goes beyond D, all products dependent indirectly upon the formation of C may likewise fail to develop. One of the best-known examples in humans concerns a number of disorders produced by blocks at different points in the metabolism of phenylalanine (Fig. 3.12). Phenylalanine is an amino acid whose transformation into tyrosine is mediated by the enzyme phenylalanine hydroxylase. When this enzyme is absent, phenylalanine converts, in part, to phenylpyruvic acid. These two substances accumulate and eventually lead to phenylketonuria (PKU), a disease that results in severe mental retardation. Fortunately, newborn babies can now be screened for this defect. If the tests are positive, the severe effects of the disease can be avoided by placing the infant on a dietary regime very low in phenylalanine.

In the absence of a block between phenylalanine and tyrosine, the latter, through a series of intermediate steps involving the enzyme tyrosinase, is transformed into the skin pigment, melanin. Tyrosinase deficiency (a block at this point in the pathway) leads to the absence of melanin, and resulting albinism.

Figure 3.12 Diagram of the metabolism of phenylalanine and tyrosine in man. The thickened arrows indicate the probable blocks, because of deficiency of the indicated enzyme, in several inborn errors of metabolism. In each case the normal allele is responsible for production of the enzyme, and affected individuals are homozygous for an abnormal gene which appears to be recessive to its normal allele. (From Max Levitan and Ashley Montagu, *Textbook of Human Genetics,* 2nd Ed. Copyright © 1971, 1977 by Oxford University Press, Inc. Reprinted by permission.)

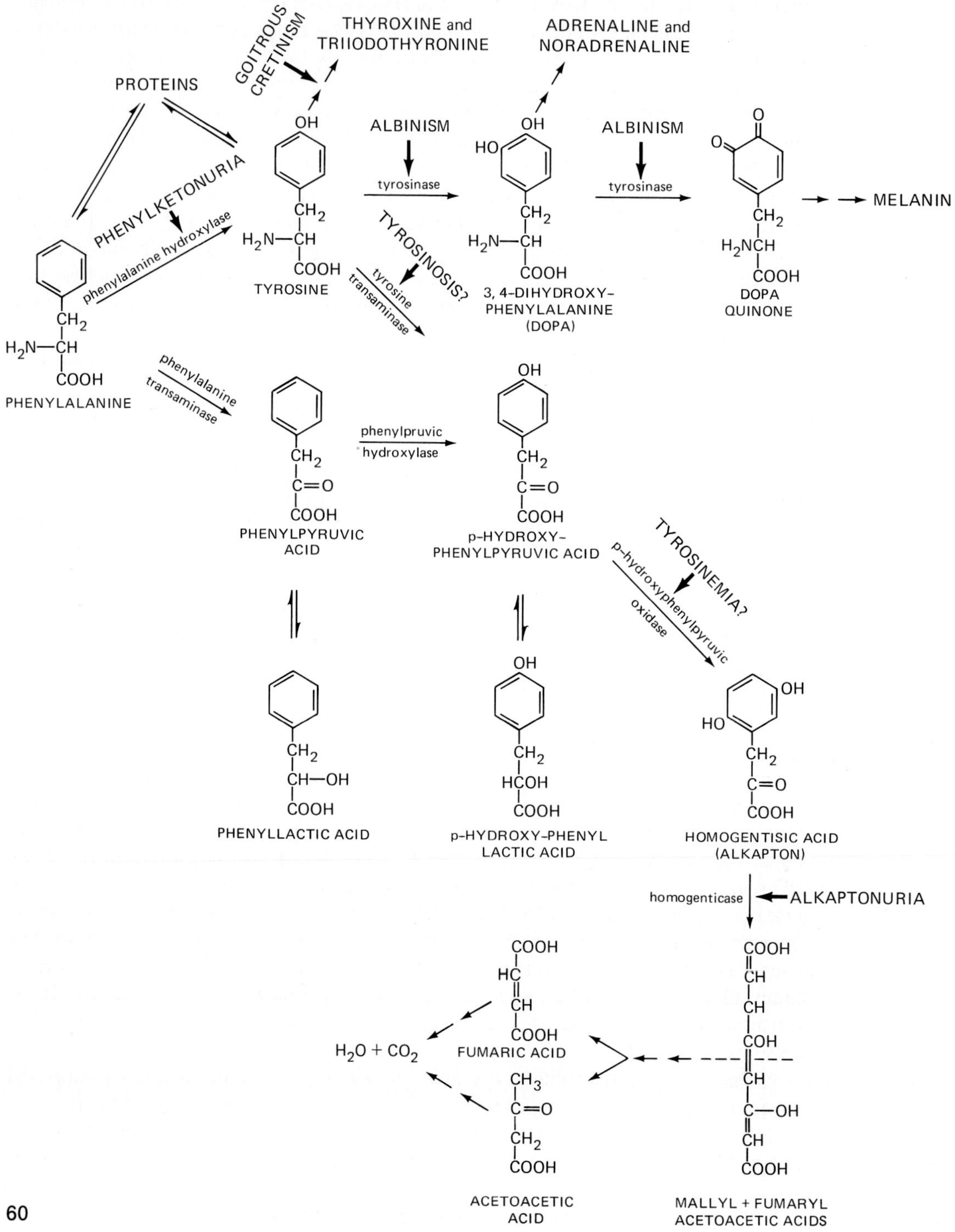

Similarly, tyrosine conversion in a different pathway to thyroxine and triiodothyronine may be blocked, leading to thyroid deficiency and goitrous cretinism. Tyrosine is normally converted by the enzyme transaminase to p-hydroxyphenylpyruvic acid and then by the action of p-hydroxyphenylpyruvic acid oxidase to homogentisic acid. A gene mutation that deactivates the enzyme p-hydroxyphenylpyruvic acid oxidase leads to tyrosinanemia, a disease characterized by severe liver damage which may be quickly fatal in infancy. Those who survive, furthermore, may have cirrhosis of the liver, resistant rickets, and other symptoms.

In the normal individual, homogentisic acid is converted to maleylacetoacetic acid by means of the catalytic action of the enzyme homogentisic acid oxidase, and through a series of steps, the final breakdown products in phenylalanine metabolism are carbon dioxide and water. But yet another metabolic block sometimes occurs between homogentisic acid and maleylacetoacetic acid, leading to a condition called alkaptonuria. Individuals with this condition are usually quite healthy, although in later life they appear to be especially prone to a certain form of arthritis.

A metabolic block between B and C in the preceding diagram can have other consequences. It can lead to an accumulation of B, the immediate precursor; it can lead to an accumulation of A, a remote precursor of the blocked reaction; or, it can lead to an accumulation of both. As the main purpose of this short discussion is to demonstrate the manner in which gene mutations can produce metabolic blocks and various inherited disorders, we shall not belabor the point by tracing more metabolic pathways. Instead, the interested reader is referred to the excellent discussions of metabolism in Sutton (1962), Harris (1975), Brock (1972), and Stanbury, et al. (1972).

What causes gene mutations? As in the brief discussion of chromosomal mutagens, nearly all gene mutation research has been performed experimentally on nonhuman organisms, and it can only be inferred that these mutagenic agents affect human DNA in a similar manner. For the most part, the mutagenic agents listed in Chapter 2 (Table 4) also produce gene mutations. More complete lists may be found in Auerbach and Kilbey (1971) and Miller and Miller (1971).

Summary

Research in biochemistry and genetics since the early 1950s has led to the undeniable conclusion that genes are composed of the nucleic acid DNA. DNA is composed of sugar molecules, phosphate groups, and four different nucleotide bases called adenine, guanine, thymine, and cytosine. Each of these bases when coupled with a sugar and phosphate group forms a nucleotide which, in addition to hundreds or thousands of other nucleotides, results in a polynucleotide chain. Since adenine and guanine in one chain always pair with thymine and cytosine, respectively, in another chain, DNA actually occurs as a double rather than a single polynucleotide chain. Furthermore, it is arranged as a double helix in which the sequential order of different nucleotides is specific for each gene. Three DNA bases together lead to complementary strands of messenger RNA which, in turn, specifies the amino acids that comprise the fundamental units of proteins.

Gene mutations occur when alterations take place in the sequential order of DNA base pairs. Such changes, among others, include the deletion of a base, substitution of a wrong base, and insertion of an additional base. While some gene mutations may be lethal or detrimental, others can theoretically result in specification of the same original amino acid and thus be completely undetectable. However, gene mutations that result in phenotypic changes are usually harmful.

Recent advances in biochemistry have led to methods for the detection of gene mutations in humans. As discovered by electrophoresis, fingerprinting, and amino-acid-sequence analysis, one of the clearest examples of such a mutation is an amino acid substitution which causes a change in the hemoglobin molecule that leads to sickle-cell anemia. Other gene mutations are responsible for inborn errors of metabolism. These metabolic defects often arise upon the alteration of an enzyme that is a necessary catalyst in a certain chemical reaction vital to a specific developmental or physiological process.

4 Gene Interaction and Human Inheritance Patterns

Introduction

Geneticists who study the course of a gene or genes through several generations have relied traditionally upon organisms such as fruit flies, small mammals, certain plants, and various kinds of bacteria. The advantages of utilizing these sorts of organisms in basic genetic research are numerous: they have short generation intervals, their matings can often be controlled according to the wishes of the investigator, they can be raised under ecologically controlled conditions, and they can be grown in large numbers.

Human families and human populations, conversely, possess none of these qualifications. However, extrapolations from the results of experimental genetics to humans and subsequent observation and study of human family histories have demonstrated beyond doubt that most of the basic rules of inheritance are shared by most living organisms. The study of human pedigrees has always been less precise than analogous investigations on experimentally controlled laboratory populations, but the analysis of innumerable human pedigrees has provided a great deal of informative and invaluable data about human genetics.

Phenotypic Expression of Genes

Before discussing human inheritance patterns, it is useful to review a few fundamental concepts about gene action. These concepts, like those outlined at the conclusion of Chapter 2, have led to several terms that form part of the common genetic vocabulary.

Among others, G. R. Fraser has emphasized the point that it is "a truism to say that a mutant allele is not dominant or recessive as the case may be; the qualification properly belongs to its effects" (1972:645). Although this is worth repeating periodically, it is not a new concept. It has been known for many years that alleles of a gene are not inherently dominant or recessive. Rather, the terms "dominant" and "recessive" refer to the phenotypic state produced by certain alleles. To state that allele A is dominant over allele a, in other words, means that the heterozygote Aa will possess whatever characteristic is determined by A. Referring to alleles as dominant or recessive (or by other terms discussed below) is only a shorthand way of expressing the effect that an allele has on the phenotype.

A dominant allele, therefore, is one that usually manifests itself phenotypically when in either homozygous or heterozygous form. A recessive allele, conversely, manifests itself phenotypically only when the dominant allele is absent. Sometimes, however, two alleles at homologous loci are both represented phenotypically, as in the heterozygote of the MN blood group system. In this case, three genotypes, $L^M L^M$, $L^M L^N$, and $L^N L^N$ (the capital letter L denotes the discoverer of the MN system, Dr. Karl Landsteiner) and three distant phenotypes, M, MN, and N, will result from the two alleles. Since both alleles express themselves phenotypically in the heterozygous state, they are said to be co-dominant. In other cases, homologous loci may be occupied by any of several different alleles, as in the ABO blood group system. In this system, the alleles I^A and I^B (the capital letter I stands for isoagglutinogen, a normally occurring antigen) are co-dominant, and both are dominant to I^O. Thus the three alleles can produce six genotypes ($I^A I^A$, $I^A I^O$, $I^B I^B$, $I^B I^O$, $I^A I^B$, and $I^O I^O$) but only four phenotypes (A, B, AB, and O).

There is rarely a clear demarcation between dominance and recessiveness, because characterizations of the phenotype may be changed as new information emerges. The genetics of sickle-cell anemia and sickle-cell trait illustrate this point quite well. It was shown in the last chapter that $Hb^A Hb^A$ homozygotes are normal, $Hb^A Hb^S$ heterozygotes have the sickle-cell trait, and $Hb^S Hb^S$ homozygotes have sickle-cell anemia. If the phenotype is described by the presence or absence of sickle-cell anemia, then inheritance of the Hb^S allele can be explained as a simple Mendelian recessive (as Neel originally suggested in 1949).

Since heterozygotes have the sickle-cell trait but not anemia, Hb^A could be described as an incomplete dominant because it does not completely mask the effects of Hb^S (McKusick 1969). However, electrophoretic methods have shown that heterozygotes possess nearly (up to 40%) equal amounts of both hemoglobins. If this criterion is used to describe the phenotype, then Hb^A and Hb^S can be described as two co-dominant alleles (Stern 1973). It is important to realize that it is often quite difficult to distinguish between incomplete dominance and co-dominance because different alleles manifest themselves in various gradations.

Until now, alleles have been discussed as if they had one clear, conspicuous phenotypic effect. However, it is not uncommon for some alleles to have more than one effect on the phenotype. This phenomenon is termed **pleiotropism.** As an example, in 1962 (Field, et al.; Gerritsen, et al.) a substance called homocystine was detected in the urine of children who were mentally retarded and afflicted with other abnormalities. This defect, called homocystinuria, is caused by a deficiency of the enzyme cystathionine synthetase (Uhlendorf and Mudd 1968). The defect occurs from a block in the metabolic pathway involved with the conversion of methionine to cysteine (Harris 1975) and is inherited as a simple autosomal recessive. Although an excess of urinary homocystine is a diagnostic feature of this disease, a wide range of additional phenotypic abnormalities are observed to vary between affected individuals. A few examples include scoliosis (an abnormal curvature of the vertebral column), enlarged liver, mild to severe mental retardation, and a number of eye defects (myopia, glaucoma, cataracts, etc.). In this case, and for nearly all other known metabolic defects, pleiotropism refers to the multiple symptomatic manifestations of a single allele.

Not all individuals with homocystinuria possess the full range of abnormalities given above, nor do the abnormalities always assume the same form. Some individuals may be more mentally retarded than others; some may and others may not have scoliosis or enlarged livers, and so forth. In other words, individuals with the same genetic defect may react to this defect in different ways. When this occurs, the gene (or trait) is said to show variable **expressivity.** In other genetic disorders, some individuals with the requisite genotype fail to show any of the expected phenotypic effects. The gene is then described as incompletely penetrant because we cannot detect with available methods the "penetration" of the gene products into the phenotype. The degree of penetrance is usually expressed quantitatively as the percentage of individuals with a particular gene who also have its associated trait. To say that gene A is 95% penetrant means conversely that 5% of the individuals with the gene will not show the trait.

We have seen above that some differences in genetic interpretation can arise for the inheritance of Hb^S because of phenotypic definition. There is even more ambiguity in calculating levels of penetrance for various alleles, especially if penetrance is defined as the appearance of *any* of the phenotypic manifestations of an allele. As new refinements are developed in the methods for detecting gene products, levels of penetrance are bound to change.

Variable expressivity and penetrance reflect the generally accepted conclusion that the development of phenotypic traits either depends upon, or is influenced by, genes at other loci (in addition, of course, to external environmental variables). The "genetic environment" or "genetic background," as it is sometimes called, may be as critical for the development of a phenotypic trait as the responsible gene itself. Genes that indirectly influence the expression of other, or "main" genes, are often referred to loosely as genetic modifiers. Although little definitive evidence has been gained about modifiers in humans, there is at least one well-known example of a gene that inhibits the reaction of another gene. Such a gene is called a suppressor, and the example referred to is called the "Bombay" phenotype. Further comments about this condition are deferred until later in this chapter (see "The ABO Blood Groups") because additional background information is necessary for an adequate discussion.

Linkage and Recombination

It was shown in Chapter 2 that genes on different chromosomes assort independently of each other. However, genes on the same chromosome do not follow this rule because (barring recombination and chromosomal mutations) the integrity of chromosomes is maintained during meiosis. Genes on the same chromosome are often linked together, and one might therefore expect that offspring would receive intact from their parents some of these combinations of linked genes. Herein lies one of the major reasons for searching for linkage relationships. If a particular genetic disorder in a certain family is closely linked to an apparently unrelated subclinical defect or to a normal variant, then the latter might be used to predict the onset of the former in related individuals. In a few instances, as will be outlined later, genes appear to be so closely linked that they are inherited together most of the time.

However, the observation that children always differ from their parents (and from their sibs) in innumerable characteristics suggests the operation of other factors. After all, given the fact that we have only 23 pairs of chromosomes, how is it possible that no two children from the same parents (barring identical twins) are ever genetically identical? This is assured mostly by recombination, or crossing over, a meiotic process during which parts of paired maternal and paternal homologous chromosomes are exchanged.

When homologous chromosomes begin to synapse, they are characterized by areas of attachment to each other at certain points along their lengths. These points are called chiasmata (singular, **chiasma**), and indicate the points of exchange of chromatid segments (Fig. 4.1). Crossing over between chromatids may occur at two or more places and, thus, a number of double or triple crossovers may involve two, three, or all four chromatids (Fig. 4.2).

Ernst Mayr has stated that " . . . recombination is . . . the most important source of genetic variation" (1963:179). A few very conservative figures from Stern (1973) might assist in an appreciation of the meaning of Mayr's statement. If an individual has 23 chromosome pairs, and if each pair is marked *only* by one different pair of alleles, then by segregation the total number of different kinds of gametes would be 2^{23}, or 8,388,608. This number may seem large, but it is an infinitesimal fraction of the number of possible combinations when recombination is considered. If it is assumed that 10% of our loci are heterozygous (a very conservative estimate!), and that our chromosome set contains *only* 10,000 loci, then 9,000 of the genes will be common to both mother and father. In other words, 1,000 of the loci would be characterized by different alleles contributed by the parents.

Dividing this by 23, an average of roughly 40 different loci would be heterozygous on each of the 23 chromosome pairs. If only single crossovers were allowed, the gametes in any individual could contain 80 different combinations for any single pair of chromosomes. If it is further assumed that crossing over in one pair of chromosomes is unrelated to that in a different pair, and that each pair of chromosomes segregates independently of other pairs, then the product of the combinations in each of the 23 pairs gives the total number of possible combinations. Thus, under these assumptions the number—80^{23}—represents a minimal estimate, since only single crossovers were considered. Compared to the previous figure (8,388,608), the number $80^{23} = (8,388,608)^3 \times 10^{23}$. The magnitude of this number is virtually impossible to appreciate, and the probability that two identical gametes (and hence two genetically identical individuals) will ever be independently formed is vanishingly remote.

The genetics of **linkage** in humans, compared to our knowledge of linkage genetics in experimental organisms, is still largely unknown. The findings on crossing over in other animals, plants, and microorganisms, however, suggest strongly that most living organisms, including humans, share a number of common features. First, the actual genotypic construction has nothing to do with the occurrence of crossing over. It can occur, for example, between double homozygotes (AB/AB or ab/ab) or between double heterozygotes (Ab/aB or AB/ab). The latter, however, are able to produce new combinations of these loci and, hence, observable crossovers.

Second, the double heterozygotes AB/ab and Ab/aB represent two structural phases. The double-dominant and double-recessive combination AB/ab is often said to be in the "cis" or "coupling" phase, and the mixed dominant-recessive combination Ab/aB is called the "trans" or "repulsion" phase. Third, in both phases the frequency of crossing over is about equal. It is usually measured by determining

Figure 4.1 Synapsis, crossing over, and chiasma formation: **a,** tetrad with four chromatids in synapsis; **b,** chiasma formed as chromosomes separate after crossing over; **c,** resulting chromosomes after crossing over and the disappearance of the chiasma. (From Paul Amos Moody, *The Genetics of Man.* 2nd Ed., with the permission of W. W. Norton and Co., Inc. Copyright © 1967, 1975 by W. W. Norton and Co., Inc.)

Figure 4.2 Double crossing over: **a,** two strands; **b,** three strands; **c,** four strands. Note that the two-strand double crossing over results in two chromosomes that have undergone two exchanges and two chromosomes that have undergone no exchanges; that the three-strand double crossing over results in four chromosomes that had undergone *1, 2, 1,* and no exchanges, respectively; and that the four-strand double crossing over results in four chromosomes, each of which has undergone one exchange only. (From Curt Stern, *Principles of Human Genetics.* 3rd Ed. W. H. Freeman and Co. Copyright © 1973.)

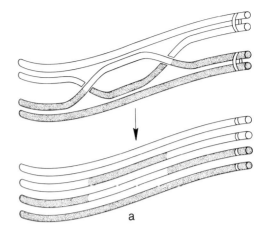

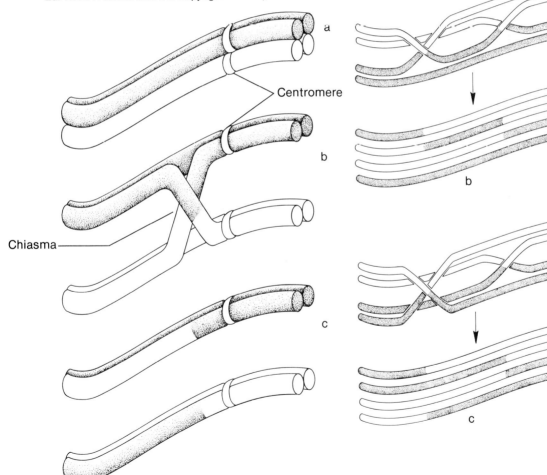

Centromere

Chiasma

67

the number of recombinant loci and expressing this number as a percentage of the parental loci. Thus, a crossing over frequency of 25% between two loci means that we expect 25% of the gametes to have new crossover combinations and, conversely, 75% to represent the original combinations. In general, the extent to which crossing over occurs between two loci is a function of the distance between the loci on the chromosomes. Linkage, therefore, is sometimes expressed in terms of loci that are very close together (close linkage), those that are separated by intermediate distances (moderate linkage), and those that are separated by relatively great distances (loose linkage). The genetic consequences are different for all three situations.

Loci that are very closely linked generally produce few recombinants, and when the linked genes are so close that recombinants cannot be found, linkage is virtually indistinguishable from allelism. One of the better-known examples in humans concerns a long-standing controversy as to whether the antigens in the Rh blood group systems are controlled genetically by a series of **multiple alleles** at a single locus (Wiener 1961) or by a series of closely linked genes (Race and Sanger 1975). As both points of view will be scrutinized later, it need only be mentioned now that the argument will be resolved if and when crossing over between the hypothesized linked genes is demonstrated. Unequivocal evidence of such a crossover has not yet been found, although Steinberg (1965) found one case in which either a crossover or a new mutation offers the best explanation.

Because the demonstration of autosomal linkage in humans is of great importance to clinical genetics, a number of investigators have attempted to develop different methods for linkage detection. Examples of these may be found in Haldane (1934, 1946), Fisher (1935), Penrose (1953), Smith (1953), and Ott (1974). In recent years, the Lod Score method has perhaps been the most rewarding technique. The mathematical formulation of this method is beyond our present scope, but those who are interested may find its full description in Morton (1955, 1957).

Until about 1961, very few autosomal linkages in humans had been confirmed. Those that had been found all involved substances in the blood, including blood group antigens, serum proteins, and red cell enzymes. These substances have well-established inheritance patterns and readily serve as genetic "markers" which can be identified with relative ease and high confidence. Thus the ABO blood group locus showed a close linkage to the nail-patella syndrome (Renwick and Lawler 1955) to xeroderma pigmentosum (El-Hefnawi et al. 1965), and to the enzyme adenylate kinase (Rapley et al. 1968).

In 1951, Mohr began the work that eventually demonstrated linkage between the Lutheran (*Lu*) blood group locus and the secretor (*Se*) locus. The secretor gene determines the presence of a water soluble antigen which is found in nearly all of the body fluids and organs, but not in the red blood cells or serum. Somewhat later (Renwick et al. 1971), this linkage was extended to include the locus (*Du*) responsible for myotonic dystrophy, a disease characterized by a slow but progressive muscular atrophy. This led Renwick (1971) to suggest the possibility that in families of myotonic dystrophy, determination of the secretor genotype in a fetus at a very early stage would aid considerably in genetic counseling of the parents. Yet another blood group, Duffy (*Fy*), was closely linked to a rare dominant disorder of the eye called congenital zonular pulverulent cataract (Renwick and Lawler 1963).

Among the serum proteins, the iron-binding beta-globulin transferrin (*Tf*) is closely linked to the red cell enzyme pseudocholinesterase (E_1) locus (Robson et al. 1966), and albumin (*Alb*) to the locus controlling the group-specific component (*Gc*) (Weitkamp et al. 1966). Many more linkages have been confirmed or tentatively identified since about 1970, most of which are between loci for various enzymes. A recent listing of these, including assignments of the various loci to their respective chromosomes when possible, may be found in McKusick and Chase (1973). Our understanding of linkage in humans has also been enhanced, albeit in a negative way, by a number of recent studies (e.g., Chautard-Freire-Maia 1974; Ott et al. 1974) which have demonstrated the absence of linkages between a wide variety of genetic markers.

Pedigree Analysis

Suspicions of linkage between the loci for two traits frequently arise as a result of examining a pedigree. Throughout the history of genetics, pedigree analysis has been a time-honored method for drawing inferences about the inheritance of certain traits. A pedigree is a graphic representation of the individuals belonging to two or more generations in a kindred (or family), and the individuals in the pedigree are identified by (1) sex, (2) generational affiliation, and (3) their relationship to the trait under study. At first glance, the pedigrees encountered in a scientific periodical such as *The American Journal of Human Genetics* might lead to the conclusion that there are no universally accepted rules on pedigree construction and nomenclature. This is to some extent true, but most pedigrees have a number of similar features. Some of the generally accepted conventions may be outlined by listing a few rules and constructing a hypothetical pedigree in the following manner.

    1. Pedigree analysis usually begins with the person who has the trait. This person is called the **proband,** or propositus (if female, proposita), and may be marked by an arrow. Males are denoted by a square, females by a circle. When the trait is present in the individual, the square or circle may be blackened; otherwise, it is left open.

    2. When a mating is encountered, males are placed on the left, females on the right, and a horizontal line is drawn connecting the two. Offspring are denoted by a vertical line as follows:

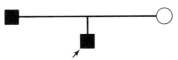

    3. Brothers and sisters, or sibs of the proband, are indicated in chronological order of birth from the left, if possible.

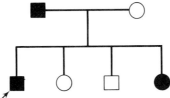

4. The appropriate symbols for sex are used for the designation of **monozygotic** (identical) and **dizygotic** (fraternal) twins as illustrated below for III 1-2 and III 3-4 respectively.

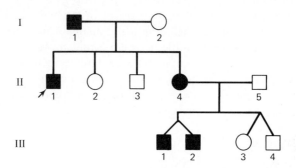

5. Finally, each generation is numbered consecutively from the top by roman numerals, and each individual in every generation is numbered consecutively from the left by arabic numerals as indicated above. In this fashion, every individual can be readily identified without use of his or her actual name. In the last pedigree above, for example, the monozygotic twins of the proband's sister (II-4) are referred to as III-1 and III-2.

Many other devices are commonly used to indicate individuals with combinations of different traits or different manifestations of a certain disorder. For example, an investigator might have a special purpose that requires separation of three forms of a particular disease. The choice of symbols is arbitrary, but this could be accomplished by denoting the affected individuals as follows:

For these, and for individuals who are denoted as having multiple traits, a legend explaining each symbol must be included with the pedigree.

Single Locus Autosomal Dominance

The inheritance pattern of single locus autosomal dominant genes is often called simple dominance and has several general characteristics. These can be described with reference to Figure 4.3, a very large, seven-generation pedigree of Mackinder's brachydactyly (Battle et al. 1974). The condition is transmitted as a fully penetrant autosomal dominant with variable expressivity. The primary phenotypic characteristics include shortened middle segments and strikingly reduced or absent distal segments of the fingers, abnormalities of the nails and unusual fingerprint patterns, and bony variations in the toes. The individuals in this pedigree were found normal in health and intelligence, and the degree of physical impairment was surprisingly slight.

The first generalization about simple dominance is that the trait appears in each generation. Barring mutation, the offspring will not have the trait unless it also appears in one or both parents. Conversely, two normal parents can produce only normal offspring. Second, the trait is expected, on the average, to appear in equal frequency in males and females. The pedigree in Figure 4.3 satisfies this expectation. In Table 4.1 are the numbers of normal $(+/+)$ and affected $(Bd/+)$ offspring of

Figure 4.3 Pedigree of Mackinder's brachydactyly in a seven-generation Ontario kindred. ♂, male (+/+); ♀ female (+/+); ♂, male (Bd/+); ♀, female (Bd/+). (Courtesy of Battle et al., *Ann. Hum. Genet.* 36: 415–424, 1973.)

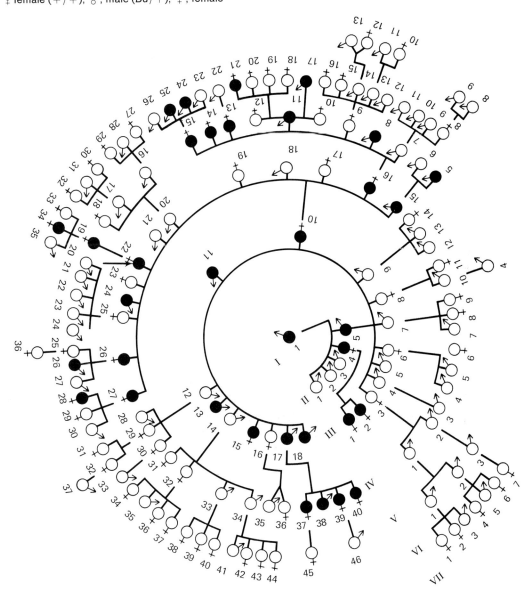

affected males and females. In no instance is there a significant difference between the numbers of affected versus normal offspring from affected males or females.

In the case of a rare dominant, the great majority of individuals with the trait will be heterozygous. In accordance with Mendelian rules, matings between heterozygotes and normal individuals will be expected to produce half normal and half affected offspring.

Table 4.1 Comparison of Numbers of Normal ($+/+$) and Affected ($Bd/+$) Offspring from Parents with Mackinder's Brachydactyly (From Battle et al. 1974). The first two comparisons involve the number of affected and nonaffected offspring of both sexes from affected males and females respectively. The third is a comparison of the total number of affected and nonaffected males and females from affected parents.

Genotypes of Offspring	Offspring of $Bd/+$ Males (1)		Offspring of $Bd/+$ Females (2)		Total (3)		Grand Total
	♂	♀	♂	♀	♂	♀	
$Bd/+$	8	7	6	13	14	20	34
$+/+$	10	7	11	9	21	16	37
Totals	18	14	17	22	35	36	71

(1) $\chi^2 = 0.10$, with ldf, $P > 0.5$
(2) $\chi^2 = 2.17$, with ldf, $P > 0.1$
(3) $\chi^2 = 1.72$, with ldf, $P > 0.1$

Single Locus Autosomal Recessiveness

It has already been shown that simple recessive traits will appear only in the homozygote. Thus two parents, both of whom are homozygous recessive (e.g., $aa \times aa$) will produce only type a sperm and ova and consequently all offspring will be aa. Matings between aa and Aa heterozygotes will, on the average, give rise to $1/2$ aa offspring, while matings between two heterozygotes will produce $1/4$ aa offspring.

Pedigrees of simple recessive traits, therefore, not only outline the inheritance of the recessive allele but are also associated with the allele frequency in the population and the extent of mating between relatives (see Chapters 5 and 7). This is because the frequency with which the recessive allele is in the heterozygous or homozygous form is a function of its frequency in the population. If the recessive trait is rare, then the frequency of Aa individuals will be uncommon and the frequency of aa persons even more rare. Thus few matings will occur between these two types of individuals. When aa and AA genotypes occasionally mate, only Aa offspring will result. When these offspring mate, again mostly to AA individuals, half of their progeny will be heterozygous and all will be phenotypically normal. In this fashion the recessive allele may not express itself for generations, and we may be totally unaware of its existence. Thus, whereas dominant alleles are expressed phenotypically in every generation in a pedigree, recessive alleles often skip generations. A pedigree of one type of albinism, a trait dependent on a recessive allele, is given in Figure 4.4.

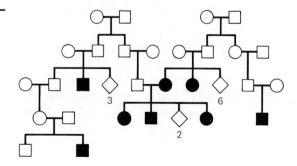

Figure 4.4 Recessive inheritance of albinism in the Hopi Indians. (From C. M. Woolf and F. C. Dukepoo, Hopi Indians, Inbreeding, and Albinism, *Science*. 164: 30–37, Fig. 9, 4 April 1969. Copyright 1969 by the American Association for the Advancement of Science.)

Sex-Linked Inheritance

Simple autosomal dominant and recessive traits are not associated with the sex of the individual, because the alleles responsible for such traits are located on any of the 22 autosomes. The term **sex-linked** is used to denote the inheritance of traits whose loci are on either the X- or Y-chromosome, but it does not imply that these alleles are related in any way to the development of the many features that distinguish males from females.

We have already seen that females have two X-chromosomes and males an X and a Y. The term **heterogametic** may be used to designate an individual with a single X-chromosome, and **homogametic** to the XX condition. The heterogametic sex is called **hemizygous** for X-chromosomal genes that have no homologous alleles on the Y-chromosome. Evidently, only small parts, if any, of the X- and Y-chromosomes have any synaptic affinity during meiosis and, thus, only a few homologous loci exist. Genes thought to be at these loci have been called partially, or incompletely, sex-linked, but attempts to demonstrate the existence of traits controlled by such genes have been equivocal. Morton (1957), for example, has shown that several traits which were supposed to be partially sex-linked can be adequately explained by autosomal inheritance.

That nonhomologous genes are located on both the X- and Y-chromosomes is not in doubt. The variety of sex chromosome karyotypes (see Chapter 2) with a Y-chromosome, produced by primary or secondary nondisjunction, are male. Those with no Y-chromosome in any combination appear to be female. From this it can be inferred that the Y-chromosome possesses genetic material associated with male characteristics. Since the normal female has no Y-chromosome, the genetic material on it is exclusively male and is said to be holandric.

In principle, **holandric inheritance** should be the simplest pattern to detect. Since only males have the Y-chromosome, the trait should be found only in males. If the gene is fully penetrant, furthermore, it would be expressed phenotypically in every male in the kindred. It is interesting, however, that holandric inheritance has yet to be demonstrated in humans. The only possibility is a trait called hairy pinnae, or hypertrichosis of the ear, in which individuals possess long, rather stiff hairs on the rims of the ears (Dronamraju 1960). Even in this instance, however, there is some doubt of Y-linkage (Stern et al. 1964). In light of the absence of demonstrated Y-linked traits in mammals (Moody 1975), including those that have served for years as experimental animals in genetic research, it may be assumed that phenotypic traits associated with Y-linked genes are quite rare.

The same cannot be said for X-linked genes. In 1971, McKusick listed 86 confirmed and 64 suspected X-linked traits. These numbers increased in two years (McKusick and Chase 1973) to 92 and 65 respectively, and over 100 have now been confirmed (McKusick 1974). Like autosomal inheritance patterns, pedigrees of X-linked traits indicate both dominant and recessive inheritance and include both common and rare traits.

A female may be homozygous or heterozygous for a given X-linked gene because she has two X-chromosomes. But the hemizygous male, having only a single X-chromosome, expresses the trait because there is no homologous allele on his Y-chromosome. Obviously, sons receive their Y-chromosome from their fathers and their X-chromosome from their mothers, while daughters receive an X-chromosome

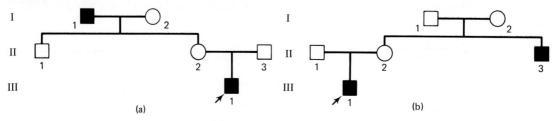

Figure 4.5 Two hypothetical pedigrees of X-linked recessive inheritance.

(a)

(b)

from each parent. If a father possesses an X-linked trait, therefore, he transmits this to his daughter rather than his son. Thus, the definitive feature of X-linked inheritance is the absence of father-to-son transmission.

The definitive features of X-linked recessive inheritance are fairly straightforward. Suppose a trait is due to the X-linked recessive allele *a*, which occurs at a low frequency in a population. The heterozygous *Aa* females will on the average transmit an *a* to half their sons, who express the trait. The females will also transmit an *a* to half their daughters, most of whom will be *Aa* since they receive an *A* from their fathers. Thus there will be more affected males than females, in addition to the occurrence of the trait in alternate generations. In other words, this pattern goes from an affected father to a heterozygous daughter to an affected grandson (Fig. 4.5*a*). Although this is a common pattern, males with an X-linked recessive trait may be related in other ways as well. In the pedigree in Figure 4.5*b*, for example, the proband is the nephew of another affected male who received the allele from the proband's maternal grandmother.

One of the better known examples of rare X-linked recessive trait is hemophilia A, or classic hemophilia (Fig. 4.6). This is a disease characterized by a blood coagulation defect and subsequent prolonged bleeding time. The **coagulation** of blood is a complex process requiring at least 13 different substances. The genetic defect in hemophilia A is responsible for either a nonfunctional form or a deficiency in one of the substances, called Factor VIII. For a full discussion of this and other coagulation disorders, see Denson (1972).

X-linked dominant traits are far less common than recessives, but the rules for their inheritance are similar. Female heterozygotes as well as males will express an X-linked dominant trait, and more females than males will be affected. Affected fathers, of course, cannot pass the trait to their sons but will always transmit it to their daughters. Regardless of sex, half of the offspring from a heterozygous mother will, on the average, express the trait.

One of the best-known X-linked traits is a deficiency in the enzyme **glucose-6-phosphate dehydrogenase** (G6PD). The enzyme itself catalyzes the oxidation of glucose-6-phosphate to 6-phosphogluconate, one step in the pentose shunt metabolic pathway described in detail by Giblett (1969) and Harris (1975). Progress toward the genetic explanation of G6PD deficiency began when it was observed that the red blood cells in a number of American blacks were destroyed (**hemolysis** occurred) upon administration of primaquine, an anti-malarial drug. Dern and his colleagues (1954) showed that these individuals had an inherited red blood cell

Figure 4.6 The pedigree of a kindred with hemophilia A (classic hemophilia). Some females were affected (e.g., III 1) and there is apparent male-to-male transmission. However, affected males such as III 4 received the hemophilia gene from the carrier mother. (From Victor A. McKusick, *Human Genetics.* 2nd Ed., 1969. Prentice-Hall, Inc., Englewood Cliffs, N. J. Based on L. Gilchrist, *Proc. Roy. Soc. Med.* 54:813, 1961.)

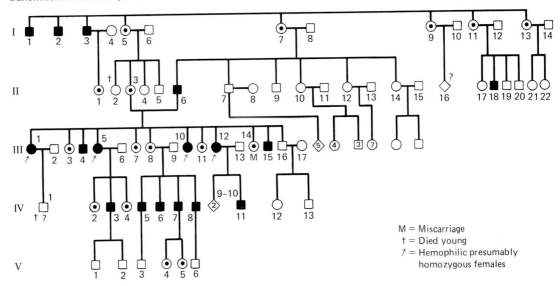

M = Miscarriage
† = Died young
↗ = Hemophilic presumably homozygous females

abnormality, and two years later (Carson et al. 1956) the abnormality was associated causally with a deficiency of G6PD. Shortly thereafter, several investigators (e.g., Szeinberg et al. 1958) independently found that a different form of G6PD deficiency was responsible for a disease called favism. This is an acute hemolytic anemia, most often present in Middle Eastern and Mediterranean populations, brought about by ingestion of fava beans (or inhalation of the plant pollen) and certain drugs.

Since the late 1950s, an enormous amount of work has clarified the geographical distribution and biochemical basis of the disease. It is the most common genetically determined enzyme abnormality known, affecting over 100 million males (Motulsky et al. 1971), and it reaches frequencies as high as 70% in a population in Northern Iraq (Szeinberg 1963). Over 100 different G6PD variants have been described (Livingstone 1973), and the agents causing hemolysis in G6PD-deficient people now include a wide variety of both anti-malarial and anti-bacterial drugs.

Systems of Multiple Alleles

Inheritance patterns of two alleles at a single locus have occupied most of our attention until now. At the beginning of this chapter, however, it was mentioned that some genes regularly appear in more than two allelic forms, as in the ABO blood group system. When a gene may assume more than two allelic forms, the group of these alleles is called a multiple allelic system.

Without doubt, the most thoroughly investigated multiple allelic systems concern certain substances in the blood, and the genetics of a few of these will be examined in this section. You should bear in mind that no new rules of transmission must be learned to understand the genetics of multiple alleles. As an alternative expression of a gene, any allele of a group of multiple alleles at a single locus is subject to the rules discussed earlier. The number of possible genotypic combinations, of course, increases as the number of alleles increases. We have already seen that only three genotypes are possible when a gene has only two alleles, namely the two homozygotes and the heterozygote. For most multiple allelic systems, the number of possible genotypes can be determined by substituting the number of alleles at the locus (n) into the equation.

$$\frac{1}{2}(n^2 + n).$$

The possible number of genotypes in a three-allele system is thus $1/2 (3^2 + 3) = 6$; for five alleles $1/2 (5^2 + 5) = 15$; and so forth.

The ABO Blood Groups

Blood contains a variety of suspended particles. Within a fluid composed of water, salts, carbohydrates, dissolved gases, and proteins are the red and white cells and the **platelets,** which are highly modified white cells. The red and white cells are called **erythrocytes** and **leukocytes** respectively, and the platelets are sometimes referred to as **thrombocytes.** One cubic millimeter of normal human blood contains approximately 4,500,000 to 5,500,000 erythrocytes, 5,000 to 8,000 leukocytes, and 300,000 thrombocytes. Several functions of these and other blood substances have been identified, but a great deal has yet to be learned about the functions of all constituents of the blood.

Several of the different kinds of leukocytes (Carpenter 1965), for example, counteract the effects of injury and invading disease organisms. By their role in clot formation, thrombocytes assist in sealing injured areas and preventing excessive blood loss. Many proteins in the blood have specific capacities to bind certain minerals and other substances for transport to and usage by cells—e.g., ceruloplasmin and copper, transferrin and iron, the hemoglobin heme group and oxygen. Others appear to have **antibody** functions including the various classes of immunoglobulins. Giblett (1969) should be consulted for a lucid description of these known functions.

In freshly drawn blood, the fluid may be separated from the cells by allowing a clot to form at room temperature and then removing it. This leaves a slightly opaque, straw-colored solution called the serum. When whole blood is treated with an anti-coagulant chemical, such as heparin, and the cells removed by centrifugation, the remaining fluid is called the plasma. Plasma is serum that contains fibrinogen, one of the proteins involved in the clotting process. By rather simple methods, then, the cells and proteins may be separated and studied independently.

When one individual's erythrocytes are mixed with another individual's serum—a process called cross-matching—one of two phenomena will occur. Either the cells will disperse in the serum, meaning that the mixture is compatible, or the erythrocytes will clump together or agglutinate. **Agglutination** is due to the interaction between an antigen (agglutinogen) and an antibody (agglutinin). Antigens are substances (usually proteins) that stimulate the formation of antibodies, with which

Table 4.2 Phenotypes, Genotypes, and Antigen-Antibody Relationships in the ABO Blood Group System (Adapted from Race and Sanger 1975.)

Phenotype (blood group)	Genotype	Red Blood Cell Antigens	Serum Antibodies
O	$I^O I^O$	—	anti-A, anti-B
A	$I^A I^A$, $I^A I^O$	A	anti-B
B	$I^B I^B$, $I^B I^O$	B	anti-A
AB	$I^A I^B$	A, B	none

they can react observably. If an individual is injected with a foreign material such as—but not limited to—red blood cells, substances will appear in the serum that react with the foreign material. These substances are called antibodies, and the individual who develops these antibodies is said to be immunized.

The formation of an antibody by an antigen from a member of the same species (from one person to another) is called **isoimmunization.** When two different species (human to rabbit) are involved, the process is called **heteroimmunization.** If an antigen from one person causes antibody formation in another, the antigen is referred to as an **isoagglutinogen.** The discovery early in this century that some people contain serum antibodies that agglutinate the erythrocytes of others led to the use of the symbol I (isoagglutinogen) to denote the various alleles in the ABO blood group system.

There are several well-established subgroups and a few rare variants of both A and B described in detail by Race and Sanger (1975). For purposes of illustrating inheritance of the ABO blood groups, however, we need consider only three alleles, I^A, I^B, and I^O. To begin, the ABO system is unlike many other blood groups because antibodies against the antigens are normally occurring substances. Of course, no individual normally possesses an antibody against his or her own antigen because agglutination of one's own cells would be fatal. In this three-allele system, the six possible genotypes and their antigen-antibody relationships are given in Table 4.2. Because I^A and I^B are co-dominant and I^O is recessive to both, only four phenotypes are possible.

That these three alleles occur at a single locus is not in doubt, although it was first proposed (von Dungern and Hirschfeld 1910) that genes at two different loci were involved. A particularly lucid account of the demise of this "two-locus" theory may be found in Moody (1975), who outlines Bernstein's (1925) early mathematical proof that ABO inheritance could not be adequately explained on the basis of two independent loci.

With this brief description of the genetics of the ABO system, we may return to the discussion of genetic modifiers for an example of a suppressor gene. In 1952, Bhende and his colleagues coined the term "Bombay" to describe a phenotype whose red blood cells did not group as A, B, or AB, and whose serum contained anti-A, anti-B, and another antibody called anti-H. As we have seen, this individual would normally be classed phenotypically as group O and genotypically as $I^O I^O$. However, an examination of this individual's pedigree indicated that blood type O was clearly impossible. Somewhat later, other researchers (Levine et al. 1955; Aloysia et al. 1961)

Table 4.3 ABO Phenotypes of Mother, Father, and the Possible and Impossible Blood Groups of Children from All Mating Combinations (Adapted from Schiff and Boyd 1942.)

Known Mother	Alleged Father	Possible Children	Children Not Possible by Alleged Father
O	O	O	A, B, (AB)*
O	A	O, A	B, (AB)
O	B	O, B	A, (AB)
O	AB	A, B	O, (AB)
A	O	O, A	B, AB
A	A	O, A	B, AB
A	B	O, A, B, AB	—
A	AB	A, B, AB	O
B	O	O, B	A, AB
B	A	O, A, B, AB	—
B	B	O, B	A, AB
B	AB	A, B, AB	O
AB	O	A, B	AB, (O)
AB	A	A, B, AB	(O)
AB	B	A, B, AB	(O)
AB	AB	A, B, AB	(O)

*Parenthesis indicate offspring who could not have been the mother's children

also identified $I^A{}_1$ and $I^A{}_2$ (subgroups of I^A) and I^B alleles in the offspring of parents who failed to express these alleles as normally expected for the ABO blood group system. In other words, the I^A and I^B allele products were apparently being suppressed.

It was subsequently found that the suppression was associated with another locus, the *H* locus. The *H* gene is responsible for the *H* substance, and the majority of people are either *HH* or *Hh*. The normal production of the A and B antigens depends upon the presence of this substance, which cannot be formed by the very rare individuals who are genotypically *hh*. Neither can such individuals form the A or B antigens, even though they possess either or both alleles. Thus they appear to be blood group O, but are fully capable of transmitting either the I^A or I^B alleles to their offspring. The offspring, if *Hh*, then fully express either the A or B antigen.

Recognition of the multiple alleles at the ABO locus has contributed much to our knowledge of human genetics and to our understanding of small evolutionary changes in human populations. The ABO groups also are important in more practical matters, including determination of compatible versus incompatible blood transfusions and in the solution of some legal cases in paternity suits.

It was stated above that serum antibodies are normally occurring substances in the ABO system. Any transfusion of red cell antigens into a person with antibodies against these antigens is termed incompatible. In an incompatible transfusion, such as type A cells into a type B person (whose serum contains anti-A), the donor's erythrocytes may be agglutinated by the patient's antibodies. Type AB individuals have no serum antibodies and are sometimes called "universal recipients," while type O people are often called "universal donors." Even though type O people have anti-A and anti-B isoagglutinins, the concentration of these antibodies is ordinarily low and, hence, diluted by the recipient's blood. In any event, the safest transfusions are between individuals with the same ABO type.

The ABO blood groups are used in some states in combination with other well-known blood groups, including the Rh and MNSs systems, for the resolution of disputed paternity cases. In Table 4.3 are the possible and impossible offspring blood group phenotypes from all parental combinations. Clearly, a type O mother claiming that her type B child was fathered by a type A man would probably lose her case. Had the man been type B, little would have been proven other than the fact that he *could have been* the father. But the ABO system, in conjunction with many other systems, increases the chance of proving innocence and, conversely, decreases the chance that another man was involved.

The Rh Blood Groups

In 1940, Landsteiner and Wiener discovered another red cell antigen. They obtained red blood cells from rhesus monkeys (*Macaca mulatta*) and used them to immunize rabbits and guinea pigs. It was found that the resulting antibodies agglutinated not only rhesus monkey cells, but human red cells as well. Among white inhabitants in New York City, slightly less than 85% of their sample of 379 individuals reacted positively, and were termed Rh-positive (Rh+). The cells in the remaining 15.4% were not agglutinated by the antibodies, and these individuals were called Rh-negative (Rh−). Shortly thereafter, Landsteiner and Wiener (1941) suggested that inheritance of the antigen was under simple genetic control. Those with the antigen (Rh+) were either homozygous dominant *RR* or heterozygous *Rr*, and those lacking the antigen (Rh−) were homozygous *rr*. Since then, however, extensive research has shown the Rh blood group system to be one of the most complex systems known, the details of which may be found in Race and Sanger (1975) and Wiener and Wexler (1958).

Several nomenclatural systems have been proposed for designating the Rh genotypes and phenotypes. Only two of these will be described here, because each represents a fundamentally different interpretation for inheritance in the system. One interpretation postulates that the Rh groups are controlled by either a series of three closely linked genes, or sites within a gene (Race and Sanger 1975). The other (Wiener 1966) holds that the Rh groups are controlled by eight alleles at one locus, each allele having its own agglutinogens.

Three antisera (sera containing antibodies) are needed to demonstrate how the Rh system works. These are called (1) anti-Rh_0, or anti-D, (2) anti-rh', or anti-C, and (3) anti-rh'', or anti-E. As seen in Table 4.4, the reactions among different individuals are of eight kinds, implying eight different phenotypes. The first four phenotypes listed have red cells which do not react with anti-Rh_0, and these individuals are classed as Rh−. The last four phenotypes do react with anti-Rh_0 and are Rh+. Finally, the alleles responsible for the red blood cell agglutinogens are given in the second column. This is basically the multiple allelic system of Wiener.

Based on Race and Sanger's observations (1950), R. A. Fisher found no evidence of crossing over between these alleles and formulated the theory that the Rh system was controlled by three very closely linked genes. In this theory, the three

Table 4.4 Eight Rh Phenotypes, Their Respective Alleles, and Their Reactions with Anti-Rh$_O$, Anti-rh′, and Anti-rh″ Antisera.

Phenotypes (Red Blood Cell Agglutinogen)	Alleles	Reactions with Antisera*		
		Anti-Rh$_O$ (D)	Anti-rh′ (C)	Anti-rh″ (E)
rh	r	−	−	−
rh′	r'	−	+	−
rh″	r''	−	−	+
rh$_y$	r^y	−	+	+
Rh$_O$	R^O	+	−	−
Rh$_1$	R^1	+	+	−
Rh$_2$	R^2	+	−	+
Rh$_z$	R^z	+	+	+

* + = cells that react with antiserum
 − = cells that do not react with antiserum

Table 4.5 Nomenclature in the Rh Blood Group System: The Eight Multiple Alleles Contrasted with the Eight Gene Complexes

Multiple Allele Designations	Gene Complex Designations
r	dce
r'	dCe
r''	dcE
r^y	dCE
R^O	Dce
R^1	DCe
R^2	DcE
R^z	DCE

genes *C*, *D*, and *E* and their *c*, *d*, and *e* alleles are inherited as a unit with *C* occurring between *D* and *E*. The eight different combinations are given in Table 4.5 with Wiener's multiple allelic equivalents.

The information in Tables 4.4 and 4.5 coupled with the observation that the presence of an antigen which reacts with an antiserum is dominant over its absence, allows us to determine the possible genotypes for both systems. Rh⁻ individuals whose red blood cells do not react with any of the antisera, for example, are *rr* or *dce/dce*. Those whose red blood cells react only with anti-rh′ are genotypically *r′r′* or *r′r*, corresponding to *dCe/dCe* or *dCe/dce*.

It can be seen in Table 4.4 that the red blood cells in all Rh⁺ individuals react with anti-Rh$_O$. To determine the possible genotypes of each Rh⁺ phenotype, for example Rh$_O$, any allele that produces no reaction with anti-rh′ and anti-rh″ can occur in combination with R^O. The possible genotypes, then, include R^OR^O (*Dce/Dce*) and R^Or (*Dce/dce*). As you determine the rest of these genotypes for yourselves, the complexity of the Rh system becomes apparent. People with the Rh_Z phenotype, for example, could be any one of the following genotypes:

R^ZR^Z (DCE/DCE) R^Zr'' (DCE/dcE) R^2r' (DcE/dCe)
R^ZR^2 (DCE/DcE) R^Zr' (DCE/dCe) R^1r^y (DCe/dCE)
R^ZR^1 (DCE/DCe) R^Zr (DCE/dce) R^1r'' (DCe/dcE)
R^ZR^0 (DCE/Dce) R^2R^1 (DcE/DCe) R^0r^y (Dce/dCE)
R^Zr^y (DCE/dCE) R^2r^y (DcE/dCE)

Further complicating the Rh system is the presence of a number of antigenic variants of those just discussed, in addition to compound antigens. These are lucidly discussed by Race and Sanger (1975) and need not be outlined here.

The ABO and perhaps the Rh blood group systems are only two examples of multiple alleles. On the red blood cells are many other antigens and enzymes which, in conjunction with plasma proteins, are routinely analyzed by biological anthropologists and human geneticists in studies of human populations. In later chapters, it will be shown how these "genetic markers" (Tables 4.6 and 4.7) are used to elucidate certain aspects of human population structure and evolution.

Polygenic Inheritance

Until now, the discussions of inheritance have been centered around characteristics controlled by the action of single genes or alleles of a gene. It is implied (see Appendix I) that continuous characteristics, such as stature, weight, and skin color are also influenced genetically. These characteristics are affected by genes at more than two different loci (polygenes) and are said to be **polygenic.** Polygenic traits are usually more easily modified by environmental factors than discontinuous traits. Stature and weight, for example, are particularly susceptible to nutritional variables, diseases, and other factors, and skin color is temporarily modified to varying degrees by exposure to sunlight. This **phenotypic plasticity,** as it is sometimes called, coupled with the fact that several or many different loci may be genetically involved, leads to considerable difficulty in genotypic determinations. It becomes even more difficult to specify the genotype when the number of involved loci increases. For human stature and weight, for example, we have no idea of the number of loci that affect the development and final expression of these traits. Methods are available, however, that provide estimates of the heritability of quantitative traits. These are described briefly at the end of this chapter.

A Model of Polygenic Inheritance
Imagine a hypothetical population in which stature is controlled by two pairs of genes, and suppose a person who is 170 cm tall mates with another who is 150 cm tall. For the sake of simplicity in the model, make the following assumptions:

1. The tall individual has the *AABB* genotype, and the short individual has the *aabb* genotype.

2. The *aabb* genotype confers upon its carrier a stature of 150 cm, and each capital letter allele, which we may term an effective allele, increases stature by an

Table 4.6 Blood Group Antigens in Humans (Courtesy of R. R. Race and R. Sanger, *Blood Groups in Man* (6th Ed.), Blackwell Scientific Publications, Oxford.)

System	Antigens Detected By	
	Positive Reaction with Specific Antibody	*Positive Reaction with One Antibody, Negative with Another**
A_1A_2BO	A_1, B, †H	A_2, A_3, A_x, and other A and B variants
MNSs	M, N, S, s, U, M^g, $\tilde{M}_1$, M′, Tm, Sj, Hu, He, Mi^a, Vw (Gr), Mur, Hil, Hut, M^v, Vr, Ri^a, St^a, Mt^a, Cl^a, Ny^a, Sul, Far	M_2, N_2, M^c, M^a, N^a, M^r, M^z, S_2
P	P_1, P^k, †Luke	P_2
Rh	D, C, c, C^w, C^x, E, e, e^s, (VS), E^w, G, ce(f), ce^s(V), C̲e̲, CE, cE, D^w, E^T, Go^a, hr^s, hr^H, hr^B, $\bar{R}^N$, Rh33, Rh35, Be^a, †LW	D^u, C^u, E^u, and many other variant forms of D, C, and e
Lutheran	Lu^a, Lu^b, Lu^aLu^b (Lu3), Lu6, Lu9, ‡Lu4, Lu5, Lu7, Lu8, Lu10–17	
Kell	K, k, Kp^a, Kp^b, Ku, Js^a, Js^b, Ul^a, Wk^a, K11, ‡KL, K12–16	
Lewis	Le^a, Le^b, Le^c, Le^d, Le^x	
Duffy	Fy^a, Fy^b, Fy3, Fy4	
Kidd	Jk^a, Jk^b, Jk^aJk^b (Jk3)	
Diego	Di^a, Di^b	
Yt	Yt^a, Yt^b	
Auberger	Au^a	
Dombrock	Do^a, Do^b	
Colton	Co^a, Co^b, Co^aCo^b	
Sid	Sd^a	
Scianna	Sc1, Sc2 (Bu^a)	
Very frequent antigens	Vel, Ge, Lan, Gy^a, At^a, En^a, Wr^b, Jr^a, Kn^a, El, Dp, Gn^a, Jo^a, and many unpublished examples	
Very infrequent antigens	An^a, By, Bi, Bp^a, Bx^a, Chr^a, Evans, Good, Gf, Heibel, Hey, Hov, Ht^a, Je^a, Jn^a, Levay, Ls^a, Mo^a, Or, Pt^a, Rl^a, Rd, Re^a, Sw^a, To^a, Tr^a, Ts, Wb, Wr^a, Wu, Zd, and many unpublished examples	
Other antigens	I, i, Bg (HL-A), Chido, Cs^a, Yk^a	
Xg	Xg^a	

*Recognizable only in favourable genotypes.
†A genetically independent part of the system.
‡Place in system not yet genetically clear.

Table 4.7 Some Genetic Markers in Man (Courtesy of J. H. Renwick, *Brit. Med. Bull.* 25: 65–73 (1969). By permission of the Medical Department, The British Council.)

Autosomal Loci		Commonest allele in Europe	
		Allele	*Approximate Frequency*
Scored by difference in antigenic properties	Erythrocytes:		
	ABO	O	0.66
	MNSs	Ns	0.39
	P	P_2	0.52
	Rhesus	r	0.40
	Lutheran	Lu^b	0.96
	Kell	k	0.95
	Lewis	L	0.75
	Duffy	Fy^b	0.59
	Kidd	Jk^a	0.52
	Dombrock	Do	0.60
	Leucocytes:		
	HLA	HLA^u	0.10
	Serum or Plasma:		
	Gm	$Gm^{-1,-2,3}$	0.61
	Inv	Inv^{-1}	0.92
	Ag Lipoprotein	Ag^y	0.77
	Lp Lipoprotein	Lp	0.81
Scored by difference in charge shown by electrophoresis	Erythrocytes:		
	Acid phosphatase	AcP^B	0.60
	Phosphoglucomutase$_1$	$PGM_1{}^1$	0.76
	6-Phosphogluconate dehydrogenase	$6PGD^A$	0.98
	Adenylate kinase	AK^1	0.95
	Adenosine deaminase	ADA^1	0.94
	Leucocytes:		
	Phosphoglucomutase$_3$	$PGM_3{}^1$	0.75
	Serum or Plasma:		
	Haptoglobin	Hp^2	0.60
	Protease inhibitor	Pi^M	0.98
	Cholinesterase$_2$	$E_2{}^{-5}$	0.96
	Group-specific component	Gc^1	0.72
	Complement C′3	$G3^2$	0.77
Scored by difference in sensitivity to enzyme inhibitor	Cholinesterase$_1$	$E_1{}^u$	0.97
Scored on secretory property	Secretor	Se	0.52

Figure 4.7 A hypothetical mating between two individuals whose statures are 170 cm. (genotype = *AABB*) and 150 cm. (genotype = *aabb*), and production of a heterozygous offspring whose stature is 160 cm.

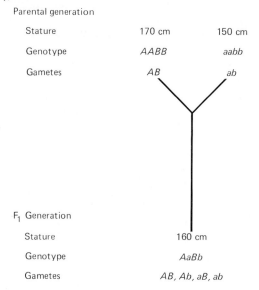

Parental generation

Stature	170 cm	150 cm
Genotype	*AABB*	*aabb*
Gametes	*AB*	*ab*

F₁ Generation

Stature	160 cm
Genotype	*AaBb*
Gametes	*AB, Ab, aB, ab*

identical amount. Since the difference between the tall and the short person is 20 cm, each of the four effective alleles in the *AABB* genotype increases stature over 150 cm by 5 cm. The *AABB* genotype, then, is 150 cm + (5 cm) (4) = 170 cm.

When the tall and the short individuals mate, all offspring will be heterozygous *AaBb* and, hence, 160 cm tall (Fig. 4.7). Suppose now that an F₂ generation is produced by matings between *AaBb* genotypes. As seen in Figure 4.7, the F₁ offspring produce four different genetic combinations. When mated, they produce F₂ offspring which appear, on the average, in the proportions given in Figure 4.8.

Through independent assortment, the F₂ generation consists of 16 individuals ranging from 150 cm to 170 cm in the ratio

1 (150 cm) : 4 (155 cm) : 6 (160 cm) : 4 (165 cm) : 1 (170 cm).

The 1 : 4 : 6 : 4 : 1 ratio, incidentally, represents the coefficients of the binomial ($p + q$) when expanded to the fourth power. As shown in Appendix I (Fig. A.8), a histogram showing the five classes and the number of individuals in each class would approximate the normal distribution (Fig. 4.9). From the discussion of the binomial distribution (see Appendix I), furthermore, it becomes obvious that the normal distribution will be ever more closely approximated when the number of hypothetical gene pairs increases.

In this model, then, the F₁ hybrids are all an intermediate 160 cm tall, and the F₂ offspring display considerable variation. However, all are within the two parental extremes. By relying on the simple Mendelian rules of segregation and independent assortment, the observed phenotypic variation is best explained by assuming two pairs of genes with equal and additive effects.

Figure 4.8 Matings between F_1 generation offspring from Figure 4.7, and the genotypes and statures of the F_2 progeny.

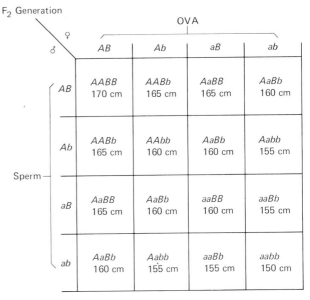

F_2 Statures: 170 cm   165 cm   160 cm   155 cm   150 cm

Ratio: 1   :   4   :   6   :   4   :   1

Figure 4.9 Histogram of the F_2 generation cross given in Figure 4.8, in which the superimposed line represents the normal distribution.

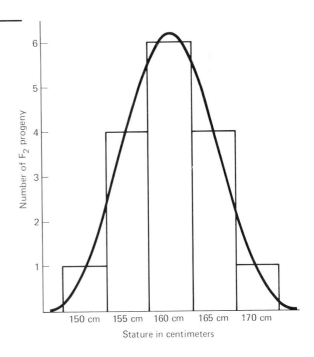

Inheritance of Skin Color

One of the earliest attempts to demonstrate the genetic basis of a continuous characteristic in humans was performed by C. B. Davenport in 1913. Concentrating on the inheritance of skin color differences, Davenport examined data from matings between people with dark and light skins. Similar to the intermediate stature in the F_1 offspring in the model in Figure 4.9, he found that the majority of F_1 hybrids fell into a single class that was intermediate between the darkest and lightest individuals (Table 4.8). In addition, the differences in skin color in the seven individuals in the first and third classes from those in the second class were rather slight. These differences could easily have been due to minor genetic factors responsible for the variation commonly seen in any single black or white population. It is also evident in Table 4.8 that the offspring of the F_1 hybrids occur in all classes in what appears to be a left-skewed normal distribution.

An examination of the first four columns in Table 4.8 suggests an hypothesis whereby skin color has its genetic basis in two independent loci, each locus having two alleles (A^1 and A^2; B^1 and B^2). In this interpretation (see the last column in Table 4.8) those with the least pigmentation (color class 0) possess the $A^1A^1B^1B^1$ genotype; those with the most pigmentation (color class 4) are $A^2A^2B^2B^2$. Matings between two individuals with these genotypes will, according to the principle of segregation, produce heterozygous $A^1A^2B^1B^2$ offspring. Assuming that the A^2 and B^2 alleles have an equal and additive effect on increase in skin pigmentation, these F_1 hybrids will all be intermediate between their parents' skin color. Matings between these F_1 hybrids will, in turn, produce children having from none to four effective alleles according to the principle of independent assortment. These five classes of children will be distributed normally, as predicted by the model, and will range in relative pigmentation from color class 0 to color class 4.

The unresolved problem that Davenport faced, as do other investigators today, was how to precisely divide the color classes. For any continuous characteristic, the division is arbitrary because there are an infinite number of points along a continuum. The equipment that Davenport used in 1913 to discern the five classes of skin color was primitive compared to the modern reflectance spectrophotometers. The latter measure skin color by reflecting light of different wavelengths from the melanin pigment, and have been used by later investigators to clarify the genetic basis of skin

Table 4.8 Results of Davenport's (1913) Study on the Inheritance of Skin Color: Skin Color Distribution in Black/White Hybrids and Hypothetical Genotypes of Each Color Class. Note that the superscript 1 causes lightness and 2 causes darkness.

Pct. of Black Component	Color Class	Distribution of F_1 Hybrids	Offspring of F_1 Hybrids	Genotypes Assigned to Each Color Class
0–11	0	—	3	$A^1A^1B^1B^1$
12–25	1	2	10	$A^1A^1B^1B^2$, or $A^1A^2B^1B^1$
26–40	2	22	13	$A^1A^1B^2B^2$, or $A^1A^2B^1B^2$, or $A^2A^2B^1B^1$
41–55	3	5	5	$A^1A^2B^2B^2$, or $A^2A^2B^1B^2$
56–78	4	—	1	$A^2A^2B^2B^2$

color. Although we know neither the number of loci involved nor the effects of genetic modifiers (if any), the studies by Harrison and Owen (1964) and Stern (1970) support models based on three to six pairs of genes at different loci with additive effects. There is little doubt that Davenport's original two-locus hypothesis is inadequate, but to his credit goes the original demonstration of the polygenic nature of skin color.

The Components of Phenotypic Variance

It was mentioned earlier that quantitative traits are particularly susceptible to environmental influences. Thus individual variation in stature, for example, arises not only from genetic differences, but also from environmental differences. For some traits, furthermore, an interaction may exist between the genotype and a certain environment. In these instances, a certain genotype may interact in a different manner to diverse environments, so that analysis of the trait must deal with the interaction rather than the genes of the environment alone. The statistical methods outlined in Appendix I are used to describe and compare quantitative data but, with the exception of the analysis of variance, they are incapable of partitioning quantitative variation into its respective components.

It is shown in Appendix I that the variability of quantitative traits is expressed statistically by the variance, which can be denoted here by the symbol V. When phenotypic variance (V_P) is due to genotypic and environmental variability, and variability due to genetic-environmental interaction, then

$$V_P = V_G + V_E + V_{GE},$$

where V_G is the genotypic variance, V_E the environmental variance, and V_{GE} the interaction between genetic and environmental factors.

A number of sources may contribute to genotypic variance: alleles with dominant effects; genes that influence the action of other genes (**epistasis**); genes with additive effects, as in the polygenic systems just discussed. Genotypic variance, therefore, may be subdivided into the components

$$V_G = V_D + V_I + V_A,$$

where V_D, V_I, and V_A denote the variance due to dominance, epistatic interaction, and additive genes respectively. Inserting these into the equation for phenotypic variance, we obtain

$$V_P = V_D + V_I + V_A + V_E + V_{GE}.$$

In experimental populations of organisms of known genotypes for certain traits, the values of some of these components can be estimated within certain limits. For example, variability in a certain trait between genotypically identical individuals will be limited to that caused by environmental factors. As an illustration, suppose you had two populations, one of which was genetically uniform and the other genetically diverse for a certain trait. Suppose that you measured the trait in a sample of individuals from both populations, determined the variances, and compared them.

Assume in this comparison that the phenotypic variance in the genetically uniform population was 75% less than in the genetically diverse population. Since V_P was reduced by 75%, you could conclude that the remaining 25% was variance caused by either V_E, V_{GE}, or by a combination of both.

Heritability

If the individuals from the two populations developed in identical environments, thus deleting V_E and V_{GE}, the remaining variance (V_G) would be responsible for the total phenotypic variance. This fraction of V_P is usually called heritability and is denoted by the symbol h^2. If we ignore V_{GE} for the moment, then the following relation exists:

$$V_P = V_G + V_E.$$

Dividing by V_P, we obtain

$$\frac{V_G}{V_P} + \frac{V_E}{V_P} = 1,$$

where the first fraction, $V_G/V_P = h^2$ and the second fraction, $V_E/V_P = e^2$. The latter is that part of the total phenotypic variance when all genetic components are deleted.

Heritability values range from 1 (when no environmental component exists) to zero (when no genetic component exists). To say that $h^2 = 0.50$ for a certain trait does not mean that the trait relies on 0.50 heredity and 0.50 environment for its expression. Rather, this estimate means that half the *total population variance* is due to genetic differences between the members of the population. Some examples of heritability estimates for characteristics in nonhuman mammals are given in Table 4.9.

Table 4.9 Some Approximate Heritability Estimates in Nonhuman Mammalian Characteristics (After Falconer 1960.)

Cattle	h²
White spotting in Friesians	0.95
Percent butterfat	0.60
Milk-yield	0.30
Pigs	
Thickness of back fat	0.55
Body length	0.50
Weight at 180 days	0.30
Litter size	0.15
Sheep	
Length of wool	0.55
Weight of fleece	0.40
Body weight	0.35

Twin Studies

Because human populations are not appropriate for experimental laboratory conditions, the most useful approach toward delineation of variance components and calculation of heritability estimates involves the study of twins. In these studies, twins are assumed to be of two types: (1) monozygotic or identical (abbreviated by MZ) twins, in which two genetically identical individuals arise from a single ovum fertilized by a single sperm cell; and (2) dizygotic or fraternal (DZ) twins, which arise from separate fertilization of two different ova. DZ twins have the same degree of genetic similarity as, for example, a full brother and sister.

Twin studies are especially valuable because they provide the ability to determine the variance of the differences between partners of twin pairs. Given the genetic identity between MZ twins, for example, there is no genetic component in the intrapair difference. Thus the variance, when present, must be due to other than genetic factors. A convenient way to score intrapair twin differences and thus to partition genetic and environmental factors is by classifying the twins by concordance and discordance for the trait. Concordance means that the characteristic is present in both twins; discordance means that only one of a twin pair shows the trait. The heritability of the trait may then be expressed as a percentage value according to Holzinger's (1929) formula,

$$\frac{\% \text{ concordant (MZ)} - \% \text{ concordant (DZ)}}{100 - \% \text{ concordant (DZ)}}.$$

This formula has been used extensively for evaluation of concordance in MZ vs. DZ twins for qualitative traits, such as various diseases. In a different formula, the same principle utilizes the variances for heritability estimates of quantitative traits (Osborne and DeGeorge 1959).

$$\frac{\text{Variance DZ} - \text{Variance MZ}}{\text{Variance DZ}}.$$

Several examples of percentage concordance for various traits in human MZ and DZ twins are given in Table 4.10.

It should be repeated again that estimates of heritability tell us only the extent to which *variation* in a trait is genetically determined and nothing about inheritance of the trait itself. It must also be clearly understood that heritability estimates have validity only for the population from which they were derived, and only at a certain time. Different populations exist in different environments, and these environments, as well as the genetic composition of the population, change through time. The heritability of a particular trait is therefore subject to considerable interpopulation variation, in addition to temporal variation in a single population.

Table 4.10 Percentages of Concordance and Discordance for Several Characteristics in Monozygotic and Dizygotic Twins (After Lerner 1968.)

Characteristic	Percentage Concordance	
	MZ Twins	*DZ Twins*
Incidence of schizophrenia	69	10
Tuberculosis	54	16
Cancer	10	5
Clubfoot	32	3
Measles	95	87
Scarlet fever	64	47
Rickets	88	22
Electrocardiogram	39	25
Shape of stomach	24	19
Type of body sway	45	34
Blood pressure	63	36
Pulse rate	56	34

Summary

Alleles are frequently called dominant or recessive, but both terms actually refer to phenotypic states. Hence, the gene products of a dominant allele will be expressed in both homozygous and heterozygous forms, while the product of a recessive allele is expressed only in the homozygous state. However, there are numerous dominant and recessive alleles that are not always phenotypically expressed as expected, even in individuals known by pedigree analysis to possess such alleles in specific combinations. Gene products may thus fail to "penetrate" into the phenotype, or they may be expressed phenotypically among different individuals in different ways. These deviations are thought to arise during development because of various interactions with the products of other alleles at different loci.

Independent assortment is a process that involves genes on different chromosomes instead of those on the same chromosome. These are sometimes linked together, and if the linkage is close, the genes involved may be inherited as a group. Combinations of genes on certain chromosomes can be broken up during meiosis by recombination, a process that reshuffles genes and ensures that no two individuals other than identical twins will be genetically identical.

The traditional method for establishing inheritance patterns of various traits has been pedigree analysis. Simple autosomal dominant traits appear in each generation and never occur among offspring unless also present in one or both parents. They also occur equally among both sexes, and matings between heterozygous and normal individuals will, on the average, result in half of the children bearing the trait. Simple autosomal recessive traits often skip generations. All offspring from two homozygous parents will possess the trait, whereas matings between a homozygous recessive and a heterozygous parent will, on the average, give rise to half affected offspring. Alleles on the X-chromosome can also be either dominant or recessive.

Males inherit such alleles from their mother and, when dominant, will always show the trait. Since they inherit their father's Y-chromosome, however, lack of father-to-son transmission is the characteristic feature of X-linked inheritance. That genes also occur on the Y-chromosome is evident from the association between the Y-chromosome and male characteristics, but there is no phenotypic trait that can unequivocally be associated with a Y-linked allele.

Some traits, including the ABO blood groups, are controlled by several alleles at a single locus. In this system, the *A* and *B* alleles have no dominance relationship to each other, but both are dominant to *O*. A similar system, but with eight multiple alleles, has been suggested for the Rh blood group system. However, inheritance at this locus can also be explained by a set of three very closely linked genes at different loci on the same chromosome. Both blood group systems have played important roles in expanding our knowledge of the genetics and evolution of human populations, and both are important for more practical matters such as maternal-fetal incompatibility reactions, transfusion reactions, and resolution of paternity suits.

Most traits controlled by a pair of alleles or by multiple allelic systems are qualitative in nature, but other traits such as stature, weight, and skin pigmentation are quantitative. These characteristics are influenced genetically by several genes and their alleles at different loci, and most are more susceptible to environmental influences than simple qualitative traits. There are no quantitative traits in humans for which the number of relevant genes is known, but for skin pigmentation the best current evidence suggests three to six pairs of genes at different loci with additive effects. For other traits, heritability estimates have been used to indicate how much of the variation in the trait is genetically determined. However, such estimates cannot clarify inheritance mechanisms per se.

5 Fundamentals of Population Genetics

Introduction

The emphasis up to this point has been on the biology and genetics of the individual, but a major conceptual shift must now be made in order to consider the biology and genetics of populations. It will become evident that there are a few rough but useful analogies between populations and individuals, but it will also become obvious that the rules governing the genetics of populations are considerably different from those that apply to the genetics of individuals.

Mayr (1963), Dobzhansky (1970), and other evolutionary biologists use the term "population thinking" to denote a fundamentally distinct way of conceptualizing the biology of populations. In light of Mayr's contention that the change from typological thinking to population thinking represents one of the great conceptual revolutions in biology, it seems pertinent to begin this chapter by commenting briefly on this point.

The basic idea of typology was formally codified by the famous Greek philosopher Plato (427–347 B.C.) in his concept of the *eidos,* or type: the observed variability in nature only imperfectly reflects reality. The only fixed and permanent objects in nature are reality, and consist of ideal abstractions or "essences" which underlie all observed variation. Diametrically opposed to this view is that of the modern population biologist: there are no ideal types; reality is the observed variation in nature.

Typological principles in the natural sciences have been rejected to the extent that "to call someone a typologist is to employ a mild form of invective, and to describe someone's systematic work as typological is to condemn it outright on fundamental grounds" (Sokal, 1962:232). The difference between typological and population thinking, and the reason why biology has rejected typological principles is clearly outlined in the rather extensive quotation from Mayr.

> The populationist stresses the uniqueness of everything in the organic world. What is true for the human species—that no two individuals are alike—is equally true for all other species of animals and plants. Indeed, even the same individual changes continuously throughout his lifetime and when placed into different environments. All organisms and organic phenomena are composed of unique features and can be described collectively only in statistical terms. Individuals, or any kind of organic entities, form populations of which we can determine the arithmetic mean and the statistics of variation. Averages are merely statistical abstractions, only the individuals of which the populations are composed have reality. The ultimate conclusions of the population thinker and of the typologist are precisely the opposite. For the typologist, the type

(eidos) is real and the variation an illusion, while for the populationist the type (average) is an abstraction and only the variation is real. No two ways of looking at nature could be more different. (1959b:2)

The Mendelian Population as a Unit of Study

In biology and genetics the **Mendelian population** is defined as "a community of individuals of a sexually reproducing species within which matings take place" (Dobzhansky 1970/310). The cohesiveness of a Mendelian population—the unity that allows it to be studied as a concrete entity—is brought about and maintained by interbreeding among its members, who thereby share a common gene pool. Mendelian populations are distributed in space and through time; they occur in various sizes; and they occupy different environmental zones within the geographical range of the species.

The smallest Mendelian populations are units that undergo relatively little interbreeding with other such groups and whose members mate at random with others in the same population. The largest Mendelian population, at least theoretically, is the **biological species.** A biological species is generally considered to be a group of actually or potentially interbreeding natural populations which is reproductively isolated from other such groups (Mayr 1940). Populations of a species inhabit various parts of the entire species range and are prevented from interbreeding with populations of other species by the possession of biological and behavioral characteristics that either prevent mating or prevent the production of fertile or viable offspring (see Chapter 8 for a more complete discussion of species concepts, their applications, and reproductive isolation).

Mendelian populations are far more easily defined in theory than in practice. This is particularly true for human populations. It is an observed fact that the geographic distribution of human populations is not random. Although they inhabit nearly all of the world's land surface, humans are organized into groups and, for various reasons, generally prefer to mate within their own group (endogamy). There are numerous social and cultural factors responsible for this tendency: religious, class, caste, and racial prejudice, linguistic differences, economic status, and so forth. These sociocultural barriers tend to maintain the unique biological properties of different populations by restricting genetic exchange between groups. This process of genetic exchange, called differential migration, has important implications for human evolution and will be discussed in detail in Chapter 6.

Because all but identical twins are genetically unique, and since individuals comprise populations, all populations are also genetically unique. The differences between human populations involve both quantitative and qualitative characteristics and are often visibly apparent, as between Norwegians and Melanesians, for example. Other populations—especially those that more freely exchange their genes and cultural inventories and which live in similar environmental and geographical zones—may show only slight statistical differences.

The study of human population genetics almost always has evolutionary ramifications. Since an individual's genotype is determined at fertilization and remains invariant throughout life, the individual per se cannot evolve. However, the individual carries the genetic material which, by recombination and mutation, gives rise upon mating to offspring with different genotypes. These offspring, in turn, may respond to environmental stimuli in a slightly more efficient manner than their parents. To the extent that certain genotypes tend, on the average, to leave more offspring than others, the frequency of genes represented by the more favorable genotypes will increase in the population. A generally accepted conception of evolution concerns cumulative changes in the gene pools of populations through generations. Thus populations rather than individuals are the basic evolutionary units.

The study of human population genetics is ultimately based upon some fundamental characteristics of population genetic variation. A few of these features are given below.

1. All individuals possess both **quantitative** and **qualitative traits.** As discussed in Appendix I, quantitative traits are described by statistics of location and dispersion, while qualitative traits are usually represented by percentage values (frequencies).

2. Genetically influenced traits in several adjacent populations often vary independently. The frequency of one variable, for example, might increase regularly from one population to another, while that of a different variable can either decrease or remain constant.

3. As a result of migration, traits in neighboring populations tend to intergrade imperceptibly. When populations are separated by geographic or cultural barriers that restrict genetic exchange, however, trait frequencies may show sudden differences.

4. Changes in traits in a series of adjacent populations often tend to be regular. This is due to the combined effects of migration, which tends to level out the existing differences, and environmental changes, which tend to exaggerate the differences. Such geographical character gradients are called **clines.**

5. When traits are clearly associated with environmental factors, they are said to possess an "adaptive value" (see Chapter 6). Some characteristics, on the other hand, seem to be due purely to chance. In most cases, this means simply that no adaptive value has been identified.

6. The genetic characteristics in human populations tend to change rather slowly through time.

The Effective Population Number

To study the genetics and evolution of populations requires the identification and description of the breeding population (N), because these individuals are responsible for the genetic nature of the following generation. The breeding population is not given by the total number of individuals as determined by census data, but rather includes only the breeding members—the progenitors. The estimation of N, which is invariably much smaller than the total population number, requires a careful survey of the demographic information on age structure, mating patterns, and reproductive histories. When N can be estimated—which is especially difficult in small and technologically unadvanced societies that retain no written records of these events—the population geneticist usually refines this estimate in order to assess the effect of various processes that alter gene frequencies. This refinement involves calculation of the effective population size (N_e).

The effective population size is N reduced to a value equivalent to the number of breeding individuals in an "ideal" population. In such an ideal population, the N breeding individuals are distributed evenly by sex—half males and half females—and mate at random. This means, of course, that a random gamete in the population has an equal chance of arising from any parent, and that any gamete has an equal chance of fertilizing or being fertilized by any other gamete. In an ideal population, furthermore, the rate of decay of variability is assumed to be $1/2N$ per generation. Rate of decay, also called the rate of loss of heterozygosis or the rate of fixation of loci, may be summarized as follows.

All small breeding populations consist in part of genetically related individuals. These related breeding individuals will contribute to an increase in homozygosity to a greater extent than would a large ideal population whose breeding members were all unrelated. Put another way, the breeding population will not be comprised solely of unrelated gametes, but instead will be slightly less heterozygous than an ideal population. It follows that the next generation will receive fewer unrelated gametes, and the probability of any gamete mating with an unrelated gamete will be correspondingly reduced. This loss of heterozygosity for any pair of alleles will theoretically occur at the rate of $1/2N$ per generation until every individual in the population has the same set of alleles. These alleles are then said to be fixed. Although theoretically possible, such populations are not found in nature. Even if they did exist and were well adapted to particular environmental conditions, their ultimate fate would probably be extinction. If everyone possessed the same allele set, they could not undergo the genotypic reorganization necessary for response to changing environmental conditions.

Only very rarely can an investigator directly determine the effective size of a population. Thus, several mathematical formulae have been developed (Wright 1931, 1938) for the reduction of N to N_e, depending upon certain conditions that tend to increase the number of genetically related individuals in the population. In each case, the practical result is that N_e is substantially less than N. Four of these conditions include (1) when the sexes are distributed unevenly, (2) when the size of the population varies cyclically, (3) when mating occurs between relatives (inbreeding), and (4) when all individuals are not equally fertile. It is inappropriate to derive the mathematical formulae for each of these cases (for this, see Li 1955; Crow and Kimura 1970). However, the first condition may be outlined as an instructive example of how the effective population size is derived.

Suppose in a population that there is an unequal distribution of sexes. Let N_m and N_f represent, respectively, the number of males and females in the parental generation, so that $N_m + N_f = N$. From Appendix I, the probability that different individuals in the offspring generation obtained the same two genes from a male in the parental generation is $1/4$. The probability that these two genes came from the *same* male is $1/4N_m$. The probability that they came instead from the *same* female is $1/4N_f$. Therefore, the probability that they came from the same individual, regardless of sex, is

$$\frac{1}{4N_m} + \frac{1}{4N_f} = \frac{1}{N_e}.$$

Solving for N_e, we obtain

$$N_e = \frac{4N_m N_f}{N_m + N_f}.$$

For example, suppose that the breeding members of a hypothetical population consisted of 340 females and 85 males ($N = 425$). The effective population size is found by substituting these values into the equation above.

$$N_e = \frac{4(85)(340)}{85 + 340} = 272.$$

Two points are revealed by an inspection of this equation. First, when the number of males and females are equal, then $N = N_e$. Second, inequality in numbers, such as 8 ♂ and 10 ♀, will always have the effect whereby $N > N_e$. You may substitute these numbers into the equation to assure yourself of these two points. In this example, then, it may be stated that the rate of decrease in heterozygosis in the 425 individuals will be the same as if there were only 272 individuals in the breeding population.

Phenotype, Genotype, and Gene Frequencies

Classical population genetics emphasizes the study of gene frequencies and the various processes that change gene frequencies. The alleles for any specific genetic marker cannot, of course, be directly observed. Rather, their presence is inferred from examination of the phenotypic characteristics they affect. For some characteristics, the phenotype and genotype frequencies are identical, as in the MN blood group system. For this trait there are two alleles, L^M and L^N, which in combination form three phenotypes (M, MN, and N). These phenotypes correspond to the three genotypes $L^M L^M$, $L^M L^N$, and $L^N L^N$. The genotype frequencies are determined simply by dividing the number of individuals of each of the three genotypes by the total population size. Consider, for example, a population of 224 individuals whose MN blood group phenotypes were distributed as follows:

Phenotypes	Genotypes	No. of Individuals
M	$L^M L^M$	84
MN	$L^M L^N$	110
N	$L^N L^N$	30
	Total	224

The following are the genotype frequencies.

$$L^M L^M = 84/224 = 0.38$$
$$L^M L^N = 110/224 = 0.49$$
$$L^N L^N = 30/224 = 0.13$$
$$\text{Total} \quad 1.00$$

If the genotype frequencies are known, then the gene frequencies can be easily calculated. For an autosomal locus in a diploid population, as in the above example, there must be a total of 448 alleles in the population because every individual carries two alleles. Let p = the frequency of L^M, and q = the frequency of L^N. The two allele frequencies can now be found by substituting the numbers given above into the formula

$$p = \frac{\text{total number of } M \text{ alleles in the population}}{\text{total number of alleles}}.$$

Notice in this population that there are 278 L^M alleles. The 84 homozygous $L^M L^M$ individuals contribute 168, and the heterozygotes 110. The gene frequency of p, therefore, is

$$p = \frac{168 + 110}{448} = 0.62.$$

Similarly,

$$q = \frac{60 + 110}{448} = 0.38,$$

and, of course, $p(0.62) + q(0.38) = 1$.

The calculation of allele frequencies for a codominant trait like the MN blood group system is quite simple, because the heterozygote is detectable and can be directly counted. In these cases, it is generally true that the frequency of either allele is equal to the genotype frequency of the homozygote plus one-half that of the heterozygote.

The calculation of allele frequencies for multiple allelic systems, however, depends upon the dominance relationships of the allelic combinations. The ABO blood group system provides a case in point because, as pointed out in the preceding chapter, the O allele cannot be detected in the heterozygous state and, thus, cannot be directly counted. To illustrate how the I^A, I^B, and I^O allele frequencies are found, suppose that the 224 individuals in the same population were also tested for their ABO blood types and were distributed as follows:

Phenotypes	No. of Individuals	Phenotype Frequencies
A	79	0.3527
B	38	0.1696
O	97	0.4330
AB	10	0.0447
Totals	224	1.0000

The frequency of each of the three alleles is represented by the trinomial expansion $(p + q + r)^2$, where $p = I^A$, $q = I^B$, and $r = I^O$. Therefore,

$$p^2 \;+\; 2pr \;+\; q^2 \;+\; 2qr \;+\; 2pq \;+\; r^2 \;=\; 1.$$
$$(I^A I^A) \quad (I^A I^O) \quad (I^B I^B) \quad (I^B I^O) \quad (I^A I^B) \quad (I^O I^O)$$

The combined phenotypic frequencies are

Types A and O ($p^2 + 2pr + r^2$): $0.3527 + 0.4330 = 0.7857$

Types B and O ($q^2 + 2qr + r^2$): $0.1696 + 0.4330 = 0.6026$

Type O (r^2): 0.4330.

Taking the square roots of these frequencies, we obtain the following:

Types A and O: 0.8664

Types B and O: 0.7763

Type O: 0.6580.

Now, the square root of the combined frequencies of types A and O subtracted from 1 will provide an estimate of the frequency of B (q).

$$q(I^B) = 1 - 0.8664 = 0.1136.$$

The frequency of A(p) is derived in a similar fashion.

$$p(I^A) = 1 - 0.7763 = 0.2237.$$

And type O (r) is simply the square root of the phenotype frequency

$$r(I^O) = 0.6580.$$

Note that $p + q + r = 0.9953$ instead of 1, as expected. This sometimes happens because error may be introduced into these values whenever p and q are based on an estimate of r. In such a case, the estimates may be improved by applying simple formulae developed by Bernstein (1930).

In practice, allele frequencies are always determined on a sample of a population. Rarely, if ever, will every individual in a population be examined or tested for the full set of genetic traits commonly used in population studies. In general, accuracy in deriving allele frequencies in a finite population increases as the sample size increases. For extremely small populations and even smaller samples, the estimate may not adequately reflect the true population frequency. It is desirable, therefore, to express some degree of confidence in such estimations. This is usually done by calculating a statistic called the standard error of the mean, symbolized by SE.

The standard error of the mean provides a statement of the chances that the true population frequency is within a certain range of the frequency observed in the sample. For alleles that can be counted directly, SE is given by

$$SE = \sqrt{\frac{pq}{N}},$$

where p and q represent the respective allele frequencies, and N is the total number of alleles in the sample. If the frequency of an allele $p = 0.50$, for example, and $SE = 0.10$ (the usual notation being $p = 0.50 \pm 0.10$), then in 67.4% of the samples the true value of p is expected to lie between 0.40 and 0.60 (from Appendix I, $\pm 0.674 \sigma$ contains 0.50 of the area under the normal curve).

The standard error for the allele frequencies for the MN blood group system in the hypothetical population above is, then

$$SE = \sqrt{\frac{(0.62)(0.38)}{448}} = 0.023.$$

We may infer from this that in 67.4% of the cases the frequency of L^M will lie between 0.60 and 0.64. The true population frequency, similarly, will lie between 0.57 and 0.67 for 95% of the time (in other words, for $\pm 2\,SE$).

Random Mating and Genetic Equilibrium

The concept of random mating, or **panmixis,** is of fundamental importance in population genetics. It means simply that matings take place without regard to specific genotypes. Clearly, therefore, the choice of a mate with a certain genotype is dependent upon the frequency of that genotype in the population. For some genes, populations are in random mating proportions. For other genes they are not. Any human population, for example, may mate totally at random for genes affecting nonvisible traits such as red cell enzyme **polymorphisms.** Simultaneously, they may not mate at random for genes affecting skin color, intelligence, or hereditary diseases.

For our purposes here, random mating can be considered synonymous with random combination of gametes. For clarification, suppose that a large population consists of equal numbers of males and females who mate at random for an autosomal locus with two alleles, A (p) and a (q). Assume further that the frequency of $p =$ that of q for both sexes. Under these assumptions, the results of random mating are given in Table 5.1.

After one generation, then, the genotypic proportions are $1/4$ (p^2) : $2/4$ (pq) : $1/4$ (q^2). Eliminating the common denominator and setting the three genotypes to unity, we obtain the expression

$$p^2 + 2pq + q^2 = 1.$$

This squared binomial represents equilibrium conditions described by the **Hardy-Weinberg principle,** so named in honor of the two co-discoverers Hardy (1908) and Weinberg (1908). A more extended discussion of this important principle will follow shortly.

Suppose now that these F_1 offspring mate at random for the same locus. Since both sexes occur in the proportions $1/4\ AA : 2/4\ Aa : 1/4\ aa$, and since mating

Table 5.1 Random Combination of Gametes and Their Genotypic Proportions for an Autosomal Locus with Two Alleles

	Male gametes	
	1/2 A (p)	1/2 a (q)
Female gametes — 1/2 A (p)	1/4 AA (p^2)	1/4 Aa (pq)
Female gametes — 1/2 a (q)	1/4 Aa (pq)	1/4 aa (q^2)

Table 5.2 Mating Types and Their Expected Frequencies for an Autosomal Locus with Two Alleles

	Male genotypes		
	1/4 AA	2/4 Aa	1/4 aa
Female genotypes — 1/4 AA	1/16 AA × AA	2/16 Aa × AA	1/16 aa × AA
Female genotypes — 2/4 Aa	2/16 AA × Aa	4/16 Aa × Aa	2/16 aa × Aa
Female genotypes — 1/4 aa	1/16 AA × aa	2/16 Aa × aa	1/16 aa × aa

Table 5.3 Relative Proportions of the Genotypes of Offspring Produced by the Matings in Table 5.2

Mating Types	Frequency of This Mating	Offspring Genotype Proportions		
		AA	Aa	aa
AA × AA	1/16	1/16	—	—
AA × Aa	4/16	2/16	2/16	—
AA × aa	2/16	—	2/16	—
Aa × Aa	4/16	1/16	2/16	1/16
Aa × aa	4/16	—	2/16	2/16
aa × aa	1/16	—	—	1/16
Totals	1	1/4	2/4	1/4

is determined by the genotypic frequency in the population ($p = 0.50 = q$), any AA male has a 1/4 chance of mating with either an AA or an aa female and a 2/4 chance of mating with a female heterozygote. The same probabilities exist for females. The matings and their expected frequencies, therefore, will occur as given in Table 5.2.

The mating types and their relative frequencies in Table 5.2 may be rearranged as shown in Table 5.3. These individuals will, on the average and according to Mendelian principles, produce offspring whose genotypes and relative proportions are given in the last three columns of Table 5.3. When the proportions of each offspring genotype are summed, it is found that the offspring, like their parents, will be expected to occur in the same $1/4\ AA : 2/4\ Aa : 1/4\ aa$ ratio.

Table 5.3 may be viewed in yet another way—from the standpoint of genotype frequencies, or the "p's" and "q's". This is outlined in Table 5.4 which demonstrates again that in a random mating population the genotype frequencies in the offspring will be the same as in their parents.

Recall that the frequencies of AA, Aa, and aa are given respectively by p^2, $2pq$, and q^2, and note in Table 5.4 the mating type frequencies. The mating $AA \times AA$, for example, is $(p^2)(p^2) = p^4$; the mating $AA \times Aa$ is $(p^2)(2pq)$, and because it can occur in two different ways ($AA\ \male \times Aa\ \female$ and vice versa) we multiply it by two.

$$2[(p^2)(2pq)] = 4p^3q.$$

It is equally easy to show that the sum of all mating types equals unity.

$$p^4 + 4p^3q + 2p^2q^2 + 4p^2q^2 + 4pq^3 + q^4$$
$$= p^2(p^2 + 2pq + q^2) + 2pq\,(p^2 + 2pq + q^2) + q^2(p^2 + 2pq + q^2)$$
$$= p^2 + 2pq + q^2$$
$$= (p + q)^2 = 1.$$

It may also be shown that the offspring genotype frequencies are identical to those of the parents by summing each of the last three columns in Table 5.4.

Table 5.4 Mating Types, Their Frequencies, and Offspring Frequencies for an Autosomal Locus with Two Alleles in a Random Mating Population

Mating Types	Frequencies	Offspring Probabilities			Offspring Probabilities × Mating Frequencies		
		AA	Aa	aa	AA	Aa	aa
$AA \times AA$	p^4	1	—	—	p^4	—	—
$AA \times Aa$	$4p^3q$	1/2	1/2	—	$2p^3q$	$2p^3q$	—
$AA \times aa$	$2p^2q^2$	—	1	—	—	$2p^2q^2$	—
$Aa \times Aa$	$4p^2q^2$	1/4	1/2	1/4	p^2q^2	$2p^2q^2$	p^2q^2
$Aa \times aa$	$4pq^3$	—	1/2	1/2	—	$2pq^3$	$2pq^3$
$aa \times aa$	q^4	—	—	1	—	—	q^4
Totals	1				p^2	$2pq$	q^2

$$AA = p^4 + 2p^3q + p^2q^2 = p^2(p^2 + 2pq + q^2) = p^2(1) = p^2$$

$$Aa = 2p^3q + 2p^2q^2 + 2p^2q^2 + 2pq^3$$

$$= 2p^3q + 4p^2q^2 + 2pq^3 = 2pq(p^2 + 2pq + q^2) = 2pq(1) = 2pq$$

$$aa = p^2q^2 + 2pq^3 + q^4 = q^2(p^2 + 2pq + q^2) = q^2(1) = q^2.$$

Thus, $AA\ (p^2) + Aa\ (2pq) + aa\ (q^2) = 1$.

The concept of **genetic equilibrium** may now be defined by stating that a population is in equilibrium when it undergoes random mating and the relative gene frequencies remain the same from generation to generation.

The Hardy-Weinberg Principle

Populations, however, are not always in genetic equilibrium. The detection of departure from equilibrium for any particular locus requires application to the alleles in question of the squared binomial $(p + q)^2$ or multinomial $(p + q + r + \ldots , n)^2$, depending upon the number of alleles at the locus. Such an application involves the Hardy-Weinberg principle, which forms one of the cornerstones of population genetics. As shown below, this principle has applications other than just describing equilibrium conditions. Notably, it may be used to predict genotypic frequencies when gene frequencies are known and random mating is assumed. Also, it may be used to calculate the number of heterozygous carriers of a genetic disorder when the number of homozygous affected individuals is known.

The Hardy-Weinberg principle requires several assumptions when used to describe equilibrium conditions. First, it assumes that no forces are operating to disrupt gene frequencies. These forces (see Chapter 6) include mutation, selection, random genetic drift, and differential migration, all of which may alter a population's genetic equilibrium. It also assumes random mating, and for it to be exactly true, the population must be infinitely large (Crow and Kimura 1970).

Applications

For an example of how the Hardy-Weinberg principle is used to determine a population's departure from equilibrium, return to the earlier example where the distribution of MN blood group genotypes was as follows:

Genotype	Number	Genotype Frequency
$L^M L^M$	84	0.38
$L^M L^N$	110	0.49
$L^N L^N$	30	0.13
Totals	224	1.00

Recall also that the allele frequencies of p (L^M) and q (L^N) were calculated respectively as 0.62 and 0.38. If the population is in equilibrium for this locus, then substitution of these two allele frequencies into the squared binomial should provide expected frequencies that are not significantly different from those actually observed.

$$(p + q)^2 = p^2 + 2pq + q^2$$
$$(0.62)^2 + 2(0.62)(0.38) + (0.38)^2$$
$$0.3844 + 0.4712 + 0.1444.$$

These represent the expected frequencies for each of the three genotypes. The expected numbers of individuals for each is obtained by multiplying the frequencies by the total number of individuals.

Expected Genotype Frequency Multiplied by N		Expected Number of Individuals
(0.3844)(224)	=	86
(0.4712)(224)	=	106
(0.1444)(224)	=	32
	Total	224

It can be seen that there is fairly good agreement between the expected and observed numbers of individuals, although they are different. The significance of this difference may be determined by the Chi-square test (see Appendix I).

$$\chi^2 = \frac{(84 - 86)^2}{86} + \frac{(110 - 106)^2}{106} + \frac{(30 - 32)^2}{32}$$
$$= 0.32, \text{ and with 1df, } P > 0.5.$$

Because this difference is not statistically significant, the population cannot be regarded as having departed from equilibrium for this locus.

We may also ask if the population is mating at random for the MN blood groups. Suppose that the 224 individuals tested were mates (112 matings), and that the six different mating types occurred as follows:

Mating Type and Number

Mating Type and Number		Mating Type and Number	
$L^M L^M \times L^M L^M$ 15		$L^M L^N \times L^M L^N$ 24	
$L^M L^M \times L^M L^N$ 44		$L^M L^N \times L^N L^N$ 18	
$L^M L^M \times L^N L^N$ 10		$L^N L^N \times L^N L^N$ . . . . _1_	
		Total 112	

The expected numbers of each mating combination are derived by utilizing the allele frequencies for $L^M (p = 0.62)$ and $L^N (q = 0.38)$.

Mating Type	Expected Frequency	Expected Number
$L^M L^M \times L^M L^M$	$p^4 = 0.1478$	17
$L^M L^M \times L^M L^N$	$4p^3 q = 0.3623$	41
$L^M L^M \times L^N L^N$	$2p^2 q^2 = 0.1110$	12
$L^M L^N \times L^M L^N$	$4p^2 q^2 = 0.2220$	25
$L^M L^N \times L^N L^N$	$4pq^3 = 0.1361$	15
$L^N L^N \times L^N L^N$	$q^4 = 0.0208$	_2_
	Total	112

Note that the expected number for each mating type is obtained by multiplying each expected frequency by the total number of matings (112). Again, testing the observed and expected numbers by Chi-square,

$$\chi^2 = 1.93, \text{ with 1df, P} > 0.1.$$

As before, the difference between observed and expected numbers is not statistically significant. Thus the population has not deviated from random mating for this locus. Note that only one degree of freedom was used. In nearly all Chi-square tests of frequencies involving two alleles at a single locus, only one degree of freedom is used because variation in the frequency of one allele automatically determines the frequency of the other. For most tests on allele frequencies, degrees of freedom are determined by subtracting the number of alleles from the number of possible phenotypes.

It was noted at the beginning of this discussion that the Hardy-Weinberg principle can also be used to predict genotypic frequencies. For example, assume that 20% of the same 224 individuals were homozygous recessive for an allele k. Suppose also that this was one of two alleles at a certain locus, and that there were no laboratory techniques for distinguishing the heterozygote Kk. Under the assumption of random mating, we expect $p^2 (KK) + 2pq(Kk) + q^2(kk)$ individuals. Since 20% of the population is kk (q^2), $q =$ the square root of $0.20 = 0.447$. Because $p + q = 1, p = 1 - 0.447 = 0.553$, and the frequency of the heterozygote, given by $2pq$, is $2(0.553)(0.447) = 0.494$.

In the same fashion, the number of heterozygous carriers of the rare recessive disease phenylketonuria (PKU) and other recessive disorders can be determined from the frequency of affected persons in the population. In some populations, PKU occurs on the average in 1 of every 10,000 individuals. If p = the frequency of the normal allele A, and q = the frequency of the recessive allele a, then

$$q^2 = \frac{1}{10,000}$$

$$q = \sqrt{\frac{1}{10,000}} = 0.01$$

$$p = 1 - q = 1 - 0.01 = 0.99.$$

The frequency of heterozygous carriers in the population, then, is $2pq = 2\,(0.99)\,(0.01) = 0.0198$. Therefore, nearly 2 of every 100 people are carriers of the recessive allele for PKU. For this condition, and for all other rare recessive disorders, the number of carriers is always much greater than the number of affected individuals. In conjunction with inbreeding, this important point will receive additional attention in Chapter 7.

The Meaning of Departure from Equilibrium

As discussed and applied above, the Hardy-Weinberg principle states:

> In the absence of disrupting factors (mutation, migration, sampling effect, selection, and linkage) the allele and genotype frequencies at any locus in a panmictic population will be repeated faithfully from generation to generation; should the frequencies be perturbed for any reason, they will come to the expected equilibrium values after one generation of random mating. (Giesel 1974:14).

This principle, therefore, describes equilibrium conditions in a static, random mating population. In reality, all human populations undergo gene frequency changes for some alleles from generation to generation. In addition, human matings are usually not random, at least for visible genetic characteristics.

It will be shown in Chapter 7 how two nonrandom mating patterns, **inbreeding** and **assortative mating**, provide the principal departures from random mating. For now, suffice it to state that such mating patterns will alter gene frequencies only when associated with some selective process. Otherwise, they affect only the relative genotypic frequencies. Both inbreeding and **positive assortative mating** (individuals with similar phenotypes mating with each other) tend to increase the frequency of homozygotes at the expense of the heterozygotes. Negative assortative mating (mating between dissimilar phenotypes), to the contrary, tends to increase the frequency of the heterozygote at the expense of the two homozygotes.

The forces causing changes in gene frequencies and, hence, departure from equilibrium in random mating populations, are the basic evolutionary factors (Wright 1955) responsible for the origin and maintenance of the genetic variation necessary for a population's existence. These forces are generally classified as follows:

I. Deterministic, or directed factors
   A. Selection
   B. Differential migration
II. Stochastic, or random factors
   A. Mutation
   B. Genetic Drift

These four factors form the central topics of the following chapter, but a few remarks in the context of the Hardy-Weinberg principle are desirable here.

1. Selection. An implicit assumption in the Hardy-Weinberg equilibrium is that individuals with different genotypes contribute equally to the next generation. If this does not happen, that is, if individuals of a certain genotype are less capable of reproducing fully fertile and viable offspring than those of another genotype, alleles of the latter will tend to increase in the gene pool. Thus both zygotic and gene frequencies may deviate from equilibrium.

2. Differential migration. Migration, or admixture, refers to genetic exchange between populations. Another assumption in the Hardy-Weinberg equilibrium is that the population is closed, which means that all individuals in the population are offspring of members of the same population. Genetic equilibrium for a particular locus in a certain gene pool may be upset if emigrants from a second population mate with members of the first population.

3. Mutation. As shown in Chapter 3, mutations are changes from one allele into another. If allele A slowly but consistently mutates to A', then the frequency of A' will tend to increase and thus lead to a frequency change. Such changes will not occur, of course, if mutations regularly occur in both directions (A to A' and vice versa).

4. Genetic drift. The Hardy-Weinberg equilibrium assumes an infinite population size, which means that there would be no error variance in gene frequencies. In reality, all populations are finite and some are quite small. A certain amount of random fluctuation in zygotic frequencies, and hence gene frequencies, may occur because of sampling error. This is especially true for small populations in which random fluctuation may result in the complete loss of an allele.

When a population deviates from Hardy-Weinberg expectations, an opportunity arises for an examination of these evolutionary forces. Of these four, mutation is the only process capable of generating novel genetic material. Both mutation and migration, however, produce genetic variability in populations by introducing genes, gene complexes, and chromosomal structures that were previously nonexistent. In the context of enabling a population to respond to changing environmental conditions, neither mutation nor migration can act upon the variability already within a population. This role is fulfilled by natural selection and, to a lesser extent, genetic drift. The raw materials for **evolution,** then, are provided by mutation and migration. New genes eventually lead to new phenotypes, and the action of natural selection on these new phenotypes adapts a population to its own ecological conditions.

Summary

In thoroughly rejecting the concept that variation in nature imperfectly reflects ideal types, modern population biologists have adopted the view that only variation has reality. This switch from typological thinking to population thinking represents one of the great conceptual revolutions in the natural sciences, and the study of populations is ultimately concerned with providing explanations for the origin and maintenance of such observed variation.

Mendelian populations are reproductive communities of individuals who share in common gene pools. That each population is genetically distinct from all others is assured by the genetic distinctness of each of their component individuals, but the process of interbreeding among these individuals gives each population its own identity. Historically, human populations have tended to retain their identity because of various sociocultural barriers that limit interpopulation genetic exchange. However, genetic changes within populations occur when, for numerous reasons, certain genotypes leave, on the average, more offspring than others. Since such changes are evolutionary by definition, the population can be considered the basic evolutionary unit.

Because the genetic composition of any generation of individuals depends upon the breeding members of the preceding generation, the study of small changes in gene frequency necessitates estimation of the effective population number. This figure is calculated mathematically rather than observed directly, and is always somewhat less than the actually observed number of adult individuals because not all of these are breeding members of the population.

The detection of small gene frequency changes in human populations has traditionally centered around genetic marker systems, such as the various blood group loci, and begins with the premise that the population is in genetic equilibrium for the locus concerned. Genetic equilibrium occurs when a population mates at random, and the gene frequencies remain unchanged from one to the next generation. The determination of whether a population has departed from equilibrium is accomplished by the mathematical theorem called the Hardy-Weinberg principle, which states that allele and genotype frequencies in a random mating population will undergo no change through generations and, even if altered, will once again reach equilibrium values after one generation of random mating. The population described, as such, is static inasmuch as no genetic change occurs. Further, it can hardly exist in nature, since no real population is invulnerable to the evolutionary processes (natural selection, differential migration, mutation, and genetic drift) responsible for gene frequency change. Nevertheless, the Hardy-Weinberg principle is a most fundamental principle of population genetics which, by detecting departure from genetic equilibrium, stimulates an examination of the evolutionary forces responsible for the change. It can also be utilized for more practical purposes, as in estimating the frequency of heterozygous carriers of rare recessive disorders.

6 Changes in Gene Frequency

Introduction

At this point, the conservative nature of heredity should be apparent: DNA tends to duplicate itself faithfully and, thereby, lends considerable stability to individuals and, ultimately, to populations. But the simple fact that all populations are different has led to the overriding concern of biological anthropology: to describe and interpret the evolutionary meaning of such observed geographic variation. Because the evolution and maintenance of human populations depend upon the simultaneous interactions among social, biological, and environmental parameters, the study of genetic variation would ideally strive to integrate the principles of population genetics, ecology, and cultural anthropology.

Unfortunately, there are enormous difficulties in attempting to inter-relate genetic, demographic, environmental, and social variables for the purpose of building an inclusive model of human population genetic structure. This is reflected in Levin's comment that "a precise mathematical description may involve hundreds of parameters, many of which are difficult to measure, and the solution of many simultaneous non-linear partial differential equations, which are usually insoluble, to get answers that are complicated expressions of the parameters which were uninterpretable (1968:5). This does not imply that investigations designed to explain genetic differences between populations are doomed from the outset. Indeed, population geneticists have developed widely applicable mathematical models that allow generalizations about (1) the genetic composition of a population at a given time, (2) the factor or factors associated with particular changes in gene pools, and (3) the rate of change in allele frequencies under certain conditions. The models presented in this chapter are limited to changes in the frequency of one or two alleles under diverse conditions and, for clarity, must often be described in elementary algebraic terms.

Nongenetic Modification of the Phenotype

The physical variation of an individual and the ability to respond to certain environmental changes is both genetic and nongenetic. A few comments about the latter are appropriate before considering changes in gene frequency. We begin by repeating that an individual's phenotype is shaped during development by (1) genes and their interactions and (2) the interplay between the genotype and all relevant environmental factors.

The phenotypes of two genetically identical individuals (MZ twins) may vary when they develop under different environmental conditions. Newman, Freeman, and Holzinger (1937), for example, have shown that the stature of two MZ twins differs when one is raised under conditions of adequate nutrition and good medical care, and the other, in a state of generalized undernutrition and poor medical care. However, a male Pygmy of the Mbuti tribe (average stature = 144.03 cm) in the central African Ituri forest, when reared under the same environmental conditions as a Nuer in the southern Sudan [(average stature = 184.88 cm) (Hiernaux 1968)], will still have a Pygmy's stature. This is because an individual's genotype determines the norm of reaction of the individual to all environments. The **norm of reaction** of a genotype is defined as "the range of developmental responses to all environments that can occur in carriers of that genotype." The genotypes of Pygmies, like those of all other human populations, determine the range of response for stature in different environments. But even under the most ideal conditions, the upper limit of their range for stature is far less than the average stature of the Nuer.

Nongenetic variation, sometimes called "phenotypic plasticity" (Mettler and Gregg 1969), is itself subject to the effects of natural selection because the norm of reaction is established by the genotype (Mayr 1963). However, phenotypic modifications by the environment do not constitute evolutionary change because they are not incorporated into the genotype, and, hence, cannot be transmitted from one generation to the next.

An example of this point is Takahashi's study (1966) of stature increase from 1934 to 1964 in Japanese schoolchildren from the northeastern part of the main island of Japan. As indicated in Figure 6.1, the stature of these children increased regularly until about 1937. It tended to level off from 1937 to 1941, and then decreased sharply from 1941 to 1946. In few and perhaps no instances has there been as sharp an increase in stature as for this group since 1946, although the trend toward increased stature has been occurring in most western industrialized societies for the past century.

Takahashi points out the fact that the Sino-Japanese incident erupted in 1937, and Japan entered World War II in 1941. Commensurate with those events was a drastic decline in the nation's food supply, including deficiencies in proteins, calcium, total calories, and other aspects associated with normal growth. At the end of World War II and the onset and continuation of milk supplements in school lunches from 1947, growth in height began the rapid increase clearly seen in Figure 6.1.

The most plausible explanation for the general trend toward stature increase in this and other societies is better nutrition and improved hygienic conditions rather than evolutionary change. This view accords well, furthermore, with the theoretical expectation (Cavalli-Sforza and Bodmer 1971) that natural selection is responsible for only a small portion of the general increase in stature.

Homeostasis

It must not be assumed from this discussion that the phenotype is without evolutionary importance. Natural selection operates on the phenotype, and the adjustment by the organism to external conditions—the matter of survival and

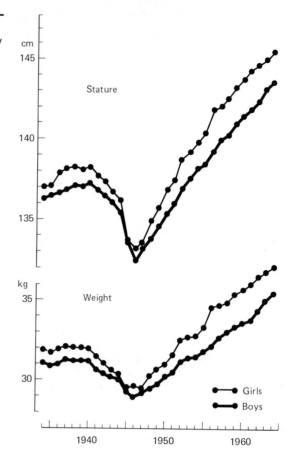

Figure 6.1 Secular trend of height and weight of 12-year-old schoolchildren in Sendai, Japan. (Courtesy of E. Takahashi, *Human Biology* 38:114, No. 2, Fig. 2, 1966.)

reproduction—depends upon phenotypic characteristics. Biologists and naturalists have known for many years that organisms in natural populations generally have phenotypic traits which enable them to respond to regularly recurring environmental stimuli in a fashion conducive to survival and successful reproduction. Such phenotypic responses take many forms. Certain species of animals living in arctic habitats, including arctic hares and ptarmigans, undergo a change from dark to white coat color in the winter. Because of this adaptive change (see Cott 1940, for a classic discussion of adaptive coloration in animals), these animals are presumably less vulnerable to predation and, hence, more successful in exploiting their habitats.

The ability of living organisms to maintain a relatively constant internal environment under varying and sometimes stressful environmental conditions is a fundamental and necessary attribute of life. Almost a century ago, Claude Bernard (1878–1879) suggested that the body's cells live in a constant *milieu interieur,* and that the fixity of the *milieu interieur* was an essential condition of life (Dubos 1965). This concept was subsequently expanded by the renowned American physiologist, W. B. Cannon (1932), who introduced the term "homeostasis" to refer to the "totality of steady states maintained in an organism through the coordination of its complex physiological processes" (Lerner 1954:1).

For biological purposes it is convenient to view homeostasis and homeostatic mechanisms in three somewhat different ways, although the concept of homeostasis per se can be applied to social, ecological, and other systems. These three viewpoints include **physiological homeostasis,** developmental homeostasis, and genetic homeostasis.

1. Physiological homeostasis. This is Cannon's basic concept. Some of the more obvious examples in humans include the maintenance of relative constancy in body temperature, blood volume and pressure, respiratory rate, renal and endocrine function, and in the concentration of minerals such as calcium, potassium, and sodium (Sargent and Weinman 1966).

2. Developmental homeostasis. This refers to phenotypic flexibility, which has been subdivided by Thoday (1953) into developmental and behavioral flexibility. According to Mayr (1963) and Dobzhansky (1970), the former leads to the development of diverse phenotypes under different environmental conditions. The tanning of human skin is a case in point, because it constitutes a conspicuous adaptive change (i.e., protection against sunburn) that requires some time to develop. In this context, temporary adaptation to environmental fluctuations may be brought about by behavioral flexibility. Human populations effectively alter nearly every aspect of their environments and, hence, are largely insulated from environmental changes. They therefore demonstrate behavioral flexibility to a much greater extent than any other animal.

Both physiological and developmental homeostasis enable an organism to respond effectively to environmental stresses. The complex homeostatic mechanisms in an individual serve to maintain a relatively steady physiological state under adverse conditions, and these mechanisms are shared by all populations of a species. They sometimes overlap between different species, but every species possesses certain characteristic homeostatic properties. Such properties limit the species to a particular environmental niche. The chimpanzee is a tropical animal, for example, and cannot survive in polar regions. Likewise, numerous species of reptiles, insects, birds, and mammals are limited geographically to certain ranges of environmental temperature, humidity, altitude, and so forth (Mayr 1963). In most instances, the species border is the point beyond which the specific homeostatic mechanisms no longer effectively function.

3. Genetic homeostasis. This term was first introduced by Lerner (1950), who later defined it as "the property of a population to equilibrate its genetic composition and to resist sudden changes" (Lerner 1954:2). Just as physiological and developmental homeostasis determine the extent to which an individual may respond to environmental variables, genetic homeostasis determines the population's range of response to selection.

Mutation

In the context of changes in gene frequency, several generalizations pertain to mutation.

1. To reiterate, mutations are the only source of new genetic material. Although a population's genetic variation arises mostly by recombination and migration, only mutation can produce a new allele.

Figure 6.2 Distribution of viabilities of new mutations. Solid line, from data. Dotted lines, extrapolations. Farther to the right would be a hump caused by the grouping together of all lethal mutations, regardless of time of death. (From *Proc. Sixth Berkeley Symp.*, Vol. 5 (1972), L. Le Cam, J. Neyman, and E. Scott, eds. Copyright 1972 by the Regents of the Univ. of California. Reprinted by permission of the Univ. of California Press.)

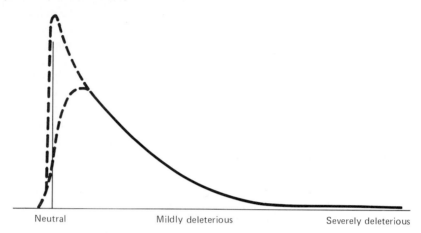

Neutral   Mildly deleterious   Severely deleterious

2. Mutations are random. They occur regardless of any specific selective pressures; there is no significant correlation between the occurrence of a new mutation and a given environmental variable. Also, there is no way of predicting the locus of the next mutation.

3. The frequency of new mutations is generally quite low, although it can increase as a result of mutagenic agents. As noted by Stevenson and Kerb (1967), an estimate of about 1×10^{-6} mutations per cistron per generation is a widely accepted estimate for the rate of mutations with lethal or visible effects.

4. The majority of new mutations have **deleterious** effects. However, Crow (1972) and others have suggested that the viabilities of new mutations range along a continuum from slightly beneficial to lethal. This implies (Fig. 6.2) that some new mutations are nearly, if not totally, neutral under particular selective regimes.

5. The phenotypic effects of new, slightly beneficial mutations are exceedingly slight, and many generations will be required for the new allele to increase to fixation (Fisher 1930; King 1972).

In light of the last three statements, the question of what happens to a newly arisen mutation is especially interesting. It is known that gene mutations constantly arise, although at low rates, in all human populations. It is also known that in some cases, such as the sickle-cell gene, mutations become fixed at rather high frequencies through time. In this instance, as discussed later, such a mutation becomes fixed because it confers an advantage to its heterozygous carriers. In other cases, at least in principle, mutations can be fixed in a population by chance (random genetic drift) even if they are of no particular selective advantage. The probability of fixation by random genetic drift of an essentially neutral mutation is only $1/2 N$, where $N = $ the number of individuals in the population. However, this probability is expected to be higher for advantageous and lower for disadvantageous mutations.

Many years ago, R. A. Fisher (1930) showed theoretically that family size is a primary determining factor in the increase or decrease of a new mutant allele in future generations. He found mathematically that the probability of survival of a new mutation in one generation is 0.6321; in the third generation is 0.3741; in the fifteenth generation is 0.1127; and decreases to 0.0153 in the 127th generation. After n generations (when n is high), the probability of survival of a mutant allele is approximately $2/n$. Thus the probability of survival of a new mutation with no particular selective advantage is, for most practical purposes, nonexistent when the number of generations is high.

It can be shown mathematically that mutation is an evolutionary process capable of changing gene frequencies (Li 1955), but such changes occur very slowly. If irreversible mutations are considered, i.e., when A mutates to a (but never the opposite) at a rate of 10^{-5}, then a will increase in frequency through time until A disappears. But how much time is involved? Nearly 70,000 generations would be required to reduce the frequency of A from, say, 0.80 to 0.40; another 70,000 generations to reduce 0.40 to 0.20; and so forth, until A disappeared from the population. A reduction in the frequency of A from 0.80 to 0.025 would require approximately (5) (70,000) = 350,000 generations. If we assume the length of a human generation at 20 years, then by irreversible mutation alone such an evolutionary change would require about 7,000,000 years. This length of time does not accord well with the rates of evolutionary change actually observed in nature, and we may assume that mutation is far less effective than selection, migration, or genetic drift in changing gene frequencies.

Selection

Modern definitions of **natural selection** are usually similar to Wilson and Bossert's, "the differential change in relative frequency of genotypes due to differences in the ability of their phenotypes to obtain representation in the next generation" (1971:47). There is little doubt that natural selection is the most important cause of gene frequency change, and it is important to explore the concept in more detail before examining some of its mathematical and genetic aspects.

Over 100 years ago, Charles Darwin showed that the driving force behind natural selection was the tendency for all living organisms to produce far more offspring than could survive to reproductive age. It was common knowledge then, as it is today, that plants and animals of various species produce hundreds, thousands, and sometimes millions of eggs. Under ideal conditions—when all eggs are fertilized and develop into fully fertile and viable offspring—the increase in size of a population in a few generations can be astronomical. One hundred common flour mites, for example, would increase their numbers to 28 billion in the space of ten weeks (Solomon 1969).

Darwin also knew that all species, including slow breeding mammals with long generation times, are capable of expanding their numbers exponentially. He stated in 1859:

> The elephant is reckoned to be the slowest breeder of all known animals, and I have taken some pains to estimate its probable minimum rate of natural increase: it will be under the mark to assume that it breeds when thirty years old, and goes on breeding till ninety years old, bringing forth three pair of young in this interval; if this be so, at the end of the fifth century there would be alive fifteen million elephants, descended from the first pair. (1859:64)

As a matter of observed fact, our planet is not overrun with elephants, flour mites, or any other species (with perhaps the exception of *H. sapiens*). The reason, of course, is because the vast majority of offspring do not survive to reproduce. They are eliminated by both biotic and abiotic environmental factors. These are called limiting, or selective, factors, and they operate continuously in all populations. Obvious selective factors include available food supply, predators and parasites, overcrowding, disease, and nearly all aspects of the physical environment. Some of these variables are humidity, available light, seasonal or permanent changes in temperature, catastrophic occurrences, and so forth. It will be shown later that such selective factors tend to (1) eliminate individuals whose phenotypes are disadvantageous and (2) preserve individuals whose phenotypes are advantageous. The survival of an individual and the genetic transmission to the next generation depends, therefore, upon how well that individual copes with the various selective factors in the environment. Few biologists have summarized Darwin's concept of natural selection more clearly than Dobzhansky in the following set of logical statements:

1. Any organism needs food and other resources in order to live.
2. The resources are always limited.
3. The number of individuals of any species is therefore also limited.
4. Any species is capable of increasing in number in an exponential progression.
5. Sooner or later the state will be reached when only a part of the progeny will be able to survive.
6. The statistical probability of survival or elimination, despite accidents, will depend on the degree of the adaptedness of individuals and groups to the environment in which they live.
7. This degree of adaptedness is in part conditioned by the genetic endowment.
8. Therefore, carriers of some genotypes will survive, or will be eliminated, more or less frequently than will the carriers of other genotypes, and the succeeding generations will not be descended equally from all the genotypes in the preceding generations, but relatively more from the better adapted ones.
9. Therefore, the incidence of better adapted forms will tend to increase and the incidence of the less well adapted ones to decrease. (1962:128)

Finally, two very important points must be emphasized. First, natural selection is not evolution, although these two concepts are sometimes confused. Natural selection is only a process which, in conjunction with other processes, leads to evolutionary change. Second, natural selection is the differential reproduction of genotypes, and not differential survival. Obviously, individuals must survive in order to reproduce. But the importance for evolutionary change is the differential contribution of genotypes to the progeny of all future generations (Mayr 1963). This differential ability of genotypes to leave offspring is, by definition **Darwinian fitness.**

Fitness and the Selection Coefficient

It is relatively simple to estimate the fitness (designated by W, and often called the adaptive value) of individuals of contrasting genotypes in certain selective regimes. Suppose two alleles at one locus can be identified in all individuals of a population.

Suppose also that the genotypes *AA*, *Aa*, and *aa* survive disproportionately as a result of a hypothetical selective factor. These data may be ascertained by a direct census.

	Genotypes		
	AA	*Aa*	*aa*
Number of individuals before selection	8600	9500	4700
Number of individuals after selection	8300	7200	900

The survival rate of each genotype, represented by the symbol λ, may be determined by dividing the number of individuals after one generation of selection by the number before selection.

$$\lambda_{AA} = \text{the survival rate of } AA = 8300/8600 = 0.97$$
$$\lambda_{Aa} = \text{the survival rate of } Aa = 7200/9500 = 0.76$$
$$\lambda_{aa} = \text{the survival rate of } aa = 900/4700 = 0.19$$

If the genotype with the highest survival rate is used as a standard for comparison, then the relative fitness of each genotype is found by dividing its survival rate by the highest survival rate (in this case, λ_{AA}). The result, as shown below, is that fitness (W) can range only between 1 and zero.

$$W_{AA} = \text{the relative fitness of } AA = 0.97/0.97 = 1$$
$$W_{Aa} = \text{the relative fitness of } Aa = 0.76/0.97 = 0.78$$
$$W_{aa} = \text{the relative fitness of } aa = 0.19/0.97 = 0.20$$

Clearly, the intensity of selection varies among the three genotypes. This intensity is given by the selection coefficient (s) and is defined as $(1 - W)$. For each genotype, therefore, the coefficient of selection reflects the proportionate reduction in fitness compared to the most fit genotype.

$$s_{AA} = \text{the selection coefficient of } AA = 1 - W_{AA} = 0$$
$$s_{Aa} = \text{the selection coefficient of } Aa = 1 - W_{Aa} = 0.22$$
$$s_{aa} = \text{the selection coefficient of } aa = 1 - W_{aa} = 0.80$$

Types of Natural Selection

Natural selection operates on phenotypes in various ways, and four general types of natural selection can be distinguished on the basis of how they change gene frequencies. These are (1) **stabilizing,** (2) **balancing,** (3) **directional,** and (4) **diversifying selection.**

1. Stabilizing (or normalizing) selection. It was stressed earlier that the success of a population is closely related to its harmonious interactions with the environment. In other words, populations generally consist of individuals with phenotypic traits that are adapted to varying degrees to existing environmental conditions. If environmental variables were to become constant and to remain so for a considerable time, then selection would result in highly adapted individuals in a population in which gene frequencies for most loci would be close to equilibrium. The role of stabilizing selection is to maintain this highly adapted state. However, other processes such as mutation, migration, and recombination continually produce less well-adapted forms. Stabilizing selection tends to eliminate these individuals because

they produce fewer offspring on the average and, thus, contribute fewer genes to the next generation than the better-adapted individuals.

Another way of visualizing the effects of stabilizing selection is presented in Figure 6.3. This is a hypothetical frequency distribution of a phenotypic trait, in which the frequency of individuals is given on the vertical axis and the phenotypic variation on the horizontal axis. Stabilizing selection discriminates against phenotypes at both extremes of the distribution. Although the variance of the trait increases every generation because of mutation, migration, and recombination, stabilizing selection simultaneously reduces the variance and results in a concentration of phenotypes around the mean. The population, therefore, tends to become more homogeneous for the trait and its associated genes.

The operation of stabilizing selection in a human population is evident in the data of Karn and Penrose (1951). They recorded over an 11-year period the birth weights of nearly 14,000 babies born in a London hospital. As shown in Figure 6.4, the birth weights in this sample are distributed much like other quantitative characteristics. Most of the birth weights occur near the mean, and the frequency of both high and low weights falls away from the mean in both directions. Fortunately, the hospital also kept records on the survival of these babies. After finding that 4.47% of all babies died before reaching 4 weeks of age, Mather (1964) plotted the mortality rates by birth weights. As the dotted line in Figure 6.4 indicates, a sharp increase in mortality occurred at both extremes of the distribution, and the lowest mortality was near the mean birth weight. It appears in this group, therefore, that stabilizing selection reduces the variance for birth weight and retains the expression of this variable near its optimal value.

2. Balancing selection. It has been mentioned that most new mutations are deleterious, and some appear to be sublethal or lethal regardless of their environment. Homozygotes with the dominant sublethal defect, epiloia, for example, generally die at an early age (Gunther and Penrose 1935) in spite of external conditions. Other mutations, however, may be harmful in one environment but beneficial in another. If environments remained constant, then stabilizing selection would tend to deplete genetic variation. But environmental conditions are notoriously variable, especially through time, and populations must possess a store of genetic variation for adequate response to such fluctuations. Adaptively beneficial genetic variation is either maintained or increased by the process called "balancing selection." The maintenance of genetic variation in a population by balancing selection may result in normal individuals with sharply distinct characteristics. This phenomenon, called "genetic polymorphism," was first outlined by Ford (1940), who later defined it as "the occurrence together in the same locality of two or more discontinuous forms of a species in such proportions that the rarest of them cannot be maintained merely by recurrent mutation" (1964:84).

There are numerous examples in human populations of two or more alleles at a locus being maintained in a balanced state at relatively high frequencies, that is, as a balanced polymorphism. However, there are many other genetic polymorphisms that are not balanced (Berg and Bearn 1968; Steinberg 1969), but are, rather, in a transient, or changing state. Balanced polymorphisms are usually due to balancing selection, which often involves selection for the heterozygote and against

Figure 6.3 The results of detrimental (↓) and advantageous (↑) selection pressures on parts of the population frequency distribution curves of a hypothetical quantitative characteristic. Numbers of individuals are on the vertical axis; character variation is on the horizontal axis.

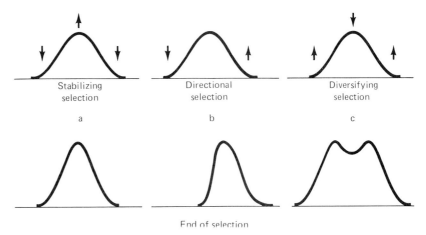

Beginning of selection

Stabilizing selection

a

Directional selection

b

Diversifying selection

c

End of selection

Figure 6.4 The distribution of birth weight among 13,730 children, and the rates of early mortality of the various birth weight classes. The hatched histogram shows the proportions of the population falling into the various classes in respect to birth weight. The broken line is the curve of mortality in relation to birth weight, the values actually observed for the classes of birth weight being represented by the points to which the curve is an approximation. M marks the mean birth weight and O the birth weight associated with the lowest mortality and, hence, to be regarded as the optimum weight. (Courtesy of K. Mather, *Human Diversity*, 1964. The Free Press.)

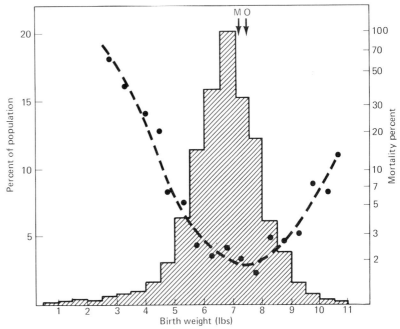

the homozygote. When this occurs, the terms "heterozygote superiority" or "heterotic balance" are used to describe the system.

The classic example of a balanced polymorphism involves falciparum malaria as a selective force and the sickle-cell allele (see Chapter 3 for a discussion of the genetics of sickle-cell anemia and the sickle-cell trait). The frequency of the Hb^S allele is highest in geographical areas of endemic falciparum malaria, including West and Central Africa. In these areas, both Hb^S and Hb^A homozygotes are at a selective disadvantage compared to the heterozygote. Hb^S/Hb^S individuals have a poor expectation of life due to the effects of sickle-cell anemia, and Hb^A/Hb^A individuals are particularly susceptible to falciparum malaria.

For various physiological reasons (Sheagren et al. 1970; Luzzatto et al. 1970), however, heterozygous Hb^S/Hb^A individuals are relatively resistant to malaria. The differences in mortality rates from falciparum malaria between normal individuals and those with the sickle-cell trait are considerable, and every study has shown that mortality in the latter is far lower than in the former (Livingstone 1971). In malarial regions, then, the fitness of the heterozygote exceeds that of either homozygote. The reason that homozygotes are continually produced every generation, in spite of their lower fitness, is because matings between two heterozygotes will on the average result in one-fourth of the progeny being Hb^S/Hb^S and one-fourth Hb^A/Hb^A.

In geographical areas where malaria is not endemic, such as North America, the Hb^S allele occurs in much lower frequencies and the polymorphism is no longer balanced. The strong selective pressure against the Hb^S homozygote still remains, and there is no good evidence for a difference in fitness between the heterozygote and the normal homozygote. Under these conditions selection is directional, and providing there is no immigration of individuals with the Hb^S allele, the frequency of this allele is expected to eventually decrease to extinction. How long will this take? Assuming a frequency of the Hb^S allele among United States black populations of 0.05 (Motulsky et al. 1971), Li and Nei (1972) have estimated average extinction times of 130 generations when N_e (the effective population size) = 1,000, and 518 generations when N_e = 10,000. Assuming 25 years per generation, the average extinction time for this allele is approximately 3,250 years when N_e = 1,000, and 12,950 years when N_e = 10,000.

3. Directional selection. We have seen that stabilizing selection results in highly adapted genotypes in stable environments. This implies that the mean population fitness values are closely attuned to existing conditions. However, there is no guarantee that the favored adaptations will be advantageous to future generations under different environmental conditions. When a population is exposed to different external conditions, some phenotypic variants that were at a disadvantage under previous conditions may be favored by the new conditions. Because selection tends to maximize the mean fitness of the population, the genes responsible for the most advantageous phenotypes will tend to increase and, hence, lead to a new phenotypic optimum. Directional selection establishes a new optimum composed of phenotypes that were previously toward one end of the phenotypic distribution (Fig. 6.3b). Like stabilizing selection, directional selection eventually decreases the variance. But unlike stabilizing selection, it shifts the mean to a new point in the distribution.

The classic example of directional selection is industrial melanism in the peppered moth, *Biston betularia* (Kettlewell 1961, 1965; Ford 1964). Before the

Figure 6.5 *Biston betularia,* the Peppered Moth, and its black form, *carbonaria,* at rest on **a,** lichened tree trunk in unpolluted countryside and **b,** soot covered oak trunk near Birmingham, England. (From Lawrence S. Dillon, *Evolution.* 2nd Ed., 1978. The C. V. Mosby Co., St. Louis, From The Experiments of Bernard Kettlewell, Univ. of Oxford, England.)

nineteenth century, specimens of this moth were observed to be a mottled grayish-white and black. This presumably conferred a selective advantage to the moth, for it was camouflaged against predators when resting on lichen-covered tree trunks (Fig. 6.5*a*). In 1848, a melanic (dark) form of the moth was collected, and today many populations of *B. betularia* consist of high frequencies of the black forms. It has been observed, furthermore, that populations with the highest frequencies of the dark form are positively correlated with English industrial areas and increased levels of industrial pollutants. Trees in these areas are blackened with soot, and the dark forms enjoy the same selective advantage as the lighter forms in nonpolluted areas. (Fig. 6.5*b*). The most prominent predators of this moth are birds, which hunt by sight, and directional selection has favored the color variants that blend best with the background coloration.

There are numerous examples of directional selection in domesticated animals, plants, insects, and microorganisms, but not in human populations. Most instances involve either intentional or unintentional artificial manipulation of the organisms' environment. Animal and plant breeders often select for an extreme expression of a particular characteristic (usually judged beneficial by human standards) such as increased yield per acre and improvements in disease resistance in food plants, increases in egg and milk production and personality characteristics in domestic dogs and cats. In attempting to control or eradicate populations of harmful insects such as flies and mosquitoes, we have inadvertently selected for strains resistant to compounds such as DDT, dieldrin, and a variety of organophosphates. Reviews on this subject have been given by Keiding (1967) and Brown (1967). Needless to say, the evolutionary versatility of what we regard as pests has far exceeded our ingenuity in developing adequate and long-lasting controls.

4. Diversifying selection. This type of natural selection, illustrated in Figure 6.3c, is essentially the converse of stabilizing selection. By favoring both extremes of the distribution and acting against the values around the mean, diversifying selection increases the variance but leaves the mean unchanged. A population may respond to selection for two or more optimal phenotypes in two different ways: (1) it may become polymorphic and show discontinuities in the pattern of variation, or (2) individuals for certain phenotypic optima may cluster in local "subpopulations," which are adapted to local conditions. Whether the subpopulations diverge completely will depend upon an intervening period of geographic separation, directional selection for different phenotypic optima under different ecological requirements, and subsequent reproductive isolation between the two populations (Mayr 1963).

The action of natural selection is on the entire phenotype and is a blind and automatic process. No single selective factor somehow picks out one phenotypic characteristic produced by a single allele and then changes the frequency of this allele. It has been stressed that the phenotype is an integrated expression of the entire genotype. A change in the frequency of an allele at one locus often means an indirect change in the frequency of an allele at a different locus, especially when the two loci are closely linked. These four types of natural selection are idealizations and were discussed separately only to show some of the ways in which selection can affect the relationship between a quantitative characteristic and population fitness. In the natural world, devoid of human intervention, these and other types of selection operate simultaneously upon multiple characteristics of organisms.

Changes in Gene Frequency under Different Selective Regimes

Nevertheless, our understanding of changes in gene frequency, and the rates at which they occur when selection favors or discriminates against certain phenotypes, is especially enhanced by the construction of elementary models. These represent exceedingly complex phenomena reduced to their most basic levels. Table 6.1 contains one example of such a model that describes the genetic change in only a single pair of alleles, *A* and *a*, at one locus. Those of you interested in additional models should consult Li (1955) or Crow and Kimura (1970).

Complete elimination of recessives. Suppose that the homozygous recessive genotype in a large, random mating population is lethal, so that only the homozygous dominants and heterozygotes can mate and reproduce. Assuming complete dominance, the fitness of both the homozygous dominant and the heterozygous genotype is one. Thus the proportions of the three genotypes in the population before and after selection are given in Table 6.1.

Let us examine the derivations in Table 6.1 more closely. First, the total for the frequency after selection is obtained by summing the frequencies of *AA* and *Aa* after selection.

$$p^2 + 2pq = p(p + 2q)$$
$$= p[(p + q) + q].$$

And since $p + q = 1$,

Table 6.1 Changes in Gene Frequency When the Recessive Homozygote Is Lethal

	Genotypes				
	AA	Aa	aa	Total	Freq. of a
Frequency before selection	p^2	$2pq$	q^2	1	q
Relative fitness (W)	1	1	0		
Frequency after selection	p^2	$2pq$	0	$p(1 + q)$	
Relative frequency	$\dfrac{p}{1 + q}$	$\dfrac{2q}{1 + q}$	0		$\dfrac{q}{1 + q}$

$$\Delta q = -\frac{q^2}{1 + q}$$

$$p^2 + 2pq = p(1 + q).$$

The relative frequencies after selection, or the population responsible for the next generation, are obtained by dividing the frequencies after selection for each genotype by the total: for AA,

$$\frac{p^2}{p(1 + q)} = \frac{p}{1 + q};$$

and for Aa,

$$\frac{2pq}{p(1 + q)} = \frac{2q}{1 + q}.$$

The relative frequency of a, of course, is one-half the relative frequency of the heterozygote.

$$q = \left(\frac{2q}{1 + q}\right)\left(\frac{1}{2}\right) = \frac{q}{1 + q}$$

Similarly,

$$p = 1 - q$$

$$= 1 - \frac{q}{1 + q} = \frac{1}{1 + q}$$

Now, Δq represents the change in the frequency of q from the original population frequency to the relative frequency after selection. In other words, the former is subtracted from the latter.

$$\Delta q = \frac{q}{1+q} - q = \frac{q}{1+q} - \frac{q(1+q)}{1+q}$$

$$= \frac{q}{1+q} - \frac{q+q^2}{1+q}$$

$$= \frac{q - (q+q^2)}{1+q}$$

$$= -\frac{q^2}{1+q}$$

For example, suppose a population has these original genotype and gene frequencies:

$$p^2(AA) = 0.70$$
$$2pq(Aa) = 0.28$$
$$q^2(aa) = 0.02$$
$$p_0(A) = 0.84$$
$$q_0(a) = 0.16$$

Assuming A as completely dominant and aa as lethal, then the frequency of a after selection decreases from 0.16 to

$$q_1 = \frac{q_0}{1+q_0} = \frac{0.16}{1.16} = 0.14.$$

The rate of decrease of q_0 to q_1, or $\Delta q_{0 \to 1}$, is

$$\Delta q_{0 \to 1} = -\frac{q^2_0}{1+q_0} = -\frac{(0.16)^2}{1.16} = -0.02.$$

After the homozygous recessive individuals are eliminated by selection, the relative genotypic frequencies of the breeding population responsible for the next generation are

$$AA = \frac{p_0}{1+q_0} = \frac{0.84}{1.16} = 0.72$$

$$Aa = \frac{2q_0}{1+q_0} = \frac{0.32}{1.16} = 0.28.$$

Suppose now that the next generation is produced, and that the same selective pressures operate. Recall that the relative frequencies of A and a were

$$p(A) = \frac{1}{1 + q} \text{ and } q(a) = \frac{q}{1 + q}.$$

Before selection occurs in this generation, the zygotic proportions of each genotype are

$$p^2(AA) = \frac{(1)^2}{(1 + q_0)^2} = \frac{1}{(1 + 0.16)^2} = 0.74$$

$$2pq(Aa) = \frac{2q_0}{(1 + q_0)^2} = \frac{(2)(0.16)}{(1 + 0.16)^2} = 0.24$$

$$q^2(aa) = \frac{q^2{}_0}{(1 + q_0)^2} = \frac{(0.16)^2}{(1 + 0.16)^2} = 0.02.$$

After selection, the genotypic frequencies of the population in this generation (and, hence, those responsible for the following generation) are

$$AA = \frac{p_1}{1 + q_1} = \frac{0.86}{1.14} = 0.75$$

$$Aa = \frac{2q_1}{1 + q_1} = \frac{0.28}{1.14} = 0.25.$$

The decrease in the frequency of the recessive allele is

$$q_2 = \frac{q_1}{1 + q_1} = \frac{0.14}{1.14} = 0.12.$$

And the rate of change now becomes

$$\Delta q_{1 \to 2} = -\frac{q^2{}_1}{1 + q_1} = -\frac{(0.14)^2}{1.14} = -0.017.$$

To summarize these calculations, after only two generations of selection against a recessive lethal, the allele frequency of a has decreased from 0.16 to 0.12. However, the rate of decrease has also diminished, from -0.02 to -0.017. When the initial frequency of the recessive allele is high, and when values are calculated for n generations, it will be found that q diminishes rapidly until it reaches a value of about 0.01. At approximately this value, the rate of decrease also becomes quite small. The decrease in q thereafter becomes less and less every generation because there are very few recessive homozygotes formed.

There are two aspects about selection against recessive lethals which should be mentioned. First, there is a very rapid decrease in allele frequencies from the evolutionary viewpoint because only a few thousand generations are involved.

From the standpoint of artificial selection against lethal alleles in human populations, however, it is quite inefficient. In this context, Li (1955) shows that it would require 1,500 years of compulsory sterilization to reduce the frequency of a recessive lethal allele by one-half when the original frequency is 0.02. Clearly, elimination of recessive defects by sterilization is of little, if any, practical value.

The Selection–Mutation Equilibrium

The model outlined above, along with many others that deal with different selective regimes, were developed in the late 1920s and early 1930s by R. A. Fisher, J. B. S. Haldane, and S. Wright, who are generally credited with founding the field of population genetics. Under certain conditions these models can be used to predict not only the rate and amount of genetic change, but (with additional mathematical treatment) also the number of generations required to change allele frequencies from 1 to 0, or vice versa.

For explanatory purposes, natural selection and mutation have been treated as if they operated independently. In reality, these two forces act simultaneously (with migration and genetic drift) in bringing about evolutionary change in natural populations. One of these interactions, that between selection and mutation, will be examined in this brief section.

It should be apparent that the frequency of an allele will change more rapidly when selection and mutation operate in the same direction. Similarly, a stable equilibrium may result when the elimination of alleles by selection is counterbalanced by the introduction of new alleles at the same locus by mutation. This type of equilibrium may be derived as follows. Suppose that selection eliminates a deleterious but nonlethal allele a (q) at a rate per generation of

$$\Delta q = \frac{sq^2(1 - q)}{1 - sq^2}.$$

The derivation of this expression can be found in Strickberger (1976). Suppose also that while selection decreases the value of q, mutation from A to a increases q at the rate μ per generation. The denominator in the above equation is approximately 1 when the selection coefficient is small, and thus elimination of the allele occurs approximately at the rate $sq^2(1 - q)$. Now, the gain in a because of new mutations from A to a is $\mu(1 - q)$. Since selection and mutation are operating in opposite directions, the net change in the frequency of q is

$$sq^2(1 - q) = \mu(1 - q)$$

$$sq^2 = \mu$$

$$q^2 = \frac{\mu}{s} \text{ and } q = \sqrt{\frac{\mu}{s}}.$$

This represents the equilibrium value of q; the input from mutation balances the elimination by selection. As shown in Chapter 5, the incidence of PKU in some populations is approximately 1/10,000. Because PKU is fully recessive, $q^2 = 1/10,000$, and $q = 0.01$. PKU was a lethal disorder before modern medicine, thus $s = 1$. Assuming equilibrium, the mutation rate of PKU can be estimated as

$$q^2 = \frac{\mu}{s}; \mu = sq^2 = (1)(0.0001) = 10^{-4}.$$

The same formula can be used to estimate the selection coefficient of a deleterious recessive if the incidence of the disorder and its mutation rate are known. If a certain recessive disorder occurs at a frequency of 1/20,000, and if $\mu = 10^{-6}$, then the selection coefficient is

$$s = \frac{\mu}{q^2} = \frac{10^{-6}}{1/20,000} = \frac{0.00001}{0.00005} = 0.2.$$

Migration

It has been stressed that novel genetic material is produced only by mutation. Once present in a gene pool, however, new alleles may be introduced to another gene pool by mating between members of the two populations. This phenomenon is called migration, or genetic exchange. When such exchange is continuous, some prefer the term, **gene flow.** In the context of genetic change, the effects of migration may be viewed from two rather different standpoints: (1) when it occurs between closely adjacent local populations and (2) when it occurs between geographically separated populations.

In the modern world there are no human populations completely isolated from all other populations. Before modern transportation, however, and at a time when the world's population was only a tiny fraction of today's numbers, the relative isolation of human populations was especially enhanced by physical geography. The barriers to gene flow at present are largely behavioral, and they may be even more effective than geography (Hulse 1957).

In general, the probability of gene flow is greatest between adjacent populations having a number of cultural, social, and environmental features in common. Populations that are spatially and genetically related tend to have similar gene pools, however, and gene flow is not expected to be a major factor causing gene frequency change in such groups.

The effect of gene flow between geographically separated populations, on the other hand, may be quite dramatic. Such populations possess their own local adaptations and, hence, disparate gene pools, brought about largely by selection. The introduction of new alleles by migration often alters allelic frequencies and, hence, gene complexes. If the process is continuous, the eventual result is a reduction in the genetic differences between the two groups. Gene flow also increases the genetic variation of a population, which in turn provides that population with an increased potential to adapt to changing selective factors. This point may be illustrated by a purely hypothetical case. Suppose individuals of one population (A) have the alleles a_1 and a_2 at a certain locus. Suppose also that another population (B) is characterized by two different alleles, b_1 and b_2, at the same locus. Individuals of population A will possess one of three possible genotypes (a_1a_1, a_1a_2, or a_2a_2), and individuals of population B will be either b_1b_1, b_1b_2, or b_2b_2. Let us also assume that both populations are large, mate at random for this locus, and that neither selection, mutation, nor genetic drift affect these alleles.

Unlimited gene flow between these two populations will result in a hybrid population C, which is more genotypically complex than either ancestral population. Whereas individuals in either A or B could possess only one of three possible genotypes, an individual in population C could be one of ten different genotypes (any of those of the parental populations or, additionally, the heterozygous forms a_1b_1, a_1b_2, a_2b_1, and a_2b_2).

A Static Model of Gene Flow

This hypothetical case provides an example of the simplest static model of gene flow. Suppose again that migrants from two parental populations P_1 and P_2 in the proportions m and $1 - m$ respectively establish a hybrid population H. Suppose also that the frequencies of an allele in P_1 and P_2 are respectively q_1 and q_2. The frequency of this allele in the hybrid population is q_h, which represents the frequency of q_1 and q_2 in all migrants: $q_h = q_1m + q_2(1 - m)$. This equation may be solved for m as follows:

$$q_h = q_1m + q_2 - q_2m$$
$$q_h - q_2 = m(q_1 - q_2)$$
$$m = \frac{q_h - q_2}{q_1 - q_2}.$$

If the values of q_1, q_2, and q_h are known, they can be substituted into this equation in order to derive an estimate of m. The value thus obtained represents the proportion of the hybrid gene pool derived from P_1.

Nagel and Soto (1964) and Saldahna (1968) have utilized this method to estimate the proportion of Indian ancestry in contemporary Chileans, whose genes are derived primarily from (1) Auricanians, a group of South American Indians inhabiting parts of Chile from before the Inca Empire, and (2) Europeans, mainly Spanish Castilians and Basques. In a summary of their combined data, Workman (1973) shows for various loci that roughly 36% of the genes of modern Chileans are derived from Indian ancestry (Table 6.2).

Static models of gene flow, such as that by the preceding equation, are based on two major assumptions. First, gene flow is assumed to have occurred in only one direction—from the parental to the hybrid population. Second, they assume that gene frequencies in the parental population remain unchanged by other evolutionary processes. Such models are restricted, furthermore, inasmuch as they can only provide

Table 6.2 Estimates of the Indian Contribution to the Gene Pool of Contemporary Chileans (From Workman 1973.)

Allele	Chilean (q_h)	Indian (q_1)	Spanish (q_2)	$m = \dfrac{q_h - q_2}{q_1 - q_2}$
Hp^1	0.530	0.790	0.380	0.36
r (Rh)	0.251	0.000	0.364	0.31
r (Rh)	0.294	0.119	0.384	0.34
R^1 (Rh)	0.469	0.693	0.411	0.31
A (ABO)	0.173	0.017	0.292	0.43
A (ABO)	0.187	0.071	0.286	0.46
O (ABO)	0.752	0.893	0.652	0.39
t (PTC)	0.366	0.111	0.498	0.34
M (MN)	0.561	0.630	0.511	0.41

estimates of the total proportion of genes in a hybrid population from its parental population. Clearly, these models are inappropriate for analysis of reciprocal gene flow, and they cannot be used to estimate the amount of gene flow over several generations.

However, models of gene flow that overcome some of these limitations have been developed. One of the most elementary of such dynamic models assumes that gene flow is in only one direction and occurs at a constant rate through generations. In a study of intermixture between Americans of European and African ancestry, Glass and Li (1953) utilized this method and estimated that roughly 30% of the genes in certain contemporary American black populations were derived by gene flow over 300 years (about ten generations) from American white populations. Conversely, nearly 70% of the genes in the same population were of African descent.

Genetic Drift

Genetic drift, a concept owing its mathematical formulation mainly to S. Wright (1931, 1932), is a random process that changes gene frequencies through "accidents" of biological sampling. Although it doubtlessly occurs in all populations, its effects are most apparent on small rather than large gene pools.

The meaning of the phrase, accidents of biological sampling, may be demonstrated by an example. Suppose a population consists of six males and six females whose MN blood group genotypes are

Males: $L^M L^M, L^M L^M, L^M L^N, L^M L^N, L^M L^N, L^N L^N$

Females: $L^M L^M, L^M L^M, L^M L^N, L^M L^N, L^M L^N, L^N L^N.$

Suppose also that the following matings occur, and that each mating results in two children of opposite sexes with these genotypes:

Parents		Offspring	
♂	♀	♂	♀
$L^M L^M$ ×	$L^M L^N$	$L^M L^M$	$L^M L^M$
$L^M L^M$ ×	$L^N L^N$	$L^M L^N$	$L^M L^N$
$L^M L^N$ ×	$L^M L^N$	$L^M L^M$	$L^M L^M$
$L^M L^N$ ×	$L^M L^M$	$L^M L^M$	$L^M L^M$
$L^M L^N$ ×	$L^M L^N$	$L^M L^M$	$L^M L^N$
$L^N L^N$ ×	$L^M L^M$	$L^M L^N$	$L^M L^N$

Among the parents, the allele frequencies of $M(p) = 0.58$, and of $N(q) = 0.42$, and it can be easily shown that the population is in genetic equilibrium. The gene pool of the offspring is also in equilibrium, but after only one generation, p has increased to 0.79 and q has decreased to 0.21.

This example can be extended to yet another generation by assuming again that the offspring mate at random and replace their numbers as follows:

F_1 Offspring		F_2 Offspring	
♂	♀	♂	♀
$L^M L^M$ ×	$L^M L^M$	$L^M L^M$	$L^M L^M$
$L^M L^N$ ×	$L^M L^N$	$L^M L^M$	$L^M L^M$
$L^M L^M$ ×	$L^M L^M$	$L^M L^M$	$L^M L^M$
$L^M L^M$ ×	$L^M L^N$	$L^M L^M$	$L^M L^N$
$L^M L^M$ ×	$L^M L^M$	$L^M L^M$	$L^M L^M$
$L^M L^N$ ×	$L^M L^N$	$L^M L^M$	$L^M L^N$

Notice in this second generation that the frequency of p has "drifted" even higher— to 0.92—purely by accidents of sampling. In yet another generation of mating, the L^M allele might completely replace L^N and reach fixation in the population. In the same fashion, of course, the opposite trend could also occur.

While genetic drift can alter allele frequencies quite rapidly in small populations, its effects are less immediate in large populations. Consider two populations of sexually reproducing diploid individuals, one with 500,000 and the other with 50 individuals. Suppose that the population size of each remains constant, and that two alleles (A and a) at a single locus occur in both populations with equal frequency ($p = 0.5 = q$).

The question to be asked concerns the difference in the amount of change in allele frequencies by genetic drift in the large versus the small population. Now, the variance in allele frequencies is introduced by sampling and is given by pq/N, where N is the number of individuals in the sample (see Chapter 5). Since in diploid organisms N individuals result from $2N$ gametes, the variance becomes $\sigma^2 = pq/2N$. The standard deviation (sometimes called the standard error in this case), therefore, is

$$\sigma = \sqrt{\frac{pq}{2N}}.$$

When $p = 0.5 = q$ in a population of 500,000, the standard deviation is, thus,

$$\sigma = \sqrt{\frac{(0.5)(0.5)}{1,000,000}} = 0.0005.$$

This means that the frequencies of A and a in the following generation will be 0.5 ± 0.0005. If this value is doubled (two standard deviations—see Appendix I), then in slightly over 95 cases in every 100, the allele frequency of A or a will be expected to lie between 0.499 and 0.501. From the statistical and genetic viewpoints, the population has undergone virtually no change as a result of genetic drift.

In a population of 50 individuals, however, the situation is quite different. The standard deviation is

$$\sigma = \sqrt{\frac{(0.5)(0.5)}{100}} = 0.05.$$

The frequency of A and a in the next generation is now 0.5 ± 0.05. This standard deviation is 1/10 of the original allele frequency, as opposed to 1/1,000 in the large population. Approximately 95% of the time the frequency of A or a could vary between 0.40 and 0.60, and this represents an appreciable departure from the original frequencies.

One particular situation may occur when genetic drift constitutes an effective evolutionary force. This involves the **"founder effect,"** conceived by E. Mayr (1942), who later defined it as "the establishment of a new population by a few original founders (in an extreme case, by a single fertilized female) which carry only a small fraction of the total genetic variation of the parental population" (1963:211). A founder population may be envisioned more precisely as follows. Within the geographical range of a species are many genetically different subpopulations, all of which are potentially capable of interbreeding. At the center of the species range, population density is usually greater than at the periphery. Gene flow is therefore not only greater, but also multidimensional. This leads to populations with high genetic variability and, hence, high levels of heterozygosity. However, gene flow is generally much lower in the widely separated peripheral populations and may consist only of a small influx of new genes. Thus, genetic variation is reduced and, because of inbreeding between members of these smaller populations, higher levels of homozygosity prevail.

Peripheral populations, compared to those at the center of the geographical range of the species, tend to be marginally adapted to their environmental niches. The selective pressures acting upon these populations are not only more severe, but of different kinds than those operating on central populations. Selection may favor different genotypes in peripheral populations and shift these populations into different **ecological niches.** Thus, only a fraction of the total store of genetic variation in the species will be represented in peripheral populations.

When such populations consist of only a few locally adapted breeding individuals, genetic drift can exert a strong influence in establishing gene frequencies. These frequencies may differ sharply from those in central populations. If for some reason the founder population becomes geographically isolated so that no gene flow occurs, its individuals (through many generations of selection) may become unable to interbreed with those of other populations of the parental species, even if contact is reestablished. Thus, the founder effect is potentially important for the origin of new species (see Chapter 8).

Genetic drift in human populations is not easily demonstrated. Selection, drift, migration, and mutation occur simultaneously, and it is not a simple matter to disentangle their individual effects. The effects of drift are analyzed best in a population relatively immune to gene flow, and the most appropriate variables are Mendelian systems in which (1) selection exerts no known effect and (2) the mutation rates are exceedingly low.

These criteria are met fairly well in the study of certain blood group systems in religious isolates. Steinberg et al. (1967) present one of the better examples of genetic drift in their study of several genetic markers in a highly inbred group of anabaptist Protestants. This population, originating from about 900 individuals who migrated to the United States in the late 1870s, now consists of three groups of colonies that form isolated subsects of a main isolate. Included in their study were over 5,000 individuals from colonies within two of the subsects.

Among the ABO, Rh, Kell, and MN blood group loci, the distribution of allele frequencies within the subsects was quite different. They found, for example, that the frequency of M among 44 colonies in one subsect varied from 0.36 to 0.90, and in 33 colonies in the other subsect from 0.49 to 0.84. Only the Australian Aborigines and some Micronesian populations possess lower frequencies of M, and only some Eskimos and American Indians have higher frequencies. With virtually no gene flow, mutation, or selection, the marked changes in these frequencies in such a short time period (three to four generations) can be mainly ascribed to genetic drift.

Summary

An individual's phenotype is the combined result of genotypic interactions and environmental influences, with the genotype determining the extent to which an individual can respond to both external and internal environmental factors. This is usually referred to as the norm of reaction, the range of different developmental pathways that can occur in a particular genotype in all possible environmental situations. Nongenetic variation is phenotypically plastic, which signifies its high susceptibility to environmental modification. While such variation is not directly heritable, it is dependent upon the genetically controlled norm of reaction and is therefore subject to the effects of natural selection. Natural selection exerts its effects upon the entire set of genetic and nongenetic phenotypic characteristics and, through time, has favored the evolutionary development of mechanisms that maintain stable internal conditions under fluctuating environmental stresses. These are homeostatic mechanisms, and operate to maintain relative constancy in physiological, developmental, and genetic systems.

The evolutionary processes responsible for gene frequency change in human populations include mutation, natural selection, differential migration, and genetic drift. Of these four processes, mutation is solely responsible for the generation of novel genetic material. Mutations do not arise as a consequence of particular selective agents, nor can the onset of any specific mutation be predicted. Mutations with lethal or visible effects occur at low rates. Those associated with visible phenotypic changes are usually deleterious, although some are doubtlessly neutral under certain selective conditions. And, the progress toward fixation of a new mutation with slightly beneficial effects is exceedingly slow. Thus, of the four evolutionary processes, mutation is the least effective in the context of gene frequency change.

The most important cause of gene frequency change is natural selection, an inclusive process whereby certain genotypes contribute disproportionately to the gene pools of succeeding generations. By definition, the ability of such genotypes to leave more offspring than others is called Darwinian fitness. Natural selection can be subdivided into various categories on the basis of the eventual change in population gene frequency, four of which include stabilizing, balancing, directional, and diversifying selection.

Stabilizing selection tends to discriminate against phenotypic extremes while favoring those around the mean, while the opposite holds for diversifying selection. Balancing selection, as exemplified by the gene causing sickle-cell anemia in Africa, occurs when the heterozygote possesses an advantage over both homozygotes. In directional selection, a new phenotypic optimum is produced by selection against one extreme and for the other extreme phenotype. Various mathematical models have been developed by population geneticists in order to show both the rate and magnitude of changes in allele frequencies at a single locus under hypothetical selective regimes, in addition to others that consider the effects of both selection and mutation on gene frequency change.

Differential migration refers to the exchange of genes between populations. The net result of gene flow, as it is sometimes called, is a reduction in the genetic differences between the groups and an increase in the total amount of genetic variation within the hybrid population. Mathematical models have also been developed that are capable of estimating the proportion of genes in a hybrid population that originated from both parental populations.

Genetic drift is a random process that changes gene frequency through "accidents" of biological sampling. Although this process occurs among populations of all sizes, its effects are most immediate in small rather than large groups. In particular, genetic drift may constitute a powerful evolutionary force in founder populations. These are small groups established by only a few individuals from a larger population, and they carry only a small fraction of the larger group's genetic variation. Certain religious isolates provide good examples of founder populations and have been found to differ in gene frequencies from their parental populations after only a few generations. Since such isolates often maintain relatively strong sanctions against intermating with outside groups, and because neither mutation nor selection is capable of such changes in so short a time period, genetic drift is usually invoked as a cause.

7 Mating Systems and the Distribution of Genes

Introduction

The models of genetic change discussed so far have one important feature in common: they all assume random mating for the locus or loci in question. For many loci this assumption reflects reality. In no known human population, for instance, do individuals choose their mates regularly on the basis of genetic characteristics like the blood group systems. For some visible phenotypic traits and for certain social phenomena, on the other hand, mating often does not occur at random. People frequently choose their mates preferentially by skin color, educational attainment, stature, whether both individuals are blind or deaf, and so forth. Furthermore, individuals in some small populations often mate with their near relatives for social or cultural reasons. Such practices have important ramifications for human population structure. The primary purpose of this chapter is to examine some of the genetic consequences of two kinds of departures from random mating. These are assortative mating and inbreeding.

Assortative Mating

"When mates in a breeding population have more phenotypical characters in common than would be expected by chance, that is, by random mating, the pattern is called positive assortative mating; when they have fewer than would be expected by chance, it is called negative assortative mating" (Spuhler 1967:356). In positive assortative mating, therefore, individuals with similar phenotypic traits tend to mate. In **negative assortative mating,** unlike individuals tend to mate. Since this does not occur with any regularity in human populations (except of course, for sex), the ensuing discussion will be limited to positive assortative mating.

There are at least four important genetic aspects of positive assortative mating:

1. There is virtually no evidence that it occurs for simple genetic markers, although there are numerous examples for quantitative traits.

2. Unless associated with some selective factor on fertility, it has no effect on gene frequencies. It only changes genotypic frequencies and, hence, is not a true evolutionary factor as previously defined.

3. It increases the average population homozygosity.

4. It increases the total population variance of the trait.

Genotypic Frequency Changes

The last three points may be demonstrated by a simple example similar to those given many years ago by Jennings (1916) and Wentworth and Remick (1916). Assume that a quantitative trait is controlled by a single locus with two co-dominant alleles, A and A', and that these alleles segregate in typical Mendelian fashion to produce three visible phenotypes with the genotypes AA, AA', and $A'A'$. Assume also that every member of a hypothetical population possesses one of these three genotypes, and that positive assortative mating is complete. Thus AA individuals mate only with other AA individuals, AA' with AA', and $A'A'$ with $A'A'$. A final assumption may be made purely for the sake of convenience—that the three genotypes in the parental population are distributed in $1:2:1$ Mendelian ratio. Suppose now that these individuals mate and produce the F_1 generation. What will the genotypic proportions be?

Because you began with a $1:2:1$ distribution, the matings between AA individuals will be expected to produce one-fourth of the progeny (all AA) of the F_1 generation, as will matings between $A'A'$ individuals. Matings between the AA' heterozygotes will contribute one-half of the progeny, but this fraction will consist of $1/4 AA$, $1/2 AA'$, and $1/4 A'A'$. Thus $1/8$ ($1/2 \times 1/4$) of the AA individuals in the F_1 offspring will be derived from heterozygous parents, as will one-eighth of the $A'A'$ offspring. When these fractions are added to the homozygous AA and $A'A'$ progeny from homozygous matings, the result in the F_1 generation is a $3/8:2/8:3/8$ genotypic distribution.

If the frequency of $A = p$ and of $A' = q$, the genotypic frequencies in the next generation will be

$$p^2 (AA) = p^2 + (1/4)(2pq)$$
$$2pq (AA') = 2pq/2$$
$$q^2 (A'A') = q^2 + (1/4)(2pq).$$

Under the conditions stated above, it becomes apparent that (1) the reduction in heterozygosity will be exactly one-half in each generation and (2) the concomitant increase in both homozygotes will eventually lead to a doubled variance (Crow and Felsenstein 1968). That the allele frequencies of A and A' remain unchanged should also be apparent: if $p = 0.50 = q$ in the parental generation, a moment's arithmetic will show that neither have changed in the F_1 generation (see Chapter 5).

Degrees of assortative mating are usually measured by first determining the proportion of individuals in a population who mate assortatively for a certain trait as opposed to those who do not. This yields a correlation coefficent (see Appendix I), given by r, which represents the proportion of the population who mate assortatively for the trait. When $r = 1$, assortative mating is complete; when $r < 1$, only part of the population mates assortatively. The algebraic relationships involved in partial assortative mating have been described by Crow and Felsenstein (1968) and need not be given here. Suffice it to state that under such conditions the genotypic frequencies of homozygotes increase, but at a slower rate than for complete assortative mating.

Assortative Mating in Human Populations

To what extent does assortative mating actually occur in human populations? In probably the most extensive review of preferential mating for physical characteristics, Spuhler (1968) has surveyed numerous studies on over 100 physical traits from many of the world's populations. His summary is far too extensive to repeat here, but in general r tends to be high for assortative mating by age. This is hardly surprising, for in most societies the difference in age between two mates tends to be rather low. The average value of r for age among 14 populations in Spuhler's report was about 0.80, and assortative mating by age was nearly complete ($r = 0.99$) among the Ramah Navajo Indians. For other characteristics the value of r may be quite low. The average value for assortative mating by chest circumference, for example, was approximately 0.12 among seven populations.

In another report Spuhler (1967) reviewed 25 studies on assortative mating for behavioral variables, such as intelligence scores, personality ratings, and temperament. These correlations are given in Table 7.1. Unfortunately, the extent to which the genetic structure of human populations is altered by such matings is quite unclear. We have virtually no idea of the heritability of these behavioral attributes, in addition to the fact that some of these traits are not developed until after mate selection has occurred.

By now you should have a general idea of the effects of positive assortative mating. Negative assortative mating produces essentially opposite effects, that is, it increases heterozygosity, decreases homozygosity, and reduces the population variance. The algebraic relationships for this and additional models have been described clearly by Crow and Kimura (1970), and those more mathematically inclined will profit by Wright's (1969) treatment of the subject.

Why are human geneticists and biological anthropologists interested in the effects of positive assortative mating on future generations? One important feature of positive assortative mating for both dominant and recessive phenotypes is that it increases the incidence of that phenotype. In this context, Sank (1963) found strong positive assortative mating for deafness. To the extent that congenital deafness is genetically determined (Sank and Kallman 1963, estimated that about 50% of early total deafness is of genetic origin), positive assortative mating for this condition will tend to increase its incidence.

The increase in total population variance is one of the major reasons for studying the effects of positive assortative mating. This variance-enhancing effect is particularly relevant in a large, generalized population such as the United States. Lewontin, Kirk, and Crow (1968) have noted that the overall variance in fertility in the United States (fertility is the probability of a genotype producing offspring) is undergoing a rapid decline. This decline is due to the extraordinary influence of modern contraceptive practices and advanced medical facilities. The latter have also drastically reduced the opportunity for selection by death, so that relatively little loss through death occurs before the reproductive period. In 1966, the probability that a live-born female in the United States would survive to 20 years of age was slightly higher than 0.97 (Keyfitz and Flieger 1971).

In highly industrialized societies, the greatest opportunity for selection is through differential fertility, but the decreasing variance in fertility is concomitant

Table 7.1 Assortative Mating for Intelligence Test Scores, Personality Ratings, and Other Behavioral Traits (Reprinted from *Genetic Diversity and Human Behavior*, J. N. Spuhler, ed. Viking Fund Publications in Anthropology, No. 45. Copyright 1967 by the Wenner-Gren Foundation for Anthropological Research, New York.)

Item	Source*	N pairs	r
Intelligence scores			
Stanford-Binet	Burks, 1928	174	.47 ± .04
Otis	Freeman *et al.*, 1928	150	.49 ± .04
Army Alpha	Jones, 1928	105	.60 ± .04
Progressive Matrices	Halperin, 1946	324	.76
Various tests	Smith, 1941	433	.19 ± .03
Vocabulary	Carter, 1932	108	.21 ± .06
Arithmetic	Carter, 1932	108	.03 ± .06
Mental Grade	Penrose, 1933	100	.44
Personality ratings			
Neurotic Tendency	Hoffeditz, 1934	100	.16 ± .07
Neurotic Tendency	Terman and Buttenwieser, 1935	126	.11 ± .06
Neurotic Tendency	Terman and Buttenwieser, 1935	215	.22 ± .04
Neurotic Tendency	Willoughby, 1928	100	.27 ± .05
Self-sufficiency	Hoffeditz, 1934	100	.09 ± .07
Self-sufficiency	Terman and Buttenwieser, 1935	215	.12 ± .04
Self-sufficiency	Terman and Buttenwieser, 1935	126	.02 ± .06
Dominance	Hoffeditz, 1934	100	.15 ± .07
Dominance	Terman and Buttenwieser, 1935	126	.24 ± .06
Dominance	Terman and Buttenwieser, 1935	215	.29 ± .04
Introversion-extroversion	Terman and Buttenwieser, 1935	126	.02 ± .06
Introversion-extroversion	Terman and Buttenwieser, 1935	215	.16 ± .04
Miscellaneous			
Temperament	Burgess and Wallin, 1944	316	.22
Insanity	Goring, 1909	1433	.06
Criminality	Goring, 1909	474	.20

*Cited in Spuhler, 1967.

with decreasing effectiveness of natural selection. As the average number of children per family becomes lower, "we seem to be approaching—not reaching but approaching—a situation in this country where the white population of each generation will be pretty much a genetic carbon copy of the preceding generation in frequency of genes" (Lewontin, Kirk, and Crow 1968:143). Because positive assortative mating increases population variance through the redistribution of gene combinations, it "would seem to have consequences just as relevant as any other mechanisms involving the genetic character of human societies" (Eckland 1968:72). Indeed it does, for by counteracting the reduction in population variance (see Appendix I) due to declining fertility, it constitutes one of the most important biosocial phenomena for ensuring genetic variation in human populations.

Inbreeding

That most matings occur between individuals who share a common ancestor can be easily demonstrated. The number of ancestors of each individual follows a geometric progression: two parents, four grandparents, eight great-grandparents, and so forth. If we assume an average generation length of 25 years, then 39 generations have elapsed since A.D. 1000. The total number of ancestors for any single individual would therefore be $2^{39} = 549,755,813,888$. This is well over 100 times as many people as are alive today, and perhaps 8 times greater than the number of people who have ever lived on earth (Keyfitz 1966, estimates this number at about 69 billion as of 1960). It appears safe to assume that many lines of descent must, at some point, have stemmed from a common ancestor.

In the most general terms, matings between individuals who have at least one common ancestor are said to be **consanguineous,** and offspring from such unions are said to be inbred. As stated in the previous paragraph, all matings within our (and every other) species are to some degree consanguineous and, hence, all individuals are "inbred." However, from the practical viewpoint, the effect of such remote consanguinity is not only undetectable, but meaningless. For consanguinity to have any appreciable effect on the genetics of individuals and populations, the unions must involve more closely related persons. The degree of affinity is a matter of some subjectivity, but commonness of ancestry beyond a great-great-grandparent is ordinarily not considered to have significant effects upon the composition of a gene pool.

The probability that two related mates share some genes or alleles in common is much greater than for two individuals taken at random from a population. This leads to a greater probability that offspring from a consanguineous mating will inherit the same gene or allele from each parent. Thus, the primary feature of inbreeding, like that of positive assortative mating, is an increase in homozygosity. This fundamental property of inbreeding may be associated with the enactment and passage of various laws in some states that prohibit consanguineous unions between closely related individuals. In nearly all societies, some form of social sanction usually prohibits parent-child and brother-sister matings. This "incest" prohibition is almost universal among human societies. There are a few well-known exceptions, as always, including brother-sister marriages within the royal family of the Inca Empire, Hawaii, and Egypt (Cleopatra married her 12-year-old brother, stood by while he was murdered, and then consorted with Julius Caesar and Marc Antony).

Although incest prohibitions probably arose and are maintained by sociocultural factors (Aldridge 1951) rather than biological considerations, there are good genetic reasons for their maintenance. From the genetic viewpoint, inbreeding can increase the probability of an offspring suffering from genetic defects that were not phenotypically expressed in either parent or, for that matter, in any known relative. This is due to the presence of deleterious recessive alleles and the higher probability that both related parents are heterozygous for such alleles. It is well substantiated that all of us carry a number of deleterious and sometimes lethal alleles in the heterozygous state. Morton, Crow, and Muller (1956) have estimated from data on consanguineous matings that the average number of lethal equivalents carried per person is between three and five, and Schull and Neel (1965) suggest that the average number after the first month of life is probably less than three.

The presence of three to five lethal equivalents in every individual means that deleterious recessive alleles in the homozygous state could cause death in three to five different combinations. Along with other hidden genetic defects, such deleterious and lethal alleles comprise the "genetic load" in individuals (this subject is discussed later in this chapter). For now, it may be stated that part of our genetic load is due to new mutations. Since most new mutations occur in the heterozygous state and are "recessive," they will be masked by the "dominant" allele. To the extent that these mutations are deleterious, their expression in homozygous form generally results in a reduction of fitness in the individual.

If two individuals are taken at random from a large population, the probability of their possessing the same deleterious allele is quite small (recall that every individual's genetic complement consists of an enormous number of loci). In light of the fact that inbreeding increases homozygosity for harmful alleles and, hence, decreases fertility, vigor, and fitness, it is important to be able to express the probability of homozygous offspring from consanguineous matings.

Calculation of the Inbreeding Coefficient

The degree of inbreeding in a pedigree is usually expressed by calculating the inbreeding coefficient. This coefficient (F) was originally formulated by Wright (1922). It states the probability that two alleles at one locus in an individual are identical by descent. The phrase "identical by descent" refers to the fact that an individual with related parents can receive two copies of one allele from a single ancestor.

Calculation of the inbreeding coefficient may be demonstrated by referring to Figure 7.1. There are two pedigrees here, one (a) involving a mating between an uncle and niece, and the other (b), between first cousins. In both cases, what is the inbreeding coefficient of the propositus? Alternatively stated, what is the probability that IV-1 will inherit two copies of any of the four alleles ($A_1, A_2, A_3,$ or A_4) present in the first generation?

The value of F in either pedigree is derived by following paths from the propositus through both of his parents to the allele in question in the first generation, and by multiplying the independent probabilities found therein. Suppose you wished to find the probability that IV-1 in Figure 7.1a is homozygous A_1A_1. On one side of the pedigree (IV-1 to II-1 to I-1) there are two points where there is a one-half chance of transmission of A_1. On the other side (IV-1 to III-2 to II-2 to I-1) there are three places where there is a one-half probability of an individual receiving the A_1 allele. Because these are independent events, the total probability of all five occurring is $(1/2)^5 = 1/32$. Notice that there are four alleles in the parents in the first generation. The total probability of the propositus being homozygous for any one of these four alleles (e.g., A_1) is therefore $(4)(1/32) = 1/8 = 0.125$. For an uncle-niece (or aunt-nephew) mating, then, the coefficient of inbreeding is 0.125. The value of F in Figure 7.1b for first cousins is, similarly, $(4)(1/64) = 1/16 = 0.0625$, because there are six rather than five places where a transmission probability of one-half is found.

The general formula for F, when the common ancestor is not inbred, is

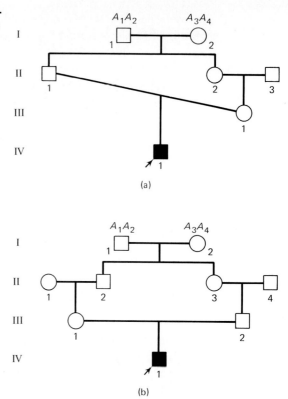

Figure 7.1 Two pedigrees involving consanguineous matings: **a,** an uncle-niece mating, and **b,** a mating between first cousins.

(a)

(b)

$F = \Sigma(1/2)^N$, where $N =$ the number of ancestors of the propositus (but excluding the propositus), beginning the count with one parent of the propositus and continuing around the lineage to the other. It must be remembered that these values are derived for each common ancestor and then summed to give F. In Figure 7.1b, the route is traced from III-1 to II-2 to I-1 to II-3 to III-2, or from III-1 to II-2 to I-2 to II-3 to III-2. Thus, according to the above formula, $F = (1/2)^5 + (1/2)^5 = 1/32 + 1/32 = 1/16 = 0.0625$. By the same procedure, it can easily be shown that $F = 1/4$ for brother-sister matings, $1/32$ for first cousins once removed, $1/64$ for second cousins, $1/128$ for second cousins once removed, $1/256$ for third cousins, and so forth.

Unfortunately, human pedigrees are often far more complicated than these simple examples. Ancestors of the propositus are themselves frequently inbred. When this occurs, the probability that the alleles in the propositus will be identical by descent is increased even more. In such cases, the general formula

$$F = \Sigma[(1/2)^N(1 + F_A)]$$

is used, where F_A represents the inbreeding coefficient of the ancestor.

Inbreeding and Deleterious Recessive Alleles

It was stated above that inbred offspring have an increased probability of being homozygous for deleterious recessive alleles. This point may be clarified by assuming in Figure 7.1b that the female denoted by III-1 is a heterozygous carrier for a rare recessive disorder such as PKU. It was mentioned in Chapter 5 that approximately 2 in every 100 individuals are carriers for this recessive allele, and the frequency of homozygous recessive individuals is approximately 1/10,000.

When one cousin in a first-cousin marriage is known to be heterozygous for any allele (in the present example, a rare recessive), the probability that the other first cousin is heterozygous for the same allele is always one-eighth. If III-1 is known to be a carrier, she could have obtained the recessive allele from her father (II-2) with a probability of one-half. If her father was heterozygous, he must have obtained the allele from one of the parents in the first generation. The father's sister (II-3) also has a one-half chance of receiving the allele, as does her son (III-2). Thus three points occur in the pedigree where there is one-half chance of an individual receiving the recessive allele, and $(1/2)^3 = 1/8$.

On the other hand, if III-1 married an unrelated man, the probability of his being heterozygous for the same allele would depend solely upon the value of $2pq$ in the population. In the present example, this is approximately 0.02. Therefore, when a known heterozygote for PKU marries her first cousin, he is more than six times as likely to be heterozygous for the same allele as an unrelated man.

This has very important ramifications for the offspring. Let P represent the dominant and p the recessive allele for PKU. One cousin (III-1) is known to be Pp, and the chance of her transmitting p to her child is clearly one-half. The other cousin has a one-eighth chance of being heterozygous. Thus the probability of his passing the recessive allele to the same child is $(1/8)(1/2) = 1/16$. The child, therefore, has a $(1/2)(1/16) = 1/32$ chance of being homozygous recessive, and afflicted with the disease.

However, when the woman mates with an unrelated man, the probability of producing a homozygous recessive offspring is $(1/2)(0.02)(1/2) = 1/200$. Hence, a heterozygous individual is about six times more likely to have offspring with PKU when mating with a first cousin than with an unrelated individual.

Inbreeding in Human Populations

In order to assess the population effects of inbreeding, human geneticists and biological anthropologists have estimated the average consanguinity in many different populations. This value is usually derived from marriages instead of progeny, and is determined from the average inbreeding coefficient of a sample of a population's constituent individuals. This quantity, symbolized by α, is defined as $\alpha = \Sigma pF$, where p represents the frequency of inbred individuals with inbreeding coefficient, F (Cavalli-Sforza and Bodmer 1971). Reid (1973) has noted that no known human population has been found for which F exceeds 0.05, and in the majority of populations examined, $F < 0.005$ (Table 7.2).

Since inbreeding leads to increased homozygosity, it follows that the frequency of recessive disorders would tend to increase in inbred populations. To the extent that such disorders decrease fertility, increase mortality and morbidity, and, in general, reduce population fitness, it is appropriate to briefly present some of the observed effects of consanguinity.

The most thorough examination of such effects has been carried out on Japanese populations. In addition to increased rates of congenital defects in offspring, Schull and Neel (1965), Schull et al. (1970), and Yanase (1966) have reported increases

Table 7.2 Average Inbreeding Coefficients in a Selected Number of Human Populations (Reprinted by permission from Russell M. Reid, Inbreeding in Human Populations. In: *Methods and Theories of Anthropological Genetics,* M. H. Crawford and P. L. Workman, eds. School of American Research Advanced Seminar Series. Univ. of New Mexico Press, Albuquerque, 1973. Courtesy of the School of American Research.)

Populations with $f < 0.00001$	Source*
The Netherlands	Polman (1951)
Panama	Freire-Maia (1968)

Populations with f between 0.00001 and 0.0001

Czechoslovakia (Brno) after 1950	Zahálková and Preis (1970)
United States (Roman Catholic)	Freire-Maia (1968)

Populations with f between 0.0001 and 0.001

Belgium	Twisselmann (1961)
Czechoslovakia (Brno) before 1950	Zahálková and Preis (1970)
Italy (Northern)	Moroni (1966)
Switzerland	Morton and Hussels (1970)
Canada (French)	Freire-Maia (1968)
Canada (Roman Catholic)	Freire-Maia (1968)
Chile (Roman Catholic)	Freire-Maia (1968)
Uruguay (Roman Catholic)	Freire-Maia (1968)
Argentina (Roman Catholic)	Freire-Maia (1968)
Cuba (Roman Catholic)	Freire-Maia (1968)
Mexico (Roman Catholic)	Freire-Maia (1968)
Bolivia (Roman Catholic)	Freire-Maia (1968)
Brazil (Roman Catholic)	Saldanha (1960)

Populations with f between 0.001 and 0.01

Japan (various)	Schull and Neel (1965)
France (Loir-et-Cher and Finistère)	Sutter and Tabah (1955b)
Hungary (Ivad)	Nemeskéri and Thoma (1961)
Italy (Sardinia and Aeolian Islands)	Moroni (1966)
Spain	Cisternas and Moroni (1967)
United States (Watauga Co., North Carolina)	Herndon and Kerley (1952)
United States (Mormon)	Woolf et al. (1956)
United States (Ramah Navajo)	Spuhler and Kluckhohn (1953)
India (Bombay)	Sanghvi, Varde, and Master (1956)
Brazil (Northeastern) from pedigrees	Yasuda (1969a)

Populations with f between 0.01 and 0.05

Japan (Hosojima)	Iskikuni et al. (1960)
India (Coastal Andhra Pradesh)	Dronamraju (1964)
India (Rural Andhra Pradesh)	Sanghvi (1966)
India (Kavanur Village, Madras)	Centerwall et al. (1969)
India (Telaga Caste, Andhra Pradesh)	Reid (1971)

Jordan and Israel (Samaritans)	Bonné (1962)
Egypt (Nubia)	Strouhal (1971), Hussien (1971)
Guinea (Fouta-Djallon)	Cantrelle and Dupire (1964)
United States (Dunkers, Pennsylvania)	Glass et al. (1952)
United States (Hutterites, South Dakota and Minnesota)	Mange (1964)
Tristan da Cunha	Roberts (1967)
Brazil (Xavante)	Neel et al. (1964)
Brazil (Northeastern) from bioassay	Yasuda (1969a)

*Cited in Reid, 1973.

Table 7.3 The Absolute and Relative Risks of Occurrences of Death and Certain Morbid Conditions among the Offspring of Unrelated Parents and of First Cousins (Courtesy of W. J. Schull, Genetic Implications of Population Breeding Structure. In: *The Structure of Human Populations*, G. A. Harrison and A. J. Boyce, eds. Clarendon Press, Oxford, 1972.)

Characteristic	Offspring of Unrelated Parents Percent	Offspring of First cousins Percent	Relative Risk Percent
Congenital defects in the newly born[2]	1.02	1.69	1.6
Simple cleft palate			5.0
Some congenital cardiac defects			3.0
Atresia ani			4.0
Anophthalmos/Microphthalmos			3.0
Oligodactyly			7.0
One or two major defects[3]	8.5	11.7	1.4
One or more minor defects	7.9	9.8	1.2
Hearing impairment[4]	10.5	13.9	1.3
Organic defect of eye	0.45	0.99	2.2
Severe visual loss without organic defect[5]	1.01	1.43	1.4
Mortality[6]	5.5–16.0	11.6–24.1	1.4–3.4

1. Where data are available from more than one study, the ranges of the various risks are recorded.
2. These figures include only those congenital defects recognizable by physical means alone at or very shortly after birth; thus they do not include many congenital heart defects or retardations of motor and mental development.
3. These values include only those defects which are incompatible with life, life-threatening, or seriously impinge upon normal functions; all such diagnoses in the first eight years of life, on the average, are included.
4. Defined as loss of at least 10 decibels in one or both ears at one or more of three frequencies, 128, 1024, and 2048 Hz.
5. Defined as vision of 20/400 or worse in one or both eyes when tested with a Snellen chart.
6. The differences to be noted here stem both from the numbers of years at risk of death and changes in mortality with time. Most recent studies suggest a relative risk closer to 1·4 than to 3·4.

in prereproductive mortality among the offspring of consanguineous marriages. Likewise, several metric variables associated with physical and mental growth and development were found to be depressed. A few of the detrimental effects are listed in Tables 7.3 and 7.4 (Schull 1972), both of which were abstracted from the extensive study by Schull and Neel (1965). Their work should be consulted for additional discussion.

Table 7.4 A Comparison of Some Selected Findings in a Cohort of Control Children and in a Cohort of Children Born to First-Cousin Marriages Studied in Hiroshima and Nagasaki (Courtesy of W. J. Schull, Genetic Implications of Population Breeding Structure. In: *The Structure of Human Populations,* G. A. Harrison and A. J. Boyce, eds. Clarendon Press, Oxford, 1972.)

Characteristic	Sex	Control Children	Offspring of First Cousins	Inbreeding Effect Percent	Change with Inbreeding Percent
Mean performance on W.I.S.C. Intelligence Test (Hiroshima)					
Verbal score	Male	58.67	55.34	2.76	4.7
	Female	57.01	53.46	2.76	4.8
Performance score	Male	57.37	54.94	2.06	3.6
	Female	55.10	52.52	2.06	3.7
School performance (average grade Hiroshima)					
Language	Male	3.09	2.95	0.10	3.2
	Female	3.28	3.10	0.10	3.0
Mathematics	Male	3.21	3.04	0.13	4.0
	Female	3.19	2.99	0.13	4.1
Physical development (Hiroshima)					
Weight (kg)	Male	26.59	26.31	2.34	0.9
	Female	26.35	25.99	2.34	0.9
Height (cm)	Male	129.7	129.1	0.47	0.4
	Female	129.8	129.1	0.47	0.4

Sexes are indicated separately only when there is a significant difference between males and females. All differences are statistically significant. For the continuously distributed characteristics, the percentage by which the depression due to consanguinity would have been overestimated through failure to consider socioeconomic concomitants has been shown. The average age of the children at the time of study was approximately 98 months in Hiroshima and 105 months in Nagasaki. The physical measurements have been standardized to age 120 months. Inbreeding effects have been computed from a regression based on the findings for both sexes.

Our Genetic Load

It should be evident from many of the preceding discussions that humans possess a variety of harmful alleles. Some of these are produced by new or recurrent mutations, some by recombination, and some are introduced by migration. Some are held in a state of balance, often by heterozygotic superiority. Other allelic combinations are maintained primarily by the selection-mutation equilibrium. In any case, certain genotypes in all populations fail either to survive or reproduce. As unfortunate as this may be, it is a side effect of the processes that maintain the genetic variation necessary for the survival and evolution of populations.

In a classic paper, H. J. Muller (1950) coined the term "genetic load" to express this "change of average fitness associated with maintaining the variability in a population" (Crow and Kimura 1970:297). Muller's paper was a carefully reasoned, but impassioned, statement declaring that deleterious and sometimes debilitating alleles produced by recurrent mutation would tend to accumulate in human populations. This accumulation would eventually result in a general reduction in population fitness and, moreover, increased suffering from genetic defects. His concern about the future of human populations is clearly evident in the following quotation:

> . . . despite all the improved methods and facilities which will be in use at that time the population will nevertheless be undergoing as much genetic extinction as it did under the most primitive conditions. In correspondence with this, the amount of genetically caused impairment suffered by the average individual, even though he has all techniques of civilization working to mitigate it, must by that time have grown to be as great in the presence of these techniques as it had been in paleolithic times without them. But instead of people's time and energy being mainly spent in the struggle with external enemies of a primitive kind such as famine, climatic difficulties, and wild beasts, they would be devoted chiefly to the effort to live carefully, to spare and to prop up their own feeblenesses, to soothe their inner disharmonies and, in general, to doctor themselves as effectively as possible. For everyone would be an invalid, with his own special familial twists. (Muller 1950:145)

H. J. Muller was a Nobel Prize-winning geneticist whose ideas were not to be taken lightly, and in subsequent years the subject of our genetic load became one of the most controversial issues in human genetics. His treatment of the subject, however, was basically qualitative and restricted to the mutational load. Since the early 1950s, many other phenomena have been identified that contribute to this concealed variability (see Crow and Kimura 1970). In addition, it has been recognized that the genetic load is not always an intolerable burden, but in certain situations may be advantageous for the continued survival and evolution of a population.

In few other instances is this as evident as with sickle-cell anemia. The nearly lethal effects of the Hb^S allele in the homozygous state were discussed in Chapter 3. Yet the mutation from Hb^A to Hb^S has been favored by balancing selection in malarial areas. This has saddled populations in these areas with a genetic load, but their average fitness is certainly greater than if all individuals possessed only the Hb^A allele. In such an event, fitness would be reduced by malaria to the extent that survival of the population would be at stake (Livingstone 1958, 1964b).

Components of the Genetic Load

In general, the phenomena that produce variation in fitness also contribute to a genetic load. This may be expressed symbolically as

$$L = \frac{W_{max} - \overline{W}}{W_{max}},$$

where W_{max} = the fitness of the optimum genotype, and $\overline{W}$ is the average population fitness. If a value of 1.0 is assigned to W_{max} (as in Chapter 6), then the genetic load becomes $1 - \overline{W}$. By looking at the genetic load in this fashion, it is possible to estimate its value in various groups instead of simply describing its effects on populations.

The factors contributing most to the genetic load in human populations have been listed by Schull and Neel (1965), Wallace (1970), and Crow and Kimura (1970). These include: the **mutational, migrational, segregational, recombinational, and incompatibility loads.**

The mutational and migrational loads occur respectively when population fitness is decreased by (1) recurrent mutation and (2) immigration of less favorable genotypes. The segregational load (often called the balanced load) is produced when, by segregation, heterozygous individuals give rise to offspring less fit than themselves. This is the load associated with heterozygote superiority and sickle-cell anemia. The recombinational load is analogous to the segregational load, but involves the production of recombinants with fitnesses lower than that of the optimum genotype. The optimum genotype, in turn, is an idealization which refers to the genotype having the highest fitness at a given time and under a given set of environmental conditions.

The incompatibility load, at least in human populations, is limited to genes responsible for certain blood groups. It usually involves an unfavorable reaction between the genotypes of a mother and her fetus. The classic example concerns alleles controlling the Rh blood group system and Rh incompatibility, which may lead to a hemolytic disease of the newborn called **erythroblastosis fetalis.**

The mechanics of this phenomenon may be outlined by assuming only two phenotypes, Rh$^+$ and Rh$^-$, where Rh$^+$ individuals are genotypically either RR or Rr and Rh$^-$ individuals are rr (see Chapter 4 for a fuller discussion of Rh inheritance). Unlike the ABO system, there are no naturally occurring antibodies against the Rh$^+$ antigen. This means that an Rh$^-$ individual will develop Rh antibodies only if Rh$^+$ cells are introduced into the bloodstream of that individual. Now, suppose that an Rh$^-$ woman marries an Rh$^+$ man. If the man is Rr, then on the average one-half of all children will also be Rr and have the Rh$^+$ antigen. If the man is RR, then all children will be Rr and have the Rh$^+$ antigen.

It frequently happens that some of the red blood cells of the Rh$^+$ fetus enter the mother's circulatory system, especially at the time of birth and in conjunction with normal birth trauma. To a lesser extent, fetal red cells may also enter the mother during the last trimester of pregnancy because the placenta is not a totally impermeable membrane. In a similar fashion, some of the mother's red cells may enter the bloodstream of the fetus. When the fetus is Rh$^+$, the cells introduced into the mother's bloodstream stimulate the formation of Rh antibodies. If these antibodies are subsequently transferred back to the fetus, the red cells agglutinate and are destroyed. This leads to hemolytic disease of the newborn.

Fortunately, not all Rh$^+$ (♂) $\times$ Rh$^-$ (♀) matings give rise to this disease. There are a number of reasons for this. First, if the mother receives the fetal antigen during the birth of a first child, the infant will suffer no ill effects. However, the second child may receive the antibodies thus formed and be affected. Second, a synthetic antibody—called RhoGAM—has been developed that can be administered to a mother shortly after birth. This antibody inhibits the ability of the mother to form Rh$^+$ antibodies, so that subsequent children will be unaffected. Third, if the mother and fetus are incompatible both for the Rh and ABO systems (there are naturally occurring antibodies in the latter), the ABO-incompatible cells will be hemolyzed before they have a chance to stimulate formation of Rh$^+$ antibodies. Additional information on this phenomenon and other related aspects of Rh incompatibility can be found in Cohen (1970a, 1970b).

Some Comments on Eugenics

Certain cultural variables increase our genetic load. The mutational load increases with the proliferation of artificial mutagens, including radiation-producing devices, chemical by-products in industrial wastes, and so forth. The migrational load is expected to increase with the breakdown of cultural barriers that inhibit matings between populations. The incompatibility load would be maintained by the accelerated use of RhoGAM and other techniques for preventing erythroblastosis fetalis in the newborn. By relaxing the effects of normalizing selection, the vast array of modern medical techniques and drugs would increase the recombinational and some of the other loads above. Simply stated, medical technology in industrialized societies prevents the elimination of genotypes which, under more rigorous conditions, would be at a severe selective disadvantage.

All of this is related to the fact that well over 1,000 dominant, recessive, and sex-linked genetic defects have been identified in the human species. It would, of course, be a boon to our species to eliminate the suffering and death caused by these detrimental genes, and it is completely understandable that a great deal of contemporary genetic research is being directed toward that goal. Unfortunately, this is not an easy task. Our information about (1) the number of genes in the human complement, (2) their chromosomal locations, (3) their linkage relationships with other genes, (4) the developmental relationships between genes and phenotypes, and other relevant aspects of our genetic constitution is severely limited. The idea of improving the hereditary qualities of future generations of *H. sapiens,* the basis of the scientific discipline called **eugenics,** has therefore been based largely upon selective breeding. For obvious reasons, the concept of selective breeding in human populations leads immediately to serious, unanswered and, perhaps, unanswerable questions of a moral and ethical nature.

From its beginnings, eugenics has been divided into two subareas. One is positive eugenics, in which the goal is to encourage people with "superior" characteristics to produce more children. The other is negative eugenics, which advocates the prevention of mating between people with "inferior" characteristics. It is easy to see the inherent danger of elitism and racism in both of these concepts. What constitutes an "inferior" or "superior" characteristic, and how will this be judged?

From a genetic and evolutionary viewpoint, a certain trait may be deleterious in one population but advantageous in another. This is certainly the case with sickle-cell anemia. Eradication of the Hb^S allele in nonmalarial populations would alleviate untold suffering; however, in malarial populations it might result in eradication of the population as well. The question of who decides "superiority" or "inferiority," not just of certain traits, but especially of groups with certain traits, can and has led to mass extermination and atrocities, such as those carried out by Nazi politicians during World War II.

In all fairness, the field of eugenics cannot be equated with racists and racism any more than Christianity can be equated with the countless murders and executions carried out historically by "good" Christians. In 1961, a special committee appointed by the board of directors of the American Eugenics Society was asked to prepare a position statement for the Society. The committee, including a geneticist, a demographer, a physical anthropologist, a behavioral geneticist, and a medical geneticist, maintained that the common interest of the Society's membership was "to promote the advancement, discussion, and dissemination of scientific knowledge of human genetics, as it relates to the welfare and improvement of individuals and populations" (Allen et al. 1961:181).

There are few rational arguments against the proposal that elimination of genetic defects is a worthwhile endeavor. Yet there are also few who advocate the application to humans of selective breeding techniques now used widely with domesticated plants and animals. The right to reproduce is one of the most universal of all individual freedoms, and it seems unlikely that any government could be successful in a long-term inhibition of this right. How, then, can human families and populations be improved?

At the present time, this is feasible through (1) the dissemination of relevant genetic information and (2) the application of knowledge and techniques for the improvement of our internal and external environments. In a lucid discussion of this problem, J. V. Neel (1970) has outlined a program with the following proposals:

1. Stabilize the gene pool numerically. This is the first and certainly the most urgent priority. The literature on the effects of rapid growth in human numbers is voluminous (e.g., Ehrlich and Ehrlich 1970) and need not be reiterated here. There is general agreement that we are rapidly approaching the point (if not already there!) where the quality of life, however it is measured, is inversely proportional to population growth. It is encouraging that the principle of population limitation is being recognized and practiced by more and more individuals and countries. It is discouraging, on the other hand, that other countries fail to recognize the urgency of population limitation, and especially that some religions are actively opposing it.

2. Protect the gene against damage. The original concern of Muller (1950) was an increase in the mutational load from radiation. More recently, there is good evidence that mutation rates will increase because of mutagenic chemicals and pollutants in the environment. Control of this problem is well within our technological grasp, and as Neel suggests: "A society that can afford to send man to the moon surely has the resources and intelligence to monitor itself properly for increased mutation rates" (1970:820).

3. Improve the quality of life through mate selection based upon genetic counseling and prenatal diagnosis. Genetics has reached a stage where the inheritance patterns of numerous diseases and abnormalities are known, and the practice of genetic counseling informs potential parents of the probability of having genetically defective offspring. Unlike many other eugenic proposals, genetic counseling has neither moral nor ethical overtones. Rather, it is a voluntary service whereby the risk of genetic disease is predicted according to Mendelian expectations, at least for simple autosomal dominant and recessive defects. For other disorders that have a less well-established genetic basis, such as diabetes, predictions are more tenuous. However, through genetic counseling, a couple can make their own decisions about their potential offspring with a knowledge of the potential risk. They can

practice birth control; they can apply for voluntary sterilization; or, they may take the chance that the offspring will be normal.

Parental concern about whether a fetus is normal can be alleviated in some cases by a prenatal diagnostic technique called "amniocentesis." This method involves withdrawal of some of the amniotic fluid, in which fetal cells are available for examination. The procedure may be performed during the first trimester of pregnancy. If the fetus is found to be defective for any of a small, but growing, list of chromosome abnormalities, a therapeutic abortion is a possible option.

4. Improve the phenotypic expression of the individual genotype. This proposal involves two subareas of research, euphenics and genetic engineering. The goal of euphenics is to manipulate environmental variables in order to maximize the potential abilities of specific genotypes. There is little disagreement that socially desirable qualities such as intelligence or artistic skills are the result of both genes and environment. It is no revelation, for example, to note that the accomplishments of Albert Einstein or Frederic Chopin could hardly be duplicated by anyone if provided with the same type of training. For many years the genetic versus environmental influence on such qualities has been vigorously disputed. At the present time the most volatile argument concerns intelligence and the claims by some (Jensen 1969) that the differences in I. Q. between American black and white populations are due to a significant genetic component.

Aside from the fact that such claims almost immediately open their proponents to charges of racism, the evidential base for these arguments is insufficient for drawing meaningful conclusions one way or the other. What is intelligence? What do I. Q. tests measure? Answers to these two questions are necessary before the environmental effect can be assessed, and the genetic component can be defined only when black and white populations share the same environmental variables relating to education, nutrition, health, and other standards of living.

Because the genetic potential of an individual cannot be reliably predicted, the application of euphenic methods is, at best, a prospect for future generations. Also for the future is genetic engineering: the utilization of techniques from biochemical genetics for directly and permanently altering the genotype of an individual. Genetic engineering holds considerable promise for the cure rather than systemic treatment of genetic disease, but the social, legal, and ethical problems involved with manipulating human genes and genotypes are enormous.

Cloning provides a case in point. Cloning is a process whereby normal somatic cells are induced to divide in the same manner as fertilized egg cells, eventually resulting in identical copies of the individual donating the somatic cells. It was pointed out in Chapter 2 that every somatic cell has the full diploid number of chromosomes, although these cells are specialized to perform highly specific and restricted functions, such as the formation of various body tissues, organs, and so forth. The nucleus of every somatic cell, however, contains all the information necessary for the production of a complete organism. This was demonstrated by J. B. Gurdon (1968) in experiments on the South African clawed toad, *Xenopus laevis*. Gurdon replaced the nucleus of an unfertilized egg cell with the nucleus of an intestinal cell. The cell responded by dividing, resulting in a tadpole that eventually developed into an identical twin of the donor toad. In later experiments involving several subclones, additional identical copies of the parental toad were produced.

In theory, then, **many** carbon copies of any chosen human could be produced in a similar fashion. Unfortunately, experimental research has progressed far more rapidly than careful consideration of the social and ethical implications. Dire predictions have been made about the ultimate results of cloning and other aspects of genetic engineering (e.g., Rivers 1974), but only calm and rational discourse will determine the utility of such methods for the improvement of future populations.

Summary

Humans mate randomly for a great many loci, particularly those controlling nonvisible characteristics such as blood types and enzyme systems. However, they often do not mate at random for visible phenotypic traits, such as skin pigmentation, stature, and deafness. In addition, certain human societies are arranged around structured kinship systems which specify that mates be chosen from within the same lineage. These practices are called assortative mating and inbreeding, respectively, both of which lead to a deviation from expectations based on random mating for the loci concerned. While assortative mating and inbreeding have important consequences for the genetic structure of populations, neither can be classified as an evolutionary process because neither is capable of directly changing gene frequencies.

Individuals who choose their mates by similarity in phenotypic characteristics more often than would be expected by chance, are said to practice positive assortative mating. This phenomenon has never been demonstrated for simple genetic markers, but does occur for quantitative traits and some behavioral characteristics that may have a partial genetic basis. Positive assortative mating changes genotype rather than gene frequencies and increases both average population homozygosity and total population variance of the trait. In the simplest algebraic model that considers complete positive assortative mating, heterozygosity is reduced by one-half in each generation and the variance in the trait will eventually be doubled. Under conditions of partial positive assortative mating, which, no doubt, is a greater reflection of reality, homozygosity still increases but at a slower rate. One of the more important effects of positive assortative mating for a certain phenotypic trait is to increase its incidence. To the extent that a disorder like deafness is genetically influenced, therefore, its frequency will increase as a result of positive assortative mating between deaf people.

Inbreeding, the occurrence of matings between individuals possessing a common ancestor, also has the effect of increasing homozygosity, because there is an increased probability that two related mates will inherit the same allele from each parent. One important fact of inbreeding involves the knowledge that if a person carrying a deleterious recessive allele mates with a relative, the probability that their offspring will be affected with the disorder increases—the closer the relative, the greater the probability.

The existence of deleterious alleles in all human populations is a result of new and recurrent mutations, recombination, and migration. Moreover, there is always a small proportion of lethal genotypes in all populations. Some have maintained that this genetic load—specifically that caused by accumulating harmful mutations—will eventually result in a significant decrease in general population fitness. However, some deleterious alleles in the homozygous state clearly provide a selective advantage to heterozygous carriers of the same allele. Such heterozygotic superiority is responsible for the high incidence of the sickle-cell gene in malarial regions, where both homozygotes are at a selective disadvantage due to sickle-cell anemia and susceptibility to malaria. In addition to the mutational load, genetic loads may be produced by (1) immigration of less favorable genotypes into a population, (2) segregation, when heterozygous mates give rise to less fit homozygous offspring, (3) recombination, when recombinants possess lower fitness levels than the optimum genotype, and (4) incompatibility. The latter is of particular interest, since it is limited mostly to the ABO and Rh blood group systems and involves a genetically mediated blood group incompatibility between a mother and her fetus.

There are few effective methods by which genetic loads can be ameliorated, since they represent normal side-effects of the processes involved in the origin and maintenance of necessary population genetic variation. Various eugenic proposals have been suggested for the elimination of genetic defects, but genetic improvement of human populations at the present time seems most feasible through stabilization of population numbers, more adequate control of artificial mutagens released into the environment, and more widespread use of genetic counseling and prenatal diagnostic methods.

8 Aspects of Evolutionary Biology and Taxonomy

Introduction

A common theme in books about evolution and paleontology concerns the gradual nature of evolutionary change. Yet in the preceding chapters, evolution was discussed in the context of gene frequency changes within a few generations. Although it may appear so, this is no contradiction. It all depends upon the different levels at which evolutionary change may be examined.

Many years ago, Goldschmidt (1940) suggested the terms **"microevolution"** and **"macroevolution"** be applied, respectively, to changes within a species and to changes in more inclusive categories, such as the genus. Furthermore, he expressed the opinion that microevolution and macroevolution were somehow qualitatively different phenomena. In other words, evolutionary differentiation between our genus (*Homo*) and other nonhuman primate genera would proceed by macroevolution. However, change within our species (*H. sapiens*) would be microevolutionary, and each of the two processes would occur independently of the other, and by a different set of rules.

Among others, Simpson (1953) criticized this notion nearly 25 years ago. He pointed out that imprecision in use and differences in definition of these terms had led to considerable confusion, and suggested that:

> These somewhat monstrous terminological innovations have served whatever purpose they may have had and that clarity might now be improved by abandoning them. . . . It is better to recognize that there are not two, three, or more sorts of evolution but that there are innumerable levels of evolution, which reflect merely how much of the whole complex tangle of the history of life is to be taken into consideration at once (1953:339).

Biological anthropologists apparently paid little heed to Simpson's argument, because they adopted and continue to use both terms in studies of both past and present populations (e.g., Johnston 1973). Fortunately, there is no longer a misconception that they represent different phenomena. Rather, microevolution and macroevolution are generally used to indicate, respectively, (1) evolution involving small changes in gene frequencies or physical characteristics within certain populations, and (2) evolutionary differentiation between groups of organisms over long periods of time. It is mainly within this second category that nomenclatural difficulties arise. For the paleontologist studying the fossil evidence of change in a group of organisms over millions of years, the single term, macroevolution, is too imprecise to designate which levels of evolution are being examined. Instead, paleontologists find it more advantageous for communicating information to other scientists to denote the particular levels under consideration. Simpson suggests this be accomplished by using the various levels of the Linnaean hierarchy (discussed later), and this suggestion will be followed for the remainder of this book.

All of this brings us to the following point. In the preceding chapters, several major components of the theory of evolution have been discussed from a microevolutionary viewpoint. The first component involved the genetic material itself, particularly the physicochemical properties of DNA, RNA, and proteins, and how these substances were associated with genes and chromosomes. The second component dealt with mutation and the origin of new alleles. The third consisted of the mechanisms responsible for genetic continuity between generations. The fourth component was concerned with genetic variation in populations, particularly in terms of the processes associated with its production and maintenance. Finally, the fifth involved changes in gene frequencies, and the different ways in which mutation, natural selection, migration, and genetic drift operate to effect such changes.

These factors form the biological basis of evolution. However, the considerable physical disparity between modern human populations and our nonhuman primate ancestors reflects an accumulation of very small, heritable adaptations to the continually changing ecological variables over millions of years. Thus, two additional dimensions, time and ecology, are necessary to obtain a more accurate picture of human evolution. We not only need to know about what happens genetically, but also about what did happen morphologically and ecologically. The study of how organisms have changed through time is the primary subject matter of paleontology, a branch of biology which utilizes fossil remains for its evidential base.

It should be very clearly understood that the only *direct* evidence for human evolution through geological time is supplied by fossils. In succeeding chapters the fossil record for human and nonhuman primate evolution will be examined in detail. However, the transition from genetics to paleontology is fraught with difficulties not immediately apparent, and the purpose of this chapter is to outline a few relevant aspects of evolutionary biology and taxonomy in order to facilitate an understanding of the major trends of human evolution.

The Species Concept

One of the central problems of biology for nearly 300 years has been the formulation of a definition of the term "species" that is applicable to all organisms. A history of the attempts to do this has been presented by Mayr (1957). Most biologists and biological anthropologists would agree that a precise definition of the term is necessary for an understanding not only of how species arise, but also for the classification of living and past groups of organisms. Unfortunately, every definition proposed thus far has certain limitations. These limitations are clearly outlined in a discussion of various species concepts by Mayr (1963), who maintains that all recent definitions of the species can be reduced to three theoretical concepts.

Different Concepts of Species

The first of these concepts is the **typological species concept.** In this case, a group of organisms is considered a species because it looks different from another group. The determination of species status for any group is thus completely subjective and depends upon the degree of difference as judged by the observer. Now, what may appear to be definitive evidence for separate species status to one observer may not be to another, and this is the fatal flaw of this concept. An example of the confusion that can result when different observers apply their own arbitrary criteria to the classification of fossil remains is evident from studies of Neandertal remains. These remains were first found in Germany in 1856, and from that time they have been classified variously as *Homo neanderthalensis, Protanthropus atavus, Homo europaeus primigenius, Homo primigenius, Palaeanthropus europaeus, Archanthropus, Anthropus neanderthalensis,* and *Metanthropus* (Campbell 1965). Not only have different observers considered these remains as different species, but also of different genera!

Other problems arise with the typological concept when extreme sexual dimorphism exists within a species. Human sexual differences are not so great as to suggest that males and females belong to two different species, but the same cannot be said of some insects, fishes, and other organisms. The male angler fish, for example, becomes fused to the female's body and appears to be a small parasite that is evolutionarily far removed from the angler fish. Furthermore, in some species of ants and wasps, the males and females are so morphologically distinct that they cannot be classified with certainty unless they are found actively copulating (Wilson 1975).

Yet another flaw in the typological species concept concerns the separation of extreme polymorphic variants within a species into separate species. To an inexperienced observer, the morphological differences between a great dane and a chihuahua might seem sufficient for assignment into two distinct species. However, both indeed belong to *Canis familiaris.* For all of these reasons, the use of morphological criteria alone is clearly inadequate for species determination. Thus modern **systematists,** scientists who are involved with "the scientific study of the kinds and diversity of organisms and of any and all relationships among them" (Simpson 1961:7), have rejected the typological species concept.

The second theoretical construct is the **nondimensional species concept,** in which populations inhabiting the same locality (**sympatric**) at the same time (synchronic) are judged as different species if they are reproductively isolated from each other. The term **reproductive isolation** means that the members of the different populations either will not or cannot produce fully fertile or viable hybrids. The reasons for reproductive isolation are numerous and will be discussed later. For now it may be noted that Mayr (1963) considers this a nonarbitrary criterion for species determination, because the presence or absence of interbreeding between two populations can be objectively ascertained.

The third concept is the interbreeding-population, or **multidimensional species concept,** in which groups of populations are considered species if they have the capacity to interbreed. Such populations are considered to be separated either geographically (**allopatric**) or temporally (allochronic). Put another way, different groups of populations are deemed the same species *if* they can surmount either the time or space barrier and interbreed with each other. These populations, then, are *potentially* interbreeding, and this aspect is the main drawback against the multidimensional concept. When populations are separated by long periods of time, potentiality becomes a fundamental concept. Although one need not agree in this instance with Russell's view that "when potentiality is used as a fundamental and irreducible concept, it always conceals confusion of thought" (1945:167), it is exceedingly difficult to judge those populations that are potentially interbreeding.

The Biological Species Concept
The limitations in each of the above three species concepts have led to the formulation of the "biological species concept," which is one of the most widely held species concepts in modern biology. Incorporating parts of the nondimensional and multidimensional concepts, Mayr maintained that "species are groups of actually or potentially interbreeding natural populations, which are reproductively isolated from other such groups" (1942:120). Thus, a biological species is a reproductive unit consisting of genetically interconnected populations that can and do coexist in the same geographical area with other species. However, such coexistence does not lead to interspecific hybridization.

Fortunately, wide acceptance of any phenomenon does not mean that the phenomenon is a fact. The biological species, as defined, is not a fact; it is simply a workable concept that does have certain limitations recognized even by those (e.g., Mayr 1963) who consider it the most applicable concept yet developed. One drawback concerns the criterion of interbreeding. To the systematist studying living populations, the presence or absence of interbreeding between populations is not always an insurmountable problem, because it can presumably be objectively determined. To the paleontologist studying small samples of fossils, however, interbreeding can never be directly ascertained. It can only be inferred by the degree to which population samples overlap in their ranges of variation for physical characteristics. The confidence attached to such inferences will depend not only upon the extent of overlapping variation, but also upon whether the samples represent geographically contiguous or separated populations.

Another limitation of the biological species concept involves potentiality. The same objections apply here as for the multidimensional concept, and it is interesting to note that Mayr (1969) has deleted the phrase, "actually or potentially," in a later definition of the biological species. Yet a third problem concerns reproductive isolation. Once again, this may be determined objectively between two groups of living populations and, hence, causes no serious difficulty for the neontologist (neontology is the study of recent organisms). The paleontologist, on the other hand, deals with changes in populations through time and must consider intermediate stages in the formation of a species. Because such changes are very gradual, the delineation of a single point in time when two populations become reproductively isolated, and hence acquire species status, is impossible.

These points lead to the conclusion that the biological species concept is more useful to the neontologist than to the paleontologist. An unfortunate fact of human paleontology is that only rarely is a sample of sufficient size to determine the range of population variation for the morphological characters being examined. Only inferences can be made, and often such inferences are difficult to justify. Usually only a few warped and fragmentary remains are recovered, especially if the material represents individuals belonging to a very early population. Thus, paleontologists have directed much time and thought toward the development of a **paleontological species concept** that incorporates the basic features of the biological species concept (see Sylvester-Bradley 1956). To a certain extent, this is apparent in Simpson's definition of an evolutionary species, "a lineage (an ancestral-descendent sequence of populations) evolving separately from others and with its own unitary evolutionary role and tendencies." (1961:153).

At least three aspects of this definition warrant further examination. The phrase "evolving separately from others" implies that the lineage was not interbreeding with other lineages. The phrase "with its own evolutionary role and tendencies" suggests that populations in the lineage were responding to selection pressures in their own particular ways. Finally, the phrase "an ancestral-descendent sequence of populations" brings the time factor into focus. This is important because species do exist through time, and a paleontological species concept that failed to signify this dimension would be quite inadequate.

There is an additional point about species that has been neglected until now. A species can be viewed in two different ways, but this has not always been recognized by individuals studying fossil or living populations. The first considers a species as a unit with great evolutionary significance; a category that can be studied profitably for the purpose of advancing our knowledge of evolutionary biology. One of the foremost proponents of this view is Ernst Mayr, who stated:

> Although the evolutionist may speak of broad phenomena, such as trends, adaptations, specializations, and regressions, they are really not separable from the progression of entities that display these trends, the species. The species are the real units of evolution, as the temporary incarnation of harmonious, well-integrated gene complexes. And speciation, the production of new gene complexes capable of ecological shifts, is the method by which evolution advances. Without speciation there would be no diversification of the organic world, no adaptive radiation, and very little evolutionary progress. The species, then, is the keystone of evolution (1963:621).

The second view of a species is as a legal unit (a **taxon**) in a hierarchic classification. The taxonomist, who specializes in the theoretical study of classification (Simpson 1961), is primarily interested in ordering complex biological phenomena so as to reflect as accurately as possible the existing order in Nature. Part of this ordering process includes assignation of a sample of a population or a group of populations to a particular taxon. One such category is the species, and the assignment of a sample to either a new or well-established species depends heavily upon the subjective decisions and experience of the practicing taxonomist. In this context, Simpson (1961) has stressed that **classification,** the actual process of placing organisms into the various taxa in a hierarchy, is an art rather than a science.

The extensive works by Simpson and Mayr on the problems of species concepts in taxonomy and systematics have had considerable influence on interpretations of evolutionary relationships between past and among present populations. However, it must be noted that their concepts are not universally shared by evolutionary biologists. An example of a fundamental disagreement with both Simpson's and Mayr's views of the species is evident in Sokal and Crovello's (1970) recent evaluation of the biological species concept. In their construction and analysis of a flow chart of the operations necessary for the recognition of the biological species *sensu* Mayr, they concluded that (1) the biological species concept is "neither operational nor heuristic nor of practical value" (1970:149); (2) Simpson's definition of the evolutionary species is "so vague as to make any attempt at operational definition foredoomed to failure" (1970:146); (3) "the localized biological population may be the most useful unit for evolutionary study" (1970:151).

To state that one of these viewpoints was absolutely correct and the other absolutely wrong would be to ignore the facts of organic diversity. For example, systematists are fully aware of the fact that the biological species concept is totally inapplicable to organisms that reproduce parthenogenetically (parthenogenesis is the reproductive process whereby offspring arise from egg cells that have not been fertilized by male gametes). In this instance, of course, the criterion of interbreeding simply does not apply. Yet the acceptance of the biological species concept, and the awareness of the components included therein, have enhanced mutual understanding of the discontinuous groups of populations that we call species. Therefore, usage of the term "species" in succeeding chapters will be in the sense of the biological species concept. Rather than pursue this topic farther, you are urged to examine Hull's (1965, 1970) excellent analyses of the controversy about the arbitrary versus nonarbitrary nature of the species.

Reproductive Isolation and Isolating Mechanisms

An interbreeding group of populations, then, is a distinct species if it is reproductively isolated from other groups of populations. In this context, reproductive isolation has a very definite meaning. It means that the members of a population have developed biological or behavioral characteristics that either (1) prevent interbreeding between them and individuals in other populations or (2) prevent the production of viable or fertile hybrids even if interbreeding occasionally occurs. Such characteristics are called **isolating mechanisms,** and they protect the genetic integrity of each species.

It must be stressed at the outset that physical separation between two groups of populations, or geographic isolation, is not an isolating mechanism. A period of geographic isolation between populations may be a necessary prerequisite for **speciation,** the process during which a group of interbreeding populations becomes reproductively isolated from other such groups. However, the mere fact that two groups of populations are separated geographically has nothing to do with whether they are reproductively isolated and, hence, of different species. Different population groups may be either sympatric or allopatric, that is, they may occur geographically in the same area or in different areas. If such groups are sympatric, and if they neither interbreed nor produce viable or fertile offspring even though cross-fertilization is geographically possible, then they are usually regarded as separate species. Some have called this "passing the test of sympatry" (Stebbins 1971).

Different Kinds of Isolating Mechanisms
As mentioned above, isolating mechanisms are either biological or behavioral, and by preventing genetic exchange allow sympatric species to retain their identity. These

Table 8.1 Classification of Isolating Mechanisms (After Littlejohn 1969.)

Premating

1. Reduction of contact.
   a. Temporal (even though populations inhabit the same regions, mating is prevented by different times of sexual maturity).
   b. Ecological (potential mates fail to interbreed because they may occupy different habitats within the same region, or because their mating seasons occur at different times).
2. Reduction of mating frequency.
   c. Ethological (incompatibilities in premating behavior prevent cross-fertilization—but only in animals).
   d. Morphological (physical differences between species in their reproductive structures either prevent or restrict the successful transfer of sperm, even though copulation may be attempted).

Postmating, but Prezygotic

3. Reduction of zygote formation.
   e. Gametic and reproductive tract incompatibility (copulation and sperm transfer occurs, but an antigenic reaction in the female prevents fertilization).

Postmating and Postzygotic

4. Reduction of hybrid survival.
   f. Hybrid inviability (fertilization occurs, but the F_1 hybrid is less successful in development and continued life than a normal individual).
5. Reduction of gene flow through hybrids.
   g. Hybrid ethological isolation (F_1 hybrids are fully fertile and viable, but may be discriminated against during pair formation for behavioral reasons).
   h. Hybrid sterility (because of abnormal segregation and other genetic reasons, fully viable F_1 hybrids may be partially or completely sterile).
   i. F_2 hybrid breakdown (although F_1 hybrids may be both fertile and viable, F_2 hybrids may be sterile or inviable).

mechanisms may be classified according to their operation before or after mating and, thus, have been called premating and postmating mechanisms. Most classifications are basically similar to Littlejohn's (1969), which appears in Table 8.1.

From the standpoint of total reproductive isolation between different species, premating mechanisms are usually the most effective barriers against interbreeding. Of these, ethological mechanisms are more prevalent than any others in animal species. Now this does not imply that humans and chimpanzees, for example, are isolated from each other solely because their reproductive behaviors are different. Instead, the total isolation between two such related species usually involves several different isolating mechanisms, especially if the two species have evolved apart for long periods of time. The only premating mechanism separating humans and chimpanzees is ethological, but it is a totally effective barrier. However, if for some unimaginable reason this barrier broke down, one or more postmating mechanisms would in all likelihood either (1) prevent fertilization or (2) block the formation of a viable hybrid. Thus Mayr has noted that isolating mechanisms are "arranged like a series of hurdles; if one breaks down, another must be overcome" (1963:107) for successful interspecific **hybridization.**

The Genetics of Reproductive Isolation

The presence of multiple isolating mechanisms in animal species is responsible for the fact that interspecific hybridization is only rarely observed in nature. Furthermore, in the few cases where fertile and viable hybrids do appear, the genetic integrity of the parental species is unaffected, because the ethologically and ecologically less well-adapted hybrids fail to any appreciable extent to backcross to members of either parental species. The eventual consequence from the viewpoint of evolutionary genetics is the same as if the hybrid never existed; the genetic variation in both parental species remains unaffected, and the hybrid represents an evolutionary dead end.

The numerous isolating mechanisms in any animal species also point to the conclusion that many different genes and chromosomal segments are involved. This conclusion is supported by direct evidence only for sterility in plants and for certain isolating mechanisms in *Drosophila*, but there is virtually no information about what genes or chromosomal segments are associated with particular isolating mechanisms in animals. Nevertheless, there are at least two reasons for the generally accepted view that all isolating mechanisms (including those of an ethological nature) have an underlying genetic basis.

First, isolating mechanisms are species-specific. All populations of a species share the same set of mechanisms, and these are peculiar to each species. Thus, it may be strongly inferred that such mechanisms are incorporated into the genotypes of the constituent individuals of a species and are inherited by progeny in accordance with established Mendelian rules. Second, it has been observed that progeny of interspecific hybrids, when they do survive, often differ in a number of factors relating to reproductive strategy. These factors include habitat preference, mating seasons, and so forth. In these progeny, segregation for these factors rarely produces expected Mendelian ratios. Instead, complex ratios and numerous intermediate types are found, which would be expected on the basis of polygenic inheritance (Stebbins 1971).

The Origin of Reproductive Isolation and New Species

It was stressed in earlier chapters that all populations of a species are to some extent genetically and morphologically distinct from all other populations of the same species. Occasionally, several populations will share a number of characteristics that differentiate the group from other populations. When this occurs, such a group of populations is often recognized taxonomically as a **subspecies.** The subspecies is defined as a group of local populations that inhabits part of the geographic range of the species and differs taxonomically from other such groups (Mayr 1963).

Now, both subspecies and populations *can* under certain conditions become reproductively isolated, but neither necessarily always represents the beginning of a new species—an incipient species—because neither is reproductively isolated from other populations of the species. A subspecies may diverge from other groups of populations, depending upon its adaptive response to a particular set of selective variables in part of the species range, and reduced gene flow between it and other groups of populations. On the other hand, it may converge with other populations and completely lose its identity, particularly if and when the partial barriers to gene flow break down. Thus, two factors are of paramount importance in the differentiation of populations: different selective pressures, and the presence or absence of genetic exchange. The origin and evolution of isolating mechanisms, and hence the origin of species, also depend upon these two factors.

The most widely held theory on how new species originate is called allopatric, or **geographic speciation.** Full evidential support of the theory may be found in Mayr's (1963) comprehensive formulation, but its essential features may be described by means of a hypothetical situation. Suppose that a certain species, consisting of many genetically distinct populations cohesively united by gene flow, occupies a certain geographic area. Suppose also that ecological variables are not uniform throughout the entire species range. Thus, it may be presumed that populations in one part of the range will be subjected to different selection pressures than populations in other areas. Suppose now that a completely extraneous event, such as a rise in sea level, a volcanic eruption, or some other natural phenomenon, totally isolates one or more populations from the species. Assume also that this period of isolation lasts indefinitely—perhaps for thousands of generations. Under these conditions, the relationship between the isolated population and the species to which it belonged can be one of two different forms.

First, the isolated population may undergo no evolutionary changes of a nature that would reproductively isolate it from the parental species. In this instance, of course, a return to sympatry would be concomitant with free genetic exchange and the production of fully fertile and viable offspring. This points out the very important conclusion that geographic isolation does not necessarily lead to speciation. It has nothing at all to do with the factors responsible for the origin and evolution of isolating mechanisms but, instead, serves only to interrupt gene flow.

In the second case, the geographically isolated population may become reproductively isolated and rank as a species itself. This would be apparent if, upon becoming sympatric with the parental species, various mechanisms prevented successful hybridization. The factors involved in this process may be summarized as follows. Suppose that geographic isolation was complete—it guaranteed that each of the two populations would undergo its own independent evolutionary development. At the outset we may safely assume that both populations were somewhat different, because no two populations are genetically identical. It may also be assumed that each population inhabited an area in which the ecological variables differed slightly, because no two physical environments are exactly the same. Now, each population may tend toward increased differentiation for a number of reasons.

First, the two populations will share neither the same mutations nor the order in which they occur. Relatively few new mutations will be incorporated into the respective gene pools, but those that are will alter the genetic background and thus have some effect on the selective value of later mutations. Second, the different ecological (selective) variables to which each population is exposed will slowly differentiate the two populations for certain gene frequencies (see Chapter 6). Since the different mutations in each population are not affected by identical selective processes, a newly established allele or gene complex associated in some way with reproductive performance or viability may eventually characterize one of the two populations. The critical point is that such an allele or gene complex has not been selected for compatibility with any particular allele in the other population. Thus, if the two populations become sympatric at a later time, they may be isolated reproductively by any of the mechanisms outlined in Table 8.1. When such mechanisms are fully developed, the two populations rank as separate species.

It must be stressed again that the origin of reproductive isolation is an *incidental* by-product of the same factors that differentiate populations within a species: mutation, recombination, and divergent selection pressures. Furthermore, it is important to note that premating mechanisms are themselves subject to improvement by natural selection. When two partially isolated sympatric populations crossbreed, relatively fewer fertile and viable offspring will be produced than by matings exclusively within each population. Selection will therefore favor those characteristics (and their genotypes) associated with mating between individuals of the same incipient species. In time, the frequency of such physical or behavioral characteristics will increase in both populations until reproductive isolation is complete.

Elements of Taxonomy

Nobody knows how many different species of animals, plants, and other organisms presently exist on earth, much less how many have existed since the origin of life. In 1969, Mayr estimated that about a million living species of animals and a half-million species of plants had already been formally described, and that estimates of undescribed species ranged from 3 million to 10 million. The organization of this vast diversity of life into a coherent classificatory scheme for facilitating communication among life scientists is the primary task of taxonomy. Without such order, it would be virtually impossible to understand anything of substance about the evolutionary and genetic relationships among both living and extinct groups of organisms.

Basic Definitions

The terminology in this and all subsequent chapters is adopted from Simpson, and unless otherwise indicated, all definitions given below may be found in the first chapter of his definitive treatise, *Principles of Animal Taxonomy* (1961).

1. Taxonomy. "The theoretical study of classification, including its bases, principles, procedures, and rules" (1961:11). It is important to remember that the subject matter of taxonomy consists of different classifications.

2. Zoological classification. "The ordering of animals into groups (or sets) on the basis of their relationships, that is, of associations by contiguity, similarity, or both" (1961:9). Thus, classification deals not only with the activity of ordering organisms, but also with the products of such activity. The ordering into groups or sets of organisms means that the subjects of classification are populations.

3. Zoological nomenclature. "The application of distinctive names to each of the groups recognized in any given zoological classification" (1961:9). The outcome of classification is, thus, formal nomenclature, and a biological unit to which a formal name is attached is called a taxon (plural = taxa).

4. Thus, a taxon is defined as "a group of real organisms recognized as a formal unit at any level of a hierarchic classification" (1961:19). As will be shown shortly, the naming of a taxon must be carried out according to the set of rules outlined in the authoritative publication, *International Code of Zoological Nomenclature*.

It should be clearly understood that classification always involves populations, but never a single individual. An individual can be identified, but not formally classified. Identification is the term referring to the procedure whereby individuals are placed into previously established classes. The process of identification, furthermore, is roughly analogous to the procedure a stamp collector might follow with an unfamiliar stamp. To locate the stamp in a catalog, the collector would examine numerous variables, such as country of origin, date of issue, whether it was a single stamp or part of a series, perforation patterns, and so forth. To identify either living or extinct organisms, the taxonomist utilizes all observable properties of the organisms being considered. Such properties include morphological, physiological, behavioral, biochemical, and ecological variables, in addition to similarities in amino acid sequences in proteins and DNA homologies.

It is an unfortunate fact that many early workers in paleoanthropology, when dealing with single specimens from which inferences about the range of population variation were unjustified, were seemingly unaware of the critical difference between classification and identification. In classification, inductive procedures are used for ordering populations into a hierarchical scheme. In identification, deductive procedures are used to locate one or more individuals in an established classification.

The application of formal names to single specimens of our remote ancestors led to "chaos in anthropological nomenclature," to use Simpson's phrase (1963). Thus, depending upon the investigator, scanty and fragmentary remains of single individuals were often given diverse names when only a catalog number was required. Such invalid terminology for fossil remains has been reviewed by Campbell (1965) and need not be repeated here. Instead, it should be noted that each taxon has only one valid name, and the *International Code of Zoological Nomenclature* contains 87 articles that determine the validity of each name. Some of the more important rules in the Code follow:

1. The formal name of any population of organisms consists of one word denoting its genus and a second word denoting its species. The first word is properly called the generic name, and the second word is the trivial name. Both words together form the specific name. For example, in *Homo sapiens* the generic word is *Homo*, the trivial word is *sapiens,* and both words together form the specific name.

The naming of a species with two Latin or latinized words is called **binominal** (not binomial) **nomenclature,** because two names are used (Latin: *binomen*). The naming of a subspecies requires that a third word be used. This results in a trinomen, as in *Homo sapiens neanderthalensis.* It is important to remember that every species must be denoted by a binomen, but the naming of a subspecies is arbitrary.

2. Specific names are always italicized. Accepted convention allows the generic name to be abbreviated after the specific name has been introduced; for example, *H. sapiens.*

3. The generic name always begins with a capital letter; trivial and subspecific names always begin with lower case letters.

4. A subgeneric name (the subgenus is a taxon directly below the genus in a hierarchical classification) is written in parentheses between the generic and trivial names, such as *Australopithecus (Paranthropus) robustus.* The subgenus does not

count as part of the binominal name of a species, nor as part of the trinominal name of a subspecies.

5. Sometimes a name such as *Homo (= Pithecanthropus) erectus* is encountered in the literature. The equal sign within the parentheses designates a synonym, that is, a different name given to the same taxon. The Code expressly forbids the use of synonyms in this manner, as well as the erection of homonyms. Homonyms are the same names given to different taxa.

6. Within the Code is the **"Law of Priority."** This law states that the oldest available name is the valid name of a taxon, provided there has been no transgression of the various articles in the Code.

Of course, there is no legal enforcement of the rules contained in the Code. Instead, it represents a set of rigorous guidelines that direct the classificatory activities of the life scientist, and strict adherence to these rules can only enhance our understanding of the relationships among groups of organisms.

The main procedures in the classificatory process have been viewed by Simpson (1963) as the five operational levels shown schematically in Table 8.2. To explain these levels, suppose you have just returned from the field after recovering a number of specimens. Suppose also that the specimens were excavated from the same

Table 8.2 Schematic Presentation of the Main Procedures in the Classificatory Process, Indicating Designations (Horizontal Arrows) at Each Procedural Level (After Simpson 1963.) See text for further explanation.

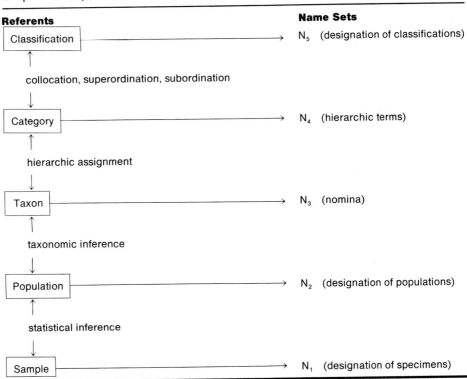

geological stratum in the same site, and that they possessed morphological similarities suggesting members of a single Mendelian population.

Your specimens, then, represent a sample that should be designated simply by assigning arbitrary catalog numbers to each specimen in the sample. This is the N_1 naming set. Such catalog numbers are associated with all relevant information about the actual recovery of the material, so that you or any other investigator may begin a study of the sample with a common data base. Now, the sample at this level has no scientific significance per se. If it is limited to only a few nondefinitive fragments representing only one or two individuals, there may be no point at all in attempting to go beyond this stage.

However, if the sample is large enough, it may be possible to draw statistical inferences about the range of variation of the population to which the sample belonged. When a population is recognized in this manner, it is best designated by reference to its spatiotemporal location. The name or set of names utilized comprise the N_2 naming set. If by taxonomic inference the population is found to belong to a previously established taxon, then the classificatory procedure ends by assigning the formal nomen (plural = nomina, the N_3 naming set) of the taxon to the population.

As will be discussed shortly, all taxa are assigned to ranked categories in a hierarchic system. Such categories are relatively few in number and are not named arbitrarily. A category is not synonymous with a taxon, but instead includes all taxa at the same level in the hierarchy. The terms given to categories include species, genus, and so forth, and these are the hierarchic terms represented by the naming set N_4.

The assignment of various taxa to their respective categories is followed by the actual construction of the hierarchy. This involves collocating the various categories and arranging them vertically (by super- and subordination) from the most to the least inclusive categories. The N_5 naming set designates such classifications according to where and by whom the classification was published.

The Linnaean Hierarchy

The hierarchy used for zoological classification is called the Linnaean hierarchy, named after Carolus Linnaeus (1707–1778). Linnaeus was regarded by Cuvier (1769–1832), himself one of the most eminent anatomists and zoologists in the history of biology, as one of the two greatest naturalists of the century (Coleman 1964). Glass suggests that "Linnaeus was born with a natural gift, almost a mania, for classifying everything, but he combined it with a deep love of nature and masterly keenness of observation" (1959:144). Linnaeus devoted much of his life to bringing order to the natural world, and eventually developed a classificatory hierarchy in the form of a five-level sequence. These levels, in addition to two others (phylum and family) that were added later from other sources, include:

Kingdom
Phylum
Class
Order
Family
Genus
Species

The most inclusive category in this hierarchy is the kingdom, and the least inclusive is the species. The use of these seven levels for classification of any group of organisms is required in modern taxonomy, but increased information about the similarities and differences among natural populations has necessitated expansion of the hierarchy. For example, until only recently it was generally held that all life belonged to two kingdoms, Animalia (animals) and Plantae (plants). However, many living organisms do not neatly correspond to the inherent features characterizing animals or plants. Thus, in the last few years systematists have expanded these two kingdoms into five (e.g., Whittaker 1969), consisting of:

1. Monera (bacteria, blue-green algae)
2. Protista (green, yellow-green, red and brown, and golden-yellow algae; protozoa, slime molds)
3. Fungi (molds, mushrooms, yeasts)
4. Plantae (all green plants developing from embryos)
5. Animalia (animals)

A full summary of these five kingdoms and their respective phyla has been presented by Margulis (1974).

The expanded hierarchy now includes intermediate levels between Linnaeus's basic categories. This system normally uses the prefixes super- to designate intermediate levels above one of the basic levels, and either infra- or sub- to denote categories below a given level. An example of a complete classification of a species such as *H. sapiens* is given in Table 8.3, along with the formal zoological nomenclature for each category.

The classification of *H. sapiens* utilizes the seven basic levels of the Linnaean hierarchy, in addition to eight other categories. Other categories, such as superclass, superorder, subfamily, tribe (beneath subfamily), subtribe, and subgenus could also be used, but in practice it has not been necessary to do so. Except for the species category, the actual number of levels in any particular classification is arbitrary. Thus classifications can and do change as new information is gained about the biological relationships among natural populations.

As mentioned earlier, all classifications proceed from the least inclusive (subspecies or species, depending upon whether a subspecies is formally recognized) to the most inclusive (kingdom). For *H. sapiens*, all modern living populations and those of the recent past are regarded as *H. sapiens sapiens*. In some classifications, *H. sapiens* includes at least one additional subspecies represented by Neandertal populations, *H. sapiens neanderthalensis*. The genus *Homo*, furthermore, includes the two species, *sapiens* and *erectus*, the latter a geographically widespread species represented by fossilized remains. Whenever a taxon consists of two or more subordinate taxa, it is said to be **polytypic**. Thus *Homo* is a polytypic genus because it includes two species, and *H. sapiens* is a polytypic species because it includes at least two subspecies.

As one goes up the taxonomic hierarchy, the biological and, presumably, the evolutionary relationships among taxa become more distant. Likewise, the diagnostic characteristics of the taxa in each category become ever more general. The inclusive nature of the various categories above *H. sapiens* may be summarized as follows:

1. Family Hominidae: includes at least two genera, *Homo* and *Australopithecus* (one of our early ancestors, represented by fossilized remains from Africa).

2. Superfamily Hominoidea: includes Hominidae, in addition to two other families, Pongidae (the great apes) and Hylobatidae (the gibbon).

3. Infraorder Catarrhini: includes Hominoidea, as well as the superfamily Cercopithecoidea (the Old World monkeys).

4. Suborder Anthropoidea: includes Catarrhini and the infraorder Platyrrhini (the New World monkeys).

5. Order Primates: includes Anthropoidea, in addition to the suborder Prosimii (lemurs, lorises, and tarsiers).

6. Cohort Unguiculata: includes Primates, and the orders Insectivora (shrews, hedgehogs, moles, etc.), Chiroptera (bats), Edentata (tree sloths, anteaters, armadillos), Dermoptera (flying "lemurs"), and Pholidota (pangolins).

7. Infraclass Eutheria: includes Unguiculata and the cohorts Glires (rodents, rabbits), Mutica (dolphins, whales), and Ferungulata (dogs, cats, sea lions, elephants, horses, cows, deer, etc.).

8. Subclass Theria: includes Eutheria and the infraclasses Pantotheria (extinct mammals from the Jurassic period) and Metatheria (the marsupials, such as kangaroos, opossums, etc.).

9. Class Mammalia: includes Theria and the subclasses Prototheria (the monotremes, such as spiny anteaters and platypuses) and Allotheria (extinct mammals from the Jurassic, Cretaceous, and Paleocene periods).

10. Subphylum Vertebrata: includes all mammals, birds, reptiles, fishes, and amphibians.

11. Phylum Chordata: includes all animals with a notochord. The notochord is a long, flexible, rodlike structure that extends for the length of the back from head to tail. In *H. sapiens* and most, but not all, other vertebrates, the notochord is replaced in the adult with the vertebral column, or backbone.

12. Kingdom Animalia: includes all multicellular animals developing from a blastula. The blastula is a stage that occurs immediately after cleavage, which in turn is the first major sequence of events after the sperm cell penetrates the egg (see Romer 1962, for a lucid discussion of cleavage and blastula formation).

The Two Taxonomies

Of considerable importance is the question, aside from coherently ordering natural populations, do classifications serve other purposes? Are classifications mere "pigeonholes" for the purpose of identification, or do they allow generalizations about evolutionary relationships? Fortunately, most, if not all, practicing taxonomists reject the idea that classification is done simply for the sake of classification. But there is currently an intense controversy about how classifications should be constructed and what they mean. At the heart of the controversy are unresolved questions about the

Table 8.3 A Formal Classification of *H. sapiens* (After Simons 1972 and Simpson 1945.)

Kingdom Animalia
  Phylum Chordata
    Subphylum Vertebrata
      Class Mammalia
        Subclass Theria
          Infraclass Eutheria
            Cohort Unguiculata
              Order Primates
                Suborder Anthropoidea
                  Infraorder Catarrhini
                    Superfamily Hominoidea
                      Family Hominidae
                        Genus *Homo*
                          Species *sapiens*
                            Subspecies *sapiens*

philosophical foundations of taxonomy itself, and these questions have led to the formation of two conflicting schools of taxonomic thought.

The first school, referred to variously as evolutionary, classical, or phylogenetic taxonomy (e.g., Simpson 1961; Mayr 1965), maintains that the most meaningful classifications—those that lead to the most useful biological generalizations—are those based upon evolutionary (phylogenetic) relationships among taxa. In this view, the evidence upon which the classification in Table 8.3 is based indicates that *H. sapiens* is evolutionarily closer to *H. erectus* than to *Australopithecus;* to the order Primates than to Chiroptera; to the cohort Unguiculata than to Ferungulata, and so forth.

The second school, called numerical taxonomy, was defined by its principal spokesmen, Sokal and Sneath, as "the numerical evaluation of the affinity or similarity between taxonomic units and the ordering of these units into taxa on the basis of their affinities" (1963:48). Numerical classification is based solely upon resemblances and differences in various characteristics among organisms rather than phylogenetic relationships between taxa, and advanced statistical techniques in conjunction with high-speed computers are utilized to construct and order classes. Because numerical classification is thoroughly nonphylogenetic, evolutionary relationships that are suggested by classes so constructed are incidental to other goals. These goals are to achieve a high degree of objectivity and repeatability in estimating resemblances between different forms of organisms. Thus, classifications would become very stable, definitive, and not subject to continual change.

On the surface, there might appear to be no real substance to the differences between the two schools. It would certainly be ideal to have natural classifications that were at once stable, objective, repeatable, and reflective of actual phylogenetic relationships. However, several philosophical and methodological issues appear to be irreconcilable between the two schools. These issues are:

Evolutionary taxonomy

1. The construction of various classes utilizes characteristics that show evolutionary trends and branchings. Therefore, some characteristics can be deleted because they provide little "useful" information. In creating natural taxa, characteristics are disproportionately weighted by their relative importance.

2. The ideal natural classification reflects the actual phylogenetic relationships between taxa.

3. Depending upon the sufficiency and reliability of evidence, the evolutionary history of natural populations can be determined with a high level of confidence.

4. For the most part, classification is an art.

Numerical taxonomy

1. Phylogenetic considerations play no part in the selection of characteristics for the construction of taxa. All possible characteristics should be used for classificatory purposes, and each characteristic is given equal weight.

2. The taxa in an ideal classification should have maximum information content and must be based solely upon similarity in compared characteristics.

3. For the vast majority of organisms, the fossil evidence necessary for phylogenetic generalizations is either very scarce or nonexistent, and it is likely to remain that way. Since we will never be able to fully document the evolutionary history of most organisms, principles of taxonomy cannot be based on phylogeny.

4. Classification is an empirical science, not an art.

The arguments about phylogenetic versus numerical taxonomy have been presented forcefully by advocates of each viewpoint, and those of you wishing to follow these arguments in greater depth should consult Hull (1965, 1967), various articles in Heywood and McNeill (1964), Mayr (1965), Pratt (1972), Sokal and Camin (1966), and Wagner (1969). Rather than pursuing this topic farther, the position adopted herein is that classification does indeed have a systematic relationship to phylogeny. This relationship is a fundamental tenet in evolutionary taxonomy and must be clearly understood. Very few have expressed it as well as G. G. Simpson in this extensive quotation:

> We propose to *define* taxonomic categories in evolutionary and to the largest extent phylogenetic terms, but to use evidence that is almost entirely nonphylogenetic when taken as individual observations. . . . The well-known example of monozygotic ("identical") twins is explanatory and is something more than an analogy. We *define* such twins as two individuals developed from one zygote. No one has ever seen this occur in humans, but we recognize when the definition is met by *evidence* of similarities sufficient to sustain the inference. The individuals in question are not twins because they are similar but, quite the contrary, are similar because they are twins. Precisely so, individuals do not belong in the same taxon because they are similar, but they are similar because they belong to the same taxon. (Linnaeus was quite right when he said that the genus makes the characters, not vice versa, even though he did not know what makes the genus.) That statement is a central element in evolutionary taxonomy, and the alternative clearly distinguishes it

from nonevolutionary taxonomy. Another way to put the matter is to say that categories are defined in phylogenetic terms but that taxa are defined by somatic relationships that result from phylogeny and are evidence that the categorical definition is met. (1961:69)

Summary

The development of a species concept applicable to all organisms, both living and extinct, has been a central problem in evolutionary biology for centuries. Such a definition is necessary for understanding the origin of diverse groups of organisms, in addition to bringing some classificatory order to organic nature. Although an all-inclusive concept has never been developed, some are far more descriptive of reality than others.

Specifically, the typological species concept has been thoroughly rejected because it defines a group as a species on the basis of the subjective evaluation of the observer. Because different observers emphasize different morphological criteria, use of the typological concept has led to nomenclatural and, hence, classificatory chaos. A second construct is the nondimensional concept, which considers sympatric and synchronic groups as different species if they are unable to produce fully fertile or viable hybrids. Yet a third concept is multidimensional, which holds that allopatric and allochronic populations are species if they have the capacity to successfully hybridize.

Probably the most widely accepted concept has been derived in part from the nondimensional and multidimensional concepts. This is called the biological species concept, which defines species as "groups of actually or potentially inter-breeding natural populations which are reproductively isolated from other such groups." While this construct is particularly useful for the differentiation of living species, the matter of "actually or potentially interbreeding" prevents its rigorous application to extinct fossil groups. Nevertheless, elements of this definition have been incorporated into the paleontological species concept, "a lineage (an ancestral-descendent sequence of populations) evolving separately from others and with its own unitary evolutionary role and tendencies."

Reproductive isolation between two species is not synonymous with geographic separation but, rather, means that the populations of both species possess certain sets of biological and behavioral characteristics that either prevent interbreeding or the production of fertile or viable hybrids if occasional interbreeding occurs. Such characteristics are called isolating mechanisms, and they almost certainly have an underlying genetic basis. Isolating mechanisms are species-specific, are shared by all populations of a species, and thus are very likely inherited according to established Mendelian rules. According to the widely accepted theory of geographic speciation, two sympatric populations may, after an intervening period of geographic separation and consequent interruption of gene flow, evolve distinct characteristics that serve to reproductively isolate them from each other in the event of a return to sympatry. When this occurs, each can be classified as a related, but distinct, species.

As a category to which populations of organisms can be assigned, the species is the only nonarbitrary taxon utilized by taxonomists for classifying groups of organisms. The primary task of taxonomy, the theoretical study of classification, is to organize living diversity into a coherent and orderly framework in order to facilitate communication among all life scientists. To this end, the *International Code of Zoological Nomenclature* is a set of highly specific rules that outline the procedures to be followed in a zoological classification. In such a classification, populations are arranged into the Linnaean hierarchy. This is a set of different levels, each one of which is more inclusive as one goes up the hierarchy. The most inclusive level is the kingdom (such as Animalia and Plantae), and the least, a group of similar populations within a single species called the subspecies.

2

The Origin and Evolution of the Human Species

9 Our Closest Living Relatives: The Order Primates

Introduction

The study of the biology of living and past nonhuman primates is called "primatology," a term first appearing in print in 1941 (Schultz 1971). It is a fascinating discipline with a history of only a few decades, although academic interests in primates are almost as old as the biological and medical sciences themselves. Primatology differs from many other broad disciplines emphasizing the study of certain groups of organisms, such as entomology (the study of insects), because the focus of primatology is on a relatively low categorical level (the order Primates) in the Linnaean Hierarchy. The number of identified species of primates is quite small when compared to species diversity encompassed by many other disciplines, whatever classification one chooses to follow. For example, Simons (1972) maintains that 206 extinct and 154 extant primate species are contained within 148 currently accepted living and extinct genera. By contrast, entomology is concerned with the Class Insecta, which contains somewhat less than a million identified species (Mayr 1969). Approximately 12,000 of these are different species of ants alone (Wilson 1975)!

We probably know more about the order Primates than any other order of comparable size, but the reasons for this knowledge are not limited to the fact that other orders are far more diverse and hence more difficult to understand. Instead, all available evidence demonstrates conclusively that nonhuman primates are **phylogenetically** closer to *H. sapiens* than any other group of animals. These close evolutionary relationships are reflected in obvious anatomical ways, but modern research has also demonstrated remarkable genetic, biochemical, ecological, neurological, and behavioral similarities between *H. sapiens* and certain other primate species. Thus, concentrated investigations on nonhuman primates in these and other areas provide important extrapolations for humans. Such information is useful not only for more meaningful anthropological interpretations about human evolution and behavior (e.g., various articles in Buettner-Janusch 1962), but also for matters with more practical consequences. Among the more important of these is the widespread experimental use of primates for medical purposes, such as the careful testing on primates that prevented the thalidomide disaster from reaching epidemic proportions in the United States. An indication of the value of primate research in medicine may be found in Beveridge (1969), Montagna and McNulty (1973), and Meldrum and Marsden (1975).

Of more immediate interest here is the role that primatology plays in biological anthropology, and how anthropologists utilize primatological data to shed light upon their hypotheses. The most important area centers around comparative primate studies, which, in conjunction with paleontological evidence, has led to countless interpretations about human evolution. Such studies have traditionally been limited almost exclusively to comparative primate anatomy (e.g., Le Gros Clark 1959), but in recent years these studies have been extended to include aspects of behavior, genetics, and biochemistry.

For now, it may be noted that comparative anatomists have been interested in the relationship between anatomical form and function for nearly 300 years. This relationship involves several concepts that are basic to comparative evolutionary studies, three of which are analogy, **homoplasy,** and **homology.** Although these three concepts often refer to similarities in various characteristics between different organisms, they do have important differences.

Structural characteristics, whether overtly similar or not, are said to be analogous if they share a common function (Fig. 9.1). Analogous characteristics are usually superficial and do not imply similarity in either their genetic basis, embryological origin and development, or anatomical construction. For example, the scales of fishes and snakes are analogous because they presumably serve a similar protective function. Likewise, the wings of bats and some flying insects are analogous because of similar locomotory patterns. However, these organisms are evolutionarily far apart. These structures are not similar in their embryological origin, and they are dissimilar in their microscopic structure. Moreover, different physiological mechanisms are responsible for their operation.

Scales on fishes and snakes are also an example of homoplasy, a term often used to denote structures that are only visually similar. Thus, such characteristics can be analogous, homoplasic, or both. Analogies and homoplasies indicate only that the most fit organisms are those whose genotypes allow them to respond most efficiently to various selective factors, and similar selective variables may lead to similarities in function and appearance of structures in totally unrelated species. However distant the evolutionary relationships may be, terrestrial vertebrates have legs; animals that utilize the air as a medium for locomotion have wings, and so forth.

Neither analogies nor homoplasies are of particular interest for comparative primate studies because they reflect nothing about the ancestral relationships between different primate species. Characteristics shared by different species that indicate a common ancestry are called "homologies," and the analysis of such features is fundamental to comparative anatomy. Homologies may or may not be obviously similar, but upon detailed investigation their equivalency is reflected by close similarities that can be genetic, embryological, developmental, anatomical, physiological, or topographical.

Although a bat's wing and a human arm may appear analogous at first glance, close inspection reveals that they are actually homologous structures. Not only do the number and types of bones and muscles in a bat's wing approximate those in a human arm, but they develop embryologically in a similar fashion; they operate by similar physiological mechanisms; and they appear roughly in the same position relative to the body. Thus, comparative analysis of structural complexes often leads to results that might not be apparent solely from visual inspection. For example, it is generally accepted that humans are more closely related to bats than dogs, a conclusion without much visual basis. Humans and bats belong to different orders

Figure 9.1 Venn diagrams showing the differences between homologies, homoplasies, and analogies. (Courtesy of Carl Gans, *Biomechanics. An Approach to Vertebrate Biology,* 1974. J. B. Lippincott Co., Philadelphia.)

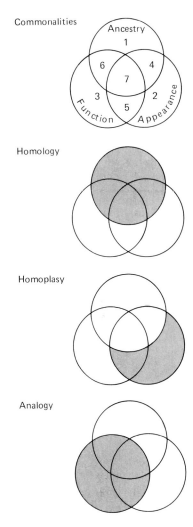

within the cohort Unguiculata, but dogs belong to an entirely different cohort (Ferungulata).

The conceptual basis underlying comparative studies for evolutionary interpretations is quite straightforward. Although very small genetic changes in populations can occur relatively quickly, evolutionary changes in adaptive complexes such as structural characteristics proceed very slowly. Thus modern species that have stemmed from the same ancestral form will possess certain features in common. The greater the number of homologous characteristics shared by two groups of animals, the closer their evolutionary relationship.

The inherent simplicity in this line of reasoning is very appealing, but a number of criticisms have been leveled at some of the inferences drawn from comparative primate studies. One of the more important of these criticisms concerns the widespread disagreement on how such evidence is to be interpreted. This problem may be phrased briefly as follows. Suppose that a number of gross structural characteristics, such as arms, legs, shoulder girdles, etc., are being compared between two groups of newly discovered primates for the purposes of classification. Suppose also that the result of these comparisons suggests that the two groups are closely related species. Assume now that a variety of new techniques and methods becomes available, and that comparisons may be made in far greater detail than before. The outcome of these comparisons is predictable: the two groups will display a greater number of differences than originally demonstrated.

The realization that these two hypothetical primate groups differ in many ways could often lead to the tendency called "splitting" (as opposed to "lumping"), especially when anatomical evidence is unaccompanied by paleontological or biochemical evidence. Briefly, splitters place more taxonomic importance on dissimilarities than lumpers, and their classificatory schemes reflect this tendency. Based upon the same evidence, then, a splitter might place the two groups into two different species (or genera), while a lumper might classify them as two subspecies. Obviously, the problem involves the relative importance, or "weight," that different observers attach to certain characteristics. Unfortunately, there is presently no universal agreement on how to weight characters nor, more importantly, whether it is philosophically defensible in the context of taxonomic theory (see the brief discussion of the two schools of thought on this in Chapter 8).

Another criticism, less important than that above but nevertheless quite relevant, has been restated periodically by Simpson (e.g., 1945, 1963). This involves an unfortunate lapse into subjectivity by some anthropologists and biologists who are engaged in the classification of either human or nonhuman ancestors of *H. sapiens*. For reasons perhaps best understood by psychologists, otherwise objective biological scientists sometimes abandon their sense of perspective when attempting to classify populations phylogenetically related to *H. sapiens*. The practical effects of this, as alluded to in the previous chapter, are (1) considerable taxonomic confusion and (2) even more confusion in interpretations of our evolutionary relationships to other primate species.

General Adaptations of the Order

These criticisms notwithstanding, comparative biological studies have led to almost incontrovertible conclusions about our relationships to other primate species. For example, there is little doubt that *H. sapiens* is more closely related to the anthropoid apes (the gorilla, chimpanzee, orangutan, and gibbon) than to the New and Old World monkeys. Furthermore, it appears probable that humans have a closer relationship with the chimpanzee and gorilla (perhaps in that order) than the chimpanzee does with the orangutan or gibbon. Before the evidence for these and other findings is given, however, it is desirable to outline briefly some of the diagnostic characteristics of the order.

Primates are mammals, of course, and they share a number of definitive features with other orders in the class Mammalia. Some of the more notable features include:

1. The maintenance within well-defined limits of a constant body temperature.

2. The evolution of a **heterodont dentition** and a two-stage tooth series—the **deciduous** (milk) and the permanent dentitions. Heterodonty is a species-specific characteristic, and refers to the possession of a dental complement composed of teeth that differ both functionally and morphologically (e.g., incisors for biting, molars for chewing). The other alternative is **homodonty** (typical, for example, of reptiles), in which all teeth in the complement are similar in shape and function.

3. The evolution of **viviparity,** the process whereby the mother retains and nourishes the fertilized egg for a considerable period of time and provides extended postnatal care and nourishment of the newborn. One of the most unique features of Mammalia, from which the class was named, is the presence of mammae. These are the milk-producing glands that supply the newborn with the nutrients and other substances required for early growth and development.

4. The evolution of a larger, more complex, and highly organized brain.

Mammals possess many other distinctive features, such as true hair, a relative reduction in the number of bones of the skull, a single bone on each side of the lower jaw, the presence of a diaphragm separating the chest and abdominal cavities, the almost universal presence of seven neck vertebrae, and so forth. A full description of mammalian biology may be found in Young (1957) and need not be further elaborated here.

The wide diversity within the order Primates makes it difficult to provide a list of traits characteristic of all primate species. Hence, some of the features listed below also appear in other mammals, and some do not appear in certain primate species. However, at least part of the general biological pattern of Primates can be viewed in the context of two basic functional complexes. The first is currently held to represent either (1) evolutionary trends associated with early primate arboreality or (2) basal mammalian adaptations related to visually directed predation, while the second is associated with learning and socialization. The first three sets of features below are associated with the first complex, and the latter four with socialization and learning (see Napier and Napier 1967; Jolly and Plog 1976).

1. Retention of a pentadactyl (five digits) hand and foot, and extraordinarily mobile limb structures.

2. The development of nails, rather than claws, on the fingers and toes. The mobility of the fingers and toes is particularly suited for gripping, and both the hands and feet serve locomotory functions. The hands, furthermore, are used for exploratory behavior, and such behavior is greatly enhanced by the development of highly sensitive tactile pads on the digits.

3. A highly developed sense of vision, with a concomitant reduction in the **olfactory** sense. In particular, the changes in the visual sense involved: (a) larger, more closely set and better-protected eyes; (b) an improved retina and the development of color vision, and (c) stereoscopic vision and a corresponding elaboration of the part of the brain involved with interpretation of visual input.

4. A reduction in litter number and an increase in rearing time. This allows increased infant dependence upon the mother and a greater opportunity for learning.

5. A relative increase, as compared to other mammals, in those parts of the brain involved with association and learning.

6. A trend toward longer individual life expectancies.

7. A tendency toward the organization of groups to which all individuals belong and in which certain members have fairly well-circumscribed functions.

Classification of the Order

It should be clearly understood that the expression of these general trends varies widely among different primate species. In later chapters we will often return to these trends in order to examine the many ways that primates have responded to evolutionary processes. For now, however, let us turn to the formal classification of the order (Table 9.1).

The two suborders in this classification, the Prosimii and the Anthropoidea, contain 55 genera and 167 species. This is a fairly standard classification and differs only slightly from those given by Simons (1972), Napier and Napier (1967), and other authors. For reasons outlined in the preceding chapter, it is by no means the "last word" in primate classification. Primate taxonomy is in a constant state of flux, to put it mildly, and all classifications will doubtlessly be revised as new information emerges.

The Prosimii are frequently called the "lower" and the Anthropoidea the "higher" primates, although the adjectives "lower" and "higher" have no apparent evolutionary meaning and could well be abandoned. This distinction has probably been made to reflect the almost certain conclusion that *H. sapiens* is more closely related to species in Anthropoidea, and there seems always to have been an unfortunately anthropocentric tendency to regard humans as having reached some sort of "pinnacle" of evolutionary progress.

In any case, the prosimians and the New World monkeys (the Cebidae and Callithricidae) have relatively distant phylogenetic relationships to *H. sapiens*. Because the main focus of this book is on human rather than nonhuman primate evolution, most of the discussions in subsequent chapters will center around the Old World primates in the infraorder Catarrhini. The group of primary interest, furthermore, includes members of the superfamily Hominoidea.

A Survey of Primate Characteristics

The Prosimii
Table 9.1 lists five living families in the Prosimii: Lemuridae, Daubentoniidae, Indriidae, Lorisidae, and Tarsiidae. Included in the first three of these families are 12 genera and perhaps 20 species of lemurs (Fig. 9.2) that are geographically native to the island of Madagascar. The Lorisidae is composed of six species of bushbabies and two potto species in Africa (Figs. 9.3 and 9.4), and three species of lorises (Fig. 9.5) in the Far East. Within the Tarsiidae are three species of tarsiers (Fig. 9.6) that occur in the East Indies.

Like the suborder Anthropoidea, prosimians are widely diverse and thus, overall generalizations about this suborder are difficult to make. There is general agreement, however, that the entire group has not diverged from primitive Eocene (a

Table 9.1 Classification of the Living Primates. Since the total number of species is quite large, their names have been purposely omitted. The number of species in each genus and the vernacular name is given in parenthesis after each genus.

Order Primates
  Suborder Prosimii
    Infraorder Lemuriformes
      Superfamily Lemuroidea
        Family Lemuridae
          Subfamily Lemurinae
            Genus *Lemur* (common lemur-4)
                  Hapalemur (gentle lemur-3)
                  Lepilemur (sportive lemur-1)
                  Varecia (variegated lemur-1)
          Subfamily Cheirogaleinae
            Genus *Cheirogaleus* (dwarf lemur-2)
                  Microcebus (mouse lemur-2)
                  Phaner (fork-marked lemur-1)
                  Allocebus (no vernacular name-1)
        Family Indriidae
          Subfamily Indriinae
            Genus *Propithecus* (sifaka-2)
                  Indri (indri-1)
                  Avahi (avahi-1)
        Family Daubentoniidae
            Genus *Daubentonia* (aye-aye-1)
    Infraorder Lorisiformes
      Superfamily Lorisoidea
        Family Lorisidae
          Subfamily Lorisinae
            Genus *Loris* (slender loris-1)
                  Nycticebus (slow loris-2)
                  Arctocebus (golden potto-1)
                  Perodicticus (potto-1)
          Subfamily Galaginae
            Genus *Galago* (bushbaby-6)
    Infraorder Tarsiiformes
      Superfamily Tarsiioidea
        Family Tarsiidae
          Subfamily Tarsiinae
            Genus *Tarsius* (tarsier-3)
  Suborder Anthropoidea
    Infraorder Platyrrhini
      Superfamily Ceboidea
        Family Cebidae
          Subfamily Aotinae
            Genus *Aotus* (night monkey-1)
                  Callicebus (titi-3)
          Subfamily Pithecinae

Figure 9.2 *Lemur catta.* (Courtesy of J. Buettner-Janusch, *Physical Anthropology: A Perspective,* 1973. By permission of John Wiley and Sons, Inc., New York).

Continued

Table 9.1 Continued

              Genus *Cacajao* (uakari-3)
                    Pithecia (saki-2)
                    Chiropotes (bearded saki-2)
         Subfamily Alouattinae
              Genus *Allouatta* (howler monkey-5)
         Subfamily Cebinae
              Genus *Cebus* (capuchin monkey-4)
                    Samiri (squirrel monkey-2)
         Subfamily Atelinae
              Genus *Ateles* (spider monkey-4)
                    Brachyteles (woolly spider monkey-1)
                    Lagothrix (woolly monkey-2)
         Subfamily Callimiconinae
              Genus *Callimico* (Goeldi's marmoset-1)
      Family Callithricidae
              Genus *Callithrix* (marmoset-3)
                    Saguinus (tamarin-16)
                    Cebuella (pygmy marmoset-1)
                    Leontideus (lion tamarin-3)
Infraorder Catarrhini
    Superfamily Cercopithecoidea
      Family Cercopithecidae
         Subfamily Cercopithecinae
              Genus *Macaca* (macaque-13)
                    Cercocebus (mangabey-4)
                    Papio (baboon-5)
                    Theropithecus (gelada baboon-1)
                    Cercopithecus (guenon-17)
                    Allenopithecus (Allen's swamp monkey-1)
                    Erythrocebus (patas monkey-1)
                    Miopithecus (talapoin-1)
                    Mandrillus (mandrill-2)
         Subfamily Colobinae
              Genus *Presbytis* (langur-13)
                    Pygathrix (douc langur-1)
                    Rhinopithecus (snub-nosed langur-2)
                    Simias (Pagai Island langur-1)
                    Nasalis (proboscis monkey-1)
                    Colobus (colobus-1)
                    Procolobus (olive colobus-1)
  Superfamily Hominoidea
    Family Hylobatidae
      Subfamily Hylobatinae
         Genus *Hylobates* (gibbon-7)
                Symphalangus (siamang-1)
    Family Pongidae
      Subfamily Ponginae
         Genus *Pongo* (orangutan-1)
                Pan (chimpanzee-2)
                Gorilla (gorilla-1)
    Family Hominidae
      Genus *Homo* (human-1)

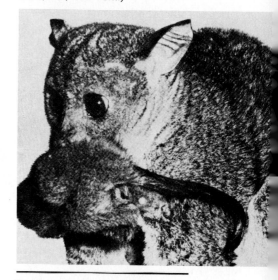

Figure 9.3 An adult female *Galago* with her infant. (Courtesy of J. Buettner-Janusch, *Physical Anthropology: A Perspective,* 1973. By permission of John Wiley and Sons, Inc., New York.)

Figure 9.4 *Perodicticus potto,* an African loris. (Courtesy of J. Buettner-Janusch, *Origins of Man,* 1966. By permission of John Wiley and Sons, Inc., New York.)

Figure 9.5 The skeletal structure of *Loris tardigradus*.

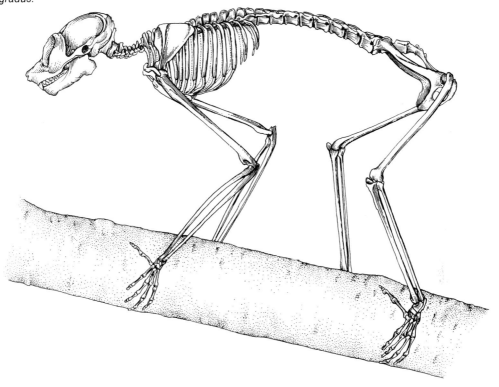

Figure 9.6 A female *Tarsius* from Borneo. (Courtesy of J. Buettner-Janusch, *Origins of Man,* 1966. By permission of John Wiley and Sons, Inc., New York.)

geological epoch dating from approximately 36 to 58 million years ago) primates to the same radical extent as anthropoid groups. For example, except for tarsiers, the prosimians have retained the rhinarium, an area of naked and moist skin surrounding the external nostrils. As in dogs, cats, and other mammals, the rhinarium may signify a more efficient olfactory apparatus, inasmuch as the direction and intensity of certain smells may be recognized at considerable distances (Le Gros Clark 1959). Likewise, some prosimians have retained sensory receptors that are far more typical of mammals than of other Anthropoid primates. It has already been mentioned that digital pads serve as efficient receptors for **tactile** stimuli, especially among the anthropoids.

In addition to these pads, lemurs possess a full mammalian-like set of vibrissae. **Vibrissae** are tactile hairs, such as a cat's whiskers, with large bulbous roots in direct association with nerves. In lemurs, they occur on the face, above the eyebrows, on the cheeks, on the chin and jaw, and slightly above the wrist on the inner side of the forearm. Such vibrissae are also present in lorises and tarsiers, although reduced in size and number and distributed somewhat differently. Since many prosimian species are both nocturnal and arboreal, information about the proximity of various objects that cannot be easily seen would be especially advantageous. It seems not unreasonable to suppose that natural selection would favor the retention of such characteristics in animals with nocturnal and arboreal habits.

In their locomotory behaviors, many, but not all, prosimians have a basic pattern that has possibly been in existence since the Eocene. This has been called vertical clinging and leaping (Napier and Walker 1967). Animals within this category rest by clinging vertically to a branch or trunk, and utilize their powerful hindlimbs in leaps (sometimes over 25 feet) from one place to another. That this is an ancient form of locomotion has been inferred by the skeletal structures of *Notharctus* and *Smilodectes,* two Eocene prosimians from North America that bear remarkable postcranial skeletal resemblances to the modern Malagasy lemurs.

Vertical clinging and leaping is found among several Lemuriformes (including *Lepilemur* and *Hapalemur*) and all three indriid genera (*Propithecus, Indri,* and *Avahi*). It is also the locomotory behavior of *Tarsius* and of some of the Lorisiformes, notably *Galago.* However, it is only one of several prosimian locomotory modes which, for that matter, probably represent only the extremes in the behavior ranges for any given group. Another is quadrupedalism, which may be subdivided into (1) slow and cautious climbing and (2) running and walking along branches. The genera of the Lorisidae (the slender and slow lorises and the pottos) are the slow climbers, while *Lemur, Cheirogaleus, Phaner,* and *Microcebus* represent the faster-moving arboreal quadrupeds. At least one prosimian does not fit nicely into any of these categories. This is the aye-aye (*Daubentonia*), which moves quadrupedally on the ground, rests like *Lemur,* and climbs vertically like *Lepilemur.* Napier and Napier (1967) have suggested that the aye-aye, thus, has a modified vertical clinging form of locomotion.

One of the more important prosimian evolutionary trends has been the development of an acute visual sense. It is obviously important for any arboreal animal to be able to judge distances accurately, especially one that leaps from one branch or tree to another. Such spatial judgments depend upon the organization of the retina and the degree to which the visual fields of both eyes overlap.

The retina contains light-sensing photoreceptors (rods and cones) and nerves through which light stimuli are transmitted to the brain's visual centers. With the exception of purely nocturnal forms, all mammals have rods and cones. Rods are highly sensitive, function at relatively low light levels, and are usually concentrated toward the periphery of the retina. They play the major role in peripheral and "twilight" vision, even though their discriminatory powers are fairly low. By contrast, cones are more sensitive to bright light, are concentrated toward the retinal center, and are far more efficient than rods for the discrimination of distances, color, and the texture of various objects.

Nearly all anthropoid species possess retinas with only very few rods at the center. This central area is called the *macula lutea* (sometimes called the "yellow spot"), in the center of which is a small depression referred to as the fovea. There are no blood vessels and only a single layer of cones in the fovea, and therefore the light that reaches this area is far more unobstructed than that which has to pass through other retinal layers and blood vessels to reach other cones. In short, the fovea represents that part of the retina with highest visual acuity.

As expected, the concentration of rods and/or cones is associated with the rhythm activities of the particular species. **Nocturnal** genera, such as *Loris, Nycticebus,* and *Cheirogaleus* have rod-type retinas, while diurnal and **crepuscular** (a term sometimes used to distinguish animals whose rhythm activities take place during dusk and early morning) species possess both rods and cones. Interestingly, *Tarsius* is the only known prosimian with a true fovea (Polyak 1957), in spite of this animal's rod-type retina (Wolin and Massopust 1970) and exclusively nocturnal rhythm pattern. Why *Tarsius* has retained a fovea remains unknown, but Le Gros Clark (1959) has suggested that it may simply be a structure carried over from very early tarsioid ancestors with diurnal habits.

It was mentioned above that another critical factor in the ability to judge distances is the extent to which the visual fields of the eyes overlap. Such overlap allows light from the same object to penetrate both eyes simultaneously, a prerequisite for stereoscopic vision. For an animal to possess full stereoscopic vision, two conditions must be met. First, the eyes must be placed on the skull in such a manner that their optical axes are parallel. Second, the optic nerves that transmit impulses to the brain must be aligned so that visual centers in both halves of the brain receive these impulses. Such an alignment in humans is illustrated schematically in Figure 9.7.

With exception of some feline species, in no other mammalian order is this characteristic as well-developed as it is in Primates (high degrees of orbital frontation are, of course, typical of some nonmammalian genera, such as owls). Most mammals have eyes that occur somewhat laterally on the skull and, hence, may have only limited binocular vision. In the horse, for example, the field of overlapping vision is only about 57°, as compared to about 120° in humans and apes (Walls 1963). In general, the trend toward orbital (not optical, for the optical axes may be parallel even when the orbital axes are not) frontality and convergence of the orbital axes has been more pronounced in Anthropoidea than in Prosimii, although there are some exceptions. The angle subtended by the axes of the orbits in anthropoid families usually varies around 30°, even though the optical axes are parallel or very close to it. In the Lemuridae, on the other hand, the orbital angle is roughly 60° to 70°.

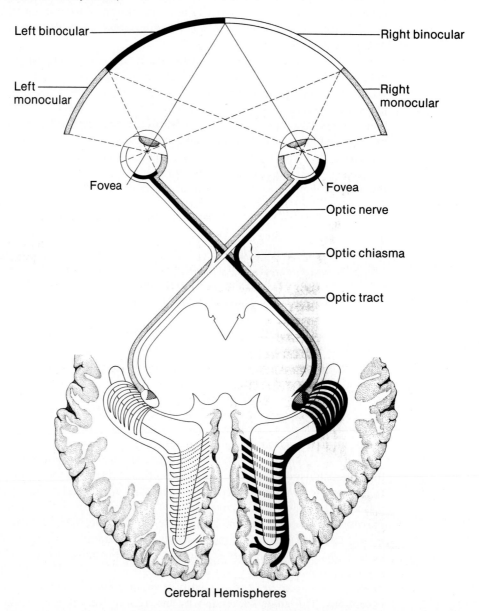

Figure 9.7 Composite diagram showing the projection of the visual field upon the retinas, and the relationship of the retinas to the cerebral hemispheres. (Courtesy of G. J. Romanes, The Central Nervous System. In: *Cunningham's Textbook of Anatomy.* 10th Ed., 1964, G. J. Romanes, ed. Redrawn with permission from Oxford University Press.)

Left binocular

Right binocular

Left monocular

Right monocular

Fovea

Fovea

Optic nerve

Optic chiasma

Optic tract

Cerebral Hemispheres

In addition to retinal morphology and the degree of orbital frontality, the retention of the snout and the higher dependence on the sense of smell both suggest that most prosimians are not as capable as anthropoids in discriminatory visual skills. This may, in turn, be related to the lowered manual dexterity of prosimians as compared to most anthropoids. One anthropoid characteristic that differs strikingly from prosimians is the manual manipulation and intense inspection of objects, especially food.

The natural diets of prosimians are incompletely known and cannot always be inferred directly from the foods accepted by captive animals. For example, lorises, pottos, and *Lepilemur* appear to be insectivorous in the wild, but are quite omnivorous in captivity. Tarsiers and perhaps *Cheirogaleus* are mostly insectivorous, feeding on grasshoppers, beetles, mealworms, and occasionally small lizards and some vegetable matter. In addition to the indriids, all lemurs but *Lepilemur* are probably natural vegetarians. Only the bushbaby seems to be naturally omnivorous. The aye-aye has the most unique diet of all prosimians, or at least the most specialized method of obtaining food. This animal apparently uses acute hearing to locate wood-boring larvae, removes the wood with its rodentlike incisors, and probes for the larvae with an extremely elongated third finger.

Many other general characteristics of prosimians could be described here, and, indeed, entire books have been written on certain aspects of their biology and behavior (e.g., Charles-Dominique and Martin 1972; Martin, Doyle, and Walker 1974). For example, prosimians generally have shorter life spans than anthropoids, which at least implies less time for the transfer of learned behavior from one generation to the next. Prosimians have diversified skeletal structures that reflect their particular locomotory and feeding behaviors, and they exhibit certain dental features quite unlike anything found among anthropoid genera. These and other attributes of prosimians are discussed in an introductory textbook by Buettner-Janusch (1973). A more advanced treatment of their morphology, vital statistics, and geographic distribution appears in Napier and Napier (1967), and Simons (1972) offers a detailed account of prosimian paleontology.

The Anthropoidea

One of the chief reasons for the anthropologist's interest in prosimians is the likelihood that anthropoid primates evolved from prosimianlike ancestors. Unfortunately, the fossil evidence is not conclusive about whether the three superfamilies in Anthropoidea—Ceboidea, Cercopithecoidea, and Hominoidea—arose independently (**polyphyletically**) or as a single group that later diverged (**monophyletically**). However, the differences among the earliest fossils representing these three superfamilies lead to the suggestion that they did not arise from the prosimians in existence about 50 million years ago. The evidence for this suggestion will be deferred until later.

A general characterization of all anthropoid species is fraught with the same kinds of difficulties as for prosimian species, again because of the considerable diversity within the suborder. This is especially true when *H. sapiens* is considered as an anthropoid primate, for we are at least as aberrant when compared to other anthropoids as the aye-aye is to other prosimians. Nevertheless, all anthropoid species do possess similarities representing certain evolutionary trends, some of which are given in this chapter.

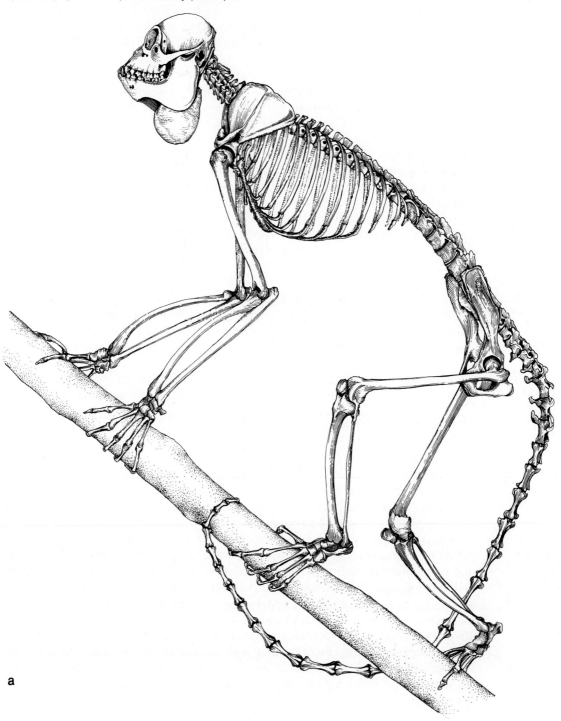

Figure 9.8 The skeletons of two New World monkeys of the family Cebidae, the howler monkey (*Alouatta*) **a,** and the squirrel monkey (*Samiri*) **b.**

a

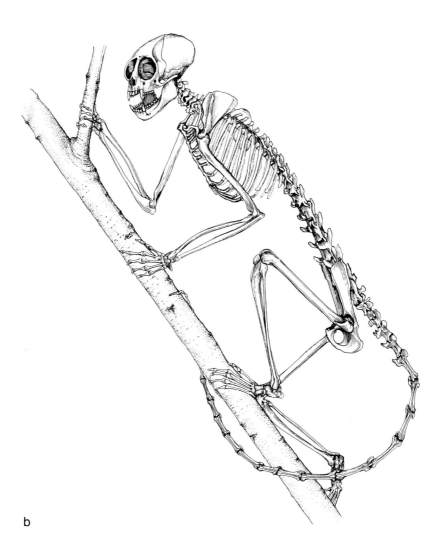

b

From Table 9.1, Anthropoidea is divided into two infraorders. The first is Platyrrhini (the New World monkeys), which is further subdivided into two families. These are the Cebidae (Fig. 9.8) and the Callithricidae (Fig. 9.9). The second infraorder, the Catarrhini, contains four families. These are the Cercopithecidae (Fig. 9.10), the Hylobatidae (Fig. 9.11), the Pongidae (Fig. 9.12), and the Hominidae. Reflecting only one of many basic differences between the two infraorders, the terms "platyrrhine" and "catarrhine" refer to the placement of the nostrils. Platyrrhine primates have relatively widely separated nostrils that face somewhat laterally, and catarrhine primates have less widely separated nostrils that project downward.

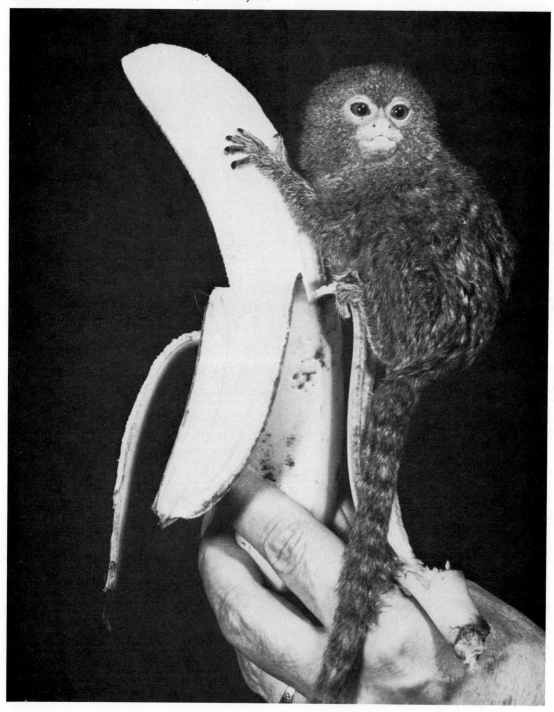

Figure 9.9 The pygmy marmoset (*Cebuella pygmaea*) from South America. (Courtesy of C. A. Bramblett, *Patterns of Primate Behavior,* 1976. Mayfield Publishing Co., Palo Alto, Calif. From Photo Researchers, Inc., New York.)

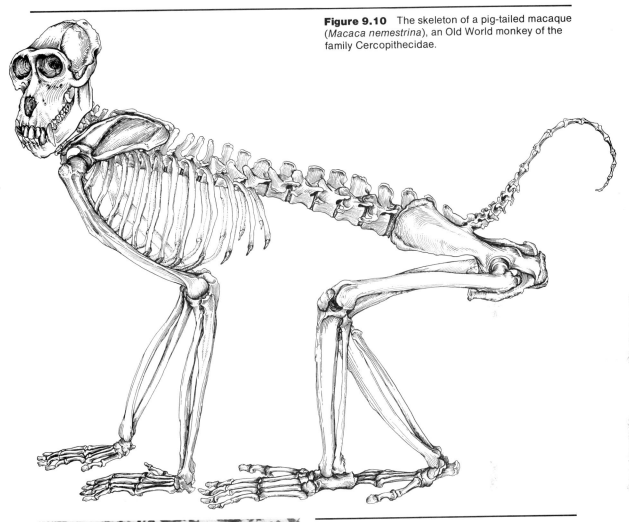

Figure 9.10 The skeleton of a pig-tailed macaque (*Macaca nemestrina*), an Old World monkey of the family Cercopithecidae.

Figure 9.11 The gibbon (*Hylobates*) from India. (Courtesy of C. A. Bramblett, *Patterns of Primate Behavior*, 1976. Mayfield Publishing Co., Palo Alto, Calif. From Photo Researchers, Inc., New York.)

Figure 9.12 Front and side views of the skeleton of the western lowland gorilla (*Gorilla gorilla*) from Africa.

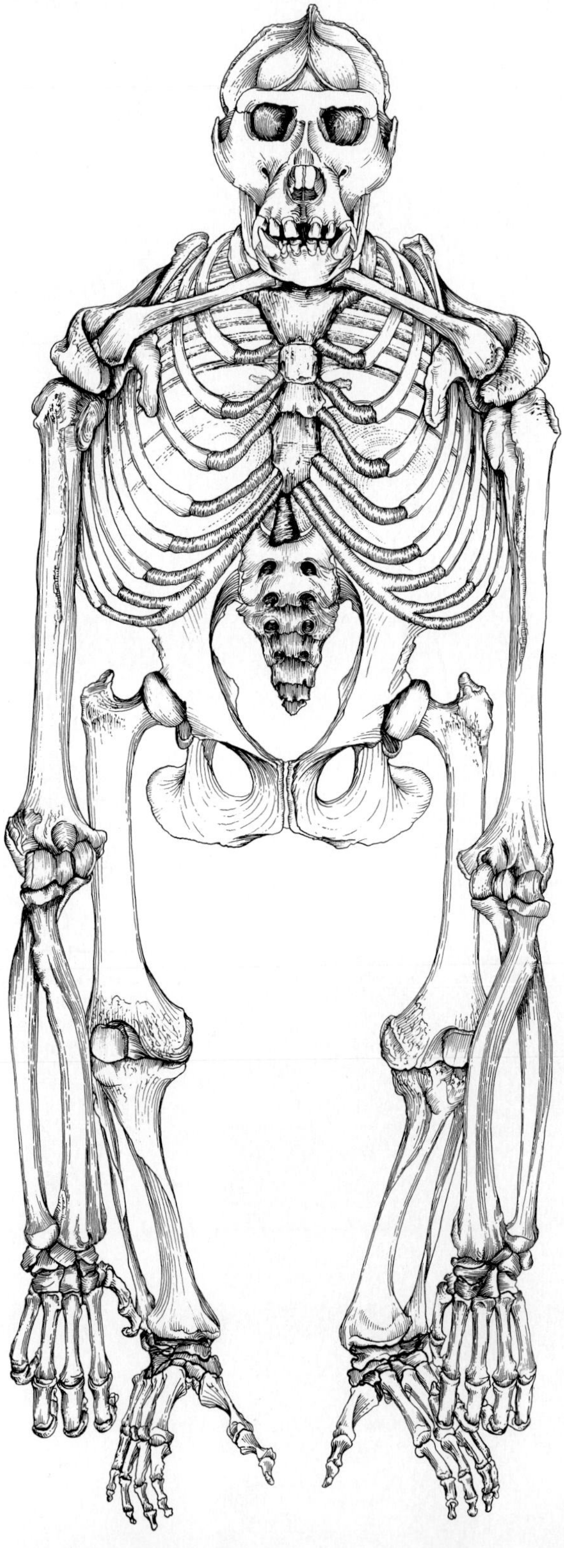

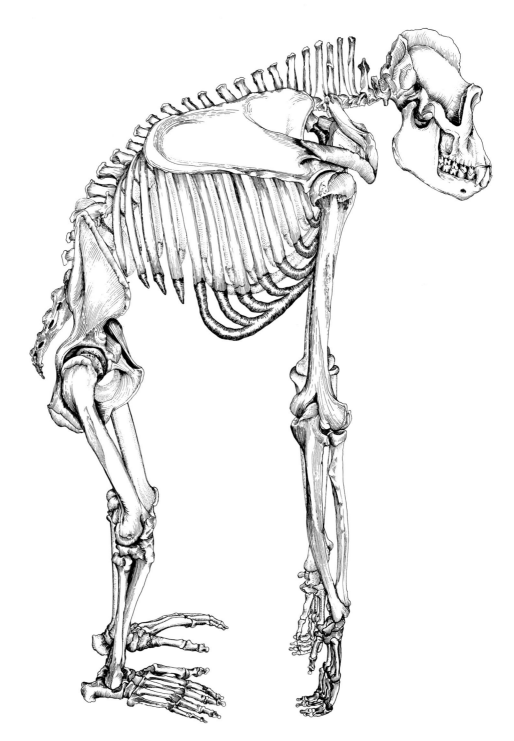

There are other broad differences (see below) that distinguish New from Old World primates, but there are also fundamental features shared by these two infraorders that distinguish them from prosimians. In conjunction with a decreased dependence upon the sense of smell and increased dependence upon the visual sense, anthropoid primates have shorter snouts, no naked rhinarium, more forwardly directed orbits, and concomitant differences in the brain that are associated with interpretation of visual and olfactory stimuli. Also, anthropoids generally have a *macula lutea* in the center of the retina, and only one platyrrhine monkey (the nocturnal *Aotus*—the night monkey) has a predominately rod-type retina.

There are many structural differences between prosimian and anthropoid postcranial skeletal characteristics, notably those related to locomotor activities. For example, none of the latter practice vertical clinging and leaping, and none are slow climbers. A few anthropoid genera fit roughly into the category of running and walking along branches, including the marmosets, some of the Cebidae, and a few Old World monkeys. However, the locomotor patterns of all other anthropoids are quite different from those of prosimians. These patterns may be categorized as follows:

1. New World semibrachiation. This is a quadrupedal and arboreal category practiced by the howler monkey (*Alouatta*) and all genera of the subfamily Atelinae (*Ateles*, *Brachyteles*, and *Lagothrix*). These animals utilize their arms, legs, and prehensile tails to swing beneath branches, and they walk and run quadrupedally when on the ground.

2. Old World semibrachiation. This is the mode of locomotion of the langurs and colobus monkeys (subfamily Colobinae). It also is an arboreal form of **quadrupedalism** that involves swinging by the arms and climbing. Like the New World forms in the first category, these primates walk (but also leap) quadrupedally upon descending to the ground.

3. Terrestrial quadrupedalism. Within this category are two different types of locomotion, ground-walking/running and knuckle-walking. The main difference between the two types concerns the way that the forelimb contacts the ground. Various genera within the subfamily Cercopithecinae, including some species of *Macaca*, *Papio*, *Theropithecus*, *Erythrocebus*, and *Mandrillus*, make contact with the palmar surface of the fingers and are classed as the ground-runners and walkers. The knuckle-walkers, including *Pan* and *Gorilla*, support the weight of the front part of the body on the backs (the dorsal aspect) of the last two segments of the second through the fifth fingers.

4. Brachiation. Two different subclasses of **brachiation** can also be recognized. The first is modified brachiation, observed only in the orangutan (*Pongo*). This animal swings by the arms and hands, but its large body size requires use of the feet for additional support. In a sense, the orangutan "clambers," and when on the ground places the weight of the front part of the body on the dorsal side of the hands. The second category is called true brachiation, in which the entire weight of the body is suspended by the arms and hands when swinging from one branch to another. This is the locomotory mode of gibbons and siamangs (family Hylobatidae), which also walk bipedally on branches and on the ground.

5. Erect **bipedalism.** This final locomotor pattern is characteristic only of *H. sapiens,* who stands, walks, and runs solely on the hindlimbs.

That these diverse locomotor patterns are reflected by anatomical differences should be obvious: the limb structure of a terrestrial quadruped like the baboon, for example, is hardly suitable for vertical clinging and leaping, brachiation, or erect bipedalism. Such anatomical adaptations will be examined more closely in the next chapter, especially as to their morphology, ideas on how they arose, and their functional relationships with certain ecological variables.

Compared to prosimians, anthropoid primates also have generally larger and more complex brains, more complex and diverse vocalizations and gestures, more elaborate developmental stages in placental structure, and far more complicated levels of social organization. Additional comparisons between prosimians and anthropoids might be made, but would serve little purpose here. Those of you interested in more specific details should consult Napier and Napier (1967), Simons (1972), and Hill (1972). Rather than pursue this further, then, let us turn to some of the generalized characteristics of genera within the suborder Anthropoidea.

It was mentioned earlier that all of the living New World primates are included within the Cebidae and the Callithricidae. It was also stated that one of the differences between New and Old World forms was nasal morphology. Another fundamental difference is the presence in some New World genera of a fifth grasping organ—a prehensile tail. No Callithricidae genera possess such an organ, but it is a characteristic structure in all genera in the subfamilies Alouattinae and Atelinae. It is never found in Old World primates.

Yet another difference concerns the **dental formulas** of the two infraorders. As will become evident in later chapters, analyses of dental characteristics have played major roles in evolutionary interpretations. One such characteristic is the dental formula, which states in a shorthand manner both the numbers and types of teeth that are normally present in the upper (maxilla) and lower (mandible) jaws.

The four different kinds of teeth in anthropoid primates are called incisors, canines, premolars, and molars. For an example of how to determine a dental formula, consider your own **maxilla** and **mandible.** If you bisect both with an imaginary plane into right and left halves, and if you have erupted the full complement of teeth, you will note that there are eight teeth on each side of both jaws. Each half consists of a central incisor (I1), a lateral incisor (I2), a canine (C), a first and second premolar (P1 and P2), and a first, second, and third molar (M1, M2, and M3). Since we have the same numbers and types of teeth in both the maxilla and mandible, our dental formula is

$$\frac{2.\ 1.\ 2.\ 3.}{2.\ 1.\ 2.\ 3.}\ .$$

Because the count of the different kinds of teeth begins with the imaginary plane (the median plane) at the front of the mouth, the formula above states that *H. sapiens* is characterized by 2 incisors, 1 canine, 2 premolars, and 3 molars on both sides of each jaw. The total number of teeth in the complement, of course, is 32.

The dental formula of all catarrhines is the same as ours. However, the cebid monkeys have one additional premolar. Thus the formula

$$\frac{2.\ 1.\ 3.\ 3.}{2.\ 1.\ 3.\ 3.}\ .$$

They differ from Callithricidae genera, which have one less molar. Hence the formula

$$\frac{2.\ 1.\ 3.\ 2.}{2.\ 1.\ 3.\ 2.}$$

A final difference between the New and Old World monkeys is the lack of true opposability of the pollex (the thumb) in the former, and its presence in the latter. Humans have a completely opposable pollex, as do other Old World anthropoid species. In such a hand, the pollex is capable of rotation at the carpometacarpal joint (the carpometacarpal joints are those formed by the wrist bones—the **carpals**—with the long bones—the **metacarpals**—that can be felt in the back of the hand). This rotation allows the end of the pollex to make contact with the ends of the other four digits. In contrast, the New World monkeys (and the Prosimii) have only pseud-opposable thumbs. These do not rotate at the carpometacarpal joint, but rather are capable of movement in only one plane (for additional information on this topic, see Napier 1961, and Bishop 1964).

Very little is known about the geological record of the Platyrrhini, and even less about their evolutionary relationships to the Catarrhini. However, the available fossil evidence indicates almost certainly that both infraorders have been geographically confined to their respective hemispheres for at least 30 million years. It thus is appropriate to ask why the Old and New World monkeys share so many characteristics in common. The traditional viewpoint (e.g., Buettner-Janusch 1973) is that (1) the New World monkeys arose from Eocene prosimians that (2) belonged to a different group that gave rise to both the Old World monkeys and modern prosimians, and (3) that the similarities between Catarrhini and Platyrrhini have arisen because of parallel evolutionary processes. In this explanation, the similarities between the two infraorders would be due to similar selective pressures in the respective environments and an ultimate evolutionary origin from a very early common ancestral form.

In direct contrast to this view is one advanced by Sarich (1970) and further supported by Cronin and Sarich (1975). In a comparative immunochemical study of certain proteins among New and Old World monkeys, they concluded that both groups had a common ancestor long before the divergence of lineages leading to modern prosimian genera. This common ancestor had already reached the evolutionary grade of a "monkey," or at least nearly so. Thus, the observed characteristics shared by catarrhines and platyrrhines are supposedly not due to parallel evolutionary changes, but rather to their possession by the common ancestral form. At the present time, we simply do not know which, if either, of the two viewpoints is correct. The matter of the origin and evolution of New World anthropoids is only one of the many intriguing problems of primatology that will doubtlessly be illuminated by additional immunochemical, geological, and paleontological information.

A number of general features of the Catarrhini have already been outlined in the above discussions, and the following chapters will stress various aspects of these primates in far greater detail. Thus, only a few additional remarks about the Old World monkeys and apes are necessary in this brief and very general survey of living primate characteristics.

The Cercopithecidae, one of the largest families of Primates, is composed of nearly 70 species that are widely distributed throughout Africa and Asia.

Figure 9.13 A typical bilophodont molar, illustrating the enamel crests between the two mesial cusps and between the two distal cusps. The tooth is a left second mandibular molar from a baboon.

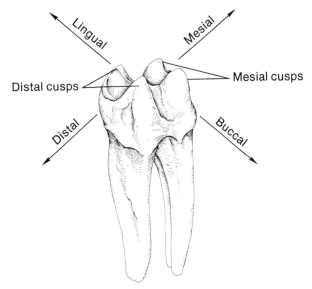

This family is divided into two subfamilies, the Cercopithecinae (47 species) and the Colobinae (20 species). As a natural taxon, the Cercopithecidae (monkeys) differs from families included in the Hominoidea (apes and humans) in several respects. First, the former have **bilophodont molars,** and the latter do not. Such molars have enamel crests connecting each of the two front (mesial) cusps and each of the two back (distal) cusps (Fig. 9.13).

A second fundamental difference involves the shape of the thoracic region of the postcranial skeleton. As seen in Figure 9.14, the human rib cage is much flatter in a dorsal-ventral direction than, for example, that of a macaque. Also shown in Figure 9.14 are differences in the shoulder girdle, the functional complex composed of the **clavicle** (collarbone), **scapula** (shoulder blade), and **sternum** (breastbone). The differences in size, shape, and relative location of these bones are associated with different locomotory patterns. Old World quadrupedal monkeys have relatively smaller clavicles and sternums, and their scapulas are positioned on the sides of the rib cage. In contrast, scapulas of hominoids are typically placed on the back of the rib cage.

A third difference, although neither as pronounced nor as definitive as either of the above two, concerns the vertebral elements forming the tail. Monkeys, apes, and humans have such bones (termed caudal vertebrae), but no hominoids have external tails. Most but not all Old World monkeys have external tails, the most notable reductions occurring in *Mandrillus* and some species of *Macaca (M. sylvanus,* the Barbary ape; *M. nemestrina,* the pig-tailed macaque; and *M. speciosa,* the stump-tailed macaque). Such reduced tails may represent a minor evolutionary trend associated with increased utilization of the forelimbs for climbing and decreased use of

Figure 9.14 Top views of the thoracic skeleton and pectoral girdles of a macaque and a human.

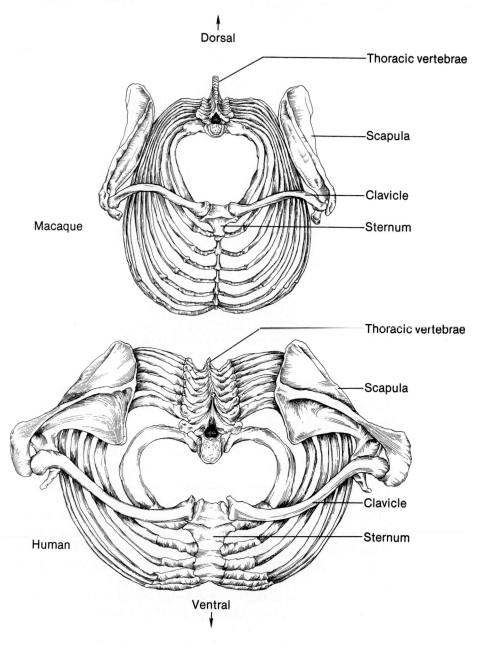

Dorsal

Thoracic vertebrae

Scapula

Clavicle

Macaque

Sternum

Thoracic vertebrae

Scapula

Clavicle

Sternum

Human

Ventral

the tail as an organ of balance during leaping (additional information on this may be found in Wilson 1972).

A fourth feature that not only differentiates Hominoidea from Cercopithecoidea, but which is more fruitfully assessed from the viewpoint of the order Primates, involves certain changes in the brain. As one compares the different genera of primates from prosimians to humans, one finds that the **cerebral cortex,** the **cerebellum,** and other parts of the brain become progressively differentiated, elaborated, and reorganized. These changes represent an evolutionary specialization of certain centers of the brain called **encephalization,** defined by Noback and Moskowitz as "the evolutionary process whereby the higher centers increasingly dominate the functional activities of the lower centers" (1962:210).

The so-called higher centers are cortical areas for which some function has been established, and of basic interest here are those functions relating mostly to the input and interpretation of sensory impulses and to motor activity function. The cerebral cortex itself is a variably thick (several millimeters) layer of grey matter on the external surface of the cerebral hemispheres. It consists mainly of neural cell bodies with long, delicate processes called axons. These axons extend into the white matter of the brain below and transmit impulses away from the cell body. The cerebral cortex also varies in structure and texture, depending upon its location and function, and in humans occurs in its most richly folded and furrowed state (Fig. 9.15).

These folds (gyri; singular = gyrus) and furrows (sulci; singular = sulcus) have the effect of increasing the surface area of the brain without a concomitant increase in brain volume. Aside from minor individual variations, furthermore, the major gyri and sulci that are associated with known functions may very well be species-specific. In general, the progressive elaboration of the cerebral cortex from prosimians to humans is directly associated with progressive abilities in perception and reaction to environmental stimuli. This elaboration and expansion of the cortex has enhanced the visual and tactile senses, but a simultaneous reduction in the olfactory area of the cortex has occurred among those primates relying least upon the sense of smell. For hearing, on the other hand, there seem to have been no outstanding neural trends. Also in the cortex are "association areas," which are interrelated with sensory and motor projection areas, and which serve a storage function (i.e., memory) for past stimuli. These areas are most highly developed in humans, less so in apes and monkeys, and even less in other primates.

In addition to cortical elaboration, other parts of the brain have undergone progressive differentiation. Accommodating the visual cortex are the occipital lobes, which have become increasingly expanded in a posterior direction and overlie more of the brain beneath in humans than in all other primates. Likewise, the temporal lobes have become particularly elaborated in Hominoidea. These areas are associated with sound discrimination, and probably expanded in conjunction with increasingly complex vocalizations and vocal communication. The frontal lobes have also followed this trend toward relative expansion, culminating in almost vertical foreheads in modern *H. sapiens.*

One of the many functions of areas in the frontal lobes appears to be involved with certain behavioral characteristics (e.g., Milner 1974), but other

Figure 9.15 Superior **a,** lateral **b,** and inferior **c,** views of an adult human brain.

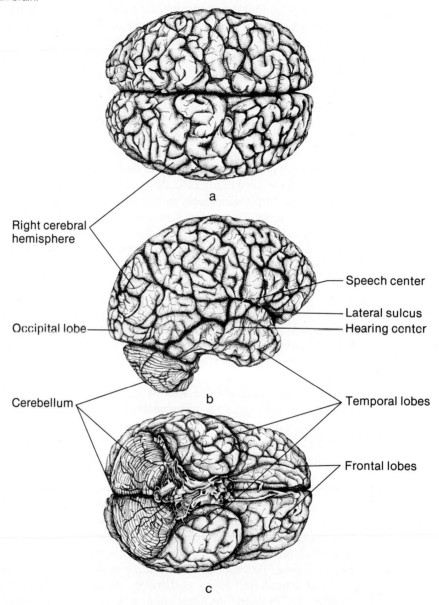

Right cerebral hemisphere

Occipital lobe

Cerebellum

Speech center

Lateral sulcus

Hearing center

Temporal lobes

Frontal lobes

a

b

c

functions have yet to be clearly defined. Finally, the middle and lateral lobes of the cerebellum have become expanded, and its connections with the motor area of the cortex have become progressively elaborated. The cerebellum is that part of the brain located directly beneath the occipital lobes. Included among its many functions are (1) the regulation and design of rapid movements, programmed by the cortex, before their initiation and (2) control of body equilibrium, locomotion, and limb movements (De Long 1974; Ito 1974; Kornhuber 1974).

Summary

Primatology, the biobehavioral study of living and extinct nonhuman primates, is intimately related to biological anthropology because of the close phylogenetic relationships between nonhuman primates and the human species. These ties consist of similarities in anatomical, genetic, biochemical, ecological, neurological, and behavioral systems. Although experimentation on primates with respect to medical technology and allied areas has led to advances of considerable applicability to humans, aspects of comparative primate anatomy, behavior, and biochemical genetics have been especially useful in analyses of human evolutionary processes. In particular, valuable insights into the origin and evolution of the human species have been gained through comparative studies of anatomical homologies, those characteristics that humans share with nonhuman primates owing to commonness of ancestry.

All primates are mammals, and all share a set of basic mammalian characteristics. Some of these features are (1) the acquisition of homeostatic mechanisms for maintaining constancy in body temperature within certain limits, (2) the evolution of a two-stage dental development, with teeth that are differentiated morphologically according to differences in function, (3) the evolution of extended maternal retention and nourishment of the fertilized egg, along with milk-producing glands and relatively long-term postnatal care and nourishment of the newborn, and (4) the evolutionary development of a more complexly organized and larger brain.

Within Mammalia, the order Primates is distinguished by a set of characteristics that were acquired either before Primates came into existence or shortly thereafter. Some of these include retention of pentadactyly in the hand and foot and extraordinary limb mobility, the substitution of nails for claws on the digits, a reduction in olfactory sensitivity, and an enhanced optical apparatus that involved stereoscopic color vision and elaboration of the brain's centers for visual intepretation. Evolutionary trends associated with socialization and learning include litter number reduction and an increase in rearing time, an increase in the areas of association and learning in the brain, an increase in average life expectancy, and a tendency toward the development of group social organization.

Although classifications may differ slightly, primates can be categorized into two suborders, the Prosimii and the Anthropoidea, which as a group consists of 55 genera and 167 species. The Old World Prosimii, consisting of lemurs, bushbabies, pottos, lorises, tarsiers, and the aye-aye, show a number of morphological features that suggest far less evolutionary change since the Eocene than has occurred among anthropoid groups. Many prosimians are both nocturnal and arboreal, and many, but not all, practice the vertical clinging and leaping mode of locomotion. This mode may be Eocene in origin, inasmuch as inferences derived from the skeletal remains of the Eocene *Nothartcus* and *Smilodectes* are valid. Based upon retinal morphology, degree of orbital frontality, retention of the snout, and a highly efficient olfactory sense, prosimians possess a visual sense that is highly acute but probably less efficient than anthropoids.

The anthropoids consist of the New and Old World monkeys, the great apes, and *H. sapiens*. Compared to the prosimians, anthropoid primates, as a group, have a decreased dependence upon the scnsc of smell and an increased visual sense, both of which are associated with changes in the brain with respect to the interpretation of these stimuli. Anthropoid primates do not locomote by vertical clinging and leaping, but rather fall into several locomotory classes: New and Old World semibraciation, terrestrial quadrupedalism, modified and true brachiation, and in the case of humans, erect bipedalism. New and Old World anthropoid primates differ in nasal morphology, the existence of a prehensile tail in some New World forms—but in no Old World forms, in their dental formulas, and by a lack of true thumb opposability in New World monkeys.

That the two infraorders within Anthropoidea have evolved within their respective hemispheres for at least 30 million years is strongly suggested by current evidence. The similarities between the New and Old World Anthropoidea are probably due to a common prosimian ancestor, perhaps in the Eocene, and parallel evolutionary processes.

Several fundamental differences occur between the Cercopithecidae (the Old World monkeys) and the Hominoidea (the apes and humans). These include basic differences in molar morphology, in the shape of the thoracic skeleton and the size, shape, and location of the bones comprising the shoulder girdle, and in the greater differentiation, elaboration, and reorganization of the cerebral cortex, the cerebellum, and other areas of the brain among the hominoids.

10 Aspects of Nonhuman Primate Sociobiology and Ecology

Introduction

The evolutionary trends characterizing primates have been constantly maintained and refined since the Eocene. The remarkable success of natural primate populations can be ascribed partially to genes, gene complexes, and physiological and morphological adaptations. However, their success also stems from the evolutionary development of social systems, which, in turn, are intimately associated with prevailing biological and ecological factors. Primate societies may not be completely unique among other mammalian social systems in their complexity (Eisenberg 1973), but they are among the most variable and diverse of any within Mammalia. The ultimate function of such flexible social structures is to help assure species survival in fluctuating ecological conditions.

Nonhuman primate social structures are nowhere near as complex or variable as those of the human species, but this does not mean that the behavioral attributes contributing to primate social structures are invariant and predictable. While such attributes can be described for any given group, they may not apply to another group of the same species that occupies a different habitat. Thus, primate social structures should not be viewed as species-specific adaptations. In some instances, such as territoriality in the gibbon (*Hylobates lar*), certain aspects of social behavior appear to have been established for a comparatively long time and assume a "standardized" form (Ellefson 1968). In other species, like the olive baboon (*Papio anubis*) and the gray langur (*Presbytis entellus*), considerable flexibility in social organization occurs as an apparent consequence of different habitat variables (Hall and DeVore 1965; Yoshiba 1968). Because different degrees of intraspecific variation typify most primate social systems, and since this variation is related to habitat differences, it has been quite difficult to develop a unifying theory of primate social organization and evolution.

Nevertheless, a great deal of data on various primate societies have been gathered in recent years, and some of this information has led to hypothetical reconstructions of the early development of human social systems (see Jay 1968, for a general discussion). The reconstructions of particular interest to biological anthropology are those that consider the integrated effects of ecology and biology on social structure, and in the rest of this chapter some examples of such effects will be given for various nonhuman primate species in different evolutionary grades of social structure. However, it is appropriate before beginning these discussions to define some elementary terms. The definitions of the five terms that follow are those given by Wilson (1975) in his definitive treatise on sociobiology.

1. **Communication.** "The action on the part of one organism . . . that alters the probability pattern of behavior in another organism . . . in a fashion adaptive to either one or both of the participants" (1975:176). Wilson uses the term "adaptive" to indicate that natural selection has operated to some extent on the genetic programming of either or both signal and response. Communication is the ensuing relationship between signal and response, rather than solely one or the other. It follows, therefore, that no communication takes place unless the probability of response is altered by the signal. Some difficulties in this definition do arise, specifically concerning its limits. A person may climb a tree in response to a lion's attack signal. The person's behavioral patterns in such an event have certainly (and wisely) been altered, but communication has not taken place. Perhaps perception has. To avoid these types of definitional difficulties, therefore, communication should be thought of as occurring between members of the same species.

2. **Coordination.** "Interaction among units of a group such that the overall effort of the group is divided among the units without leadership being assumed by any one of them" (1975:10). One function of males in nearly all species of social primates is to challenge and, if possible, rebuff predators (see "Predator Defense," below). Males join together for mutual defense of females and infants in some groups, and females assist the males in other groups. Such defensive strategy is an example of coordination.

3. **Hierarchy.** "The dominance of one member of the group over another, as measured by superiority in aggressive encounters and order of access to food, mates, resting sites, and other objects promoting survivorship and reproductive fitness" (1975:11). Among many primates, there is little doubt that agonistic encounters play a role in the establishment of dominance hierarchies. However, the threat behaviors related to such encounters are widely diverse among different groups. They also occur at different frequencies and have different effects upon social hierarchies, and it is important to note that hierarchies are established on more than just agonistic behavior. Furthermore, the term "dominance" has been used too often in conjunction with single rank-orders established and maintained by threats. Alison Jolly (1972) has recognized this problem and suggests that a more descriptive term is needed. She suggests something like "status ranking" or "role playing."

4. **Group.** "A set of organisms belonging to the same species that remain together for any period of time while interacting with one another to a much greater degree than with other conspecific organisms" (1975:8). The difference between a group and a Mendelian population (see Chapter 5) is that the former is a social unit and the latter, a biological unit. A group designates subsets of a society and is especially useful for reference to different levels within organized social systems. This is a highly flexible term that refers to collections of individuals that are organized for some particular reason or that share a collective function. The functions of various groups, such as bands, troops, and multi-male units may be related to defense, hunting and foraging, reproduction, and so forth.

5. **Society.** "A group of individuals belonging to the same species and organized in a cooperative manner" (1975:7).

Some Advantages of Being Social

Predator Defense

When faced by a predator, a healthy male baboon is superbly equipped to defend himself and, in combination with other adult males, other individuals in his troop. However, no matter how large and aggressive the baboon may be, his chances of survival against a predator (e.g., a lion) are drastically reduced when alone as compared to when allied with other males in the troop. The only reason for mentioning this age-old concept of "strength in unity" is to point out one of the selective advantages of social organization. This advantage, of course, is defensive superiority, and above all other examples of cooperative behavior, it occurs in the greatest number of animal species.

There are many ways in which different primates and groups of primates defend themselves and their groups against predators. Some (but not all) groups are characterized by organized defense, although this type of behavior appears to be the rule for those societies with multi-male groups. The proposition that such social groups have evolved as an adaptive response to sustained predation has been suggested by Chance (1961). If this did occur, then the relationships between ecology, social structure, and biology become clear.

Suppose that sustained predation on early primate groups constituted a strong selective pressure. How could this lead to an increase in the social complexity of the group, and what ensuing biological effect would it have? Although the responses to such a selective factor could vary, it might be supposed that there would be a selective advantage for both the most proficient fighters and for mutual defense. Thus, the physical attributes related to defense, such as those observed in male savanna baboons (DeVore 1963), would be favored. As part of their physical equipment, males are large, strong, agile, and aggressive, and they possess extraordinarily long maxillary canines. These features, in turn, could have had a direct effect on the males' aggressive behavior toward each other, as well as to predators. Finally, the genetic structure of the group could also have been affected, because highly aggressive males tend to occupy the upper levels of dominance hierarchies and contribute their genes disproportionately to the gene pool of the next generation.

This hypothetical sequence of events may contribute to our efforts to understand the social integration of certain primate groups. For the most part, such groups are semiterrestrial and occupy open habitats, such as African savannas and grasslands. Baboons provide a good example. However, similar relationships do not apply to all primate societies. Furthermore, modern field studies have shown that sustained predation on living primate groups is so minimal that it hardly constitutes a strong selective pressure. For example, Rowell (1969) studied a baboon population over a five-year period and did not witness any predation on healthy animals of either sex, or of any age. This was in spite of the fact that lions, leopards, and hyenas occupied the same territory.

It may be possible that baboons, much like chimpanzees and gorillas, have developed defensive behavior to the extent that they are relatively immune from predation (excluding humans). In any event, it is interesting that primates themselves occasionally attack and eat other primates. Chimpanzees have been observed, although infrequently, eating young baboons, and baboons have been seen eating vervets. However, the fact that vervets do not fear baboons, nor do the latter fear chimpanzees, probably indicates the rarity of hunting behavior in these primates.

There is little doubt that cooperation in defensive behavior is highly adaptive for large and intermediate-sized semiterrestrial primates. However, it is only one of many different characteristic defense mechanisms. Some primates hide, others give alarm signals to their group and then flee, others may try to bluff with barks, bristled hair, and fake charges, and yet others are apparently content to defend only themselves and their harems. For example, lemurs, squirrel monkeys, and vervets all alert members of their groups to potential danger by issuing calls that vary according to whether the intruder is airborne or on the ground (Baldwin 1968; Struhsaker 1967). The terrestrial cercopithecoid monkey, *Theropithecus gelada,* displays a defensive behavior more akin to that of wildebeests than to other monkeys. Organized loosely into roaming "herds," males protect only themselves, their harems, and their infants.

It is difficult to make overall generalizations about defensive strategies in primate groups because of their widely diverse behaviors. About as close as one can come to a general primate characteristic is that males in socially organized groups usually play the role of defender. This position seems particularly true of the apes and monkeys, among which the dominant males ordinarily "lead" the defense. It might also be generally found that primates prefer not to engage in actual physical combat, either among themselves or against predators. Rather, field investigations have shown consistently that the males of social primates nearly always attempt to frighten predators by mob action, fake charges, and various threat displays. The frequency of actual attacks is low, and they occur most often when infants are threatened.

Reproduction and Early Survival

It should not be assumed from the last sentence that males in all primate species either tolerate or protect their infants. Some instances where males have been observed to ignore their newborn infants include a species of lemur (Ulmer 1957), the lion-tailed macaque (Bertrand 1969), the rhesus monkey (Kaufmann 1966), the patas monkey (Hall and Mayer 1967), and the Indian langur (Jay 1963). Among other species, such as the bonnet macaque, mothers of newborn prevent any contact by males (Simonds 1965). In this context, it may be stressed once again that these behavioral attributes vary according to habitat. In particular, behavioral responses toward infants (and other factors) in free-ranging species often differ drastically from those displayed by caged animals of the same species. For example, Bertrand (1969) observed captive male rhesus monkeys protecting infants, and experimental intervention in another group of macaques (*M. nemestrina*) had a clear effect upon male response to infants (Kaufmann and Rosenblum 1967).

These observations notwithstanding, adult males in many free-ranging societies of monkeys and apes actively protect infants. These include, but are not limited to, several different macaque species (MacRoberts 1970; Bertrand 1969; Itani 1963), and the hamadryas, chacma, and olive baboons (Kummer 1967; Hall and DeVore 1965). Interestingly, this function in chimpanzees and gorillas is carried out almost exclusively by the mother, and males are sometimes not even tolerant of infants (van Lawick-Goodall 1969; Schaller 1963). Regardless of whether the mother or father, or both, fulfill this protective function, it comprises only one part of the total behavioral repertoire of primate parents toward their infants. Other aspects include playing and grooming, retrieval, touching, approaching, carrying, and caring for (for several pertinent reviews, see Mitchell and Brandt 1972; Loizos 1969; and Mason 1965). The upshot of such behavior is generally to ensure not only survival of the infant, but also its social integration.

As Wilson (1975) and other evolutionary biologists have noted, the production of offspring in evolving animal species generally takes two forms. One, which is characteristic of insects and most reptiles, is devoid of parental care. Eggs are simply laid in abundance, and the probability of offspring survival is roughly proportional to the number of eggs deposited and how well they are concealed. The second option, which characterizes birds and mammals to varying degrees, requires an investment of time in either (1) incubation of eggs, (2) bearing live young, or (3) assisting the embryo during the birth process and immediately thereafter.

Furthermore, mammalian reproductive characteristics can be roughly divided into two subcategories. The first is an altricial complex, which includes the following features: (1) nest building, (2) production of large litters, (3) less complete development at birth, (4) short gestation and lactation periods, (5) early sexual maturity, (6) short life spans, and (7) unelaborated social systems. Mice provide a good example of altricial mammals. The second, which is almost universal among nonhuman primates, is the precocial complex. By and large, the definitive features of this complex are opposite of those listed above. Litter number is reduced, newborn infants are relatively well-developed, gestation and lactation periods are long, a long developmental period precedes sexual maturity, life spans are considerably extended, and elaborate social systems prevail.

These features clearly indicate a high level of investment toward offspring by primate parents. Parental investment, as defined by Trivers is "any investment by the parent in an individual offspring that increases the offspring's chance of surviving (and hence reproductive success) at the cost of the parent's ability to invest in other offspring" (1972:139). It includes biological factors, like gestation and lactation periods, in addition to the time spent during infantile and juvenile phases when the young are being taught to perform as full-fledged members of the society. Furthermore, much of the "social training" of young primates occurs by alloparental care—the assistance of parents by other societal members of either or both sexes in the care and rearing of the offspring. In no other mammalian order is this expressed as richly as in Primates.

Most of the precocial attributes of primates lead to one factor of fundamental importance—low reproductive turnover. As a matter of observation, single births are characteristic of all anthropoid species except the marmosets and tamarins. Obviously, any factor or set of factors that contribute to the probability of survival and reproduction of these single newborn will be selectively advantageous. The important point is that much of the parental investment is interwoven into each social system, and the determinants of alloparental behavior are nearly, if not entirely, of social origin. Although difficult to demonstrate, it may well be that elaborate primate societies have developed as adaptations to low reproductive turnover.

Although slightly out of the present context, it is interesting to speculate on the ecological factors that might have led to precocial characteristics in Primates. As

Martin (1975) has suggested, the distinction between precocial and altricial complexes may have involved MacArthur and Wilson's (1967) concept of r- and K-selection. They have stated that

> in an environment with no crowding (*r selection*), genotypes which harvest the most food (even if wastefully) will rear the largest families and be most fit. Evolution here favors *productivity*. At the other extreme, in a crowded area, (*K selection*), genotypes which can at least replace themselves with a small family at the lowest food level will win, the food density being lowered so that large families cannot be fed. Evolution here favors *efficiency* of conversion of food into offspring—there must be no waste. (1967:149)

In this theory, food availability is an all-important factor for the determination of reproductive rates. Such rates should be high (as should infant mortality rates) when food supply fluctuates to any great extent, and low (with decreased mortality among infants) when the supply is reasonably stable.

Now, consider the fact that the majority of primate species, including those fossil species for which there is associated floral and faunal evidence, live in either subtropical or tropical forest habitats. Although tropical forests are indeed seasonal (especially regarding periods of rainfall) and hence all food sources are not always available, there is less temperature fluctuation and more potential food sources in these habitats than in temperate zones with marked temperature changes. Therefore, food supply is relatively more stable in the former than in the latter, where it is usually patchy and unpredictable. With this in mind, Martin hypothesizes that

> the precocial complex characteristic of living primates can therefore be regarded as an outcome of a reproductive strategy involving efficiency of exploitation of available food sources rather than high reproductive turnover. A relatively large brain size and a long period of mother-infant interaction, which permits social learning of such aspects of the environment as appropriate food sources, combined with the behavioral flexibility of a long-lived adult, would have contributed to the success of such a strategy. (1975:54)

Use of Food Resources
The natural distribution of food and its procurement are major factors affecting the evolutionary development of primate social systems, because natural selection will favor those social attributes involved with increasing the safety and efficiency of food exploitation. Although the details of foraging strategies vary widely among primates, the natural availability of food may help explain why individuals of some species are organized into single-family groups, and why members of other species tend to cluster into groups larger than the single family. Consider these two alternatives: (1) an environment throughout which food is evenly distributed and relatively abundant and (2) an environment in which the distribution of food is uneven and unpredictable, except for scattered patches where it is either permanent or at least predictable.

In the first case, a small territory with ample food is easily defended, and the monogamous pair bond is likely the best defensive strategy. Primates in this category are characteristically highly territorial vegetarians, and do not display particularly complex social systems (see Table 10.1, "Parental Family"). Primate

Table 10.1 Evolutionary Grades of Primate Societies and Their Ecological Correlates. Each Grade Is Based upon Male Involvement (After Eisenberg et al. 1972, and Wilson 1975.)

Solitary Species	Parental Family

A. Insectivore-frugivore
    Lemuridae
        Microcebus murinus
        Cheirogaleus major
    Daubentoniidae
        Daubentonia madagascariensis
    Lorisidae
        Loris tardigradus
        Perodicticus potto
 	
B. Folivore
    Lemuridae
        Lepilemur mustelinus
 	
C. Arboreal frugivore
    Pongidae
        Pongo pygmaeus
	A. Frugivore-insectivore
	    Callithricidae
	        Saguinus oedipus
	        Cebuella pygmaeus
	        Callithrix jacchus
	    Cebidae
	        Callicebus moloch
	        Aotus trivirgatus
	
	B. Folivore-frugivore
	    Indriidae
	        Indri indri
	    Hylobatidae
	        Hylobates lar
	        Symphalangus syndactylus

Uni-Male Troop	Age-Graded Male Troop

A. Arboreal folivore
    Colobinae
        Colobus guereza
        Presbytis senex
        Presbytis johnii
        Presbytis entellus
 	
B. Arboreal frugivore
    Cebidae
        Cebus capucinus
    Cercopithecidae
        Cercopithecus mitis
        Cercopithecus campbelli
        Cercocebus albigena
 	
C. Semiterrestrial frugivore
    Cercopithecidae
        Erythrocebus patas
        Theropithecus gelada
        Mandrillus leucophaeus
        Papio hamadryas
	A. Arboreal folivore
	    Colobinae
	        Presbytis cristatus
	        Presbytis entellus
	    Cebidae
	        Alouatta villosa
	
	B. Arboreal frugivore
	    Cebidae
	        Ateles geoffroyi
	        Saimiri sciureus
	    Cercopithecidae
	        Miopithecus talapoin
	
	C. Semiterrestrial frugivore-omnivore
	    Cercopithecidae
	        Cercopithecus aethiops
	        Cercocebus torquatus
	        Macaca sinica
	
	D. Terrestrial folivore-frugivore
	    Pongidae
	        Gorilla gorilla

Continued

Table 10.1 Continued

Multi-Male Troop

A. Arboreal frugivore
   Indriidae
      Propithecus verreauxi
   Lemuridae
      Lemur catta
B. Semiterrestrial frugivore-omnivore
   Cercopithecidae
      Cercopithecus aethiops
      Macaca fuscata
      Macaca mulatta
      Macaca radiata
      Papio cynocephalus
      Papio ursinus
      Papio anubis
      Macaca sinica
   Pongidae
      Pan troglodytes

groups foraging in the second type of environment will tend to either collapse or abandon rigidly delimited feeding territories and forage in groups larger than the single family unit. Such groups, including baboons and macaques, range freely in rather extensive territories but are not particularly territorial. They are generally either frugivorous or omnivorous, and possess among the most complex of all primate social structures.

Kummer (1971) may be correct in suggesting that environmental severity is positively correlated with the degree of coordination within a group adapted to such conditions: the more severe the environment, the greater the amount of coordinated group behavior. Although difficult to quantify, an impression is gained from Schaller (1963) that social behavior in gorillas is far less strictly coordinated than, for example, that in hamadryas baboons. Even less coordination is seen among chimpanzee groups, which by all reasonable standards are organized more loosely than any other hominoid species.

This does not imply that troops of gorillas are lacking in social organization. Indeed, they travel and forage in small troops, possess well-structured dominance hierarchies, and so forth. But unlike hamadryas baboons, they live in a lush tropical forest with relatively concentrated and unlimited food sources, and each individual is able within certain limits to choose where and when to eat and drink. The same option is not open to the individual hamadryas baboon. Living in a most severe habitat, each individual in a troop relies upon other members for defense and protection. In addition, prior knowledge among the troop's leaders plays a vital role in guiding the troop to the most reliable sources of food and water.

Evolutionary Grades of Primate Societies and Their Ecological Correlates

In the last several paragraphs, special emphasis has been placed upon how a few ecological variables can affect primate social behavior. It has also been stressed that differences in habitat, especially those relating to food supply and predation, can cause intraspecific variation in social structure. As a matter of field observation, such variation appears to be much greater among those species that have adapted to a wide range of habitats as opposed to those that have adapted more uniformly to a restricted habitat. In the latter, a greater degree of uniformity in social structure prevails. However, a number of investigators (e.g., Crook and Gartlan 1966; Eisenberg et al. 1972) have maintained that knowledge of the range in variation in troop structure often affords discernment of a generalized, or "modal" pattern for any single species.

This line of reasoning has led to classifications of evolutionary grades of social structure, such as that given in Table 10.1. In this classification, each grade is based upon the degree of male involvement, because the positions of males in primate societies are associated in various ways with dominance hierarchies, territoriality, group composition and size, and other social attributes. Beginning with the "solitary species," furthermore, each grade listed in the table represents an increased level of social complexity. These social grades must not be confused with phylogenetic groups, as evidenced by the placement of *Pongo, Gorilla,* and *Pan* (all genera within the subfamily Ponginae) in the first, fourth, and fifth grades respectively. In the following sections, some of the social attributes of species within each grade are discussed.

The Solitary Species

For obvious reasons, no individual in a sexually reproducing species can live an entirely solitary existence. Thus the term, "solitary," is relative, and signifies only that very little social interaction occurs between conspecific individuals within the same age range and of either sex. Thus, the only social unit that lasts for any appreciable amount of time is formed by a mother and her dependent offspring. A good example of the typical lack of male involvement among solitary species is represented by the orangutan (see MacKinnon 1974, for a recent field study of the orangutan). When a juvenile male reaches 10 to 11 years of age, it leaves its mother and becomes totally solitary. It forages alone, wanders over a wide range before establishing its own home range, and has essentially no contact—social or otherwise—with other males of the species.

Occasionally, a male is seen with a female and her offspring, but male-female contact is normally restricted to a quite brief and simple copulatory period. Nothing even approaching a male dominance structure has been observed, and only indirect evidence suggests that males are aggressive toward each other. It is possible, for instance, that their very large and extensible vocal pouches are utilized to deliver calls which either inform or threaten other nearby males. This idea is supported in part by the loudness of the call (audible to humans for at least a kilometer), as well as by the fact that orangutans are otherwise extraordinarily silent animals. Also, females lack such pouches.

The other primates listed in Table 10.1 as solitary species are prosimians, and in all but a few key attributes, differ strikingly from orangutans. The lesser mouse lemur (*Microcebus murinus*) provides a case in point. This animal differs from orangutans in its rhythm patterns (nocturnal vs. diurnal), diet (omnivore vs. frugivore), locomotory mode (arboreal quadruped vs. modified brachiator), vocal repertoire (rich and varied vs. highly restricted) and, of course, in its physical characteristics and phylogenetic affinities. Like orangutans, however, mouse lemurs are essentially solitary animals.

Although females tend to nest in small groups and appear to be compatible while rearing the offspring, no semblance of social structure among these groups has been recognized. Male-female contact is not completely limited to copulatory activity as among orangutans, instead, single males often accompany a female in estrus. The core area of a reproductive male includes an average of about four females, and the surplus males generally congregate on the peripheries of these areas. Males probably defend their territories to some extent, but do not appear to be particularly aggressive toward one another. Like orangutans, lesser mouse lemurs are completely solitary in their foraging activities.

Parental Family

Under the most rigid definition of parental family structure, nonsexual social behavior occurs only between a bonded male and female and their offspring. This type of structure has been infrequently observed among primates, but with some degree of variation, a few species do appear to fall into this category. The variation hinges mainly upon the male's involvement in rearing offspring and ranges from (1) those species in which offspring are reared predominantly by adult males, to (2) those in which interactions between adult males and their offspring are limited, to (3) those where adult males play essentially no part in the rearing of offspring.

The species listed in Table 10.1 under "Parental Family" reflect this trichotomy. The tamarins (*Saguinus oedipus*) and marmosets (*Cebuella pygmaeus* and *Callithrix jacchus*) represent the most extreme expression of male involvement with the young. Adult males display a conspicuous paternalistic behavior toward their infants (normally twins), and the mother's functions are limited mainly to nursing and some cleaning (Hampton et al. 1966; Stellar 1960). Otherwise, infants cling to their fathers at all times for a period of several weeks.

Dusky titi monkey (*Callicebus moloch*) and night monkey (*Aotus trivirgatus*) males display a similar pattern, although their predominance over infant rearing is less than among tamarins or marmosets. Infant titi monkeys are often cleaned by their mother, and if the male adult is nearby, they may go voluntarily to their mother. The night monkey infant is cared for by both parents, but the male adopts this function almost exclusively after the infant is about nine days old (Moynihan 1964). After that time, the mother's role is relegated to nursing. Finally, little participation in infant rearing has been reported for indris (*Indri indri*), gibbons (*Hylobates lar*), or siamangs (*Symphalangus syndactylus*). Nevertheless, all of these species are classed in the same evolutionary grade of social organization because of their tendency to form a group consisting of a bonded pair of each sex and their offspring.

The strength of attachment between these bonded pairs in nature has been clearly described by Mason for *Callicebus moloch:*

> The behaviors that characterize the relationship between a mated pair are remarkable for their subtlety and variety. There is the close coordination of behavior during feeding, progressions, and confrontations with other groups; there is tail-twining and frequent and prolonged bouts of social grooming; there is nuzzling, hand-holding, foot-grasping, and lip-smacking; there is obvious evidence of distress when a monkey is separated from its mate; and there is the unequal division of parental labor in which the male carries the infant at most times. . . . (1968:216)

Some of these attributes are shared by other parental family species. For example, mutual grooming is an important part of their social behavior, as is mutual foraging. Dominance is generally not exerted by either sex of any of these species, although some evidence indicates a slight degree of dominance among *Aotus* males. Of those species observed in nature, all have a wide-ranging vocal repertoire, and at least the gibbons, siamangs, night monkeys, and titi monkeys are strongly territorial and aggressive toward other conspecific families.

The Uni-Male Troop

The increased complexity of the uni-male troop over the parental family structure arises because of the additional number of adult females, their offspring of both sexes in different age classes, and the reciprocal behavioral attributes between these individuals and toward the single adult male. For stability in the uni-male troop, there are social mechanisms that promote tolerance between adult females, and in some (e.g., *Papio hamadryas*) groups such stability is enhanced further by the adult male's behavior in preventing his females from leaving the troop. Although the behavioral mechanisms leading to the formation of new troops are not known for all species, in one case (again, *P. hamadryas*), a new troop can begin upon the capture of a subadult female from an established troop by a solitary male.

An example of a species with a uni-male troop configuration is the patas monkey (*Erythrocebus patas*). Most of our current knowledge about the natural behavior of these primates has come from K. R. L. Hall's study (1965a) of groups in the Murchison Falls National Park, Uganda. Patas monkeys are large (♂ = about 25 to 30 lbs; ♀ = about 15 lbs) terrestrial quadrupeds distributed widely over west and east African grasslands and savannas. In the Ugandan habitat, Hall observed uni-male groups, all-male groups, and solitary males. All-male groups and solitary males presumably represent those individuals that had been driven off from other troops.

In the troops with a single adult male, the total number of animals ranged from 9 to 31. The number of adult females in these same troops varied from 2 to 12, and the average adult male/female ratio was about 1 : 7. Hall could not determine precisely the home range of each of his nine troops, but they were quite extensive. In one case, for example, the home range of a troop with 1 adult male, 12 adult females, and 18 other individuals covered about 5,200 hectares (almost 13,000 acres). Patas monkeys will also travel relatively great distances in search of food, sometimes as far as 12 kilometers per day in times of scarcity. In addition, the separate troops are very widely spaced and have little contact with each other.

The social behavior observed in uni-male troops of patas monkeys is drastically different from that recorded among, for instance, single-male units of hamadryas baboons. In the latter, the male "herds" his females, punishes them when they tend to wander, and in general exerts complete authority over all individuals in his unit. By contrast, adult male patas monkeys display no dominance over adult females. Instead, the adult male assumes the functions of a breeder (when and with whom is determined by ranking females) and sentry, and exhibits no aggressive behavior toward females. As a matter of fact, females are sometimes highly aggressive toward the male, and will on occasion (usually when he attempts to copulate with one of them or threatens an infant) threaten or attack him. Females tend to "lead" the group, possess a highly structured dominance hierarchy of their own, and are largely responsible for internal cohesion of the troop.

Typically, the behavioral attributes vary widely among different species classified in the uni-male-troop grade of social organization. It may have been noticed in the preceding paragraph that groups of hamadryas baboons were called units instead of troops. The number of adult females in such units corresponds fairly closely to that in a patas troop, but the relationships between different hamadryas baboon units are completely dissimilar to those between patas troops. An adult male and his permanent group of females constitutes the basic social element in hamadryas baboon societies, and this is the unit as referred to above. However, these units are not relatively isolated, like those of patas monkeys. Rather, a second level of social organization occurs when a small number of units occasionally combine for purposes of cooperative foraging and defense. These groups are called bands, and their formation has no influence whatever upon integrity of the units of which they are composed. Yet a third level of organization, the troop, occurs when several bands collect together in a common sleeping place.

In patas monkeys and hamadryas baboons, then, are two species that have evolved contrasting modes of behavior within a uni-male-troop social configuration. Of course, the common thread running through both species and, for that matter, the uni-male arboreal folivores and frugivores in Table 10.1, is the evolutionary development of highly polygynous mating systems. But another feature held in common by patas monkeys and hamadryas baboons (and *Theropithecus gelada,* the gelada baboon) is the patchiness and unpredictability of their respective habitats. An intriguing problem concerns how similarities in ecology could have contributed to similarities in social structure.

In one interpetation, Hans Kummer (1971) has suggested that variation in size of baboon groups—from the one-male unit to relatively large bands—is directly associated with efficiency in utilization of food that typically appears in variable clusters:

> In hamadryas baboons, the correlation between group size and resource unit is relatively clear. In their Danakil habitat, the flowers and beans of small acacia trees are the main food source. One regularly observes that an isolated tree is picked by a single one-male group, about five animals. . . . The groves of ten or more large acacias on the larger river beds are usually occupied by one band at a time. In the dry season, waterholes become the critical resource unit. These

river ponds are then situated miles apart, but most of them carry enough water for a hundred or more baboons. Though hamadryas troops rarely assemble on their daily route, and never assemble to drink during the rains, they do assemble at waterholes in dry months. (1971:44)

The Age-Graded Male Troop

The age-graded male troop represents an intermediate level of social organization between the uni-male and multi-male structures, and differs from the former mainly in the increased tolerance of the adult male toward other younger males in the troop. In other words, young males are not banished from the group at an early age, but, rather, are allowed to mature to a greater extent. Similar to the uni-male troop, however, the age-graded system is still fundamentally polygynous. Because of the additional males, age-graded societies tend to be larger, occupy more extensive home ranges, and disperse more widely during day-to-day foraging.

In general, internal cohesion in age-graded male troops seems less strong than in uni-male troops, hence the possibilities for the generation of new troops may be greater. These new troops may be formed when a young male (and perhaps female) split unequally from the parental group. This process had been dubbed "apoblastosis" by Carpenter (1940), who described several generalized forces that act upon a young male to separate him from the parental group. Although these forces were based upon Carpenter's observations on gibbon behavior, they probably apply in general to most primate societies.

First, the attachments with the parent group may become weak. In particular, maternal attachments are diminished after weaning and by the birth of intermediate offspring. Attachment to individuals of the same age class in play relationships also lessens as the juvenile male matures. Second, the young male may experience frustration as a consequence of being unable to satisfy certain increased motivations. One of the most important of these motivations is an increasingly strong sex drive, but the juvenile is normally prevented from satisfying these urges by the dominant adult male. Third, young males become antagonistic toward each other, and especially toward adult males. And fourth, the young male may be tempted to leave the group by incentives from individuals from other groups. One of the strongest incentives occurs when the young male encounters a female that has become temporarily isolated from her own group, thus representing a potential mate.

As with uni-male troops, a great deal of behavioral variation exists among species with age-graded male societies. Although the social structure of any of several species could be described as an example of an age-graded male society, there are good reasons for choosing the eastern mountain gorilla (*Gorilla gorilla beringei*). This species is phylogenetically close to *H. sapiens;* it is the only anthropoid primate with such a social system; its social organization has been extensively documented; and it has been falsely maligned for many decades.

For many years the subspecific classification of gorillas has been disputed, mostly from the standpoint of whether two or three subspecies should be recognized. Since this is a relatively subjective matter of minor concern here, we may arbitrarily follow Napier and Napier (1967) and others who maintain the existence of three subspecies. These include the western lowland gorilla (*G. gorilla gorilla*), the eastern lowland gorilla (*G. gorilla graueri*), and the eastern mountain gorilla. The geographical distribution is different for each, and may be found in Napier and Napier (1967).

The total range of the eastern mountain gorilla covers approximately 35,000 square miles, but the populations are concentrated in an area encompassing about 8,000 square miles. Geographically, they are found in central equatorial Africa along the eastern border of the Congo just north and slightly east of Lake Kivu, which in turn is about 50 miles north of Lake Tanganyika. This is an area of exceptionally high average humidity and lush vegetation, and since gorillas are exclusively vegetarian, they enjoy an almost unlimited food supply. The natural and continuous abundance of food is probably the most important factor leading to the rather small home ranges of individual groups (10 to 15 square miles), in addition to the remarkably short distances traveled each day during foraging activities. Schaller (1963) measured these distances in feet, which for seven groups varied between 300 to 6,000 feet with an average distance of 1,742 feet.

Occurring in cohesive groups of 2 to 30 individuals, a "typical" group might consist of (1) a central core composed of a single dominant (silverbacked) adult male, all females, and the young, and (2) extra subordinate and subadult (black-backed) males, who tend to remain on the troop periphery. Single males and small male groups also occur, and the former have been observed to follow at a relatively short distance other well-established troops with whom they have no definable social affinity.

One of the more striking features of gorilla social behavior, at least when compared to that of other anthropoid primates, is their almost completely nonchalant temperament. The various adjectives commonly used to describe the actions and reactions of other primates, such as "boisterous," "noisy," and "aggressive," rarely apply to gorillas. These animals are aloof, independent, and reserved in nearly all aspects of their behavior, including dominance, play, sex, intergroup contact, grooming, and so forth. A few selected quotations from Schaller's remarkable work (1963) should indicate their stoic behavior:

1. Dominance Interactions

> A silverbacked male sits on a log, a juvenile beside him. He leans over and gives the juvenile a light push with his forearm. The juvenile moves over one foot. Five minutes later, the male rises and faces the juvenile, who ignores the male even when touched lightly with the forearm. The male then suddenly pushes the juvenile sharply, and the juvenile rapidly clambers to one side while the male descends from the log. (1963:241)
>
> A juvenile sits under the dry canopy of a leaning tree trunk during a heavy rainstorm. A female walks toward the juvenile who rapidly vacates its seat, while she appropriates the dry spot. Shortly thereafter the silverbacked male arrives and pushes the female with the back of his hand on the lower part of her back until she is out in the rain and he under cover. (1963:241)

2. Play

> An eight-month-old bumbles around by the reclining dominant silverbacked male. With a wide overhand motion it swats the male on the nose, but he

merely turns his head. The infant then runs downhill and turns a somersault over one shoulder and ends up on its back, kicking its legs in bicycle fashion and waving its arms above the head with great abandon. A ten-month-old infant watches these proceedings while propped against the rump of the male. Suddenly the ten-month infant rises, hurries to a sitting juvenile, and pulls the hair on its crown with one hand. When this brings no response the infant yanks at the hair with both hands, but the juvenile remains oblivious. The infant desists, sits briefly, suddenly rolls forward over one shoulder, and with arms and legs flailing like a windmill rolls over and over down hill and disappears in the vegetation. (1963:250)

3. Sexual Behavior

A peripheral male stands looking down the slope. A female appears behind him, clasps him around the waist and mounts him, thrusting about 20 times. The male at first pays no attention, but after about 10 seconds turns his head and looks at her. Suddenly he swivels around and sits. With his right hand he reaches over, grabs the female by the hip and pulls her to him. She sits in his lap, facing away from him, her body supported by still arms propped on the ground, as the male thrusts about 10 times. The dominant male, who has been resting 15 feet away, slowly rises and walks toward the pair. The copulating male immediately desists and ambles 10 feet uphill. The dominant male sits beside the female one minute, then moves and rests 15 feet away. The other male reoccupies his former spot, and the female approaches him. He reaches out with both hands, swivels her around and again pulls her onto his lap. He thrusts rapidly, about two times per second. After about 70 thrusts he begins the copulatory sound. . . . The female waves her head slowly back and forth, and, at about the hundredth thrust, suddenly twists sideways and sits beside the male, who then rolls over and rests on his abdomen for ten minutes. (1963:284)

It should be noted that this was only one of three separate periods of copulatory activity between these two animals, and that this activity (between initial contact and orgasm) lasted for about an hour. The actual mounting time, however, was for about 4 1/2 to 5 minutes. Furthermore, in 466 hours of observation among free-ranging gorillas, Schaller saw only two copulations, and no instances of play mounting, homosexualism, or deviant sexual behavior (as he defined the latter two terms).

4. Intergroup Contact

The two groups nested 500 to 600 feet apart . . . both sat and fed slowly, most of them out of sight of each other. Group VII ignored the proximity of group V, and only when several animals in the latter group quarreled loudly did several members of group VII lift their heads to look in the direction of the sound. After resting, both groups fed toward each other. . . . A blackbacked male of group V just lies on a log, head propped on his hand, observing group VII. Two silverbacks of group V jerk up their heads intermittently from their feeding to glance at group VII, which is spread over a slope 200 feet away. The silverbacked male of group VII thumps the ground and beats his chest several times; only one male in group V beats his chest once. (1963:117)

5. Grooming Behavior

> A lone female sits. A juvenile ambles up, thrusts its head into the bend of her elbow, and retains that position while the female grooms its head for about 15 seconds. The juvenile then wanders off. (1963:246)
>
> Two juveniles sit 10 feet apart. One rises, walks over and faces the other, then swivels around and backs its rump close to the face of the sitting one. It stands still for several seconds. Nothing happens. But when it looks over its shoulder seemingly to determine the cause for the delay, the other juvenile begins to groom the rump. (1963:247)

Although adult males are extremely tolerant of infants, the sole responsibility for their care, feeding, transportation, and protection lies with the mother. Infants are usually weaned by about one year of age, and can travel with the troop by themselves by about 18 months. Nonetheless, the close and reciprocal social ties between mother and infant last until the infant is about three, when it is fully integrated into the troop. Finally, gorillas are rather silent animals unless disturbed. The actual number of basic vocalizations is small, but apparently their vocal repertoire is enhanced by differences in pitch, pattern, and intensity. Their system of communication is certainly adequate, but no less rich than that of the majority of other social mammals and primates.

The Multi-Male Troop

The multi-male troop should be viewed as a logical extension of the age-graded male troop, and does not differ profoundly from it. The primary difference, and that which makes multi-male societies more socially complex, is the existence and full integration into the troop of a number of adult males of approximately equal ages. Of course, young males also exist, hence, age-graded series are also part of multi-male configurations. For troop harmony and cohesion, adult males possess behavioral interactions that promote tolerance toward each other and cooperation in such matters as predator defense, foraging, and hunting activities. For example, the cooperative tactics displayed by male chimpanzees when preying upon other animals (e.g., young baboons) are unmatched by those of any other nonhuman primate species (Telecki 1973). In some multi-male societies, well-established dominance hierarchies exist simultaneously among the adult males and among the subadult males. The males in the former are usually dominant as a class to those in the latter.

Most of the multi-male troops listed in Table 10.1 are intermediate-sized primates adapted to semiterrestrial foraging in African savannas and forest fringes. Because they are often composed of many individuals, such troops may have evolved as efficient defensive strategies against predators. It is reasonable to suppose that protection of a relatively large number of females, juveniles, and infants against a lion pride, a leopard, or a hyena is far more successful when carried out by cooperating adult and subadult males.

The classic examples of multi-male troops are those of baboons, particularly olive (*P. anubis*), chacma (*P. ursinus*), and yellow baboons (*P. cynocephalus*). These baboons now carry formal specific designations, but taxonomic nomenclature may have to be revised in the future. Field observations have shown them fully capable of hybridization, hence, they may simply represent geographical population variants of a single polytypic species. Thus the term "common baboon" is frequently used in the vernacular sense to refer to all three groups.

Beginning primarily with the pioneer observations by Washburn and DeVore (1963, 1965), common baboons have been studied far more extensively than any other primate species (see Baldwin and Telecki 1972, for a recent bibliography of baboon field studies). They are relatively large, semiterrestrial monkeys that inhabit a wide variety of habitats throughout most of subsaharan Africa. The most widely distributed are yellow baboons (Hall 1965b), and those occurring south of Nairobi, Kenya, in the Nairobi National Park and the Masai-Amboseli Game Reserve provide an adequate reflection of some aspects of baboon ecology and social behavior.

The sizes of baboon troops at Amboseli are remarkably variable. Altmann and Altmann (1970), for example, observed troops with from 16 to 198 animals, with an average number of about 51. In over 50 determinations of the size and composition of 20 different troops, they found the following average age and sex distribution: 22.9% adult males; 30.0% adult females; 4.1% subadult males; 23.3% juveniles, and 19.3% infants. The average adult sex ratio was about four females to every three males. This is only an average, however, and in most troops there were only about half as many males as females. The variation in sex ratio was considerable, and the Altmanns even noted some troops in which the adult males outnumbered the females. Troops of yellow baboons are peculiar among those of other baboons in this regard, and this is particularly interesting in light of the fact that the maturation rate of females is roughly twice as fast as that of males.

The Amboseli baboons aggregate in the evenings around groves of trees for sleeping. Periods of intensified social activity occur shortly after they descend in the mornings, and include agonistic behavior, sexual interactions, infant relations, grooming, and greeting. A similar "social hour" occurs in the evening shortly before they ascend into their sleeping trees. Most of the time between these "social hours" is spent in feeding. In at least one group (called the "Main Group" by the Altmanns), the average distance traveled per day during foraging was 3.67 miles.

The estimated home range of the Main Group was a bit over nine square miles, although all parts of the range were not equally utilized. About one-fourth of the total range was used during all nighttime and three-fourths of all daytime activities. The reasons for favored use of only a small part of the total range are probably related to relative abundance of food and water, and to ease in obtaining these resources. Yellow baboons at Amboseli, like all other common baboons, showed no convincing evidence of territorial defense of their home ranges.

Predator defense by these baboons is rapid and complex, and varies according to the predator: adult baboons often flee from leopards—and always from Masai tribesmen and their dogs—but not from jackals or tawny eagles. Against large felids, such as leopards and cheetahs, common reactions include immediate and loud vocalizations, and scattering in diverse directions by all animals in the vicinity. The dominant adult males do not necessarily stand their ground and face the predator. Rather, they may be interspersed between the predator and the rest of the troop because of a slower start, a slower run, and a tendency to stop and turn more quickly than others. Contrary to earlier opinion, adult females, subadult males, and juveniles will sometimes chase and rout certain predators: ". . . two jackals approached an adult female, Shorty, on the edge of the group; Shorty was carrying an infant on her belly at the time. She fled into the group. A large young juvenile baboon then trotted toward the jackals, but ran off when the jackals turned and faced him. The jackals then left the area" (Altmann and Altmann 1970:176).

Dominance relationships in Amboseli baboons are complex and exist among males, females, and juveniles. In an extensive study of these relationships, Hausfater (1975) has noted the following generalizations:

1. Females of all ages and nonadult males exhibit strongly consistent dominance relationships through time, but those between adult males are slightly less consistent. Because of agonistic behavior, adult male rankings changed on the average of once every 21 days. However, agonistically induced changes in female ranks did not occur during the entire course (400 days) of Hausfater's study.

2. For the most part, all animals in their respective age and sex classes (excluding infants) could be arranged in linear dominance orders, and individuals in the older age classes were generally dominant to those in the younger classes.

3. Within all age classes, males were dominant to females.

Each of these five evolutionary grades of primate social structure represents an ascending level of behavioral complexity among the groups' members. The last two classes (age-graded and multi-male troops) are variations on the uni-male theme, specifically in terms of increased adult male tolerance of other males in the group, and both classes may have derived from the uni-male troop. In general, uni-male troops are found among arboreal species; age-graded male troops among both arboreal and semiterrestrial species; and multi-male troops primarily among semiterrestrial species.

Primate social behavior and subsequent social structure cannot be profitably viewed apart from ecological variables, such as predation and essential resource availability. Such variables directly affect infant interactions, territorial defense, dominance relationships, communication, and other behavioral patterns that ultimately form the different forms of primate societies.

Summary

Natural species of primates owe much of their evolutionary success to their particular social systems, which are among the most variable and diverse found within Mammalia. Each of these social structures is harmoniously attuned to extant biological and ecological factors and, as among other groups of mammals, is not necessarily species-specific: different subspecies of a single species occupying different habitats may diverge considerably in their social attributes. A unifying theory of nonhuman primate social organization has been very difficult to formulate, partially because of this diversity, but also because the integrated effects of relevant biological and ecological variables must be taken into consideration.

Group cooperative behavior provides numerous advantages in assisting species survival. One such advantage is organized predator defense, which typifies many, but not all, primate societies. One hypothesis dealing with the evolution of cooperative defense in response to sustained predation and its effect on social structure can be outlined as follows. If predation is viewed as a selective agent, considerable advantage would accrue to those individuals possessing the most efficient physical attributes for defense. These characteristics would likely influence certain aspects of behavior, including aggression toward each other and toward predators, and would probably represent a major factor in the establishment of dominance hierarchies. The genetic structure of the group would in turn be affected, since in some primate societies the most aggressive males occupy the upper levels of dominance hierarchies and, thus, exert strong individual control over mating within the group.

Such cooperative behavior in defense applies mostly to large and intermediate-sized semiterrestrial primates such as baboons, but represents only one means by which primates defend themselves against predators. The range of other mechanisms (e.g., fleeing, hiding, bluffing, vocalization) is so great as to deny the existence of a generalized group response toward predators typical of all primates.

In addition to predator defense, group cooperative behavior is also advantageous with respect to reproduction and early survival and in the utilization of food resources. Primates have reduced litter numbers, relatively well-developed newborn infants, long gestation and lactation periods, and long developmental periods before reaching sexual maturity. The probability of offspring survival is maximized under these conditions not only by a high degree of parental investment, but also by assistance by other members of the social system. Such alloparental behavior is nearly, if not entirely, of social origin. And as for food resources, any social attribute that increases the safety and efficiency of food exploitation will be selectively advantageous. Hence, different primate species have developed more or less complex social organizations related to the defense of territories in which the distribution of food is (1) even and relatively concentrated and (2) uneven and unpredictable.

Primate social organizations, although exceedingly diverse, can be classified in terms of increasing levels of social complexity. In one such classification, the grades are based upon the degree of male involvement, since males are associated with such social attributes as dominance hierarchies, territoriality, and group composition and size. In the lowest grade, called the solitary species, very little male involvement exists, and the primary social unit is formed by a mother and her dependent offspring. Very little social interaction occurs between conspecific individuals of similar ages or of different sexes. The second level is the parental family, in which the male may (1) be mainly responsible for rearing of the offspring, (2) possess only limited interactions with the offspring, or (3) play no part in the offspring rearing. The main social group is composed of the bonded male and female and their offspring. The third level of complexity is represented by the uni-male troop, in which social interactions occur between a single male, several adult females, and their variously aged offspring. Usually, the male is dominant over the mutually tolerant females. Among patas monkeys, however, females possess their own dominance hierarchy, while the male is reduced to the role of breeder.

The fourth and fifth levels are termed the age-graded male troop and multi-male troop respectively. The former is an extension of the uni-male troop, and differs from it in that the adult male exhibits greater tolerance toward the younger males in the troop. Such social systems usually tend to be larger and occupy more extensive ranges than uni-male troops. Multi-male troops are, in turn, extensions of the age-graded male system. In these, several males of similar ages are fully integrated into the system. In addition, the males possess behavioral interactions toward each other that promote troop harmony and cohesion, and they cooperate in predator defense, foraging, and hunting.

11 Bones and Muscles

Introduction

Without fossils, human paleontology would consist only of unsubstantiated inferences and hypotheses and would clearly not be a scientific endeavor. The fundamental data upon which paleontological investigations depend are ultimately derived from fossils; specifically, in the context of where they are found, their chronological age, their association with other fossils of the same and different species, and their relationships to preceding, contemporaneous, and succeeding populations. These kinds of data on fossil hominids frequently allow considerable confidence to be attached to inferences about functional morphology, encephalization, diet, and locomotion, in addition to less tangible subjects like demographic parameters, the manufacture and use of tools, and certain aspects of social organization. However, the initial analysis of hominid fossils always involves description, which, in turn, requires a comprehensive anatomical knowledge. Before outlining the major features of human paleontology in the next several chapters, therefore, a few relevant aspects of human muscular and skeletal anatomy are necessary.

Selected Aspects of Human Anatomy

Terms of Location

By convention, the location of any anatomical structure and its position relative to another structure are described with reference to the anatomical position. This standard position occurs when a person stands upright with the face forward, the arms at the sides, and the palms of the hands directed forward. A body in this position may be divided into a number of different imaginary planes. The most important is called the **median plane,** which divides the body vertically into right and left halves. Because this plane closely approximates the sagittal suture, which separates the two bones (the parietals) that form part of the top and part of both sides of the skull, any other plane parallel to the median plane is called a **sagittal plane.** Any plane that bisects the body vertically, but at right angles to a sagittal plane, is called a **coronal plane.** This name derives from the coronal suture, which is approximately at right angles to the sagittal suture and separates both parietals from the frontal. Finally, the body can at any point be sectioned at right angles to both the sagittal and coronal planes. These are called transverse, or **horizontal planes.**

The location of an anatomical structure relative to another, or of two parts of a single structure, is often described in conjunction with one of these imaginary planes. The terms "anterior" and "posterior" refer, respectively, to front and back, the former being in front of some imaginary coronal plane and the latter in back of the same plane. Thus it may be stated that the vertebral column is posterior to the sternum. If a coronal plane is allowed to bisect a single vertebra, furthermore, then one part of the bone may be described as being either anterior or posterior to another part.

In a similar fashion, the term "medial" is used to denote a structure that lies closer to the median plane than another; those lying farther from the median plane are called "lateral." The term used to designate a structure that is higher (i.e., toward the head) than another is "superior," and its opposite term is "inferior." And the terms "proximal" and "distal" are used to denote the end of a structure that is closer to and away from the center of the body, respectively. The proximal end of the bone of the upper arm (the **humerus**), for example, is that which takes part in the shoulder joint; the distal extremity forms part of the elbow joint.

Comparative anatomists use a few different terms of location. The human sternum is obviously anterior to the vertebral column, but in a quadrupedal mammal or primate it is inferior to the vertebrae. Thus for quadrupeds (and for certain structures in humans), the belly area is called "ventral" (anterior) and the back is "dorsal" (posterior); toward the head is termed "cranial" (superior) and toward the tail is "caudal" (inferior).

The human skeleton (Figs. 11.1 and 11.2) is sometimes divided for classificatory purposes into axial and appendicular bones. Axial bones enter into the formation of various body cavities, hence serving a protective function. Such bones include the vertebral column, sacrum and coccyx, the skull and mandible, the ribs and sternum, and the hyoid (the small bone that can be felt just above your "adams apple"). Altogether, adults normally possess 74 axial bones, 21 of which comprise the skull (22, if the mandible is included). The appendicular bones are mainly the limb bones, including those of the shoulder girdle, the arms and hands, legs and feet, and the two hip bones (*os coxae*). Most of these serve as levers for limb muscle action, and they number 126 in the normal adult. When added to the 6 small bones of the middle ears, the total number of bones in the adult skeleton is normally 206.

The skeletal system serves at least five primary functions. First, by its rigidity it protects the vital and soft organs of the body, including the brain, heart, lungs, and liver. Second, it provides the entire body with rigidity. Third, it serves as attachment sites for muscles, ligaments, and tendons. By their muscle attachments, bones serve as levers in pulley systems, thus allowing muscles to produce movement. Fourth, the sites for red blood cell production are located in the interior of certain bones. And fifth, bones store and release vital minerals and salts.

It will become evident, later, that many inferences about the functional aspects of fossil species can be drawn not only from the general size and shape of particular bones, but also from the various markings on bony surfaces. Strong attachments of tendons and ligaments are usually marked by raised "lumps" called **tuberosities** and tubercles. The numerous ridges, crests, and lines are associated with the attachment of aponeuroses (sheetlike tendons) and intermuscular septa, the fibrous tissues that separate muscles from each other.

Figure 11.1 Front view of an adult human skeleton.

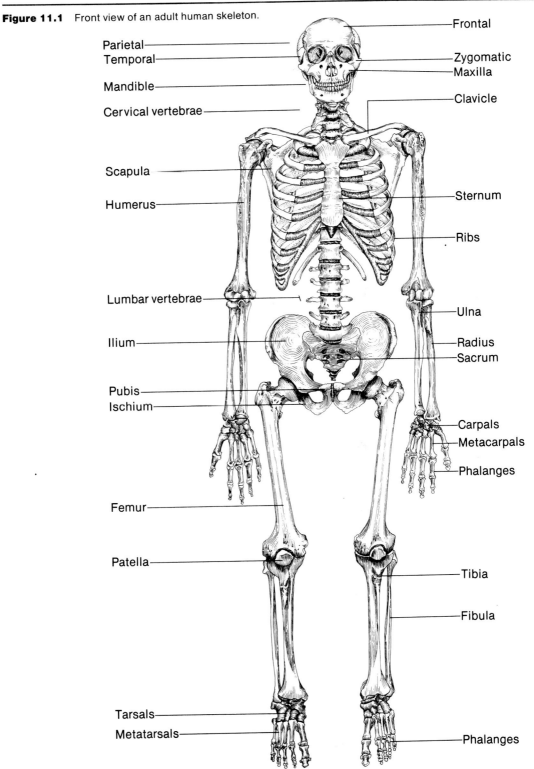

Parietal

Temporal

Mandible

Cervical vertebrae

Scapula

Humerus

Lumbar vertebrae

Ilium

Pubis

Ischium

Femur

Patella

Tarsals

Metatarsals

Frontal

Zygomatic

Maxilla

Clavicle

Sternum

Ribs

Ulna

Radius

Sacrum

Carpals

Metacarpals

Phalanges

Tibia

Fibula

Phalanges

Figure 11.2 Side view of an adult human skeleton.

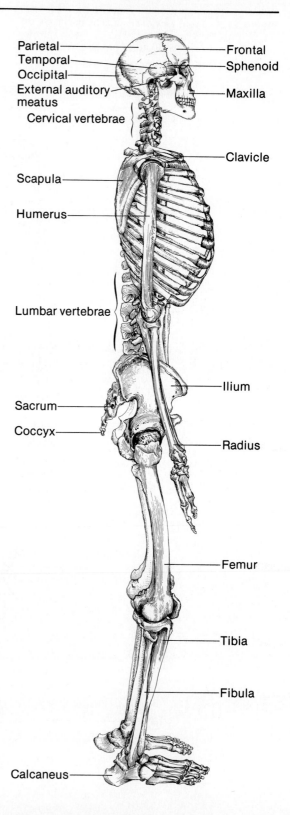

Parietal

Temporal

Occipital

External auditory
meatus

Cervical vertebrae

Frontal

Sphenoid

Maxilla

Clavicle

Scapula

Humerus

Lumbar vertebrae

Ilium

Sacrum

Coccyx

Radius

Femur

Tibia

Fibula

Calcaneus

A smooth bony surface indicates either no strong attachment of another structure or an attachment of more "fleshy" fibers. The holes (**foramina**) in bone serve mainly for the passage of blood vessels and nerves, and the grooves (sulci), depressions (fossae), notches, and similar features either house important structures or serve other highly specific functions. It is important to recognize that the skeleton is a system in itself, and also that it is inseparably integrated with other nonskeletal anatomical systems. And it is particularly important, especially for evolutionary and taxonomic investigations, to realize that every species has its own unique skeletal characteristics.

Of the three different types of muscles (voluntary, involuntary, and cardiac), we are concerned here only with the first type. Voluntary muscles are those that can be consciously activated or deactivated, in contrast to involuntary muscles like those lining the stomach or intestines. These operate without conscious intervention. Voluntary muscles are also called striated muscles—because of their striated microscopic appearance—and skeletal muscles—because most of them are attached to the skeleton.

Voluntary muscles produce movement at joints by contracting, never by pushing, and nearly always operate in conjunction with the action of other muscles. A muscle that effects any given movement is called a prime mover, but the occurrence of such a movement usually requires the simultaneous relaxation of another muscle (the antagonist). Furthermore, the movements created by prime movers and their antagonists are often assisted by other muscles that (1) serve a stabilizing function (fixation muscles) and (2) prevent power wastage if the prime mover passes over an intermediate joint (synergists). For a muscle to exert a contractive force, it must be securely anchored at a minimun of two areas or points. For the limb muscles, the proximal area of attachment is called the origin, and the distal area the muscle's insertion. However, for many muscles the distinction between their areas of origin and insertion is unclear. In these instances it is more convenient to speak simply of their particular attachment sites.

Any movement produced by a set of muscles has an opposite movement. Hence some structures are raised, with reference to the position of other structures, by levators, and lowered by depressors. Muscles that move a part of the body away from the central axis are abductors, and those that move the same part toward the central axis are adductors. Parts are rotated downward or backward by pronators, but upward or forward by supinators. Thus the primary types of movement are—

1. **Flexion** and **extension** (e.g., bending and straightening the arm at the elbow).

2. **Abduction** and **adduction** (e.g., raising and lowering the arm from the side of the body).

3. **Pronation** and **supination** (e.g., rotating the lower arm so that the palm of the hand faces posteriorly and then anteriorly).

4. **Lateral** and **medial rotation** (e.g., pivoting the head to the side and then back toward the midline).

5. **Circumduction** (e.g., straightening the arm and swinging the hand in a circular motion). This motion occurs when a bone circumscribes a conical space, with the apex of the cone at the articular cavity.

Although the names of muscles often appear bewildering, and the naming of muscles a haphazard process, there is an element of consistency in that their names usually reflect something about their size (e.g., vastus), location (e.g., dorsi), shape (e.g., triangularis), function (e.g., extensor), or some other characteristic feature. Names of muscles are frequently a combination of words, and by convention the first term is capitalized, as in the Extensor carpi radialis longus. The word "carpi" refers to the carpus, the small bones of the wrist; "radialis" refers to the radius, the lateral of the two bones of the forearm; and "longus" means long, which implies that a shorter (brevis) extensor is also present. Hence a very liberal translation of this Latin term means "the longer of two muscles on the radial side of the forearm that extends the wrist."

Bones and Muscles of the Skull

For the sake of descriptive convenience, the skull may be divided into two separate parts. One part is the facial skeleton, most of the bones of which can be seen in a frontal view of the skull (Fig. 11.3). The other is comprised of bones that enclose the brain (Figs. 11.4 and 11.5). In the adult, all bones of the skull are united by immovable articulations called sutures and synchondroses. Since the lower jaw articulates with the skull by means of a movable joint on either side, it is usually described separately. Although arbitrary, this practice is followed here.

A general but most important function of the facial bones is to surround and protect the eyes, mouth, and nasal cavity. The largest bones of the face are the paired maxillae, which join together along the median palatine suture at the roof of the mouth. When articulated, they form the horseshoe-shaped upper alveolar arch, into which the upper teeth are inserted. The maxillae articulate along their posterior margins with the horizontal parts of the two palatine bones. The four bones together

Figure 11.3 Frontal view of an adult human skull.

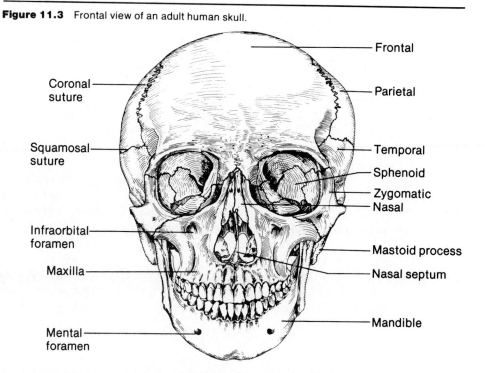

224

Figure 11.4 Side view of an adult human skull.

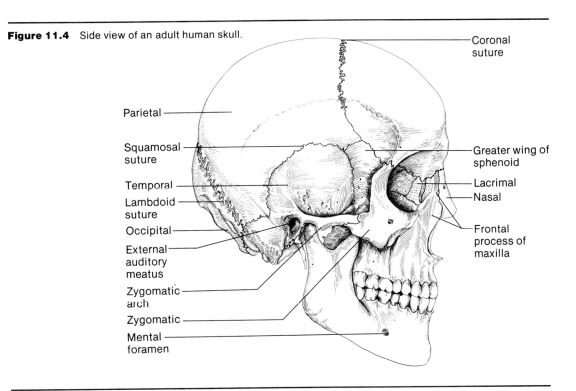

Coronal suture

Parietal

Squamosal suture

Temporal

Lambdoid suture

Occipital

External auditory meatus

Zygomatic arch

Zygomatic

Mental foramen

Greater wing of sphenoid

Lacrimal

Nasal

Frontal process of maxilla

Figure 11.5 Inferior view of an adult human skull.

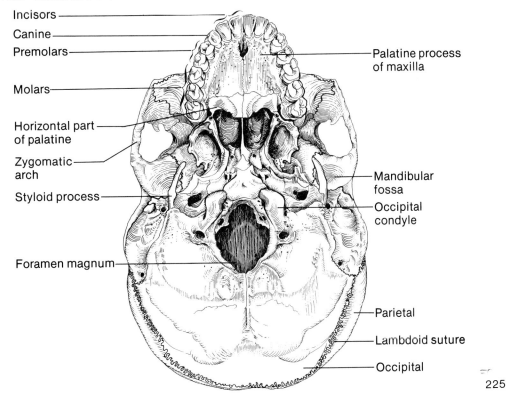

Incisors

Canine

Premolars

Molars

Horizontal part of palatine

Zygomatic arch

Styloid process

Foramen magnum

Palatine process of maxilla

Mandibular fossa

Occipital condyle

Parietal

Lambdoid suture

Occipital

225

contribute to a horizontal bridge of bone whose inferior surface is the hard palate. The superior surface of this structure is the floor of the nasal cavity.

The two maxillae also surround the opening of the nasal cavity, except for its superior border. This border is formed by the two nasal bones, which in turn articulate with each other and form the "bridge" of the nose. Each nasal bone is bounded laterally by a medial and superior extension of the maxilla called the frontal process. This process articulates at its superior extremity with the **frontal,** and it forms about half of the medial and a smaller part of the lower orbital border. Most of the frontal bone is concerned with enclosing the anterior part of the brain, but it also contributes to the facial skeleton by forming the superior borders and walls of the orbits. The greatest part of the floor of the orbit, as well as the lateral walls of the nasal passage, are formed by the maxillae. The remainder of the orbital floor and part of its lateral wall is contributed by the **zygomatic,** the bone with which the maxilla articulates laterally.

When disarticulated, each maxilla is a surprisingly light bone. This is due to the fact that most of the maxillary body is simply a shell around a large cavity, the maxillary sinus. How, then, do the maxillae withstand the enormous pressure placed upon them during biting and chewing? To a large extent, this is accomplished by a bilateral system of skeletal buttresses that extend superiorly from the canines, premolars, and molars. The first buttress runs superiorly from an area around each canine and first premolar through the frontal process, thus transmitting a line of force from these teeth to the frontal.

The second buttress is formed by the maxilla and zygomatic, in which lines of force run from an area around the second premolar and first molar through the lateral part of the maxilla and medial part of the zygomatic. From this point the line of force divides, one branch extending superiorly through the zygomatic to the zygomatic process of the frontal. The other line runs horizontally through the bony arch (the zygomatic arch) that ends just anterior to the opening of the ear (the external auditory meatus). The third buttress occurs behind the third molar and is formed by the pterygoid processes of the sphenoid. The line of force here runs from an area around the third molars to the cranial base.

Unlike the maxillae, the mandible (Figs. 11.6 and 11.7) is a heavy, solidly constructed bone. In the adult, the mandible can be divided into a body and two rami. The body lodges the lower dentition. Extending upward from the posterior part of the body are the two mandibular rami, each of which has (1) an area for articulation with the skull called the mandibular condyle and (2) a sharply pointed, rather triangular projection in front of the condyle called the coronoid process.

The dietary inferences about the fossil remains discussed in the succeeding chapter were drawn not only from dental wear patterns, but also from the size and shape of the attachment areas of the masticatory muscles. There are four such muscles on each side, the **Temporoparietalis, Masseter, Medial pterygoid,** and **Lateral pterygoid.**

The Temporoparietalis is a very thin, fan-shaped muscle whose broad end arises from the side of the skull in an area circumscribed by the temporal lines (Fig. 11.8). It descends beneath the zygomatic arch, where the small end of the "fan" inserts into the coronoid process of the mandible. The Temporoparietalis is primarily an elevator of the mandible and exerts considerable force during biting.

Figure 11.6 Lateral view of an adult human mandible.

Mandibular condyle — Mandibular notch
Coronoid process

Ramus

Mental foramen

Body

Mental protuberance

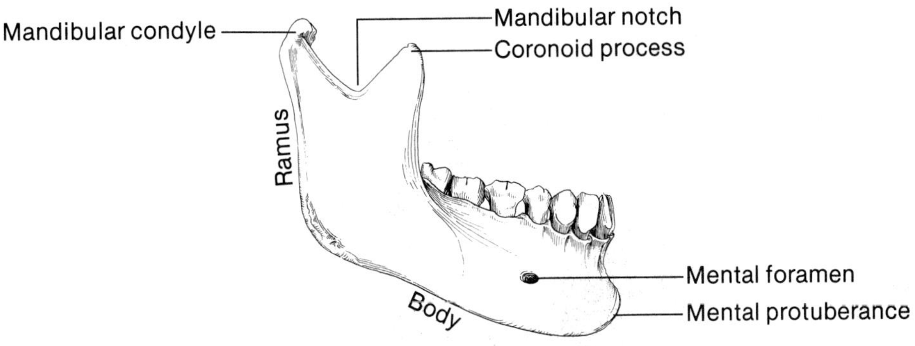

Figure 11.7 Occlusal view of an adult human mandible.

Mandibular condyle

Coronoid process

Molars

Premolars
Canine
Lateral incisor
Central incisor

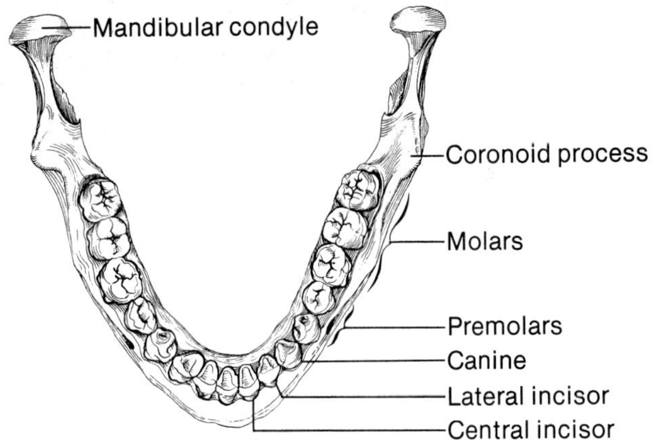

Figure 11.8 Lateral view of an adult human skull, showing the approximate locations of two important muscles of mastication, the Temporoparietalis and the Masseter.

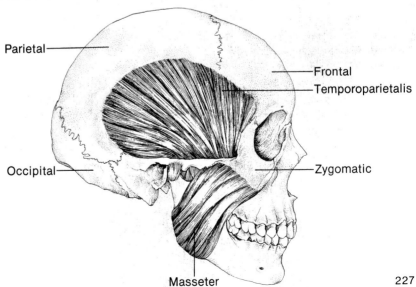

Parietal

Frontal
Temporoparietalis

Occipital

Zygomatic

Masseter

In closing the jaw during biting or crushing, the Masseter (Fig. 11.8) operates in conjunction with the Temporoparietalis. It is a thick, quadrangular, and very powerful elevator that has its origin along the anterior portion of the zygomatic arch. Its insertion covers about one-third of the lateral side of the mandibular ramus.

The Medial pterygoid is an anatomical and functional counterpart of the Masseter that is located on the inner side of the mandibular ramus. It also serves as a powerful elevator whose general shape and orientation parallel the Masseter. It arises from the pterygoid fossa of the sphenoid, just behind the third molars, and inserts into the mandible at the junction of the body with the ramus. In addition to its function as an elevator, the Medial pterygoid produces a lateral motion of the jaw during chewing. The Lateral pterygoid arises from the lateral pterygoid plate of the sphenoid, but runs roughly horizontally back to its insertion into the neck beneath the mandibular condyle. Hence, during contraction it pulls the condyle forward, protruding the jaw. The alternating movement of both Lateral pterygoids produces a grinding movement during chewing.

In sum, then, the mandible is drawn upward for biting by the combined actions of the Temporoparietalis, Masseter, and Medial pterygoids on both sides. The mandible can and does fall downward simply by gravitation, but other muscles (the Mylohyoid and Digastric) can assist in depressing the mandible should there be some form of resistance. For the side-to-side movement required in chewing, the left Medial and Lateral pterygoids contract, pulling the mandible to the right, and the same muscles on the right side pull it to the left.

The relatively huge brain of modern *H. sapiens* is obvious in a lateral view of the skull (Fig. 11.4). Much of that discussed above can also be seen in this view, but some features become more clear. The zygomatic arch ends just above the outer opening of the ear, the **external auditory meatus,** and directly in front of this bony canal, on the temporal bone, is the mandibular fossa. This is a rather deep fossa with which the mandibular condyle articulates (see Figure 11.5). Behind the external auditory meatus is the mastoid process, a strong projection honeycombed with air spaces that serves as the origin for the Sternocleidomastoideus. This very powerful neck muscle extends obliquely down the side of the neck and inserts inferiorly into the clavicle and sternum. Simultaneous contraction of the muscles on both right and left sides flexes the head and neck, and contraction of only one side lifts the chin to the opposite side.

Directly between the two mastoid processes, at the base of the skull, is the **foramen magnum** (Fig. 11.5). It is through this opening that the brain communicates with the spinal cord, thus innervating the body. The outline of the bones comprising the cranial vault can be traced by drawing a line backward from the most posterior point on the foramen magnum, up over the occipital bone in the midline, along the sagittal suture until it meets the frontal bone, and downward over the frontal to a point where the frontonasal suture meets the median plane. Such an outline is roughly parallel to the temporal lines, which mark the origin of the Temporoparietalis, and to the squamosal suture, which separates the temporal superiorly from the parietal.

The vault bones, then, include (1) the single frontal, separated posteriorly from the parietals by the coronal suture; (2) the paired **parietals,** separated medially from each other by the sagittal suture and inferiorly from the two temporals by the squamosal sutures; (3) each of the paired temporals, which articulates (*a*) anteriorly with the greater wing of the sphenoid and with the zygomatic at the middle of the zygomatic arch, (*b*) superiorly with the parietal, and (*c*) posteriorly and inferiorly with the occipital, and (4) the **occipital,** which is separated from both parietals and temporals by the lambdoid suture. The occipital also articulates with the sphenoid at its most anterior point on the cranial base.

The bones of the cranial vault have often been represented as hard, curved plates that more or less "float" on the surface of an expanding brain, especially during the period of initial brain growth. To some extent this may be a useful concept, although it is grossly oversimplified. The vault bones are kept in close association with each other by different forms of sutures, the functions of which are critical for normal growth and development of the brain and skull. These functions may be summarized as follows. First, they prevent the bones from separating under the influence of unusual external stress. Second, they allow the occurrence of relative motion during the early stages of cerebral expansion. And third, new bone is laid down at the sutural margins during expansion of the cerebral capsule. These functions have little meaning after the skull and brain have reached their full growth, and the vault bones eventually fuse together in most, but not all, adults (see Bennett 1967, for a brief review of experimental investigations on factors initiating sutural fusion).

When viewed from its inferior aspect with the mandible removed (Fig. 11.5), many of the cranial features mentioned above become more obvious. Such features include the alveolar arch, the hard palate, the pterygoid processes of the sphenoid, the zygomatic arches, the mandibular fossae, and the foramen magnum. On both sides of the foramen magnum, anterior to its center, are the **occipital condyles.** These smooth, oval, articular surfaces are convex from front to back and correspond to concave articular facets on the first cervical vertebra (the atlas). The gliding motion between the occipital condyles and the superior facets of the atlas is analogous to that of a rocking chair: it allows the head to be "nodded" back and forth.

The area behind the foramen magnum, in the suboccipital region, is quite rough and marked by several transverse lines. These are called nuchal lines, and they extend outward in gentle anterior curves from the median nuchal line of the occipital. The nuchal lines mark the attachment sites of several important muscles at the back of the neck. Occurring bilaterally, these include the Splenius capitis, the Semispinalis capitis, the Obliquus capitis inferior, the Obliquus capitis superior, the Rectus capitis posterior major, and the Rectus capitis posterior minor. These muscles all extend the head, thus lifting the chin in the median plane during bilateral contraction. Unilateral contraction lifts the chin, but tilts it to the side opposite the contracting muscles. The reverse process, i.e., turning the chin back down and to the median plane, is accomplished by bilateral groups of flexors on the ventral side of the neck.

Bones and Muscles of the Trunk

The foregoing descriptions have been limited mostly to the cranial bones represented in the fossil record. Many bones, such as the lacrimals, inferior nasal conchae, ethmoid, and vomer, were not discussed intentionally. Because these bones are particularly susceptible to rapid decomposition, the details of their structure in early hominids remain unknown. Similarly, the following discussions about postcranial bones and muscle are restricted primarily to features about which some paleontological information exists.

Figure 11.9 contains an anterior view of the vertebral column, the thoracic cage, and the **pectoral** (shoulder) **girdle.** The human vertebral column contains 24 separate bones, including 7 cervical (in the neck), 12 thoracic (those with which the ribs articulate), and 5 lumbar vertebrae. Each of these vertebrae consists of two parts: (1) the body, which along with its associated intervertebral disc serves a weight-bearing function; and (2) the vertebral arch, each half of which arises posteriorly from the lateral side of the body. The vertebral arch serves at least two important functions. First, it surrounds a large foramen (the vertebral foramen) behind the body. The respective vertebral foramina are continuous throughout the entire articulated column, thus forming the vertebral canal and a solid, bony protection for the spinal cord on its posterior and lateral sides. Second, the transverse processes and spinous processes on the lateral and posterior sides of the arches, respectively, offer attachment sites for numerous muscles of the back.

The bones of the thoracic cage (Fig. 11.9) include 12 pairs of ribs and the sternum, which, in turn, has three separate components. These are the manubrium, body, and, at its distal extremity, an irregularly shaped structure called the xiphoid process. Dorsally, the ribs articulate directly with the tips of the transverse processes and the bodies of the thoracic vertebrae. Ventrally, the first ten ribs on both sides are either directly or indirectly (ribs no. 8, 9, and 10) connected to the sternum by intervening spans of costal cartilage. Such a composite structure allows the voluntary act of inspiration (inhalation) by simultaneously increasing the capacity of the thoracic cage in its transverse, anteroposterior, and vertical diameters. Unfortunately, relatively little is known about the thoracic cage in fossil hominids. Because the compact bone surrounding their internal structure is relatively thin compared to other bones of the postcranial skeleton, the ribs and sternum deteriorate rapidly and are only infrequently recovered in paleontological excavations.

The deep, or intrinsic, muscles of the back may be divided into two groups, one overlying the other. The deeper of these two groups consists of numerous smaller muscles (e.g., the Semispinalis cervicis, the Semispinalis thoracis, and the Multifidus) that are collectively called the **Transversospinalis.** These are illustrated on the left side in Figure 11.10. On the right side of the same figure is a more superficial group of muscles, the **Erector spinae,** which divides into three columns as it extends cranially from its attachment areas on the sacrum and ilium. In general, the muscles of both groups are responsible for extending (or straightening) the vertebral column and, under unilateral contraction, bending the column to the same side as the contracting muscles. Some of these muscles, notably the Multifidus and other smaller, oblique muscles associated with it, also provide a twisting motion to individual vertebral groups.

The intrinsic back muscles are in operation during walking and running, although they contribute nothing per se to the actual forward motion. The vertical muscle groups on one side usually, but not always, contract as the foot on the same side leaves the ground. This action is probably related to the maintenance of balance, inasmuch as the same muscle groups regulate vertebral posture. Since such posture during relaxed standing can be maintained by relatively little back muscle action, most of the intrinsic muscles of the back remain essentially inactive in this

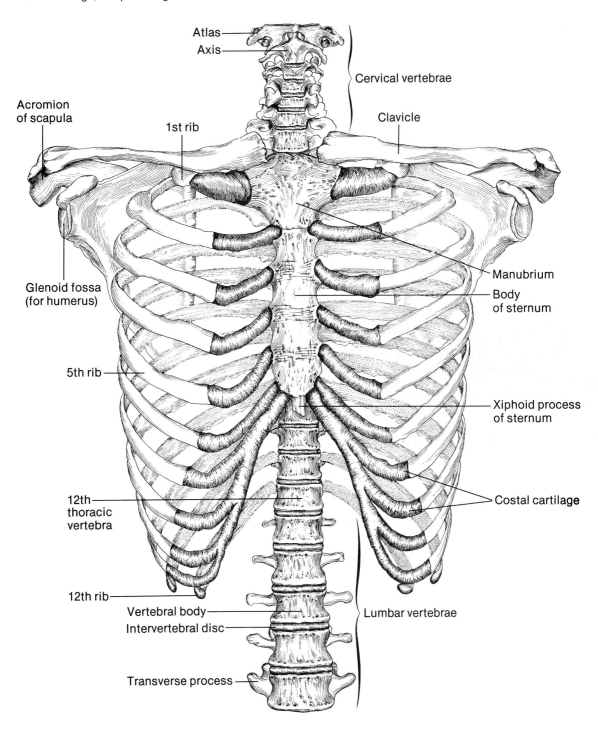

Figure 11.9 Anterior view of the vertebral column, thoracic cage, and pectoral girdle in an adult human.

Atlas

Axis

Cervical vertebrae

Acromion of scapula

Clavicle

1st rib

Manubrium

Glenoid fossa (for humerus)

Body of sternum

5th rib

Xiphoid process of sternum

12th thoracic vertebra

Costal cartilage

12th rib

Vertebral body

Intervertebral disc

Lumbar vertebrae

Transverse process

Figure 11.10 Dorsal view of the deepest muscles of the back. The muscles on the left side of an imaginary vertical plane through the center of the vertebral column are the deepest and are overlain by those on the right side.

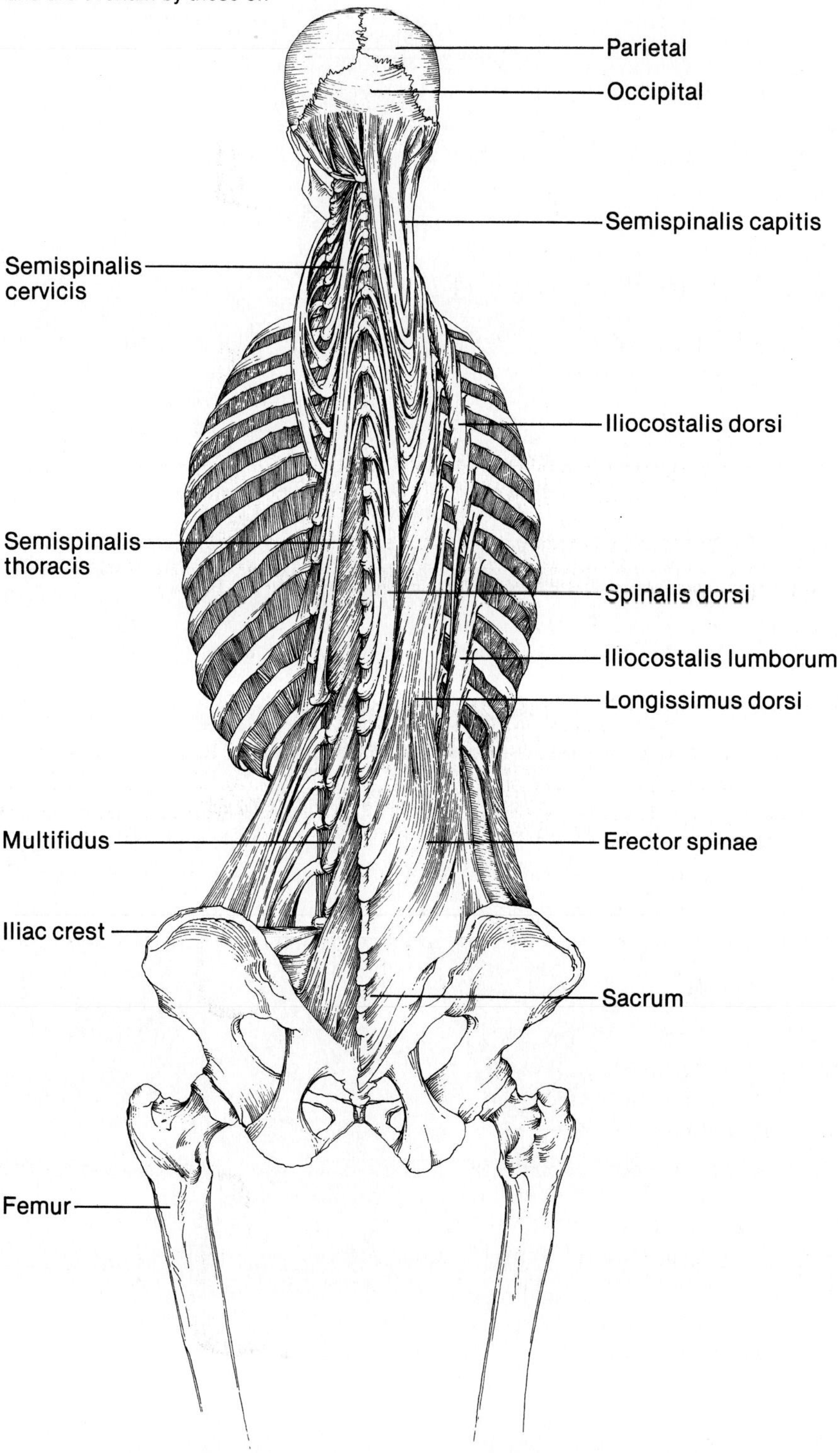

Parietal

Occipital

Semispinalis capitis

Semispinalis cervicis

Iliocostalis dorsi

Semispinalis thoracis

Spinalis dorsi

Iliocostalis lumborum

Longissimus dorsi

Multifidus

Erector spinae

Iliac crest

Sacrum

Femur

position. However, they respond almost immediately when balance is threatened by a motion such as bending slightly at the waist.

The Pectoral Girdle and Upper Limb

The parts of the pectoral girdles of early hominids that have been recovered yield highly important information about the critical shift from quadrupedalism to erect bipedalism during hominid evolution. The pectoral girdle (Fig. 11.9) serves as a structure by which the arm is attached to the skeleton, and it is comprised of the clavicle (anterior) and scapula (posterior). Articulating medially with the manubrium, the clavicle can be viewed as a horizontal strut that suspends the scapula on its lateral extremity. The clavicle passes directly over the first rib, at the base of the neck and, by its lateral scapular articulation, forms a "hood" over the glenoid fossa of the scapula. The glenoid fossa articulates with the head of the humerus and, in anatomical position, faces laterally, slightly forward, and slightly upward. Except for the area around the glenoid fossa, the scapula is a thin, triangular plate of bone. In anatomical position, it is placed on the back of the thoracic cage between the second and seventh ribs. Its most lateral extension, the acromion, is the easily palpated "point of the shoulder."

Both the pectoral girdle and the humerus (Fig. 11.11) are capable of considerable mobility. Since their movements are very closely coordinated, it is convenient to describe the major shoulder and upper arm muscles in terms of three different groups. The muscles in the first group are those that pass from the axial skeleton to the pectoral girdle (Figs. 11.12 and 11.13), and including the following:

1. Trapezius. Covering the upper half of the back of the trunk and part of the back of the neck, this muscle imparts several different motions to the scapula. When all parts of the muscle operate simultaneously, the scapula is rotated. When only its upper fibers contract, the scapula is drawn cranially (as in "shrugging" the shoulders). The horizontal fibers in the middle adduct the scapula, drawing it toward the midline. And the lower fibers can operate alone to draw the scapula caudally.

2. Levator scapulae. This muscle is located on the dorsolateral part of the neck and assists in raising the scapula and rotating it slightly in order to tilt the glenoid fossa caudally.

3. Rhomboideus minor and Rhomboideus major. These arise from the spinous processes of the last cervical and first four thoracic vertebrae and insert into the vertebral border of the scapula. They adduct the scapula and turn the glenoid fossa downward, thus assisting in arm adduction.

4. Serratus anterior. The Serratus anterior originates from the anterior and lateral parts of the first eight or nine ribs, extends dorsally very close to the chest wall, and inserts into the entire length of the vertebral border of the scapula. This muscle operates as a powerful protractor of the scapula, and it also provides an upward movement of the glenoid fossa when raising the arm above the head.

The muscles of the second group extend from the pectoral girdle to the humerus, and include the following:

1. Teres major. This muscle originates from the bottom, or inferior angle, of the scapula and inserts just below the head of the humerus on its anterior side. It is a medial rotator, extensor, and adductor of the arm.

2. Subscapularis, Supraspinatus, and Infraspinatus. These three muscles comprise a functional group that counteracts forces tending to displace the head

Figure 11.11 Anterior, **a,** and posterior, **b,** views of a right humerus from an adult human.

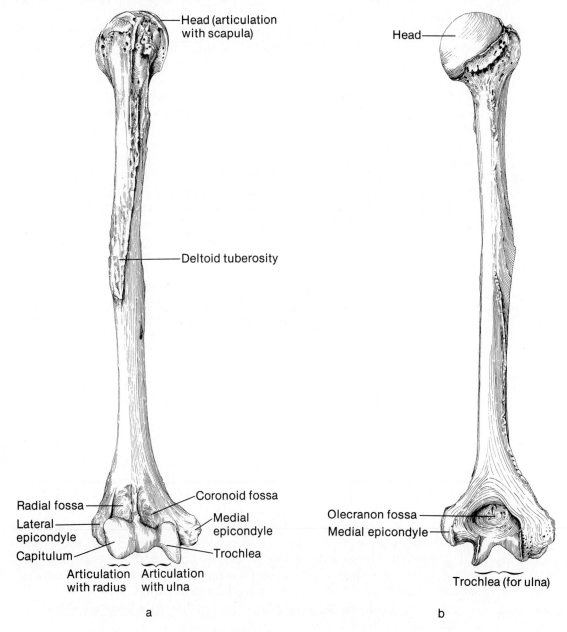

Head (articulation with scapula)

Head

Deltoid tuberosity

Radial fossa
Lateral epicondyle
Capitulum

Coronoid fossa
Medial epicondyle
Trochlea

Articulation with radius   Articulation with ulna

a

Olecranon fossa
Medial epicondyle

Trochlea (for ulna)

b

of the humerus from the glenoid fossa. Each of these three inserts into an area next to the head of the humerus. They originate from the body of the scapula, the Subscapularis anteriorly and the other two posteriorly. In addition to their "protective" function, the Subscapularis is a medial rotator, the Supraspinatus an abductor, and the Infraspinatus a lateral rotator of the arm.

Figure 11.12 Dorsal view of the muscles connecting the upper limb to the axial skeleton. Note that the muscles on the right side of an imaginary vertical plane through the center of the vertebral column underlie those on the left side of the same plane.

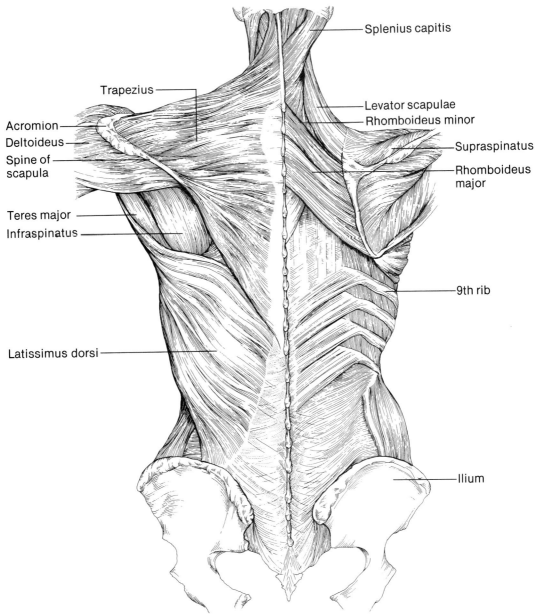

3. Deltoideus. The Deltoideus is a large, powerful muscle that abducts the arm and forms the "roundness" of the shoulder. Arising from (*a*) the lateral part of the clavicle, (*b*) the lateral border of the acromion, and (*c*) part of the dorsal spine on the scapula, it extends over the head of the humerus and inserts into the deltoid tuberosity on the humeral shaft (Fig. 11.11).

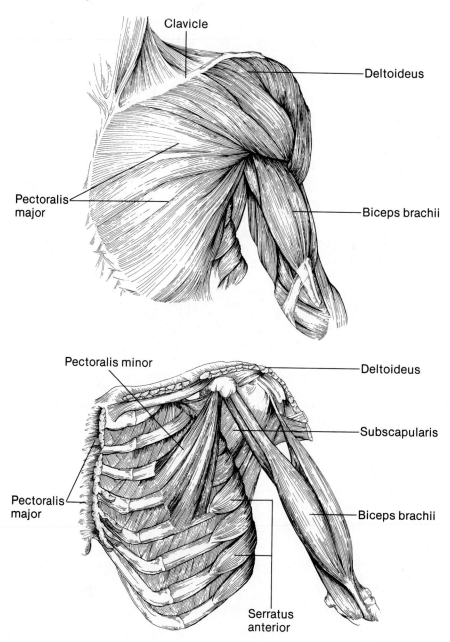

Figure 11.13 Ventral aspect of the deep (lower view) and superficial (upper view) muscles that connect the scapula to the thoracic cage.

Clavicle

Deltoideus

Pectoralis major

Biceps brachii

Pectoralis minor

Deltoideus

Subscapularis

Pectoralis major

Biceps brachii

Serratus anterior

The final group of muscles includes the Pectoralis major and Latissimus dorsi, both of which connect the axial skeleton to the proximal part of the humerus. The Pectoralis major is a superficial muscle that arises from two heads on the front of the upper trunk. One is the clavicular head, originating from the medial half of the clavicle and inserting into an area just below the head of the humerus. The other is the sternal head, which originates along the lateral side of the sternum and inserts into an area on the humeral shaft very close to the clavicular head. The Pectoralis major is a powerful adductor, but also a medial rotator of the arm.

The Latissimus dorsi arises in the middle of the lower part of the back, specifically along the posterior half of the iliac crest, the spinous processes of the upper sacral vertebrae, and the spinous processes of all lumbar and the last six thoracic vertebrae. As it extends cranially, it swings laterally across the lower ribs and ultimately inserts just beneath the humeral head on the anterior side. It is an extensor, adductor, and medial rotator of the arm.

Articulating with the distal portion of the humerus, thus forming the elbow joint, are the two bones of the forearm (Fig. 11.14). These are the ulna (medially) and radius (laterally), both of which articulate distally with certain bones of the wrist (the carpals). Movement at the elbow joint is brought about primarily by three muscles, the Brachialis, the Biceps brachii, and the Triceps brachii. The primary flexor of the elbow joint is the Brachialis, which is lodged beneath the Biceps brachii. The latter is the large, powerful muscle on the anterior side of the upper arm. It does assist the Brachialis in flexion, especially when resistance is encountered, but it is also an important supinator of the forearm. On the back of the upper arm is the Triceps brachii, the only important extensor of the elbow joint.

Each hand (Fig 11.15) contains 27 bones: 8 carpals, 5 metacarpals, and 14 **phalanges** (bones of the fingers and thumb). Numerous muscles in the forearm are responsible for flexion, extension, adduction, and abduction of the wrist, carpometacarpal, and interphalangeal joints. The extraordinary deftness of the fingers and thumb is provided by the coordinated action of 18 small muscles in the hand.

Bones of the Pelvis and Lower Limb

The bony pelvis (Fig. 11.16) is made up of the two *os coxae,* the sacrum, and the coccyx. The pelvic girdle is comprised of the right and left *os coxae,* each of which consists of three bones that are separated by cartilage in early life, but which fuse together during development. Joining together in the **acetabulum** (the cuplike socket that receives the head of the femur), these three bones are—

1. The **ilium,** which is the expanded, curved, and somewhat "fan-shaped" bone above the acetabulum.

2. The **ischium,** which descends nearly vertically from the acetabulum and bears the upper body weight when sitting upright.

3. The **pubis,** which curves anteriorly and medially from the acetabulum until it meets the other pubis in the midline.

The two pubic bones are attached in the midline by a tough band of fibrocartilage that essentially prevents any movement between the two bones. Dorsally, each ilium articulates with the sacrum. But the opposing articular surfaces are interlocking, and only a slight amount of motion is possible. Thus the sacrum can

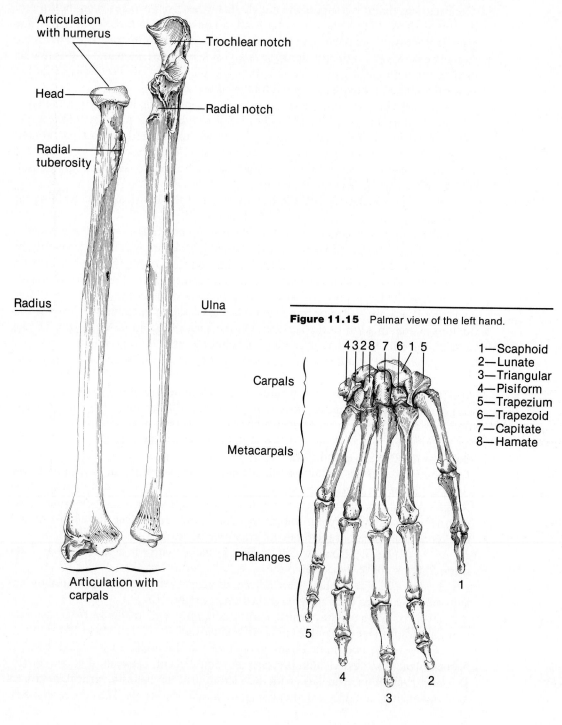

Figure 11.14 Anterior view of the right radius and ulna of an adult human.

Articulation with humerus

Trochlear notch

Head

Radial notch

Radial tuberosity

Radius

Ulna

Articulation with carpals

Figure 11.15 Palmar view of the left hand.

Carpals

Metacarpals

Phalanges

4 3 2 8 7 6 1 5

1—Scaphoid
2—Lunate
3—Triangular
4—Pisiform
5—Trapezium
6—Trapezoid
7—Capitate
8—Hamate

Figure 11.16 The bony pelvis of an adult male.

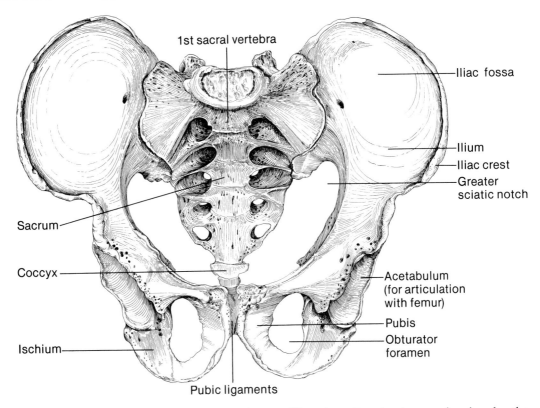

1st sacral vertebra

Iliac fossa

Ilium

Iliac crest

Greater sciatic notch

Sacrum

Coccyx

Acetabulum (for articulation with femur)

Pubis

Obturator foramen

Ischium

Pubic ligaments

be viewed as a wedge between the two ilia, where it rests at an angle whereby the superior surface is more anterior than the coccygeal extremity. Because there is considerable weight placed on the first sacral vertebra, a tendency thus exists for the sacrum to be rotated or tilted in a counterclockwise direction. Such a tilt is prevented by very strong ligaments that "bind" the three bones together. In particular, the short fibers of the interosseous ligament join the sacrum to the ilia directly behind their articular areas. The downward pressure on the sacrum actually tightens these ligaments and brings the two ilia toward the midline. As the pressure increases, therefore, the interlocking articular areas are pressed ever more tightly together.

The hip joint, the articulation between the head of the femur and the acetabulum, is not only one of the most secure joints of the body, but also the best example of a ball-and-socket joint. The acetabulum itself is a hemispherical surface facing laterally and downward. The femoral head (Fig. 11.17), mounted on a short neck that lies at an angle of about 125° from the femoral shaft, is normally contoured so that it accurately fits the acetabular socket. Such a joint is necessary for the wide range of movements required for erect bipedal locomotion—flexion, extension, abduction, adduction, and medial and lateral rotation. Obviously, the joint must also be very strong, because during locomotion each joint must withstand the entire weight of the body (except for the leg and foot that are in stance phase). Most of the strength of the joint stems from its surrounding fibrous covering. On the anterior side,

Figure 11.17 An adult human femur in an anterior,
a, and posterior, **b,** view.

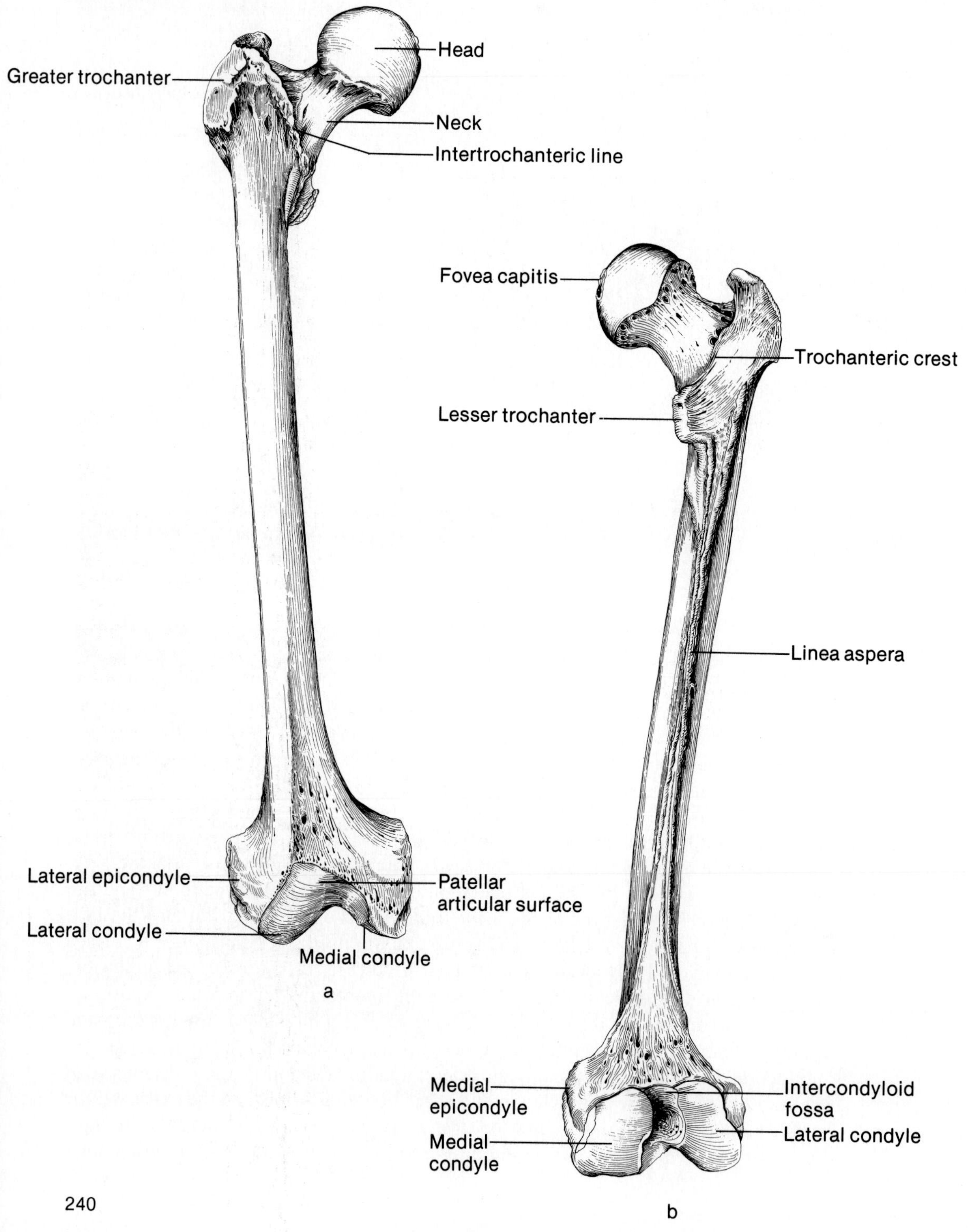

Head

Greater trochanter

Neck

Intertrochanteric line

Fovea capitis

Trochanteric crest

Lesser trochanter

Linea aspera

Lateral epicondyle

Patellar
articular surface

Lateral condyle

Medial condyle

a

Medial
epicondyle

Intercondyloid
fossa

Medial
condyle

Lateral condyle

b

extending the entire length of the intertrochanteric line (Fig. 11.17) to the anterior inferior iliac spine, is the very thick and strong iliofemoral ligament. One of the strongest capsular ligaments in the body, this prevents the femur from being overly extended. Strengthening the joint posteriorly are two accessory ligaments, the ischiofemoral and pubofemoral ligaments. Neither of these two, however, approaches the strength of the iliofemoral ligament.

The **femur** is the longest and heaviest bone in the body and transmits its own weight and that above it directly to the tibia (Fig. 11.18). The **tibia** is the medial of

Figure 11.18 Anterior view of the right tibia and fibula in an adult human.

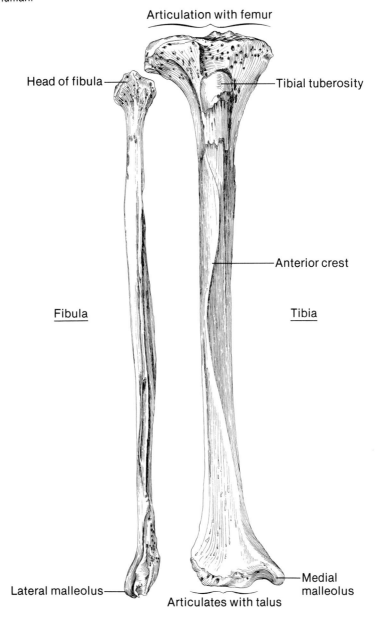

Articulation with femur

Head of fibula

Tibial tuberosity

Anterior crest

Fibula

Tibia

Lateral malleolus

Medial malleolus

Articulates with talus

241

two bones of the lower leg, and it alone conveys body weight to the foot. The lateral bone is the fibula, which has no weight-bearing function. Along its length are attachment sites for numerous muscles and tendons, but its primary purpose is to lend lateral security to the ankle joint. The so-called "anklebones," for that matter, are the distal extemities of the tibia and fibula.

Each foot (Fig. 11.19) contains 7 tarsals, 5 metatarsals, and 14 phalanges. The foot is similar to the hand only inasmuch as both have several bones that constitute a proximal part (carpals and tarsals), a middle part (metacarpals and metatarsals), and a terminal part (the phalanges). However, the hand differs radically from the foot, a consequence that is best explained in the context of adaptation to bipedal locomotion. Natural selection has favored highly mobile components in the hand; hence the bones, muscles, ligaments, tendons, and joints are arranged in a fashion conducive to extreme manual dexterity. By contrast, the functions of the human foot are concerned only with weight-bearing and locomotion. Hence a few functionally related differences are—

1. The tarsals are far less capable of movement than the carpals.

2. The phalanges of the foot are shorter than those of the hand, and their mobility is similarly reduced.

Figure 11.19 A human right foot viewed from above.

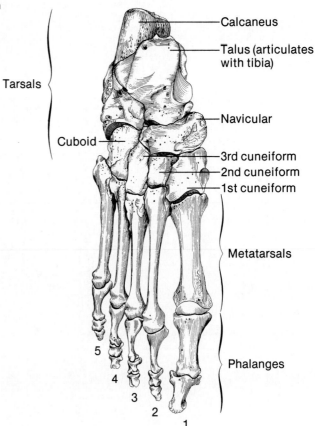

Tarsals

Cuboid

Calcaneus

Talus (articulates with tibia)

Navicular

3rd cuneiform
2nd cuneiform
1st cuneiform

Metatarsals

Phalanges

5
4
3
2
1

3. The first metatarsal is parallel to the other four and is a short, thickset bone with little mobility. It is directly involved with weight-bearing. Its counterpart in the hand, the first metacarpal of the thumb, is also short and strong. However, it occurs at an acute angle from the metacarpal of the index finger, and its articulation with the trapezium (one of the carpals) allows flexion, extension, abduction, adduction, and opposition. The latter movement occurs when the thumb is brought across the palm of the hand.

4. Whereas the carpals are small in relation to the rest of the hand, the tarsals form the major bulk of the foot. Whereas the carpals occur in a continuous line from the radius and ulna to the fingertips, the tarsals are placed at a right angle to the lower leg.

5. The articulated tarsals and metatarsals form both a longitudinal arch and a series of transverse arches, each of which serves to distribute body weight over a larger area than would be possible in their absence. No such structures exist in the hand.

Muscles of the Pelvis and Lower Limb

The lower limbs provide balance and stability to the rest of the body, and, compared to the pectoral girdle and upper limbs, their range of motion is quite limited. The primary function of the most massive muscles of the lower limb is locomotion, and the most powerful of these muscles are located on the back of the hip, in front of the femur, and behind the tibia. These are the muscle groups called into action when the body is raised from the sitting to standing position.

A convenient way to describe the lower limb muscles is by dividing them into various groups according to either their function or location. For this, we may adopt Basmajian's (1976) six-part division.

1. Muscles crossing the front of the hip joint. Two muscles are in this group, the Psoas major and Iliacus. The Psoas major arises from the transverse processes and sides of the bodies of the last thoracic and all lumbar vertebrae. The Iliacus arises from the superior two-thirds of the iliac fossa, the concave part of the ilium on the internal side. From these origins, both muscles extend downward, fuse together, pass over the front of the hip joint, and insert by a common tendon into the lesser trochanter of the femur. Both muscles are flexors, abductors, and lateral rotators of the hip joint. Since they share a common function and the same tendinous insertion, they are sometimes referred to as a single muscle called the Iliopsoas.

2. The three **gluteal muscles** and the Tensor fasciae latae. The gluteal muscles are all large and powerful, their relative sizes being indicated by their full names—Gluteus maximus, Gluteus medius, and Gluteus minimus. The Gluteus maximus is one of the largest, most coarse-grained muscles of the body and is placed entirely behind the hip. As seen in Figure 11.20, it originates partially from the posterior part of the back of the ilium, but mainly from the ligaments that attach the sacrum to the ilium. Running inferiorly and laterally from this area, it inserts into the femoral shaft in a continuous line that begins just beneath the greater trochanter and extends along the linea aspera on the posterior side. The line finally ends in an area slightly below the lateral condyle of the tibia. The Gluteus maximus functions as a powerful extensor of the hip joint in movements such as rising from a sitting position, climbing, walking upstairs, and running, but it normally plays no significant role

Figure 11.20 Origin and insertion of the Gluteus maximus. Note that the muscles illustrated in the right view underlie those at the left.

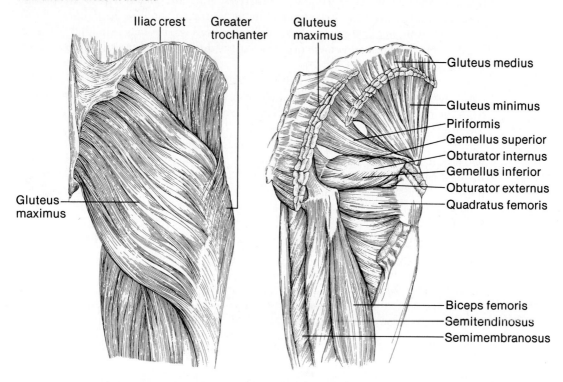

during level walking. This muscle also acts as a powerful lateral rotator of the thigh when the latter is extended, but it cannot rotate the flexed thigh.

The Gluteus medius, most of which is covered by the Gluteus maximus, is a broad and thick muscle that originates on the outer surface of the ilium. It is very wide at its origin, but as it descends downward and laterally, it converges into a flattened tendon that inserts into the greater trochanter of the femur. The Gluteus medius is an abductor and medial rotator of the thigh. The Gluteus minimus is beneath the anterior part of the Gluteus medius and originates on the lower part of the outer surface of the ilium. It also inserts into the greater trochanter and possesses the same actions as the Gluteus medius. The Tensor fasciae latae arises on the most anterior part of the outer surface of the iliac blade, runs downward, and inserts into the same area as the Gluteus maximus on the femur and tibia. Although it may assist other muscles in abduction, medial rotation, and flexion of the hip joint, its primary function is to brace the knee joint and thus prevent it from "buckling" when the other leg is off the ground (see Fig. 11.21 for an illustration of the origins of the gluteal muscles and the Tensor fasciae latae).

3. The six lateral rotators. These are six small muscles (Piriformis, Obturator internus, Gemellus superior and Gemellus inferior, Quadratus femoris, and Obturator externus) that pass more or less horizontally behind the hip joint. From their origins on the sacrum (Piriformis), inside the *os coxae* (Obturator internus,

Figure 11.21 Areas of origin of the gluteal muscles and the Tensor fasciae latae on a right ilium.

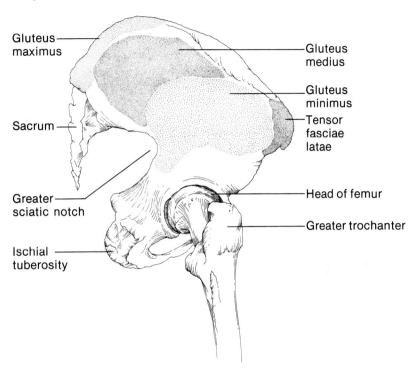

Gluteus maximus

Gluteus medius

Gluteus minimus

Tensor fasciae latae

Sacrum

Greater sciatic notch

Head of femur

Greater trochanter

Ischial tuberosity

Gemellus superior, and Gemellus inferior), on the ischial tuberosity (Quadratus femoris), and on the outer side of the *os coxae* (Obturator externus), all but the latter insert into the greater trochanter of the femur. The Obturator externus inserts into a pit just below and medial to the greater trochanter. All six muscles rotate the thigh laterally.

4. Muscles of the thigh. These muscles may be subdivided into groups according to their relative location and action as follows:

a. Muscles at the front of the thigh, the extensors. This group includes the Sartorius and the Quadriceps femoris, the latter of which consists of the Rectus femoris, and the Vastus medialis, Vastus lateralis, and Vastus intermedius (Fig. 11.22). In humans, the Sartorius is the longest muscle of the body, but by itself it produces very little motion. The Rectus femoris reaches vertically from the anterior inferior iliac spine to the superior border of the patella (kneecap), and it serves two functions. First, it assists in flexion of the thigh, since it passes over the hip joint. And second, it extends the lower leg by pulling on the patella, which in turn is connected to the tibia by strong patellar ligaments. Flexion of the thigh and extension of the lower leg are the two movements that, in combination, advance the limb during walking or running.

The Vastus medialis and lateralis both originate on the linea aspera of the femur, while the Vastus intermedius arises from the anterior part of the upper

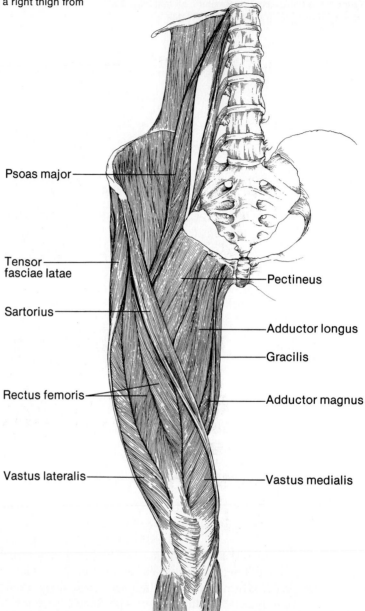

Figure 11.22 Extensor muscles of a right thigh from a human.

Psoas major

Tensor fasciae latae

Sartorius

Rectus femoris

Vastus lateralis

Pectineus

Adductor longus

Gracilis

Adductor magnus

Vastus medialis

femoral shaft. All three insert into parts of the patella, and in conjunction with the Rectus femoris form the primary extensors of the lower leg.

b. Muscles on the medial side of the thigh, the adductors. The five adductors are the Gracilis, Pectineus, Adductor longus, Adductor brevis, and Adductor magnus. The first four muscles originate on the front of the pubic bone, and the Adductor magnus from the ischiopubic ramus. Except for the Gracilis, their insertions lie along the femoral shaft, beginning beneath the lesser trochanter and

Figure 11.23 Adductor muscles of a right thigh from a human.

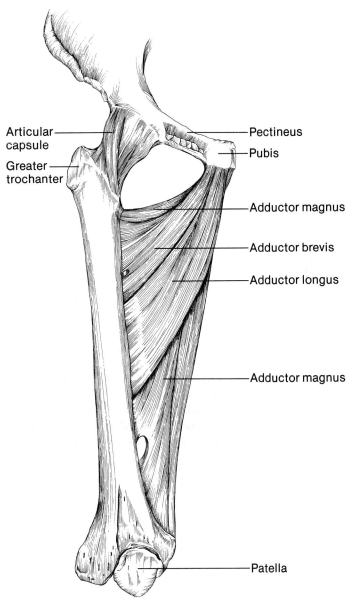

Articular capsule

Greater trochanter

Pectineus

Pubis

Adductor magnus

Adductor brevis

Adductor longus

Adductor magnus

Patella

continuing down the length of the linea aspera. The Gracilis inserts into the tibial shaft beneath the head. Thus the origin of all five muscles is both superior and anterior to their insertion, and all five lie on a plane anterior to the hip joint. Contraction of these muscles, therefore, results in thigh adduction as well as flexion. Because their insertion lies on the back of the femoral shaft, they also assist in medial rotation (Fig. 11.23).

c. Muscles on the back of the thigh, the flexors. Collectively called the hamstrings, the three muscles in this group include the Biceps femoris, Semimembranosus, and Semitendinosus. All three have their origin on the ischial tuberosity, and each inserts into a different area behind and below the knee joint. They flex the lower leg during walking and running in the following manner. When initiating a step, the hamstrings contract and momentarily assume the weight of the calf. This is followed immediately by hip flexion and hamstring relaxation, the latter allowing extension at the knee joint in the advancing limb. The hamstrings also assist in other movements. After flexion of the calf, the Biceps femoris is capable of lateral rotation, and the Semimembranosus and Semitendinosus are medial rotators.

Like the muscles discussed above, those of the human calf and foot are designed for bipedal locomotion. However, there are only a few skeletal remains of the tibia, fibula, and foot bones of early bipedal hominids. Hence descriptions of the musculature of these structures is not mandatory for the chapter that follows. Let it suffice to state that dorsiflexion, the movement whereby the angle between the tibia and the ends of the toes is decreased, is accomplished by five muscles on the lateral side of the tibia. The opposite movement, plantarflexion, is brought about by muscles located mostly on the back of the calf. Some of these muscles also take part in inversion (turning the sole inward) and eversion (turning the sole outward) of the foot.

Summary

Evolutionary interpretations of the fossil remains of early hominids, especially those pertaining to subjects such as diet, encephalization, and locomotion, rely upon a fundamental knowledge of skeletal and muscular anatomy. As indicated by their primary functions, these two anatomical systems are intricately interrelated. In addition to its function as a site for red blood cell production and reservoir for certain minerals and salts, the skeletal system protects the vital organs of the body. It provides the body with necessary rigidity. And it serves as a complex structure to which muscles are attached. Bones also serve as levers, which, in combination with their attached muscles, form pulley systems for the production of movement.

The attachment sites of muscles on bone correspond to various kinds of markings (e.g., tuberosities, ridges, crests, and lines) on bony surfaces, which, in turn, differ according to strength of muscle attachments and specific kinds of muscle action. Knowledge of these factors in living individuals, in combination with information about the range in size and shape of musculoskeletal structures, allows inferences to be drawn about similar functions in early hominids. Occasionally, such inferences are based upon relatively small fragments of fossilized bone.

Information about early diets is obviously based upon bones and muscles of the skull, primarily those of the face and lower jaw and the enclosed teeth. Of particular importance in the maxillae is the evolutionary development of a system of bilateral buttresses that transmit through other cranial bones the enormous pressure experienced during chewing and biting. The muscles involved in chewing movements also occur bilaterally, and they include the Temporoparietalis, Masseter, and Medial and Lateral pterygoids. Of these four pairs, the first three draw the mandible upward for biting, and the latter pair produce side-to-side chewing movements.

Relative degrees of encephalization in early hominids involve analysis of both cranial capacity and morphological details of the bones forming the skull vault. These include the paired parietals and temporals, in addition to the frontal, occipital, and other bones of the cranial base. The relative position of the foramen magnum, the large opening at the base of the skull through which the spinal cord passes, has been studied in great detail with respect to the early acquisition of erect bipedalism.

Erect bipedalism and the extraordinarily mobile upper limb typical of the human species depend upon the uniquely human musculoskeletal arrangement in the back, pectoral girdle, pelvic girdle, and lower limb. In particular, two groups of powerful back muscles (the Transversospinalis and the Erector spinae) serve to maintain trunk balance during bipedal locomotion, and the bones of the pectoral girdle (the clavicle and the scapula) are arranged in such a manner as to maximize free suspension and range of movement of the arm.

This mobility arises as a consequence of two groups of muscles: one set that passes from the axial skeleton to the pectoral girdle, and the other set that extends from the pectoral girdle to the humerus. In the pelvic girdle, likewise, the ball-and-socket joint formed by the head of the femur and the acetabulum allows flexion, extension, abduction, adduction, and medial and lateral rotation. These movements are necessary for bipedal locomotion, as is the unique system of arches in the foot that serve to efficiently distribute total body weight. The most massive muscles of the lower limb are for locomotion, and occur in front and behind the hip joint, and on the front, back, and side of the thigh. They also provide stability and balance to the rest of the body when it is in the erect position.

12 The Earliest Primates

Introduction

Knowledge about the biological relationships among different primate taxa is gained primarily from the combined information from studies in comparative anatomy and paleontology. While the former field of study offers indirect evidence from which evolutionary relationships may be inferred, the latter provides direct evidence for either nullifying or strengthening such inferences. Hence the final solution of any phylogenetic sequence, particularly with respect to closely intermediate evolutionary stages, will ultimately depend upon adequacy of the fossil record.

It will become quite obvious in this and succeeding chapters that the fossil record is not and will probably never be so complete as to regard the evolutionary history of any primate species a closed book. Thus, while we may be unable to trace the precise evolutionary line of a certain species or genus, sufficient remains have been recovered for the formulation of reasonable hypotheses about the general evolutionary stages of major primate taxa. On this point, Le Gros Clark's comment of 20 years ago is still pertinent:

> So far as the evolution of the Primates is concerned, it is still necessary to rely to a large extent on hypotheses based on an inadequate fossil record, particularly in discussions on the origin and differentiation of some of the earlier representatives of the order. But hypotheses are not to be disparaged because they are hypotheses; on the contrary, they are quite necessary preliminaries in the pursuit of any scientific inquiry, for only by the construction of hypotheses is the opportunity given of putting them to the test by further observation and discovery. (1959:3)

Theories on the Origin of Primate Characteristics

Several attempts have been made to embody primate characteristics into a comprehensive theory capable of explaining the functional significance of the evolutionary features outlined in Chapter 9. Two of these theories are briefly discussed below. The first, which has been widely accepted until recent times, is generally called the arboreal theory. It was formulated over 50 years ago by G. E. Smith (1924) and F. Wood Jones (1916), and contributed to by E. T. Collins (1921). The second is the visual predation theory, developed and proposed by Cartmill (1970, 1972) in response to that which he deemed inadequate in the arboreal theory.

The Arboreal Theory

This theory assumes that Mesozoic primate ancestors were themselves either partly or completely arboreal and possessed a variety of features necessary for a successful existence in trees. It also presumes that the earliest primates were arboreal, that this habitat was relatively unexploited, and that natural selection continuously maintained and refined those traits associated functionally with arboreal life. Under such assumptions, it is relatively easy to postulate the functional significance of some of the characteristics within the order Primates. In no particular order, these postulates are—

1. There would be readily apparent advantages for a tree-dwelling animal to possess elaborate visual and tactile receptors and a highly developed eye-hand coordination. Any arboreal environment may be considered a multidimensional matrix in which depth perception and the sense of touch are critical not only for agile movement but also for an animal's survival. Thus the selective advantage for sure footing and keen visual abilities led to a corresponding elaboration and enlargement of the associated centers in the brain.

2. Smith felt that the sense of smell had relatively little importance for arboreal primates, and this reduced function led to olfactory degeneration. This suggestion, incidentally, represents a point of contention in the theory. Evolutionary biologists have known for many decades that loss of function of a species characteristic does not result automatically in disappearance or reduction of the characteristic. The basic idea that disuse leads to atrophy was one part of a broad theory of evolution formulated over 150 years ago by Lamarck, and it has long since been abandoned (see, for example, Simpson 1964, and Gillispie 1959, for additional information on Lamarckian and Neo-Lamarckian thought).

3. Animals that live in trees must be able to climb, and natural selection favored animals whose forelimbs were capable of efficient grasping. Simultaneously, a selective premium existed for hindlimbs that could both propel and support the body. Among terrestrial quadrupeds, propulsion and support are functions assumed by both the fore- and hindlimbs, and the snout is used for biting, grasping, etc. In Jones's view, the assumption by the forelimbs of grasping functions previously undertaken by the snout resulted in a gradual recession of the latter structure. Furthermore, this indirect reduction in the length of the facial skeleton resulted in more closely set orbits.

4. Orbital convergence was seen by Collins (and most authorities today), however, not as an indirect result of shortening of the snout. Rather, it arose as a consequence of selection for visual overlap. We saw in Chapter 9 that visual overlap is necessary for stereoscopic vision and hence depth perception, and such spatial judgment is obviously vital to animals that leap from branch to branch.

The Visual Predation Theory

These salient features of the arboreal theory have been criticized most recently by Cartmill (1972), who suggests that the evolutionary trends in Primates have resulted from rather different selective pressures. His displeasure with the theory centers around two key elements. The first is whether two different lineages, such as primates and tree squirrels, can stem from a common arboreal ancestor, remain arboreal, and yet develop drastic structural differences while adapting to a similar environment. The second is the question of whether mammals ancestral to the earliest primates were arboreal or terrestrial.

Arboreal squirrels and primates are considerably different in those characteristics presumably associated functionally with life in the trees. In contrast to primates, tree squirrels have no opposable first digit. They have claws instead of tactile pads and nails. They have a well-developed sense of smell and a prominent snout, and they have displayed little, if any, evolutionary tendency toward orbital convergence and visual overlap.

Since squirrels and primates are both mammals, it is reasonable to assume that they shared a common ancestor at an earlier time. One might thus expect that one of these lineages would be more reminiscent of the ancestor than the other, and, further, that one lineage would have had to adapt differently to similar conditions than the other. Jones considered this problem and suggested that ancestral mammals were already arboreal and possessed some primate characteristics. Whereas some of these mammals gave rise to the first primates, which retained the traits, other mammalian orders returned to the ground and adapted structurally to terrestrial life. At a later time, a few of these terrestrial orders returned to the trees and underwent a secondary adaptive change to arboreal life. However, they retained some of the essential features of terrestrial quadrupeds. Thus the tree squirrel has claws, a highly efficient olfactory apparatus, etc., but it exhibits none of the characteristic primate trends.

Cartmill refutes this argument of arborealism to terrestrial quadrupedalism to arborealism:

> Squirrels retain pentadactyl hands and feet, functional clavicles, and unfused long bones in the forearm and leg. They appear to have the morphological potential for developing grasping hands and feet like those of primates; they have simply not done so. If arboreal life favors these adaptations, there is no reason why they could not have appeared among the sciurids. (1972:107)

Now, squirrels do indeed possess such physical traits, but the argument as presented is weakened by the concept of "morphological potential." The term itself is far too vague to have much meaning—perhaps any quadrupedal primate has the "morphological potential" to become an erect biped like *Homo,* but simply has not done so. Squirrels might never have had genes or gene complexes in any way comparable to those of primates, specifically the genetic material involved in arboreal traits in the latter.

However, Cartmill does point out two elements of the arboreal theory that are open to serious question. The first is that there exists no fossil evidence supporting the hypothesis that mammals ancestral to primates were arboreal. As a matter of fact, pre-Eocene fossils that have been recovered display claws instead of nails and, by implication, padded digits. Coupled with the observation that Eocene lemuroids had primatelike digits, this offers support to the suggestion that mammalian primate ancestors were terrestrial. The second is a lack of direct evidence indicating a causal association between arborealism and olfactory degeneration. To the contrary, the olfactory apparatus is well-developed in many arboreal mammals but reduced in some predatory arboreal marsupials. And for over 70 million years, some arboreal marsupials have been successful in their environment without undergoing any remarkable diminution in the sense of smell.

Cartmill considers these problems answered by the visual predation-theory. In this explanation, the characteristics of Primates were initially established in a small animal that utilized highly developed visual skills to prey upon insects located at the ends of branches in a tropical rain forest. The main aspects of the theory may be summarized by briefly describing the adaptive significance of grasping hands and feed, orbital convergence and olfactory degeneration, and clawless digits.

Many insects and other invertebrates feed upon new leaves, fruits, and nuts that appear primarily on terminal branches. The heavy concentration of small organisms in these areas therefore constitutes a readily available food supply for any insectivorous animal capable of its utilization. Ask yourself the question: What sorts of characteristics would be particularly advantageous to an animal foraging in such an environment? First, body weight must be light enough so that it is not overly hazardous to move about on slender branches. Second, grasping hands and feet provide advantages related to locomotion, safety, and feeding. For relatively slow and cautious movement among twigs and terminal branches, grasping feet allow an animal to securely grip one branch while reaching in any direction for another. Should the supporting branch break, the animal can pull itself to safety by the forelimbs. Furthermore, the body can be supported by the hindlimbs during feeding, thus freeing the forelimbs to obtain food. Third, the replacement of claws with nails and padded digits may be related to locomotor efficiency. As judged from observations on other arboreal mammals, those with claws are far more proficient on large branches and tree trunks than on slender branches. Modern primates such as *Microcebus* and *Loris* (but not the vertical clingers and leapers), on the other hand, are less adept on broad structures than they are on slender ones.

Fourth, orbital convergence is necessary for stereoscopic vision, but this may not have arisen by selection for arboreal locomotion. Cartmill (1972) indicates convincingly that there is no significant correlation between arboreality and orbital convergence among arboreal and terrestrial genera within several mammalian groups. For example, terrestrial squirrels actually have a greater degree of orbital convergence than their tree-dwelling counterparts, yet the latter are superbly efficient arboreal acrobats. Thus he suggests that the increase in visual overlap and stereoptic integration were adaptations for feeding rather than for leaping from branch to branch, a suggestion that seems quite warranted in light of the modern data. Insects are both quick and evasive, and a selective premium would exist for the visual acuity to compensate for prey movement and to accurately strike the prey.

Finally, many arboreal mammals have undergone no apparent olfactory degeneration. This observation, coupled with recent demonstrations of the fundamental importance of olfactory signals in several prosimians, some ceboids, and a few Old World anthropoids, contradicts the view of olfaction given in the arboreal theory. Reduction in the sense of smell, observed mainly in tarsiers and anthropoids, is more aptly explained, therefore, as an incidental by-product of orbital convergence. Stated simply, movement of the orbits toward the midline has significantly reduced the space necessary for a highly developed olfactory apparatus.

The Dating of Fossil Remains

As with any theory, neither of these two theories can be proven or disproven beyond doubt. Indeed, Cartmill's theory appears to have more explanatory power. As such, it can receive more thorough validation, and thus better confirmation, through the recovery and analysis of relevant fossil remains. Since fossils lend themselves to evolutionary interpretations only when reasonably dated, a great deal of effort has been expended toward the development of reliable dating methods. Some of these methods have subsequently led to the establishment of a chronological frame of reference into which dated fossils may be placed.

Dating methods fall into two general classes. The first is usually called **relative dating,** which describes the chronological position of a fossil as compared to another fossil or event. To state that fossil A is older or younger than fossil B provides neither direct information on the actual age of fossil A, nor information as to how much younger or older it is. This sort of information is provided by the second class, which is called absolute dating, or to use Oakley's (1964) term, **chronometric dating.** A chronometric date of fossil A might be 10,000 B.P., which states the number of elapsed years from some common point of reference (in this case, "before the present"). Relative dating may be of utmost value to archeology, as claimed by Hole and Heizer (1969), but each class of dating is extremely important for fossil studies. Chronometric dates are necessary for the establishment of an overall chronological framework, as well as for the determination of evolutionary rates. The primary value of relative dating, on the other hand, is that fossils can be placed in their proper sequence relative to each other.

Relative Dating

Most relative dates ultimately depend upon the stratigraphic position of the fossil. Stratigraphy proper is the study of the spatial and temporal relationships of layered deposits in the earth's crust (Dunbar and Rodgers 1957), and at its fundamental base is the fact that deeper deposits are older than those above them. It follows that the lower of two fossils found at different stratigraphic levels in an undisturbed site is, to some extent, older than the other. If the age of the stratigraphic levels is unknown, then all that can be determined is the temporal relationship between the two fossils. Nothing can be said about the actual age of the two fossils or about the difference in age between them because deposits are generally laid down at different rates. It may take thousands of years of continual occupation of a site, for example, to leave a deposit of the same thickness as that which may result in a few days from a volcanic eruption or flood.

Another way of obtaining a relative date is by cross-dating. Cross-dating involves comparing artifacts (potsherds, projectile points, etc.), artifact assemblages, or key fossils from one site to those of known age from another site. There are two implicit assumptions behind this procedure. The first is that material items in any culture persist for only a limited amount of time before being changed or replaced. The second hinges on the first: similarity in artifact form or design indicates a certain measure of chronological contemporaneity. Yet a third kind of relative dating involves the comparison of fossil remains from one stratum to other fossils found in the same stratum. Several analytical methods are available for such comparisons, notably those that determine the relative content of fluorine, nitrogen, and uranium in the fossils.

The fossilization of bones and teeth through time is primarily a result of the deposition of minerals, such as lime and silicates, into the porous part of bone. However, the mineral part of bone, occurring in a hydroxyapatite form, also undergoes change. Such an alteration does not involve mineral replacement, but, rather, a chemical change in the hydroxyapatite. The small quantities of fluorine existing in ground water occur as soluble fluorides that are progressively absorbed by hydroxyapatite crystals. These crystals undergo a chemical change that results in a far more stable compound called fluorapatite, thus "locking" the fluorine atoms within the bone. Assuming that bones from the same stratigraphic level will acquire approximately the same amount of fluorine, this content can then be determined by a chemical test or by X-ray crystallography. Theoretically, older bones that might have been washed into the formation from a different locality and/or younger bones that might have been intentionally buried would show different fluorine levels. Thus one fossil can be dated relative to another—the more the fluorine, the older the fossil.

In contrast to progressive fluorine accumulation, the organic part of bone undergoes a progressive loss of nitrogen. The organic matrix of bone is made up mostly of collagen, an extemely stable protein that degrades very slowly through time. For example, Towe and Urbanek (1972) have found structures resembling collagen from floating marine organisms (graptolites) that existed approximately 450 million years ago during the Ordovician period. Likewise, Akiyama and Wyckoff (1970) have determined the amino acid composition of collagen from fossils from the Jurassic period (about 150 million years ago), and others (Matter and Miller 1972; Ho 1967; Wyckoff et al. 1964) have studied amino acid compositions of vertebrate and invertebrate collagens from the Cretaceous period and Pleistocene epoch. The degradation of collagen is concomitant with a loss of nitrogen, and, as with fluorine dating, chemical tests are used to determine nitrogen content.

Like fluorine, traces of uranium occur in ground water, and in a roughly similar fashion, they become progressively absorbed into bone mineral. Relative dates can sometimes be obtained by measuring the amount of radioactive decay, a constant and regular process during which uranium eventually converts into lead. The straightforward nature of relative dating by fluorine, nitrogen, and uranium analysis is quite appealing and, when used in combination, can assist in determining the relative chronological sequence of several fossils from the same stratum. However, their unlimited use is restricted because of several serious drawbacks.

For example, because bones and teeth apparently absorb fluorine at different rates, misinterpretations can occur in dating the remains of a single individual. Furthermore, fluorine absorption is directly dependent upon the amount of soluble fluorides in ground water. Since there is considerable geographic variation in natural fluoride levels, comparisons of fossils from different areas for the purpose of cross-dating are, at best, impractical (see, for example, McConnell 1962, for a criticism of the fluorine method). Similarly, the rate of nitrogen loss probably varies from site to site; therefore the effect of extraneous conditions such as temperature, humidity, and soil acidity or alkalinity on the rate of chemical degradation of collagen is poorly understood.

Chronometric Dating

Paleoanthropologists nearly always ask two fundamental questions about a newly recovered fossil: (1) Has it been accurately dated? and (2) How old is it? Depending upon the antiquity of the specimen, a number of chronometric techniques can be used to answer the second question. Most of these methods, such as tree-ring dating (**dendrochronology**), artifact-sequence dating, and measurement of the thermoluminescent glow of prehistoric potsherds, are appropriate only for highly restricted time periods in the not-too-distant past. Thus they are very useful to archeologists but not to the biological anthropologist, who often deals with much older specimens without any evidence of material culture.

The most useful methods for determining the ages of both minerals and organic matter are based upon the regular disintegration of radioactive isotopes of certain elements, such as uranium 238 (U^{238}) and 235 (U^{235}), rubidium 87 (Rb^{87}), potassium 40 (K^{40}), and carbon 14 (C^{14}). The decay of such isotopes is accompanied by measurable amounts of alpha, beta, and gamma radiation, and the eventual decay product of each is an isotope of a different element. For example, U^{235} transmutes to lead 207 (Pb^{207}), Rb^{87} to strontium 87 (Sr^{87}), K^{40} to argon 40 (Ar^{40}), and C^{14} to nitrogen 14 (N^{14}) The times involved in the natural decay of elemental isotopes vary enormously—from billionths of a second in some to billions of years in others. However, each isotope has its own characteristic disintegration rate, and these rates are not known to be affected by environmental conditions.

A major factor leading to the utilization of radioactive elements for dating purposes was the discovery of the half-life of several isotopes. These are given in Table 12.1. The half-life of an isotope is the amount of time required for half of its atoms to decay, and this term is normally used to express the disintegration rate. Thus one-half of K^{40}, for example, will transform into Ar^{40} in 1.33 billion years; half of that which remains will similarly change into Ar^{40} in another 1.33 billion years, and so forth. This information, along with modern equipment to measure the ratio of Ar^{40} to K^{40}, allows calculation of the age of the mineral in which fossil specimens are found. Analyses of different radioactive isotopes in various minerals according to this basic principle have led to the construction of the geologic time-scale presented in Table 12.2.

It can be seen in Table 12.1 that isotopes of uranium, rubidium, and potassium have exceedingly long half-lives, while that of C^{14} is comparatively very short. Note also that effective dating with isotopes of uranium and rubidium begins on material at least 10 million years old, and with K^{40}, on material at least 100,000 years of age. These three methods are applicable only to the dating of minerals; hence dates on fossils derived by these means are actually inferences based on association between the fossils and the deposits in which they are discovered. However, the dating of more

Table 12.1 The Major Radioactive Isotopes Used for Dating, Their Decay Products, Half-Lives, and Effective Dating Ranges

Parent Isotope	Decay Product	Half-Life (Years)	Effective Dating Range (Years)
U^{238*}	Pb^{206}	4.5×10^9	$10^7 - 4.6 \times 10^{9**}$
U^{235}	Pb^{207}	0.71×10^9	$10^7 - 4.6 \times 10^9$
Rb^{87}	Sr^{87}	4.7×10^{10}	$10^7 - 4.6 \times 10^9$
K^{40}	Ar^{40}	1.33×10^9	$10^5 - 4.6 \times 10^9$
C^{14}	N^{14}	5,730	0–50,000

*These symbols refer respectively to the elements Uranium (U), Lead (Pb), Rubidium (Rb), Strontium (Sr), Potassium (K), Argon (Ar), Carbon (C), and Nitrogen (N).
**The date 4.7×10^9 is currently thought to represent the age of the earth.

recent material by the C^{14} method is carried out directly on organic remains, such as wood, charcoal, bone, shell, etc. Since this technique has literally revolutionized our knowledge of prehistory, it merits brief but special attention.

The underlying principle of C^{14} dating may be phrased as follows. The small but continuous bombardment of atmospheric nitrogen by natural radiation converts a nitrogen proton into a neutron. This results in the C^{14} isotope, which in combination with oxygen forms $C^{14}O_2$, a special form of carbon dioxide that is assimilated (along with ordinary C^{12}) by all living organisms during the normal

Table 12.2 The Geological Timetable (From Lawrence S. Dillon, *Evolution,* 2nd ed. St. Louis, 1978, The C. V. Mosby Co.)

Eras	Periods	Epochs	Years Since Beginning (Millions)	Important Radio-isotopic Dates (Millions)	Method	Source
Cenozoic	Quaternary	Recent	0.025			
		Pleistocene	2	2.0	K-Ar	Biotite, Olduvai Gorge
	Tertiary	Pliocene	13	12 ± 0.5	K-Ar	Biotite, Nevada
		Miocene	25	25 ± 1	K-Ar	Glauconite, Austria
		Oligocene	36	33.1 ± 1	K-Ar	Biotite, Texas
		Eocene	58	55 ± 6	Rb-Sr	Glauconite, New Jersey
		Paleocene	63	59 ± 2	U^{238}-Pb^{206}	Pitchblende, Colorado
Mesozoic	Cretaceous		135	134 ± 4	K-Ar	Glauconite, Germany
	Jurassic		181	180 ± 5	K-Ar	Biotite, Indonesia
	Triassic		230	195 ± 5	K-Ar	Biotite, New Jersey
Paleozoic	Permian		280	280 ± 5	Rb-Sr	Biotite, England
	Pennsylvanian		310	315 ± 5	K-Ar	Biotite, France
	Mississippian		345	344 ± 10	Rb-Sr	Biotite, England
	Devonian		405	395 ± 5	Rb-Sr	Biotite, England
	Silurian		425	410 ± 15	K-Ar	Glauconite, Ohio
	Ordovician		500	490 ± 10	Rb-Sr	Biotite, Nova Scotia
	Cambrian		600	610 ± 61	K-Ar	Glauconite, U.S.S.R.
Archean (Oldest Life)			3,100	3,100		Cherts, South Africa
Age of Earth			4,700	4,750 ± 50	U^{238}-Pb^{206}	Galena, Ontario

oxygen-exchange process. As long as a plant or animal is alive, it continues to absorb at a constant rate both radioactive C^{14} and nonradioactive C^{12}. When the organism dies, no additional carbon atoms are assimilated and C^{14} immediately begins to decay. Beta particles are emitted during this disintegration process. The age of a specimen, therefore, can be determined by counting the number of beta radiations per minute (cpm) per gram of the substance in question. Since it has been established that new C^{14} emits about 15 cpm/g and that C^{14} has a half-life of 5,730 years, a sample that emits about 7.5 cpm/g is expected to be about 5,700 years old. Likewise, a specimen emitting about 3.7 cpm/g is expected to be about 10,500 years old, and so forth. By measuring the amount of C^{14} still existing in organic remains, then, the time of death of the organism can be ascertained.

Only a minimal survey of dating methods has been presented here. Virtually no attention has been given to the limitations and inherent problems of the various techniques. These and other special situations have been discussed in several articles in books edited by Brothwell and Higgs (1970), Michael and Ralph (1971), and Bishop and Miller (1972), and in a recent synthesis of dating methods by Michels (1972).

The foregoing considerations on the origin of primate characteristics and the geologic time scale have been given as preparation for examining the direct evidence of primate evolution—the fossil record. More often than not, the preservation and subsequent recovery of fossil material is strongly dependent upon time—the older the remains, the more fragmentary and scarce they are. Thus in many instances, especially those representing the earliest primate fossils, broad inferences are often made on the basis of exceedingly small and fragmented specimens. At times the specimen is only a small part of a single individual, such as a mandibular fragment or a few teeth.

Those of you who have read the first few pages of Appendix I will correctly conclude that a single specimen cannot, by its very nature, have any of the characteristics of a good sample. It cannot be free of bias, adequate, or homogeneous, and is therefore not amenable to statistical treatment. Yet, very often, all that is found is a fragment of bone, a tooth, or part of a skull. This is the bane of paleontology. The phylogenetic meaning of such meager evidence can be extracted only through carefully reasoned and objective study by those with a thorough knowledge of all relevant factors. These include date of the specimen, associated flora and fauna, and morphological characteristics of other fossils to which it might be evolutionarily related.

Primate Radiation in the Paleocene

Quite often, a new fossil provides data that can lead only to tentative conclusions. Such appears to be the case with *Purgatorius* (Van Valen and Sloan 1965), an extinct genus considered by many to represent the earliest known primate. Two species of *Purgatorius* have been named, the earliest of which (*P. ceratops*) is of late Cretaceous age and represented by a single molar. The later form, *P. unio,* dates from the Paleocene and is known from a sample of 50 isolated teeth. Both were discovered in Cretaceous and Paleocene sediments, respectively, in western North America

Table 12.3 A Classification of the Earliest Known Primates. The Age and Geographic Distribution of Each Genus Are Given in Parentheses.

Suborder Prosimii
  Infraorder Plesiadapiformes
    Superfamily Plesiadapoidea
      Family Plesiadapidae
        Genus *Pronothodectes* (Paleocene; North America)
            Plesiadapis (Paleocene-Eocene; Europe and North America)
            Chiromyoides (Paleocene; Europe)
            Platychaerops (Eocene; Europe)
            Saxonella (Paleocene; Europe)
      Family Carpolestidae
        Genus *Carpolestes* (Paleocene; North America)
            Carpodaptes (Paleocene; North America)
            Elphidotarsius (Paleocene; North America)
      Family Paromomyidae
        Genus *Paromomys* (Paleocene; North America)
            Palaechthon (Paleocene; North America)
            Palenochtha (Paleocene; North America)
            Plesiolestes (Paleocene; North America)
            Purgatorius (Cretaceous-Paleocene; North America)
            Phenacolemur (Paleocene-Eocene; North America)
      Family Picrodontidae
        Genus *Picrodus* (Paleocene; North America)
            Zanycteris (Paleocene; North America)

(Montana). Much speculation has appeared about the evolutionary status of *Purgatorius,* the shift from a Cretaceous insectivore to a primitive primate with a frugivorous diet and primate origins (e.g., Szalay 1968, 1972; Cartmill 1975). However, the evidence is simply insufficient at the present time to assess this animal's phylogenetic relationships to other primates.

It seems widely accepted, on the other hand, that *Purgatorius* and five additional Paleocene and Paleocene-to-Eocene genera belonged to the family Paromomyidae. Paromomyidae, in turn, represents one of four families within the superfamily Plesiadapoidea. A classification of these early primates is given in Table 12.3. Note in this table that the known geographic distribution of Paleocene primates is restricted to western Europe and North America. The existence of at least one genus (*Plesiadapis*) in both areas indicates the possibility that the two continents were connected by land. Furthermore, since primates are naturally successful in warm climates, it is not unreasonable to assume that the Paleocene climate during which these animals lived was warm, if not tropical.

There is no dearth of Paleocene primate fossils, but the majority of existing material is highly fragmentary and consists of isolated teeth and a few small postcranial fragments. Nevertheless, the number of identified specimens, in addition to the wide geographic distribution, points strongly to the conclusion that these primates were a well-established and morphologically diversified mammalian group. Whatever their ancestral group, it is almost certain that the evolutionary transition from mammalian insectivore to primate occurred sometime before the end of the Cretaceous.

Unfortunately, very little is known about the entire skeletal structure of Paleocene forms. Hence inferences about locomotion and diet must be viewed with considerable caution. However, some strong inferences have been drawn from the remains of species of *Plesiadapis,* the most widespread (and, by implication, the most successful) and best preserved of any Paleocene genera. It has been suggested (Wood 1962) that *Plesiadapis* was in Rodentia ancestry, but dental characteristics and anatomical details of the skull in the ear region offer persuasive arguments for its primate status. An almost complete skull (Fig. 12.1) and a relatively large portion of the postcranial skeleton have been found in northern France (Russell 1964), and additional remains of a smaller species of the same genus were recovered in Colorado. Based upon both discoveries, a reconstruction of the full skeleton may be seen in Figure 12.2.

Although inferences from *Plesiadapis* cannot be applied "across-the-board" to its contemporaneous genera, a number of characteristics are especially informative as to the evolutionary grade of Paleocene primates. Some of these features are—

1. The size of different species was variable, from that of a large rat to a small cat.

2. There was no **postorbital bar.** This is a bony ring occurring on the lateral side of each orbit, which, in later forms such as the Eocene *Adapis,* offered lateral protection for the eye.

3. The orbits have undergone no forward rotation and lie on the lateral sides of the skull.

4. Compared to later forms, the braincase is very small. In addition, the facial skeleton (particularly the snout) is large relative to the braincase. As evident from the snout, the olfactory apparatus was highly developed.

5. Simons (1972) suggests that the locomotor pattern may have been "preadaptive" to the vertical clinging and leaping or springing modes observed in later forms, because the forelimb was apparently capable of extreme flexion. However, the presence of claws instead of flat nails and, presumably, padded digits, suggests that this animal was, instead, some form of arboreal quadruped.

6. The enlarged, rodent-like incisors, along with the almost rudimentary canines, suggest specialized functions for the former and less importance for the latter. This and related evidence has led Szalay (1972) and others to the conclusion that Plesiadapis (and other Paleocene genera with canine reduction and incisor specialization) was primarily an herbivore-frugivore and, if nothing else, less insectivorous than other Cretaceous insectivores.

Important insights into the evolutionary grade of Paleocene primates have been gained from these fossil remains, and it would be intuitively satisfying to state confidently that the plesiadapids were directly ancestral to Eocene primates. Unfortunately, such a statement cannot be made. To the contrary, their peculiar specializations and the absence of distinctive primate trends indicate just the opposite. They could not have been in a direct evolutionary line to later primates but, rather, became extinct during the Eocene. It is an intriguing, although undemonstrable,

Figure 12.1 Superior view of the skull of *Plesiadapis,* a geographically widespread Paleocene primate. (Reprinted with permission of Macmillan Publishing Co., Inc., from E. L. Simons, *Primate Evolution.* Copyright © 1972 by Elwyn L. Simons.)

Figure 12.2 A reconstruction of the skeleton of *Plesiadapis.* (Reprinted with permission of Macmillan Publishing Co., Inc., from E. L. Simons, *Primate Evolution.* Copyright © 1972 by Elwyn L. Simons.)

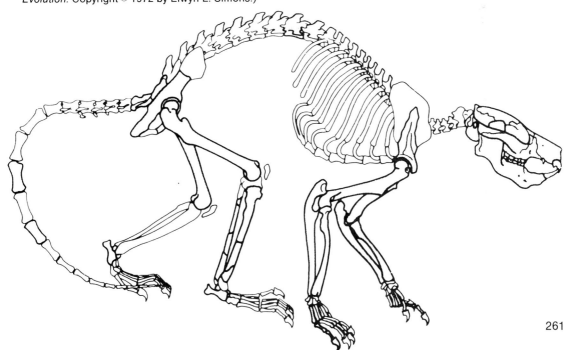

proposition that they were unable to compete for similar resources with the true rodents, which were undergoing their own rapid radiation at the same time.

Eocene Prosimians

Some authorities are still hesitant about assigning various Paleocene fossils to Primates (e.g., Picrodontidae), but such reservations are almost nonexistent for Eocene forms. Simons (1972) calls them the "first primates of modern aspect," Buettner-Janusch (1973) states flatly that "they are primates," and most, if not all, primate paleontologists agree. For reasons discussed in Chapter 8, however, there is less consensus of opinion on their classification. Thus the hierarchy given in Table 12.4 is subject to revision upon the discovery of new evidence and reinterpretation of existing material.

That there was an explosive radiation of prosimians during the Eocene is evident from the generic diversity indicated in Table 12.4. Note that at least 32 genera within 3 families (Adapidae, Tarsiidae, and Anaptomorphidae) have been formally classified. In addition, there are four other genera whose taxonomic placement is still uncertain. Two of these (*Hoanghonius* and *Lushius*) probably belong to the Anaptomorphidae, and the other two (*Amphipithecus* and *Pondaungia*) are frequently assigned to the superfamily Hominoidea (although this placement is uncertain).

One of the clearest indications that Paleocene primates were not ancestral to Eocene forms is that a few representatives of the former existed simultaneously with the latter, and the two were very different. The evolutionary characteristics of modern primates seem to have occurred rather suddenly among Eocene primates, but there is a complete absence of fossil evidence that would illuminate the earlier origin and development of such features. In general, and compared to Paleocene forms, Eocene primates had larger brains (a factor which was probably associated with the shift in the location of the foramen magnum more toward the anterior part of the base of the skull); the snout was shorter; the orbits were encircled by a bony rim; their incisors were small and unspecialized; they had nails instead of claws; their forelimbs had longer and freely mobile digits; their hindlimbs were longer; and their hallux was both greatly elongated and highly mobile.

These basic features lead to a multifaceted portrait of Eocene prosimians. They were clearly arboreal (some of them were vertical clingers and leapers, and others quadrupeds) and had an increasingly strong reliance upon visual skills. Their incisors indicate a diet consisting mostly of vegetable matter, and their limb structure suggests that the hands were at least capable of object manipulation. Their increased brain size, although still very small and primitive compared to modern prosimians, indicates the occurrence of a certain degree of encephalization. The elaboration and complexity of their brains, of course, cannot be precisely determined. However, it is tempting to think that bigger brains, in addition to the other characteristics given above, signify "the adoption of a distinctive primate survival strategy . . . based upon the fine coordination of sharp wits, keen eyes, and skillful manipulatory hands, and also the slow, careful rearing of the young, one or two at a time" (Jolly and Plog 1976:119).

Table 12.4   A Classification of Eocene Prosimians (After Simons 1972.)

Suborder Prosimii
   Infraorder Lemuriformes
      Superfamily Adapoidea
         Family Adapidae
            Subfamily Adapinae
               Genus *Adapis*
                     Pronycticebus
                     Protoadapis
                     Periconodon
                     Anchomomys
                     Caenopithecus
                     Lantianius
                     Agerina
            Subfamily Notharctinae
               Genus *Notharctus*
                     Pelycodus
                     Smilodectes
   Infraorder Tarsiiformes
      Superfamily Tarsiioidea
         Family Tarsiidae
            Subfamily Microchoerinae
               Genus *Nannopithex*
                     Necrolemur
                     Microchoerus
                     Pseudoloris
         Family Anaptomorphidae
            Subfamily Anaptomorphinae
               Genus *Absarokius*
                     Tetonius
                     Tetonoides
                     Uintalacus
                     Anemorhysis
                     Trogolemur
                     Anaptomorphus
                     Uintanius
            Subfamily Omomyinae
               Genus *Omomys*
                     Loveina
                     Hemiacodon
                     Washakius
                     Shoshonius
                     Teilhardina
                     Utahia
                     Stockia
                     Ourayia
                     Rooneyia

It should be stressed that these are only general features of a basic Eocene prosimian plan and that there is considerable diversity both within and between the three families given in Table 12.4. The anatomical characteristics of certain genera that reflect this diversity have been examined thoroughly by Stehlin (1916), Gregory (1920), and Gazin (1958), and the taxonomic meaning of these differences has been assessed recently by Simons (1961, 1963, 1972). A brief summary of some of the more important features in each family appears below.

The Adapidae

Two North American genera (*Notharctus* and *Smilodectes*) and one European genus (*Adapis*) have provided the most information about this family. The general cranial and postcranial skeletal anatomy of all three genera (Fig. 12.3) is reminiscent of modern Malagasy lemurs, although *Smilodectes* and *Notharctus* can safely be excluded from direct lemur ancestry. Either *Adapis* or other European adapid genera are more reasonable contenders for this title. Although the question is still entirely open, the recovery of Eocene adapids from Africa would doubtless shed considerable light on this problem.

In any event, these lemurlike primates display notable evolutionary advances over earlier forms such as *Plesiadapis*. *Smilodectes*, in particular, had more convergent orbits, an expanded frontal region of the skull, and elongated hindlimbs relative to the forelimbs. This primate also had fully opposable first digits on the fore- and hindlimbs, and these limbs were heavier and more robust than those in modern

Figure 12.3 Fossil remains of Eocene primates: **a,** a lateral view of the skull of *Notharctus;* **b,** a reconstructed postcranial skeleton of the same genus; **c,** a lateral view of the skull of *Adapis;* and **d,** a lateral view of the skull of *Smilodectes.* (Reprinted with permission of Macmillan Publishing Co., Inc., from E. L. Simons, *Primate Evolution.* Copyright © 1972 by Elwyn L. Simons.)

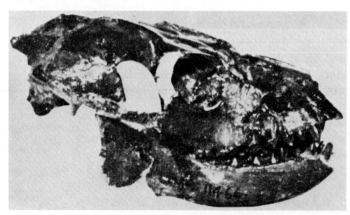

a

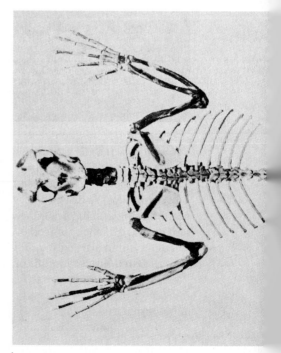

b

Lemur. However, some of the skeletal features that make it tempting to associate *Notharctus* and *Adapis* evolutionarily with the modern Malagasy lemurs include—

1. Structural similarities in the foot, notably the absence of pronounced calcaneal elongation. The calcaneus is the largest bone of the foot and ends posteriorly in the heel. In a slow and cautious climber, such as the slow loris or potto, relatively little leverage is needed, and hence the calcaneus is very abbreviated. It is not as short relative to other foot bones in either *Notharctus* or *Adapis* but, instead, bears a strong resemblance to the calcaneus in modern lemurs such as *Propithecus*. Since the latter is a vertical clinger and leaper, this resemblance and the apparently long and powerful hindlimbs in both Eocene genera suggest that they either practiced vertical clinging and leaping or another similar locomotor mode.

2. A free tympanic ring in the auditory bulla. The auditory, or **petrosal, bulla** is that part of the temporal bone containing the small ossicles and other structures that form the middle ear. One of these structures is called the **tympanic ring** (Fig. 12.4). Stretched across this ring and attached to the walls of the bulla is the tympanic membrane—the eardrum. The relationship between ring and bulla is very important; it not only distinguishes primates from other mammals, but it also differentiates between certain groups of primates. The arrangement observed in *Adapis* and *Notharctus* is like that depicted in Figure 12.4b, which is characteristic of Lemuriformes.

3. Approximately the same degree of snout elongation and orbital frontality.

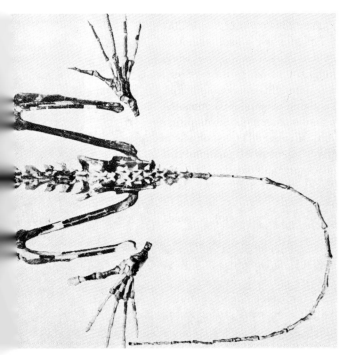

c

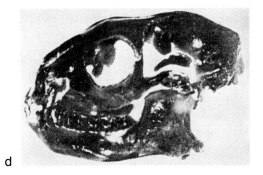

d

Figure 12.4 Schematic drawings of the various relations of the tympanic ring to the tympanic bulla: **a,** primitive mammalian condition, in which the ring is exposed and the floor of the tympanic cavity is unossified; **b,** the lemuriform type, in which the ring is enclosed within an osseous bulla; **c,** the lorisiform and platyrrhine type, in which the ring is placed at the surface and contributes to the formation of the outer wall of the bulla; **d,** the catarrhine type, in which the ring is produced outwards to form a tubular auditory meatus. (Courtesy of Edinburgh University Press, from W. E. Le Gros Clark, *The Antecedents of Man,* 1960.)

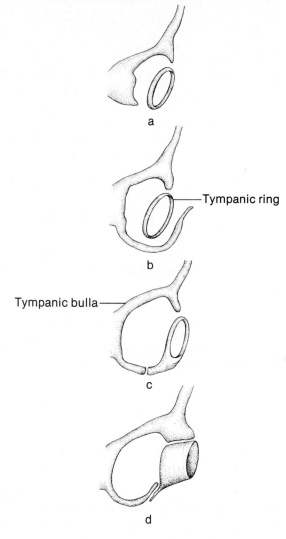

The Tarsiidae

The Tarsiidae contains two subfamilies, the extant Tarsiinae with one genus (*Tarsius*), and the fossil Microchoerinae with four genera. The Microchoerinae date roughly from middle Eocene deposits in south-central France. The four genera in this subfamily are placed in the Tarsiidae because they possess many features in common with modern East Indian tarsiers. For example, the fossil forms have the same maxillary dental formula (2. 1. 3. 3.) as today's *Tarsius*. The mandibular formula is still being disputed, although it clearly differs from *Tarsius*. In the latter it is 1. 1. 3. 3., but Simons (1972) feels that 2. 1. 2. 3. is the most probable formula for Microchoerinae mandibles.

Figure 12.5 A reconstruction of the skull of *Necrolemur,* found in Eocene deposits in France. (Reprinted with permission of Macmillan Publishing Co., Inc., from E. L. Simons, *Primate Evolution.* Copyright © 1972 by Elwyn L. Simons.)

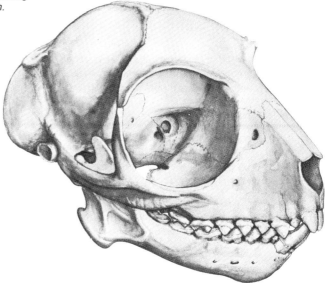

The mandibular formula notwithstanding, other features justify the taxonomic placement within Tarsiidae. The orbital region in each genus indicates very large eyes. This, in turn, implies either crepuscular or nocturnal rhythm patterns. The olfactory sense had probably undergone some diminution, as presumed from a shortened snout and relatively small interorbital space. As in *Tarsius,* the postorbital bar had expanded and partially enclosed the orbital cavity. These features can be seen in Figure 12.5, a reconstruction of the skull of *Necrolemur.*

Compared to the adapids, the foramen magnum in *Necrolemur* had shifted even more forward, the forebrain had become larger, and there was a greater degree of orbital frontality. Thus this primate at least had the potential for depth perception. The only modern primate with tibiofibular fusion (the tibia and fibula are the two bones of the lower leg) is Tarsius. Found in the same location with *Necrolemur* cranial bones were fused tibias and fibulas of about the proper proportions expected for this animal. If they indeed belonged to *Necrolemur,* and if we can infer that it had elongated calcaneii such as those in *Nannopithex,* then *Necrolemur* was probably adapted for leaping or hopping.

No intermediate fossils between microchoerine genera and *Tarsius* have been recovered. Because of this, and since a number of cross-specializations in dental characteristics have been observed in the fossil genera, most authorities maintain that none of the microchoerines were directly ancestral to modern species of *Tarsius.* Thus we have no unequivocal evidence of fossil *Tarsius* in the Eocene, and it may be presumed that *Necrolemur* and its allied genera represent an evolutionary lineage that became extinct.

The Anaptomorphidae

Anaptomorphidae contains two subfamilies, Anaptomorphinae and Omomyinae, with eight and ten genera, respectively. While the anaptomorphines are exclusively North American, omomyine fossils have been recovered from North America, Europe, and Asia. Of all early Cenozoic primates known, there is little doubt that the omomyines were not only the most morphologically diversified but also the most geographically widespread. In addition, they are usually considered to be the most likely group from which Oligocene anthropoids were derived. The anaptomorphines, on the other hand, appear to have become extinct.

Tetonius (Fig. 12.6) is known better than all other anaptomorphines, and an indication of the evolutionary grade of other genera in this subfamily may be gained by extrapolation. *Tetonius* was clearly tarsioid, as indicated by tooth structure, orbital enlargement, and other details of cranial anatomy. However, existing evidence is insufficient for claims of direct ancestry to modern tarsiers. Furthermore, neither *Tetonius* nor any other New World anaptomorphine was in a lineage leading to the New World monkeys. This is ruled out by their respective dental formulas. In the former, the formula was

$$\frac{2.\ 1.\ 2.\ 3.}{2.\ 1.\ (2.\ or\ 3.\ ).\ 3.} .$$

in the latter it is

$$\frac{2.\ 1.\ 3.\ 3.}{2.\ 1.\ 3.\ 3.} .$$

Although *Tetonius* left no known descendants, one of the most important contributions to our knowledge of early Eocene primate radiation has been gained by a study of the natural cast (endocast) of its olfactory and cerebral chambers. This is the earliest primate endocast known, the anatomical details of which were described by Radinsky (1967). In sum, the external morphology shows that (1) relative to the rest of the brain, the olfactory bulbs were larger than those of any living primate, but reduced as compared to contemporaneous mammals; and (2) the temporal and occipital lobes had already undergone considerable expansion. The enlargement of these two areas corresponds to enhanced optic and auditory functions which, as discussed earlier, were critical factors in the rapid radiation of Eocene primates. The dental formula typical of omomyines is

$$\frac{2.\ 1.\ 3.\ 3.}{2.\ 1.\ 3.\ 3.} .$$

the same as among the living Cebidae. The only basis for which the omomyines might be excluded from ancestral status to either Ceboidea, Cercopithecoidea, or Hominoidea is a single incisor specialization: the incisors were larger than the canines. Otherwise, there is little about the morphological details of the teeth, the dental

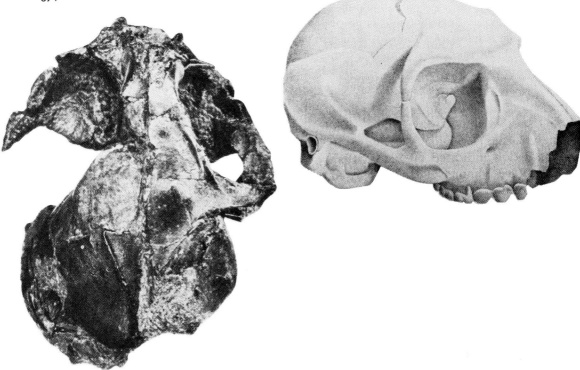

Figure 12.6 Superior view of the skull of *Tetonius homunculus,* an early Eocene tarsioid primate from North America. The scale at the upper right is 10 mm long. (From L. B. Radinsky, The Oldest Primate Endocast, *Am. J. Phys. Anthrop.* 27: 385–388, 1967. By permission of the Wistar Institute of Anatomy and Biology.)

Figure 12.7 Lateral view of the skull of *Rooneyia,* an Oligocene primate from North America. (Reprinted with permission of Macmillan Publishing Co., Inc., from E. L. Simons, *Primate Evolution.* Copyright © 1972 by Elwyn L. Simons.)

formula, or the geographic distribution that would remove the omomyines as possible ancestors to any of the three taxa above.

The recent description of the remarkably complete early Oligocene omomyine genus *Rooneyia* (Wilson 1966) and a later study of its endocast (Hofer and Wilson 1967) support this suggestion. Discovered near the United States-Mexico border in southwest Texas, *Rooneyia* (Fig. 12.7) is associated with a formation dating back 35 million years. This fossil skull is of particular interest because it possesses a combination of prosimian and anthropoidlike characteristics. For example, the developmental stage of the cerebral hemispheres and the large orbits suggests an enhanced visual system similar to that in modern prosimians. On the other hand, it has a more well-developed postorbital bar than *Necrolemur,* to which it bears an overall resemblance. Furthermore, *Rooneyia* is the only New World primate with an ossified auditory canal. Both of these traits, in addition to the size of the olfactory bulbs relative to the rest of the brain, appear to be incipiently anthropoid. Finally, Hofer and Wilson (1967) conclude that certain features of the brain approach a developmental level similar to that of early simian forms.

Summary

Various theories have been advanced to explain the evolutionary development and functional significance of modern primate characteristics. One of these is termed the arboreal theory, which maintains that the earliest primates and their immediate ancestors had already adapted successfully to arboreal life. Characteristics conducive to survival and reproduction in a tree-dwelling species, or those that would be favored by natural selection, include (1) elaborate visual and tactile receptors, a highly developed eye-hand coordination, and an increase in the centers of the brain associated with these sensory organs; (2) forelimbs capable of efficient grasping; and (3) convergence of the orbits, leading to visual overlap and stereoscopic vision. In addition to olfactory degeneration and reduction in the length of the facial skeleton, both of which are presumed to have occurred because of loss of function, these evolutionary trends characterize modern primates.

The second is the visual predation theory, which holds that the same trends can be traced back to a small animal with highly developed visual skills for predation on insects at the ends of small branches in a tropical rain forest. For an animal in such a habitat, the features of selective advantage would include small body size, grasping hands and feet, the replacement of claws with nails for enhanced locomotory efficiency, and orbital convergence with stereoscopic vision. In this theory, stereoscopic vision arose as an adaptation for feeding instead of arboreal locomotion, while olfactory degeneration is seen as an indirect result of orbital convergence.

Direct support of either of these two theories can be gained only by examination of the fossilized skeletons of very early primates of known chronological age, which can often be determined by either relative or chronometric dating methods. The chronological position of one fossil with respect to another fossil or event is established by relative dating methods, while chronometric methods provide direct information on the actual age of the fossil. Relative dating techniques may be based upon principles of stratigraphic deposition, on comparison of artifacts from one site to those of known age from another site, or on the comparison of the relative content of fluorine, nitrogen, and uranium in fossils from one stratum to that contained in other fossils from the same stratum. None of these methods is capable of actual age determination. The most useful chronometric methods for dating specimens of great antiquity are based upon the regular disintegration of certain elemental isotopes. With modern equipment and knowledge of half-life times, these methods can be used to derive an actual age (within limits) of the minerals contained in fossilized bone and hence an age of the bone itself.

As inferred from a single molar, primates may have existed as early as the late Cretaceous period. The discovery of many other fossils of Paleocene primates over a wide geographic range in North America supports this conclusion, and it is widely accepted that the evolutionary transition from mammalian insectivore to primate occurred sometime during the Cretaceous. Paleocene primates were small and had no postorbital bar. They had laterally situated orbits, large snouts, and small brains; possessed claws instead of nails; and had large rodentlike incisors, but small canines. These forms probably became extinct in the Eocene.

The earliest primates similar to modern species have been discovered in Eocene deposits, and their almost explosive radiation is reflected by the existence of three different families containing at least 32 genera. Although quite diverse, these were prosimians which, in comparison to Paleocene forms, had larger brains, more forwardly located foramen magnums, shorter snouts, a bony rim around the orbits, small and unspecialized incisors, nails instead of claws, and longer forelimbs and hindlimbs with mobile digits. These arboreal forms relied heavily upon visual skills; they were probably vegetarians who could manually manipulate objects; and perhaps most important, they had begun the characteristic primate trend toward encephalization.

13 The Origins of Anthropoids, Hominoids, and Hominids

Introduction

At the onset of the Oligocene, the earth's climate underwent a sharply accelerated cooling process. The temperatures of the warm northern seas became lower, and, at least in Britain and western North America, the subtropical floral assemblages of the Eocene began to be replaced with trees more typical of temperate climates. Aridity was fairly widespread in various parts of the world, and grasslands encroached upon what had previously been tropical and subtropical forests. A shrinking body of water called the Tethys Sea separated Europe from Africa, and on the southern border of this sea—in what is now an almost featureless Egyptian desert—was a rain forest.

Within this forest (about 60 miles southwest of the present city of Cairo) was a geographical area now called the Fayum. About 30 to 35 million years ago, the Fayum was part of a lush riverine delta (see Cachel 1975, for a brief paleoenvironmental description of the area) that harbored within its estuaries, wet lowlands, streams, and forested edges a faunal assemblage, which included catfish, turtles, crocodiles, and large riverine mammals. Along the banks of the many streams was a dense forest that gradually gave way to inland grasslands, which were inhabited by numerous grazing animals. It is also from the Fayum that the only known Oligocene catarrhines have been found, most of which have been recovered during the extensive excavations by Simons (1962, 1965a, 1974) and his colleagues. These primates are unequivocally the earliest known catarrhines, and there is general agreement that they comprise the ancestors of modern cercopithecoid monkeys, apes, and humans.

These Oligocene forms had clearly surpassed the earlier prosimians in several of the trends previously discussed. Notably, they had smaller and narrower snouts, greater reduction in the olfactory lobes, and the postorbital bar behind each orbit had become an almost completely closed orbital plate. Such elaborations of the basic trends among Eocene prosimians are almost certainly indicative of increased reliance on vision over olfaction.

The postcranial remains of Oligocene primates from the Fayum are scanty, but Conroy's study (1976) of foot and arm bones suggests that they practiced arboreal quadrupedalism in a fashion roughly analogous to that of the modern squirrel monkey (*Samiri*) or the howler monkey (*Alouatta*). The largest of these primates was *Aegyptopithecus zeuxis,* which has been estimated as no larger than an adult gibbon (about 25 lbs). The unspecialized nature of the teeth of these early primates suggests an omnivorous diet, perhaps including fruits, leaves, and insects. One of the more important aspects of Oligocene primates is that they provide an opportunity to observe a very early grade of anthropoid evolution; hence a few phylogenetically significant characteristics of each genus are discussed below. More comprehensive anatomical and dental descriptions may be found in Simons (1972).

Oligocene Anthropoids from the Fayum

Apidium and *Parapithecus*

Apidium (Fig. 13.1) and *Parapithecus* each contain two species. *A. phiomense* and *P. fraasi* were discovered by Markgraf in 1907 and 1908, respectively, and described later by Osborn (1908) and Schlosser (1911). The second species of *Apidium (A. moustafai)* was discovered during an expedition led by Simons and described by him shortly thereafter (1962). *P. grangeri* was found even more recently, again by Simons's crew, and formally described by Simons in 1974.

The morphological and dental similarities between *A. phiomense* and *A. moustafai* indicate congeneric status, but the latter is a smaller, more primitive, and earlier form. Indeed, many have suggested that *A. moustafai* and *A. phiomense* belonged to the same lineage, the former being replaced by the latter. Similarly, there is little doubt that *P. fraasi* and *P. grangeri* belong to the same genus. The earliest of the two is evidently *P. fraasi*, which is about 15 to 20% smaller than *P. grangeri*.

Figure 13.1 A reconstruction of the face of *Apidium phiomense*. (From E. L. Simons, A Current Review of the Interrelationships of Oligocene and Miocene Catarrhini. In: *Dental Morphology and Evolution*, A. A. Dahlberg, ed. The University of Chicago Press. Copyright © 1971 by The University of Chicago.)

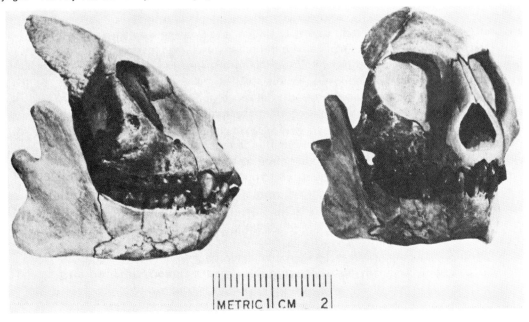

There are numerous details of the dentition that distinguish *Apidium* from *Parapithecus* at the generic level, but their many similarities have prompted various investigators to assign them to common higher levels. For example, Simons (1972) includes them within the subfamily Parapithecinae, while others have claimed that they belong to the family Parapithecidae. Such classificatory disagreements notwithstanding, a few of the features shared by both genera include the following:

1. Both had complete fusion of the two frontal bones at an early age. Taking part in the formation of the upper walls of the orbits, the forehead, and the anterior portion of the cranial vault, the frontals are two bones that are separated by the frontal, or **metopic suture.** In anthropoid primates, this suture fuses very early during development and results in a single frontal bone. However, closure of the frontal suture is delayed in prosimians. The juvenile remains of both *Apidium* and *Parapithecus* with closed frontal sutures are clearly those of anthropoid primates.

2. This anthropoid status is further indicated by their mandibles, which are fused together in the midline. Such fusion between the halves of the mandibles at an early age is another anthropoid characteristic.

3. Both *Parapithecus* and *Apidium* had relatively small canines, and each had the following dental formula:

$$\frac{2.\ 1.\ 3.\ 3.}{2.\ 1.\ 3.\ 3}\ .$$

This formula occurs in no other Old World anthropoid species, including others from the Fayum. This signifies that, since *Apidium* was partially contemporaneous with the other Fayum forms (with the exception of *Oligopithecus*), neither it nor *Parapithecus* would have belonged directly to any lineage represented by the other Oligocene genera. Indeed, the formula is identical to that of some New World monkeys. However, other morphological and dental criteria rule out any possible ancestral relationships between Fayum anthropoids and cebids. To postulate an ancestor-descendant relationship from *Apidium* and *Parapithecus* to Cercopithecoidea, on the other hand, would necessarily involve a gradual reduction and eventual loss of the extra premolar. Such situations have been documented in the fossil record for many evolutionary lineages. However, *A. phiomense* displays no evidence of size reduction in the third premolar, at least up to the time of its disappearance as shown by the fossil record. Thus it appears unlikely that *Apidium* gave rise directly to the known Old World monkeys in the Miocene.

Aeolopithecus

Aeolopithecus, which was discovered by Simons in 1964, is known from a single mandible. It has the 2. 1. 2. 3. catarrhine dental formula, relatively large canines, and a greater degree of premolar heteromorphy than the other Fayum primates. The molars increase in size from the first to the second, but the third is considerably reduced and the smallest of the series. Although the dental formula is compatible with a possible ancestry to later catarrhine primates, the third molar reduction is atypical of cercopithecoid monkeys and argues against any such affiliation. As a matter of fact, the reduced third molar in *Aeolopithecus* is reminiscent of a similar pattern observed in modern gibbons. This, along with evidence of a short face, is one of the factors leading to Simons's classification (1972) of *Aeolopithecus* within the Hylobatidae. However, other primates not closely related to gibbons also have short faces. Thus it seems tenuous to assume gibbon ancestry for *Aeolopithecus* until additional remains are recovered.

Aegyptopithecus, Propliopithecus, and *Oligopithecus*

The largest, best preserved, and most completely known Oligocene primate from the Fayum is *Aegyptopithecus zeuxis* (Fig. 13.2), which dates at about 28 million years B.P. A few of the salient morphological and dental characteristics include moderately well-developed canines, a long and forward-projecting snout, complete orbital frontation, a dental formula of

$$\frac{2.\ 1.\ 2.\ 3.}{2.\ 1.\ 2.\ 3.},$$

a **sagittal crest,** and orbits that are completely closed posteriorly. These and other morphological details of the skull are functionally associated with both stereoscopic vision and strongly enhanced muscles of mastication. The cranium of *A. zeuxis* indicates some forebrain expansion, especially as compared to prosimians, but the

---

Figure 13.2 Lateral view of the skull of *Aegyptopithecus zeuxis.* (From E. L. Simons, A Current Review of the Interrelationships of Oligocene and Miocene Catarrhini. In: *Dental Morphology and Evolution,* A. A. Dahlberg, ed. The University of Chicago Press. Copyright © 1971 by The University of Chicago.)

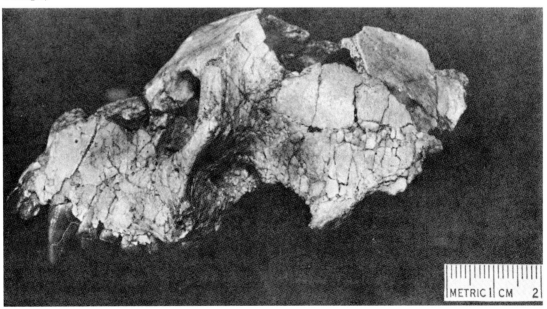

entire braincase is quite small as compared to the size of its facial skeleton. Although the braincase is smaller than that of any living ape, the entire skull is approximately equal to that of the modern gibbon. The teeth are relatively very large and, importantly, molar sizes increase from the first to the third. This pattern is typical of orangutans and gorillas.

As inferred from dental, morphological, and chronological data, *A. zeuxis* may well belong directly to a phylogenetic lineage that includes *Dryopithecus*. As will be shown, this is one of the most important pongid genera from the Miocene. The major differences between these two genera include facial architecture, a few dental details, and, to a lesser extent, overall size. However, the existence of such a lineage is perhaps most strongly suggested by their dental similarities. The evolutionary meaning of *A. zeuxis* as it may relate to human evolution has been aptly phrased by Simons:

> . . . both *Aegyptopithecus zeuxis* and *Dryopithecus africanus* can be shown from cranial and dental studies to be plausible stages related to or in the ancestry of the modern chimpanzee. Inasmuch as the chimpanzee is possibly the closest relative of man among animals, the implications of these relationships are obvious. Somewhere along a line of ancestry in or near this one, the first hominids branched off. We cannot be certain when this was, but the oldest undoubted hominids are much younger than either of these two skulls. Thus the possibility exists that one or both of them represent a stage in human ancestry. (1972:217)

Propliopithecus was first found in 1908, again by Markgraf, and consists of two parts of the mandible of a single individual. Since that time only a single second molar has been recovered. The amount of information gained from such meager remains is small, but the following features can be observed: the molar sizes are roughly equal; the mandibular dental formula is 2. 1. 2. 3.; the canines are relatively small; and the tooth sockets of the incisors indicate teeth that were oriented more vertically than at a slight outward angle as reflected in monkeys and apes.

Although only a rough estimate, most investigators feel that these remains date from about 30 million years B.P. If so, then it is about 2 million years earlier than *Aegyptopithecus*. The generalized nature of the teeth of *Propliopithecus* is such that several alternative views of its phylogenetic position have been advanced. In one interpretation, Simons and Pilbeam (1972) feel that *Propliopithecus* and *Aegyptopithecus* are simply two samples of different chronological age drawn from the same evolving lineage. Thus the former would be a contender for the earliest known dryopithecine, and hence the basal group from which pongids and hominids ultimately arose. In light of the sparse remains of *Propliopithecus*, however, this viewpoint cannot be adequately reinforced until more material becomes available.

The remains of *Oligopithecus* are also scanty and consist only of the left half of a single mandible. The age of the fossil is fairly well-established at 32 million years B.P., making it the earliest Oligocene primate from Africa. It has a mandibular dental formula of 2. 1. 2. 3., thus associating it with the Old World Anthropoidea, but it also shows several dental traits that resemble the Eocene Omomyidae. Unfortunately, the remains are simply insufficient for the construction of reasonable phylogenetic hypotheses.

In sum, the Oligocene primates from the Fayum seem to constitute two natural anthropoid groups. The first consists of two monogeneric lineages, including *Parapithecus* and *Apidium*, each of which contains two time-successive species. There is no solid evidence that either genus left any post-Oligocene descendants. The origin of both genera is also unknown, although their morphological and dental similarities are suggestive of a common ancestor.

The second group is composed of *Aegyptopithecus, Propliopithecus,* and perhaps *Oligopithecus,* the heterogeneity of which is indicative of the extensive hominoid radiation in the Oligocene. Phylogenetically, probably one and perhaps three distinct lineages are represented. However, the nature of their ancestors and post-Oligocene descendants awaits clarification upon the recovery and analysis of additional fossil material.

There is less-than-general agreement about the phylogenetic affinities and hence the zoological classification of these Oligocene primates. In one interpretation, Simons (1972) has advocated the placement of *Parapithecus* and *Apidium* in the family Cercopithecidae, *Aeolopithecus* in Hylobatidae, and *Aegyptopithecus, Propliopithecus,* and perhaps *Oligopithecus* in the Pongidae (see Table 13.1). This implies phylogenetic affinities of the first two genera to the Old World monkeys, of the third genus to the gibbons, and of the latter two genera to the pongids. Many other investigators, however, feel that the available evidence is still inconclusive for the construction of a formal classification. Yet others may agree with Delson, who suggests that "*Parapithecus* (and *Apidium*) may have been the ecological vicar of cercopithecids (or at least of '*Miopithecus*') in the Fayum region, but it seems unlikely that they were phyletically related to modern species" (1975a:186).

Nevertheless, there is some consensus of opinion on other aspects of Fayum primates. First, the nine species (see Simons 1972) included in the five recognized genera (*Oligopithecus* is still in question) are certainly anthropoids, which argues convincingly for a considerable anthropoid radiation either during the late

Table 13.1 An Example of a Classification of Oligocene Primates from the Fayum of Egypt

Infraorder Catarrhini
    Superfamily Cercopithecoidea
        Family Cercopithecidae
            Subfamily Parapithecinae
                Genus *Parapithecus*
                        Apidium
    Superfamily Hominoidea
        Family Hylobatidae
            Subfamily Pliopithecinae
                Genus *Aeolopithecus*
        Family Pongidae
            Subfamily Dryopithecinae
                Genus *Aegyptopithecus*
                     Propliopithecus
                     Oligopithecus (?)

Eocene or very early Oligocene. Second, a similarly early hominoid radiation is indicated by the undoubted affinities of *Propliopithecus* and *Aegyptopithecus* to the Pongidae. Third, the primary importance of these Oligocene species is that they represent intermediate forms between the Eocene prosimians and the larger, more advanced Miocene monkeys and apes.

Pongid Evolution in the Miocene: The Dryopithecinae

There is a gap of a few million years between the known Oligocene primates of the Fayum and the fossil apes of the Miocene. The Miocene is usually defined as an epoch dating from about 23 to 13 million years B.P., although there is a current tendency (e.g., Delson 1975b; Campbell 1976) to extend the upper boundary to approximately 5 million years B.P.

In any event, dramatic changes occurred on the earth's surface during the Miocene, including extensive tectonic movements, increased volcanic activity, cooler temperatures, and drier conditions. During this epoch the fold mountains of the Near East and the mountains preceding the formation of the Himalayas were thrust upward, and similar geologic disturbances led to the formation of the Great Rift Valley in Africa. The Tethys Sea decreased to a series of shallow basins, and the drier atmospheric conditions in southern Europe resulted in the replacement of temperate forests with grasslands. It is also from this epoch, specifically from about 20 to 6 million years ago, that a geographically widespread and extinct subfamily of Pongidae is known. This subfamily is called the Dryopithecinae. One of its genera, *Dryopithecus,* is represented by the numerous remains of at least seven species (Table 13.2) from Europe, Africa, and Asia. Careful analyses of the bones and teeth of *Dryopithecus* have led most paleontologists to the conclusion that both hominids and modern pongids had a common ancestry within this group.

Table 13.2 Classification of *Dryopithecus* (After Simons and Pilbeam 1965.)

Order Primates
    Infraorder Catarrhini
        Superfamily Hominoidea
            Family Pongidae
                Subfamily Dryopithecinae
                    Genus *Dryopithecus*
                        Species *fontani*
                                indicus
                                sivalensis
                                africanus
                                nyanzae
                                major
                                laietanus

Figure 13.3 Occlusal views of two molars: **a,** a typical bilophodont molar from a baboon mandible and **b,** a left mandibular molar from a highland gorilla showing the Y–5 cusp pattern.

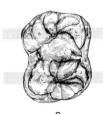
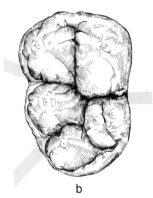

a   b

Some Basic *Dryopithecus* Features

One of the classic characteristics of *Dryopithecus* involves the number and arrangement of cusps on the lower molars. This is usually called the Dryopithecus, or Y-5, pattern. Although it may occur in a slightly modified form, it has persisted for over 20 million years and is shared by modern gibbons, the great apes, and humans. In cercopithecoid monkeys there are four cusps on each of the first and second upper and lower molars, two cusps in the front and two in the back. Each of the front cusps, as well as those in the back, is connected by an intervening enamel ridge. This is called the bilophodont pattern. By contrast, the lower molars in hominoids have five cusps instead of four. Furthermore, each cusp is separated from the others by grooves. The pattern of grooves separating the cusps assumes the shape of a modified Y, with the branches of the Y facing toward the cheek (Fig. 13.3).

Dryopithecines had sectorial instead of nonsectorial (as in Hominidae) lower first premolars. Their premolars were relatively large but laterally compressed, and had a cutting edge that, in combination with the overlapping upper canine, may have served a shearing function. The sizes of their canines were variable; there was a progressive size increase from the first to the third molar; and their incisors were small in comparison to those of modern pongids. Variation in body size of the different species of *Dryopithecus* ranged from approximately that of a large gibbon (about 25 lbs) to nearly that of a small gorilla (about 150 lbs). Unfortunately, the few postcranial remains recovered thus far allow only tentative statements about locomotion.

African Dryopithecines

The three species known from Africa include *Dryopithecus africanus, D. nyanzae,* and *D. major,* all of which date from the early Miocene. Discovered in a number of sites in Kenya, around Lake Victoria, *D. africanus* is by far the best known of any dryopithecine species. Its remains include cranial (Fig. 13.4), dental, and postcranial fragments. *D. africanus* was roughly intermediate in size between a large gibbon and a pygmy chimpanzee, perhaps 30 to 40 lbs (Simons and Pilbeam 1965).

Figure 13.4 *Dryopithecus africanus,* a Miocene hominoid from Kenya. (Reprinted with permission of Macmillan Publishing Co., Inc., from E. L. Simons, *Primate Evolution.* Copyright © 1972 by Elwyn L. Simons.)

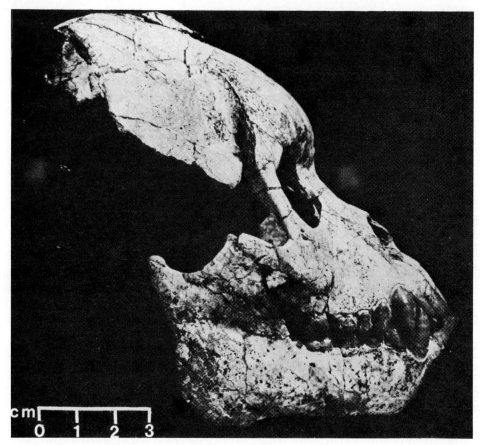

In its essential dental details, *D. africanus* bears a close resemblance to the modern chimpanzee (*Pan troglodytes*). The skull, furthermore, is quite like that of the pygmy chimpanzee (*P. paniscus*), although it has only a very rudimentary development of the supraorbital ridges. The humerus of *D. africanus* (see Napier and Davis 1959), at least in its distal portion, is also very similar to that of *Pan,* but the structure of the proximal half of the same bone seems to be intermediate between that of arboreal quadrupeds, or semibrachiators, and the chimpanzee. The radius is curved laterally, as in *Pan,* and the forearm length relative to the upper arm length is well within the range of variation for *Pan.* In addition, the capability for suspensory posture and arm-swinging in *D. africanus* is evident in the wrist joint and elbow joint. For all of these reasons, Pilbeam (1972), Simons (1972), and others consider *D. africanus* to be at least close to the lineage leading to the modern chimpanzee.

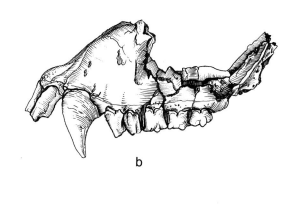

Figure 13.5 Occlusal, **a,** and lateral, **b,** views of the maxilla and dentition of *Dryopithecus major.*

b

a

Remains of *D. major* (Fig. 13.5) have been discovered in Kenya and Uganda. This species was the largest of the three African forms, with adult males estimated at about the size of a large chimpanzee or a small female gorilla. The phylogenetic relationships of *D. major* are still obscure because the fossil material is very scarce. In 1965, Simons and Pilbeam stated confidently that this species was "almost certainly a species ancestral to modern *Gorilla gorilla*" (1965:134), but they softened this viewpoint later by commenting, "It seems reasonable at present to consider *D. major* a probable gorilla ancestor" (Simons and Pilbeam 1972:50). In direct contrast is the opinion of Groves, who suggests that since gorillalike morphology is highly adaptive, "it becomes unnecessary to postulate . . . that the Miocene *Dryopithecus major* is actually ancestral to the gorilla, and that the gorilla and chimpanzee separated so long ago" (1971:50).

The size of the third African species, *D. nyanzae,* was apparently intermediate between *D. africanus* and *D. major.* A few dental characteristics bear a resemblance to *Aegyptopithecus,* but other dental and facial criteria point to a relationship that may be closer to *D. major* than to *D. africanus.* Unfortunately, the evolutionary lineage to which *D. nyanzae* may be associated is even more obscure than that for *D. major.*

Eurasian Dryopithecines

Neither of the two European species, *D. fontani* and *D. laietanus,* dates before approximately 16 million years B.P. (middle Miocene). Judging from the various sites where teeth and some maxillary and mandibular fragments have been recovered, the former was a geographically widespread species. Parts of the maxillae and mandibles of *D. fontani* were first found in France, but isolated teeth of this species have subsequently been located in Germany, Austria, and Czechoslovakia. In addition, limb bone fragments that may be assignable to *D. fontani* have been discovered in Germany, Austria, and France. *D. laietanus,* on the other hand, is a poorly known specimen from middle to late Miocene deposits in Spain.

D. fontani and *D. nyanzae* appear to be closely similar in dental morphology, estimated body size, and, inasmuch as the fragmentary material allows, in their postcranial skeletons. Simons and Pilbeam (1972) have suggested that these are the remains of a generalized "quadrupedal" form, with some capability of suspensory posture and locomotion. Although quite primitive as compared to modern apes, which is expected for a pongid in existence about 14 million years B.P., *D. fontani* does show certain resemblances to the modern pongids. Such similarities include relatively large, interlocking canines, sectorial lower first premolars, a fairly rapid eruption sequence of the molars, and a progressive increase in molar size (as in *Gorilla*) from the first to third molars.

The Asian species, *D. indicus* and *D. sivalensis,* are younger than the African dryopithecines, but roughly contemporary with the European species. The majority of fossils representing these Asian species has been found in India and Pakistan. Although their chronological distribution ranges from middle Miocene to middle Pliocene (about 16 to 6 million years B.P.), most of the known fossils are associated with faunas of the late Miocene and early Pliocene (about 14 to 9 million years B.P.). It is possible, although not presently demonstrable, that these species represent African dryopithecines that migrated to Eurasia during the middle Miocene.

D. indicus was nearly the size of a modern gorilla. The remains consist of isolated teeth and parts of the mandibles and maxillae, which have been recently described by Simons and Pilbeam (1971). Based upon the unusually large and broad teeth, cusp morphology and wear pattens, dental eruption sequences, and anatomical features of the jaws, they postulated *D. indicus* to be close to the ancestry of an extinct genus named *Gigantopithecus.*

Gigantopithecus

Gigantopithecus was a remarkably large animal (perhaps 600 lbs) whose species inhabited parts of India during the middle Pliocene (*G. bilaspurensis*) and parts of China (*G. blacki*) until about 500,000 years B.P. Both species had extemely small (relative to the premolars and molars) and nonprocumbent incisors, relatively small and nonprojecting canines, bicuspid lower premolars, high-crowned molars with complex chewing surfaces, and massive mandibles.

These features are consistent with the conclusion that this animal was a powerful chewer; hence it has been widely assumed that *Gigantopithecus* was adapted to ground feeding in an open country habitat. Since such a habitat is essentially the same as that postulated for the earliest hominids (see Jolly 1970), it has also been suggested that *Gigantopithecus* was ancestral to the hominids: "On balance, it seems to me that *Gigantopithecus* is a most attractive potential ancestor for *Paranthropus* and, through the latter, of the other hominids also" (Robinson 1972:255). However, Pilbeam (1972) and others deny hominid status for *Gigantopithecus,* primarily along two lines of reasoning.

One involves **canine** function. In spite of the similarities between *Gigantopithecus* and hominids in relative tooth proportions and in nonprojecting canines, canines in the former were worn and probably served a chewing function. In hominids, canines are not worn flat, but remain sharp and pointed for a cutting function. The second reason involves the fact that there are other chronologically contemporaneous fossil species that are more probable ancestors to hominids. Thus until the fossil evidence becomes more complete, we may consider *Gigantopithecus* as an extinct and aberrant ape that, in contrast to other apes, was peculiarly adapted to ground feeding in open country.

Concluding Comments

It is hardly surprising that most authorities view the phylogenetic relationships of dryopithecine species with considerable caution. Given the fragmentary and incomplete nature of the fossil evidence, such reserve is necessary. What, then, can be concluded about this extinct Miocene and early Pliocene genus? And of what importance is it to our understanding of hominid evolution?

One important point is that *Dryopithecus* was a highly successful, geographically widespread, and morphologically variable pongid genus that possessed no peculiarly hominid characteristics. Even though we cannot be confident about the precise phylogenetic affiliations of the various species, there is no morphological or dental evidence detracting from the possibility that dryopithecines represent modern pongid ancestors.

Another matter of importance concerns the widely accepted opinion that the first hominids arose from the Dryopithecinae. The available fossil evidence allows neither a precise determination of when such a divergence occurred, nor the dryopithecine genus from which hominids evolved. However, if *Ramapithecus* (see below) is accepted as the earliest known hominid, then the 14-million-year K/Ar date (Evernden and Curtis 1965; Bishop et al. 1969) for the earliest *Ramapithecus* species (*R. wickeri*) becomes quite significant. It implies that hominid differentiation from the Pongidae took place at least 15 to 20 million years ago, and perhaps even as early as the Oligocene-Miocene boundary.

Ramapithecus and the Origin of Hominids

For obvious reasons, the origin of the Hominidae has always been a point of central interest and controversy among paleoanthropologists. Simply stated, we wish to know what sort of animal our earliest hominid ancestor was and where this animal first evolved. We also want to know from what lineage it arose and the nature of the various extraneous factors involved with its initial differentiation. A survey of the literature indicates that *Ramapithecus* is a most likely candidate for the earliest hominid, although this is not a universally shared opinion. Recovery of more complete skeletal remains would doubtlessly resolve much of the current controversy, but at present our information is limited to jaw fragments and teeth. Differences in interpretation of this meager evidence by various investigators have thus led to diametrically opposed statements, such as the following two:

> . . . examination of the *Ramapithecus* material . . . has convinced me that there is not one specifically hominid feature known in this form and that in all respects it is more pongid than hominid. I do not believe that it is a hominid or that it was ancestral to hominids . . . let it suffice here to say that the canine, upper incisor, P_3, the upper precanine diastema, and the nature of the wear on the upper and lower teeth all indicate closer resemblance to pongids than to hominids. (Robinson 1972:255)

In contrast, Tattersall notes:

> . . . the dental mechanism quite evidently played a crucial role in the hominid/pongid divergence, and *Ramapithecus* falls quite unequivocally on the hominid side of the divide. Irrespective of what its mode of locomotion or other unknown characteristics may have been, *Ramapithecus,* as known, had crossed the hominid threshold in the critical area of dental adaptation, and was plausibly ancestral to later hominids, or, at the very least, shared an ancestor with the ancestral hominid which was not pongid. For these reasons alone we are fully justified in classifying *Ramapithecus* within the Hominidae. (1975:28)

Tattersall's view is adopted here with the reminder that additional confidence in the hominid status of *Ramapithecus* is totally dependent upon the discovery of more fossil material.

There are at least two known species of *Ramapithecus,* one of which is from northwest India and Pakistan (*R. punjabicus*), and the other (*R. wickeri*) from Ft. Ternan, Kenya. Other isolated teeth and jaw fragments probably assignable to *Ramapithecus* have been discovered in Germany, Greece, Hungary, and China. These latter finds presently contribute only marginally to our information about the genus, although they do indicate that it was a very geographically widespread animal.

It is currently thought that the Asian species is slightly younger than the African. Based upon faunal correlations (the problems of which have been recently reviewed by Conroy and Pilbeam 1975), *R. punjabicus* is thought to have existed about 14 to 10 million years B.P. The Ft. Ternan specimen, on the other hand, has been dated chronometrically between 14.0 and 12.5 million years B.P. Along with paleogeographic and paleontologic evidence, the slight difference in dates is compatible with the speculation that *R. wickeri* and *R. punjabicus* represent two time-successive species of the same evolving genus.

Morphological Considerations

Only maxillary and mandibular fragments have been recovered, some, but not all, of which contain teeth. At least 13 specimens are known, 11 of *R. punjabicus* and two of *R. wickeri* (inventories of these have been furnished by Khatri 1975, and Conroy and Pilbeam 1975). Because the material is very limited, it is convenient to describe the salient dental features on a tooth-by-tooth basis.

1. Maxillary central (I^1) and lateral (I^2) incisors. Although only an isolated upper incisor from Ft. Ternan has been found, the maxillary fragments from India provide some inferences as to the general size and shape of these teeth. Judging from each tooth socket (alveolus), the central incisors were approximately the same size as the laterals. Both were small, as in hominids, and the empty alveoli indicate that they were implanted more vertically than in the Pongidae.

2. Maxillary canines (C). The only upper canine, again, comes from Africa, but one complete and one partial canine alveolus are known from India. It can be inferred from the latter that the canines, as compared to those among pongids, were small in their mesiodistal (front to back) dimension and rather compressed in the labial (outside)-lingual (inside) dimension. The canines in both Indian and African species had relatively short roots, as in other hominids, but the crown morphology of the latter is more similar to pongids than to hominids.

3. Maxillary first (P^3) and second (P^4) premolars. Both premolars are markedly bicuspid, and in P^3 the largest cusp (on the labial side) is not overly projecting. Both upper premolars, in contrast to the rest of the dentition, are reminiscent of those of the small dryopithecines.

4. Maxillary molars (M^1, M^2, and M^3). The molar occlusal surfaces of *Ramapithecus* are flat and broad, in contrast to the relatively constricted surfaces among dryopithecines. The sides of the molars in the former are steep; in the latter they slope. Enamel thickness of *Ramapithecus* molars is apparently greater than among dryopithecines, and the general contours of the molar crowns are square rather than elongated. To these distinctive hominid characteristics may be added the possibility that the eruption sequence (M^1 to M^2 to M^3) in *Ramapithecus* was slower than among pongids. This has been suggested (Conroy 1972; Tattersall 1975) on the basis of the marked differential wear on the three molars, the severity of which decreases from the first to the third molar.

It should be noted, on the other hand, that dietary peculiarities could produce the same phenomenon. A different kind of molar wear has also been observed, which, in general, might be more characteristic of Hominidae than of Pongidae. Called **interstitial wear**, it occurs between adjacent teeth, rather than on the occlusal surfaces. The phylogenetic significance of such wear remains in question (e.g., Wolpoff 1971a), however, because the factors responsible for its production are imprecisely known.

In the mandibles, most of the dental features listed above have either been observed or inferred to have existed from empty alveoli. Thus the incisors and canines were comparatively small; the molars were broad and rather square, steep-sided teeth showing heavy and disproportionate wear on their occlusal surfaces; and there was advanced interstitial wear. In the Ft. Ternan mandible, P_3 is only "semi-sectorial" (Andrews 1971), which would correspond to the relatively small upper canines. It is not as fully bicuspid as P_4, but rather had a main cusp and a smaller, accessory cusp on the distal part of the tooth.

The maxillae and mandibles of the African and Indian species appear quite similar and have led to a number of reconstructions of the palate, (Fig. 13.6), dental arcades (Fig. 13.7), and facial regions (e.g., Simons 1965b; Walker and Andrews 1973). There is little doubt that, at least when compared to an ape, the lower facial region of *Ramapithecus* is both deeper and shorter. As reconstructed by Walker and Andrews (1973), the tooth rows in the molar regions were nearly straight, and the palate and mandible were long and narrow. However, Tattersall (1975) feels that this mandibular reconstruction is too compressed laterally and should be a bit wider. In any case, the nearly parallel dental rows are in sharp contrast to the diverging rows in modern humans.

Figure 13.6 Occlusal view of the reconstructed palate of *Ramapithecus wickeri*. (Courtesy of A. Walker and P. Andrews, Reconstruction of the Dental Arcades of *Ramapithecus wickeri. Nature* 244: 313–314, 1973.)

Figure 13.7 Occlusal view of the reconstructed mandible of *Ramapithecus wickeri*. (Courtesy of A. Walker and P. Andrews, Reconstruction of the Dental Arcades of *Ramapithecus wickeri. Nature* 244: 313–314, 1973.)

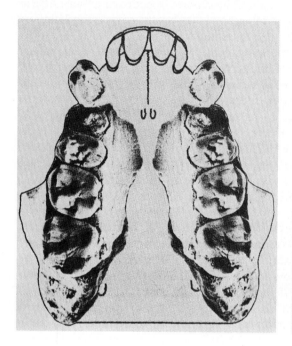

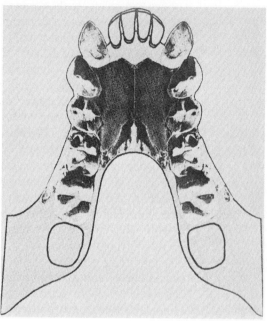

Functional Interpretations

The foregoing characteristics of the jaws and teeth portray *Ramapithecus* as having a short, flat, and deep face. The upper and lower jaws were heavily constructed; the anterior dentition (the incisors and canines) was reduced in size; and the size of the molar occlusal surfaces was increased. These features, in conjunction with advanced occlusal and interstitial wear, lead to the conclusion that the dietary apparatus of *Ramapithecus* was that of a powerful chewer. The presumed thickness of the enamel also supports this contention, and the extensive dental wear leads to the reasonable hypothesis that whatever was being eaten by this animal was tough and gritty.

The interpretation of these observations and their associated inferences, specifically as to the evolutionary grade of *Ramapithecus,* is best accomplished in conjunction with a theory of hominid differentiation. Described below are the primary features of one such theory, developed by Jolly (1970) from observations on the gelada baboon (*Theropithecus*), the common baboon (*Papio*), and the mandrill (*Mandrillus*). Jolly begins with two basic assumptions. The first is that the Dryopithecinae was the ancestral group giving rise to both the hominids and African pongids, and that in the chimpanzee and Hominidae can be seen different evolutionary trends away from this common ancestor. The second is that different evolutionary trends have occurred in *Theropithecus* and *Mandrillus,* both of which diverged from a *Papio*-like cercopithecine ancestor (or, less likely, that *Theropithecus* and *Papio* diverged in different directions from a common ancestor).

It is to be expected that chimpanzees and hominids have many common characteristics, which they do. Likewise, *T. gelada* is expected to (and does) possess many similarities to *Papio*, its closest living relative. Because of their distant phylogenetic relationships, however, there are no obvious reasons to suspect close similarities between *T. gelada* and early hominids. Furthermore, any superficial resemblances that do exist would be examples of evolutionary **parallelisms**, presumably in response to similarities in selective factors operating upon both species.

Table 13.3 presents a list of adaptive characteristics that Jolly considers a functional complex related to diet. Column A represents characteristics that distinguish early Hominidae from *Pan* and other Pongidae. Column B lists the characters distinguishing *T. gelada* from *Papio* and *Mandrillus*. Column C lists features of Hominidae not present in *T. gelada*. And Column D represents features of the *Theropithecus* complex not present in Hominidae. Note that in 14 of 27 characters (those with the rectangles) the Hominidae and *Theropithecus* have diverged in the same direction from *Pan* (and the other Pongidae) and *Papio* (and *Mandrillus*), respectively.

Jolly had two primary reasons for using *T. gelada* in this evolutionary analogy. First, it is completely terrestrial. Second, it has a highly specialized diet, and most, if not all, of the above 14 parallelisms are functionally associated with diet. In contrast to the diet of the common baboon, the gelada baboon subsists on small and tough objects. These include the blades and rhizomes of grass, insects, seeds (which form a primary part of the diet), and other hard, spherically shaped items that must be crushed and rolled between the molar surfaces. Since such food is obtained from the ground, it is invariably gritty. This fact in itself explains the advanced occlusal wear on the molars. To account for the reduction in the anterior dentition, especially the incisors (which are not utilized in the preparation of these foods), Jolly states:

> Natural selection will favour the genotype producing a structure of such size and complexity as to confer the greatest *net* advantage. In a monkey or hominoid adapting to a gelada-like diet, each unit of tooth-material allotted genetically to a molar will bring a greater return in food processed than a unit allotted to an incisor. Thus selection should favour the genotype which determines the incisors at the smallest size consistent with their residual function. (1970:14)

Most of the 14 parallelisms have been either inferred to have existed or actually observed in the *Ramapithecus* fossils. Because of the remote phylogenetic affinities between *Ramapithecus* and *T. gelada*, these parallelisms can be explained only in the context of similar selective pressures operating on both genera. At least this would appear to be the case if the assumption can be made that dental and facial morphology is strongly correlated with masticatory function. Therefore, the immediate conclusion is that the dietary regimes of *Ramapithecus* and *Theropithecus* were similar. Furthermore, in this respect, *Ramapithecus* had already made the shift away from the pongid pattern.

Beyond these critical dental adaptations, nothing definitive can be added about the hominid status of *Ramapithecus*. Since this animal lived in a forested environment but apparently fed on the ground, it could be surmised that it was partly arboreal and partly terrestrial, or in a state of transition between the two. However, the absence of postcranial remains prevents anything other than speculation about its locomotory habits.

Table 13.3 Adaptive Characters of the Villafranchian Hominidae and *Theropithecus* (From Jolly 1970.) See text for explanation.

	A	B	C	D
1. Cranium and mandible				
a. Foramen magnum basally displaced	X	—	X	—
b. Articular fossa deep, articular eminence present	X	—	X	—
c. Fossa narrow, post-glenoid process appressed to tympanic	X	X	—	—
d. Post-glenoid process often absent, superseded by tympanic	X	—	X	—
e. Post-glenoid process long and stout	—	X	—	X
f. Basi-occipital short and broad	X	X	—	—
g. Mastoid process regularly present	X	X	—	—
h. Temporal origins set forward on cranium	X	X	—	—
i. Ascending ramus vertical, even in largest forms	X	X	—	→
j. Mandibular corpus very robust in molar region	X	X	—	—
k. Premaxilla reduced	X	X	—	—
l. Dental arcade narrows anteriorly	X	X	—	—
m. Dental arcade of mandible parabolic, 'simian' shelf absent	X	—	X	—
n. Dental arcade (especially in larger forms) V-shaped; shelf massive	—	X	—	X
2. Teeth				
a. Incisors relatively small and allometrically reducing	X	X	—	—
b. Canine relatively small, especially in larger forms	X	X	—	—
c. Canine incisiform	X	—	X	—
d. Male canine 'feminised', little sexual dimorphism in canines	X	—	X	—
e. Third lower premolar bicuspid	X	—	X	—
f. Sectorial face of male P_3 relatively small and allometrically decreasing	—	X	—	X
g. Molar crowns more parallel-sided, cusps set towards edge	X	X	—	—
h. Cheek-teeth markedly crowded mesiodistally	X	X	—	—
i. Cheek-teeth with deep and complex enamel invagination	—	X	—	X
j. Cheek-teeth with thick enamel	X	—	X	—
k. Canine eruption early relative to that of molars	X	X	—	—
l. Wear-plane on cheek-teeth flat, not inclined bucco-lingually	X	—	X	—
m. Wear on cheek-teeth rapid, producing steep M1–M3 'wear-gradient'	X	X	—	—

Summary

The earliest known fossils of catarrhine primates, recovered from Oligocene deposits in the Egyptian Fayum, date from about 30 to 35 million years ago. There is widespread agreement among paleontologists that either these or similar species were ancestral to the modern cercopithecoid monkeys, apes, and humans. The evolutionary trends initiated among earlier prosimian genera, especially those related to increased reliance on vision over olfaction, became even more fully expressed in these Oligocene primates. In particular, they had greater orbital convergence, smaller and narrower snouts, greater reduction in the olfactory lobes of the brain, and increased bony protection around the orbits. Studies of the foot and arm bones and the dentition suggest that these primates were arboreal quadrupeds with an omnivorous diet.

That anthropoids underwent a considerable radiation during the late Eocene or very early Oligocene is indicated by the existence in the Fayum of at least nine species contained within five genera. There is little consensus as to whether any of the known Oligocene anthropoids were directly ancestral to modern nonhuman primates. However, they do represent an early grade of anthropoid evolution that is clearly intermediate between Eocene prosimians and the more advanced monkeys and apes of the Miocene. This is exemplified by *Aegyptopithecus zeuxis*, which had a 2.1.2.3. dental formula, a pattern of molar-size increase typical of modern gorillas and orangutans, complete orbital frontation, well-developed canines, orbits that were completely closed posteriorly, and a forebrain somewhat larger than among prosimians. However, the overall size of the brain was smaller than that of any living ape, and the snout was relatively long and forward-projecting. It has been postulated that *A. zeuxis* belonged to the same lineage as *Dryopithecus*, a Miocene pongid genus in the subfamily Dryopithecinae. Both modern hominids and pongids probably arose from genera within this subfamily.

One of the more notable characteristics observed in *Dryopithecus* is the Y-5 cusp pattern on the lower molars, a feature that has been shared by modern gibbons, the great apes, humans, and their ancestors for over 20 million years. Based upon dental features and additional morphological criteria of the mandibles and maxillae, different species of *Dryopithecus* throughout Africa and Eurasia are considered by some authorities to have been at least close to the lineages leading directly to the modern chimpanzee, the gorilla, and to the extinct pongid species *Gigantopithecus*. However, precise phylogenetic affiliations of the various *Dryopithecus* species will remain equivocal until more complete fossils are recovered.

Dryopithecines were not hominids, but it is widely accepted that the first hominids arose from this group. If this indeed did occur, and if the fragmentary remains of the 14-million-year-old *Ramapithecus* are accepted as the earliest known hominid, then differentiation from the Pongidae could have occurred as early as the Oligocene-Miocene boundary. *Ramapithecus* had a short, flat, and deep face with heavily constructed jaws. The reduction in size of the anterior dentition, increased molar occlusal surfaces, and heavy interstitial and occlusal wear portray *Ramapithecus* as a powerful chewer of tough and gritty foodstuffs. It may have had a diet not dissimilar to that of the gelada baboon, a fact that would represent an important shift away from the pongid pattern.

14 Pliocene and Pleistocene Hominids

Introduction

One of the more prophetic statements in paleoanthropology was made by Raymond Dart in the last sentence of his initial report on the first specimen of a group of early hominids, subsequently recovered from sites in South and East Africa. Dart concluded by saying: "In Southern Africa . . . we may confidently anticipate many complementary discoveries concerning this period in our evolution" (1925:199). Since the discovery of this specimen in 1924, an incomplete skull and natural endocast of a child (Fig. 14.1) that Dart named *Australopithecus africanus,* literally hundreds of complete and fragmentary bones and teeth of different species of early African hominids have been found. Indeed, because these are the earliest undoubted representatives of Hominidae, no other group (excluding modern human populations) of primates has attracted a comparable amount of interest and attention from paleoanthropologists.

This is not to imply that universal agreement has been reached about the phylogenetic position and classificatory status of these fossil species. Quite to the contrary, the paleontologists who specialize in the analysis of eary hominids have historically differed in their assessments of the evolutionary importance of skeletal and dental characteristics (see Chapter 8). This is not to disparage their interpretative skills, but rather to point out that their differences in opinion have predictably led to a number of contrasting yet fully viable hypotheses. These hypotheses are not concerned with whether these fossils are hominids, but rather with their evolutionary relationships to each other, and especially to *H. sapiens.* Thus, although different interpretations have been advanced, it should be recognized that not one will be generally accepted until the fossil record becomes more complete.

More about the dates of the various fossils will be given later, but for now it is sufficient to mention that these hominids range in age from about 5.5 million to 1 million years B.P. However, depending upon the confirmation of dates and the recovery of additional specimens, there is a possibility that the earlier figure will be extended to beyond 9 million years B.P. In particular, the crown of an upper molar that appears to be hominid was recently discovered in the Lake Baringo basin in west-central Kenya in fossiliferous sediments dated tentatively between 12 and 9 million years B.P. (Bishop and Chapman 1970).

The geological formations associated with the South African remains are entirely different from those in which the East African species are appearing (Fig. 14.2). The major sites in the former are (1) cave deposits filled with sandy breccia, a

Figure 14.1 Lateral view of the infant skull of *Australopithecus africanus* from Taung. (Reprinted with permission of Macmillan Publishing Co., Inc., from D. R. Pilbeam, *The Ascent of Man.* Copyright © 1972 by David R. Pilbeam.)

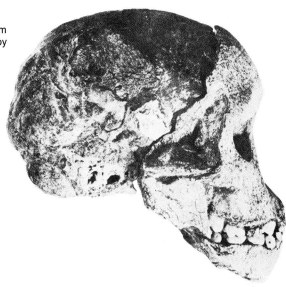

Figure 14.2 A map showing the approximate locations of East and South African sites that have yielded early fossil hominids.

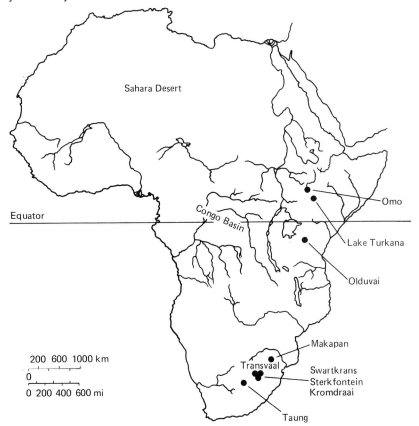

general term signifying a coarse-grained sedimentary rock made up of small angular fragments and (2) limestone quarries and their attendant rock dumps. However, the fossils found in the East African Rift Valley in Kenya, Ethiopia, and Tanzania are associated with old volcanic lake sediments. These sediments not only include an extensive faunal assemblage, part of which has been correlated to the South African sites, but also contain material that is amenable to K/Ar dating.

Early Hominids from South Africa

The type specimen of *A. africanus* that Dart described over 50 years ago was found in a limestone quarry near Taung, in Cape Province, South Africa. For various reasons, not all of which were scholarly, Dart's conclusion that *A. africanus* was a hominid, and thus at least close to human ancestry, was rejected by nearly all of his peers (see Le Gros Clark 1967, for a stimulating discussion of this period in paleoanthropology). His main supporter was Robert Broom, a South African paleontologist who expressed agreement with Dart in a series of publications in the middle and late 1920s. About ten years after Dart's report on *A. africanus*, Broom discovered the cranium of an adult at Sterkfontein, a site near Krugersdorp, Transvaal. He first named this specimen *A. transvaalensis* (Broom 1936), but later changed this designation to *Plesianthropus transvaalensis*. Sterkfontein has since yielded many additional specimens, the latest of which was found 40 years to the day after Broom's first visit to the site (Hughes and Tobias 1977).

Broom continued his search for fossil hominids, and two years after the discovery of *P. transvaalensis* he found additional fossils at Kromdraai, a site in the same vicinity as Sterkfontein. These were thought to represent a different genus and species named *Paranthropus robustus* (Broom 1938). This discovery preceded by a decade the recovery of even more fossils at Swartkrans, yet a third site in the same general vicinity. The fossils from this area were designated *Paranthropus crassidens* (Broom and Robinson 1949). In the meantime, Dart recovered still more fossil hominid fragments from Makapansgat, a fifth site, northeast of the three and about 200 miles north of Johannesburg, South Africa. These and later finds at the same site were named *Australopithecus prometheus*.

By 1950, the most widely used nomenclature for these South African hominid fossils was that given by Broom (1950). In his classification there were two species of the genus *Australopithecus* (*A. africanus* and *A. prometheus,* although the latter was curiously placed in a different subfamily), two species of the genus *Paranthropus* (*P. robustus* and *P. crassidens*), and a third genus (*Plesianthropus transvaalensis*). However, many authorities, including those who were intimately involved with the discovery and actual analysis of the specimens themselves, questioned this classification. In the same year as Broom's classification, for example, the noted systematist E. Mayr (1950) proposed an arrangement in which both fossil and recent hominids were placed into *Homo*. This single genus, furthermore, contained only three species—*transvaalensis, erectus,* and *sapiens.* Four years later, J. T. Robinson (one of Broom's students, and co-discoverer of many fossil hominid specimens) objected to both, saying: "Broom's classification is that of a determined splitter and Mayr's that of an equally determined lumper" (Robinson 1954:181). In the same article, Robinson proposed this classification:

Family Hominidae
    Subfamily Australopithecinae
        Genus *Australopithecus*
            Species *africanus africanus* (Taung)
                africanus transvaalensis (Sterkfontein, Makapansgat)
        Genus *Paranthropus*
            Species *robustus robustus* (Kromdraai)
                robustus crassidens (Swartkrans)

It should come as no surprise that neither Robinson's nor anyone else's scheme received general acceptance. Without going into the multitude of different proposals formulated during the next 20 years, it may simply be noted that differences of opinion still abound today. Tobias (1967), for example, formally suggested rearranging the South African forms into one genus (*Australopithecus*) with two species (*A. africanus* and *A. robustus*). And Robinson himself (1972) has recently proposed sinking the genus *Australopithecus* into *Homo,* while retaining the genus *Paranthropus* in a separate subfamily Paranthropinae.

These diverse proposals are not due to a lack of adherence to standard systematic principles, as they once were. Instead, the astounding proliferation of fossil specimens in the last decade, particularly from sites in East Africa, demands continual reanalysis of known fossils and their integration into a coherent evolutionary framework. Stated candidly, it would be amazing if no differing opinions existed.

Because they have been found in materials unsuitable for known chronometric techniques, South African specimens have always presented a dating problem. Only relative dates have been available and most of them are based upon faunal correlations (e.g., Cooke 1963; Howell 1955). The traditional views of the ages of some of these sites relative to each other have recently been challenged in accordance with paleoclimatic interpretations (Brain 1958) and new geomorphological evidence (Butzer 1974; Partridge 1973).

The prevailing view up to the early 1970s was that Taung was the earliest of the five South African sites, followed, in order from oldest to youngest, by Sterkfontein, Makapansgat, Swartkrans, and Kromdraai (Tobias 1973). However, there are now good reasons to question this interpretation. The latest provisional age estimated by Butzer and Partridge (cited above), even though their methods were entirely different, suggest the following:

Makapansgat and Sterkfontein:	2.5 to 3.0 million years
Swartkrans:	2.0 million years
Kromdraai:	1.5 to 2.0 million years
Taung:	0.8 million years

Finally, a few comments about cranial capacity are in order before discussing the fossils from South Africa, because this variable has been strongly emphasized throughout the history of paleoanthropological studies. In a brief chapter entitled "Crossing the Rubicon 'Twixt Ape and Man," Sir Arthur Keith stated: "What sign can we use to mark the end of apehood and the beginning of manhood? The essential mark of man lies neither in his teeth, nor in his postural adaptations, but in his brain, the organ of his mentality" (1949:205). Keith went on to reason that this "Rubicon" lay somewhere between the highest cranial capacities for gorillas and the lowest for aboriginals, and adopted a figure between 700 cc and 800 cc. Now Keith was a very influential figure during the time, and it became commonplace for human paleontologists to place a great deal of taxonomic importance on differences in cranial capacity of fossil hominids. As a matter of fact, the early South African fossils were often denied hominid status because the absolute sizes of their endocasts were considerably below 700 cc.

The conception of a cerebral Rubicon separating apes from humans was thoroughly rejected by a number of authors in the 1950s (e.g., Dart 1956) and 1960s (von Bonin 1963) and has recently been restated by Holloway (1975). As shown by Tobias (1971), the brains of early hominids are smaller than those of some chimpanzees and gorillas. Likewise, the cranial capacity of the largest gorilla is essentially the same as that of the smallest Indonesian *H. erectus* (Tobias 1967). Further, it is a well-documented fact that modern human microcephalics may have brain volumes equal to or less than those of gorillas and the largest male chimpanzees. Yet these disadvantaged individuals still possess the ability for symbolic language—one of many human species-specific characteristics far different from anything observed in our closest primate relatives—and do not behave otherwise as gorillas or chimpanzees.

Even though gross brain size is probably the crudest variable for studies in human brain evolution, it is an important feature because of its relationships to various features of brain reorganization (e.g., estimates of neural density, neuron size, and other variables associated with behavioral variation). Clearly, there has been a striking increase—about threefold—in absolute brain volume from early hominids like *A. africanus* to modern *H. sapiens*. The average value in the former, as estimated from a few natural endocasts, is about 450 cc. The average in modern human populations is about 1400 cc, with a range of variation from about 1000 cc to 2200 cc. However, detailed studies by Holloway (1966, 1968) and others on various aspects of brain morphology and reorganization have led to the widely held conclusion that evolutionary modification of the primate brain toward the "human pattern" occurred at least 3 million years ago (Holloway 1975).

Taung

The remains from Taung consist of the undistorted facial skeleton, mandible, the dentition, and remarkably well-preserved endocast of a juvenile *A. africanus* whose age at death corresponds roughly to that of a modern 4- to 6-year-old child. Additional specimens will, unfortunately, not be recovered from Taung, as the site has long since been destroyed during mining operations for limestone.

The estimated endocranial volume of the Taung specimen is 414 cc, but Holloway (1975) has projected the adult volume at 440 cc. The position of the lunate, or parieto-occipital sulcus is often taken as indirect evidence that brain reorganization has progressed a long way toward the human condition at this early evolutionary stage. This sulcus is a deep fissure separating the parietal and occipital lobes. In the Taung specimen, as in modern humans, this sulcus occurs far more posteriorly than among apes. Its relative posterior location signifies an expanded parietal association area, which, in turn, is thought to be involved with speech production and the ability to utilize other behavioral symbols.

The teeth of the Taung juvenile are clearly hominid and in many respects are very much like those of modern human juveniles. All teeth are deciduous with the exception of the upper and lower first molars, which were in the process of eruption when this individual died. Likewise, the teeth were heavily worn and the anterior dentition severely damaged. Nonetheless, a few notable dental observations can be made.

1. The eruption sequence appears to conform closely to that of the Hominidae, not the Pongidae.

2. Relative to the sizes of the mandible and maxillae, the teeth were larger in overall size than is normal for modern human juveniles.

3. Although damaged, the upper deciduous canines were rather small and spatulate, another characteristic corresponding closely to the human condition.

4. The lower deciduous canines are also small and probably did not project much above the occlusal plane. In addition, they possessed a small distal cusp.

5. The lower first deciduous molar was multicuspid. This is a marked deviation from the unicuspid configuration among pongids.

6. The dental arcade is more parabolic than the U-shaped arcade in apes.

7. The heavy attrition on the deciduous molars is indicative of the combined transverse and rotatory chewing movements typical of modern humans.

Sterkfontein

Many more remains have been recovered from Sterkfontein than from Taung. Several individuals are represented by both cranial and postcranial material, and early stone tools have been recovered (Robinson 1961; Robinson and Mason 1957, 1962) from part of the site called the West Pit (formerly known as the Extension Site). At least 21 individuals had been identified by 1954 (Robinson 1954), and a number of new specimens have been found during uninterrupted excavations since 1966 (Tobias and Hughes 1969). Nearly all of the fossils recovered so far may be considered part of another population of *A. africanus,* and most have been excavated from the original Sterkfontein site. The major exception, which will be discussed shortly, is a newly discovered skull that has been described and tentatively assigned to *Homo* by Hughes and Tobias (1977).

The average endocranial volume of the *Australopithecus* sample, as estimated by Holloway (1973a) on four crania, is 442 cc. Although obtained from a very small sample, this value is entirely consistent with the projected value given above for the Taung specimen. Morphologically (Figs. 14.3 and 14.4), adults had fairly small brow ridges as compared to pongids. Their faces were deep, but projected forward. They had a moderately high forehead with a large, rounded braincase. The nuchal region was far more lightly developed than among pongids, and the nuchal lines were oriented inferiorly rather than posteriorly. As compared to pongids, this indicates a reduction in the muscles at the back of the neck (see Chapter 11). In

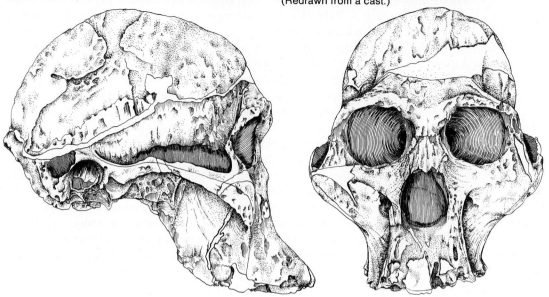

Figure 14.3 Side view of STS–5, *Australopithecus africanus* from Sterkfontein. (Redrawn from a cast.)

Figure 14.4 Frontal view of STS–5, *Australopithecus africanus* from Sterkfontein. (Redrawn from a cast.)

conjunction with the relatively anterior position of the occipital condyles, this reduced musculature strongly suggests that the head was positioned on the vertebral column in a fashion more characteristic of an habitually upright biped than a quadrupedal pongid.

Two decades ago Robinson (1956) showed that the teeth of the Sterkfontein fossils were completely hominid in their morphological details. As in modern humans, the small and spatulate incisors are not separated by a gap from the canines. These teeth, in turn, were small and, unlike pongid canines, did not project appreciably above the occlusal plane. Like the Taung juvenile, each jaw is strongly developed and forms a typically hominid parabolic dental arcade.

That *A. africanus* was a powerful chewer is suggested by several observations. First, the molars are very large. In fact, they are larger in absolute size than those in modern humans, although they are quite similar morphologically. Second, the considerable molar attrition is flat, again indicating both transverse and rotatory chewing movements. Third, the areas for insertion of the masticatory muscles, as compared to humans, are strongly developed. And fourth, the masticatory stress columns discussed previously are also strongly developed.

A. africanus has long been thought to have been omnivorous (see Robinson 1962), and the possible association with stone tools found at part of the site called the West Pit has often led to the hypothesis that these were made and used for the preparation of both meat and vegetables. However, serious doubt has now been cast upon the assumption that *A. africanus* was the maker and user of these tools. This doubt revolves around the recent skull, mentioned above, that Hughes and Tobias

(1977) assigned to *Homo,* and perhaps to the East African species *H. habilis.* In the West Pit breccia under excavation were two geological formations: one called Member 5 (of the Sterkfontein formation) and the other, an adjacent stratum, called Member 4. Although Member 5 occurs directly above Member 4, there was a chronological gap of 0.5 to 1.0 million years before the onset of deposition of Member 5.

While the earlier of the two formations contains all of the individuals unequivocally designated as *A. africanus,* it has produced no stone artifacts. Until the new skull was found, Member 5 had yielded only a few teeth and jaw fragments that were in some taxonomic dispute, but it contained an abundance of stone implements. Thus Hughes and Tobias now postulate that (1) this 2.0 to 1.5 million-year-old representative of *Homo* was the maker and user of the Sterkfontein tools; (2) that *A. africanus* was earlier in time than early *Homo;* and (3) that this discovery provides solid supportive evidence for the hypothesis that *A. africanus* was the most probable ancestor to *H. habilis* and later species of the genus *Homo.*

A. africanus from Sterkfontein is represented by a few very important postcranial remains that have been carefully studied by Robinson (1972). Included in this small sample is (1) an almost complete pelvis and the lower 15 vertebrae of a single mature female adult, (2) the greater part of an ilium of another adult, perhaps male, (3) a proximal end of an adult femur and the distal end of two other adult femurs, (4) part of a scapula around the glenoid fossa, and pieces of an associated humerus, (5) a single wrist bone, the capitate, and (6) a few ribs.

A visual inspection of Figures 14.5 and 14.6 leads to the immediate conclusion that the general features of the pelvis are far more like those in humans than in pongids. As in humans, the hip bones are short and broad and possess a deep and strongly developed greater sciatic notch. This notch is either absent or at least never strongly developed in pongids. Although the ischial tuberosity of *A. africanus* is more pongidlike in the area of the ischium that it covers, the ischium itself is close to the human condition in its functional length. Overall, as Robinson puts it, the Sterkfontein *os coxae* ". . . manifestly and without doubt sorts with modern man rather than with the pongid group" (1972:16).

Judging from the remains illustrated in Figures 14.5 and 14.6, *A. africanus* was rather small and lightly built. Although it is hazardous to estimate either height or weight from the available evidence, the remains suggest that this individual was 4 ft to 4 ft 6 in tall and weighed from 40 to 60 lbs. Because the pectoral girdle is most important for reconstructions of the locomotory behavior of early hominids and hominoids, a number of attempts have been made to interpret the scapular fragment and upper part of the humerus in terms of their functions. Very often these interpretations are formulated after analysis by advanced statistical procedures whose applications to single specimens might well be open to serious methodological questions.

Nevertheless, Campbell (1966) suggested that the form of the scapula placed it in the semibrachiating or brachiating class. Moreover, Oxnard stated that "the architecture of the scapular fragment includes, to an extent greater than that of any living primate save the small-bodied gibbon, and certainly more than the large-bodied orang-utan, morphological specializations directed towards the bearing of tensile forces in the shoulder region as in suspension of the body by the arms" (1968a:215).

Figure 14.5 Side view of the lumbar vertebrae, sacrum, and innominate of *Australopithecus africanus* from Sterkfontein. (From J. T. Robinson, *Early Hominid Posture and Locomotion.* The University of Chicago Press. Copyright © 1972 by John T. Robinson.)

Figure 14.6 Front view of the reconstructed pelvis of *Australopithecus africanus* from Sterkfontein. (From J. T. Robinson, *Early Hominid Posture and Locomotion.* The University of Chicago Press. Copyright © 1972 by John T. Robinson.)

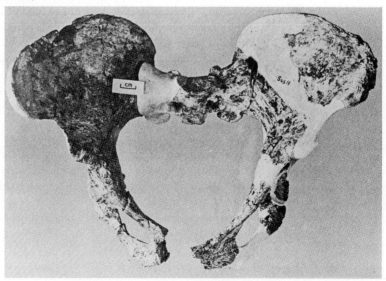

Furthermore, in a new interpretation, Ciochon and Corruccini suggest that *A. africanus* ". . . frequented an arboreal environment to a greater degree than previously considered or at least did so in its immediate evolutionary past" (1976:81). They offer the analogy with certain savanna-dwelling baboons, who forage in an open savanna during the day but spend their nights in the shelter of trees.

It should be emphasized that these investigators are not quibbling about the primary locomotory behavior of *A. africanus*. There is an absolutely solid body of evidence from the vertebral column, pelvis, and lower limb that these individuals were habitually erect bipeds. Instead, the differences in interpretation center more around what kind of locomotion was practiced by their immediate ancestors. We shall not pursue that matter here, but the position adopted by Robinson (1972) on the usefulness of the Sterkfontein scapular fragment does deserve comment. After analyzing the pectoral girdle fragments in great detail and carefully considering previous interpretations, he concludes that because of the great variability in scapular shape both within and between taxa, the bone *by itself* is of little use for either classificatory purposes or hypotheses about locomotory behavior of fossil species.

Whether this point of view is correct will ultimately depend upon refinements in analytical methods, but most of all upon the recovery of enough specimens to constitute a sample large enough to provide adequate information about the actual population variation. Robinson's second contention, however, seems most reasonable. This is that very little can be learned about the locomotory behavior of *A. africanus* by studying this single, very incomplete specimen. About all that can be presently said is that the scapula is not typically hominid, at least as compared to modern human scapulas, and that it may be the most "unhominidlike" bone of any of the known skeletal fragments.

A number of features in the vertebrae, pelvis, and lower limb indicate erect bipedal locomotion and posture in *A. africanus*. The individual illustrated in Figures 14.5 and 14.6 had a distinctly hominid lumbar curve, although it also had six lumbar vertebrae instead of the usual five among modern humans. Still, this condition is much more like that among humans than among our closest pongid relatives. Gorillas and chimpanzees usually have four lumbars, but about one-third of those examined by Schultz (1968) had only three. Humans normally possess five, but a little less than 5% have six. The extremely short lumbar region in gorillas and chimpanzees, coupled with their very long iliac blades, has contributed to a far less laterally flexible trunk than in humans or *A. africanus*. While such lateral flexibility—bending sideways at the waist—is apparently of no special adaptive significance to quadrupedal primates, it is essential to an erect biped for the maintenance of balance.

One of the major requirements for efficient bipedalism—whether during standing, walking, or running—is the capacity for maintaining body balance. The trunk must not only be balanced in an anteroposterior direction, which is accomplished by the powerful muscles of the lower and middle back and the abdomen, but also in a lateral direction. Such lateral balance is provided by the combined action of the back muscles and those that attach to the upper part of the ilium.

In the pongid pelvis, the ilia are separated posteriorly by a relatively narrow sacrum, and there is no appreciable anteromedial curvature of the iliac blades.

In *A. africanus* and in modern humans, however, the ilia are separated by a relatively wide sacrum. Furthermore, the iliac blades are wider in an anteroposterior direction and tend to curve medially as they extend anteriorly from their sacral articulation. Put in other words, the ilia form a wide "semicircle" from the sacrum to their most anterior extremity. This arrangement, a typically human condition, affords an advantageous structure for the attachment of the lateral trunk muscles that assist in controlling lateral balance. As Robinson (1972) has shown, there is no doubt that *A. africanus* had already achieved this stage.

Also similar to the human condition, and related to the efficiency of bipedal locomotion, was the construction of the ilium between the acetabulum and iliac crest. The outer layer of bone in this area was thicker, forming a buttress that evolved in conjunction with the considerable strain placed on the ilium by alternating muscle action during bipedal walking. Finally, additional confirmatory evidence of bipedal locomotion exists in the shape of the distal end of the femur. Full extension of the lower leg is indicated, and the structure and shape of the femoral condyles show that weight was transmitted through the knee joint in a human rather than pongid pattern (for a recent review of Australopithecine locomotion, see Lovejoy 1974).

Makapansgat

Representing five or six individuals, the remains of *A. africanus* from Makapansgat consist of a fragmentary cranium, parts of the skull and face of other individuals, several mandibular and maxillary fragments with some teeth, other isolated teeth, the left ilium and right ischium of two juveniles, another left ilium of an immature individual, a small piece of a clavicle, and a small piece of the shaft of a humerus. The original discovery of parts of an occipital and both parietals, designated *A. prometheus* by Dart (1948), was followed by the discovery of a more complete female skull in 1958 (Dart 1962). In 1954 Robinson proposed formally that the first remains found were those of *A. africanus,* and it is now widely accepted that all specimens from Makapansgat belong to this species.

The 1958 skull (Fig. 14.7) shows only minor differences from the most complete skull from Sterkfontein. The estimated cranial capacity is 435 cc (Holloway 1973a), and the morphological differences between this and the Sterkfontein specimen are no more than might be expected between two similar populations of the same species. Close resemblances are also present in premolar morphology and in the size and shape of the mandibles, maxillae, and teeth.

Swartkrans

Investigators familiar with the fossils might not share identical taxonomic and evolutionary viewpoints about the Swartkrans hominids, but, with few exceptions, most would agree that these specimens are quite different from *A. africanus.* This difference can quickly be appreciated by a visual comparison of the Sterkfontein *A. africanus* skull in figure 14.3 with the Swartkrans skull in Figure 14.8.

Originally given the generic designation *Paranthropus* (Broom 1949; Broom and Robinson 1949), the robust forms that constitute one of two kinds of hominids from Swartkrans are now considered by many authorities to be a separate species of *Australopithecus* called *A. robustus.* A notable exception to this practice is Robinson's (1972), which maintains that these robust forms and a few other fossil

Figure 14.7 An incomplete skull from Makapansgat, representing *Australopithecus africanus*. (Courtesy of P. V. Tobias and A. R. Hughes.)

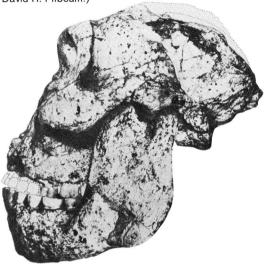

Figure 14.8 Lateral view of the *Australopithecus robustus* skull from Swartkrans. (Reprinted with permission of Macmillan Publishing Co., Inc., from D. R. Pilbeam, *The Ascent of Man.* Copyright © 1972 by David R. Pilbeam.)

specimens from East Africa and Java belong to *Paranthropus*. Furthermore, he combines *Paranthropus* with *Gigantopithecus* into a separate subfamily, Paranthropinae, as distinct from Homininae. Within the latter is placed *Homo,* which includes *Australopithecus,* the later *H. erectus,* and all past and present populations of *H. sapiens.* Robinson's reasons for this classification are given in great detail in his 1972 monograph, but to avoid nomenclatural confusion, the name *A. robustus* will be used in the following discussions of most of the remains from both Swartkrans and Kromdraai.

More hominid fossils have been recovered from Swartkrans than from any other South African site, the most recent being part of a pelvis (Brain, Vrba, and Robinson 1974) encased in the pink breccia blasted out nearly 25 years ago by Broom and Robinson. The remains of *A. robustus* recovered from 1949 to 1965 have been listed by Day (1965), and specimens found up to 1970 are enumerated by Brain (1970). Without outlining these finds piece-by-piece, let it suffice to state that *A. robustus* is now represented by the cranial and postcranial remains of over 60 individuals.

The second hominid species from Swartkrans, originally called *Telanthropus capensis* (Broom and Robinson 1949), is represented by a relatively few mandibular remains, a maxillary fragment, and part of a radius and metacarpal. Recently, a facial part of the cranium that had been classified as *Paranthropus* and stored in the Transvaal Museum has been fitted perfectly to part of a palatal fragment thought to be *Telanthropus.* Broom and Robinson (1949, 1950) knew shortly after the first discovery that *Telanthropus* was more human than *Australopithecus,* and Robinson (1961) later reclassified the fossil as *H. erectus.* Considerable controversy ensued, culminating in the recent analysis of the conjoined fragments by Clarke and

Howell (1972). They demonstrated conclusively the earlier interpretation of Robinson. Although they have reservations about assigning specific status to this fossil, especially in light of other discoveries from East Africa, there appears to be little doubt that Swartkrans has the distinction of being the only site in South Africa where *A. robustus* and *Homo* were contemporaneous.

As implied by the specific name, *A. robustus* was a relatively large, powerfully built species. In comparison to *A. africanus,* the following differences may be noted:

1. The cranial vault is quite low, and there is no appreciable development of the "forehead." Given the rather greater development of the frontal sinuses in *A. robustus,* the implication is that the brain of *A. africanus* had undergone greater upward expansion in the frontal and parietal regions.

2. *A. robustus* may have had a slightly larger absolute endocranial volume, but this observation is based completely upon Holloway's (1975) estimate of 530 cc on the single specimen from Swartkrans. The other crania are so badly crushed that reasonable estimates are impossible to derive. However, if additional *A. robustus* endocasts are found, and if their mean endocranial volume remains significantly greater than that of *A. africanus,* then it is important to understand the meaning of such a greater volume. There are currently two rather diametrically opposed views about this, each of which depends upon reliable estimates of both endocranial volume and body weight. One is by Robinson (1972), the other by Pilbeam and Gould (1974).

Robinson feels that endocranial volume in *A. africanus* was proportionately much greater than in *A. robustus* because the latter had a much greater body weight. This contention, coupled with the first difference given above, led him to state that *A. africanus* ". . . had already embarked upon the hominid brain expansion but that *Paranthropus* had not" (1972:220). By a completely different analytical technique, Pilbeam and Gould find that (1) the australopiths ". . . did little more than increase in size during its evolution" (1974:892); (2) ". . . *A. africanus* exhibits 'advanced' dental and cranial features primarily because it is small" (1974:894); (3) ". . . all australopithecines had brains equally expanded beyond the ape grade" (1974:896); and, finally, (4) "as for cranial capacity, . . . australopithecines may simply represent the 'same' animal displayed over a wide range of body size" (1974:898).

Perhaps the main reason for the divergence in these two views is that there is not enough fossil material for even a reasonably accurate estimate of body weight in *A. robustus.* Simply stated, estimates of this important variable are little more than educated guesses. Likewise, the sample sizes for estimation of endocranial volume are so small as to be statistically meaningless (for *A. africanus,* $n = 6$; for *A. robustus,* including the East African fossils, $n = 4$). As critical as this question may be for understanding the respective places of *A. africanus* and *A. robustus* in human evolution, as well as their relationship to each other, it would seem that its satisfactory resolution hinges upon the recovery of additional specimens.

3. The dentition of *A. robustus* tends to be larger, especially in absolute molar size, than that of *A. africanus.* For both species, however, there is some overlap in the observed ranges of variation for all teeth.

4. Along with the larger molar sizes in *A. robustus* are differences in skull morphology that are functionally related to more powerful masticatory muscles.

Hence the zygomatic arch (for attachment of the Masseter) is much more heavily constructed; there is always a central, or sagittal crest that served as an attachment site for the larger Temporoparietalis; and there is some marginal evidence for larger pterygoid plates, signifying larger and more powerful Medial pterygoids.

Again, Robinson's (1972) interpretation of the meaning of these differences has been vigorously disputed by Pilbeam and Gould (1974). In Robinson's dietary hypothesis, *A. robustus* was a foraging herbivore whose dietary-associated behavior was very different from that of *A. africanus*. The latter is considered omnivorous and is thought to have behaved more like a primitive hunter-gatherer. Now it is presumed that a change from the ape to human grade of organization involved a switch from a herbivorous diet (as in gorillas) to an omnivorous diet (as in later hominids). Hence Robinson maintains that *A. robustus* had made no demonstrable change in this direction, but *A. africanus* was in the process of doing so. Pilbeam and Gould, on the other hand, find that ". . . the positive allometry of tooth area in australopithecines affords no evidence for differences in diet and behavior." (1974:898).

5. The pelvic fragment of *A. robustus* (Fig. 14.9), although badly crushed and distorted, suggests that *A. robustus* may have been heavier than *A. africanus*. Inferences drawn from its shape suggest that *A. robustus* already had a wide sacrum and lumbar curvature like that of *A. africanus,* and there is no good reason to suppose that it lacked lateral balance control. However, the ischium of the

Figure 14.9 The pelvic fragment of *Australopithecus robustus* from Swartkrans. (Redrawn from a cast.)

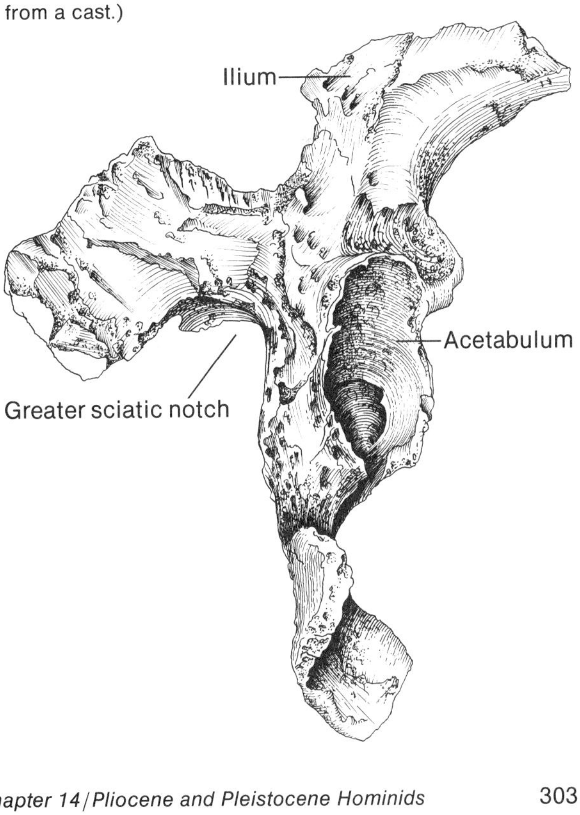

Ilium

Acetabulum

Greater sciatic notch

Figure 14.10 Posterior, **a,** and anterior, **b,** views of the proximal end of the right femur of *Australopithecus robustus* from Swartkrans. (Redrawn from a cast.)

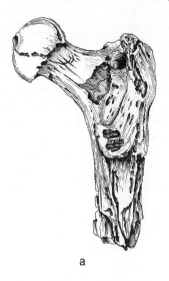

a   b

former was relatively longer than that of the latter, and apparently the hip joint (as judged from the acetabulum and proximal end of the femur shown in Figure 14.10) was smaller. The relatively long ischium is one feature that led Robinson to the conclusion that *A. robustus* was capable as an upright biped, but probably less effective than *A. africanus* in this locomotory pattern.

Kromdraai

The rest of the known specimens of *A. robustus* in South Africa come from Kromdraai, which is generally considered younger than Swartkrans. Both cranial and postcranial remains have been found, but the number of individuals represented by these remains is very small. Of some interest is a distal part of a humerus and proximal part of an ulna of probably the same individual whose skull was the type specimen of *Paranthropus robustus.* Although these fragments are very small and of limited usefulness, those which do exist bear a striking resemblance to the modern human elbow joint.

Of even greater interest is a fragmentary talus, the second largest bone of the foot that articulates with the distal extremity of the tibia and fibula. This was first reported by Broom (1943), subjected to close anatomical scrutiny a few years later by Le Gros Clark (1947), and has been analyzed more recently with advanced statistical methods by Day and Wood (1968). The talus is distinctive because its characteristics are neither fully pongid nor human. Although it was a bipedally adapted foot, the hallux was not fully and habitually adducted as in ourselves. It may have been capable of limited grasping, but, in any case, the morphology of this bone suggests that bipedalism in *A. robustus* was perhaps not as efficient as in later hominids and modern humans. As Robinson has noted in this context: "It clearly must have had appreciable capability as an erect biped, (but) it was not as effectively specialized in this direction as was (*A. africanus*) since it still had a long ischium and therefore still used its propulsive mechanism at least partly in a power-specialized manner" (1972:251).

Overview of the South African Hominids

Arranged in order from the oldest to the youngest, the five sites in South Africa that have yielded fossil hominid remains include Sterkfontein and Makapansgat (2.5 to 3.0 million years), Swartkrans (2.0 million years), Kromdraai (1.5 to 2.0 million years), and Taung (0.8 million years). It appears that at least three hominid species are represented: *A. robustus* from Swartkrans and Kromdraai; *A. africanus* from Makapansgat, Sterkfontein, and Taung; and *Homo* from Sterkfontein and Swartkrans.

The East African fossils must be considered with these from South Africa for an overall assessment of African hominid evolution from about 5.0 million to 1.0 million years ago, and both groups will be considered together later in this chapter. However, it may be instructive to examine some of the possible phylogenetic explanations based solely upon the South African evidence.

1. If it is assumed that the Taung juvenile is *A. africanus*—an assumption that might not be warranted given the fact that the skull has never yet been subjected to full description and analysis—then *A. africanus* occupied parts of South Africa from about 3.0 to 0.8 million years ago. However, the chronological gap of about 1.5 million years between Taung and the other *A. africanus* specimens from Sterkfontein and Makapansgat would suggest that the Taung specimen represents an isolated relic population of *A. africanus* that existed comtemporaneously with *Homo* (whether *habilis* or *erectus*). The mere fact that we have no specimens of *A. africanus* dating from 2.5 to about 1.0 million years B.P. could be explained on the basis of inadequate sampling.

In any event, *A. africanus* would have been contemporaneous with both *Homo* and *A. robustus* from about 2.0 to 1.5 million years B.P. *A. robustus* would probably have become extinct sometime after 1.5 million years B.P., and *A. africanus* would have dwindled to extinction several hundred thousand years later. From what species did *Homo* arise? Clearly, *A. robustus* may be ruled out for all of the reasons discussed above. The most reasonable contender for this title appears to be *A. africanus*, or at least an earlier hominid that could have been ancestral to both *A. africanus* and *Homo*. If this is indeed what happened, then *Homo* would represent a lineage that either evolved directly or split away from that containing *A. africanus*. This differentiation would have occurred sometime before 2.5 to 3.0 million years ago.

2. If it is supposed that the Taung juvenile is a late representative of *A. robustus*, then a different interpretation must be considered. Only two lineages would have been in existence after about 2.5 million years B.P. One of these lineages is that to which *A. robustus* belongs, and it probably became extinct shortly after 1.0 million years ago. The other is *Homo*, which eventually led to the two time-successive species, *H. erectus* and *H. sapiens*. It may be postulated that both *A. robustus* and *Homo* arose from an ancestral lineage that also gave rise to *A. africanus*, which, in turn, became extinct sometime after about 2.5 million years B.P. The time when *Homo*

differentiated is speculative, but it probably would have taken place before 3.0 million years ago. Thus it may be that the Taung juvenile is a very important key to understanding hominid evolution in South Africa.

Early Hominids from East Africa

Until about 1960, the evidence for hominid evolution in Africa was limited to specimens from South Africa. The first important hominid fossil discovered outside this region was found in 1959 by L. S. B. Leakey and M. D. Leakey at Olduvai Gorge in Tanzania, and was announced by the former in the same year (L. S. B. Leakey 1959). Since that time, several other sites in East Africa have yielded the fossil remains of early hominids. In Kenya these include Chemeron, Chesowanja, Kanapoi, Lothagam Hill, and Lake Turkana (formerly Lake Rudolf); in Tanzania, Peninj; and in Ethiopia, the Omo Valley (R. E. F. Leakey 1973a).

A major difficulty in attempting a synthesis of early hominid evolution in East Africa concerns the relative profusion of new discoveries each year. One would be remiss not to mention that what follows below will doubtless need revision in the next few years because many new and important fossils have not yet been fully analyzed or subjected to comparative studies. For this reason, the five specimens from Hadar, in the central Afar, Ethiopia, are not included here. These have been described anatomically by Johanson and Coppens (1976), who date these specimens biostratigraphically from 3.0 to 4.0 million years B.P. Similarly, the 35 new hominid fossils from Lake Turkana (Day et al. 1976) are awaiting comparative analysis.

Olduvai Gorge

Olduvai Gorge is a deeply eroded canyon in northern Tanzania that contains a chronologically continuous sequence of stratigraphic beds. At the base of the sequence is Bed I, which overlies an ancient basalt flow dating very close to 1.85 million years B.P. Although still uncertain, the onset of deposition of Bed II probably began about 100,000 years later, and the higher sediments in Bed II appear to date around 1.5 to 1.0 million years ago. Two other beds, Bed III and Bed IV, complete the stratigraphic sequence up until about 300,000 to 400,000 years ago.

The fossil remains of at least 48 individuals have now been recovered from various Olduvai horizons. While most of these specimens have yet to be fully interpreted, the works of L. S. B. Leakey et al. (1964) and Tobias (1967) clearly indicate the presence of two hominid lineages throughout most of Bed I and a substantial part of Bed II. One of these lineages (represented by the remains of five individuals) was composed of extremely robust forms, the type specimen of which was originally named *Zinjanthropus boisei* (L. S. B. Leakey 1959). In an extensive analysis of the *Zinjanthropus* cranium, however, Tobias (1967) concluded that this was a hyper-robust australopithecine and named it *A. boisei*. This nomenclature has been accepted by many but is used here more for convenience than conviction. The reason for this comment will follow shortly. The other lineage, represented by the remains of 15 individuals in Beds I and II, is an ultragracile species called *Homo habilis*. Although there are some nomenclatural disagreements—Pilbeam (1972), for example, prefers the designation *A. habilis*—*H. habilis* is the term accepted here.

The skull of *A. boisei*, found in the lower part of Bed I, has been dated at close to 1.8 million years B.P. The recovery of additional specimens in the upper parts of both Bed I and Bed II indicates that *A. boisei* inhabited the Olduvai region for perhaps 500,000 years, but this is only about one-fourth of the known temporal span of this species. In particular, a number of isolated teeth found by Howell and his colleagues in the Lower Omo Valley in Ethiopia apparently belonged to *A. boisei,* or at least to a very similar robust australopith. These specimens date approximately 300,000 years earlier than those at Olduvai (about 2.1 million years B.P.), and the species persisted in the Omo Valley until about 1.0 million years ago (Howell 1976). Likewise, a form "likely to be the same species as *A. boisei*" (R. E. F. Leakey 1974:655) spanned a period of time from 2.8 million to a bit less than 1.0 million years B.P. at Lake Turkana, and Leakey has even suggested a Pliocene origin for this species.

The *A. boisei* skull (Fig. 14.11), otherwise called Olduvai Hominid 5 (or simply OH 5), is that of a very massive, robust, and efficient herbivore. The adaptations for powerful chewing can be seen in the large molars and premolars and their correspondingly increased occlusal surfaces, as well as in the cranial and facial architecture related functionally to masticatory stresses. Thus, the facial buttresses are massively constructed; there is an extraordinarily large area on the side of the skull and a sagittal crest, both of which denote a more powerful Temporoparietalis; the shortened face is mechanically related to an increased capability for exerting force through the incisors and canines; the increased height of the ascending ramus of the mandible is highly indicative of more powerful Medial pterygoids and Masseters; and the shape of the zygomatic arch where the Masseter originates is also indicative of a larger, more powerful muscle.

Figure 14.11 Frontal view of *Australopithecus boisei,* originally called *Zinjanthropus.* (From P. V. Tobias, The Cranium and Maxillary Dentition of *Australopithecus [Zinjanthropus] Boisei, Olduvai Gorge* Vol. 2., 1967. By permission of Cambridge University Press, New York.)

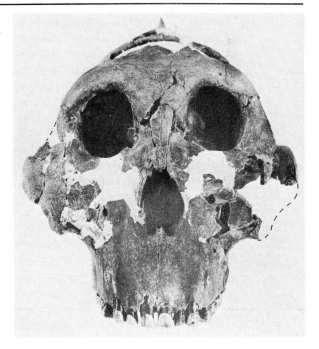

The endocranial volume of OH 5 is estimated to be 530 cc (Holloway 1975), the same as for the endocranial cast of *A. robustus* from Swartkrans. Tobias (1967) has argued that in spite of the obvious visual differences in cranial conformation between *A. boisei* and *A. africanus,* the brains of both were essentially similar in size and external form. Further, he suggests that the seeming failure of the *A. boisei* braincase to rise appreciably above the orbits was due to the lower level at which the calvarium joined the facial skeleton.

If *A. boisei* did indeed have a stage of cerebral development similar to *A. africanus,* then one might assume that *A. boisei* was the maker and user of the various assortment of Oldowan tools (scrapers, choppers, etc.) found at the same Bed I level as the fossil specimens. However, a contemporary of *A. boisei* was *H. habilis,* who apparently had toolmaking capabilities. Thus Mary Leakey is probably correct in her assertion that ". . . on the evidence now available it seems unlikely that . . . (*A. boisei*) . . . was responsible for more than tool using, or possibly for simple modification of objects without employing another instrument for the purpose" (1976:455).

The morphology of *A. boisei* inextricably links it with *A. robustus,* but the uncertain phylogenetic nature of this link has led to different classificatory opinions. Tobias (1976) feels that the physical differences are sufficient for both groups to be considered as a single superspecies. Since a superspecies is a monophyletic group composed of two or more distinct species that occupy different geographical areas, this viewpoint would have to assume that both forms were descended from a common robust australopith. Each would have adapted ecologically and ethologically to the selective pressures in its own particular environment, with *A. boisei* representing the most extremely specialized species.

A different interpretation—that which is favored here—is that each of these two forms is simply a geographical variant of *A. robustus.* R. E. F. Leakey, for one, has suggested that "there may be some merit in treating . . . (*A. boisei*) . . . as a subspecies of *A. robustus*" (1976:576). However, one could argue rather convincingly that there is no real need for formal subspecific differentiation between the two forms. One reason for this is that because of individual variation within populations and the overlapping ranges of variation between adjacent populations (Mayr 1963), it is not always possible to assign individuals to subspecies. For neither of these forms is the number of known specimens sufficient for more than a guess about their intra- and interpopulation variation. Thus it seems most reasonable to view both as geographical variants of *A. robustus,* just as we presently consider such widely diverse populations as Australian aborigines and Apache Indians as geographical variants of *H. sapiens.*

As mentioned above, the second lineage at Olduvai Gorge is that represented by *H. habilis,* a taxon proposed by L. S. B. Leakey et al. (1964). Within this same lineage, but at the upper levels, is *H. erectus.* The type specimen of *H. habilis* (OH 7) was recovered from a level slightly beneath that of the earliest *A. boisei,* but the temporal span of both species at Olduvai is essentially the same.

That *H. habilis* was morphologically intermediate between *A. africanus* and *H. erectus* is apparent, and there is some evidence suggesting evolutionary change from the earliest to the latest *H. habilis* specimens in a direction toward *H. erectus.* Now, transitional forms such as this are very difficult to classify, especially if they are presumed to bear an ancestor-descendant relationship to later and earlier species. In other words, is *H. habilis* to be classified as an advanced australopith or a primitive *Homo?*

Paleoanthropologists are currently rather evenly divided on this question, although the majority probably feel that the original hypothesis of L. S. B. Leakey et al. (1964) on the evolutionary position of *H. habilis* is implausible. Briefly, Leakey and his colleagues viewed *H. habilis* as a non-australopith-derived group that was directly ancestral to *H. sapiens.* Interestingly, *H. erectus* was not considered as an intermediary stage in this evolutionary line.

In any case, Pilbeam (1972) maintains that, on the balance of all available evidence, *H. habilis* should be designated *A. habilis.* Howells feels that ". . . a full species may not be necessary for the transitional phase between *Australopithecus* and *Homo* . . . because its original sense (Leakey, Tobias, and Napier 1964) was in definition of a species which was not thus transitional at all, but outside of any direct line from *Australopithecus* to *Homo erectus*" (1973b:53). Yet others are very adamant about placing *H. habilis* into the genus *Homo:* "Beyond doubt, the new specimen represents the genus *Homo* as defined by Leakey, Tobias, and Napier and differs fundamentally from the australopithecines" (M. D. Leakey et al. 1971:312). This quotation, incidentally, was made at the conclusion of a report describing the cranium (OH 24) recently found in the lower part of Bed I, hence dating around 1.8 million years B.P. (Fig. 14.12).

Figure 14.12 Four views of Olduvai Hominid 24. (Courtesy of M. D. Leakey et al., New Hominid Skull from Bed I, Olduvai Gorge, Tanzania. *Nature* 232: 308–321, 1971.)

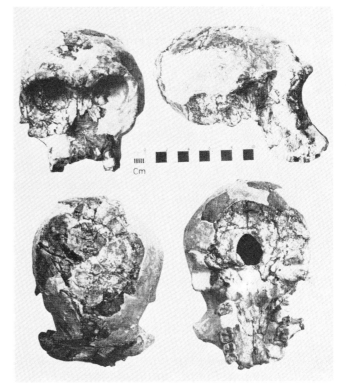

Without further belaboring these nomenclatural disagreements, the position adopted here is similar to that expressed by Clark: "If the intermediate position of the *Homo habilis* fossils between *Australopithecus africanus* and *Homo erectus* is confirmed, it is not of too great significance whether they are classified as an advanced australopithecine or a lowly form of *Homo,* although the cultural evidence seems to favor inclusion with *Homo*" (1976:16). We may go one tentative step further by including the *habilis* fossils within *Homo* and thus accepting the taxon *H. habilis,* primarily to indicate that the organized and systematic manufacture and use of stone tools by this species constituted an adaptive zone different from that occupied by *A. africanus.*

From the morphological standpoint, the placement of *H. habilis* into *Homo* rather than *Australopithecus* poses a more difficult problem, because both cranial (on OH 24 and other specimens) and postcranial characteristics (see Day 1976a) indicate intermediacy between *A. africanus* and *H. erectus.* Some of the more important characteristics are as follows:

1. Compared to *A. africanus,* the cranial conformation was different in several respects. The *H. habilis* skull is more expanded in the parietal areas; the occipital region projects posteriorly to a greater extent, at least when measured from a vertical plane through both external auditory meati; the frontal region is not constricted postorbitally to the same degree as in *A. africanus;* and the mandibular fossae are very deep, as in modern humans.

2. The endocranial volume of *H. habilis,* as far as the number of available specimens indicates, was about 30% greater than in *A. africanus,* but about 32% less than in *H. erectus.* From three specimens (OH 7, 13, and 24), Holloway's (1975) estimates are 687 cc, 650 cc, and 590 cc, respectively ($\overline{X} = 642$ cc). This mean value is about 200 cc greater than that derived from the South African *A. africanus* crania.

3. The morphology of the left clavicle of OH 48 indicates a range of shoulder girdle movements essentially the same as for modern humans (Napier 1965). Although Oxnard (1968b) associates the same clavicle with an ability to suspend the body by the arms (as in apes), Day's (1976a) more recent anatomical comparisons with the clavicles of gorillas, chimpanzees, and modern humans tend to confirm Napier's earlier conclusions.

4. Although detailed anatomical descriptions of the hand bones of the type specimen of *H. habilis* have not yet appeared, Napier's (1962) and Day's (1976a) combined conclusions were that *H. habilis* was capable of a powerful grip, strong finger flexion, and thumb opposability.

5. Along with the clavicle, an almost complete left foot (Fig. 14.13) was found at the same level as the type specimen. In their original description of the foot, Day and Napier (1964) outlined five primary skeletal adaptations associated with the striding gait of modern humans:

a. Arched conformation of the foot as a whole, both in the long and transverse axes.

b. An adducted position of the great toe.

c. Level proportions commensurate with the weight to be lifted and the forces to be transmitted during bipedalism.

Figure 14.13 Articulated fossil foot from Bed I, Olduvai Gorge, Tanzania. (Courtesy of M. H. Day and J. R. Napier, Fossil Foot Bones. *Nature* 201: 967–970, 1964.)

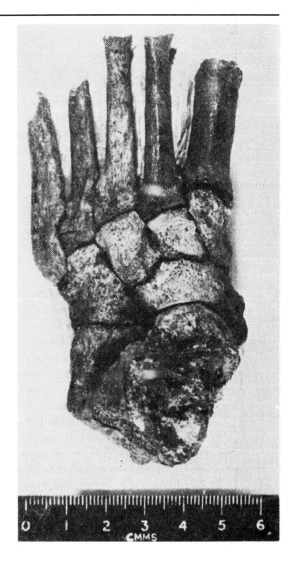

d. Particular robustness of the marginal metatarsals.

e. A stout posterior pillar of the combined medial and lateral arches situated beneath the talus and bearing a horizontal shelf for the support of the talar neck.

Because the Olduvai foot conformed in nearly every aspect to these five requirements, there is no question that *H. habilis* was an habitually erect biped.

To briefly summarize the evidence from Olduvai Gorge, there are two chronologically contemporaneous lineages ranging in time from about 1.8 to around 1.3 million years B.P. One lineage, represented by the robust *A. boisei*, was probably a highly specialized geographical variant of *A. robustus* that eventually became extinct sometime after about 1.0 million years ago. The other lineage, a relatively large-brained but gracile, stone-tool manufacturing, bipedal species called *H. habilis,* was a direct descendant either of *A. africanus* or of an ancestral species common to both. *H. habilis,* in turn, gave way to *H. erectus* (see Chapter 15), which is represented at Olduvai by about 0.8 million years B.P.

The Omo Valley

In 1966, F. C. Howell and his colleagues began a major interdisciplinary study of the fossiliferous sediments in the lower Omo River Valley in southern Ethiopia. Since then, the fossil remains of Hominidae have been found in 93 localities in two formations (Howell and Coppens 1976). These are the Usno (2 localities) and Shungura (91 localities) Formations, each of which dates at 3.3 million years B.P. at its lowest level. While the Usno Formation has a comparatively short time span (3.3 to 2.97 million years), the span of the Shungura Formation is much longer (3.3 to 0.8 million years). Most of the fossil specimens consist of teeth and small cranial fragments, but a few partially complete mandibles and long bones have also been recovered.

Over 90% of the total sample has been gained from nine members of the Shungura Formation. From the oldest to the most recent, these members are labeled B, C, D, E, F, G, H, K, and L. The fossils from these strata have been dated by the conventional K/Ar technique and paleomagnetic measurements, and fall between 2.9 and 1.0 million years B.P. (Howell 1976). Thus at Omo the record of hominid evolution in East Africa goes back about 1.5 million years before the start of the sequence at Olduvai Gorge. As at Olduvai, however, the fossils from Omo belong to two lineages, one represented by robust australopiths and the other by *Homo.* In addition, a gracile australopith very much like *A. africanus* from Sterkfontein occurs at the lower levels.

The specimens from the Usno Formation and from members B, C, D, E, F, and the lower part of G from the Shungura Formation are remarkably similar to the South African *A. africanus,* probably differing only as a geographical variant of the same species. The remains of the Omo *A. africanus* date from about 2.9 to 2.5 million years B.P., thus being chronologically contemporaneous with the South African species, and they persisted at Omo in a somewhat changed form until about 1.9 million years ago. At about 1.84 million years B.P., fossils from the upper part of member G (Boaz and Howell 1977) and from member H were morphologically very similar to *H. habilis* as defined by Leakey, Tobias, and Napier (1964). Furthermore, by about 1.3 to 1.4 million years B.P., *H. erectus* is represented by various cranial fragments in member K.

This adds strong support to the interpretation from Olduvai Gorge that *H. habilis* evolved into *H. erectus* somewhere between 1.5 to 1.0 million years ago in East Africa. Because there is no chronological overlap between the most recent specimens of *A. africanus* and the earliest specimens of *H. habilis,* it is tempting to follow Pilbeam's suggestion that these two species "are merely different parts of a single evolving lineage changing through time principally in brain size and tooth structure" (1972:148). However, such a suggestion cannot be made solely on the basis of the insufficient evidence from Omo. It must be considered in conjunction with additional material recently discovered at Lake Turkana (see below).

The fossils comprising the second lineage at Omo are chronologically contemporaneous with the known time span formed by *H. habilis* and *H. erectus.*

Found in certain units of members E, F, and G of the Shungura Formation, and dating to about 2.1 million years ago, these specimens present a craniofacial morphological pattern essentially no different than that of *A. boisei*. They have been tentatively assigned to this species by Howell (1969a, 1976).

Lake Turkana

In 1968, R. E. F. Leakey and his colleagues conducted an initial reconnaissance of fossiliferous sedimentary outcrops in an extensive locality slightly east of Lake Turkana in northern Kenya. They recovered 110 specimens within three years of the first descriptions of hominid fossils (R. E. F. Leakey 1970, 1971, 1972), and since 1973 new fossils have been gained at a relatively astonishing rate (138 specimens have now been enumerated by Leakey and Isaac 1976, and by R. E. F. Leakey 1976). The known remains now represent most parts of the cranial and postcranial skeletons of individuals belonging to two distinct genera: *Australopithecus* and *Homo*.

The deposition of sediments at Lake Turkana occurred over a period of about 4 million years, and constitute several natural units with the following time spans (R. E. F. Leakey and Isaac 1976):

Galana Boi Beds:	5,000 to 11,000 years
Goumde Formation:	about 0.7 million years
Koobi Fora Formation:	1.0 to 3.5 million years
Kubi Algi Formation:	3.5 to 4.5 million years

The majority of hominid fossils are associated with a number of stratified tuff beds within the Koobi Fora Formation, but no hominid specimen has yet been discovered that dates earlier than about 3.0 million years. Thus our attention may be centered upon the fossils recovered from the tuffs in this formation, dated as follows:

Chari Tuff:	1.22 million years
Karari Tuff:	1.32 million years
Ileret Tuff Complex:	1.48 million years
Koobi Fora Tuff:	1.48 and 1.57 million years
Okote Tuff Complex:	1.70 and 1.56 million years
KBS Tuff Complex:	2.54 and 2.61 million years
Tulu Bor Tuff:	3.18 million years

The fragmentary adult cranium (Cat. No. KNM-ER 1470) discovered in 1972 is without doubt the most important and controversial specimen from Lake Turkana (Fig. 14.14). The sediments with which this skull is associated are overlain by the KBS Tuff Complex, and preliminary paleomagnetic dating indicates an age of about 3.0 million years B.P. (Wood 1976). If so, this would be the oldest hominid cranium known, and it is particularly interesting because many of its morphological characteristics seem to align it with *Homo* rather than *Australopithecus*. If the proposed assignment of this specimen to *Homo* (R. E. F. Leakey 1973b) holds up under the scrutiny of forthcoming comparative analyses, then the origin of the *Homo* lineage will have been extended in time by about a million years over that indicated by the fossils from Omo and Olduvai.

Figure 14.14 Front view of the KNM–ER 1470 cranium from Lake Turkana in East Africa. (Courtesy of Robert Campbell. Copyright © by National Geographic Society.)

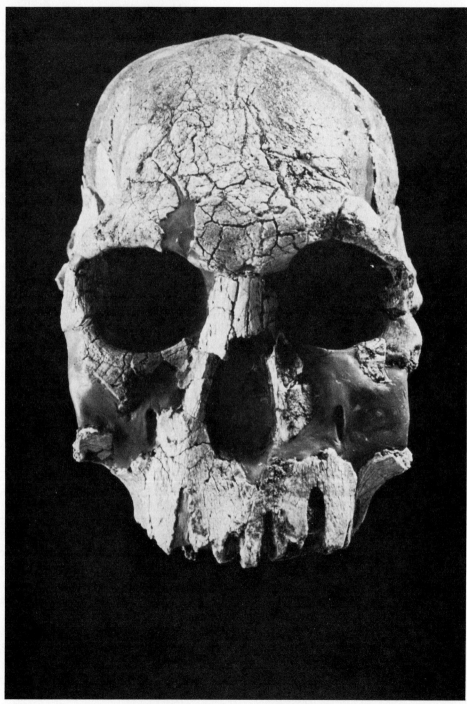

The KNM-ER 1470 cranium, described briefly by R. E. F. Leakey (1973b), and in more detail later by Day et al. (1975), displays several interesting features. Notably, the general shape of the skull is unlike that of either *Australopithecus, H. habilis,* or *H. erectus.* The occipital region is rounded in sagittal profile; the parietal eminences are strongly pronounced; the nuchal region of the occipital is quite lightly marked, indicating a reduced nuchal musculature; and the cranial capacity has been estimated at 770 cc (Holloway 1975). Unfortunately, no tooth crowns were preserved and the zygomatic arches are missing. However, a reduction in the masticatory muscles is at least suggested by the absence of marked temporal lines and the associated inference of less powerful Temporoparietalis muscles. The dental arcade is typically parabolic, and the remarkably broad palate conforms to those of other early *Homo* specimens rather than to the narrower *A. boisei* palates. In addition, Wood (1976) concludes from a few measurements that the premolars were not similar to those of the robust australopiths.

The major controversies about the taxonomic affiliation of KNM-ER 1470 stem from two sources: accuracy of the date and the unusually large endocranial volume. As for the date, R. E. F. Leakey and Isaac (1976) have found no evidence detracting from the original estimate of 2.9 million years B.P. (R. E. F. Leakey 1973b), and they emphasize that the cranium is associated with strata just above the Tulu Bor Tuff.

Part of the problem with this specimen's endocranial volume concerns the relative taxonomic weight that can be attached to this variable. Since there is presently no satisfactory answer to this problem (see Chapter 8), many investigators disagree about the taxonomic meaning of endocranial volume. Thus Walker (1976) places no special emphasis upon this variable in his plea for exercising proper taxonomic caution for KNM-ER 1470, noting merely that its volume falls in the lower part of the *Homo* range. Yet it is well above the known range for *Australopithecus* (428 cc–530 cc), and this may be one of the reasons why Wood has taken the stance that

> rightly or wrongly, it has been the absolute volume of the cranial cavity rather than any consistent changes in vault shape that has chiefly influenced decisions about inclusion of specimens in the genus *Homo,* and until detailed investigations of the endocranial cast have been made, the cranial capacity of the vault of KNM-ER 1470 will have to be used as a guide to its affinities (1976:492).

The salient points leading to Wood's contention that the KNM-ER 1470 cranium belongs to *Homo*—the view adopted here—may be summarized as follows. The mean endocranial volume from six *H. erectus* specimens from Java is 859 cc (range = 750 cc–975 cc), and from five *H. erectus* crania from China, the mean is 1,043 cc (range = 915 cc–1,225 cc). From the statistical viewpoint (see Appendix I), then, the endocranial volume of KNM-ER 1470 is within one standard deviation of the Javanese *H. erectus* mean. However, the former is nearly 2.0 million years older than the latter, and the only other specimens that even approach the age of KNM-ER 1470 are from Olduvai Gorge. These are Olduvai Hominids 7, 13, 16, and 24, and date no older than about 1.8 million years B.P. Provisionally assigned to *H. habilis,* their mean endocranial volume is 637 cc. Since the endocranial volume of KNM-ER 1470 is over 100 cc greater than the Olduvai mean, and since it is about a million years earlier, some have expressed doubt about the correctness of assigning the Olduvai Hominids to *H. habilis.* However, the difference between KNM-ER 1470 and the Olduvai Hominid mean is only on the borderline of statistical significance (see the discussion of the t-test in Appendix I), and this is hardly sufficient for taxonomic reassignments.

In any event, the volume of the KNM-ER 1470 cranium is significantly greater than that of either the robust or gracile australopiths. Thus, to the extent that this variable reflects brain size, and inasmuch as brain size may be utilized to taxonomically differentiate these early hominids, KNM-ER 1470 is probably the earliest known representative of *Homo.*

The very early existence of *Homo* at Lake Turkana is not limited to KNM-ER 1470. The cranial vault (KNM-ER 1590) of a juvenile with similar characteristics was recovered beneath the KBS Tuff, and an adult male innominate, clearly *Homo,* was found in the "Lower Member" (R. E. F. Leakey 1976). The Lower Member, as defined by Vondra and Bowen (1976), is part of the Koobi Fora Formation below the upper contact of the KBS Tuff. Other specimens, including mandibles, isolated teeth, cranial parts, and a number of postcranial bones (see Day 1976b), offer additional evidence for the conclusion that *Homo* existed in East Africa at least in the area of 2.9 million years ago.

Unfortunately, most of the specimens recovered from Lake Turkana localities are not assignable to *Homo* but rather to a robust australopith. Very likely these were populations of *A. robustus* (or *A. boisei,* depending upon acceptance of specific differentiation between the South and East African groups). Rather than reiterate their morphological features (see Walker 1976), let it suffice to state that this lineage (1) was contemporaneous with *Homo* throughout the known span of the latter's existence at Lake Turkana and (2) underwent essentially no changes in craniofacial morphology during this period.

Other East African Sites

Although the vast majority of East African Plio/Pleistocene hominids have come from Olduvai Gorge, the Omo Valley, and Lake Turkana, a few isolated discoveries have been made at other sites. One of the more interesting is a mandibular fragment with a first molar from Lothagam Hill, a Pliocene site west of Lake Turkana that dates about 5.0 million years B.P. If this specimen represents a gracile form of *Australopithecus,* as has been suggested (Patterson et al. 1970), then the australopith lineage would be at least 2.0 million years older than indicated by the evidence from Omo, Sterkfontein, and Makapansgat. However, with the lack of supporting evidence it would seem prudent to withhold formal classification of this specimen.

Similar reservations can be placed upon the fossils obtained from Chemeron and Chesowanja, the former to the west and the latter to the east of Lake Baringo in Kenya's Rift Valley. The greater part of a right parietal from Chemeron dates between 2.0 and 3.0 million years B.P., and some craniofacial fragments from Chesowanja probably date around 1.0 million years ago. Although the affinities of both are equivocal, several characteristics suggest *Australopithecus* affiliations (Martyn and Tobias 1967; Carney et al. 1971).

Also attributed tentatively to *Australopithecus* are specimens recovered from Kanapoi and Peninj. Kanapoi, a site on the southern end of Lake Turkana, has yielded the distal end of a left humerus that may be over 4.0 million years old. This specimen probably belongs to *A. africanus* (Patterson and Howells 1967), although

Pilbeam (1972) feels that it is more reasonably assigned to *A. boisei*. Likewise, the well-preserved mandible from Peninj (1.4 to 1.6 million years B.P.) is generally accepted as that of a robust australopith.

An Interpretation of Plio/Pleistocene Hominid Evolution in Africa

The evidence presented above has led to several different interpretations about the phylogenetic history of South and East African hominids, but as mentioned earlier, none has received general acceptance. Hence what appears below should not be taken as the final word on the subject, but rather as a plausible interpretation based upon existing data. The underlying assumptions and final outcome are only slightly different from the view given by Tobias (1976).

There is an almost complete dearth of fossil material from the latest *Ramapithecus* (about 10 million years ago) to the earliest hominid with clear affinities to either *Australopithecus* or *Homo*. Likewise, the Lothagam mandible and the distal end of the Kanapoi humerus provide only marginal evidence for maintaining the existence of *A. africanus* between 4.0 and 5.0 million years B.P. Hence our information is restricted mostly to fossils dating between about 1.0 to 3.0 million years ago, and these fossils seem to fall naturally into the following three groups:

1. *Australopithecus robustus: A. robustus* and *A. boisei* are considered here as geographical variants of the same species (*A. robustus*). This robust form was apparently derived some time before 3.5 million years ago from a more gracile ancestor with strong affinities to *A. africanus* and makes its first appearance about 2.9 million years ago at Lake Turkana. It also appears in East Africa at Omo (2.1 million years) and Olduvai (1.8 million years) and in South Africa at approximately the same time at Swartkrans and Kromdraai. *A. robustus,* at least by the evidence from Omo and Lake Turkana, did not become extinct until after about 1.0 million years ago.

2. *Australopithecus africanus.* These populations were well-established by about 3.0 million years B.P. in both South Africa (Sterkfontein and Makapansgat) and East Africa (Omo). *A. africanus* persisted in South Africa for at least another 500,000 years and, depending upon the status of the Taung juvenile, perhaps for another 1.5 million years.

3. *Homo.* The earliest evidence of *Homo* is from Lake Turkana (KNM-ER 1470). The date of about 2.9 million years B.P. implies a separation from an australopithlike ancestor sometime before 3.5 million years ago. At Omo, these large-brained, but gracile, hominids appear a bit before 2.0 million years B.P. and *H. habilis* is represented at Olduvai roughly between 2.0 and 1.5 million years. It may be surmised that *H. habilis* changed into *H. erectus* before about 1.0 million years ago, at which time specimens of the latter are found both at Olduvai, Omo, Swartkrans, and at other sites discussed in the next chapter.

In this interpretation, schematically illustrated in Figure 14.15, there were at least two very important and interrelated evolutionary changes in *Homo* from the initial differentiation from a gracile, australopithlike ancestor to *H. erectus* and, ultimately, to *H. sapiens*. The first was an increase in cranial volume, but more important, an increase in cerebral complexity. And the second involved the purposeful manufacture, use, and increased reliance upon tools.

Figure 14.15 A hypothetical diagram of the evolutionary relationships among African fossil hominids during the Plio/Pleistocene. (Modified from Tobias, 1976.)

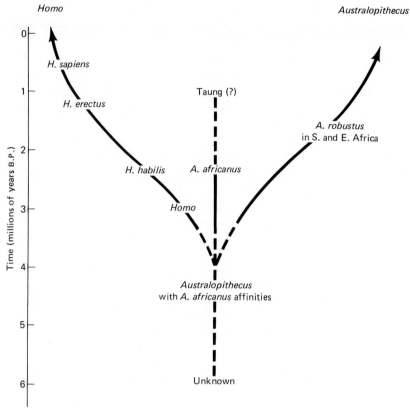

Summary

The earliest undoubted hominid fossils have been recovered from numerous sites in South and East Africa, and, although differences of opinion abound with respect to their evolutionary relationships to each other and to modern humans, most investigators agree that the initial differentiation of *Homo* occurred on this continent. Furthermore, the time of this differentiation appears to have been sometime before about 3.5 million years ago. In South Africa, fossils have been discovered at Sterkfontein, Makapansgat, Swartkrans, Kromdraai, and Taung. These remains appear to represent three different species, including *Australopithecus robustus* (from Swartkrans and Kromdraai), *A. africanus* (from Makapansgat, Sterkfontein, and Taung), and *Homo* (from Sterkfontein and Swartkrans). In East Africa, the principal sites include those in Olduvai Gorge (*A. boisei*, which is probably a regional variant of *A. robustus, Homo habilis,* and the later *H. erectus*), the Omo Valley (*A. africanus* and *Homo*), and Lake Turkana (*Australopithecus* and *Homo*).

The critical evolutionary changes that distinguished *Australopithecus* from contemporary pongid genera were (1) an increase in cranial capacity relative to body weight, and internal reorganization of those parts of the brain involved in behavioral symbolism, (2) the use and, in some cases, purposeful manufacture of stone tools, (3) the acquisition of fully efficient erect bipedalism, and (4) morphological changes in the dentition that approach the modern human pattern.

Of all fossil species recovered from Africa, *A. robustus* (and hence *A. boisei*) is least likely to have been directly ancestral to *H. sapiens*. The species was geographically widespread, occurring at Lake Turkana nearly 3.0 million years ago, at Omo about 2.1 million years ago, and at Olduvai Gorge, Swartkrans, and Kromdraai about 1.8 million years ago. *A. robustus* was a relatively large, powerfully built species with a low cranial vault of perhaps equal capacity to that of *A. africanus*. It had a tendency toward large molar dimensions and cranial structures that were probably associated with strong masticatory muscles. These considerations, in addition to some postcranial evidence that *A. robustus* may have been a less efficient biped than *A. africanus*, rule this species out as a human ancestor. Instead, it probably differentiated from a more gracile ancestor with affinities to *A. africanus* about 3.5 million years ago, existed contemporaneously with both *A. africanus* and *Homo*, and became extinct sometime after about 1.0 million years ago.

A. africanus, depending upon the status of the Taung juvenile, occupied parts of South Africa from about 3.0 to 0.8 million years ago and was well-established in East Africa equally as early. This species was a fully efficient biped, with an average cranial capacity of about 450 cc, that probably manufactured and used stone tools. If the relatively late Taung specimen belonged to this species, then *A. africanus* would have been contemporaneous with *Homo* for a considerable length of time. Initial differentiation of the latter could have occurred from an earlier hominid ancestral to both *A. africanus* and *Homo*, or *Homo* could have split from the *A. africanus* lineage sometime before 2.5 to 3.0 million years ago. If the Taung specimen is a late representative of *A. robustus*, on the other hand, then it could be postulated that *Homo* and *A. robustus* both evolved from an ancestral lineage from which *A. africanus* also arose. The time of differentiation of *Homo* from such a common ancestor would have been before 3.0 million years ago.

As evidenced by the KNM-ER 1470 skull, *Homo* may have been present in East Africa by about 3.0 million years ago. Cranial capacity of this specimen has been estimated at about 770 cc, which is significantly greater than that of any known australopith, but well beneath the average volumes of both the Javanese and Chinese *H. erectus*. Cranial capacity of the later (1.8 to 1.3 million years B.P.) specimens from Olduvai Gorge, often called *H. habilis*, average about 637 cc. If the date of the KNM-ER 1470 skull is correct, then *Homo* would have branched off from an australopithlike ancestor before about 3.5 million years ago. Similar specimens of gracile forms appear at Omo shortly before 2.0 million years B.P., and *H. habilis* is well represented at Olduvai Gorge by about 1.8 million years.

Although enmeshed in taxonomic controversy, the latter species is at an intermediate position between *A. africanus* and *H. erectus* in cranial conformation, endocranial volume, and in a number of postcranial morphological features. It has been postulated that *H. habilis* gave rise to *H. erectus* shortly before about 1.0 million years ago, at which time the latter spread rapidly throughout Africa, parts of Europe, southeast Asia, and China.

15 The Genus *Homo*

Introduction

According to biochemical data on modern humans and pongids and the available fossil evidence, the conclusion that Africa was the continent where the hominids first diverged from the Pongidae seems well-founded. Yet this point is not altogether assured (Campbell and Bernor 1976). As shown in Chapter 13, *Ramapithecus* was geographically widespread before ten million years ago. If Simons's (1977) contention that *Ramapithecus* was the hominid that gave rise to *Australopithecus* is valid, then the apparent confinement of the latter to Africa could reflect little more than inadequate sampling from other Old World regions.

Nevertheless, the evidence for *Australopithecus* outside of Africa is currently equivocal. Therefore, if *Ramapithecus* is disregarded for the moment, there is no solid evidence of hominid occupation of other parts of the Old World until the final part of the lower Pleistocene (about 1.5 million years B.P.). Beginning at about this time and continuing for another million years or so was a stage in human evolution from which the populations are collectively classified as *Homo erectus*. Although a number of divergent opinions were offered shortly after the recovery of *H. erectus* remains, this species is now generally acknowledged as the immediate ancestor of the early *H. sapiens* populations that, in turn, gave rise to modern humans.

Homo Erectus

Some General Comments

As a segment in an evolving lineage, *H. erectus* is characterized by a number of significant elaborations of the basic evolutionary trends initiated millions of years earlier. Some of the more important changes are—

1. *H. erectus* had a much larger brain than either *Australopithecus* or *H. habilis*, and even the unusually large KNM-ER 1470 cranium would have fallen only into the lower part of the *H. erectus* range for endocranial volume. Conversely, the greatest *H. erectus* endocranial volumes are within the lower part of the *H. sapiens* range.

2. The relatively larger brain was associated with a marked reduction in the size and rugosity of the facial skeleton, a relationship that has prompted Howells (1973b), Jolly and Plog (1976), and others to remark that the braincase dominated the face and jaws, instead of the converse being true. *H. erectus* was very clearly not

adapted for powerful chewing, as opposed to *A. robustus,* who was. Rather, the dimensions of the molar occlusal surfaces are well within the range for modern humans. Likewise, the attachment sites for the masticatory muscles, and by inference the muscles themselves, were almost delicate by comparison to the same structures among some earlier hominids.

3. The stature of *H. erectus* varied geographically but averaged less than in modern groups and more than in *Australopithecus.* The structural relationships between the postcranial bones and their respective functions were essentially the same as in modern humans.

4. The unusually large supraorbital tori, the relatively low but broad vault, the massive occipital torus, and the remarkable thickness of the cranial and post-cranial bones were unique specializations of *H. erectus.* The functional meaning of these features has yet to be satisfactorily explained.

Were it not for differences in average endocranial volume, shape relationships of the skull and facial skeleton, and a few poorly understood differences in the postcranial skeleton, there would be little justification for specific differentiation between *H. erectus* and *H. sapiens. H. erectus* presents a taxonomic problem similar to *H. habilis,* although the name of the former is so ingrained in anthropological literature that few advocate any nomenclatural changes. Nonetheless, it should be emphasized that both are groups of populations within a continuously evolving lineage, and the placement of either into a taxon distinct from its immediate ancestor and descendant is an arbitrary matter.

The closeness of *H. erectus* to early populations of *H. sapiens* lies not only in morphological similarities, but also in the manner in which the nonbiological components of culture were used to cope with the environment. These early humans manufactured and used stone tools, but they were consciously built from materials most suitable for a given purpose, e.g., those which would provide the sharpest cutting edge. Because there was a heavy reliance upon such implements, the absolute number of tools increased. However, it is more significant that *H. erectus,* especially among later populations, apparently learned that different kinds of tools allowed more efficient resource exploitation. Hence these individuals modified their tools to serve specific functions, and, although specializations in tool form characterized different regional groups, the patterns of manufacture were remarkably consistent throughout all *H. erectus* populations.

The basic kinds of tools and how they were manufactured formed a tradition—the Acheulean tradition—whose precise origin is unknown, but which dates back to at least 1.2 million years B.P. to Bed II at Olduvai Gorge (M. D. Leakey 1975). The tradition lasted until about 50,000 years ago, thus outlasting the *H. erectus* stage of human evolution and extending well into early *H. sapiens* populations. It is beyond our present purpose to discuss the archeological details (the interested reader will profit from the authoritative treatment of paleolithic industries by Bordes 1968), but it may be mentioned that the most characteristic Acheulean core tool was a bifacially flaked hand axe. Almost as common was a bifacial cleaver, made either from a stone core or from a large stone flake. Other tools fashioned from stone include blades, scrapers, and denticulates (stone objects with roughly serrated edges that may have been used for preparing fibrous vegetable matter). In addition, fragmentary evidence from the early Acheulean site of Torralba in Spain and the late Acheulean site of Kalambo Falls in Zambia shows that wooden tools or weapons were also manufactured (Braidwood 1975).

Increased tool diversity among *H. erectus* populations was associated with a subsistence pattern probably begun earlier, but elaborated to the extent that it represented an almost radical departure from that of previous hominids. This pattern was big game hunting, a method of obtaining food that irrevocably changed both the behavioral and biological characteristics of *H. erectus* and all subsequent human populations (Washburn and Lancaster 1968). Some of the more important changes that were directly linked to hunting large animals are paraphrased below from Campbell (1966).

1. Males had to cooperate for a successful hunt.

2. Home bases or semipermanent campsites were formed by the group's females, who would not have participated fully in hunting because of pregnancy, nursing, and care of young children.

3. Completely efficient bipedalism would have been at a selective premium because of the long distances traveled.

4. Great ingenuity was required in the manufacture of implements used for catching, killing, and butchering large animals.

5. Females were supplied meat by males, a behavioral pattern that would have certainly strengthened the division of labor between the sexes. The absence of males from the home base during the hunt would have had a similar effect.

6. The sharing of food between all members of the group would have contributed to intragroup cohesion and, perhaps indirectly, to the development of rudimentary speech patterns by which plans for and outcomes of the hunting activities could be communicated.

7. Hunting large animals, especially those organized into herds, is basically a matter of strategy. Thus perception, memory, and prediction would have been strongly selectively advantageous in the context of the location, movements, and accessibility of specific animals.

The adoption of hunting, then, involved a broad range of relatively new behavioral patterns relating to technical skills, male cooperation, male-female sharing, sexual division of labor, advanced mental prowess, and other aspects of rudimentary social organization. In addition, *H. erectus* was undoubtedly the first user of fire. There is no good evidence that these individuals learned how to make fire—such methods were apparently acquired thousands of generations later and formed part of the regular equipment of Neandertal and Cro-Magnon populations (Oakley 1961). Nevertheless, the use of fire for warmth, cooking, predator defense, and other purposes enabled *H. erectus* to subsist outside tropical and semitropical climatic zones. Thus the geographic distribution of their fossil remains now includes parts of southeast Asia, China, Africa, and a few European localities.

The original discovery of *H. erectus,* a braincase from Trinil in eastern Java, was made in 1891 by Eugene Dubois. He found a femur a year later and, since the two specimens were from the same formation, considered both as part of the same individual. Dubois was an anatomist and knew immediately that the femur was not essentially different from a modern one. The cranial vault, however, was obviously not modern. It had a low and flattened appearance (platycephaly), very heavy supraorbital tori, a strongly projecting occiput, and an endocranial volume much less than that expected among modern crania. Thinking that he had at long last found the "missing link" between apes and humans—an erect, bipedal ape-man—Dubois (1894) gave it the appropriate name *Pithecanthropus erectus* (literally, an erect ape-man).

Given the time period and the fact that these were the first fossils ever discovered that seemingly demonstrated an evolutionary relationship between apes and humans, it is not surprising that Dubois's interpretation was greeted with considerable scientific skepticism and total religious rejection. Stung by criticism from both sides, Dubois responded by locking the specimens in strongboxes and preventing their further inspection for the next 30 years (for an historical account of this, see Weidenreich 1946).

The status of *P. erectus*—not as a "missing link," but, rather, as the earliest human known at the time—was confirmed only after other discoveries were made in Java (von Koenigswald 1937, 1938) and China. The first fossils from the latter were found by Davidson Black in the late 1920s and early 1930s (bibliographic data on his original reports may be found in Black 1931). They were originally named *Sinanthropus pekinensis* and exhaustively described and compared to other hominids in a series of monographs by Weidenreich (1936a, 1936b, 1938, 1941, and 1943a).

By the early 1940s, then, most of these middle Pleistocene hominids were divided into two genera, each with a single species. However, the differences between the two groups were not such that even specific distinction was warranted, much less separation at the generic level; hence in 1944 Mayr concluded that the Javanese and Chinese fossils were only subspecifically distinct. And in 1950 he formally proposed the dissolution of both genera, including them in the single taxon *H. erectus*. The nomenclature is now accepted by the vast majority of paleoanthropologists.

Southeast Asian Remains

The Javanese deposits containing hominid fossils are divided into three lithostratigraphic units, each of which corresponds roughly to a different faunal assemblage. From the oldest to the youngest, the units and their respective faunas are (1) Putjangan (Djetis), (2) Kabuh (Trinil), and (3) Notopuro (Ngandong). Unfortunately, dating these faunal zones and their associated *H. erectus* remains has always been difficult. However, some relatively recent data (Day and Molleson 1973; Jacob 1972; von Koenigswald and Ghosh 1973) suggest a temporal span for the Trinil fauna of between 0.5 and 1.0 million years B.P., and an early date of at least 1.9 million years B.P. for the underlying Djetis Beds. The Ngandong fauna is much more recent, although very difficult to date. The deposits in which this fauna is represented probably began about 250,000 years ago, thus during the time of early *H. sapiens.*

Only two *H. erectus* individuals are known from the Djetis Beds. One of these, commonly called *H. erectus* IV, consists of the posterior half of an adult skullcap and the inferior parts of both maxillae. When compared to the *H. habilis* crania, the bones are much thicker and heavier and the cranial shape broader, longer, and lower. This apparently indicates a relative expansion in the temporal and parietal lobes. By inference, enlargement in these regions may have been concomitant with certain behavioral changes (such as increasingly complex vocalizations associated with speech). The endocranial volume is usually estimated (e.g., Tobias 1971) at around 750 cc. The occipital torus is massive, and forms the point of an acute angle (when viewed in lateral profile) between the occipital squama and the nuchal region. The strongly developed nuchal lines indicate neck musculature much more massive than among earlier *Homo* populations.

Although it was distorted by crushing, it is clear that the palate was both large and long. The teeth show surprisingly little attrition. The size decrease in the molars follows the typically human order (M2 > M1 > M3). And the mesiodistal molar diameters are slightly greater than those in *H. sapiens,* but considerably reduced compared to the early australopiths. The morphological details of the teeth (Tobias and von Koenigswald 1964) are very similar to OH 13 (*H. habilis*). In addition, *H. erectus* IV had a maxillary **diastema** between the lateral incisors and canines. This gap was very slight relative to that among pongids, but quite pronounced as compared to modern humans.

The second individual from the Djetis Beds, a 2 to 3-year-old infant, is represented only by the frontal, parietal, occipital, and temporal bones. Relatively little information can be derived from these remains, but there are a few notable features compared to the skull of a modern infant of equivalent age. The occipital region had already become angulated, but without an occipital torus; the frontal region was beginning to show some postorbital constriction; and there is some indication of more heavily constructed supraorbital tori.

The main problem in assessing the evolutionary position of the Djetis fossils concerns their chronological age. To assume that these remains are nearly 2 million years old requires an explanation of how they could be descendants of *H. habilis,* who was present at Olduvai Gorge at the same time. One hypothesis holds that *H. erectus* evolved in Asia, presumably from an as-yet-undiscovered australopithlike ancestor, and that hominid evolution on this continent was ahead of that in Africa. Migrating Asian populations would account for the seemingly sudden appearance of *H. erectus* (perhaps represented by KNM-ER 3733, discussed below) about 1.3 to 1.6 million years ago in East Africa at Lake Turkana (R. E. F. Leakey and Walker 1976).

Given the existing evidence, however, there are few good reasons for formulating such a hypothesis. It is far more plausible, in light of the almost unbroken chronological sequence of African fossils from *Australopithecus* to *H. erectus* (spanning a time period from about 3.0 million to about 500,000 years B.P.), that some African populations of *Homo* dispersed to Java. These groups could have been in the *H. erectus* stage only if the dates for the Djetis specimens are too early, which is very possible. Otherwise, migrating African populations may have been not unlike those represented by the KNM-ER 1470 skull. Once transplanted to Java, they would have had nearly a million years—50,000 or more generations—to respond genetically to a different set of selective factors and hence become phenotypically somewhat different from *H. erectus* in both Africa and China. Such phenotypic differentiation could easily occur during that number of generations, especially among populations that were very likely small and relatively isolated from other such groups.

H. erectus specimens from the Trinil layers include six fragmentary crania, five from Sangiran (Fig. 15.1) and one from Trinil, some basicranial fragments,

Figure 15.1 Lateral view of the Sangiran calvaria from the Trinil layers in Java. (Redrawn from a cast produced by the Wenner-Gren Foundation for Anthropological Research.)

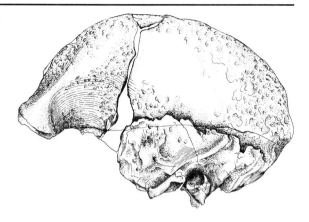

a number of isolated teeth, three mandibles, and several femora. To judge by comparison between the adult Djetis cranium and the Trinil specimens, *H. erectus* appears to have become generally less robust through time. Endocranial volume continued to increase, the average being close to 900 cc if the most recent specimen found by Sartono (1971) is included. The endocranial volume of this individual (*H. erectus* VIII) was almost surely over 1,000 cc, although all estimates are still provisional.

The Trinil femora are in nearly all aspects like those in modern individuals. Based upon their length, the stature of the males was probably no more than about 5 ft 8 in. This value is, of course, well within the range of variation in modern groups, and it represents an increase in height over *H. habilis* of about 12 inches. The nature of the selective factors for stature increase remains speculative. It has been suggested (e.g., Pilbeam 1972) that these changes were associated in some way with an increase in group range size and increased hunting efficiency, but this view would be contingent, in large part, upon the hunting methods employed by *H. erectus*.

About 20 years ago, Brues (1960) showed convincingly that large body size would be selectively advantageous if bludgeoning were the primary weapon technique:

> Bludgeoning does not require any very specialized application of energy. Within reasonable limits, the destruction wrought on the victim will depend on the total amount of energy absorbed; that is to say, a four-pound club moving at the rate of ten feet per second will probably smash as much skull as a two-pound club moving at the rate of twenty feet per second, and so on, unless the velocity is so low that the blow simply pushes. Thus the effectiveness of the bludgeon can remain the same with two factors reciprocally varying, namely, the weight of the object accelerated and the velocity which it attains. In this case neither momentary force nor speed of action need be at a maximum; rather, the total amount of energy embodied in the moving weapon, and therefore the total amount of muscular work performed, determines the effectiveness. Thus the determining factor in terms of body structure will be the aggressor's total bulk of muscle, rather than specific proportions or leverages. (1960:462)

In a similar fashion, she also showed that linear body build would be at a selective premium among those populations using projective weapons: ". . . within a group in which the spear had become a standard weapon, there would be selection in favor of the individuals who, because of linearity of build, were able to attain the maximum in range and accuracy with it, and thereby enjoy a better food supply" (1960:464).

Because *H. erectus* possessed neither the bow and arrow nor the spear-thrower—both were inventions that appeared many thousands of years later—it may be reasonably assumed that animals were killed either by bludgeoning or with a sharply pointed object (e.g., a wooden spear), or by a combination of both. However, it seems rather unlikely that these individuals relied solely upon bludgeoning, especially in light of their abilities in manufacturing stone tools for cutting, chopping, scraping, and so forth. It also seems unlikely that clubs would be efficient means of dispatching large animals such as elephants and rhinoceroses.

Compared to its immediate ancestors, *H. erectus* increased not only in stature, but also in muscularity. Thus it may be premature to attribute these changes to increased hunting efficiency. To the contrary, it could be argued that the most efficient hunters during this stage of human evolution were those with smaller body builds (and therefore less energy expenditure), extraordinary endurance, and above all, advanced mental facilities. In any event, the underlying factors associated with these physical changes in body build remain completely unsubstantiated.

Specimens from China

The first Chinese *H. erectus* fossil was a lower molar, discovered over 50 years ago at Choukoutien, near Peking. Since then the remains of nearly 50 individuals have been recovered from Locality 1 at the same site. Although the Choukoutien deposits have never been accurately dated, there is little doubt that Locality 1 is less than a million years old. Based on faunal correlations and other evidence, Pilbeam (1975) suggests an age of about 600,000 to 700,000 years B.P. However, Howells (1973b) cites an unpublished estimate (derived by a relatively new dating technique called amino acid racemization) on the same deposits of 300,000 years B.P.

The earliest *H. erectus* specimens, on the other hand, were found in Lantian County, Shensi Province, east-central China. These include a skull cap and maxilla (Woo 1965) excavated from deposits that probably date between 1.5 and 1.0 million years B.P. In combination, then, the Chinese sites span about the same period of time as the hominid-bearing localities in Java.

As expected among geographical variants of the same species, the total morphological pattern of the jaws, teeth, crania, and postcranial bones from China is very similar to the Javanese and African specimens. However, there are a few notable differences, particularly between (1) the earliest and later Chinese populations and (2) the Chinese and Javanese fossils. In general, the Lantian fossils resemble the early Javanese *H. erectus* more closely than do the Choukoutien specimens. Thus the vault bones of the former were thick and heavy. The brow ridges were massive, and the platycephaly marked. Angulation of the projecting occipital torus was rather sharp, while the mandible lacked a pronounced chin. The endocranial volume, moreover, has been placed at between 750 and 800 cc.

Figure 15.2 Lateral view of the skull of *H. erectus* from Choukoutien, China.

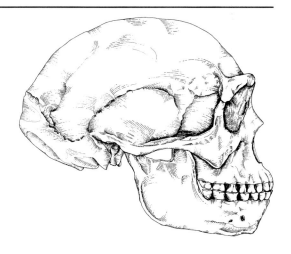

The cranial features of the Choukoutien people, compared with those from both Java and Lantian, seem to reflect some progressive evolutionary changes during the intervening period of several hundred thousand years. Their brains became larger, but perhaps not significantly so. Endocranial volumes ranged from a little less than 900 cc to around 1,300 cc, averaging a bit over 1,000 cc. Although these estimates were derived from a small sample, this is an increase of about 100 cc over the Trinil specimens. Furthermore, increased endocranial volume is, to a slight extent, reflected by a few subtle differences in cranial shape. The Choukoutien skulls are expanded somewhat more in the parietal regions, and there appears to be a greater development of the forehead in lateral view (Fig. 15.2). Although no complete facial skeleton has been found, a number of fragments indicate that the face was broad, short, and large relative to the rest of the skull. The maxillary dentition, which was larger than that among modern human populations, contributed to a slightly protruding mouth.

Postcranial remains from Choukoutien are poorly represented, but enough has been found to conclude that these individuals were shorter than the individuals from Java. Males probably averaged around five feet or a bit taller, and females about six inches less. The cortical bone was thicker and heavier than in both preceding hominids and modern humans, giving an overall impression of a short but stocky body build.

Unfortunately, the fossils from Choukoutien are not in direct association with manufactured implements. However, various levels yielding fossilized human remains have also produced a wealth of stone artifacts, and there is no reason to suppose that a species other than *H. erectus* was responsible for their manufacture and use. The earliest tools were fashioned from materials such as quartz and coarse chert, and, admittedly, were relatively crude. But they were made from material intentionally carried to the site. In addition, they were associated with traces of fire, and there was a basic pattern in their style. There is no doubt at all that *H. erectus* in China had developed a culture of some complexity.

To the extent that the animal bones found in the same levels may be taken as an indication of diet, the animals eaten most often by *H. erectus* (about 70% of all bones recovered) were two species of deer. In addition, the remains of antelopes and sheep, horses and camels, water buffalos, elephants, rhinoceroses, and wild boars were found in these deposits. Various carnivores were also represented: cave bears, leopards, saber-tooths, and hyenas. The weapons used to dispatch this diverse assortment of animals remain unknown—the best guess would be a wooden spear with a fire-hardened tip. Crude pit-traps may also have been used. In any case, it makes little difference whether these animals were killed intentionally for food, or in order to protect the group. What is important, particularly at this early stage of human evolution and in light of the relatively unsophisticated items of material culture, is that these people must have relied very heavily upon intragroup cooperation and some form of rudimentary verbal communication for their existence.

Fossils from Africa and Europe

For many years it was assumed that the geographic distribution of *H. erectus* was limited to southeast Asia and China, but relatively recent discoveries have dispelled this notion. As early as 1954, Arambourg (1954) and Arambourg and Hoffstetter (1954) discovered three mandibles and a parietal at Ternifine, in Algeria. The size and shape of the mandibles, the details of the teeth, and the general configuration of the parietal are all very similar to the remains from Choukoutien. Hence these remains have been transferred from their original taxon (*Atlanthropus mauritanicus*) to *H. erectus*. Additional evidence of *H. erectus* in North Africa includes mandibular fragments from Sidi Abderrahman in Morocco, and some very fragmentary parts of a juvenile mandible and maxilla found near Rabat, also in Morocco. The latter are very difficult to assess taxonomically, but Le Gros Clark (1964a) and others suggest that these specimens bear certain morphological affinities to archaic groups of *H. sapiens*.

A better African representation of *H. erectus* is in East Africa, particularly from the upper part of Bed II and Bed IV at Olduvai Gorge and from Lake Turkana. Two crania (OH 9 and OH 12) are known from Olduvai. OH 9, discovered by L. S. B. Leakey (1961), is from upper Bed II (dating from about 900,000 to 1.0 million years B.P.) and displays strong similarities to the Javanese specimens (Fig. 15.3). The endocranial volume has been estimated at 1,067 cc (Holloway 1937b). OH 12, found in 1963 in Bed IV (L. S. B. Leakey and M. D. Leakey 1964), is a very fragmentary cranium with an estimated endocranial volume of 727 cc (Holloway 1973b).

Also from Bed IV is OH 28 (dating between 700,000 and 800,000 years B.P.), which consists of the shaft of a left femur and the major portion of a left *os coxa* (M. D. Leakey 1971). Since this is the only known pelvic fragment of *H. erectus*, no comparisons with other specimens are possible. However, after a detailed anatomical, metric, and radiological examination, Day (1971) found the femur remarkably similar to those from Choukoutien. OH 28 is also unique in that it is the first *H. erectus* fossil in direct association with a lithic industry. This is clearly early Acheulean, characterized by hand axes, bifacial cleavers, choppers, scrapers, and other tools.

The most complete *H. erectus* skull ever found, again strikingly like those from Choukoutien, is KNM-ER 3733 from Lake Turkana (R. E. F. Leakey 1976). As seen in Figure 15.4, the skull consists of the vault bones and a large part of both maxillae, zygomatics, and nasal bones. Typically, the supraorbital tori are very large; the nuchal plane and occipital squama are sharply angled; and the postorbital

Figure 15.3 Lateral view of the OH 9 calvaria, the remains of *H. erectus* from Olduvai Gorge, East Africa. (Redrawn from a cast produced by the Wenner-Gren Foundation for Anthropological Research.)

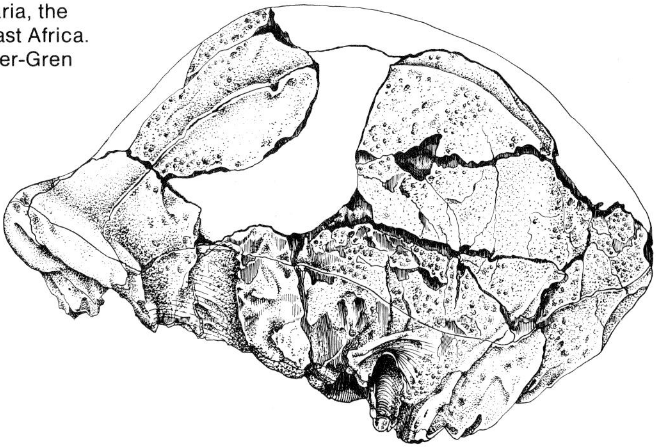

Figure 15.4 Lateral views of **a,** KNM-ER 406 (a robust australopith) and **b,** KNM-ER 3733 (*H. erectus* from Lake Turkana). (Courtesy of A. Walker and P. Andrews, *Australopithecus, Homo Erectus* and the Single Species Hypothesis. *Nature* 261: 313–314, 1973.)

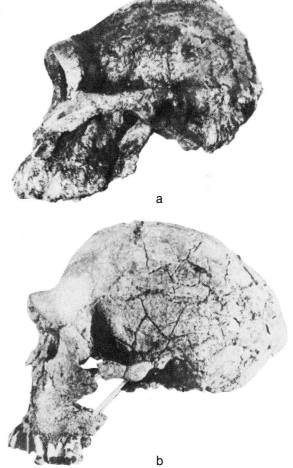

a

b

constriction is rather slight. Although a formal estimate of endocranial volume has not been given, R. E. F. Leakey and Walker (1976) consider it on the order of 800 to 900 cc.

Evidence for European *H. erectus* is very scarce, consisting only of a controversial mandible from Mauer in southern Germany, four deciduous teeth and an adult occipital from Vértesszöllös in Hungary, living and butchery sites at Torralba and Ambrona in Spain (Howell 1965, 1966), the occupation sites of Terra Amata at Nice and Le Vallonnet in southeastern France (de Lumley, Gagniere, and Pascal 1963), and the well-preserved Petralona skull from Greece (Hemmer 1972).

The earliest indication of European *H. erectus* comes from Le Vallonnet, which dates between 1.3 and 0.7 million years B.P. (de Lumley 1975). The stone artifacts from this site were made of limestone, quartzite, and flint, and include flakes, choppers, scrapers, and worked pebble tools. In addition, there is some evidence of intentionally cut and flaked animal bones. Terra Amata is much younger, dating between 450,000 and 380,000 years B.P., and provides more information than Le Vallonnet about the material culture of *H. erectus*. Consisting of a number of successive, but nonpermanent, living floors, this site is interpreted by de Lumley (1975) as a temporary camp where nomadic Acheulean hunters paused, built their shelters, and manufactured a variety of stone implements.

Oval shelters were built by laying either branches or hides on poles and anchoring these to the ground with stones. These shelters measured from about 23 to 49 feet long and 13 to 20 feet wide, and usually had a hearth built in their center. Each hearth also had a small wall of stones or pebbles built on the northeast side—that of the prevailing wind. If it is assumed that these short walls were arranged as small windbreaks, then the presence of drafts within the shelter would imply that branches rather than hides were used in their construction. In any case, the evidence is clear that tools were manufactured in the shelters. In the center of the huts were small areas devoid of flakes, but around which waste flakes were abundant. Very likely these bare areas represent the spot where the man sat while fashioning his tools.

Unfortunately, no human remains have been found at either Le Vallonnet or Terra Amata. The same is true for Torralba and Ambrona, two sites excavated from 1961 through 1963 (Howell et al. 1963). These closely adjacent sites, located about 200 kilometers northeast of Madrid, Spain, were apparently kill/dismemberment areas and secondary butchering/meat-processing areas occupied by *H. erectus* about 400,000 years ago. Elephants, horses, aurochs (wild European oxen), a few deer and rhinoceroses, and meager remains of carnivores, small mammals, and birds were found in association with Acheulean tools. In most instances the bones were split and fractured and in some cases appear to have been flaked in "recognizable" forms (Howell 1966). These findings, in addition to the clear indication that fire was used, have led to the reasonable conclusion that *H. erectus* hunters used fire to drive groups of animals into bogs where they could be more easily killed with stones, wooden spears, or both.

The mandible from Mauer and the partial occipital from Vértesszöllös, both of which date somewhere between 400,000 and 600,000 years B.P., are the oldest human remains known from Europe. Both have been the subject of considerable controversy, and their taxonomic assignment to *H. erectus* will probably not be fully accepted until additional material is located. While certain details of the dentition of the Mauer mandible differ from other chronologically contemporaneous specimens in different areas, such as smaller tooth size relative to mandibular size, other features point toward *H. erectus* affiliation. In particular, the mandible lacks a chin, is massively constructed, and has a broad ascending ramus. These features, coupled with its age and association with animal bones broken in a fashion similar to those found at Choukoutien, argue for its inclusion into *H. erectus* (Le Gros Clark 1964a).

The four occupation horizons at Vértesszöllös have yielded substantial remains of early mammals (Kretzoi and Vertes 1965), in addition to several thousand stone artifacts. While about half of these are debris from stone tool manufacture, about 20% are recognizable implements. Included are choppers and chopping tools, flake tools, side scrapers, denticulates, borers, and retouched flakes (Howell 1966). Interestingly, the artifact assemblage is in many ways similar to that from Choukoutien. The tools are nearly always quite small, and there is a complete absence of handaxes and bifacial cleavers. Hearths have also been discovered, which, with those from Terra Amata, represent the oldest yet known.

The Vértesszöllös occipital presents some intriguing problems because (1) it belonged to a skull that was probably larger than that of any other known *H. erectus* individual and (2) it presents morphological features resembling both *H. erectus* and *H. sapiens*. Thus Thoma (1966, 1972a) estimated endocranial volume at close to 1,400 cc and placed the specimen in *Homo (erectus seu sapiens) paleohungaricus*. This was an attempt to recognize the intermediate nature of the fossil, but according to the rules of zoological nomenclature (see Chapter 8), this name actually reflected a new species (*paleohungaricus*) belonging to an intermediate subgenus (*erectus seu sapiens*) of *Homo*. Wolpoff (1971b) quickly concluded that the volume was less (no more than 1,325 cc, and within the expected range of variation for *H. erectus*), and that the total morphological pattern was closer to *H. erectus* than to *H. sapiens*. However, Thoma (1972b) reaffirmed his previous estimate a year later. What may be concluded from this? In light of the small amount of fossil material involved and the extremely tenuous nature of estimating endocranial volume from part of an occipital, it would seem prudent to withhold formal taxonomic assignment of this specimen until additional evidence is available.

The Petralona cranium was discovered in 1959 and originally thought to be an example of archaic *H. sapiens*. However, the fauna with which it was associated suggests a much earlier date—perhaps contemporaneous with the Mauer mandible. With an estimated endocranial volume of about 1,250 cc, the external cranial morphology is consistent with that observed in other *H. erectus* crania (Hemmer 1972). Unfortunately, a detailed anatomical description of this specimen has yet to appear.

A Brief Summary of *Homo Erectus*

The formal morphological diagnosis of *H. erectus* quoted below was written by Le Gros Clark before the discovery of the African fossils. But inasmuch as any species can be legitimately defined on the basis of common anatomical criteria, these features are still descriptive of *H. erectus*:

> *Homo erectus*—a species of the Hominidae characterized by a cranial capacity with a mean value of about 1,000 cc; marked platycephaly, with little frontal

convexity; massive supra-orbital tori; pronounced post-orbital constriction; opisthocranion coincident with the inion; vertex of skull marked by sagittal ridge; mastoid process variable, but usually small; thick cranial wall; tympanic plate thickened and tending toward a horizontal disposition; broad, flat nasal bones; heavily constructed mandible lacking a mental eminence; teeth large, with well-developed basal cingulum; canines sometimes projecting and slightly interlocking, with small diastema in upper dentition; first lower premolar bicuspid with subequal cusps; molars with well-differentiated cusps complicated by secondary wrinkling of the enamel; second upper molar may be larger than the first; limb bones not distinguishable from those of *H. sapiens*. (1964a: 114–115)

Compared to the australopiths, the more notable biological and cultural changes among *H. erectus* populations included (1) larger body size, (2) increased endocranial volume, (3) completely modern erect bipedalism, (4) reduction in the relative size of the dentition, (5) elaboration, if not the development, of complex verbal communication, (6) more expertise in the manufacture and use of tools and a concomitant increase in the number and variety of implements, (7) use of fire, (8) adoption of a subsistence pattern based in part on the hunting of large animals, (9) significant advances in group cooperation and other aspects of social organization, and (10) a much wider geographic distribution.

Homo Sapiens

By all reasonable standards, *H. erectus* came a long way toward modern *H. sapiens*. However, many changes accrued from the latest *H. erectus* to the Neandertal populations (*H. sapiens neanderthalensis*) that emerged about 100,000 years ago (see "The Neandertals," below, for definitional comments). Comparisons of the skeletal structures between these two groups indicate that the primary physical changes were limited almost exclusively to the skull. Thus, compared to *H. erectus*, the masticatory complex of Neandertal was smaller relative to the rest of the skull. The supraorbital tori were still very large, but perhaps not as relatively massive as before. Although the forehead had not become as vertical as among modern humans, the frontal region was more expanded and postorbital constriction was less. Platycephaly was not as pronounced, and the external occipital protuberance was relatively high. The occipital torus was heavily developed, but angulation between the nuchal area and the occipital squama was not as pronounced. And finally, the face was both prominent and high. Added to these differences is yet an additional increase in endocranial volume, the average population values being essentially the same as among modern human populations.

The Earliest Homo Sapiens
The fossil record for the period between about 400,000 to 100,000 years ago was nearly nonexistent for many years. Only two fragmentary skulls were known, one from Steinheim, north of Stuttgart, Germany, and the other from Swanscombe, along the Thames River, in England. The number of specimens from this time period is still lamentably low, but a few recent discoveries are beginning to shed some light on the transitional change from *H. erectus* to *H. sapiens*.

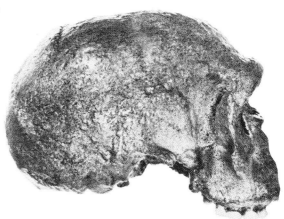

Figure 15.5 A lateral view of a cast of the Steinheim skull. (Reprinted with permission of Macmillan Publishing Co., Inc., from D. R. Pilbeam, *The Ascent of Man.* Copyright © 1972 by David R. Pilbeam.)

The Steinheim and Swanscombe specimens both date from approximately 250,000 years B.P. The Steinheim skull (Fig. 15.5), probably a female, is only moderately platycephalic and has a fairly well-developed forehead. The supraorbital tori are strongly developed, prompting Le Gros Clark (1964a) to suggest that their structure seems to have foreshadowed the massive tori among the later Western European Neandertals (sometimes called the Classic Neandertals). The occipital region is much more well-rounded than in *H. erectus*, and the facial skeleton was moderately constructed. Estimated endocranial volume is slightly less than 1,200 cc, which would be within the low part of the range for female Classic Neandertals, but well above the *H. erectus* average.

The Swanscombe remains (see articles in Ovey 1964, for a complete anatomical description) consist only of the occipital and both parietals. These remains, also from a female, are very similar to the specimen from Steinheim. The endocranial volume is about 100 cc greater, and analysis of the endocranial cast (Le Gros Clark 1964b) indicates no feature that would differentiate it from a modern cast.

The evolutionary position of the Steinheim and Swanscombe specimens was debated at some length during the early 1960s. In his analysis of various measurements, Coon argued that they were little different from some modern groups: "If these women were not *sapiens,* neither are many of the living female Australian aborigines and New Caledonians, whose skulls Steinheim and Swanscombe resemble in grade, but not in line (1962:497). However, a subsequent multivariate statistical analysis by Weiner and Campbell (1964) showed convincingly that some features were not modern. This points toward the conclusion that both were a primitive form of *H. sapiens,* and perhaps even ancestral to the later Western European Neandertals.

Also roughly contemporaneous with Steinheim and Swanscombe is the mandible from Montmaurin in southern France. The mandible bears some morphological resemblances to the Mauer mandible, although it is a good deal smaller. The shape of the mandible indicates a projecting face, however, and for this reason it very likely associates with Classic Neandertal. Additional evidence for the continuity between *H. erectus* and Neandertal populations in Europe comes from Arago Cave

Figure 15.6 Front and side views of the skull from Arago Cave, Tautavel, France. (Courtesy of H. and M.-A. De Lumley. Reproduced by permission of the American Association of Physical Anthropologists, from *Yearbook of Physical Anthropology* 17: 166–167, 1973.)

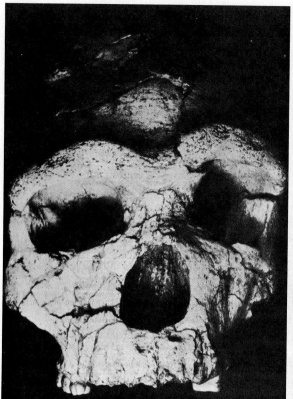

and La Chaise-Abri Suard, both in France. In 1969 and 1971, de Lumley and de Lumley (1971) discovered a number of isolated teeth, a few phalanges, parts of a parietal, two mandibles, and the anterior part of a skull (with an almost complete facial skeleton—see Figure 15.6) in deposits dated at about 200,000 years B.P. In some characteristics, such as pronounced prognathism, extraordinarily massive supraorbital tori, marked postorbital constriction (but not to the same extent as in *H. erectus*), and a low receding frontal bone, the skull is clearly archaic compared to Neandertal. However, certain features of the face and frontal distinguish it from *H. erectus*. Thus the de Lumleys (1974) consider it intermediate between *H. erectus* and the Western European Neandertals.

A great deal of hominid fossil material, dating around 120,000 years B.P., has been gained from the Abri Suard. Of special interest are two cranial vaults, a temporal, and an occipital (Krukoff 1970; Piveteau 1970). Affinities to *H. erectus* are suggested by the relatively thick cranial bones, marked platycephaly, and well-developed occipital torus. However, the small mastoid processes and other characteristics of the occipital and temporal are reminiscent of Western European Neandertals. The sample of prehistoric remains dating between about 100,000 to 70,000 years

B.P. is little better than just mentioned, although more confidence can be attached to their Neandertal affiliations. Of most importance are the sites of Saccopastore (near Rome), Ehringsdorf (in central Germany), and Fontechevade (in western France), but a number of other sites have yielded scattered hominid remains (see Mann and Trinkaus 1974).

The Saccopastore remains, dating to about 70,000 years B.P., include a female skull (Sergi 1944), found in 1929, and a male skull, discovered in 1935 (Blanc 1958). Features held in common with Classic Neandertals are strongly developed supraorbital tori, moderate platycephaly, a large maxilla, and small mastoid processes. However, both crania possess a well-rounded occipital, such as that found among modern humans. In addition, endocranial volumes have been estimated at about 1,200 cc and 1,300 cc for the female and male, respectively. These are relatively low values for either Neandertals or modern *H. sapiens.*

Although the cranial vault found at Ehringsdorf had an estimated endocranial volume of about 1,450 cc, it was probably also female. This cranium, reconstructed by Weidenreich about 50 years ago, is clearly more modern than those above in several respects. These include a relatively high vault, well-developed mastoid processes, and a convex and quite vertical forehead. However, the size of the supraorbital tori and the low occipital region approximate those found in Classic Neandertals.

The cranial fragments from Fontechevade are probably a bit older than the Ehringsdorf specimen. Consisting only of (1) the top of an adult cranial vault with parts of the frontal and (2) a smaller piece of a frontal bone of a different and perhaps immature individual, these specimens have been controversial since the time of their first description (Vallois 1949). The disagreements have arisen primarily because the bones are strikingly modern in appearance, inasmuch as modernity may be judged from such fragmentary material.

In particular, the controversy hinged upon marginal evidence that neither of these individuals possessed the massive supraorbital tori expected among Classic Neandertals. Thus it was suggested that the Fontechevade specimens represented a population more like the later (but morphologically modern) Cro-Magnon people than the Neandertals. This would, in turn, mean that modern groups of *H. sapiens* existed in Europe over 70,000 years ago—fully 30,000 years earlier than the evidence indicates elsewhere—and that they were contemporaneous with Neandertal during that period of time. The endocranial capacity, estimated at 1,450 cc, is consistent with either Neandertals or modern populations and therefore adds nothing toward solution of the problem. The thickness of the cranial bones, however, probably associates better with Neandertal.

There is no substantial evidence from other European sites suggesting the existence of two subspecific lineages—one leading to Neandertal and the other to Cro-Magnon. Thus, in light of the fragmentary nature of the specimens and inherent lack of diagnostic morphological features (see Trinkaus 1973, for a re-evaluation of the Fontechevade fossils), the hypothesis suggesting two contemporaneous subspecific lineages is presently unwarranted.

The Fontechevade remains notwithstanding, fossils from Morocco (Jebel Irhoud) and Israel (Jebel Qafzeh and Mugharet es-Skhul) present problems that are not affected by specimen inadequacy. The crania (Fig. 15.7) from these sites

Figure 15.7 Skulls from Jebel Irhoud, **a;** Jebel Qafzeh, **b;** and es–Skhul, **c.** (From W. W. Howells, *Evolution of the Genus Homo.* Copyright © 1973 by Cummings Publishing Company, Inc., Menlo Park, California.)

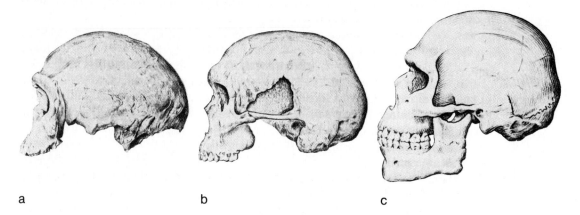

a   b   c

are younger than those discussed earlier, Jebel Irhoud dating at about 45,000 years B.P., Jebel Qafzeh a bit earlier, and es-Skhul at about 40,000 years B.P. However, they are still contemporaneous with Western European Neandertal populations. All three are associated with the Levalloiso-Mousterian culture, the same as among many Western European Neandertals, and each of the three can be distinguished morphologically from the other two. But, most interesting, none of these crania can be classed unequivocally as Neandertal.

Discovered in 1962 by Ennouchi (1962a, 1962b, 1963), the specimens from Jebel Irhoud now include several fragmentary crania. Most (e.g., Mann and Trinkaus 1974) maintain, on traditional morphological grounds, that these crania align quite closely with the Western European Neandertals, indicating the presence of such populations in North Africa. However, at least Piveteau (1967) and Howells (1973b) disagree with this view, the latter stating: ". . . the face is generally modern in appearance, rather short, and recessed well under the brows, though prognathic in the mouth region—evidently, the teeth were large. . . . Such people could easily be direct descendants of Steinheim, as far as all these features go" (1973b:89).

The remains from Jebel Qafzeh (Vallois and Vandermeersch 1972; Vandermeersch 1966, 1969, 1970) are among the most complete skeletal remains known from this time period, and they are morphologically fully modern or very nearly so (complete anatomical descriptions have yet to be published). The supraorbital tori are much less strongly developed than those of Classic Neandertals. The forehead is both rounded and vertical, and the occipital torus, although present, is much reduced. Furthermore, the chin is well developed, the face, nonprojecting, and the dental details are decidedly modern.

The Mugharet es-Skhul crania were discovered, along with the remains of two individuals from a neighboring cave called Mugharet et-Tabun, on Mount Carmel near Haifa, Israel (McCown and Keith 1939). While the et-Tabun specimens are about 10,000 years older than those from es-Skhul (Higgs 1961) and are clearly

Neandertal, the es-Skhul crania must be considered as archaic *H. sapiens sapiens*. The latter do indeed show a few minor Neandertal-like details in morphology, such as fairly well-developed supraorbital tori and generally robust cranial features. However, the high-vaulted and rounded crania are much more modern than the Jebel Irhoud specimens (but less so than those from Jebel Qafzeh).

The combinations of anatomical characteristics observed in many of the specimens discussed above have led to numerous controversies about the origin of modern *H. sapiens*. In particular, these disagreements have usually revolved around the position of Neandertal populations in the lineage leading to anatomically modern humans. Before discussing the various hypotheses advanced to explain the evolutionary relationships between these two groups, however, a few comments about the Neandertals themselves are in order.

The Neandertals

A problem that has continually occurred in most discussions on Neandertals is definitional: What is meant by the word "Neandertal"? Probably the most frequently cited definition—given the period when these populations were thought to represent a separate species (*H. neanderthalensis*)—is purely anatomical:

> The skull is distinguished by an exaggerated development of a massive supra-orbital torus, forming an uninterrupted shelf of bone overhanging the orbits (with complete fusion of the ciliary and orbital elements); absence of a vertical forehead; marked flattening of the cranial vault (platycephaly); relatively high position of the external occipital protuberance and the development (usually) of a strong occipital torus; a massive development of the nasomaxillary region of the facial skeleton, with an inflated appearance of the maxillary wall; a heavy mandible, lacking a chin eminence; a pronounced tendency of the molar teeth to taurodontism (that is, enlargement of the pulp cavity with fusion of the roots); a relatively wide sphenoidal angle of the cranial base (about 130°); angular contour of the occiput; certain morphological details of the ear region of the skull (including the rounded or transversely elliptical shape of the auditory aperture, the conformation of the mastoid process, and of the mandibular fossa); a slightly backward disposition of the foramen magnum; and a large cranial capacity (1,300–1,600 cc). (Le Gros Clark 1964a:60–62)

This definition is satisfactory as far as it goes, as may be others that are based solely upon anatomical criteria (e.g., Thoma 1965). However, it must be noted that it applies only to the Western European Neandertal populations. Ranging in time from about 75,000 to 32,000 years B.P., these populations probably stemmed from earlier, more widespread "Neandertaloid" groups (F. C. Howell 1952). Not only were they geographically highly restricted and nearly completely isolated from other contemporaneous populations, but in a number of minor features they were physically different from these other populations. Thus a definition of "Neandertal" based upon anatomical criteria of Western European Neandertals is too restrictive to be of much utility, because it is incapable of expressing the normal geographic variation of the species.

Others have attempted to define Neandertal in a cultural context: "Neandertal man and period seems to be . . . the man and period of the Mousterian culture" (Hrdlicka 1927:251). And still others (Brace and Montagu) have incorporated culture and anatomy into the definition: "Neanderthal man is the man of the Mousterian culture prior to the reduction in form and dimensions of the Middle Pleistocene face" (1977:330).

The major difficulty in defining Neandertal, or for that matter any segment of a biological or cultural evolutionary continuum, involves the arbitrariness of partitioning that segment. This does not necessarily mean that one is doomed to failure when defining Western European Neandertals—a group that is morphologically, culturally, and temporally about as discrete a group as one could wish to find. However, it does mean that the definition will become more tenuous as the number of transitional specimens (e.g., Jebel Qafzeh, es-Skhul, and others) increases. Admittedly, the definition given above by Le Gros Clark does apply to specimens recovered from western Europe, parts of the Near East, central Asia, and perhaps North Africa before about 32,000 years ago. But the usefulness of the definition is couched only in terms of facilitating communication between investigators, and it may have shortcomings even in this respect.

The morphological definition does not apply to the specimens from Swanscombe, Steinheim, or to the other European remains dating before about 75,000 years B.P. Nor is it strictly applicable to other contemporaneous populations that were widespread throughout the Old World. Nevertheless, there has been a tendency for over 50 years to label all of these diverse populations "Neandertal," doubtless because of the early conviction (Hrdlicka 1927; Weidenreich 1928) and later acceptance by some investigators that such populations represented a phase—the Neandertal phase—of human evolution between *H. erectus* and *H. sapiens*.

Indeed, human populations underwent numerous evolutionary changes from *H. erectus* to modern *H. sapiens*, but not all populations went through the same changes at the same times. To assume this and thus to postulate such a discrete evolutionary phase would be to deny the facts of human spatio-temporal distribution, physical variation, and differential adaptation to the diverse and changing Pleistocene environments. F. C. Howell (1957) recognized this over 20 years ago in his rejection of simple rectilinear models of human evolution during this period: "The concept of a Neanderthal phase or stage of man's evolution is no longer useful since there was marked variability from one such group to another. Frequently . . . the application of the designation Neanderthal has obscured rather than clarified the real nature and importance of the human skeletal materials" (1957:343).

Unfortunately, very few paid heed to F. C. Howell's commentary. Thus W. W. Howells strongly reemphasized the same point nearly 20 years later.

> . . . to label . . . (the phase). . . "Neanderthal" is to discourage attempts to examine distinctions among late Pleistocene populations, distinctions which might be of great importance, while at the same time to suggest that the Neanderthals . . . as they are traditionally thought of, are the specific source of modern man. We simply do not know that all men of this morphological zone or phase were like Neanderthal man proper . . . the common practice of using "Neanderthaloid" to name and classify, rather than simply to describe . . . is carelessly to state a conclusion in the terminology itself. (1973b:104)

With these comments in mind, then, it hardly appears useful or even desirable to have a single descriptive term or phrase that covers the spectrum of fossils representative of the time period mentioned above. In its usual context, the word "Neandertal" describes only a relatively few populations in Europe that shared a constellation of morphological and cultural characteristics. The words "Neandertaloid," "Neandertalian," and similar adjectives frequently used to describe specimens outside this geographical area and physically somewhat different, serve only to state that the fossils are in some respects similar to Western European Neandertals. Unfortunately, this has created a tendency to view Western European Neandertals as (1) the group from which contemporaneous populations elsewhere migrated and (2) a peculiar sort of ideal type to which individuals from other populations can only approximate.

Whereas the first viewpoint is indefensible on the basis of the fossil record, the second is unjustifiable from the standpoint of taxonomic theory (see the brief discussion of typological thinking in Chapter 8). For that matter, one of the primary reasons for the traditionally heavy emphasis upon Western European Neandertals stems from the simple fact that these fossils are more numerous than those from other areas—a chance circumstance related to extraneous factors of preservation and intensity of excavation rather than to relative population density. In sum, W. W. Howells's advice on this problem seems especially pertinent: "It would be of benefit if the careless use of "Neanderthal" were scrupulously avoided . . . rather than embraced as a basic premise for investigation . . ." (1974:26).

Selected Topics on Neandertal Biology and Culture

Although Europe was sparsely inhabited as early as 600,000 years B.P., and probably earlier, human penetration into the subarctic zone and effective exploitation of the resources in this area were not fully realized until about 80,000 years ago. Certain changes were obviously necessary for successful subsistence in this previously unpopulated and inhospitable region. Without doubt, most of these changes involved social and technological innovations that contributed to a higher probability of survival, but there is every reason to assume that certain biological adaptations also occurred.

The single physical change of particular interest to anthropologists concerns the highly distinctive craniofacial morphology of the Western European Neandertals, and especially the environmental factors with which the shape of the various skeletal components may have been associated. These populations were apparently isolated for a long period of time by glaciers to the north and impassable Alpine tundra to the east (Howell 1952). There may have been a southern "corridor" along the northern Mediterranean coast, but for all practical purposes the Western European Neandertals were isolated for a few thousand generations in a fluctuating, but essentially arctic, climate. Given the set of selective factors in this extreme environment, the time involved, and the lack of sophisticated technology (as among modern Eskimos) for ensuring survival, it is reasonable to assume that selection would favor those phenotypes that provided the most efficient anatomical and physiological protection against cold exposure.

In 1962, Coon adopted this assumption in a lucid hypothesis that attempted to explain certain peculiarities in the shape of the Neandertal face and skull, and a decade later Steegmann (1972b) partially verified the hypothesis in an experimental study of the relationships between cold exposure and facial shape among Hawaiians of European and Japanese descent. Coon reasoned that the prominent, broad, and projecting Neandertal nose was adapted for increased warming and moistening of the cold arctic air, thereby decreasing the chance of overcooling the lungs.

Although Steegmann (1975) has shown that a narrow and high nose humidifies and warms the air more efficiently than a broad one, the wide opening of the Neandertal nose was necessarily attendant with the relatively broad intercanine breadth. Coon also postulated that the unusually large infraorbital foramina, at least in the remains from La Ferrassie and La Chapelle, were capable of a six- to sevenfold increase in facial vascular supply as compared to modern Europeans. This increase would assist in preventing facial frostbite. Finally, Coon placed the greatest emphasis upon the forward position of the nose and face relative to the brain. Since normal brain function is dependent upon the maintenance of temperature within very close tolerances, an increase in the distance between (1) the brain's major arteries and (2) the exposed face and nasal passages would lessen the chance of the brain being chilled.

Another interesting possibility is that the Western European Neandertals may have had lightly pigmented skin. There is no hard and fast evidence for this, but indirect information of several kinds lends some plausibility to the idea. Consider these points: Neandertals lived in a northern climate; they must have remained heavily clothed most of the time; and those who did not inhabit caves resided in semipermanent shelters. From this comes the obvious conclusion that these people were chronically underexposed to sunlight, in general, and ultraviolet light, in particular.

Now, ultraviolet light is essential for the production of vitamin D, which is formed beneath the surface of the skin by a reaction between ultraviolet radiation and the body's natural cholesterol. Vitamin D does not occur naturally elsewhere, except in certain fish oils, and there is no evidence (fishhooks, etc.) of fish being a major part of the Neandertal diet. By its role in maintaining proper calcium metabolism, the relative amount of synthesized vitamin D is especially important for normal skeletal growth and development. Inadequate calcium deposition associated with vitamin D deficiency often leads to rickets, a disease characterized, in part, by irregularities in the joints and vertebral column and distortions of the shafts of long bones (see Sandstead 1973, for other symptoms).

Given the arctic conditions, it seems at least plausible that the amount of vitamin D synthesized by Neandertals would be less than optimal: only the face and the hands could have been exposed for any length of time, and even these periods would have had to be limited to avoid cold injury. Vitamin D production would have been even less if their skins possessed a heavy melanin content, because large amounts of melanin tend to "filter" out ultraviolet radiation. Under these conditions, and in light of the fact that certain disorders associated with vitamin D deficiency can lead to permanent skeletal deformities, it could have been selectively advantageous for Western European Neandertals to evolve lightly pigmented skin (for more about these relationships, see Loomis 1967, and Blum 1961, 1968). Additional support for this notion has been given recently by Post and his colleagues (1975), who found that people with heavily pigmented skin are more susceptible to cold injury than those with lighter skin pigmentation.

Compared to *H. erectus,* Neandertals were sophisticated hunters and gatherers, and, as harsh as the western European environment may have been, the regional flora and fauna upon which they subsisted was adequate, if not abundant. Although much of Europe was glaciated during the time of Neandertal occupation, a number of relatively short intervals occurred during which milder climatic conditions prevailed. By about 70,000 years B.P., the animals hunted for food included the woolly rhinoceros, wild cow, horse, and deer. About 20,000 years later the woolly mammoth appeared and was hunted and eaten by Neandertals. However, large animals provided only part of their diet. In other regions with more moderate climates, such as Shanidar Cave in northern Iraq, the evidence indicated utilization of sheep, goat, wild cow, pig, tortoise, bear, fox, deer, marten, and gerbil (Kennedy 1975). Although much of the Neandertal diet was meat, fossil pollen extracted from various sites shows that plants of different kinds were also eaten.

The implements with which Neandertals hunted and prepared their food probably evolved out of the late Acheulean tradition, but they were more advanced in manufacturing technique and functional variation. This time period is represented by the Mousterian industry, but the implements often show features similar to both preceding and succeeding periods. Thus artifact assemblages are sometimes called "Mousterian of Acheulean Tradition," "Levalloiso-Mousterian," or other phrases more descriptive of the particular tools. The manufacture of points, scrapers, and other implements from flakes that were struck from carefully prepared stone cores is called the Levallois technique, one of two stone-tool manufacturing methods used by these people.

The other, called the discoidal technique, also involved striking flakes from a core. However, this core produced a greater number of flakes that were both smaller and more uniform in size. In any case, the most common flake tool of Neandertals was a multipurpose side scraper that was probably used to prepare hides, sharpen wooden spears, and so forth. Various pointed tools, bifacially flaked hand axes, denticulate flakes, and end scrapers were also common. Far less numerous are perforators, blades, and burins, which are small tools utilized for engraving or, perhaps, minor cutting duties.

Finally, any doubt about the "humanness" of Neandertals can be quickly dispelled by a brief glimpse into their belief systems, two aspects of which are particularly noteworthy. The first concerns intentional burial of the dead, and the other an apparent veneration of the cave bear. Both practices argue strongly for the contention that rudimentary ideas about religion originated with Neandertals, but of course we can only speculate about their actual meanings.

The interment procedures of these groups varied from one region to another, as they do today. Some of those buried had stone slabs placed over their heads and shoulders; some were flexed, and others extended; and many were accompanied with material items such as animal bones, flint flakes, bone splinters, and assorted stone tools. However, the most convincing example of burial ritualization comes from Shanidar Cave (Solecki 1971). In the burial place of an adult male in the back of the cave was an unprecedented amount of pollen that could not have been deposited naturally. Analysis of the pollen produced two remarkable findings:. not only was the pollen distributed in concentrated clusters, but also it was derived from a number of brightly colored flowering plant species (e.g., hollyhock, groundsel, grape hyacinth, bachelor's button). Given the location of the burial, the most reasonable explanation is that masses of flowers were picked and intentionally placed in the grave.

Evidence of veneration of the cave bear has been gained from several dispersed sites, including Drachenloch Cave in the Swiss Alps and Regourdou in southern France. At Drachenloch, a cubical stone pit measuring slightly over three feet to a side, contained seven bear skulls. In addition, more skulls were placed in niches along the walls in deeper parts of the cave. All skulls in the pit, which was covered with a heavy stone slab, were oriented with their muzzles toward the cave entrance. A similarly massive stone slab covered a pit near Rigourdou, in which about 20 skulls of the cave bears were found. These animals were larger than modern adult grizzly bears and must have been formidable adversaries to hunters armed only with lances and stones. Thus it may be surmised that they were killed mainly to remove them from habitable caves or for defensive purposes, but we can only speculate about why Neandertals preserved their skulls in such ritualistic fashions.

One of the most puzzling enigmas about Western European Neandertals and other contemporaneous groups is their relatively abrupt disappearance about 35,000 years ago and their almost immediate replacement by anatomically modern Cro-Magnon populations. The hypotheses that attempt to explain this so-called Neandertal "extinction" are intimately involved with the nature of the transition between Neandertals and modern humans and the origin of modern populations. Hence both of these subjects are discussed at the beginning of the following chapter.

Summary

Australopithecus was apparently widespread in South and East Africa, but there is no good evidence that it spread beyond this continent. There is, however, solid paleontological evidence that australopiths gave rise to *Homo erectus* in Africa by about 1.5 million years B.P., and during the next million years or so this species radiated geographically to Europe, Southeast Asia, and China. There is general agreement that *H. erectus* was the immediate ancestor of early *H. sapiens* populations that subsequently evolved into modern humans.

The extent to which *H. erectus* had evolved toward modern *H. sapiens* can be indicated by the following: (1) larger brains than any previous hominids, with the greatest endocranial volumes within the lower part of the range for modern humans; (2) a great reduction in the masticatory complex as compared to earlier hominids, with molar dimensions also in the range for modern *H. sapiens;* (3) greater stature than *Australopithecus;* and (4) the use and manufacture of stone tools, but intentional modification of these implements for serving different functions.

Such similarities notwithstanding, *H. erectus* differed from *H. sapiens* in certain shape relationships of the skull and facial complex. In particular, *H. erectus* was characterized by unusually large supraorbital tori, a massive occipital torus on a relatively low and broad vault, and extraordinary thickness of the cranial and postcranial bones.

The tools recovered from various sites indicate clearly that *H. erectus* had embarked upon a subsistence pattern quite different from that of earlier hominids. The pattern was oriented around the hunting of big game, which, in turn, had profound behavioral and biological consequences. Among these were changes related to the improvement of technical skills, male cooperation and sharing between the sexes, sexual division of labor, and significant mental advances in the areas of perception, memory, and prediction. That *H. erectus* populations had developed a rudimentary culture is evident from a basic stylistic pattern of tool manufacture, group cooperation during hunting activities, the building of temporary camps with shelters and hearths, and the use of fire for cooking, warmth, and predator defense. This important achievement enabled *H. erectus* to be the first hominid to subsist outside tropical and semitropical climatic zones.

Unfortunately, few fossils have been discovered that represent the transitional period (from about 400,000 to 100,000 years ago) during which *H. erectus* evolved into the earliest *H. sapiens*. From those that do exist, it can be determined that, in comparison to *H. erectus,* the occipital region became more rounded, the facial skeleton less massively constructed, and endocranial volume was well above the *H. erectus* average.

The earliest *H. sapiens* for which abundant fossil and archeological remains exist were the Neandertals, which appeared about 100,000 years ago and are usually considered different from modern humans only at the subspecific level (*H. sapiens neanderthalensis*). In general, Neandertals had smaller masticatory complexes, more expanded frontal regions with less postorbital constriction (but still with massive supraorbital tori and remarkably thick cranial and postcranial bones), less pronounced platycephaly, less pronounced angulation between the nuchal region and occipital squama, and endocranial volumes that were no different from those among modern human populations. Neandertal populations in different geographical areas varied morphologically, with perhaps the most distinct cranial and facial phenotypic characteristics occurring among the Western European Neandertals. However, there is no doubt that all Neandertal populations possessed culture, however defined. They were far more sophisticated than *H. erectus* in their hunting techniques and technological capability, and ample evidence indicates that rudimentary ideas about religion originated among these people.

3

Topics on Modern Human Biology

16 Modern Population Origins and Diversification

Introduction

One of the major unsolved problems of human paleontology concerns the absence of fossil remains after about 35,000 years B.P., of the peoples traditionally called Neandertal. The problem is confounded by the evidence of what seems to be a sudden replacement by anatomically modern humans, almost as if the Neandertals had been "hybridized" out of existence or otherwise systematically eliminated by these later groups throughout the Old World. Equally as interesting is the observation that these latter populations were already regionally differentiated to the extent that some remains can be identified morphologically with modern inhabitants of the same areas.

The remains of an adult male from Niah Cave in northwest Borneo provide a good example. Dated at about 38,500 years B.P., this specimen predates the oldest anatomically modern Europeans by several thousand years, and is perhaps the oldest known modern human remains. Although acknowledging that this specimen is a "mere pinpoint" of evidence, Howells (1973c) and others are convinced of the correctness of Brothwell's (1960) findings—that these remains are classifiable as Tasmanian (or Melanesian or Australian). In any event, the Niah Cave skeleton establishes the presence of modern humans in southeast Asia at a time when Neandertals were still living in western Europe.

Another facet of the problem, perhaps even more perplexing than Neandertal disappearance, is the matter of the spatio-temporal emergence of modern *H. sapiens.* Several investigators have attempted to explain these enigmas by formulating various hypotheses, most of which can be subsumed under these titles: the Neandertal phase hypothesis, the pre-*sapiens* hypothesis, and the pre-Neandertal hypothesis. However, the controversies about this period of human evolution have continued unabated for over 50 years, and there is currently no completely acceptable solution in sight.

The Transition from Neandertal to Modern Humans

The Neandertal Phase Hypothesis

Originally offered by Hrdlicka (1927), amplified later by Weidenreich (1943b, 1947), and supported in its essence, more recently, by Coon (1962), Brace (1964), and Brose and Wolpoff (1971), this hypothesis holds that modern human populations evolved directly from regional groups contemporaneous with Western European Neandertals.

Hrdlicka did not define these groups in particular, but instead maintained only that local evolution would vary from one region to another according to prevailing differences in selective factors. Weidenreich's (1947) elaboration also held that Neandertals evolved into modern *H. sapiens* and, moreover, that such changes occurred simultaneously, but at different rates in different areas. He also suggested that beginning with the onset of the *erectus* stage, four regional lineages interconnected by gene flow passed through a "Neandertalian" stage and ultimately culminated in the Australian, African, Mongolian, and Eurasian races. Since Weidenreich neglected the Western European Neandertals in his scheme, it may be presumed that he considered them as having become extinct.

In an extension of Weidenreich's explanation, Coon (1962) began by postulating the present existence of the following five human subspecies:

1. Caucasoid: Europeans, wherever they occur, Middle Eastern white populations, most people from India, and the Ainu of Japan.
2. Mongoloid: most populations in eastern Asia, Indonesians, Polynesians, Micronesians, American Indians, and Eskimos.
3. Australoid: Australian aborigines, Melanesians, Papuans, some tribes in India, and south Asian and Oceanic Negritos.
4. Congoid: African black populations and Pygmies.
5. Capoid: Bushmen and Hottentots in Africa.

Coon maintained that these five subspecies had existed for a long period of time, and displayed some traits that had developed in their *H. erectus* ancestors. Furthermore, each subspecies was traced to certain *erectus* specimens: Caucasoid to a form either similar to or represented by the Mauer mandible, Mongoloid to the Chinese *H. erectus,* Australoid to the Javanese *H. erectus,* and Congoid to the so-called "Rhodesian man" (now usually acknowledged as an archaic *H. sapiens*). As for the Capoids, Coon believed that they stemmed from larger North African ancestors who were driven south by Caucasoids at the end of the Pleistocene. Once in southern Africa (perhaps 8,000 to 9,000 years ago), they underwent a general reduction in body size for reasons not fully understood. Hence these *erectus* populations were also subspecifically differentiated, and each of the five evolved independently into *H. sapiens.* However, the "threshold" through which they passed "from a more brutal to a more *sapient* state" (Coon 1962:657) occurred at different times, the Caucasoids being first and the Congoids last (on the order of only 40,000 to 50,000 years ago).

Finally, Brose and Wolpoff refuted Howell's comment that "beginning some 35,000 years ago new peoples with new ideas and new designs for living displaced and eventually replaced antecedent Neanderthal peoples and their Mousterian way of life" (1969b:XXI), and suggested instead that "*in situ* transitions of both hominids and their industries took place throughout the Old World within the period of the last glaciation. These transitions did not occur at the same time" (Brose and Wolpoff 1971:1184). Following some of Brace's earlier arguments (1962, 1964), they concluded that an important impetus for this direct transition was related, in part, to a more efficient lithic technology. In particular, the development of easily made flake tools eliminated the necessity of using the anterior dentition as a tool in assisting the hands for holding or working with hides or wooden objects. They supposed that this constituted a relaxation of selection and, accordingly, that a mutation effect (see Brace

1963, for more of this subject) would have contributed to a diminution in facial and dental architecture. The importance of the decrease in these structures, incidentally, is reflected in Brace's amendation of Hrdlicka's definition of Neandertal: "Neanderthal man is the man of the Mousterian culture prior to the reduction in form and dimension of the Middle Pleistocene face" (1964:18)

The Neandertal phase hypothesis has not been immune to criticism, and is by no means generally accepted. For example, Vallois (1958) objected on the basis of the amount of time involved in the transition between Neandertals and their *H. sapiens* successors. Indeed, this has been a major stumbling block when Western European Neandertals are assumed to have evolved into upper Paleolithic Europeans, because they would have had only 400 generations or less to do so. Although evolutionary changes in small populations can occur rapidly, such changes are normally very small. This length of time is simply not sufficient to account for the relatively large structural changes in craniofacial architecture between the two respective groups.

Dobzhansky (1963) disagreed with Coon's hypothesis, but from the viewpoint of an evolutionary biologist. In sum, he felt that

> The possibility that the genetic system of living men, *Homo sapiens*, could have independently arisen five times, or even twice, is vanishingly small. A biological species can be likened to a cable consisting of many strands; the strands—populations, tribes, and races—may in the course of time subdivide, branch or fuse; some of them fade away and others may become more vigorous and multiply. It is, however, the whole species that is eventually transformed into a new species. The populations, or races, in which these evolutionary inventions have occurred then increase in number, spread, come in contact with other populations, hybridize with them, form superior new gene patterns that spread from new centers and thus continue the process of change . . . man is, and apparently always was, a wanderer and a colonizer, and as people come in contact gene exchange takes place. But if this is true, the assumed separate evolution of the five subspecies becomes a practical impossibility. (1963:365)

The most convincing rebuttal of Brose and Wolpoff has been given by Howells (1974). The latter sees no methodological justification for the presumption by Brose and Wolpoff that all human populations between the end of the Riss Glaciation (somewhat less than about 200,000 years ago) and the advent of anatomically modern humans can be classified as Neandertals. According to Howells, this contention is based upon misuse of certain basic statistical concepts, i.e., a confusion of the difference between inter- and intrapopulation variance (see Appendix I):

> . . . the authors fail to comprehend the need to seek distinctions in levels of variation. . . . In fact, by implication, their approach rejects such distinctions: by demonstrating individual variation to be considerable for such a "population" as the western Neanderthals, it suggests that one scale of variation is sufficient to account for the world-wide variation in their "Neanderthal" supergroup, and thus, in addition, for the basis of transition anywhere between components of this group and anatomically modern *Homo sapiens*. Theoretically, this is a sizable flaw. (Howells 1974:27)

Thus such an all-inclusive definition of Neandertal would discourage examination of (1) the morphological variation within regional populations and (2) both the magnitude and meaning of the differences between human populations during this time period.

The Pre-*Sapiens* Hypothesis

Of the three, the pre-*sapiens* hypothesis has the fewest supporters. In essence, this formulation considers Neandertals as not having made any significant contribution to the modern European gene pool. Rather, its adherents (e.g., Vallois 1958; L. S. B. Leakey 1972) hold that *H. sapiens* had become differentiated much earlier. The main opposition to this hypothesis is simply that the fossil evidence for a "pre-*sapiens*" ancestor is very tenuous. The specimens from Swanscombe and Fontechevade have been frequently included in such a group, but the recent work by Weiner and Campbell (1964) on the Swanscombe remains casts considerable doubt on this interpretation: "On the basis of all the morphological and metrical features examined by us we would allocate Swanscombe not to the strict *sapiens* category or the 'pre-*sapiens*' lineage of Vallois but to the Neandertaloid 'intermediate' group which contains the Steinheim, Ehringsdorf, Skhul V and Krapina specimens" (1964:202). Similarly, the Fontechevade remains are too fragmentary to provide the kind of information necessary for the hypothesis.

The only fossils that might be seriously considered as early *H. sapiens* are from Africa: those discovered in Kenya in 1932–1933 by L. S. B. Leakey in the Kanjera Lake deposits, and the Omo I skull (R. E. F. Leakey et al. 1969) from southern Ethiopia. Tentatively dated at about 60,000 years B.P., the Kanjera remains have recently been restudied by Tobias (1962) and affirmed as *H. sapiens*. Because he found no indication of massive supraorbital and occipital tori and since the facial structure was relatively delicate, Tobias noted later that "it had undergone the reduction in form and dimension of the middle Pleistocene face" (1964:30).

However, Tobias also noted that only 5 of the 42 fragments were found *in situ* in undisturbed deposits. Since the 42 specimens were scattered throughout an area of about 100 yards in diameter, the possibility arose that they were not temporally homogeneous. In addition, the original middle Pleistocene age ascribed to the fossils by L. S. B. Leakey (1970) is probably much too early: Oakley (1964) estimates their age at about 60,000 years B.P. Therefore, the position of the Kanjera remains as a middle Pleistocene *H. sapiens* is open to serious question.

The Omo I skull is indeed modern in appearance, resembling in many ways the material from Mugharet es-Skhul and Swanscombe, but it is beset with the same reservations about its age as the Kanjera fossils. A Th^{230}/U^{234} date of fossil mollusks associated with the remains was estimated at about 130,000 years B.P. Because this dating method may not be accurate when applied to mollusks, however, there is considerable doubt as to the actual age of the Omo I specimen (Butzer et al. 1969). In light of these considerations, then, it would seem that the pre-*sapiens* hypothesis suffers from a serious lack of evidential support.

The Pre-Neandertal Hypothesis

This final view of human evolution in the upper Pleistocene considers two "Neandertal" groups. One is usually called the "Progressive" Neandertals, and is thought to have been widely distributed throughout Europe, North Africa, and parts of the Middle East during the early part of the upper Pleistocene. These populations are represented by the fossils from Steinheim, Ehringsdorf, Saccopastore, Mount Carmel, Krapina, and other sites. Beginning about 80,000 years ago, some of these populations became isolated by glaciers in western Europe and adapted morphologically to an essentially arctic climate. These isolates, termed the Western European or "Classic" Neandertals, are represented by fossils from France (e.g., La Chapelle-aux-Saints, La Ferrassie, La Chaise, La Quina, Le Moustier), Germany (Neandertal), Belgium (Bay-Bonnet, Engis, La Naulette, Spy), and Italy (e.g., Monte Circeo). Other sites yielding the remains of both Classic and Progressive Neandertals have been listed by Howell (1957) and Mann and Trinkaus (1974).

Supporters of the pre-Neandertal hypothesis (e.g., Howell 1952, 1957) maintain that Progressive Neandertals located in areas other than western Europe were evolving in response to their own local selective pressures at the same time the Classic Neandertals were developing the distinctive craniofacial morphology discussed earlier. However, they were evolving, instead, toward anatomically modern humans, and some specimens (such as Jebel Qafzeh and es-Skhul) have been cited as examples of morphologically transitional forms (Howell 1957).

In sum, the pre-Neandertal and pre-*sapiens* hypotheses are similar, but the supposed time when the Neandertals branched off from the line leading to modern human populations occurs earlier in the latter. While the matter of Western European Neandertal extinction poses no special problem to supporters of the Neandertal phase hypothesis (with the exception of Weidenreich and Coon), it is probably fair to state that most authorities regard this as an unanswered question.

One of the more prevalent views, unsubstantiated by any solid evidence but intrinsically appealing in its simplicity, is that Western European Neandertal populations were replaced locally (but not liquidated by wholesale genocide) by the Cro-Magnons. As Kennedy (1975) notes, the migration of the latter into western Europe was probably initiated by the quest for new hunting areas, and there are at least two reasons to suppose that the Neandertals would have been at a disadvantage in the ensuing intraspecific competition for the same resources.

First, the technology of the Cro-Magnons was clearly superior. While Neandertals did manufacture points that were probably hafted to a spear and used mostly for thrusting, the Cro-Magnon developed the spear-thrower. By increasing distance, velocity, and accuracy, this advanced weapon gave the Cro-Magnon a substantial edge in hunting technology. Second, the archeological evidence from caves, inhabited first by Neandertals and later by their replacements, indicates a greater population density among the latter. Now we can only speculate about the levels of social organization of Neandertals and Cro-Magnons. They may have been organized into bands, or in the case of the Cro-Magnon, into more complex groups such as the pan-tribal sodalities described by Service (1971). In any event, if larger group size is positively correlated with more complex social bonds, then the Cro-Magnon may have had both organizational and strategic advantages over the Neandertals during periods of conflict.

Whatever the actual circumstances may have been, it is often assumed by those who view Neandertal extinction as a real phenomenon that some Neandertal/Cro-Magnon hybrids were produced in the process. The historical literature is replete with examples of colonial populations displacing native groups, and when this occurs, some females of the latter are almost inevitably retained and give birth to hybrid children. Thus Birdsell (1975) comments that estimates of the frequency of Neandertal genes still present among modern European populations range from about 5 to 15% of the total gene pool.

The Partitioning of Modern Humanity

Estimates of world population size during any period from the first appearance of hominids until about the middle of the eighteenth century are extremely crude. For example, Coale (1974) notes that global population in the mid-1700s can only be calculated with an uncertainty factor of about 20%, and that the margin of error increases when earlier periods of time are considered. Hence we have virtually no idea of the actual numbers of *Australopithecus, H. erectus,* or late Pleistocene *H. sapiens* for any given time interval. About all that can be definitively stated, and this only in the context of increasingly wide geographic distribution, is that humans increased their numbers. However, the increase was very slow for a long period of time.

For the sake of argument, we may suppose that *H. erectus* numbered in the thousands or tens of thousands after a relatively brief period of time after their differentiation from *Australopithecus.* From this time until the advent of agriculture and animal domestication (about 8,000 years ago), world population remained quite low. For over 99% of the history of our species, people were hunters and gatherers, a mode of subsistence, which, even in the most hospitable of environments, would have allowed a population density of about one person per square mile. In extreme environments, such as semiarid or arctic regions, population density would have hardly been greater than about one person per every 50 to 100 square miles.

This was changed irrevocably by the shift to settled agriculture and animal domestication, which, for reasons related directly to increased food production and storage, enabled an ever greater number of people to inhabit restricted land areas. However, these achievements did not immediately lead to rapid population expansion. The relative stability in numbers during the next several thousand years was associated, doubtlessly, with the inability to cope adequately with disease, famine, and other factors contributing to high mortality levels.

By about 8,000 years B.C., there were probably 8 million people on Earth, and by A.D. 1 this number had expanded to about 300 million. These figures are only informed guesses, but such an increase over 8,000 years represents an annual growth rate of approximately 0.36 per 1,000. The annual growth rate increased slightly—to about 0.56 per 1,000—between A.D. 1 and A.D. 1750. By this time there were 800 million people, and it was also at this time that human population growth began to rapidly accelerate. This extraordinary increase has been ascribed to a variety of changes in material culture and socioeconomic reorganization that occurred during the Industrial Revolution (Childe 1951).

By 1800 the annual growth rate had increased to about 4.4 per 1,000, and world population to 1 billion. And in the next two 50-year intervals (from 1800 to 1850, and 1850 to 1900), the annual growth rate increased to 5.2 and 5.4 per 1,000, respectively. World population went from about 1.3 billion in 1850 to 1.7 billion in 1900, and even more phenomenal increases have occurred since then. There were 2.5 billion people in 1950 (growth rate = 7.9 per 1,000), and 25 years later—in 1975—the annual growth rate had doubled to over 17 per 1,000. Current estimates of world population are now fairly accurate and center around 4 billion. As seen graphically in Figure 16.1, the increase in annual growth rate and population number has been exceedingly gradual for most of our existence. However, in the last 200 years population increase has been so stupendous that, if we follow the mathematical reasoning of Keyfitz (1966), the 4 billion people alive today represent about 6% of all the people who have ever lived on Earth.

If numerical increase over a relatively short span of time is an adequate criterion for evolutionary success, then *H. sapiens* must be judged the most successful of any large mammal that has ever existed on Earth. Yet such large numbers of people, distributed over nearly all of the Earth's land surface and exposed to a bewildering variety of different selective factors, have made analysis of human infraspecific variation enormously difficult.

For the last two centuries, since Blumenbach's (1776) early racial classification, the traditional approach toward understanding modern human diversity has involved subdividing humanity into various races. However, not one of the dozens of classifications that have been proposed has been generally accepted. Furthermore, the biological validity of this basic approach itself has been challenged seriously in recent years (see, for example, Livingstone 1964a; Ehrlich and Holm 1964). The controversy centers around the question of whether human variation is best explained by clines or by naturally occurring subspecies. Whereas a cline denotes a progressive change in some trait through contiguous populations, i.e., a geographic character gradient (Huxley 1938), a subspecies is defined as "an aggregate of local populations of a species inhabiting a geographic subdivision of the range of the species, and differing taxonomically from other populations of the species" (Mayr 1963:672). A brief discussion of both concepts follows below.

Clines

The concept of the cline was formally introduced by Huxley (1938). Along with other investigators, he realized that formal subspecific names and descriptions were often incapable of revealing the full extent of variation within species, and, furthermore, that simple subspecies identification was not necessarily useful in determining the mechanisms responsible for infraspecific variation. This became evident after a series of thorough studies of morphological character variation revealed that traits did not always change abruptly between groups of populations. Rather, they were often observed to change gradually from one end of the species range to the other.

This phenomenon posed considerable problems for taxonomists who defined subspecies as groups of populations whose trait frequencies differed significantly from other such groups. Formal subspecific differentiation at the extremes of a species range was not usually as difficult as for that of adjacent population groups that were only slightly different, but in both cases the formal naming of different subspecies along the line of progressive character changes was a totally arbitrary process. Hence, under these conditions, the establishment of subspecies often tended

Figure 16.1 Graphs representing an overview of the human population from a million years ago to the present. Note that population size and annual rate of increase are constant for most of the evolutionary history of the species. World population numbers have accelerated rapidly only since about 1750, a time period representing about 2% of human history. However, about 80% of the increase in human population numbers has occurred during this period, with the most dramatic rise in the rate of increase occurring only during the last several decades. (From A. J. Coale, *The History of the Human Population.* Copyright 1974 by Scientific American, Inc. All rights reserved.)

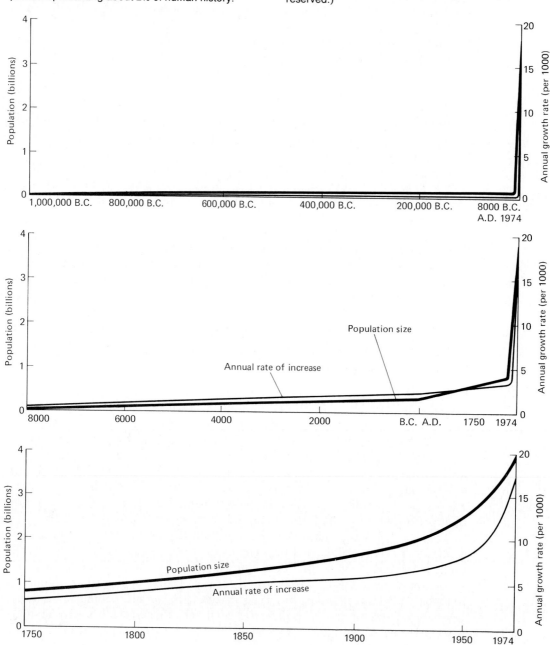

to (1) give a false impression of the biological homogeneity within the defined subspecies and (2) overemphasize the named groups versus those which were not named.

In light of these difficulties, Huxley suggested the cline as a useful auxiliary taxonomic device for describing infraspecific variation: "It is in no way intended that specification by clines should replace any of the current taxonomic methods. It would constitute a supplementary method which, it is suggested, would correct certain defects inherent in the naming of areal groups, notably in stressing continuity and regularity of variation as against mere distinctness of groups" (1938:219). It should be stressed that Huxley did not wish to abandon the subspecies concept, but rather to use clines to clarify the taxonomic relationships between populations.

However, he also maintained that, in instances where a well-defined character gradient extended throughout a series of populations over a considerable geographic range, the cline itself could be used as a taxonomic category. Nomenclaturally, such a cline would be denoted by the abbreviation *cl.* followed by a hyphenated Latin name. An example of this procedure was given later by Huxley (1943) for the Burmese squirrel (*Callosciurus sladeni*). These squirrels had been previously divided into four subspecies (*shortridgei, fryanus, careyi,* and *harringtonii*), mainly on the basis of coat color differences. However, the discovery of intermediate forms between two of these suggested that coat color varied clinally. Thus, in Huxley's view, the proper nomenclatural designation would be *Callosciurus sladeni cl. shortridgei-harringtonii.*

It is probably fortunate, given the nomenclatural confusion that would have inevitably resulted, that Huxley's proposal did not gain acceptance among practicing taxonomists and zoologists. Nevertheless, Huxley's emphasis on clinal variation and the subsequent demonstration of the near-universality of this phenomenon among sexually reproducing animal and plant species have resulted in an extremely useful method for describing and understanding infraspecific genetic variation.

Theory of Cline Formation

Theoretically, any genetically determined morphological or physiological trait or any allele frequency is subject to clinal variation. Such traits may be either polygenic or under simple genetic control. Clines are ultimately associated with environmental selective factors, although it is usually difficult to identify the particular selective agent responsible for maintaining a given cline. In adjacent continental areas or closely spaced island chains, the environmental factors in each local area usually intergrade with neighboring conditions to form environmental gradients. These gradients can be defined in terms of the climatic and edaphic factors that are generally associated with differences in latitude and altitude. Thus environmental gradients exist for temperature, humidity, solar intensity, relative day-length, soil acidity or salinity, substrate color and composition, and numerous other climatic and topographical features.

Because these features also act as selective factors, the phenotypic characteristics that they affect would also be expected to vary along gradients. However, contiguous populations usually exchange genes, a process that tends to diminish the differences thus produced. Therefore, clines are produced and maintained by the combined action of selection, which adapts populations to their own local habitats, and gene flow, which tends to "smooth" out these local adaptations and thereby reduce the differences between contiguous populations.

Clines are not necessarily always smoothly changing gradients. For example, when gene flow is interrupted by geographic or social barriers, the regularity of a pre-existing cline may also be interrupted. The reason is that normalizing selection, in the absence of gene flow, will tend to bring trait values toward their phenotypic optima. These optima may differ, depending upon the prevailing set of selective factors in each habitat. Thus, when gene flow is only partially obstructed, a cline may be interconnected in a "stepped" fashion. But when gene flow is completely prevented, geographic variation in a character may be expressed as a series of discontinuous levels between adjacent populations.

All clines must ultimately be considered transient, inasmuch as environmental selective factors are also transient. Indeed, solid paleontological evidence could conceivably establish long-term clinal stability in regions where selective factors have undergone little change and where migratory patterns have remained constant. However, this has yet to be demonstrated. In this context, the theoretical conditions required for clinal stability and maintenance (Haldane 1948; Fisher 1950) are interesting, although for practical purposes they are probably inapplicable to most human clines.

For the maintenance of some clines, the difference between selection coefficients (see Chapter 6) at the extremes of the cline is surprisingly small. Consider, for example, the cline for the *A* allele in the ABO system in Japan. In this rather linear cline, the allele frequency of *A* gradually increases from 0.24 to 0.30 over a distance of about 2,000 kilometers (Nei and Imaizumi 1966). Both Haldane's and Fisher's methods provide very small but similar values (10^{-8} and 0.3×10^{-7}, respectively) which represent the difference between selection coefficients for this cline's maintenance (see Cavalli-Sforza and Bodmer 1971, for the mathematical details). The only reason for mentioning this is that clines, at least in theory, can be maintained by exceedingly small differences in selection coefficients between adjacent populations— so small, in fact, that they cannot realistically be measured.

Each cline is theoretically independent of all others, although in some instances several different clines will follow a similar pattern, owing either to migration or to a common selective factor. One such pattern concerns the allele frequencies for thalassemia and G6PD deficiency in central Sardinia (Livingstone 1969). As seen in Figure 16.2, the allele frequencies for both defects vary in the same way—high on both coasts and low in the mountainous interior. The populations among which these frequencies were observed are located in a fairly linear sequence from the southwest to the northeast coasts. Now individuals deficient in G6PD are resistant to malaria, and although the experimental evidence is presently inconclusive, the geographic distribution of thalassemia suggests strongly that carriers of the recessive allele possess malarial resistance similar to individuals with the sickle-cell trait. Since both coastal areas are infested with malaria, while the interior is not, the probable reason for the concordance between the two clines can be couched in terms of malaria as a selective agent.

Figure 16.2 The frequencies of the thalassemia and glucose-6-phosphate dehydrogenase deficiency genes in a linear series of towns in Central Sardinia. (Reprinted from Gene Frequency Clines of the β Hemoglobin Locus in Various Human Populations and Their Simulation by Models Involving Differential Selection. *Hum. Biol.* 41 (2): 1969, by F. B. Livingstone. By permission of the Wayne State University Press © 1969.)

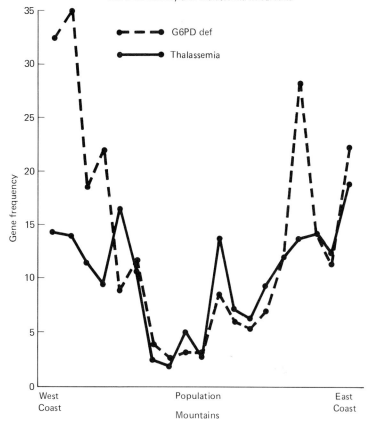

Finally, a few comments about the value of clinal analysis are in order before turning to subspecies and races. At the outset, it should be noted that clines are not appropriate for classificatory purposes. As Simpson (1961) and others have repeatedly stated, only populations can be classified. Clines are nothing more than geographic gradients in specific characters, each of which may vary in a different direction among the same populations. For this reason, and because a population represents a point along as many clines as it has variable characters, the cline is unsuitable as a taxonomic category (Mayr 1963).

One of the great advantages of studying geographic variation by clines is that gene and trait frequency variability can be graphically represented, much like the altitudinal contour lines on a geologic map. In conjunction with (1) information about migratory patterns and other aspects of population history and (2) identification of the changing selective factors along an environmental gradient, observed clinal variation in a trait is particularly amenable to explanation by mathematical methods of population genetics. In this sense, there is probably no superior method by which the evolutionary mechanisms responsible for interpopulation variation in single traits can be identified.

Yet some have objected to the use of clines for the analysis of human variation, arguing mainly that the study of variation in the frequencies of single genes or traits ignores the unity of the breeding population: The study of human variation by clines ". . . would produce a hopelessly confused picture . . . genes do not exist in isolation; they occur in a matrix of other genes. The whole genotype is carried by—although incompletely manifested in—the phenotype. By taking single genes or even single traits, out of context, you become a poor geneticist, as well as no anthropologist at all" (Damon 1977:182).

This view notwithstanding, it would seem that a greater appreciation of the ways in which groups of human populations have become different from other groups can be best acquired by first analyzing the effects of selection and migration on the expression of single traits. One understands the whole only by studying its component parts—not vice versa—and herein lies the value of clinal analysis.

Subspecies and Races

The subspecies is the only formal taxonomic category beneath the species level that is presently recognized in the *International Code of Zoological Nomenclature.* Although this category may have been used earlier, ornithologists adopted it at least as early as 1844 to designate what appeared to be distinct geographic subdivisions within recognized species of birds (Sibley 1954). Prior to that time, Linnaeus's *varietas* (variety) was the only accepted subdivision of a species. In Linnaeus's view, the species was a fixed, uniform group of individuals who replicated the ideal type of the species. Individuals who did not conform to the ideal type were called varieties. Subsequently, the term variety was applied to both individual variants and to entire populations that did not agree with the species type. Although the variety was used ambiguously and replaced later by the subspecies, the latter continued to be defined typologically.

Darwin and a few others before him were well aware of the fact that populations within a species varied geographically. Thus ornithologists in the 1800s were the first to recognize geographic groups as formal taxa, and proposed that such groups be identified by adding a third name to the standard binominal method of species nomenclature. Hence the trinomen (see Chapter 8) was born, and by the early 1900s, the subspecies category gained wide (but never total) acceptance among practicing taxonomists.

Before the subspecies came into widespread use, species were often defined on the basis of inadequate samples from only one or a few geographic regions. As a consequence, interpopulation variation within the species range was frequently overlooked, and the species themselves were considered monotypic—i.e., not consisting of various subspecies. However, as more thorough field studies were undertaken, it became evident that what had been previously described as allopatric species were actually single species interconnected by intergrading populations. Thus classificatory revisions became necessary, and the increased awareness that species were composed of populations that varied both spatially and temporally led to the concept of the polytypic species. Such a species is one that possesses two or more subspecies. The shift in species concepts, i.e., from one that was defined morphologically and typologically to the biologically defined polytypic species, is regarded by Mayr (1963) and other systematists as one of the more important conceptual contributions of modern systematics.

Most modern definitions of the subspecies are very similar to that quoted earlier by Mayr. Modern definitions of race, as evidenced by the few randomly selected samples below, are also internally consistent.

1. "A race is a division of a species which differs from other divisions by the frequency with which certain hereditary traits appear among its members" (Brues 1977:1).

2. "A race is a breeding population characterized by frequencies of a collection of inherited traits that differ from those of other populations of the same species" (Goldsby 1977:21).

3. "A race is a subdivision of a species; it consists of a population that has a different combination of gene frequencies than do other populations of the species" (Lasker 1976:344).

Obviously, it would serve little purpose to cite additional definitions. These three are sufficient to indicate that the modern concept of race, particularly as it is usually applied to *H. sapiens,* is very similar to the taxonomic concept of the subspecies. The primary difference is that, whereas subspecies are population aggregates, a race can ostensibly be a single local population (a "microgeographic" race). Otherwise, the subspecies is the same as the geographic race.

In light of the fact that most modern biological anthropologists maintain the synonymity between subspecies and geographic races, one may legitimately question why they have preferred the latter term. Unfortunately, there seems to be no readily apparent answer other than traditional usage. Indeed, some have objected strenuously to the word (e.g., Birdsell 1975) and have thought that its deletion from the scientific vocabulary would go far toward eliminating such thoroughly odious concepts as racism (e.g., Montagu 1962). This kind of solution, of course, is far too simple. Groups of populations that for social, political, or historical reasons believe in their own innate superiority over other groups will probably not be dissuaded from their beliefs by semantic magic.

In a different vein, others have denied the existence of human races (but not necessarily races in other animal species), maintaining that all variation is clinal: "For man . . . there are no races, there are only clines" (Livingstone 1964a:47). There is no doubt that much of human variation is clinal, and clines have been found that extend across entire continents. However, there are also clusters of populations that differ in sets of genetic and physical characteristics from other clusters in different areas. It solves nothing, especially concerning the promotion of interracial harmony, to deny the existence of such biological differences. In sum, Alice Brues's comment on this point seems especially pertinent:

> I believe that in a period in which the word "race" has become politically and emotionally charged, most people welcome an opportunity to discuss the perfectly simple physical differences that distinguish populations of geographically different ancestry. The very air of conspiracy with which some people avoid talking about racial differences is enough to give the impression that

these differences are in some way sinister. I do not feel this way. Racial differences need not be thought of as something puzzling or uncomfortable about strangers: they can also be something interesting about your friends. (1977:vii–viii)

Some Details about the Subspecies Category

The actual partitioning of a species into component subspecies is an arbitrary process, although some practical guidelines (see list below) for subspecific differentiation have been established. The arbitrariness of the category makes it an elusive concept, which probably explains much of the current controversy about the existence or nonexistence of human races and the obvious disagreements among those who have attempted racial classifications. Hence it is appropriate to emphasize a few salient points about the subspecies category.

1. The subspecies is a taxonomic category, *not* an evolutionary unit. It is not an incipient species in the sense that it has already acquired partial reproductive isolation from other sympatric populations.

2. The subspecies is a collective category consisting of numerous local populations that are phenotypically and genetically slightly different. Subspecific status can theoretically be based only upon interpopulation genetic differences, but, in practice, morphological characteristics with an unknown genetic basis are also used. In this regard, characteristics that vary due to phenotypic plasticity are inappropriate.

3. Each population of a species can be shown to differ genetically from all other populations, providing the measurements and statistics are sufficiently sensitive. However, subtle statistical differences between populations are not sufficient for subspecific status; otherwise, every population would possess its own formal trinomen. Hence two groups must differ "taxonomically" if they are to be formally named, a stricture in itself that can only be arbitrarily followed.

What does "taxonomically different" mean, and how is it to be determined? Unfortunately, there has never been universal agreement by taxonomists on either of these questions. Probably the greatest number of taxonomists have adopted the so-called 75% rule (Amadon 1949). As usually interpreted, this rule states that for a population or a group of populations to be recognized as a valid subspecies, 75% of the individuals in the group must differ from all ($= 97\%$) of the individuals of another recognized subspecies. If the character variation of each group is represented by a frequency distribution curve (see Appendix I), there will be a zone of overlap between the two curves. However, it will also be found (providing normality of the two distributions exists) that about 90% of the individuals of one group will differ from an equal percentage of the other group (Mayr 1969).

Other taxonomists prefer the 84% rule, which states simply that 84% of the individuals of one group must differ from 84% of the individuals of another group (Pimentel 1959). Yet others—the "splitters"—favor a 50% rule. And at the other extreme, the "lumpers" feel that subspecies cannot be formally recognized unless at least 97% of the individuals of two groups are different (Mayr 1954).

In sum, the lack of an objective definition for the subspecies has been a main source of taxonomic controversy, and all attempts to develop a more biologically oriented definition (such as that for the species) have been unsuccessful. For example, Edwards proposed the definition: "Subspecies are natural, obviously different populations, the members of which would cross-breed rather freely if they occurred sympatrically and synchronically under natural conditions, but which are distinctly separated during their mating periods with the result that they do not normally cross-breed" (1954:11). However, the greatest weakness in this definition is still the failure to specify what is meant by "obviously different."

4. Individuals cannot necessarily be assigned to a subspecies, because neighboring populations overlap in their ranges of variation. Likewise, the geographic character variation of a species is never fully expressed by a subspecies: it expresses only a fraction of that variation.

Although the subspecies category has contributed much to the study of infraspecific variation, a number of taxonomists and systematists in the 1950s became disenchanted with the concept, both as a classificatory device and as a concept for studying the processes of speciation. Contributing to this dissatisfaction was a misuse of the subspecies category and an apparent complacency in the field of systematics about the objectivity and utility of the concept. When the polytypic species concept was recognized and the subspecific trinomen accepted, the study of variation within species became a major focus of activity among evolutionary systematists.

However, it often happened that an inordinate amount of time and effort was directed toward simple description and formal classification of new subspecies. Furthermore, many of these studies tended to emphasize differences among populations instead of interpopulation relationships. Predictably, the excessive splitting of species into subspecies began to lead to a chaotic taxonomic situation. Thus the usefulness of investigations designed merely to name new subspecies was seriously questioned, particularly in terms of their contribution to the general understanding of the evolutionary processes associated with infraspecific variation.

Because the subspecies concept lacked a precise definition, some investigators felt that infraspecific variation categorized under the name of subspecies was so heterogeneous as to render the concept meaningless. Probably the most influential article illustrating this discontent was provided by Wilson and Brown (1953), who recommended abandonment of the concept as a taxonomic category and the use of vernacular names of geographic localities in future studies. In brief, their objections centered around the following four points:

1. Different characters tend to show independent trends of geographic variation (clines).

2. Phenotypically indistinguishable or similar populations can and do occur in geographically different areas, and these similarities are not due to gene flow. Such groups have been called "polytopic" subspecies, which are defined as "a subspecies composed of widely separated but phenotypically identical populations" (Mayr 1963:671).

3. Genetically different local populations, or to use Dobzhansky's (1951) term, "microgeographic races," occur regularly within recognized subspecies.

4. The arbitrary nature of distinguishing subspecies, particularly with regard to the different rules followed by different investigators.

As discussed above, these points served to crystallize much of the thought and discontent concerning the subspecies category. Clearly, they showed the fallacy of separating contiguous populations, interconnected by numerous character gradients, into formal subspecies. They also showed that the subspecies was an inappropriate topic for evolutionary discussions, since it possesses only a limited amount of the total range of inter- and intrapopulation variation of the species.

To repeat, however, the subspecies is simply a taxonomic category. It is only a convenient pigeonholing device for classifying the distinguishable geographic subgroups that occur in most species. As long as it is not confused with clines—which cannot define taxa—and if it is not deemed a unit of evolution, it continues to be a useful way of classifying groups of similar populations within geographically variable species. The only remaining consideration is the actual usefulness of the category. In this respect, Simpson feels that ". . . the conclusive answer is that most of the experienced specialists in many groups of animals (notably the higher vertebrates) find them so and regularly use them" (1961:173).

Human Races

Given this general discussion of infraspecific variation and taxonomy, we may now turn to one of the most volatile issues in modern biological anthropology: the subject of modern human racial variation and classification. At the outset, it should be noted that very few investigators (whether biologists or anthropologists) become emotionally concerned about whether races exist among nonhuman mammals. By the same token, no hue and cry accompanied Campbell's (1965) suggestion that *H. erectus* could be divided into eight geographically distinct subspecies. And even more interesting is the lack of violent opposition to the separation of *H. sapiens* into two formal subspecies—*H. sapiens sapiens* and *H. sapiens neanderthalensis.* Obviously, subspecific classification of nonhuman mammals and fossils, even if the latter were human, is immune to the kind of vitriolic criticisms leveled at classifications of living humans.

In today's social and political climate, even calm and reasoned discussions of human races and racial classifications are often met with howls of outrage. Hence it is not at all uncommon to read statements like "anybody who studies race is *ipso facto* a racist," or "there is not now, nor has there ever been a white, black, or yellow race," and so forth. Most remarks like these appear in the popular press, are written by those least qualified to comment on the subject, and are usually based upon the erroneous assumption that race classification and racism are one and the same. However, the two phenomena are decidedly different.

The race concept, even if poorly defined, is couched in terms of the biological differences among populations of a species. Definitions of racism are also fuzzy. But in a broad sense, racism is an ideological concept that is widely shared among individuals of a population—a pervasive conviction of innate superiority over other populations that is often emotionally defended for social and political gains. Nobody knows how or why racism developed, nor how to do away with it. But Osborne speculates reasonably that

> Racism and race classification . . . each had its independent origin. . . . Some form of racism has doubtless existed from the very earliest days of human social organization when diverse peoples came into contact, and was based then as now upon the fear and mistrust engendered by physical and cultural differences. Race classification, on the other hand, had its beginnings in scientific inquiry, originating and continuing in serious pursuit of a systematic body of knowledge about man. (1971:159)

A primary purpose of classification, whether above or below the species level, is to bring some semblance of order to the observed variability so that various inductive generalizations can be made about the constructed classes (Gilmour 1940). Racial classifications are based entirely upon relationships among human populations, but such relationships can take numerous forms. Hence racial classifications have been constructed upon differences in observable physical features (color of the skin, eyes, and hair; shape of the nose, lips, cheeks, and other surface features; the amount of body hair, etc.). Other classifications have utilized differences in size and shape of skeletal features. Yet others have been based upon the differences in allele frequencies of simple genetic traits—like the various human blood group systems—and more modern attempts have used combinations of morphological and genetic characteristics. Therefore, it should come as no surprise that nearly every classification that has ever been published differs somewhat.

Not only do classifications differ according to the criteria upon which they are based, but they also undergo periodic revisions as new information becomes available. For example, Coon, Garn, and Birdsell (1950) listed 30 different races, all of which belonged to six putative "stocks" (Negroid, Mongoloid, White, Australoid, American Indian, and Polynesian). A few years later, Coon (1962, 1965) argued from a phylogenetic point of view that modern *H. sapiens* was divisible into five subspecies: Caucasoid, Mongoloid, Australoid, Congoid, and Capoid. Garn (1971) also deviated from the 1950 classification and listed these nine geographic races: Amerindian, Polynesian, Micronesian, Melanesian-Papuan, Australian, Asiatic, Indian, European, and African.

Furthermore, he thought it possible to identify three sorts of racial groupings, which, from most to least inclusive, included geographic, local, and micro-races. Although he noted that the number of local races would number in the hundreds, 32 were given as representative examples. The majority of these were the same as in the 1950 classification. Garn's conception of the micro-race is synonymous with the Mendelian population, and these would literally number in the thousands. Obviously, it would be completely pointless to name each one. Finally, Birdsell (1975) chose to abandon the term "race" because of definitional ambiguities and harmful and disruptive social connotations. Nonetheless, he did recognize the existence of four different population clusters: Caucasoids, Negroids, Mongoloids, and Veddoids.

The changing opinions of these three specialists about the racial and subspecific divisions of modern humans serve to illustrate several points about racial classifications.

1. Anybody is free to propose a new classification at any time, based upon whatever criteria are deemed relevant. In this regard, it should be stressed that classifications of groups smaller than the subspecies are not regulated by any set of rules, such as those provided in the *International Code of Zoological Nomenclature*.

2. No classification is necessarily right and all others wrong. Some may simply be more useful than others, inasmuch as they allow a wider range of inductive generalizations about the constructed classes.

3. Infraspecific classifications of modern humans will inevitably change in order to reflect shifting genetic differences due to changing selective pressures or disappearance of pre-existing differences due to migration.

One particularly difficult problem is how to rationally classify human hybrids, such as those in Hawaii, for example, where about two-thirds of all live births from 1960 to 1969 were from various kinds of "interracial" crosses (C. E. Glick 1970). Modern transportation technology has all but completely erased earlier geographic barriers to migration, the result being the inhabitation of each of the world's continents by representatives of the groups often recognized as the three major human races (i.e, Negroid, Mongoloid, and Caucasoid). However, the extent to which gene flow between these groups is being significantly increased by transcontinental mobility is unknown. The actual data on "interracial" crosses in the United States is notoriously poor, and either unavailable or nonexistent for other continental areas.

In the continental United States, for example, the number of known black-white marriages in 1960 was very small, in spite of the fact that the *Emancipation Proclamation* was issued 100 years earlier. P. C. Glick (1970) estimated that the frequency of such matings was only about 4 in every 1,000. In this case, it is evident that there is very little difference between social and geographic barriers in preventing gene flow. Nevertheless, the considerable mobility in modern times can only have the effect of increasing gene flow. It may be a bit premature to suggest, as Bodmer and Cavalli-Sforza (1976) have done, that there is a trend toward greater admixture between the major human groups. However, if a breakdown in mating barriers does occur in the future, then current racial classifications will have to be either revised or abandoned.

A Short Commentary on the Usefulness of Racial Classifications

The stance adopted here is that formal classification of the world's populations into races, simply for the sake of classification, is a fruitless exercise. To judge from the absence of classifications proposed in recent years, it would appear that most biological anthropologists are in basic agreement with this view (see Baker 1974, for one exception). Furthermore, the widespread disagreements about existing classifications have severely limited, if not completely destroyed, the usefulness of the race concept in terms of understanding the origin and maintenance of interpopulation genetic variability. This is not to deny the existence of genetically distinct human populations, nor the existence of groups of populations, which, if adequately examined, might satisfy the 75% rule for formal subspecific differentiation. Rather, it only emphasizes the contention that each classification is meaningful to the classifier, but to few others.

This constitutes a singularly inappropriate state of affairs for the field of biological anthropology, which, like all other sciences, requires some precision in vocabulary for meaningful communication. In this regard, Hempel observes that

> . . . the vocabulary of science has two basic functions: first, to permit an adequate description of the things and events that are the objects of scientific investigation; second, to permit the establishment of general laws or theories by means of which particular events may be *explained* and *predicted* and thus *scientifically understood;* for to understand a phenomenon scientifically is to show that it occurs in accordance with general laws or theoretical principles. (1965:139)

Now the "things" in racial classifications are groups of people, and the "events" are supposedly the processes (e.g., natural selection, genetic drift, gene flow) responsible for the numerous relationships between such groups. However, the imprecision in defining these groups of people—these "races"—prevents analysis of the factors that distinguish them from each other. Admittedly, there is no problem at all when a race is defined as ". . . a reproductive community of individuals that share in a common gene pool" (Buettner-Janusch 1973:490). This is, of course, the standard biological definition of a Mendelian population (see Chapter 5), the unit upon which analysis of evolutionary mechanisms is best undertaken.

If, indeed, a race is a Mendelian population, then the latter term should be used for the sake of both terminological precision and consistency with usage of that throughout the rest of the biological sciences. But races are also considered as subspecies: "To be technical, the 'race' is the taxonomic (that is, classificatory) unit immediately below the species" (Garn 1971:8). If this is so, then the term "subspecies" should be used, but only after demonstrating, by generally accepted standards (e.g., the 75% rule), the taxonomic validity of distinguishing such population aggregates.

A final question, even more crucial than those involving terminological ambiguities, is whether formal subspecific classification of *H. sapiens* can contribute meaningfully to our knowledge of modern human variation. In slightly different terms, does a subspecies provide a convenient point of departure for studying the factors involved in the origin and maintenance of interpopulation differences and resemblances? For at least two basic reasons, the answer is no. First, the population rather than the subspecies is the basic unit upon which evolutionary processes operate. The subspecies is, by definition, an artificially constructed category containing a group of populations, each of which possesses its own genetic integrity as a result of adaptation to its own set of local selective factors. Second, the overall genetic differences between the so-called "major races" are not as pronounced as commonly believed.

The conspicuous surface features often used to establish racial affiliation, such as relative skin pigmentation and shape relationships in facial structure, very likely represent environmental adaptations. But such features are no more important for classificatory purposes than, for example, any of the numerous electrophoretically determined enzyme variants. For these and many other nonvisible genetic traits, the average differences between the major races are less than average intrapopulation differences. Thus description of the geographic differences in genetic traits and analysis of the causal factors associated with these differences need not proceed from, nor result in, a racial classification. That such studies can be adequately carried out on local populations will become evident in the following chapter.

Summary

Various hypotheses attempt to explain the seemingly sudden disappearance of Neandertals after about 35,000 years B.P. and the equally as sudden emergence and widespread geographic distribution of anatomically modern *H. sapiens* at about the same time. Most of these can be included in either the Neandertal phase hypothesis, the pre-*sapiens* hypothesis, or the pre-Neandertal hypothesis.

Although proponents of the Neandertal phase hypothesis have differed in some details, its essential feature is that modern human populations (or "races") evolved directly and independently from regional populations that were chronologically contemporaneous with Western European (or Classic) Neandertals. One of the strongest criticisms of this explanation is the exceedingly small probability that several subspecies could evolve independently of each other, go through parallel evolutionary changes at different rates in different areas, and culminate in the integrated genetic system represented by modern *H. sapiens*.

The pre-*sapiens* hypothesis maintains that Neandertals became extinct without making any significant genetic contribution to modern European gene pools. Instead, modern populations arose from a "pre-*sapiens*" ancestor. Relatively few adhere to this interpretation, owing to the almost complete lack of fossil evidential support. Supporters of the pre-Neandertal hypothesis maintain the existence of two different Neandertal groups: (1) the Progressive Neandertals, which were geographically widespread throughout Europe, North Africa, and the Middle East, and (2) the Classic Neandertals, which are considered as earlier Neandertal groups that became isolated by glaciers in western Europe and underwent distinctive changes in craniofacial morphology in response to prevailing selective pressures. The Progressive Neandertals in areas other than western Europe are believed to have evolved toward anatomically modern humans in their respective areas.

Although there is little consensus of opinion about the evolutionary events that transpired during this period of human evolution, there is no doubt that Cro-Magnon populations either absorbed or replaced the Neandertals within a very short period of time. Human population numbers increased regularly, but quite slowly, through the advent of agriculture (about 8,000 years B.C.), and for several thousand years thereafter, but underwent an extraordinary increase as a result of events associated with the Industrial Revolution. By expanding over nearly all of the world's available land surface, human populations have been subjected to a bewildering variety of selective factors and have responded to such pressures in countless ways. The result is that the human species has become enormously variable, and the concepts of the cline and the subspecies have been utilized to interpret this variation.

Clines are geographical gradients in character expression that are produced by the combined effects of selection and gene flow. While human populations cannot be meaningfully classified according to clines, the study of clinal variation in a particular trait provides an especially appropriate method of understanding the evolutionary mechanisms responsible for the variation. The subspecies is certainly less useful than the cline in this context. It represents, instead, a classificatory device, defined as an aggregate of local populations of a species inhabiting a geographic subdivision of the range of the species and differing taxonomically from other populations of the species. The subspecies is not considered as a unit of evolution but, rather, as an arbitrarily defined taxon beneath the species level.

Most definitions of race are closely related to (if not synonymous with) the zoological definition of the subspecies. Hence racial classifications are also arbitrary—depending upon the characteristics used—and will inevitably be transient because of shifting genetic differences due to differences in selective factors and migration patterns. The study of infraspecific variation from the standpoint of artificially constructed races is probably less profitable than from the level of the local population, because (1) the population, not the subspecies, is the basic evolutionary unit and (2) the average genetic differences between the major races are less than average intrapopulation differences.

17 Modern Qualitative Variation

Introduction

Biological diversity among modern human populations is ubiquitous, with both "single-gene" traits and polygenic characteristics frequently showing broad but fairly well-delimited patterns of geographic variation. Biogeographic descriptions of these patterns and investigations into the ecological and cultural phenomena occurring throughout their distributions have led to intriguing hypotheses about the numerous ways in which human populations have responded to evolutionary processes. For most of the history of biological anthropology, studies of geographic trait variation were simple, descriptive accounts of interpopulation differences and resemblances in external morphological features, such as stature and weight, body form, eye and hair color, relative skin pigmentation, and so forth. That the gradual geographic changes in expression of these and other visible surface features are the result of differences in past selective pressures and gene flow has never been in doubt. But for several reasons, explanations of how and why the observed changes occurred have always been elusive.

First, quantitative traits, like those mentioned above, are certainly polygenic, but there is no human quantitative trait for which a precise genetic explanation is known. This unfortunate situation, coupled with the observation that changes in both the frequencies and properties of genes are the criteria necessary for the interpretation of evolutionary problems, has limited our ability to utilize the mathematical premises of population genetics to analyze the effects of selection on quantitative characteristics.

Second, many morphological features that vary geographically are phenotypically plastic—subject to either short-term or permanent modification by external environmental stimuli without affecting the genotype. A good example of such an environmental agent that can permanently retard development is protein malnutrition, especially when it occurs during infancy. In spite of considerable efforts by many countries to ameliorate its effects, protein malnutrition continues to represent a major world health problem and a primary cause of mortality in children (Scrimshaw and Behar 1965). Some have concluded that complete rehabilitation from the effects in infancy is possible (e.g., Dreizen et al. 1967; Garrow and Pike 1967), but the most substantial body of evidence indicates a high probability that survivors of malnutrition in infancy can suffer permanent physical and/or behavioral retardation (e.g., Bass et al. 1970; Birch et al. 1971; Graham et al. 1969).

Not only can permanent retardation be traced to infantile malnutrition, but maternal protein deprivation can also have an adverse effect on critical fetal growth stages. The evidence is strongly convincing that the fetus is buffered somewhat from the external nutritional environment, but not wholly protected from maternal dietary insufficiency. This appears to hold not only for protein malnutrition (e.g., Turner 1973), although long-term effects of protein restriction on the growth of specific organs during gestation and lactation are generally unknown, but for general undernutrition and restriction of other elements as well (Fitzhardinge and Steven 1972; Hseuh et al. 1973; Newberne and Gebhardt 1973; Davis et al. 1973).

Third, polygenic traits are extremely variable in their susceptibility to environmental modification. The degree to which some adult body-size characteristics (such as linear skeletal dimensions) may be affected by nongenetic factors is certainly less, for example, than for total body weight. However, all shape characteristics of the skeleton, including those contributing to facial structure and head form, are susceptible to modification, during growth, by certain diseases, diet, and other factors that may temporarily interfere with normal growth processes.

On the other hand, phenotypic features such as hair and eye color are quite immune to change by external sources. For these reasons, studies of geographic variation in quantitative characters have not progressed much beyond the original descriptive stage. Reasonable hypotheses have been advanced to explain the observed distributional changes in a few characteristics, as will be discussed in the following chapter. But for the most part, variation in polygenic traits provides less-than-satisfactory information pertaining to evolutionary responses.

Far more illuminating insights into the causes of regional variation have been gained from data on the distribution of genetically simple biochemical polymorphisms. These traits, the so-called "genetic markers," include the red blood cell antigens and enzymes, plasma proteins, hemoglobins, and other characteristics such as PTC (phenylthiourea) taste sensitivity and urinary excretion of BAIB (β–aminoisobutyric acid). The first published reports of populations differing from each other in mean allele frequencies appeared at the end of World War I (Hirszfeld and Hirszfeld 1918–1919, 1919) and dealt with ABO frequency distributions among a large number of soldiers from various countries. The results of thousands of tests undertaken during the next 20 years were compiled by Boyd (1939), and about 20 years later, Mourant and his colleagues (1958) published the results of tests on nearly 7 million people throughout the world. The number of people who have now been tested for the ABO system is approximately 15 million. The results of these studies, along with similar data on other genetic markers, are available in the remarkably comprehensive volume by Mourant et al. (1976).

Although the ABO blood group system was discovered in 1900 (Landsteiner 1900, 1901), no other red cell antigens were found until about 25 years later. In 1927, Landsteiner and Levine discovered the MN and P systems. Thirteen years later, Landsteiner and Wiener (1940, 1941) identified the Rh system. The rate of discovery of different red cell antigens since 1940 has been astonishing: over 160 are now known (see Table 4.6, Chapter 4), all of which are inherited in Mendelian fashion, and only a very few of which can in any way be modified by external environmental

Table 17.1 A List of the Most Thoroughly Surveyed Genetic Markers in Humans

Category	Names of the Genetic Markers
Red blood cell antigens	ABO, MN, Rh, P, Lutheran, Kell, Duffy, Kidd, Diego
Red blood cell enzymes	Acid phosphatase, glucose-6-phosphate dehydrogenase (G6PD), 6-phosphogluconate dehydrogenase (6PGD), phosphoglucomutase, adenylate kinase
Red blood cell proteins	Hemoglobin
Plasma proteins	Haptoglobin, transferrin, Gc, β-lipoprotein
Plasma enzymes	Pseudocholinesterase
Other systems	PTC taste sensitivity, β-aminoisobutyric acid excretion

factors (Race and Sanger 1975, have reviewed the small number of cases in which disease has altered certain antigens in the ABO system). Similarly, the discovery of different heritable plasma proteins and red cell enzyme systems during the past 25 years has proceeded apace. Well over 30 different systems serve as genetic markers at the present time.

Not all red blood cell antigens occur in polymorphic frequencies. Many are rare, in some instances being confined to single individuals or their immediate families. For example, only 2 out of over 18,000 unrelated people tested positively for the Moen (Mo^a) antigen (Kornstad and Brocteur 1972, cited in Race and Sanger 1975). Likewise, a number of plasma proteins and red cell enzymes have been discovered too recently for large-scale population surveys to be performed. But at the present time there are approximately 70 different genetic markers that have been used for population studies. Of these, at least 22 have been surveyed fairly extensively throughout many of the world's populations (see Table 17.1). Since the data on geographic variation in these marker systems are far too voluminous to be treated comprehensively in this chapter, only a few representative examples are discussed below. Those who are interested in more complete treatments of the subject should consult Barnicot (1977) and, especially, Brues (1977).

Geographic Variation in Genetic Markers

The ABO Blood Group System

Because of its relatively early discovery, its simple mode of inheritance, and its importance in incompatibility and transfusion reactions, the ABO system is, without doubt, the most thoroughly studied genetic system in humans. As discussed in Chapter 4, the I^A and I^B alleles are codominant, with I^O recessive to both. It might also be repeated that there are well-established subgroups of I^A (I^A_1 and I^A_2), in addition to a few rare variants of both I^A and I^B (Race and Sanger 1975).

The geographic variation in frequencies of the three alleles (not distinguishing the I^A subgroups) is illustrated in the contour maps in Figures 17.1 through 17.3. These maps chart the changing gradients of indigenous populations, insofar as the frequencies of aboriginal populations of about 400 years ago—before the advent of modern transportation and the massive population movements of modern times—are accurately reflected by the frequencies of their modern descendants. Thus the frequencies in North America are for Indian populations, in Australia for Australian aboriginals, and so forth.

Since the frequencies of the three alleles must total 1.0 in every population, an increase in the frequency of one allele will be concomitant with a decrease in the frequency of one or both of the others. This rough correlation between frequencies is immediately evident between I^A and I^O in North America and Australia, and between I^B and I^O in north and central Asia. The ranges for the three allele frequencies differ considerably from one area to another. All populations have a substantial number of I^O individuals, the frequencies ranging from about 0.40 to 1.00. The lowest world frequencies of I^O are found in certain groups of Finnish Lapps (0.386), the northern Pahira in Sikkim, northern India (0.397), and a few other populations in northern India, central Asia, Japan, and Korea (these and all other allele frequencies discussed in this chapter have been taken from Mourant et al. 1976). The highest I^O frequencies occur among Indian populations from Guatemala, Argentina, Brazil, French Guiana, Peru, and Ecuador. Many Indian populations in each of these countries and throughout South and Central America and Mexico have either no I^A or I^B, or very low frequencies of one or both. It is generally assumed that the few I^A and I^B alleles are of European origin, and that Indians native to the southern half of the Western Hemisphere were totally I^O before the voyages of Columbus.

In contrast to I^O, world population frequencies of I^A range from zero to about 0.55. The least common allele is I^B, ranging from about zero to 0.30, although for both I^A and I^B, a few populations are known to have higher frequencies than these upper limits. For example, the highest recorded frequency of I^A occurs in the Blackfoot, Blood, and Piegan Indians of North America (0.58). Similarly, the frequency of I^B in several small populations in southern (e.g., the Toda and Kadve Kuhni) and northern India (the Danguria Tharu) exceeds 0.35. Probably the highest recorded frequency of I^B and, correspondingly, the lowest frequency of I^O is 0.79 and 0.17, respectively, in a small ($n = 28$) number of Htalu from Burma. And in another group ($n = 44$) from the same region, composed of a mixed Htalu-Taron population, the frequencies of I^B and I^O are 0.50 each. Now these remarkably high I^B frequencies and, in the first instance, the extremely low I^O frequency, are completely aberrant in comparison to both neighboring Burmese groups, as well as to all other populations. Such peculiarities occasionally arise in small, relatively isolated populations, and most often are ascribed to genetic drift or the founder effect.

Natural Selection and the ABO Locus

A visual inspection of Figures 17.1 through 17.3 shows patterns of variation that are far too systematic to be the result of chance. For example, there appears to have been a radiation of I^B from central Asia. However, the frequency of this allele in the New

Figure 17.1 The ABO blood group system. Distribution of the *A* gene in the indigenous population of the world. (Courtesy of A. E. Mourant et al., *The Distribution of the Human Blood Groups and Other Polymorphisms.* Reprinted with permission of Oxford University Press.)

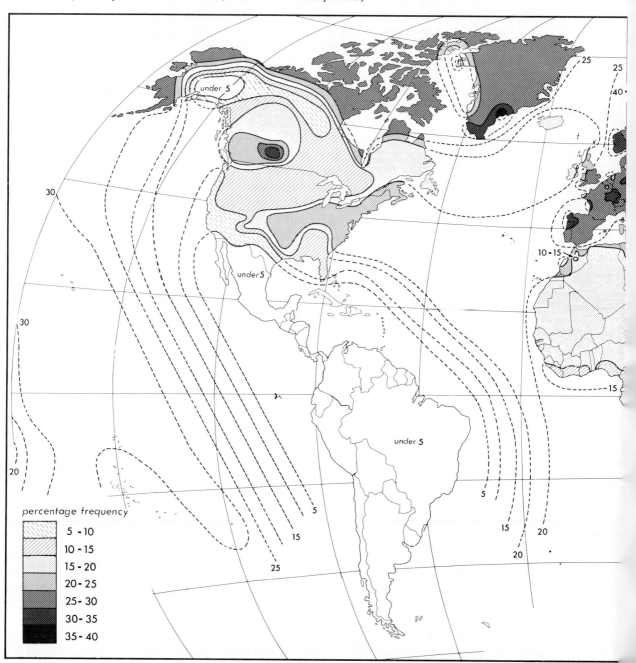

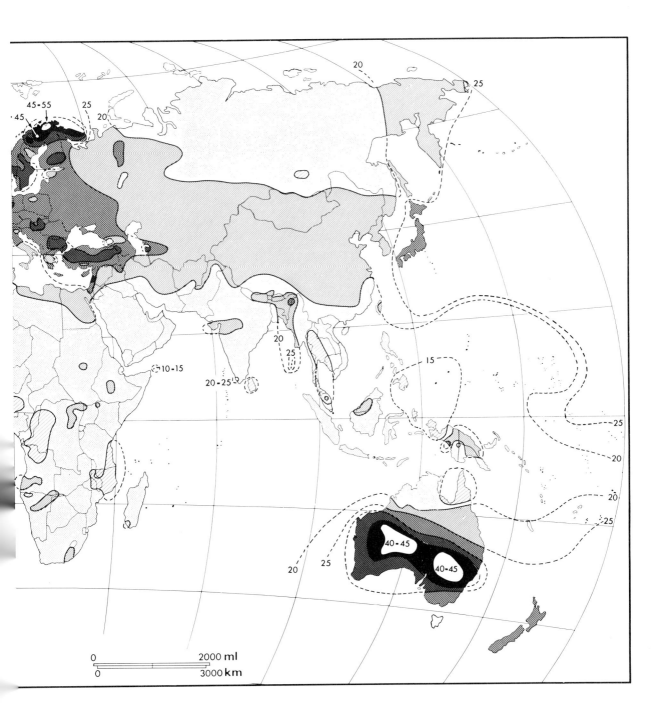

0 2000 ml

0 3000 km

Figure 17.2 The ABO blood group system. Distribution of the *B* gene in the indigenous populations of the world. (Courtesy of A. E. Mourant et al., *The Distribution of the Human Blood Groups and Other Polymorphisms.* Reprinted with permission of Oxford University Press.)

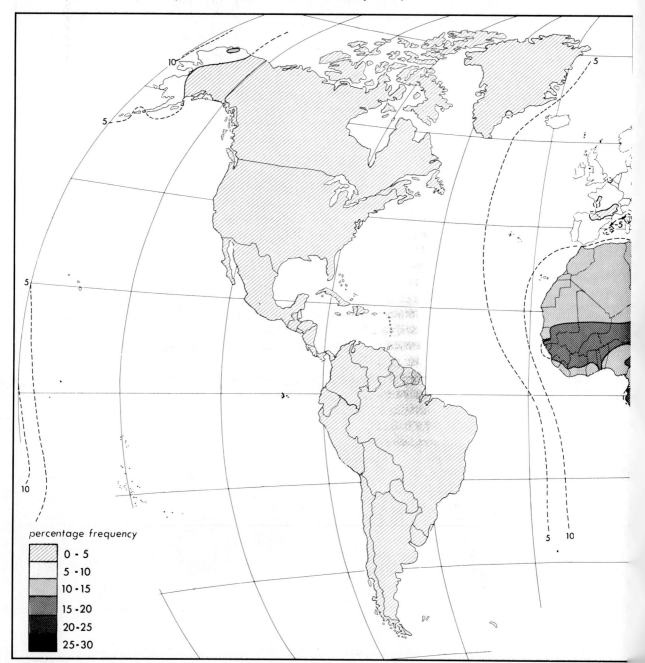

percentage frequency

0 - 5
5 - 10
10 - 15
15 - 20
20 - 25
25 - 30

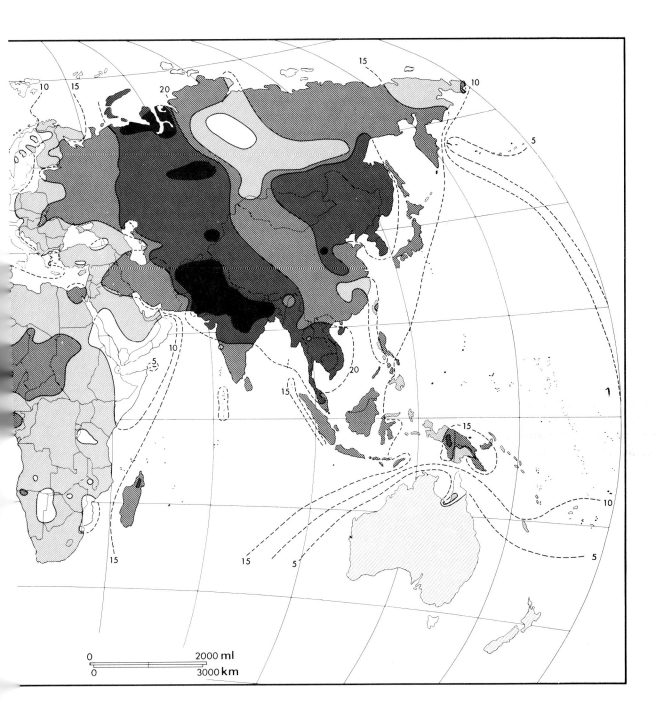

Figure 17.3 The ABO blood group system. Distribution of the *O* gene in the indigenous populations of the world. (Courtesy of A. E. Mourant et al., *The Distribution of the Human Blood Groups and Other Polymorphisms.* Reprinted with permission of Oxford University Press.)

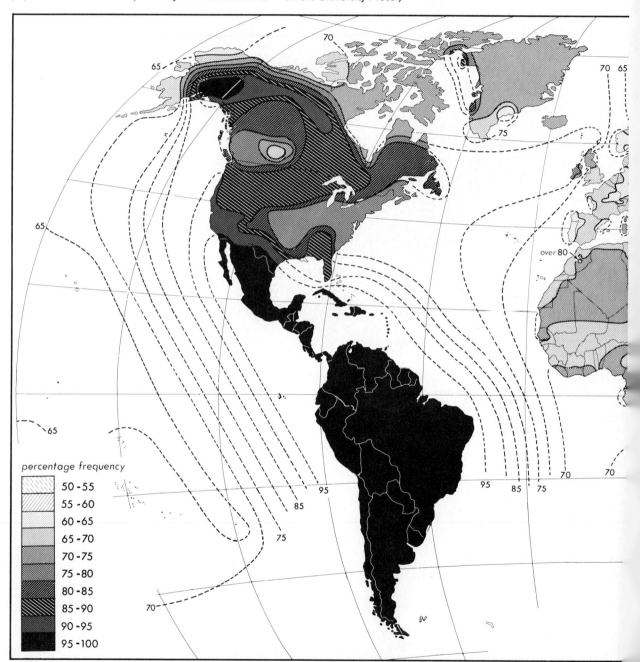

percentage frequency

	50 - 55
	55 - 60
	60 - 65
	65 - 70
	70 - 75
	75 - 80
	80 - 85
	85 - 90
	90 - 95
	95 - 100

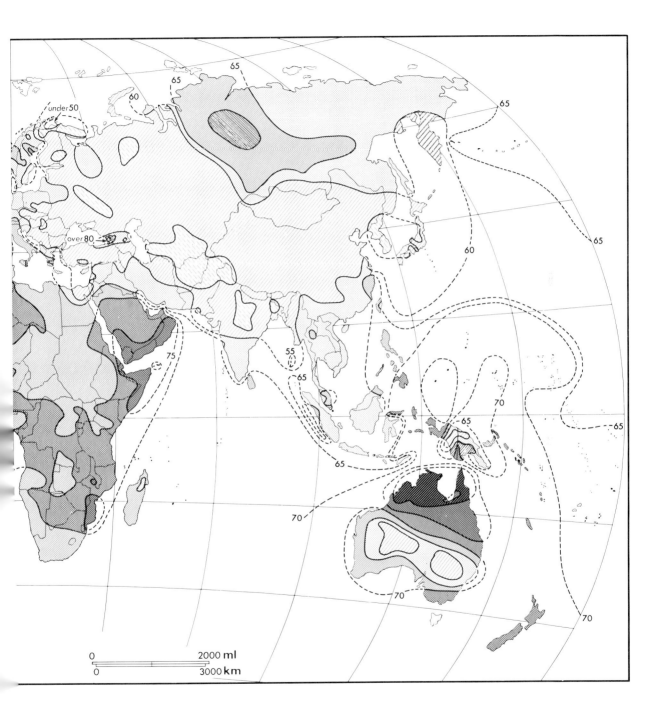

World and Australia is negligible, and it is only moderately represented in central Europe. Similarly, the I^O allele is characteristic of native New World populations, except for those inhabiting most of North America. Also, there seem to be three widely separated centers of radiation of I^A—Australian aborigines, Scandinavian Lapps, and American Indians in the northern United States and southern Canada.

In light of (1) the fact that nearly every population in the world has been tested for the ABO system, (2) the vast body of information about external phenomena that could possibly serve as selective factors, (3) a great deal of knowledge about historical and modern population movements, and (4) probably more detailed biochemical data on the ABO antigens than on any other genetically controlled trait in humans, it ought to be a relatively easy matter to explain the distributional patterns of these three alleles from the standpoint of evolutionary genetics. Unfortunately, such is not the case. It almost seems paradoxical that this system has contributed more to our understanding of human population genetics than any other, yet the most basic questions about it remain almost entirely unanswered.

For example, no positive function has ever been associated with either the ABO system or, for that matter, with any other red cell antigen. Some negative effects are known, including adverse transfusion reactions for the ABO system and hemolytic disease of the newborn due to maternal-fetal incompatibility for both the ABO and Rh systems. Yet the reason for the existence of red cell antigens in general remains unknown. Since these complex red cell polymorphisms occur in our primate relatives, in addition to more evolutionarily distant species such as cattle, horses, dogs, and chickens, it is highly probable that all vertebrates carry numerous inherited red cell antigens. This phenomenon, in itself, provides a strong argument for the existence, either in the past, at the present, or during the evolutionary history of the subphylum Vertebrata, of some kind of very fundamental functions that have been or are being favored by natural selection.

This leads to another basic question about the ABO system: Precisely what selective processes are currently maintaining the observed allele frequency distributions? The relative stability of allele frequencies among human populations suggests that the ABO system is a balanced polymorphism, because allele frequencies apparently have remained at equilibrium for very long periods of time. Now this explanation would necessitate a selective advantage of one or more of the heterozygous forms (see Chapter 6). However, there is no evidence that heterozygotes enjoy higher fitness levels than homozygotes, nor is there any indication of a systematic selective pressure that could account for the observed geographic variation in the ABO allele frequencies. In this context, Lewontin has commented that "the most glaring failure of selectionist explanation is the variety of human blood-group polymorphisms, none of which has yet been explained by natural selection although the data are more copious and reliable than for any other case and the natural history and reproductive schedules are better known than for any other species" (1974:234).

The failure to discover the function of the ABO antigens is, of course, intimately related to the inability to establish selectionist arguments for the origin and maintenance of the polymorphism. The most that can currently be said with respect to the relationships between ABO phenotypes and selection, aside from ABO maternal-fetal incompatibility, is that a number of diseases have been significantly associated with particular phenotypes. The most important of these associations are listed in

Table 17.2 Significant Associations between ABO Phenotypes and Disease (From Mayo 1975.)

Disease	Phenotypes Compared	Relative Risk
Duodenal ulcer	O : A	1.90
Gastric ulcer	O : A	1.19
Carcinoma of colon and rectum	O : A	0.90
Mammary cancer	O : A	0.92
Rheumatic heart disease	O : not −O	0.90
Pernicious anemia	O : A	0.80
Diabetes mellitus	O : A	0.93
Thromboembolism	O : A_1	0.55
Myocardial infarction	O : not −O	0.68
Atherosclerosis	O : A	0.69

Table 17.2, all of which (with the exceptions of diabetes mellitus and myocardial infarction) are consistent and well-established.

Two points about these associations should be clarified. First, the figures given under "Relative Risk" can be viewed in terms of probability: a type O person has a 1.90 greater chance of developing a duodenal ulcer than a type A person; a type O person has a smaller chance (0.90) of contracting a colon or rectal carcinoma than a type A person; and so forth. Second, these are only statistical associations and should not be taken as direct cause-and-effect relationships. For example, there is no known factor inherent in the $I^A{}_1$ allele that directly predisposes a person (as compared to a type O person) to thromboembolism, a disease of the heart brought about when a blood clot obstructs one of the heart vessels. Instead, a factor playing an important causal role in this disease is relative cholesterol level, which tends to be higher in type A_1 than in type O people.

In addition to the noninfectious diseases listed in Table 17.2, various infectious diseases have been suggested as selective agents affecting ABO phenotypes. Hence Vogel (1965) and Vogel and Chakravartti (1966) maintain that type A persons are more susceptible to both infection by and detrimental effects of smallpox; Socha et al. (1969) associated group B with infant diarrhea; Otten (1967) has discussed associations between type O people and susceptibility to bubonic plague; and Wood (1975) has attempted to show that a malarial vector, a mosquito named *Anopheles gambiae,* prefers type O hosts over types A, B, and AB. In addition, other such associations have been discussed by Vogel (1970).

To what extent can these associations be taken as selective factors leading to the distribution and stabilization of the ABO frequencies? For most of the diseases in Table 17.2, the selective effect would be either very small or nonexistent because the onset and major debilitating symptoms of the disease occur well after the reproductive period. Also, some of the disorders (such as duodenal ulcers) are strongly suspected to have reached relatively high incidences only during recent times, and thus would not have constituted an important selective factor against any of the ABO phenotypes during the long evolutionary history of the species. Of course, this might not be true for infectious diseases like smallpox, plague, or malaria, which are not known to be age-specific.

The numerous associations between ABO phenotypes and diseases, which will probably increase in number as additional investigations are performed, indicate that these phenotypes are not immune to the effects of selection. However, the associations do not explain the differential susceptibility of persons with the same blood type to a particular disease (fortunately, not everyone with blood type O develops ulcers). Because other factors are obviously involved, such as pleiotropy at the ABO locus or epistatic interactions between this and other loci, little of a positive nature can be ascribed to the importance of disease selection in maintaining the observed stability of the ABO polymorphism.

The only phenomenon that apparently does exert a systematic selective pressure on ABO phenotypes is maternal-fetal incompatibility, which, like Rh incompatibility (see Chapter 7), can lead to fetal wastage through spontaneous abortion or by hemolytic disease of the newborn. Briefly, ABO hemolytic disease is mostly restricted to offspring from a type O mother and an A_1 or B father, although other combinations are possible. In general, ABO incompatible matings are those in which the A or B antigen is present in the father but not in the mother. Hence the following matings are incompatible:

Mother		Father
O	×	A
O	×	B
O	×	AB
B	×	A
B	×	AB
A	×	B
A	×	AB

In a fashion similar to that occurring in the Rh system, with one important exception, maternal antibodies may pass through the placenta and enter the circulatory system of a fetus with opposing antigens. The ensuing antigen-antibody reaction (agglutination) results in hemolytic disease. The exception is that A and B antibodies occur normally, whereas antibodies in the Rh system are formed in response to an antigenic stimulus (such as a transfusion or earlier pregnancy). For an example, consider a type A fetus from a mating between an O mother and an A father. In this case, agglutination of the fetal red blood cells (and damage to the tissue cells, since they also contain the A antigen) is due to the interaction between the maternal anti-A antibodies and the fetal A antigen inherited from the father.

Maternal-fetal incompatibility has been proposed as the principal selective process in the maintenance of the ABO polymorphism (Chung and Morton 1961), but a number of problems remain to be solved before this hypothesis can be unequivocally accepted. The most immediate questions concern the actual number of infants suffering from hemolytic disease and whether or not the effects are deleterious enough to affect later reproductive performance. There seems to be some agreement that the disease is rare, with a frequency of only about 0.001 and, furthermore, that only about 0.008 of those at risk actually develop hemolytic disease (Cavalli-Sforza and Bodmer 1971). Most often, the disease is self-limiting, with infants who survive its initial effects being no less biologically fit than normal offspring. However, Sever (1969) did find that hemolytic disease was severe enough to require exchange transfusions in approximately 1 in every 1,654 live births in a large midwestern city. In the absence of modern medical technology, the loss of these heterozygotes (recall that most of the mothers were type O) would mean that the allele frequency of both I^A and I^B would slowly decrease relative to I^O, since removal of equal numbers of alleles at a locus will increase the frequency of that which is most common.

On the other hand, several studies have indicated that a substantial heterozygote loss due to incompatibility selection can occur at much earlier stages than in the newborn. Thus Matsunaga and Itoh (1958) found an association between ABO incompatibility and sterility, and a few years later Behrman et al. (1960) found that in a group of anatomically and physiologically normal couples who were infertile for at least five years, over 87% were ABO incompatible. By contrast, only 39% of a similar group of fertile couples were ABO incompatible.

Now this proves nothing by itself. But it does indicate an important avenue of approach for elucidating the effects of incompatibility selection: the determination of the extent to which fertilization may be prevented or inhibited by an interaction between ABO substances secreted in the female reproductive tract and A or B antigens already present in the seminal fluid of the male. On this point, Cohen concludes that

> It seems quite possible that incompatible A or B antigens in the seminal fluid of secretors, or perhaps even in the cell envelope of sperm of both nonsecretors and secretors, may react with maternal anti-A or B in the female reproductive tract, causing either inactivation and/or dysfunction of the sperm. As a consequence, perhaps, ability to fertilize the ovum is altered or some biochemical change is induced so that even if syngamy occurs, the resultant zygote is inviable or has decreased viability. Residual deleterious effects so incurred could thus be responsible for the increased loss in early gestation associated with ABO incompatibility, and may possibly provide the basis of elevated neonatal mortality. (1970a:431)

The idea that ABO incompatible loss occurs so early that (1) fertilization may be thwarted or (2) the fertilized ovum is spontaneously aborted before pregnancy is recognized is gaining wide recognition. Because there is as yet no direct way to determine the magnitude of such loss, however, the significance of ABO incompatibility in maintaining world allele frequencies is still unknown.

A final problem that has not been satisfactorily resolved is how populations have become polymorphic for the ABO system, when the polymorphism itself is responsible for incompatibility. If the polymorphism is balanced instead of transient, as most investigators currently believe, then maintenance of the observed frequencies would require some sort of heterozygote selective advantage. But as shown above, the net effect of incompatibility selection would be to reduce heterozygosity and thus eventually eradicate the polymorphism.

In 1963, Brues attempted to shed some light on this enigma with a computer simulation study of the relative selection coefficients of the six ABO genotypes. Her results indicated that worldwide frequency distributions could be explained by assuming (1) a relatively large selective disadvantage for the homozygotes, especially $I^A I^A$ and $I^B I^B$, and (2) some physiological advantages in the heterozygotes that would partially counteract the effects of incompatibility selection. Whether the assumptions are valid will depend upon finding physiological advantages enjoyed by the heterozygotes—none have been identified as yet. Thus it would appear that in spite of the intensive efforts to uncover the selective forces responsible for the origin and maintenance of the ABO polymorphism, our understanding of such forces remains severely limited.

The Rh Blood Group System

Mourant et al. put it well in their observation that "if only a dim twilight illuminates possible selective processes in the ABO system, an almost complete darkness conceals any that affect the other systems" (1976:127). In general, our information about the Rh, MN, and other blood group systems is also restricted to their genetics and frequency distributions. Chemical compositions and functions of the antigens are nearly always unknown, and, with the sole exception of Rh incompatibility, there is a near-total ignorance of selective forces that could have influenced the geographic variation in allele frequencies.

It may be recalled from Chapter 4 that the Rh blood group system has been explained genetically in terms of (1) three closely linked gene loci and (2) a system of eight multiple alleles at a single locus. There are additional variants, but these need not be described here (see Race and Sanger 1975). The designations in the "linked-gene" theory, along with the corresponding multiple allele equivalents (in parentheses) are CDE (R^z), CDe (R^1), cDE (R^2), cDe (R^0), Cde (r'), CdE (r^y), cdE (r''), and cde (r). It might also be remembered that since each of these gene-triplets (or haplotypes) occurs on a single chromosome, a person's full genotype could be CDE/cde (R^z/r), CdE/cDe (r^y/R^0), in addition to a wide variety of other combinations. In these two particular cases, the person would test as $CcDEe$, since both would produce immunologically detectable c and e antigens and there is no dominance at the C and E loci. As one additional reminder, people who contain a D in any combination are clinically Rh+, while those with two d's are Rh−.

The existence of eight **haplotypes** in the Rh system creates some difficulties in preparing contour maps of world frequency distributions. Hence a visual inspection of the frequencies (Table 17.3) from a number of widely separated populations may suffice to indicate some of the relevant points about Rh biogeography. First, four of the haplotypes (CDE, Cde, CdE, and cdE) are rather rare throughout the world, with CdE being the least common of the eight. The d allele occurs most often in the cde combination, with only Australian aborigines showing an appreciable frequency of the allele in any other haplotype (Cde). Second, the most common of any of the eight haplotypes is CDe, which occurs in low frequencies only among a few African populations. The cDE combination is the next most common, but the two remaining haplotypes containing a D are quite rare. Only certain sub-Saharan African populations have characteristically high cDe frequencies, and CDE rarely exceeds 0.05 in any population. Third, most of the world's populations are predominately Rh+, some (e.g., Bushmen and southern Chinese) being exclusively so. The highest frequency of Rh− is among the Basques. Finally, every population is polymorphic for two or more haplotypes. In this regard, the near-uniformity of small groups for certain haplotypes (e.g., 0.8246 *cDe* for Bushmen and 0.8605 *CDe* for New Hebrides Islanders) is unusual. It may be that variation has been reduced by genetic drift in such instances.

The Origin and Maintenance of the Rh System

As with the ABO system, we are plagued by ignorance about the evolutionary mechanisms associated with the origin and maintenance of the Rh polymorphism. How did the haplotypes arise, and why are four common and the others rare? What selective mechanisms could account for the fact that related populations tend to be more similar in frequency distributions, while the so-called larger "racial" groups display large differences? Why is Rh⁻ less common than Rh⁺, and what effect does incompatibility selection have on observed frequency distributions?

Although there are no clear-cut answers for any of these questions, several intriguing proposals have been advanced through the construction of rather sophisticated mathematical models. For example, Feldman and his colleagues (1969) devised one such model in an attempt to shed some light on the evolutionary origin of the major Rh alleles and the importance of Rh incompatibility selection during the evolution of the entire system. Without repeating their methods, the conclusions may be paraphrased briefly as follows.

It may be inferred with some assurance that natural selection has played an important role in the origin of the Rh system and, in particular, in the frequency distribution of the four most common haplotypes given in Table 17.3 (*CDe, cDE, cDe,* and *cde*). This seems evident because the observed differences in haplotype frequencies are generally large among unrelated populations (i.e., the major "racial" groups), but small among closely related populations. In the latter, the similarities are usually too close to invoke random genetic drift as an explanation. Likewise, the variation in

Table 17.3 Frequency Variation at the Rh Locus in a Few Selected Populations (From various sources given in Mourant et al. 1976.)

Population	CDE (R^z)	CDe (R^1)	cDE (R^2)	cDe (R^0)	Cde (r′)	CdE (r^y)	cdE (r″)	cde (r)
Blood Indians	.0346	.4841	.3721	.0000	.0000	.0000	.0165	.0927
Chippewa Indians	.0192	.3386	.4763	.0858	.0000	.0000	.0801	.0000
Apache Indians	.1565	.3959	.3093	.0000	.0670	.0000	.0297	.0416
Basques	.0143	.4032	.0431	.0726	.0271	.0000	.0035	.4362
English (London)	.0010	.4305	.1377	.0282	.0075	.0000	.0078	.3873
Italians	.0552	.3663	.1187	.1055	.0416	.0128	.0297	.2702
Swedish Lapps	.0000	.5886	.0753	.0449	.0000	.0000	.0000	.2911
Bushmen	.0000	.1397	.0357	.8246	.0000	.0000	.0000	.0000
Bantu	.0000	.0574	.0805	.5879	.0109	.0000	.0000	.2633
Pygmies	.0000	.0747	.1934	.6300	.0000	.0000	.0000	.1019
West Pakistanis	.0059	.5508	.1108	.0609	.0000	.0000	.0000	.2716
Southern Chinese	.0042	.7598	.1958	.0401	.0000	.0000	.0000	.0000
New Hebridians	.0000	.8605	.1250	.0000	.0000	.0000	.0000	.0145
Australian Aborigines	.0208	.5641	.2009	.0854	.1288	.0000	.0000	.0000

Figure 17.4 A possible evolutionary origin for the major alleles in the Rh system. The single mutated specificity appears in italics. (Courtesy of M. Feldman et al., Evolution of the Rh Polymorphism: A Model for the Interaction of Incompatibility, Reproductive Compensation, and Heterozygote Advantage. *Am. J. Hum. Genet.* 21:171–193, 1969. Reprinted by permission of the University of Chicago Press. Copyright © 1969 by The American Society of Human Genetics. All rights reserved.)

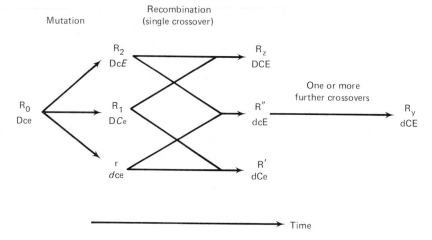

the four common haplotype frequencies cannot be adequately explained by mutation, because the great differences among relatively unrelated groups would require unreasonably high mutation rates during the evolutionary history of the species. Hence an obvious conclusion is that the Rhesus polymorphism arose initially through one or more mutations, and the newly formed heterozygotes increased in frequency because of some, as yet unknown, selective advantage.

As indicated in Figure 17.4, the haplotypes *cDE, CDe,* and *cde* may be connected to *cDe* by mutation for a single antigenic specificity, i.e., single independent mutations in *cDe* could lead to any one of these three haplotypes. This, along with supporting evidence from nonhuman primates and the world frequency distributions, suggests that *cDe* may have been the original haplotype. The four rarest haplotypes are envisioned as the result of single crossovers—a crossover in the *cDE/CDe* genotype could have led to *CDE;* in *CDe/cde,* to *Cde;* and in *cDE/cde,* to *cdE.* The rarest of the four, *Cde,* is suggested to have arisen only by further crossing over in heterozygotes involving the other three rare alleles. And the answer for the rarity of all four haplotypes is that the initial mutations that changed *cDe* to the other three common forms were relatively recent occurrences.

If indeed this chain of events did occur, which of course can never be proven, then it would mean that Rh incompatibility was an indirect development and had only secondary importance for the origin of the Rh polymorphism. Nevertheless, the role played by Rh incompatibility in maintaining stability in the system has been debated fairly extensively in recent years. Basically, the same sorts of considerations apply here as for the ABO system—how can a stable polymorphism be reached and maintained, given the disadvantage of heterozygotes produced from an Rh⁻ mother and an Rh⁺ father?

Certainly, some of these fetuses will suffer no ill effects if the parents are simultaneously incompatible for the ABO and Rh systems. In this instance, as pointed out in Chapter 7, Rh incompatible cells of the fetus will be hemolyzed by the normally present A or B antibodies in the mother before they stimulate maternal production of Rh antibodies. Hence the two incompatibilities essentially negate each other. The only way that the Rh polymorphism could reach stability via incompatibility would presumably be through reproductive compensation, the "replacement (or overreplacement) of fetuses or children dying from some disorder by subsequent surviving infants so that there is no reduction in the mean completed fertility (measured at some time after birth) of mothers or couples producing the dead fetuses or children" (Reed 1971:215).

If there is compensation in matings between Rh^- females and Rh^+ males, then heterozygote advantage need not be necessary for the maintenance of a stable Rh polymorphism. While this was shown theoretically by Feldman et al. (1969), the actual existence of reproductive compensation for the Rh system has been tacitly assumed by numerous investigators. For example, Levin (1967) suggested that human populations reproductively compensate for Rh incompatibility by either volitional or nonvolitional means. In the former, parents replace dead offspring because of their conscious desire to do so. In the latter, compensation occurs when the death of a child leads to an increased probability of survival of its sibs. This would ordinarily apply to families that, for various reasons, cannot support all of the children that are born, and it would increase the probability that a more or less constant number of children would reach reproductive age. In other situations, as in modern technological societies with abundant resources and advanced medical care, the loss of one offspring would not necessarily affect the survival probability of its sibs, and nonvolitional reproductive compensation would not occur.

Levin also presumes that the volitional form would be more characteristic of modern societies in which social factors enter into the choice of relatively small family size, but that nonvolitional compensation would be more typical of hunting and gathering groups with limited resources and extended nursing periods. Thus the change from a hunting and gathering subsistence pattern to an early agrarian economy to the present industrial state could have been associated with a concomitant change in reproductive compensation rates, which, in turn, could have been a major factor in determining how worldwide Rh frequencies have changed. One implication of Levin's suggestions ought to be apparent: the volitional compensation for Rh incompatible fetuses according to social dictates would provide an interesting example of one way in which social phenomena can bring about small evolutionary changes.

Although these comments about Rh reproductive compensation may be theoretically valid, a more pertinent question is whether the past or present occurrence of this process is supported by good evidence. Its presence could be indicated by associating Rh phenotypes with fertility, specifically by (1) demonstrating increased fertility among Rh^- women or (2) finding increased fertility among Rh incompatible matings. Indeed, Glass (1950) showed such increased female fertility in an early study of 8,421 white and 2,723 black American women, and his conclusions have been accepted by numerous investigators as evidence of Rh compensation. He found that in the black sample, the mean number of living children was 2.41 and 2.20 for Rh^+ and Rh^- women, respectively, an observation that would be consistent with no Rh reproductive compensation. However, the opposite relationship was found among the white women: the mean number of living children of Rh+ women was less than for Rh− women (1.37 as opposed to 1.453). He attributed this difference to an 8% increase in pregnancies among the Rh− women, hence supporting the notion of reproductive compensation, and suggested that selection was increasing the frequency of the *d* allele.

While several investigators have seemingly accepted these conclusions and constructed mathematical models relating to selection and compensation at the Rh locus (e.g., Feldman et al. 1969; Li 1976), others have conducted similar research and found no evidence for Rh compensation (e.g., Newcombe 1965; Reed 1968). In addition, Reed has claimed that Glass's study was performed on a biased sample: "Glass's data clearly do not represent the general population, since his two populations are strongly selected for ability to become pregnant; each woman must have had at least two pregnancies in a two- or three-year period . . ." (1971:217). Coupled with the lack of conclusive evidence for the existence of Rh reproductive compensation among other American white women, this observation led Reed to the conclusion that there is serious doubt about the importance, if not the reality, of this phenomenon. Thus it appears that much remains to be learned about the processes responsible for the origin and maintenance of the Rh polymorphism.

Human Variation and Malaria

Fortunately, other genetic polymorphisms are known for which an associated selective factor has been clearly established. Those studied most intensively are inherited red blood cell abnormalities, including the hemoglobin variants, G6PD deficiency, and thalassemia. For each of these there is a convincing body of evidence implicating malaria as the common selective factor responsible for the observed geographic variation in allele frequencies.

The importance of malaria as a systematic selective pressure throughout most of recorded history cannot be overemphasized. The disease probably became evolutionarily significant sometime after the advent of animal and plant domestication led to increased human population densities, and it has been a major cause of morbidity and mortality ever since. Malaria may have been present during the sixteenth century B.C., in Egypt, inasmuch as enlargement of the spleen and intermittent fever were observed and recorded on papyri and by hieroglyphic inscriptions, but there is little doubt of the malarial symptoms described by Hippocrates among Greeks in the fourth century B.C. Similar symptoms were seen and reported among Italians during the Roman Empire, as well as during Pre-Christian times in India and China (more on the historical aspects of malaria can be found in Garnham 1966; Gwei-Djen and Needham 1967; Jones 1967; and Russell 1955).

The impact of malaria upon modern human mortality might be best appreciated by repeating a few numbers from Livingstone's (1971) recent review. About 25 years ago, it was estimated that roughly 3.5 million people succumbed to the disease each year. In 1970, nearly 1.75 billion people inhabited previously malarial areas, and of this number over 375 million still occupy areas of endemic malaria. In addition, over 700 million live in areas where attempts to eradicate the disease are only partially effective. Obviously, there is no way of knowing whether malaria has killed more people than any of the other highly prevalent diseases, such as dysentery, the various influenza strains, or smallpox. But since it has constituted an inordinately strong selection pressure upon millions of individuals for hundreds of generations, it would be rather astonishing to find that no mutation had occurred that would increase individual resistance levels to the disease.

One of the classic examples of how a natural population acquires genetically conditioned resistance levels to disease concerns Australian rabbits and the myxomatosis virus. Some of the details of this host-parasite relationship differ from those involved with differential susceptibility to malaria, but it is instructive to use myxomatosis as a background for the following discussion of the evolutionary responses that humans have made to malaria.

In 1859, 24 wild European rabbits were introduced into the southeastern part of Australia, where they multiplied to outbreak levels over the next 20 years. Nearly all ecologically compatible parts of the continent were overrun by 1928, and in one area of about a million square miles (about one-third of the continental land area) the population density had increased to about 500 rabbits per square mile. In order to prevent total destruction of both grazing and farmlands, the Australian government initiated various measures to control this population explosion. However, none of these control measures were effective until 1950, when rabbits were inoculated with the myxomatosis virus. Having been obtained from South American rabbits that were relatively unharmed by the disease, the virus caused a rapidly fatal infection among the transplanted European rabbits.

Transmitted by two different species of mosquitoes, the disease almost immediately reached epidemic proportions. Within three years the disease had killed about 98% of the rabbits, but mortality levels fell to about 85% during the second epidemic and decreased steadily during successive epidemics. Only about 25% of the rabbits died during the sixth epidemic, and at the present time myxomatosis is a far less effective means of rabbit population control than it once was.

The reasons for this drastic decline in mortality (Fenner 1953, 1965) are fairly straightforward and probably apply in general to most situations involving mutual accommodation between hosts and their parasites. On the one hand, some rabbits possessed mutations that conferred a degree of natural resistance to the disease (Marshall 1958), which by differential reproduction accumulated in the rabbit populations. On the other hand, selection favored a less virulent viral strain because a highly lethal virus kills its host quickly, and thereby inadvertently reduces the probability that a mosquito will transmit to another host. Thus the more virulent strain has tended to be replaced by an avirulent one, which has a selective advantage because its demands are better balanced against supply in this particular ecosystem. Very likely, the accommodation between the myxomatosis virus and the South American rabbit represents an advanced phase in the evolutionary development of this host-parasite system.

There is no good reason to suppose that humans have responded any less effectively to their own parasites—especially those that have periodically caused major epidemics—although such responses are notoriously difficult to document.

Several factors contribute to this difficulty, including the general unreliability of medical records up until a few decades ago, the extraordinary length of human generations, the inappropriate nature of experimental research in this area, and so forth. Nevertheless, diseases have undoubtedly exerted major selective pressures throughout human evolution, and the genetic changes characterizing certain Old World populations in malarial regions—and their descendents elsewhere—provide the most thoroughly understood examples of disease selection.

The Hemoglobin Variants

Human hemoglobin is a tetramer that consists of two α- and two β- peptide chains. Structurally, the two α-chains make relatively little contact with each other, which is also true for the two β-chains. However, the two pairs of unlike chains contact each other at numerous points. The molecule functions as a reversible transporter of oxygen, the accomplishment of which depends upon four heme groups. Each heme group is a flat molecule containing iron atoms, and each is situated relatively far apart and at different angles from the other three within the hemoglobin molecule. About 90% of the total protein of the red blood cell is made up of hemoglobin, and its oxygen-binding capacity is such that about 21 ml of gaseous oxygen can be absorbed by 100 ml of whole blood.

Biochemically, oxygen transport is regulated by two important factors: partial oxygen pressure and pH. Since both are at high levels in the lungs, oxygen saturation of hemoglobin is at a maximum in these organs—about 96%. However, under conditions of low oxygen pressure and relatively low pH, as in the peripheral tissues, oxygen is less strongly bound. Thus it is released to respiring cells until hemoglobin oxygen saturation reaches about 65%. During its normal function as an oxygen transport mechanism, then, hemoglobin oxygen saturation levels cycle between 65% and 96% (Lehninger 1975).

Normal adult hemoglobin is packed within the red blood cell in such a way as to allow the cell to assume a biconcave disc-shaped conformation. The cell, in turn, retains this shape regardless of the degree of oxygenation. However, mutations that cause a change in the primary structure of one of the polypeptides, as in Hb^S (see Chapter 3), can lead to a distorted tertiary molecular structure. For this particular variant, Murayama (1966) has suggested that substitution of valine in place of the normal glutamic acid at the sixth position on the β-chain changes the nature of the intramolecular bond between the first and sixth positions. This change, in turn, allows adjacent hemoglobin molecules to interlock, or "stack," which subsequently leads to the formation of elongated crystalline aggregates.

Once present, these aggregates result in distortion and eventual destruction of the red cells. The process occurs in Hb^S molecules in areas of lowest oxygen tension—mainly the capillaries—and apparently takes place because oxygenation of hemoglobin leads to a change in molecular conformation that interferes with intermolecular stacking. In other words, the Hb^S molecule differs from the normal Hb^A in that the former is packed within the red blood cell so as to cause a change in erythrocyte shape upon deoxygenation.

Since the destruction of one's red blood cells is hardly selectively advantageous, it is legitimate to ask why millions of poeple in both malarial and nonmalarial environments are either homozygous or heterozygous for the Hb^S allele. As discussed earlier (Chapter 6), homozygotes develop sickle-cell anemia and have a very poor life expectancy, while heterozygotes have the sickle-cell trait. Under conditions of normalizing selection, then, the Hb^S allele frequency would be expected to decrease to quite low levels within a relatively short number of generations. Yet in some West and Central African populations the frequency of heterozygotes reaches about 30%, with allele frequencies as high as 16%. Frequencies almost this high are also found in a few populations around the Mediterranean Sea and in India, and approximately 9% of American black people have the sickle-cell trait.

The apparent explanation for the maintenance of these high frequencies involves balancing instead of normalizing selection, which requires that the heterozygote possess a selective advantage over both homozygotes. And since the sickle-cell polymorphism occurs only among populations in areas of endemic malaria or among those whose ancestry stems from such populations, it is reasonable to presume that the heterozygote advantage is somehow related to malarial resistance. That such heterozygote superiority indeed does exist has been amply documented in studies showing that (1) children with the sickle-cell trait are more likely to survive in malarial environments than normal homozygous children, and (2) heterozygous women in some populations apparently have higher fertility than homozygous normal women.

Now, malaria has been implicated in several different ways as the selective agent responsible for the advantage of the heterozygote. The most readily apparent evidence lies in the positive correlation between the geographic distribution of the Hb^S allele and malaria (see Livingstone 1973, for a recent review of the subject), although the strength of this correlation may be decreased for reasons relating to migration and to the presence of other genetic "buffers" to malaria in certain areas. Additional evidential support was provided over 20 years ago by Allison (1954), who demonstrated increased malarial resistance among heterozygotes by direct experimentation.

Thirty Luo-speaking adult males from a hyperendemic malarial region in Uganda and Kenya volunteered for this study. Fifteen were heterozygous, and the other 15 homozygous normal. All 30 were infected with *Plasmodium falciparum*, either from the bites of heavily infected mosquitoes (*Anopheles gambiae*) or through subinoculation. After 40 days, it was found that 14 of the 15 normal individuals contracted malaria, although their parasite counts were relatively low compared to those which normally occur among individuals from nonmalarial environments. Presumably, this was due to their having acquired some degree of immunity to the disease during early childhood. Of the 15 heterozygous individuals, however, only two showed malarial parasites, in spite of repeated attempts to infect them. This observation, along with the comparatively low parasite counts in the two infected individuals, clearly indicated that it was quite difficult for parasites to establish themselves in people with the sickle-cell trait.

A third line of direct evidence of heterozygote malarial resistance stems from studies of morbidity and mortality among African children, specifically in terms of observed differences in parasite rates, heavy infections, and mortality rates in Hb^S/Hb^A and normal homozygous children. In this context, Allison's (1964) survey of several earlier analyses revealed the following three generalizations:

1. In eight of ten groups, children with the sickle-cell trait had significantly lower malarial parasite counts than those without the trait.

2. The difference in the incidence of severe malarial infection in sickle-cell versus non-sickle-cell children was even more striking. Only 132 of 1,013 (0.13) heterozygous children showed heavy infections, whereas 955 of 3,858 (0.25) normal children were severely affected. Thus the incidence of heavy infection among heterozygotes is only about half that of normals.

3. Of 104 children who died from malaria, only one had the sickle-cell trait. The probability of this occurring by chance alone is less than 1 in 1,000.

In sum, the evidence is conclusive that heterozygotes are resistant to malaria, although the physiological basis for such resistance is still incompletely understood. However, at least two reasonable explanations have been advanced. One proposal (Miller et al. 1956) holds that parasitized erythrocytes in the peripheral circulation tend to adhere to capillary walls during which, under reduced oxygen tension, the sickling process occurs. Since the sickle-shaped red cell is more prone to destruction than the normal red cell, the malarial parasite contained in the former has a greater chance of having its life cycle interrupted. Another explanation, also involving death of the parasite before it achieves its full reproductive potential, is that the parasite may be unable to digest sickle-cell hemoglobin because it contains crystalline aggregates (Cavalli-Sforza and Bodmer 1971).

Perhaps the most widely accepted hypothesis concerning the initial establishment and spread of the Hb^S allele was formulated by Livingstone (1958, 1976; see also Wiesenfeld 1967). The hypothesis, a classic example of one way in which culture affects human biological evolution, involves the recent evolutionary relationships between humans, mosquitoes, and malaria. Livingstone reasoned convincingly that falciparum malaria was not a strong selective force in tropical Africa until sometime after the advent of agriculture, due in large part to the breeding habits of *A. gambiae*. Although this mosquito does have diverse breeding places, it apparently does not reproduce in water that is shaded, brackish, alkaline, or has a strong current. Thus, in an unbroken and heavily shaded tropical rain forest with a floor of highly absorbent humus, *Anopheles* had few breeding places and probably did not exist in large numbers. However, when human populations in these areas switched from an economy based upon hunting to one involving slash-and-burn agriculture, two significant changes occurred. They were especially beneficial to *Anopheles* and, in fact, ultimately led to holoendemic malaria throughout most of Africa.

First, continual clearing of the forest changed the soil texture. It became lateritic; that is, the soil nutrients were leached out by heavy rains (leaving iron and aluminum oxides, accounting for the characteristically red color of laterite). This kind of soil is relatively impervious to water, which, by accumulating periodically in small pools, provides ideal breeding sites for mosquitoes. Other breeding areas also originated around the semipermanent villages that accompanied agriculture. Second, the increase in food supply removed restraints against population increase, and population densities quickly arose to the point where humans instead of other large mammals became the primary host for *P. falciparum* (it is interesting to note that, in contrast to myxomatosis among Australian rabbits, there is no good evidence of a tendency for *P. falciparum* to become less virulent). Under these circumstances, then, the only people who were resistant to malaria were those who carried the mutant Hb^S allele, and the frequency of this allele increased to the extent that equilibrium conditions were reached fairly rapidly in these populations.

In addition to hemoglobin S, two other variants that possibly represent malarial adaptations are known: Hb^C, which is due to the substitution of lysine for glutamic acid at the 6th position of the β-chain, and Hb^E, specified when lysine replaces glutamic acid at the 26th position of the same chain. Although there is no direct evidence for malarial resistance among heterozygotes for either of these two variants, the positive correlations between their geographic distribution and areas of endemic malaria suggest that malaria selection is responsible for their occurrence. The highest frequency of Hb^C is found in a limited area of West Africa, where it occurs simultaneously with Hb^S. However, Hb^E is largely restricted to southeast Asia, both on the mainland (eastern India, Thailand, Burma, Laos, Cambodia, and Vietnam) and throughout Indonesia.

Both Hb^C and Hb^E in the homozygous state cause anemia, but it is far less severe than sickle-cell anemia. In populations where Hb^A, Hb^S, and Hb^C occur simultaneously, the Hb^S/Hb^C heterozygote is probably at a selective disadvantage to all but the Hb^S homozygote. However, the fitness values of the six possible genotypes relative to each other is open to question, since malarial intensity differs from one region to another. Nonetheless, Cavalli-Sforza and Bodmer (1971) have suggested the following order of average fitness values, noting as well that the fitness of the Hb^C homozygote would undoubtedly be above the Hb^S homozygote and probably above the Hb^S/Hb^C heterozygote:

$$AS > AA, AC > SC > SS$$

Glucose-6-Phosphate Dehydrogenase Variation

Human evolutionary responses to the ravages of malaria have not been limited to changes in the hemoglobin molecule. One particularly common resistance mechanism involves a sex-linked condition (see Chapter 4) called glucose-6-phosphate dehydrogenase (G6PD) deficiency, which occurs in varying frequencies among most Old World populations inhabiting malarial areas. As one of several enzymes involved with the metabolism of glucose in red blood cells, G6PD interacts biochemically with enzymes in a manner that prompts G6PD deficient red cells to hemolyze in the presence of certain drugs and other agents (see Harris 1975, for biochemical details). Included among these substances are antimalarial drugs, such as primaquine, and various sulfonamides and antibacterial agents. In fact, in one form of G6PD deficiency called favism, an acute hemolytic anemia may occur after ingestion of fava beans.

As judged from a statement made in the sixth century B.C. by the Greek philosopher and mathematician Pythagoras, favism has a long history. However, it was not until World War II that a series of events occurred which ultimately led to the genetic explanation of G6PD deficiency and to the underlying basis of favism. At that time, thousands of American soldiers returning from Old World malarial areas were given the antimalarial drug primaquine, a treatment that unexpectedly led to episodes of severe hemolytic anemia among many of the black servicemen. Shortly thereafter, several different laboratory tests were developed so that primaquine-sensitive individuals could be detected rapidly and accurately. It was subsequently found that nearly all individuals with either primaquine sensitivity or favism carried a mutant gene that led to a deficiency of G6PD.

The vast majority of people carry the "normal" allele, and only a few of the 100-odd G6PD variants occur in polymorphic frequencies. Likewise, the different variants do not confer equivalent effects upon their carriers: in a survey of 89 variants, Yoshida et al. (1971) noted that only 44 were associated with severe enzyme deficiency. The remaining variants cause either a moderate to mild deficiency (25) or no deficiency at all (18), and 2 variants actually lead to an increased enzyme activity. Furthermore, exogenous agents (drugs, fava beans, etc.) are necessary for the induction of hemolysis in one group of variants causing severe enzyme deficiency, but hemolytic anemia is associated with a different group of about 20 other variants regardless of such external factors (Yoshida 1973).

Although a number of G6PD variants are relevant in establishing malaria as the selective agent responsible for the high frequencies of G6PD deficiency, only four alleles need be considered here: Gd^B, Gd^A, Gd^{A-}, and $Gd^{Mediterranean}$. Since the G6PD locus is on the X-chromosome, hemizygous males and homozygous females will be either deficient or normal, depending upon their particular allele. However, heterozygous females are usually intermediate between normal and deficient males in the degree of drug response and in their levels of enzyme activity. Furthermore, because of a phenomenon called X-inactivation, female genotypes cannot always be reliably predicted from phenotypes. Briefly, any male with an X-linked gene will show the associated trait, since males have only a single X-chromosome that is always active. In females, on the other hand, only one of the two X-chromosomes is active; the other is apparently deactivated at a very early developmental stage, and deactivation of one of the two X-chromosomes in any given cell is due entirely to chance. Thus females who are heterozygous for a G6PD deficient allele will have two types of red blood cells: (1) those with a normal amount of the enzyme, because the X-chromosome carrying the allele for deficiency has been inactivated, and (2) those with an enzyme deficiency due to inactivation of the X-chromosome carrying the normal allele. Whereas males can have only one G6PD variant, females frequently have two forms that may occur in equal amounts (Beutler et al. 1962; Davidson et al. 1963).

Electrophoretic analysis of G6PD in black males often reveals three different phenotypes, Gd B, Gd A, and Gd A-. The normal form, Gd B, migrates at a slower rate than either of the other two. The mobility of Gd A and Gd A- is virtually identical, but Gd A individuals have only slightly lower G6PD activity levels than those with Gd B. Of the three, Gd A- phenotypes are the only ones with a deficient enzyme activity—from 8% to 20% of normal (Yoshida 1973)—and these individuals frequently develop episodes of hemolytic anemia when exposed to primaquine and other drugs.

Different black populations in various parts of the world are considerably variable in G6PD deficiency, but the frequencies tend to be highest in African malarial regions. As abstracted from Livingstone's (1973) recent survey, for example, nine Ugandan populations have a mean frequency of 11.4%; four Sudanese groups have a mean frequency of 12.3%; and the mean frequency among eight Angolan populations is 19.4%. In contrast, the mean frequency among 27 American black populations is 9.2%.

It now appears that the alleles responsible for the Gd B, Gd A, and Gd A- phenotypes occur at the same locus as that for Gd Mediterranean. In addition, it is quite possible that the four alleles differ from each other by only a single amino acid substitution. Such a difference between Gd B and Gd A has been reported (Yoshida 1967), although the primary structures of the other variants are still unknown. In any event, Gd Mediterranean has the same electrophoretic mobility as Gd B, but it creates a more severe enzymatic deficiency than Gd A- (less than 5% of normal). On a worldwide basis, Gd Mediterranean is most common among populations in Greece, Sardinia, Iran, Iraq, India, and Pakistan.

Most Gd A- individuals show no ill effects from enzyme deficiency unless they take any of the various drugs to which they are sensitive. Similarly, most individuals with Gd Mediterranean are quite healthy unless they ingest fava beans. However, the situation is complicated inasmuch as reaction to fava beans varies from a fairly mild to a severe, and sometimes fatal, response. Obviously, other genetic and metabolic factors peculiar to the individual are involved, but these have yet to be identified.

That the high frequencies of different G6PD deficient variants are the result of malarial selection seems well-established. This conclusion is strongly supported by the geographic distribution of G6PD deficiency in malarial areas, but even more impressive are the strong correlations between G6PD deficiency frequencies and the frequencies of hemoglobin S, thalassemia (see below), and hemoglobin E in Africa, southern Europe, and southeast Asia, respectively (Motulsky 1965). Perhaps the best evidence, however, is the experimental demonstration by Luzzatto and his colleagues (1969) that G6PD deficient red cells are much less frequently parasitized than normal red cells.

Progress is being made toward the biochemical interpretation of increased parasite resistance of G6PD red cells, but much work remains to be done in this area. At least two plausible explanations have been offered, one of which involves reduced glutathione (GSH), and the other oxidized glutathione (GSSG). Occurring in the tissues of all animals, glutathione is a simple tripeptide that, among other functions, activates certain enzymes. The first hypothesis (Motulsky 1960) stems from the early *in vitro* demonstration (Trager 1941) that glutathione is necessary for the growth of malarial parasites. Since G6PD deficient cells have a lower concentration of GSH than normal cells, optimal growth of parasites in the former would probably be inhibited. A similar inhibition of growth is proposed in the second explanation (Kosower and Kosower 1970). In their view, the inherently higher levels of GSSG in G6PD deficient cells would prevent parasite proliferation, since GSSG inhibits protein synthesis.

Thalassemia
A final example of human evolutionary responses to malaria consists of a class of chronic anemias called the thalassemias. In general, two clinical forms of thalassemia

are often recognized, thalassemia major and minor. Individuals with thalassemia major (also called Cooley's anemia and Mediterranean anemia) are homozygous for at least one of several mutant genes that cause defects in the rate of synthesis of either the α- or β-hemoglobin polypeptides (see White 1972, for a review of the biochemical nature of the various thalassemias). Symptomatically, homozygotes are usually characterized by listlessness, enlarged spleens and livers, and certain changes in cranial structure. The red blood cells may be distorted, shorter-lived than normal cells, and often possess an abnormally low hemoglobin content. Mortality is very high, with the maximum number of individuals dying in the second decade of life. The clinical picture of thalassemia minor, which occurs in heterozygotes, is ordinarily far less severe, although a rather wide spectrum of symptoms occurs. In most cases, heterozygotes develop a mild to moderate anemia as a result of ineffective red blood cell production in the bone marrow and red blood cell breakdown.

From the biochemical standpoint, the thalassemias may be classified according to the particular polypeptide that causes the hemoglobin deficiency. Hence those resulting from defects in α-chain synthesis are called the α-thalassemias; those resulting from β-chain defects are the β-thalassemias. Like the hemoglobin variants discussed earlier, there is little doubt that a number of different mutations are associated with the different kinds of thalassemia. However, all attempts to discover the precise nature of the changes in polypeptide structure have been unsuccessful.

Both α- and β-thalassemias occur at their highest frequencies in Old World malarial areas, the former being most prevalent among southern Asian populations, and the latter among Mediterranean populations (e.g., southern Italy and Greece). That the relatively high frequencies of thalassemia were due to malarial selection was first suggested by Haldane (1949), although the actual evidence for this association has never been as firmly established as for the hemoglobin variants and G6PD deficiency. Thus, while there are strong positive correlations between malaria and the frequencies of thalassemia in Sardinian and certain Italian populations, similar associations have not been found elsewhere (e.g., Greece, Malta, or New Guinea). In addition, the evidence that thalassemic red blood cells may be more resistant to malarial parasites than normal red cells is only circumstantial. In this context, Livingstone (1971) has suggested that because the thalassemic red cell is much smaller than normal and the malarial parasite completely fills the cell, later growth stages of the parasite might well be inhibited.

A Perspective on Qualitative Variation

The preceding discussions of only a few qualitative characteristics do not indicate in any way the extent of polymorphic variation in red blood cell antigens, plasma proteins, and enzymes. Although rapid progress has been made during the last two decades with respect to their discovery and genetic elucidation, there is presently no precise way to estimate the total number of these genetically controlled systems. However, there is no doubt that they number in the thousands. And since there is a large fraction of loci among the individuals of every population at which at least two common alleles occur, the total number of antigen, protein, and enzyme polymorphisms must also number in the thousands.

The simple existence of this vast number of polymorphisms is not particularly remarkable, since it also pertains to other mammalian and nonmammalian species. Likewise, the new (and mostly rare) variants that are being discovered almost daily are of only marginal interest, per se, for our understanding of human evolutionary genetics. The question of central importance is not concerned with the existence of a great store of hidden genetic variation, but rather with the circumstances involved with the initial establishment and subsequent maintenance of the various polymorphisms.

With exception of the sickle-cell and G6PD polymorphisms, both of which are rather unique situations because the selective factors responsible for their maintenance have been established, evolutionary explanations for the other well-known polymorphisms are woefully insufficient. Unfortunately, this continues to be an intractable problem despite a great deal of ingenuity in devising different research methodologies for this purpose. Obviously, any attempt to associate the frequency of a polymorphic variant with an extant selective factor will be complicated by the inconstancy of the environment. Hence the past selective agents that might have been responsible for the distribution of a polymorphic variant might presently be nonexistent, or of only minor importance. Complicating the problem even more is the fact that it is only rarely possible to determine whether the frequency of a particular allele is in the process of increasing, decreasing, or coming close to a stable equilibrium due to heterozygote advantage.

Nevertheless, the field of evolutionary genetics ultimately depends upon empirically sufficient descriptions of the genetic variation in populations. For such genotypic descriptions to be empirically sufficient—for them to lend themselves to the most meaningful evolutionary predictions and interpretations—they must also be related to their phenotypic manifestations throughout the environmental range of the population. In this context, it is difficult to disagree with Lewontin's contention that

> . . . the description must be genotypic because the underlying dynamical theory of evolution is based on Mendelian genetics. But the description must also specify the relations between genotype and phenotype, partly because it is the phenotype that determines the breeding system and the action of natural selection, but also because it is the evolution of the phenotype that interests us. Population geneticists, in their enthusiasm to deal with the changes in genotype frequencies that underlie evolutionary changes, have often forgotten that what are ultimately to be explained are the myriad and subtle changes in size, shape, behavior, and interactions with other species that constitute the real stuff of evolution. . . . A description and explanation of genetic change in populations is a description and explanation of evolutionary change only insofar as we can link those genetic changes to the manifest diversity of living organisms in space and time. To concentrate only on genetic change, without attempting to relate it to the kinds of physiological, morphogenetic, and behavioral evolution that are manifest in the fossil record and in the diversity of extant organisms and communities, is to forget entirely what it is we are trying to explain in the first place. (1974:19–20)

Summary

Geographic variation in both qualitative and quantitative characteristics occurs in distinct patterns that represent the past effects of selection and migration. For polygenically based quantitative traits, changes in allele frequencies by these evolutionary processes have defied interpretation because (1) such traits have not been defined genetically and (2) they are variably susceptible to both short- and long-term environmental modification. However, similar changes in the frequencies of alleles controlling simple Mendelian qualitative traits have been documented by field-testing techniques, and the evolutionary meaning of such changes can be enhanced with the use of classical selection models of population genetics.

Human population genetics has relied heavily upon the study of genetic markers for qualitative traits, most of which occur in polymorphic frequencies among the world's populations. Those of particular usefulness include a great many red blood cell antigens, plasma proteins, and red cell enzyme systems. About 70 of these genetic markers have been utilized for population studies, and over 20 have been extensively surveyed throughout the world. In terms of geographic variation in allele frequencies, the ABO and Rh blood group systems are better known than any other genetic marker. Geographic distributional studies reveal patterns of variation far too systematic to have resulted by chance, but the selective processes responsible for these patterns have never been discovered. One of the major reasons for this failure has been the inability to ascribe any positive function to either these two or to any other red cell antigen.

Fortunately, the origin and maintenance of a few other genetic polymorphisms by selection has been well established. In particular, malaria has been implicated as the selective agent responsible for the observed variation in allele frequencies for several hemoglobin variants, G6PD deficiency, and thalassemia. The classic example is the Hb^S allele, which is responsible for a hemoglobin abnormality that leads to sickle-cell anemia in the homozygous state. In this system, the fitness of the Hb^S and Hb^A homozygotes is greatly lowered because of sickle-cell anemia and high malarial susceptibility, respectively. But the heterozygote, who does not develop sickle-cell anemia and who is relatively resistant to malaria, is at a selective advantage. Thus, while the origin and initial establishment of the Hb^S allele can be ascribed to a new mutation that was slightly beneficial in a malarial environment, the particularly high allele frequencies in parts of West and Central Africa have been maintained as a balanced polymorphism by selection.

The high frequencies of the different G6PD variants also appear to have been maintained by malarial selection, inasmuch as (1) the geographic distribution of G6PD deficiency corresponds to malarial areas; (2) alleles for G6PD deficiency are strongly correlated to other genetically mediated resistance mechanisms to malaria elsewhere; and (3) experimental evidence has shown that G6PD deficient red cells are much less likely to be parasitized by malarial organisms than normal red cells. The evidence for the origin and maintenance of the thalassemias is not as firmly established as for the hemoglobin variants and G6PD deficiency, although the highest frequencies do occur in areas of endemic malaria. In addition, the thalassemic red blood cell is smaller than the normal cell, which could inhibit later growth stages of the parasite and thus serve as a malarial resistance mechanism.

18 Human Adaptation

Introduction

That the biological integrity and persistence of populations ultimately depend upon both natural and artificial environmental variables is a truism for all living organisms, including *H. sapiens*. It is also an obvious fact that drastically different species within any given environment achieve their basic requirements, such as food, protection, and reproductive strategy, in drastically different ways. For example, different mammals survive arctic winters by migrating southward, hibernating, developing a heavy coat of fur, or building fires within shelters of their own construction. Likewise, the responses to predators among different species in a given environment include such diverse tactics as overcompensation by extraordinarily high reproductive rates, protective coloration, rapid flight, active individual defense, and group cooperation during defense.

These observations are so obvious that they might not deserve mention, except that they lend themselves to at least two important generalizations. First, both species-specific and population-specific behaviors correspond directly to certain environmental factors. The most reasonable way to study such characteristics must, therefore, include relevant ecological variables. Second, the number of different genetic pathways involved with adaptive responses to environmental factors is, for all practical purposes, infinite. Natural selection, being a purely mechanistic process, operates on the phenotypic variation that happens to exist in any particular population. Thus the existence of similar adaptive responses among different species or populations does not necessarily reflect similar genetic processes.

The mechanisms evolved by different species to cope with environmental factors are far more variable than those characterizing populations within a single species. But the latter groups, especially those inhabiting ecologically similar regions, have also adapted to their own particular environments. This is not to say that every population will eventually become homogeneous for phenotypes with optimal survival values (see the discussion of stabilizing selection in Chapter 6). On the contrary, increased population genetic variation enhances the probability that some individuals will survive and reproduce during periods of adverse environmental fluctuation (Mayr 1963). Nor does it imply that certain genetic changes will be induced by certain environmental demands, as was maintained by the Neo-Lamarckian evolutionary school (Simpson 1964). One of the great accomplishments of modern evolutionary biology was to demonstrate the fallacy of this notion. Rather, the genetic and nongenetic characteristics of populations in different environments exist because they contribute to reproductive fitness, i.e., because they are selectively advantageous during a time period when certain ecological conditions prevail. After a requisite number of generations, such physiological, behavioral, and anatomical characteristics will tend to spread throughout the population.

The Relationship between Genotype and Phenotype

With respect to the selective forces involved with the initial establishment and subsequent increase of a genetically controlled trait in a human population, virtually everything discussed in previous chapters has been limited to traits inherited in a simple Mendelian fashion. Hence the mutation from Hb^A to Hb^S hemoglobin can be viewed as a genetic change leading to a phenotypically advantageous response to malaria. However, other responses to other environmental factors—namely, those involving differences in physiological, behavioral, and anatomical features—cannot be couched in equally as explicit genetic terms. The reason, of course, is that such complex phenotypic features are not under simple genetic control and are, at the same time, highly susceptible to nongenetic environmental modification.

That these sorts of characteristics are at least in part conditioned genetically has been well-established. With regard to a variable with both behavioral and physiological correlates, for example, Ogilvie and Stinson (1966) found that two subspecies of *Peromyscus* (the deer mouse) exhibited a difference in temperature preference. Whereas the mean thermal preference of the forest-dwelling subspecies (*P. maniculatus gracilis*) was 29.1°C, it decreased to 25.8°C in the field-dwelling subspecies (*P. maniculatus bairdii*). Because the temperature in open fields is several degrees cooler than in woodlands, the suggestion that the difference arose by natural selection is at least reasonable: each subspecies prefers either a woodland or field habitat, because it can function most efficiently in that particular thermal environment. Yet no single gene is responsible for this preference, for the physiological mechanisms associated with it, or for any behavioral variable per se. In this context, Thiessen (1972) has commented that certain genes may be identified with traits, such as enzymes and hormonal levels, that, in turn, affect behavior. Hereditary influences on behavior, on the other hand, are always indirect.

At this point it is worth remembering that selection operates upon the entire phenotype, the "biological system constructed by successive interactions of the individual's genotype with the environments in which the development takes place" (Dobzhansky 1970:36). The question of critical importance for the study of selective effects on quantitative traits, then, concerns the relationships between the genotype and phenotype, as well as the interactions between cultural and biological variables in the expression of such traits. Both areas of investigation are beset with some of the most difficult of all genetic problems, although rather new and sophisticated analytical methods have expanded our concepts in the area of human quantitative inheritance (see Morton and Rao 1978, for a recent review of the subject).

On the matter of genotypic-phenotypic interactions, it might be noted that much of our knowledge about human genetics in general has been gained from pedigree associations between certain alleles or allelic combinations and their phenotypic end-products. For example, the phenotypic manifestation observed in the large majority of children with the dominant sublethal allele for retinoblastoma is a malignant tumor of the eye; the phenotypic product in individuals with two L^M alleles is the M antigen, and so forth. Hence it is not at all surprising that during the early development of genetics as a science a widely accepted hypothesis held that different genes independently generated "unit characters," and that such "characters" accumulated during development until the organism was complete. Somewhat later, the experimental work of G. Beadle and E. Tatum led to the hypothesis that each gene produced only a single enzyme. However, more recent research has indicated that some enzymes are produced by two or more loci. In addition, these findings confirm that some loci act as templates for structural proteins rather than for certain enzymes. At present, then, the "one-gene-one-enzyme" hypothesis has given way to the view that each structural gene leads to a single protein polypeptide. And because some proteins are made up of two or more polypeptide chains, it follows that more than one structural gene may be necessary for their synthesis.

As discussed in earlier chapters, many genes influence more than a single phenotypic trait (pleiotropism), and many also interact with other genes at different loci (epistasis). It may be concluded from this that an otherwise predictable expression of a certain phenotypic trait can be inconsistent, depending upon the internal genetic environment, as well as external factors. In other words, different gene products interact with each other during development, and these interactions constitute complex networks of processes that must integrate harmoniously if the individual is to possess normal life processes and functions. Thus, with respect to the entire phenotype, the genotype determines the norm of reaction—the full range of developmental paths that can occur in all possible environments. As Dobzhansky (1970) and others have pointed out, the norm of reaction is not fully known for any genotype, whether among experimental or natural organisms. Such information is impossible to obtain, given the virtually infinite number of different environments that can either be artificially created or that naturally exist.

In light of these considerations, it should be evident that the effects of selection upon quantitative traits are far more difficult to isolate than those operating upon traits controlled by only a pair of alleles that are influenced relatively little by other genes. Contributing to this difficulty are correlated responses to selection, phenomena that have been consistently observed in experimental selective regimes applied to animals and plants, but which, without doubt, also occur in humans. The concept of correlated responses is quite straightforward, although the underlying reason for their occurrence has yet to be satisfactorily resolved.

Plant and animal breeders often observe that artificial selection over a number of generations for a particular heritable trait can produce unexpected results. Not only will the trait being selected for increase, but other traits among the population's individuals will also show changes (i.e., correlated responses). Correlated responses occur in the absence of intentional selection either for or against them; the number and severity of the responses are often directly proportional to the severity of selection; and the responses can be so detrimental (e.g., sterility) as to force the breeder to cease the selective experiment.

An intuitively appealing explanation for the occurrence of correlated responses considers (1) the polygenic nature of quantitative traits and (2) the pleiotropic effects of single genes. To paraphrase Li (1970), suppose a breeder selects for a trait denoted as A, and that this trait is influenced by genes at eight different loci

(G_1 through G_8). Suppose also that two other traits, labeled B and C, share some but not all the genes that influence A:

Trait
A $----$ G_1 G_2 G_3 G_4 G_5 G_6 G_7 G_8
B $----$ G_3 G_4 G_7 G_8 G_9 G_{10}
C $----$ G_2 G_3 G_5 G_6 G_{11} G_{12}

In this event, the expression of traits B and C could be changed as a result of selection for trait A because they are influenced by the common loci G_3, G_4, G_7, G_8, and G_2, G_3, G_5, and G_6, respectively. This explanation is probably valid as far as it goes, but as Li notes, it does have one limitation. It fails to explain why there are fewer correlated responses associated with a given change in trait A when mild selection is imposed over a long time period, as opposed to the more severe responses that accompany the same change in trait A during a shorter period of intense selection. Finally, since there is no quantitative trait for which the exact number of associated loci is known, it becomes a bit clearer why the precise nature and number of correlated responses are hardly predictable.

Some Fundamental Concepts

In sum, these comments about genotypic-phenotypic interactions indicate some of the inherent difficulties in studies designed to elucidate the genetic basis of the physiological, behavioral, and anatomical differences between human populations in ecologically dissimilar regions. Nevertheless, both experimental and field investigations have consistently shown that people respond to their environmental stressors in certain ways. Before discussing these responses, however, a few basic concepts require explanation.

Adaptation
The meaning of the term "adaptation" has been debated extensively for several decades. For example, Lewontin commented over 20 years ago that "there is virtually universal disagreement among students of evolution as to the meaning of adaptation" (1957:395), and there is presently so little agreement that even established biologists and anthropologists often deem it necessary to begin their reports with their own definition of the term (e.g., Mazess 1975a; Thomas 1975). A great deal of the disagreement probably stems from two rather disparate viewpoints: (1) the tendency, mainly among evolutionary biologists but also among many biological anthropologists, to restrict the meaning of adaptation to genetic changes in populations as a result of natural selection (i.e., genetic adaptation), and (2) the contention, mostly among those who are neither geneticists nor biological anthropologists, that adaptations occur among individuals and need not necessarily be directly reflective of selective processes.

In the first viewpoint above, the process of adaptation would seem to be synonymous with evolution by natural selection, and any adapted feature would therefore be "any transmissible characteristic of an organism that by its presence permits an interaction with the environment that causes its possessors to produce, on the average, more offspring . . . than would be produced in its absence" (Stern 1970:44). In this conception, then, there is no readily apparent difference between an adapted characteristic and one that is selectively advantageous.

In contrast to such adaptation at the "population" level, the second viewpoint stresses adjustments made by the individual or within the individual (the "infra-individual" level). Whereas individual adaptations include the diverse biological and social phenomena that provide a relative benefit in a particular environment, infra-individualistic adaptations are usually considered to be adjustments in various organ systems for the maintenance of homeostasis.

Individuals and populations respond in countless ways to environmental stressors, and these responses are by no means isolated from each other. Hence it could be argued that there is little to be accomplished by limiting the meaning of adaptation to one or the other of these two viewpoints. If, instead, the concept of adaptation is used generically, i.e., as an all-inclusive term, then it becomes far less restrictive as a rubric that can be applied to the innumerable biological and social phenomena related to the achievement of relatively beneficial adjustments to the environment. This is not an original way of looking at the meaning of the concept: others have espoused it earlier (e.g., Lewontin 1957; McCutcheon 1964; Dobzhansky 1968; Thomas 1975; Mazess 1975b). It should be stressed in this context that adaptation means more than just the ability to survive, maintain function, and reproduce. Survival is, of course, a necessity. But the maintenance of function and reproductive performance can be enhanced by relatively beneficial adjustments to the environment. Hence all three properties are the adaptive criteria to which environmental adjustments are made. And for such adjustments to be of adaptive significance requires that they be either relatively advantageous or, to some extent, necessary.

At the core of many anthropologically oriented investigations into human adaptability is the search for characteristics of adaptive significance among descendants of groups that have been exposed to extreme selective pressures for many generations. The pressures can be of a physical nature, such as high altitude, arctic, or tropical environments, and/or they may be biological, like malaria in the Old World. Moreover, the evaluation of adaptive significance can be instituted at any of the following six levels (Mazess 1975a):

1. Physicochemical
2. Cellular
3. Organ system
4. Individual
5. Population
6. Ecosystem

The arrangement of this hierarchy is based upon an increasing organizational complexity, inasmuch as the environment of each level is the dominant focus of the one preceding it. Thus the ecosystem forms the population's environment, the individual the organ's environment, and so forth. Likewise, different criteria are used to assess degrees of necessity or relative benefit at each of these levels. Obviously, the adaptive significance of a particular enzyme would be best considered in light of the enzyme's immediate environment, and the criteria for such a study should be chosen accordingly. If the individual level is considered, then traits that are beneficial to such "adaptive domains" as reproduction, nutrition, health, and growth and development have adaptive significance for the individual. And, at the population level, benefit and necessity are assessed with respect to the various demographic and genetic variables that contribute to the overall structure of the population.

It was mentioned in the preceding chapter that one of the most conspicuous failures of human population genetics has been the inability to provide solid selectionist explanations for the origin and maintenance of the various red blood cell polymorphisms. Modern research on human adaptation is plagued with a similarly difficult problem. The shortcoming is not so much concerned with finding positive correlations between a response in some characteristic and a certain environmental factor—examples of these will follow shortly. Instead, there is all too often no precise demonstration that a characteristic is of adaptive significance in a certain domain.

As an example, we may consider the widely accepted hypothesis (Roberts 1978) dealing with the relationship between climatic temperature and body form: "In order to facilitate the balance of human body heat exchange, under those conditions in which heat loss is more difficult the amount of body tissue is reduced, so that less heat is produced and the ratio of surface area to weight (i.e., the ratio of potential heat loss to potential heat production) is increased" (1978:16). Alternatively stated, the hypothesis holds that the human body tends to be more spherical in colder climates and more linear in warmer climates.

Now the general validity of this hypothesis, at least in terms of correlations between temperature and body form, has been demonstrated many times in investigations on body segments and complete individuals from highly diverse climates. But as interesting and informative as such climate-body form associations are, there still remains the unanswered question about the particular benefit to an adaptive domain. As stated above, the adaptive significance of these adjustments should be couched in terms of their conferring some relative advantage upon the individual, such as an increase in physical performance, stress resistance, or general health. That such benefits exist is highly probable, insofar as natural selection may be invoked as a teleological explanation, but the precise nature of the benefits remains to be clarified.

Other Terms

If adaptation is viewed as an all-inclusive process by which some relatively beneficial adjustment to the environment is achieved, then it is necessary to use different terms to distinguish certain responses. One of these responses is **acclimatization,** which, according to Folk, is "the functional compensation over a period of days to weeks in response to a complex of environmental factors, as in seasonal or climatic changes" (1966:24). At the outset it should be stressed that acclimatization is not a process by which environmental adjustments are made over several generations: no assumptions about changes in gene frequency by evolutionary processes are implied in the definition. Instead, acclimatization refers to the adjustments made by the individual in response to stressful or changing environmental factors. Such responses normally include changes in characteristics that are phenotypically plastic to varying degrees, in contrast to phenotypically stable traits.

Since a wide range of phenotypic characteristics acclimatize to environmental effects, it is appropriate to categorize these responses in terms of several general sets of phenotypic traits. Although different frameworks can be devised, that proposed by Mazess (1975b) seems both straightforward and useful.

1. Structural acclimatization. This category includes histological, anatomical, and morphological adjustments. A good example, the effect of training on muscle strength, has been documented by Yamakawa (1975) among young Japanese women. The sample of 50 individuals, aged 19 to 21, was divided into two groups who performed arm-curls with a barbell. The weight of the barbell was set at two-thirds of the maximum muscle strength in one group, and one-half of the maximum muscle strength in the other group. The increase in muscle strength—the acclimatization response—was marked. After a period of only 12 weeks, increases in muscle strength in the one-half weight group ranged from 120% to 125%, and in the two-thirds weight group from 140% to 150%.

2. Functional acclimatization. This category consists of at least two subcategories, both of which pertain to adjustments in the function of organ systems.

a. Physiological acclimatization. Among the most thoroughly investigated responses in this category are the prevention of heat loss by shivering and the promotion of heat dissipation by sweating. Individuals and populations may differ slightly in terms of the temperatures at which these responses begin, but the general mechanisms associated with the responses are the same for all individuals. In shivering, for example, the following sequence of events occurs (Folk 1966). After a very short period of intense cold exposure, the small vessels in the skin and its underlying layers constrict. This allows the skin to become cooler, thereby decreasing the loss of surface heat and shifting blood from the body's surface to the viscera. Heart rate increases by about 14%, and the respiratory rate accelerates. Minute muscle fibers (the Arrectores pilorum) attached to the hair follicles contract involuntarily, causing "goose pimples," a reaction that is widespread among mammals for increasing insulation by raising the hair. By these mechanisms, then, heat loss may be reduced by one-sixth to one-third. After the release of certain hormones, an increased electrical activity in skeletal muscle leads to the shivering response. This, in turn, leads to a three- to fourfold increase in metabolic rate, which, after about 20 minutes of shivering, can increase body temperature by about 0.6°C to 0.8°C.

b. Neurological acclimatization, or **habituation.** Included here are quite short-term stress responses in sensory function and neural control. According to Eagen (1963), habituation can be subdivided into both specific and general types. Specific habituation involves a certain repeated stimulus to a particular part of the body. The neurological response is frequently a reduction in sensation to the stimulus, as in the diminution of pain when a finger undergoes repeated severe cooling. In contrast to such desensitization in a single isolated region, general habituation involves a diminution in a physiological effector response to a certain stimulus. For example, vasoconstriction in the entire periphery that might occur in response to repeated cooling of a single finger would be reduced. In a sense, as observed by Stini (1975), both kinds of habituation are processes which allow normal homeostatic states to be maintained under adverse conditions, thereby preventing damage to the individual that could otherwise occur as a result of overreaction to a disruptive stimulus.

3. Psychobehavioral acclimatization. Changes in this category involve neural responses that relate to sublimation, personality alterations, adjustments in perception and cognition that directly influence behavior, and changes in activity patterns.

Although these sorts of acclimatization responses may be more similar among individuals within specific populations, they are basically individual responses. Therefore, their adaptive significance can best be assessed by demonstrating potential benefit in any of the adaptive domains pertaining to the individual.

Heat Acclimatization

Exposure to heat for longer than just a brief period initiates a series of physiological responses. The first is a rise in skin temperature, followed by dilation of the skin's blood vessels. Plasma and blood volume increase slightly, and the dilated vessels allow a greater blood flow near the surface of the skin. Since heat transfer from the body's interior is accomplished by blood flow to the surface, more heat is transported for dissipation. Some dehydration occurs, depending upon the amount of ingested water. The increased surface blood flow is associated with a fall in blood pressure, but a compensatory rise in heart rate occurs to maintain pressure.

When ambient temperature reaches about 30°C, heat loss by radiation and convection begins to be replaced by loss due to evaporation of sweat. When ambient temperature exceeds body temperature, heat loss is accomplished by sweating only. As ambient temperature becomes more severe, or if by physical labor the individual produces more heat than can be dissipated, both unpleasant (e.g., general discomfort and distress) and debilitating symptoms appear. The sweat glands may begin to improperly function; hyperventilation and sweat loss can lead to a marked loss of CO_2 and subsequent rise in blood pH; continued **vasodilation** and lowered blood pressure can threaten cardiovascular function; and muscle cramps, faintness, and collapse can occur.

Acclimatization responses to heat stress would seem clearly beneficial, especially in terms of enhancing an individual's ability to carry out normal, everyday functions in a hot environment. Such responses have been found among individuals whose ancestors have evolved in both hot and cold climates. Moreover, there is no good evidence of striking "racial" variation in the ability to acclimatize to heat. In general, repeated or continued exposure to heat for a variable, but relatively short, time period (perhaps one to two weeks) brings about a number of physiological adjustments:

1. A marked improvement in cardiovascular function. Both heart rate and heart output, which increase quickly upon initial exposure, are reduced.

2. Core temperature, which also undergoes a rapid initial increase, either reaches a plateau or rises much more slowly upon continued exposure.

3. Peripheral conductance and sweating capacity increase. Sweating begins at a slightly lower skin temperature, presumably because of an increased heat sensitivity of the sweat glands.

4. Sweat is distributed more evenly over the skin's surface, allowing more rapid and efficient heat dissipation by evaporation.

5. Salt concentration in the sweat decreases as sweat production increases. This prevents a salt deficit, especially during the first few days of heat exposure.

6. As a result of these responses, the maintenance of function and the ability to work in a hot climate are markedly improved.

Population Variation in Heat Tolerance

If it is presumed that natural selection favors the ability to acclimatize, then it might also seem reasonable to postulate that populations evolving in hot climates would consist of individuals with greater degrees of heat tolerance than those who have evolved elsewhere. Indeed, many field investigations have been designed for the expressed purpose of finding whether inherited (i.e., "racial") differences in heat tolerance exist. Most often, such studies have involved the comparison of relevant data taken from individuals from tropical versus temperate climates.

The evidence in favor of the proposition that tropical people possess greater innate degrees of heat tolerance is not as conclusive as might be expected, but it has been suggested a number of times. For example, about 40 years ago Robinson and his colleagues (1941) observed response differences between American blacks and whites who worked under hot and humid environmental conditions. The workload and time period were the same for both groups, but the core temperatures, sweat losses, and heart rates were somewhat lower among the black sample. Robinson explained these differences in terms of variation in mechanical efficiencies and surface area to weight ratios.

Seventeen years later Baker (1958) sought differences in heat tolerance (also among American blacks and whites), but he utilized eight different conditions in two climatic regimes. The imposed climates were hot and humid, and hot and dry, and the conditions included various combinations of clothing, sun, shade, walking, and sitting. By measuring initial and final rectal temperatures, total and evaporated sweat loss (no significant differences were found here), and pulse rates, Baker offered these conclusions: (1) clothed and walking, blacks had a higher physiological tolerance in hot and humid conditions; (2) whites and blacks had about equal tolerance when clothed and walking or when sitting in hot and dry conditions; and (3) sun-tanned whites had higher physiological tolerances when both groups were exposed to the sun, in the nude, under hot and dry conditions. Baker thought that these differences could be under genetic control, rather than a reflection of transient environmental effects, and suggested that the difference in rectal temperature between blacks and whites fully exposed to sunlight was due to greater absorption of solar radiation by the blacks.

Similar indications of differential heat tolerance among various ethnic groups have been reported more recently (e.g., Strydom and Wyndham 1963; Wyndham et al. 1964; Wyndham 1966). In one study (Wyndham et al. 1964), unacclimatized South African Bantus and whites were exposed to work in a severely stressful hot and humid climate. That the Bantus were more heat tolerant was suggested by their lower core temperatures, sweat rates, and heart rates. Representatives of both groups were subsequently allowed to acclimatize to a slightly higher temperature for a period of 12 days. The white sample acclimatized to these conditions, as expected, but still showed slightly higher core temperatures, sweat rates, and heart rates.

The same tests were administered to individuals from other groups (Bushmen, Australian aborigines, Saharan Arabs, and whites from different areas), with variable results. Sweat rate levels among the Australian aborigines were about the same as the unacclimatized Bantu; Saharan Arabs were similar to French and Australian whites; and the Bushmen were variable. These observations pointed out what had been learned earlier: individuals who go about their normal functions in hot environments, regardless of their ethnic affiliation, become at least partially acclimatized. But another conclusion of Wyndham and his colleagues was that given equal acclimatization, the differences in heat tolerance levels among the various groups were minimal. Hanna (1970) also found that neither Yaqui Indians nor Papago Indians, both of whom are native to the hottest part of North America, possessed heat tolerance levels above those that can be acquired by migrants from different regions.

At the present time, then, the evidence for the proposition that some groups differ in their relative heat tolerance levels is equivocal. Some have cautiously advocated the view (e.g., Hanna and Baker 1974; Austin and Ghesquiere 1976). Others have denied it (e.g., Newman 1975). Certain tropical populations may be at a slight advantage with respect to a relative decrease in sweat and salt loss and concomitant physical distress under heat stress. But as Roberts (1978) notes, it can only be speculated whether this decrease is related to water economy, sweat-gland fatigue, or to a qualitative difference in sweat-gland function between people from tropical and temperate climates.

Cold Acclimatization

The body immediately begins to lose heat upon acute cold exposure, mostly by radiation, but to a lesser extent by conduction (a primary means of loss in the event of cold water immersion), convection, and lung evaporation. The general criterion for the rate of heat loss is described by Newton's Law of Cooling:

> . . . heat loss per minute is directly proportional to the body surface and the difference between the temperature of the body core and that of the environment, and inversely proportional to the thickness of the body shell; i.e., heat flows from the body core to the external environment at a rate which increases with the surface area and the temperature drop between core and exterior, and which decreases with greater thickness of the barrier between core and exterior. (Folk 1966:101)

As described earlier for the shivering response, a temperature drop leads to **vasoconstriction,** thus providing the body with a "thicker" shell by decreasing peripheral tissue conductivity. However, further cooling leads to a cyclical response during which the skin temperature may fluctuate within a range of about 6.5°C every 20 minutes or so. Presumably, this response assists in the prevention of surface tissue damage (frostbite). Nevertheless, the transfer of internal heat to the surface continues and core temperature begins to fall. Thus the maintenance of thermal equilibrium at this point will be dependent upon an increase in heat production. This, in turn, is gained by an increase in metabolism in the viscera and muscle tissue, in addition to physical exercise and shivering. The time at which augmented heat production is initiated is strongly dependent upon ambient temperature, beginning in less than two minutes at 3°C, and in about seven minutes at 10°C (Roberts 1978).

There is no doubt at all that acclimatization to cold occurs in varying degrees in all people, but the specific responses are less clearly defined than for heat. Certainly, one of the more overt indications of increased cold tolerance is that those moving into an arctic region find the amount of extra insulative clothing needed as winter progresses to be less than that initially expected. Dietary preferences also shift, one of the most commonly reported changes being a heightened desire for fat. The mechanisms involved in the maintenance of thermal equilibrium are improved and basal metabolic rate increases.

This increase allows a higher temperature to be maintained in both the core and the extremities, but the factors responsible for the increase remain debatable. They could be related either to increased fat and/or protein intake, additional exercise and movement, a change in some endocrine function, or a combination of these phenomena. In any case, blood flow to the extremities also undergoes improvement, enhancing tactile sensitivity and the ability to manipulate objects. Thus acclimatization to cold involves complex processes that increase heat production and fat deposition, and, like acclimatization to heat, adjustments occur in the endocrine system and in both the central and sympathetic nervous systems.

Ethnic Differences in Cold Tolerance

Investigations into population variation in cold tolerance have usually proceeded from a premise similar to that applying to comparative studies in heat tolerance: populations evolving in and chronically exposed to cold may be expected, through natural selection, to develop genetically conditioned cold tolerance levels above those of tropical populations. Likewise, comparative cold tolerance studies are usually approached in one of two different ways: (1) those that seek to associate certain physical characteristics of people in cold environments with naturally occurring environmental variables and (2) those that test the physiological responses of individuals exposed to either experimentally controlled or naturally cold environments. Steegmann (1975) has referred to these two approaches, respectively, as the distributional and physiological methods.

Included in the distributional approach are investigations into possible associations between climatic variables and either gross phenotypic characteristics (e.g., stature and weight) or more specialized anatomical structures (e.g., head form, skin color, and nose shape). One of the more comprehensive analyses of the relationships between mean annual temperature and body weight and shape is that by Roberts (1978), who maintains that an organism's phenotypic form can theoretically be influenced by climate in the following ways:

1. The genotype of the organism can be directly affected, inasmuch as climatic factors can either directly affect a cytological process or serve as agents that select for any characteristic that is advantageous or lends greater efficiency to an individual in any given environment.

2. The genotype of the organism may be indirectly influenced when climate imposes a restraint on carrying capacity—and hence a restriction on population size—within any given region, because the overall effects of selection and mutation on a population depend upon its size and breeding structure. There may also

be an indirect genotypic influence when climatic factors influence the amount of gene flow.

3. The phenotype may be affected by climatic factors either by direct modification of gene products or by indirect influence on those materials (e.g., food supply) essential to normal growth and development (see Chapter 19).

Roberts utilized adult male samples from indigenous populations throughout the world to statistically test the hypothesis (quoted earlier under "Adaptation") that the surface area to weight ratio is increased in populations from hot climates and decreased in those from cold climates, in order to facilitate body heat exchange. Body weight was chosen as a measure of body size, and numerous measurements of the lower limb, upper limb, and trunk were considered reflective of body shape. The geographical pattern of these size and shape factors relative to mean annual temperature was analyzed by correlation and regression (see Appendix I), with the following general results:

1. There were significant (but by no means perfect) correlations between mean annual temperature and body morphology both between and within different continental populations. Specifically, a highly significant correlation was found between body weight and climatic temperature: average weights were lower in hot and higher in cold climates. Average sitting heights were also significantly associated with temperature, populations in cold climates having greater values than those in hot climates. The converse was found for leg length, which tends to be shorter in cold climates. With respect to other leg dimensions, both calf and thigh circumferences tend to be greater in cold climates. Individuals in cold climates also tend toward shorter arms, greater chest girths, and greater widths in the pelvic and shoulder diameters.

2. These observations, taken in their entirety, support the contention that individuals evolving in cold climates tend toward less linearity of form than those from warm climates. Hence body surface relative to weight tends to decrease with lower temperatures. These findings are at least in approximate accord with two well-known ecogeographic principles: **Bergmann's rule** and **Allen's rule,** which were formulated in 1847 and 1877, respectively, as empirical generalizations about the parallelisms between morphological and ecogeographic variation (Mayr 1956).

Both rules are related to heat conservation, and both are couched in terms of basic physical laws relating to the amount of heat that can be lost from two objects with equal mass but different surface areas. Bergmann's rule states that the body size of the subspecies within a homeothermic species will usually increase as the mean temperature of the habitats decreases. Allen's rule holds that the relative size of exposed body appendages decreases as mean temperature decreases. Physiologically, the usual rationale given for Bergmann's rule is that since body volume increases as the *cube* of a linear dimension, whereas the surface increases as the *square* of that dimension, a larger body will, thus, have a relatively smaller surface. Hence larger bodies, or at least those tending toward sphericity, should be at a selective advantage in a cold climate, because they tend to conserve heat. To the contrary, smaller body size and longer appendages should be selectively advantageous in hot climates because relatively more surface per unit of body weight is available for heat dissipation.

3. Because factors of body size and shape are significantly associated with mean annual temperature, and since these characteristics are intimately related to heat dissipation and conservation, variation in surface area to weight ratios may have arisen through natural selection, and, if so, would represent genetic adaptations.

While these findings are intriguing, there is still considerable doubt about the ultimate bases for the demonstrated associations between body size and climate. Over 20 years ago, for example, Newman and Munro (1955) investigated the relationships between climate and body size in over 15,000 young, native-born American white males of relatively recent European extraction. If genetic adaptation were to be invoked as the explanation for north-south clines in body size, then this group of individuals would not be expected to show such variation. However, after dividing the group, on the basis of birth in each of the 48 states, and correlating the average biological and environmental values, they found highly significant correlations of body weight to temperature—much the same as Roberts (1978) showed for indigenous populations.

After considering a number of possible causal factors, Newman and Munro felt that the most plausible explanation for this pattern was an increase in appetite and activity in cold weather. As mentioned earlier, this is usually considered to be an acclimatization response that is not necessarily genetic in origin. Thus it would seem that the observed differences in surface area to weight ratios have no all-inclusive explanation, but, instead, may result from a combination of genetic and nongenetic factors.

In addition to distributional studies of ethnic differences in whole body weight and shape as a result of climate, other investigations have centered around various components of the craniofacial complex. Features such as nose shape and the size of the frontal and maxillary sinuses have attracted particular attention, probably because the face is more or less constantly exposed to the environment among all populations. Furthermore, craniofacial structures are unique insofar as they rarely experience cold injury, which strongly implies that facial frostbite would be of only minor importance as a selective agent that played a role in molding facial architecture over time. This observation (Steegmann 1967, 1972b) contradicts the hypothesis formulated much earlier by Coon et al. (1950) that the "flat," fat-padded face characteristic of Eskimos and other "Mongoloids" is the selective product of frostbite in extremely cold environments.

A few articles on the associations between cold temperatures and sinus cavities have appeared, mostly with inconclusive results. For example, Koertvelyessy (1972) examined the relationships between cold climatic conditions and the occurrence and size of the frontal sinuses in 153 Eskimo crania, finding a significant reduction in sinus surface area among those in colder areas. Shea (1977) also found that the capacity of the maxillary sinus among Eskimos decreases with temperature decreases, but could offer no reason for the occurrence of such variation.

The main problem in assessing how an individual would benefit from a relatively larger or smaller paranasal sinus in any particular climate is simply that the function (if any) of these cavities is completely unknown. Some have suggested that they lighten the skull and enhance its balance; others feel that they assist in warming and humidifying inspired air; still others have suggested that they serve as "dead-air" spaces that help to insulate vital organs in close proximity; and yet others have concluded that sinus cavities are facial structures that have evolved for the maintenance of strength at the expense of weight (see Shea 1977, for a brief review and references pertaining to this subject).

One of the earliest attempts to elucidate the relationships between a morphological feature and a climatic variable dealt with the nasal index (nasal breadth relative to width). This was Thomson and Buxton's (1923) classic paper, in which mean nasal index among both indigenous living and skeletal populations was examined with respect to their particular climates. After finding that nasal index was positively correlated to mean annual temperature, to relative humidity, and to both of these climatic variables together, they concluded that mean nasal index decreases as temperature decreases (i.e., the nose becomes more narrow in colder climates).

Thomson and Buxton's correlations, as well as those obtained later by Davies (1932), led to the conclusion that air temperature was more important than humidity in observed differences in nasal index. However, several investigators in the early 1940s showed convincingly that a primary function of the nasal epithelium (the internal lining) was air humidification, and that the nasal mucous membranes of individuals in dry climates could secrete as much as a liter of water daily to raise air moisture content to 95% relative humidity at normal body temperature. Based upon these findings, Weiner (1954) postulated that to the extent that nose shape may be related to inspired air humidification, nasal index would probably be closely associated with absolute humidity. In particular, he argued logically that ". . . evaporative heat loss from the respiratory tract and moisture addition to the inspired air would both be functions of the vapor pressure gradient between the external air and the virtually saturated surfaces of the tract. The vapor pressure of the latter may be assumed to remain relatively constant so that nose shape can be directly related to external vapor pressure" (1954:617).

This line of reasoning led Weiner to utilize different measures of humidity in a reanalysis of Thomson and Buxton's data on 150 living population samples. Although it was only possible to approximate the absolute humidity in each of the regions involved, he obtained very high correlation coefficients: $r = 0.77$ for nasal index to wet bulb temperature and 0.82 for nasal index to air vapor pressure. This strongly suggests (although Weiner performed no regression analysis on this data) that (1) absolute humidity is more important than temperature as a factor influencing nose shape and (2) nasal width tends to increase as absolute air humidity increases. Support for these observations has recently been provided by Hiernaux and Froment (1976), who found that an increase in nose breadth and a decrease in nose height was associated with increasing rainfall among sub-Saharan African populations.

The existence of population differences in physiological responses to cold has been demonstrated most clearly by studies of cold exposure to the fingers, hands, and feet. The rationale for this approach is direct: if different human populations have evolved genetic adaptations to cold, these should be most apparent in those structures that are far away from the body's core and hence relatively difficult to keep warm; that have a large surface area relative to weight and thus a disproportionate tendency toward heat loss; that are vital organs for the maintenance of normal activities; and which, in comparison to other structures, are more frequently exposed to natural cold stress. The structures meeting these criteria most closely are the hands and, especially, the fingers.

The testing procedure usually involves immersing the fingers of otherwise comfortable individuals into a liquid of unvarying low temperature, the skin temperature being taken after a brief period of time to assess the specific response. In a different approach, the magnitude of heat loss in one of these appendages can be assessed by allowing it to warm cold water. But regardless of which method is utilized, the maintenance of heat under this kind of cold stress is normally taken as an adaptive response. Furthermore, significantly different responses among equally acclimatized individuals from two populations from climatically disparate regions is highly suggestive of a genetically based adaptation.

The results of numerous studies of population variation in the response of extremities to cold are conclusive: groups that are continuously exposed to cold conditions maintain higher finger and hand temperatures than groups from warmer climates. Unfortunately, the question about the ultimate source of such variation still persists. Has the ability to maintain average skin temperature been incorporated by natural selection into the gene pools of populations that have been chronically exposed to cold over many generations, or is it an extraordinarily long-term acclimatization response? Several research designs have been developed to shed some light on this question (e.g., Baker 1966; Elsner et al. 1960; Hanna and Smith 1975; Krog et al. 1960; Krog et al. 1969), a good example of which is the attempt by Little and his colleagues (1971) to evaluate the respective roles of developmental acclimatization and genetic factors in peripheral cooling responses of Quechua Indians in Peru.

Individuals representing four different populations were compared in this study. Two of the populations were genetically similar, consisting of Quechua Indians from the Peruvian highlands and from the Peruvian coast. The other two were American and British whites. While the highland Indians are habitually cold-exposed (mean annual temperature = about 8° C, with nighttime temperatures often falling a few degrees below freezing) and rarely wear protective covering on the hands and feet, the coastal group enjoys a mild temperate climate. Thus neither this group nor the American and British white samples were comparable to the highland Quechua with respect to chronic and severe cold stress. In the first part of the study, hand temperature responses to 0° air temperature for 60 minutes were recorded for individuals from all four groups. In a second part, both young and adult highland Quechua Indians and American whites were tested for foot temperature responses to cold.

The results showed that both Indian populations maintained higher extremity temperatures than either British or American whites. That the highland Quechua would do so is not particularly surprising, given their naturally cold environment. However, the higher hand temperatures among the coastal Indians is especially interesting because they have probably undergone less cold exposure during their lifetimes than either of the white groups. This would appear to provide solid support for the existence of a genetically based adaptation.

Another interesting finding was that highland Indians maintained warmer foot temperatures than hand temperatures, a pattern opposite to that observed among the white adults in this and numerous other studies. This strongly suggests an acclimatization response for two reasons. First, the natural pattern of cold exposure among all individuals within the highland Quechua population is such that only the hands and feet are routinely exposed. Since the hands can be more easily protected under severe cold stress than the feet, it follows that the greater exposure of the feet has led to a differential extremity acclimatization. Second, the inability of Indian children to maintain foot temperatures as high as adults argues for the proposition that cold responses may be enhanced by a rather long-term developmental acclimatization.

This study by Little et al. (1971) is only one of many in which differences in physiological cold response between two or more "racial" groups have implied genetic adaptations. As one additional generalization, most investigators of equally acclimatized blacks and whites of comparable background indicate that cold response in the former is less efficient than in the latter. For that matter, much of the interest in the differences between these two groups stemmed from the observation that black servicemen in Korea and Alaska were far more susceptible to frostbite than whites. Thus Iampietro et al. (1959) matched adult male blacks with white Europeans for physical characteristics and found that blacks had colder finger temperatures and less cold-induced vasodilation after 0° C water immersion for 45 minutes, and Newman (1967) obtained the same general results in a similar test. Other experiments of the same basic nature that compare the responses between these and other indigenous populations have been reviewed extensively by Steegmann (1975).

The existence of such population variation in cold responses cannot be seriously contested, although it is seldom easy to partition the causal factors into genetic versus nongenetic processes. Both are probably involved. Nevertheless, some sort of causal explanation, or at least a reasonable speculation about the occurrence of these phenomena, seems in order. The matter is somewhat complicated because genetically based adaptations to cold have probably conferred no special advantage upon individuals for thousands of years. The vast majority of today's populations adjust to cold by cultural rather than biological means, the result being that survival and function in the world's coldest climate is not dependent upon one's physiological characteristics.

However, populations of *H. erectus* in Europe and China of about 500,000 years ago, and even the later Neandertals, doubtlessly underwent long periods of chronic and severe cold stress. If it is assumed that (1) subsistence patterns based upon hunting and gathering—especially hunting—place a high premium upon use of the hands; (2) fingers are more prone toward cold injury than other appendages; and (3) some individuals would be less susceptible to cold injury because of more efficient, genetically conditioned response levels, then it seems plausible to suggest that such individuals would, through time, contribute their genes disproportionately to the gene pools of later generations. Differential cold responses in modern populations may, thus, simply represent the remnants of an earlier adaptation. It should be mentioned, finally, that this is by no means a new hypothesis: the same idea has been expressed in different terms by Coon et al. (1950), Coon (1962), and many others.

Adaptation to High Altitude

If genetic changes in human populations have been mediated by climatic selection in any way, and if these changes have been translated into morphological and physiological characteristics, then populations living at high altitudes should present many unique features. Of all regions inhabited by human populations, those at high altitudes are among the least hospitable. Such environments are typically cold, dry, and hilly, which, in conjuction with formidable geographic barriers and concomitant isolation from other populations, contributes to a marginal nutritional base. Added to these stresses is a limited availability of energy and higher levels of natural radiation, but the major stress with which to contend results from a lower partial oxygen pressure (PO_2). **Hypoxia,** or oxygen deficiency in inspired air, has been shown to exert an adverse effect upon nearly all physiological functions and organ systems during development, and virtually nothing other than very short-term artificial intervention can lessen the effects.

The fundamental reason for adverse effects of hypoxia at high altitude concerns barometric pressure, a measurement in millimeters of mercury (Hg) that expresses the total pressure of all atmospheric gases. Barometric pressure decreases as altitude increases, the approximate values being 760 mm Hg at sea level, 523 mm Hg at 10,000 feet, and 349 mm Hg at 20,000 feet. Decreases in barometric pressure are also linked to proportional decreases in oxygen pressure, which comprises about 20% of the total barometric pressure regardless of altitude. Thus the values for partial oxygen pressure (PO_2 determines the force exerted on oxygen when it diffuses through the pulmonary membrane) in dry air at sea level, 10,000 feet, and 20,000 feet are about 159 mm, 110 mm, and 73 mm Hg, respectively, although high amounts of water vapor can reduce these values by about 10 mm Hg.

At high altitudes, of course, decreased atmospheric PO_2 leads to decreased PO_2 in the small air sacs (alveoli) in the lungs. Because of compensation by an increase in pulmonary ventilation, the decrease in alveolar PO_2 relative to atmospheric PO_2 at low altitudes is somewhat less. At higher altitudes, however, there is a greater decrease in alveolar PO_2 relative to atmospheric PO_2 for the following reason. At all altitudes, water vaporization from the respiratory surfaces and carbon dioxide excretion from pulmonary blood are continuous processes that effectively reduce oxygen concentration by diluting the oxygen and nitrogen within the alveoli. But when barometric pressure at high altitudes falls to low levels, there is no comparable fall in either water vapor or carbon dioxide pressure. Water vapor pressure at normal body temperature is independent of altitude and remains at a steady 47 mm Hg. Carbon dioxide pressure also changes very little, ranging from 40 mm Hg at sea level to 24 mm Hg at 20,000 feet and above.

The way that these two gas pressures affect oxygen space may be outlined by assuming a barometric pressure of about 310 mm Hg, roughly that which might be expected at the top of Mount Everest (altitude = 29,002 feet above sea level). From that just stated, 47 mm Hg of the total pressure would be due to water vapor, the remaining gases being responsible for 263 mm Hg. In an unacclimatized individual, carbon dioxide would account for another 24 mm Hg, leaving 239 mm Hg for everything else. Since dry air consists roughly of one part oxygen to five parts nitrogen (along with several other minor components), only one-fifth of this 239 mm Hg would be due to oxygen. Thus alveolar PO_2 would only be 48 mm Hg, corresponding to an arterial oxygen saturation of about 20% to 25% (Guyton 1976a). Since loss of consciousness ensues within a few minutes when oxygen saturation content falls to about 40%, the maintenance of function at such altitudes would require use of an artificial breathing device that would supply a greater amount of oxygen relative to nitrogen.

Symptomatically, unacclimatized individuals at altitudes above 12,000 feet often experience headache, drowsiness, lassitude, mental fatigue, and, sometimes, euphoria or nausea. Each of these symptoms can be traced back to a lowered arterial oxygen saturation, and each commonly becomes more severe at higher altitudes. Hypoxia also affects night vision proficiency, due to the extreme sensitivity of the retinal rods to fluctuations in oxygen saturation. Mental proficiency, as evaluated by psychological tests and reaction times, may also be impaired.

Physiological Acclimatization to High Altitude
Within variable periods of time at high altitudes, individuals make at least six different physiological adjustments to hypoxia. These acclimatization responses include (1) an increase in pulmonary ventilation, (2) an increase in red blood cell volume and hemoglobin content, (3) a decrease in affinity of hemoglobin for oxygen, (4) an increase in tissue capillarity, (5) an increase in cardiac output and lung diffusion capacity, and (6) changes in cellular metabolism (Mazess 1975a). A few comments about these adjustments follow below.

1. Pulmonary ventilation. Located just above the heart around the aorta and carotid arteries are several chemoreceptors, which are small structures that contain sensory receptors that are specifically sensitive to oxygen deficiency. When an individual is exposed to low PO_2 and a corresponding fall in arterial oxygen saturation, these chemoreceptors become excited and stimulate certain nerves, which then elevate arterial pressure by a reflex action. In this immediate reaction to hypoxia, alveolar ventilation may be increased by as much as 65%. People who remain at high altitudes for longer periods (perhaps a year or more) increase arterial oxygen saturation by hyperventilation. That this is an acclimatization response is indicated by diminished levels of hyperventilation among both native residents and those who remain at high altitudes for longer periods of time (see Mazess 1970, and Frisancho et al. 1973b, for more on this topic).

2. Red blood cell volume and hemoglobin content. When the quantity of oxygen carried to the tissues is decreased, as in an anemic disorder or injury resulting in hemorrhage, the rate of red blood cell production automatically increases. Hypoxia stimulates an increase in both red blood cell volume and concentration (or hematocrit, i.e., the percentage of red blood cells per unit of whole blood). The concentration and volume of hemoglobin undergo a simultaneous increase, since this protein is contained within the red blood cell. The actual increase in red blood cell production is mediated by a protein called erythropoietin, which, in turn, is probably produced by the action of one of the kidney enzymes on a plasma protein after the kidney has become hypoxic. In any case, several months under hypoxic conditions are necessary for full expression of this response, at which time the normal hematocrit

value of 40 - 45 can increase to 60 - 65; blood volume increases by about 20% to 30%; and hemoglobin volume and concentration experience comparable increases. By these adjustments, more oxygen per unit of whole blood can be transported to the tissues.

3. Change in the affinity of hemoglobin for oxygen. Another rapidly developing response concerns a greater release of oxygen to the tissues. This is accomplished, in part, by an increased concentration of certain phosphate compounds within the red blood cells (notably, 2, 3-diphosphoglycerate, or 2, 3-DPG for short), but the results of this increase, as they pertain to a beneficial adjustment, are questionable. On the one hand, combination between 2, 3-DPG and hemoglobin decreases the affinity of hemoglobin for oxygen, thus allowing the latter to be delivered to the tissues at a higher PO_2. But, on the other hand, this decreased affinity also means that hemoglobin will pick up less oxygen in the lungs and thereby reduce the total amount of oxygen available for transport to the tissues.

4. Tissue capillarity. An important adjustment associated with increased blood volume and cardiac output is an increase in either the number or the size (or both) of tissue capillaries. Because blood tends toward viscosity at high altitudes, additional capillary space reduces peripheral resistance and cardiac work load. It also leads to a closer than normal contact between blood and tissue cells, thus enhancing oxygen delivery to the tissue cells.

5. Cardiac output and lung diffusion. Cardiac output increases progressively over a few days exposure to hypoxia, but assumes normal levels thereafter. For poorly defined reasons, a change in the circulatory pattern also occurs at this time. In general, a greater blood flow and oxygen delivery are provided to those organs that require high oxygen levels (e.g., the brain, heart, and muscle systems), but the flow to less oxygen-demanding tissues (e.g., the skin) is reduced. Oxygen diffusion through the pulmonary membrane can undergo a threefold increase as a result of (1) an expansion of lung capillaries and subsequent increase in the surface available for oxygen diffusion and (2) an increased pulmonary arterial pressure, which forces more blood into all of the alveolar capillaries, especially those in the upper parts of the lung that are normally rather poorly perfused.

6. Changes in cell metabolism. In addition to increased activity of certain cellular enzymes, myoglobin content is increased. Myoglobin is a relatively small globular protein that is related to hemoglobin and found in skeletal muscle tissue. Functionally, myoglobin enhances the diffusion rate of oxygen through the cell and stores oxygen for use by the cellular mitochondria. Also, anaerobic glycolysis evidently becomes more efficient. This process pertains to the formation and release of energy to the cells in the absence of oxygen.

Individual Responses to High Altitude
The physiological adjustments discussed above are ultimately related to the maintenance of homeostasis by making the most efficient use of low atmospheric oxygen at high altitudes. Hypoxia also exerts adverse effects in the various domains of the individual, especially in the areas of growth and development, nervous system performance, physical performance, and morbidity and mortality. For the assessment of the adaptive significance of these physiological responses, then, it is desirable to provide a few examples of the probable relationships between hypoxic effects at the two different levels.

The majority of studies on growth and development at high altitudes implicates hypoxia as a severe stress. Among both Peruvian children living in the Andean highlands and Sherpa and Tibetan children in the Himalayas, the effects of hypoxia have been associated with lower birth weights, slower rates of growth and longer growth periods, and variations in the adolescent growth spurt (Frisancho 1970, 1973; Frisancho and Baker 1970; Pawson 1977). That hypoxia is the agent that is most probably responsible for retardation in growth parameters has been suggested by the observation that, among Peruvian children raised at different altitudes, growth retardation increases with altitude (Baker 1969).

Perhaps the most publicized physical characteristic of high-altitude indigenous populations (although this does not apply to Sherpas and Tibetans) is the increase in chest size relative to overall body size. Obviously, lung volume is also relatively increased, but whether there is any direct relationship between increased chest size and low PO_2 at high altitudes is debatable. The genetic factors that influence body shape may be equally as important, if not more so. In refuting the idea that rapid chest growth relative to stature is a direct consequence of low PO_2 at high altitudes, Beall and her colleagues (1977) offered two alternative but related hypotheses: (1) either low PO_2 inhibits total body growth but not chest growth, or high-altitude hypoxia stimulates chest growth but inhibits linear growth, and (2) stature and weight may be under different genetic influences than chest growth, which may be relatively independent of altitudinal influences. Indeed, whether a large chest is of any benefit to a high-altitude native has also been questioned. Mazess (1968), for example, has reported that the large chests of high-altitude Peruvian natives may only increase their energy cost of breathing, a phenomenon that would seem more disadvantageous than beneficial.

Hypoxia undoubtedly affects the growth rate of every organ system in the body, which, in combination, results in the decrease in overall growth. However, each system is not affected to the same extent. Relative to the lowered total body size, therefore, some organs (e.g., the kidney) will be reduced proportionately, while others (e.g., the heart and lungs) undergo less size reduction. On the surface, at least, this suggests that hypoxia may decrease the rate of cell multiplication instead of effecting a reduction in cell size. Whatever the actual causal factors may be, most attempts to assess the relative benefits of small body size at high altitudes have been couched in terms of the various stresses characteristic of these regions. Thus it has been suggested that small body size would be advantageous in areas with a poor nutritional base and during the expenditure of energy during work.

Such suggestions are quite appealing from the viewpoint of evolutionary theory, but they have less relevance for the question of the relative benefit that individuals gain from the foregoing physiological responses. However, at least two of these responses in high altitude populations are evidently quite advantageous. The first concerns an increase in oxygen transport brought about, primarily, by changes in the cardiopulmonary system, which no doubt enhances physical performance. The second, which occurs during growth and development in high-altitude natives, but apparently never becomes maximized among newcomers, involves an increase in lung diffusion capacity. This would also increase physical performance, since oxygen transport during strenuous work at high altitudes is dependent upon lung diffusion capacity. Interestingly, native inhabitants do not appear to have the chemoreceptor sensitivity to hypoxia that is responsible for hyperventilation among nonacclimatized newcomers. This apparent disadvantage is probably compensated for by increased lung diffusion.

With respect to physical performance, high altitude severely stresses all individuals regardless of their origin. However, native highlanders are capable of greater endurance than lowlanders at high altitudes, perhaps because their low body weights entail less oxygen cost per work unit than larger individuals. Natives from high altitudes, furthermore, experience only a slight increase in aerobic capacity upon descending to sea level. This, in turn, implies that maximal performance among native highlanders would vary only slightly between high and low altitudes, although the precise reasons for this are obscure.

As previously mentioned, hypoxia also exerts adverse effects on nutrition and the nervous system, and some detrimental effects pertaining to reproductive performance and health and disease have been reported. Excellent reviews of these and other pertinent topics, specifically as they relate to human high altitude adaptation, have been presented recently by Mazess (1975a) and Stini (1975).

Summary

The action of natural selection has been firmly associated with the origin and maintenance of some traits under simple genetic control, such as sickle-cell hemoglobin and G6PD deficiency. However, the precise relationships between environmental selective factors and observed patterns of geographic variation in physiological, behavioral, and anatomical traits are far more difficult to establish. Such characteristics are not under simple genetic control, are highly plastic phenotypically, and for behavioral attributes in particular, are probably always influenced only indirectly by heredity.

The difficulty in analyzing the effects of selection on quantitative traits stems from the fact that natural selection operates upon the entire phenotype, and phenotypic traits may be influenced by numerous interacting genes at different loci. The phenotype is controlled by the genotype only insofar as the latter determines the norm of reaction, or the full range of developmental paths that may occur in an individual in all possible environments. Since the norm of reaction is not fully known for any specific genotype, it may be anticipated that the effects of selection are not always rigidly predictable. This has been confirmed in selection experiments in which selection for a certain heritable trait often produces changes in other, seemingly unassociated traits. Such unanticipated correlated responses to selection probably result from the effects that one or more genes influencing the expression of one quantitative trait will have upon the expression of a different trait.

This does not imply that human populations have responded haphazardly to their environmental stressors. Rather, field observations clearly show that populations evolving in ecologically dissimilar regions possess distinct anatomical and physiological characteristics which, it may be inferred, are genetically conditioned responses to their particular environmental selective factors. Such responses have traditionally been called adaptations, which are the innumerable genetic and nongenetic phenomena related to the achievement of relatively beneficial adjustments to the environment.

Evaluations of whether adjustments are of adaptive significance can be instituted at levels ranging in complexity from physicochemical changes within the individual to population responses to their environment. Of particular interest to human physiologists is an adaptive response called acclimatization, the functional compensation over a short period of time that an individual makes in response to a complex of environmental factors. Acclimatization responses include anatomical, histological, and morphological adjustments (as in increased muscle strength due to training), physiological adjustments (e.g., the prevention of heat loss by shivering and the promotion of heat dissipation by sweating), neurological adjustments (e.g., a neurological mechanism by which finger pain is reduced after repeated cooling), and other adjustments of a psychobehavioral nature.

Acclimatization responses to heat occur among individuals of all populations and include these physiological adjustments: (1) improvement in cardiovascular function, (2) a slow rise or plateau effect in core temperature, (3) increased sweating capacity and peripheral conductance, (4) more even distribution of sweat on the skin surface, and (5) a decrease in sweat-salt concentration. These adjustments allow a marked improvement in work ability and maintenance of function under heat stress.

Physiological responses to cold are less clearly defined than for heat, but involve the shivering response, a cyclical fluctuation in skin temperature that assists in the prevention of frostbite, an increase in basal metabolic rate for added heat production, a heightened dietary desire for fat, and improvement in extremity blood flow.

While there is only equivocal evidence for the existence of ethnic differences in heat tolerance, genetically based population differences in cold tolerance are suggested more strongly by several lines of evidence. First, individuals living in cold climates tend toward sphericity of form, and thus have less body surface relative to weight than more linear individuals in warm climates. Presumably, more spherical bodies would be selectively advantageous because of their heat conservation properties. Second, certain craniofacial morphological characteristics, including the sinus cavities and nose shape, are possibly cold-adapted structures. And third, groups that are continuously exposed to cold are capable of maintaining higher finger and hand temperatures than those who have existed for long periods in warm climates.

Although numerous stressors are found at high altitudes, that which is most important is the all-pervasive hypoxia, or oxygen deficiency in inspired air. It has been shown that hypoxia adversely affects virtually all physiological functions and organ systems during development. As with heat and cold exposure, however, individuals exposed to hypoxia will make a number of acclimatizational adjustments. These include an increase in pulmonary ventilation, an increase in red blood cell volume and hemoglobin content, a decrease in affinity of hemoglobin for oxygen, an increase in tissue capillarity, an increase in cardiac output and lung diffusion capacity, and some changes in cellular metabolism. This combination of responses allows an individual to make the most efficient use of the relatively little amount of oxygen at high altitudes.

Indications that native high-altitude populations have evolved adaptations to hypoxia include (1) small body size, which might be advantageous in areas with a poor nutritional base and in energy expenditure, (2) an increase in oxygen transport ability, (3) an increase in lung diffusion capacity, (4) great work endurance at high altitudes, and (5) only a slight increase in aerobic capacity upon descending to low altitude.

19 Human Growth

This chapter is contributed by Howard S. Barden of the University of Illinois, Circle Campus, Chicago.

Introduction and Classification of Growth

Growth is a complex process that encompasses a variety of biological phenomena. It may be very broadly defined as the morphological, physiological, and other modifications that characterize an individual's development from fertilization to adulthood. Under this broad definition, growth not only refers to the quantitative changes in height, weight, and other size parameters, but also to more qualitative aspects represented by processes of cellular differentiation. A more limited definition of growth stresses the "increase in size of a living being or any of its parts occurring in the process of development" (Stedman 1972). This definition stresses cellular growth but omits the related subject of **cellular differentiation.** Although this chapter will stress cellular growth, the fascinating subject of cellular differentiation should not be completely ignored.

Cellular Differentiation

Cellular differentiation is the process whereby cells with basically identical genetic constitutions and initial functional potentials become specialized to carry out some, but not all, processes vital to the well-being of the organism. Red blood cells, for example, specialize in the production of hemoglobin, while cells of various endocrine organs specialize in the production of specific hormones. The differentiation of a cell from an initial stage of total potentiality to one of limited functional specialization occurs during a series of complex embryological stages that follow fertilization. During the initial stage after fertilization, the zygote undergoes cleavage (Fig. 19.1), which is characterized by rapid cellular division of the zygote, but with no increase in the size of the total cellular mass. Cleavage thus produces an increasing number of successively smaller cells called blastomeres. Each blastomere contains a small portion of the heterogeneous cytoplasmic material of the mature egg.

These new cells are rearranged shortly after cleavage, and they establish precise spatial relationships to each other during a process called gastrulation. The combined result of cleavage and gastrulation is that the cells of the developing organism (1) contain different cytoplasmic substances and (2) are arranged in a precise way. Because all cells contain the same genetic material, the presence of these cytoplasmic substances is considered crucial to the initial regulation of genetic function and cellular differentiation (Wessels 1977). In addition, the rearrangement of the blastomeres at gastrulation is important because the relative position and interaction of different cell and tissue types have a profound influence on both cellular differentiation and the overall harmonious organization of the organism.

Figure 19.1 The pattern of cleavage in a mammal. An increase in cell number is achieved without a significant increase in cell mass. (Courtesy of A. S. Romer, *The Vertebrate Body.* 4th Ed., 1970. W. B. Saunders Co., Philadelphia.)

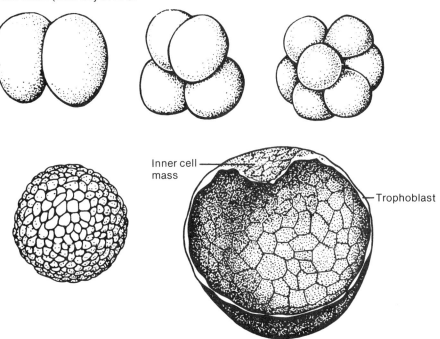

Inner cell mass

Trophoblast

Cellular Growth

Cellular growth occurs through an increase in cell number (hyperplasia), an increase in cell size (hypertrophy), or through a combination of both. In general, cellular growth refers to those increases in cell size or number that involve an increase in living substance, i.e., an increase in protein content. Thus an increase in fat or water would not constitute growth (Villee and Dethier 1971). Except for tissues such as blood, skin, and liver, which undergo continuous cell division throughout life, tissue growth generally occurs in three stages. The timing for the initiation of these stages is under strict genetic control and differs from tissue to tissue (Winick and Noble 1966).

Growth begins with hyperplasia, a period of rapid cell division during which cell size remains relatively constant. The rapid rate of cell division is reflected by an equally rapid rate of DNA synthesis. This initial stage is followed by a period characterized by both **hyperplastic** and hypertrophic cell growth. During this second stage, the rate of cell division gradually declines and the rate of protein synthesis gradually increases. The third stage is characterized solely by hypertrophic growth. DNA snythesis and cell division cease. However, protein synthesis continues and an increase in cell size results from a steady protein accumulation. Growth in a particular tissue is ended when a balance is reached between the accumulation of protein and its gradual breakdown during normal cell processes (Winick et al. 1972).

Cellular growth processes clearly do not progress at the same rate for all parts of the body. Various body organs and organ systems grow at different rates at different times. Such differential growth is of interest not only in terms of an individual's growth, but also in terms of understanding human variation both within and between populations. Differences in the size and shape of individuals result from the interaction of genetic and environmental factors. Much of the morphological variation between populations undoubtedly arises from population differences in the growth rates of various body parts relative to others, and in differences in the overall rate of body maturation.

Genetic inheritance plays a major role in influencing individual and population variability in growth. Studies utilizing identical and nonidentical twins have shown that variability in developmental processes such as skeletal maturation, tooth development, age of first menstruation, and the acceleration of growth during adolescence is under considerable genetic influence and control. For example, genes controlling hormone production and secretion are certainly significant for the control of processes of overall growth and maturation. This is not to say that environmental factors play an insignificant part during the growth process: the individual's phenotype is determined by a complex interaction of both genetic and environmental factors. However, when environmental conditions reach an optimum for the growth process, an individual's phenotype will more closely approach the genetic potential for growth. Under such optimal conditions, furthermore, variability in growth is determined to a greater extent by genetic rather than environmental factors (Harrison et al. 1977).

Recent discoveries about the genetic control of protein synthesis provide a better understanding of the basic processes of cellular growth at the biochemical and molecular levels. If cellular growth is viewed as being based upon the addition of protein substance, then it is clear that external, nongenetic factors influencing protein synthesis will also influence growth. Therefore, an understanding of the genetic control of protein synthesis greatly augments our understanding of how factors such as nutrition, disease, hormones, drugs, and various climatic and environmental stresses can affect basic growth processess by influencing the rate at which protein synthesis occurs.

Environmental factors such as nutritional adequacy and incidence of disease are primary factors influencing growth processes. Twin studies have suggested that such environmental influences have their greatest effect on growth during the prenatal growth period, a period marked by hyperplastic growth for all organs. However, those factors having a significant influence on prenatal growth exert somewhat less influence postnatally. This finding is especially reflected in linear measures, such as height and leg length, which are determined more and more by the genotype (Wilson 1976). These and other findings indicate the importance of the developmental stage of an individual or tissue relative to the timing of an environmental disturbance.

Critical Period Hypothesis
Many studies have shown that a developmental process is most vulnerable to any restrictive agent during the period of its most rapid development or growth. For most tissues, this "critical period" (Dobbing 1968) involves the period of rapid cell multiplication and differentiation. Because this critical period varies from tissue to tissue, the extent of the effect of an adverse environmental or genetic influence upon a

particular tissue is dependent upon the time of insult relative to the time of these critical periods. Experimental evidence also shows that if the rate of DNA synthesis and cell division is inadequate during the genetically restricted period of hyperplastic growth, a permanent deficiency in cell number will result.

These findings are crucially important for tissues such as the developing brain, which completes its hyperplastic phase of growth during the first year of life. Although evidence for humans is inconclusive, animal experiments strongly suggest that any external factor (e.g., poor nutrition or serious and chronic disease) that adversely affects growth during the critical period of rapid hyperplastic growth of the brain might seriously jeopardize the development of an individual's potential mental capacities (Read 1975). A comprehensive review of the findings concerning the growth and development of the brain has been presented by Brazier (1975).

The critical period hypothesis is also important in terms of tissue differentiation, for it helps explain how an organism may be seriously affected by an event that is disruptive for only a short time period during growth and development. Teratogens, substances that cause developmental abnormalities, have their greatest effect if encountered during a specific stage of development. For example, thalidomide was a sedative drug which, when administered to pregnant women during their first trimester of pregnancy, frequently caused severe developmental abnormalities of the limbs of the fetuses. Administration of the drug during a less critical stage of limb development resulted in no noticeable effect. Many other drugs and other environmental agents, such as virus infections (e.g., rubella), other diseases (e.g., syphilis), and nutritional deficiencies, have been shown to have similar effects on other organ systems (Table 19.1).

Table 19.1 Selected Environmental Agents and Their Effects on Embryonic Development (From J. E. Crouch and J. R. McClintic, *Human Anatomy and Physiology.* 2nd Ed., 1976. By permission of John Wiley and Sons, New York.)

Agent	Types of Effects on Embryo/Fetus
Aminopterin [(folic acid antagonist) (used in attempted abortion or treatment of leukemia)]	Widespread anatomical malformations
Antibiotics	Deafness, growth retardation, hemolysis
Cortisone	Cleft palate
Dicumarol	Fetal bleeding
Estrogens (diethylstilbesterol)	Masculinization of female fetus, occasionally causes vaginal cancer later in life
Herpes virus	Nervous system defects
Hypoxia	Patent ductus arteriosus
Progestational agents	Masculinization of female fetus
Quinine	Congenital deafness
Radiation	Skeletal deformities, microcephaly
Rubella virus (German measles)	Blindness, deafness, congenital heart disease, inflammation of body organs
Salicylates	Hemorrhage, anatomical malformations
Syphilis (untreated)	Blindness, deafness, congenital heart disease
Thiouracil derivatives (iodine)	Goiter
Tranquilizers (e.g., thalidomide)	Anatomical malformations

Catch-Up Growth

Growth may not be permanently retarded if environmental factors such as illness and malnutrition affect the individual or tissue during less critical stages. A child who has been malnourished may subsequently grow at an accelerated rate once adequate nutrition has been restored, and may catch up to normal-sized peers (Fig 19.2). This phenomenon has been termed "catch-up growth" (Prader et al. 1963). It appears, in part, to be related to an enhanced metabolic efficiency in utilizing available resources for growth processes (Miller and Wise 1976). In terms of the critical period concept, when the period of maximum hyperplastic growth has passed, the ability to accelerate one's growth velocity (i.e., to catch up) is diminished, and permanent growth retardation may result. Because the rate of skeletal maturation is also delayed, however, the growing period will be extended in some cases, and an adult height of normal magnitude may eventually be reached.

Overnutrition also has significant effects on growth. An overabundance of nutrients during infancy and early childhood may result in an abnormally large production of fat cells, a condition that could later predispose the individual to obesity. In addition, overnutrition appears to accelerate growth in height as well as weight, in addition to accelerating the rate of maturation (Forbes 1977; Garn et al. 1973). The common practice, in developed countries, of substituting artificial milk formulas for breast milk has been implicated as a cause for accelerated growth in infancy. In general, artificial milk formulas have protein concentrations that far exceed the level found in human breast milk (Naismith 1975).

Figure 19.2 A hypothetical growth curve superimposed on percentiles for stature, showing severe growth retardation until age 4 when catch-up growth begins and the child's growth curve returns to its normal percentile position. (Courtesy of W. A. Marshall, Growth before Puberty—Catch-Up Growth. In: *Early Nutrition and Later Development,* 1976, A. W. Wilkinson, ed. Pitman Medical Publishing Co., Ltd., Tunbridge Wells.)

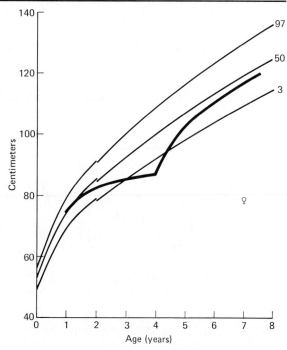

Stages of Growth

For descriptive purposes, an individual's growth period may be divided into several stages, each of which has its own distinctive characteristics (Table 19.2).

1. The ovular stage. This stage represents the initial two weeks after fertilization of the egg by the sperm, during which time the implantation of the zygote into the uterus occurs, as do cleavage and gastrulation.

2. The embryo stage. This period extends from the ovular stage until the end of the second month of gestation. During this time, rapid differentiation of cells into specialized tissues and the establishment of all of the major organ systems occurs. As different tissues grow at different rates, the organism acquires its characteristic morphological features. The embryo stage is, thus, an especially critical time in terms of the developing organism's susceptibility to drugs, infections, and other environmental insults.

3. The fetal stage. This stage extends through the remainder of intrauterine life. During this time, there is further development of the organ systems and very rapid growth resulting from rapid cell division, particularly during the second trimester of gestation. Although growth is most rapid during the second trimester, the overall size of the fetus and placenta is still quite small. Also, nutrient requirements from growth are not as great as during later stages of pregnancy. Later fetal and postnatal growth emphasize a gradual shift—from growth resulting from an increase in cell number to growth resulting from an increase in cell size.

4. Infancy. The first year of life after birth. A particularly critical period of infancy is the neonatal period, the first month after birth. Infant mortality and morbidity are highest during this period. Circulatory, respiratory, digestive, and excretory activities must be successfully initiated in order to cope with life outside the womb. In addition, components of the infant's immunological system are still immature. The infant is, thus, very susceptible to infections that are prevalent in community situations where health standards are poor.

A critical situation has developed in some underdeveloped countries where breast feeding is being replaced by bottle feeding. With bottle feeding, important immune globulins (antibodies) transmitted from mother to offspring via

Table 19.2 Periods of Growth and the Approximate Ages at Which They Occur

Growth Period	Approximate Age
Prenatal	From 0 to 280 days
Ovular	From 0 to 14 days
Embryo	From 14 days to 9 weeks
Fetal	From 9 weeks to birth
Birth	Average of 280 days
Neonatal	First 4 weeks after birth
Infancy	First year after birth
Childhood	From 1 to 10 years
Adolescence (girls)	From 8 or 10 to 18 years
Adolescence (boys)	From 10 or 12 to 20 years

the mother's milk, are lost to the infant. In addition, poorly prepared and contaminated bottles of milk or milk substitute lead to diarrhea and poor intestinal absorption of nutrients, a situation that compounds an already marginal nutritional circumstance. Because of relatively rapid growth during infancy, severe illness and malnutrition may result in permanent growth retardation.

5. Childhood. This is a period after infancy that is characterized by slow but steady growth, especially after three years of age.

6. Adolescence. The adolescent stage follows childhood and is marked, first, by a rapid increase and, then, by a decrease in overall growth (see below under "Growth at Adolescence.")

Growth Curves and Assessment of Growth

Patterns of growth are generally described by two types of growth curves: the distance or cumulative curve and the incremental or velocity curve. Each provides basic information to the growth investigator. The distance or cumulative growth curve is obtained by recording and plotting consecutive measurements of an individual over a period of time (Fig. 19.3). Any point on the curve represents the distance traveled at that time toward full adult stature, weight, or other measured parameter. The curve is steep during periods of rapid growth, while periods of slow growth show a flattened curve. At no point in time does the curve fall below an earlier point, unless an actual measurement decline has occurred.

The velocity or incremental curve (Fig. 19.4) presents the same growth data, but in a different way. Additions in growth since the last measurements, or increments, are plotted to show variation in the rate or velocity of growth over time. The curve rises when the rate of growth during one measurement period is greater than the rate of growth during the preceding period, and declines when the reverse situation holds, despite the fact that growth may still be in progress. No increase in the rate of growth is indicated by a horizontal line. The incremental growth curve graphically points out periods of most rapid growth and helps answer the clinical question about the acceptability of a child's growth rate for that particular measured time period. Because of the wide range of normal variation in growth parameters such as height, a child may be of normal stature but may not be experiencing a normal growth rate. In such cases, the incremental curve is of greater diagnostic value than the cumulative curve.

For purposes of evaluation, individual growth curves are frequently compared with standard curves derived from standard or normative data. These curves are derived from either longitudinal or cross-sectional data. Long-term growth studies that measure a sample of like-aged individuals over many years produce growth curves based on longitudinal data. When such long-term growth studies are not feasible, a large group of children representing all ages may be measured once, with the average measure for each age plotted to provide a curve based on cross-sectional data.

Although curves based on longitudinal data are the most accurate, the acquisition of such data is far more time-consuming and expensive. In addition, the problems involved with loss of part of the sample over the years of the study must be

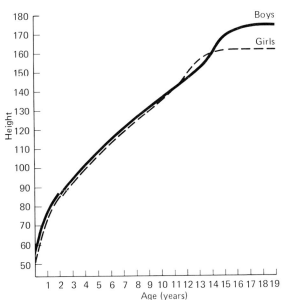

Figure 19.3 Typical individual cumulative growth curves for boys and girls. (Courtesy of J. M. Tanner, R. H. Whitehouse, and M. Takaishi, 1966, Standards from Birth to Maturity for Height, Weight, Height Velocity, and Weight Velocity: British Children, 1965. Part I. *Arch. Dis. Childh.* 41: 454–471.)

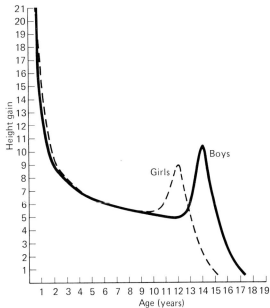

Figure 19.4 Typical individual velocity curves for height in boys and girls. (Courtesy of J. M. Tanner, R. H. Whitehouse, and M. Takaishi, 1966, Standards from Birth to Maturity for Height, Weight, Height Velocity, and Weight Velocity: British Children, 1965. Part I. *Arch. Dis. Childh.* 41: 454–471.)

considered. The major fault of cross-sectional studies is that they measure different individuals for each age category, thus revealing nothing about individual growth rates and individual variation in the timing of such developmental events as the adolescent growth spurt and attainment of peak height velocity. Within each age category, children who are maturationally advanced, and perhaps tall for their age, are grouped and averaged with children who are less advanced. As Figure 19.5 shows, a velocity curve derived from such cross-sectional data in no way reflects the typical velocity curve for each individual. Cross-sectional studies are useful for comparing the mean growth rate of individuals within one population to those of others. In such comparisons, individual variation in growth rate is not of great importance (Eveleth and Tanner 1976).

For assessing an individual's growth in terms of reference standards, standard curves with a normal distribution commonly include additional curves based either upon standard deviations (see Appendix I) from the mean curve or percentiles calculated from the standard data (Fig. 19.6). These additional curves provide a measure of dispersion of the data, and thus graphically portray the tremendous amount of normal individual variation within any population. Less variation would be present, however, if growth curves were based upon maturational age instead of chronological age. Maturational age shows a far greater correlation with such measurements as height or weight.

Figure 19.5 Individual and mean velocities during the adolescent growth spurt. The average or mean velocity curve is an inadequate representation of a typical individual velocity curve. (Courtesy of J. M. Tanner, *Growth at Adolescence.* 2nd Ed., 1962. By permission of Blackwell Scientific Publications, Ltd. Oxford.)

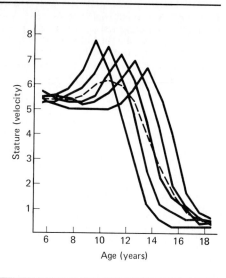

Figure 19.6 Percentile curves for measurements of height and weight for females from 2 to 18 years of age.

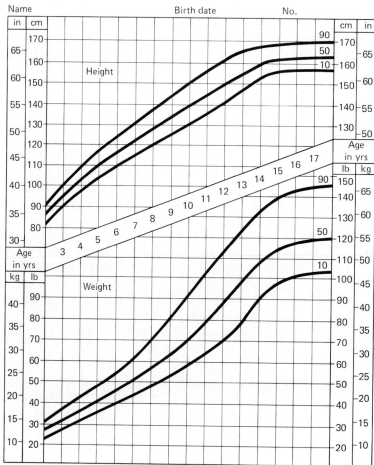

Figure 19.7 Percentiles for stature in girls with superimposed growth curves of **a,** a child whose normal growth until age 5 was disrupted by severe growth inhibition which caused the cessation of her growth by age 6 and **b,** a child who maintained her low but normal percentile position throughout the investigative period.

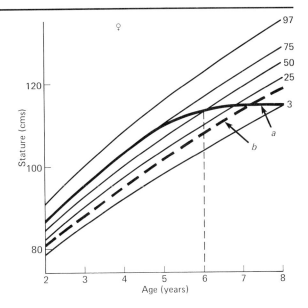

In terms of assessing one's individual growth, the position on a growth chart relative to percentiles or standard deviations is of less importance in most cases than the maintenance of that relative position over an extended time period. A child whose height may be normal for a particular age, but who has dropped from a higher percentile level to a lower one, is more suspect of having a growth disorder than one who has maintained a low but steady percentile position (Fig. 19.7).

Pre- and Postnatal Growth

The body undergoes its most rapid acceleration in growth before birth. After birth an actual deceleration occurs and continues until adolescence, when it again accelerates during the adolescent growth spurt (Fig. 19.4). If prenatal growth is measured in terms of trimesters, the first trimester is marked by rapid organ development, with growth in size being less important than cellular differentiation. The remaining two trimesters show a greater emphasis upon increase in length and weight. As Figure 19.8 illustrates, the greatest increase in length occurs during the second trimester, while weight gain is greatest during the third. The rate of growth in length and weight begins a downward trend in the latter part of gestation, and continues during infancy and early childhood. The decline in growth during the latter part of pregnancy is probably due in part to conditions of crowding *in utero*. Figure 19.9 shows that for a brief period following birth, the growth rate in weight increases to a rate similar to that at 36 weeks of gestation, the time when the *in utero* growth restriction occurs. The growth of twins also slows down when their combined weight is approximately equivalent to the weight of a 36-week-old singleton fetus (Harrison et al. 1977).

Data for prenatal growth studies have been derived mainly from selected abortuses, birth weights, and fetal monitoring techniques such as ultrasound and X-radiation. X-rays provide a means for measuring fetal size, in addition to a

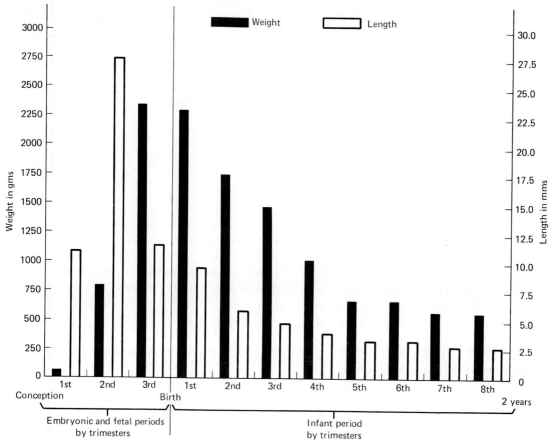

Figure 19.8 Average increment in weight and length from conception through 2 years of age. (Courtesy of I. Valadian and D. Porter, *Physical Growth and Development. From Conception to Maturity.* Copyright © 1977. Used by permission of Little, Brown and Co., Boston. Original source, S. S. Stevenson, Physical Growth and Development. In: *Textbook of Pediatrics,* 5th Ed., 1950, W. E. Nelson, ed. W. B. Saunders, Philadelphia.)

means for determining the stage of **gestation** by the appearance of bone **ossification** centers. However, X-rays are considered dangerous and are not now usually taken during a normal pregnancy. Ultrasound measurements, on the other hand, present no danger and can be repeated on a weekly or monthly basis to assess fetal growth rates. Standard fetal growth curves for normal pregnancies have recently been made available and can be used to determine normal and abnormal fetal growth rates (Brenner et al. 1976).

Birth weights are frequently examined as indicators of prenatal growth. Low birth weight children may be divided into two groups: those who are small for their gestational age (small-for-date babies), and those who are of normal weight for gestational age, but who have been born prematurely. Of these two groups, it is the small-for-date baby who reflects fetal growth retardation. Frequently, small-for-date babies retain this growth retardation throughout postnatal life, while premature

Figure 19.9 A comparison of prenatal and postnatal growth rates for weight. (Courtesy of T. McKeown, T. Marshall, and R. G. Record, Influences on Fetal Growth. *J. Reprod. Fertil.* 47: 167–181, 1976).

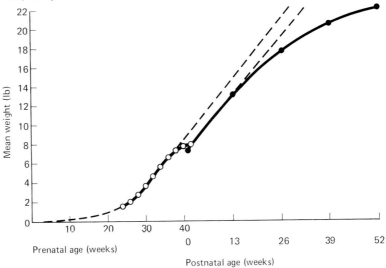

Table 19.3 Survival According to Weight Group of Premature Infants in 1945 and 1960 (From G. H. Lowrey, *Growth and Development of Children,* 6th Ed. Copyright © 1973 by Year Book Medical Publishers, Inc., Chicago. Used by permission.)

Weight Group, Gm	Survival, % 1945	1960
2,001–2,500	94	96
1,501–2,000	84	88
1,000–1,500	53	70
Under 1,000	12	23

infants of low birth weight eventually catch up to their normal peers over a ten-year period (Beck and Van den Berg 1975).

Low birth weight babies are generally defined as weighing 2.5 kg or less. Critically important from a health standpoint is the repeated finding that low birth weight babies, especially those weighing less than 1.5 kg, show strong associations with increased infant mortality and impaired physical and intellectual capacity in later life (Churchill et al. 1966; Mata et al. 1975). Table 19.3 shows the increased mortality of low birth weight babies and also the improvement in prognosis that is continuing to occur as new medical means are found to support these infants. Despite medical advances in developed countries, the high frequency of babies of low birth weight in communities of low socioeconomic status poses an enormous health problem in developing countries (Lechtig et al. 1976).

Factors That Influence Growth

Nutritional deficiency is an obvious factor contributing to both pre- and postnatal growth retardation. Nutritional deficiency of the fetus may be due to maternal undernutrition or to other factors that hinder the normal flow of oxygen and nutrients from the mother to the fetus. Various placental defects fall into this category.

Indirect indicators of maternal nutritional status that are clearly associated with fetal body, organ, and cellular growth include (1) maternal prepregnancy weight relative to height and (2) maternal weight gain during pregnancy. Infants born during periods of maternal starvation, in countries experiencing conditions of famine, consistently show somewhat lower birth weights than those born in the same countries during periods of adequate nutritional supplies (Gruenwald et al. 1967). Programs aimed at supplementing maternal nutrition during pregnancy have also led to significant increases in average birth weights (Lechtig et al. 1976). Osofsky (1975) presents a detailed review of the relationships between nutrition during pregnancy and subsequent infant and child development. Birth weights, incidentally, appear to be little affected by the size of the father.

Although both protein and calories are important for growth, several recent studies suggest that the human fetus may be better able to adapt to a maternal protein deficiency than to a marked caloric deficiency. Studies with primates have shown that maternal protein deficiency has a relatively insignificant effect on intrauterine growth, when compared to the effects of protein deficiency on animals (such as the rat) that experience multiple pregnancies and more rapid prenatal development (Cheek 1975; Riopelle et al. 1976). Diets deficient in calories, on the other hand, are significantly associated with retarded fetal growth, especially when the deficiency occurs during late gestation. The results of Naeye et al. (1973) on the effects of maternal nutrition on fetal growth support this view, as does the evidence from studies on catch-up growth. The amount of possible catch-up growth appears to be more limited by an insignificant caloric energy supply than by an insignificant protein supply (Waterlow et al. 1976). In cases of maternal diabetes, where maternal levels of blood glucose are elevated, birth weights tend to be considerably higher than normal (North et al. 1977).

Considerable interest has been directed toward the high rate of low birth weight babies born in nonindustrialized countries. One might speculate that in countries where food resources are scarce, a genetically smaller baby at birth would be better adapted to the situation of nutritional inadequacy, and that high rates of low birth weights would reflect selected genetic factors rather than nutritional factors. While such reasoning gains some support in terms of postnatal growth, population differences in fetal body and organ growth are generally not found to be significant when comparisons are made of individuals of similar nutritional status (Naeye et al. 1973).

Other factors associated with fetal growth retardation are maternal hypertension and other systemic diseases, heavy cigarette smoking—over 20 per day—(Meyer and Comstock 1972), multiple pregnancies (twins, triplets, etc.), various placental deficiencies, chromosomal abnormalities such as Down's syndrome, fetal congenital abnormalities such as congenital heart disease, and chronic fetal infections (e.g., rubella and toxoplasmosis), which frequently result in severe congenital abnormalities (Beisel 1975).

Postnatal Patterns of Growth

Distinctively varied patterns of growth are found in curves representing the postnatal growth of the body and various organ systems. These curves represent variability in the rate of hyperplasia and hypertrophy of the cells making up the organ systems. Curves for the general, neural, lymphoid, and genital systems represent four different patterns of growth (Fig. 19.10).

The general growth curve represents the pattern of growth for the respiratory, muscular, skeletal, vascular, digestive, and endocrine systems, and generally reflects the curve for increase in body size. This curve is sigmoidal, or S-shaped, with growth accelerating rather sharply during the first few years—a result of the continuation of the relatively rapid rate of growth that occurs prenatally. This early growth period is followed by one of slow but steady decline in velocity until approximately age 11 in girls and 13 in boys. The decline in velocity ends when hormonal changes at puberty initiate a short but rapid acceleration in growth—the adolescent growth spurt.

The pattern of growth of the neural system (brain, spinal cord, and peripheral nerves) is markedly different from that given by the general curve. The significant feature is the remarkably steep curve during the early years, with very little growth thereafter. This initially rapid increase in brain size reflects a continuation of the hyperplastic proliferation of brain cells begun prenatally. After the first year, hypertrophy accounts for further increases in brain size. Thus the critical period of brain growth occurs during the late gestation and early postnatal periods. Adequate

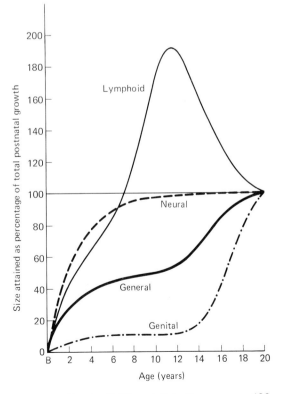

Figure 19.10 Postnatal patterns of growth of different tissues of the body. Each curve has been plotted as percent of total gain from birth to 20 years. (Courtesy of J. M. Tanner, *Growth at Adolescence.* 2nd Ed., 1962. By permission of Blackwell Scientific Publications, Ltd. Oxford.)

nutrition in the prenatal and early postnatal time periods seems vital for the realization of an individual's full brain-growth potential.

The third pattern of growth is represented by the lymphoid system, which includes the thymus, lymph glands, spleen, lymphocytes, and areas in the lining of the gastrointestinal tract. The function of this system is related to the production of antibodies (immune globulins) and the cells that constitute the cell-mediated immune system. The growth pattern of the system shows a distinctive curve that rises progressively until it reaches a maximum before puberty. This peak is followed by a decline that results in a decrease in both relative and absolute size of the lymphoid organs. At birth an infant's immune system is not fully developed, thus reliance is placed on the immune globulins that were transported across the placental barriers prior to birth or through the breast milk of the mother after birth. The initial years of lymphoid tissue growth are, thus, related to progress in the establishment of a competent immune system.

The growth curve of the genital system reflects the slow early development of the primary sex organs (testes and ovaries) and the hormonally influenced rapid growth spurt of these organs. This occurs during adolescence and corresponds to the adolescent growth spurt seen in the general growth curve. Growth curves utilizing indices of various physical measurements may be used to express changes in body proportions that occur as different parts of the body grow and mature at different rates. A curve based on the ratio of sitting height (stature minus leg length) to stature shows a downward trend, demonstrating the generally more rapid growth of the legs relative to the trunk. This begins at about 1 year of age and continues until puberty (Fig. 19.11). Figure 19.12 shows a curve based upon the ratio of hip breadth to shoulder breadth, and demonstrates a basic difference in body shape between the sexes. Beginning with the onset of pubertal changes, males show a relative increase in shoulder breadth, while females demonstrate a relative increase in hip breadth.

Figure 19.11 Sitting height/stature ratio of boys and girls aged 1 to 18. The general downward trend of the curve reflects the relatively greater growth of the legs over the trunk. At the time of puberty, the increase in leg length is relatively greater in boys than in girls. (Reprinted from L. M. Bayer and N. Bayley, *Growth Diagnosis.* 2nd Ed., 1976, by permission of The University of Chicago Press.)

Figure 19.12 The ratio of hip breadth (bi-cristal) to shoulder breadth (bi-acromial) of boys and girls aged 1 to 18. As girls approach puberty, there is a relative increase in hip breadth. For boys, shoulder breadth increases relative to hip breadth during the adolescent period. (Reprinted from L. M. Bayer and N. Bayley, *Growth Diagnosis,* 2nd Ed., 1976, by permission of The University of Chicago Press.)

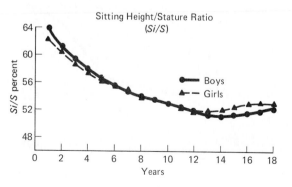

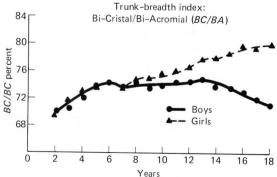

Indices of Maturity

Many investigations of growth are based upon an assessment of an individual's overall developmental maturity. As growth progresses from the time of fertilization to adulthood, an individual proceeds through a precise developmental sequence of events during which different parts of the body develop and mature at different rates. Each individual is regulated by a unique, genetically controlled timetable of development. Because individuals show considerable variability in terms of their stage of maturity relative to their chronological age, chronological age is generally a poor indicator of maturity. For some individuals, the attainment of maturity is rapid, and the overall period of growth is relatively short. Others proceed more slowly and, ultimately, grow for a longer period of time. Much research on growth has been directed toward obtaining a better definition of an individual's maturational age.

Several measures or indices of maturity have been developed to assess maturational age. These include skeletal age, dental age, and sexual age. Because sexual age indices can only be applied after the inception of puberty, the usefulness of this method is somewhat limited. Skeletal and dental age assessments, however, may be utilized throughout an individual's growth period.

Skeletal Age

Skeletal, radiological, or bone-age assessments are based upon the finding that many bones progress through a series of precise stages that can be detected with X-rays. These stages include the initial appearance, morphological changes, and ultimate fusion of primary and secondary ossification centers. The sequential pattern of the initial appearance and the changes leading to fusion of the body's numerous ossification centers generally shows only slight variability among individuals. However, the timing of these sequential events varies considerably among individuals. Therefore, the timing of the sequential stages of ossification constitutes the basis for skeletal age assessments.

Ossification is a process of bone formation that involves the deposition of bone minerals within an organic matrix. If ossification is preceded by the formation of a cartilage model, it is called endochondral or intracartilagenous ossification. The direct transformation of a connective tissue matrix into bone tissue is referred to as intramembranous ossification (McLean and Urist 1968). Most of the bones of the skeleton, including all of the bones of the thorax and limbs (with exception of the clavicle), the hyoid bone, and the majority of the cranial bones are laid down prenatally within a cartilagenous model that suggests, in miniature, the shape of the future bone. Thus these are usually called intracartilagenous bones. Figure 19.13 shows the primary and secondary ossification centers of the limbs and the times when these centers appear.

Long bones of the limbs are typically made up of a shaft (the **diaphysis**) with an **epiphysis** at each end. Until the time of fusion, the epiphyses are separated from the diaphysis. Longitudinal growth of the long bone takes place in a specialized area between the epiphysis and diaphysis called the epiphyseal cartilage plate. Ossification and replacement of cartilage with bone proceeds in all directions from the localized primary ossification centers in the diaphysis. The diaphysis eventually becomes free of cartilage cells, except for those in the area of the epiphyseal plate.

Figure 19.13 **a,** Primary ossification centers of the limbs, including hands and feet, showing the average time of appearance in fetal weeks and months. **b,** Secondary ossification centers of the limbs, showing the average time of appearance in postnatal months or years. (**a,** From G. H. Lowrey, *Growth and* *Development of Children,* 6th Ed. Copyright © 1973 by Year Book Medical Publishers, Inc., Chicago. Data from various sources. Used by permission. **b,** From J. Caffey et al., *Pediatric X-Ray Diagnosis,* 6th Ed. Copyright © 1972 by Year Book Medical Publishers, Inc., Chicago. Used by permission.)

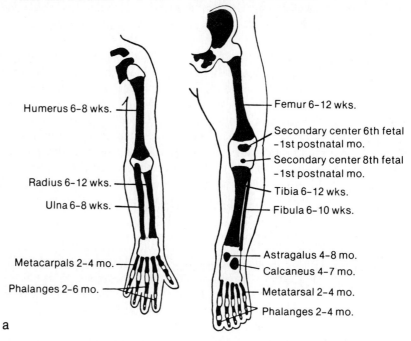

Humerus 6–8 wks.
Radius 6–12 wks.
Ulna 6–8 wks.
Metacarpals 2–4 mo.
Phalanges 2–6 mo.

Femur 6–12 wks.
Secondary center 6th fetal –1st postnatal mo.
Secondary center 8th fetal –1st postnatal mo.
Tibia 6–12 wks.
Fibula 6–10 wks.
Astragalus 4–8 mo.
Calcaneus 4–7 mo.
Metatarsal 2–4 mo.
Phalanges 2–4 mo.

a

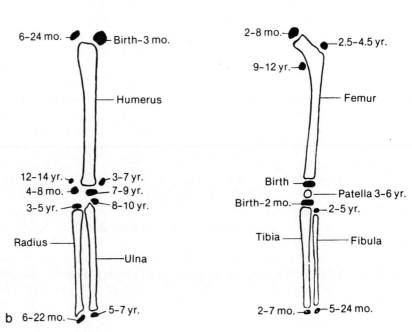

6–24 mo.
Birth–3 mo.
Humerus
12–14 yr.
3–7 yr.
4–8 mo.
7–9 yr.
3–5 yr.
8–10 yr.
Radius
Ulna
b 6–22 mo.
5–7 yr.

2–8 mo.
2.5–4.5 yr.
9–12 yr.
Femur
Birth
Patella 3–6 yr.
Birth–2 mo.
2–5 yr.
Tibia
Fibula
2–7 mo.
5–24 mo.

Figure 19.14 Schematic representation of the progressive stages in the growth and maturation of the tibia. (Modified from an original drawing by Dr. W. M. Rogers.) **a,** The mass of embryonal cartilage which is the anlage of the tibia. **b,** Initial enlargement and multiplication of the central cartilage cells and increase in cartilaginous matrix, the chondrification center which is the forerunner of the primary ossification center. **c,** The early primary ossification center, showing formation of a central belt of subperiosteal bone (early cortex) and penetration of the cartilaginous matrix by the periosteal elements; the channel of this penetration persists as the nutrient canal. **d,** Extension of ossification toward both ends of the shaft, with central resorption to form the medullary cavity. **e,** The tibia at birth, with a secondary

ossification center in the proximal epiphyseal cartilage **f,** At approximately the fourth postnatal month, showing ossification centers in both of the epiphyseal cartilages. **g,** Juvenile tibia, showing growth of all components and enlargement of the epiphyseal secondary ossification centers. **h,** Adult tibia, with complete fusion of the shaft and both epiphyses. The narrow plates of articular cartilage which cap each end of the bone persist throughout life. (1) nutrient canal, (2) epiphyseal cartilage, (3) corticalis, (4) spongiosa, (5) and (6) provisional zones of calcification or epiphyseal plates, (7) articular cartilages, (8) secondary epiphyseal ossification centers. (From J. Caffey et al., *Pediatric X-Ray Diagnosis,* 6th Ed. Copyright © 1972 by Year Book Medical Publishers, Inc., Chicago. Used with permission.)

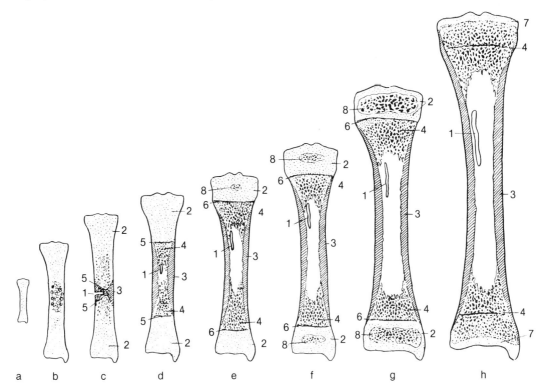

Growth is able to continue in this area as long as the proliferation of cartilage cells on the epiphyseal side of the plate is able to keep ahead of the process of ossification on the diaphyseal side. Once the proliferation of cartilage cells slows down and ultimately ceases, the cartilage cells within the plate are completely replaced by bone, and the diaphysis is fused to the epiphysis. Longitudinal growth of the bone is then no longer possible. Hormones that stimulate linear growth do so by increasing the rate of proliferation of the cartilage cells in the epiphyseal plate. However, when fusion occurs, these hormones can no longer stimulate long-bone growth. Figure 19.14 outlines the development of a typical long bone (see McLean and Urist 1968, for a detailed description of this complex process).

Several methods have been developed to determine the degree of skeletal maturation of an individual. Each method has its advantages and disadvantages in terms of reliability, simplicity, and amount of radiation involved. One popular method utilizes specially prepared radiographic atlases. These show standard radiographs that demonstrate average skeletal development for each chronological age. Hence a boy's developmental age may be determined by comparing his radiograph with the standards. For example, a skeletally advanced child of 6 years may be most like the standard for a 7-year-old. The individual's skeletal age would thus be 7 years.

Skeletal atlases have been produced for the hand and wrist (Greulich and Pyle 1959; Pyle, Waterhouse, and Greulich 1971), the foot and ankle (Hoerr, Pyle, and Francis 1962), and the knee (Pyle and Hoerr 1969). Because of its relative simplicity in assessing skeletal age, especially for the Greulich and Pyle hand-wrist atlas, this method is most frequently utilized. The hand-wrist region is preferred over other regions because of the large number of ossification centers, the spread of timing of ossification and fusion over many years, and the ability to X-ray the area without unduly exposing other large areas of the body to radiation. Figure 19.15 indicates the primary and secondary centers of ossification of the hand and wrist. Critics of the method contend that the areas encompassed within each atlas do not necessarily reflect the development of the skeleton as a whole (Garn et al. 1967; Tanner et al. 1975), and that normal variation in ossification sequences occurs commonly and leads to faulty assessments of skeletal age (Roche et al. 1970).

Figure 19.15 Time schedule for appearance of primary and secondary ossification centers and fusion of secondary centers with the shafts in the hands. (Modified from Scammon in *Morris' Human Anatomy.* From J. Caffey et al., *Pediatric X-Ray Diagnosis,* 6th Ed. Copyright © 1972 by Year Book Medical Publishers, Inc., Chicago. Used by permission.)

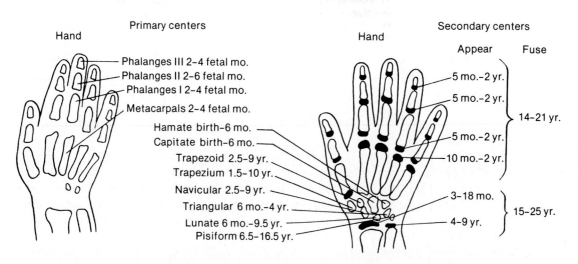

Others methods, such as the Tanner-Whitehouse system, estimate skeletal maturity by scoring each bone of the hand and wrist according to its individual stage of maturation. The scores are then summed, and the total maturation score can then be readily converted to a skeletal age by using an appropriate table of standards (Tanner, Whitehouse, and Healey 1962). A methodological revision of this technique has recently been published by Tanner et al. (1975).

As in other developmental processes, skeletal age may be affected by both genetic and environmental factors. Such factors may affect the entire organism, or they may specifically affect bone development. Those that affect the development of bone compromise the use of skeletal age as a general indicator of body maturity. Malnutrition, chronic infection, and hormonal abnormalities are among those factors that may specifically affect skeletal maturation. Sex of the individual is also associated with maturation, females nearly always being more skeletally mature than males for a given chronological age. For this reason, separate growth standards have been established for each sex. Also, the skeletal age of females appears, in general, to be less influenced by environmental disturbances such as malnutrition and disease.

Skeletal age assessments are frequently utilized in formulas that predict age at menarche and final adult height (Tanner et al. 1975; Bayer and Bayley 1976). These formulas are based upon the knowledge that sexual maturation is correlated with fusion of the long bones and cessation of long-bone growth. An assessment of skeletal age thus may indicate how far advanced a child is toward attaining sexual maturity and cessation of linear long-bone growth. A child who is small, but slow in maturing, may ultimately achieve normal adult stature. For example, children with sickle-cell anemia are small because of a marked delay in their skeletal maturation, but may eventually reach normal adult height several years later than their normal peers (Serjeant and Ashcroft 1973). Within a particular population, an individual's final adult height has little to do with the speed at which maturity was reached. Early and late maturers generally reach similar adult heights. However, individuals who mature late are usually somewhat more linear than those who mature early (Eveleth and Tanner 1976).

Dental Age
Dentition has been used as an index of maturity for many of the same reasons as has the skeletal system. Numerous centers of calcification may be observed, and the sequence of events leading to maturation follows a relatively precise pattern of change. However, there is considerable individual variation in the timing of the respective events. Assessments of dental age are based upon this variation. The sequence of events that are followed in dental development include the initial growth, calcification, and eruption of the deciduous teeth, resorption of their roots, eruption of the permanent teeth, and their gradual attrition. Most often, however, dental age assessments are based either upon the initiation of calcification or stage of calcification as determined by dental X-rays, or upon the timing of eruption of the primary and permanent dentitions. These stages of development may then be compared to reference standards for an assessment of an individual's dental maturational age [(Table 19.4) (Lowrey 1973)].

Table 19.4 Developmental Chronology of the Human Dentition. (From G. H. Lowrey, *Growth and Development of Children,* 6th Ed. Copyright © 1973 by Year Book Medical Publishers, Inc., Chicago. Used by permission.)

	Primary Dentition Calcification Begins		**Crown Completed**		**Eruption**		**Exfoliation**	
Tooth	*Maxilla*	*Mandible*	*Mandible (Mo.)*	*Maxilla (Mo.)*	*Maxilla (Mo.)*	*Mandible (Mo.)*	*Maxilla (Yr.)*	*Mandible (Yr.)*
Central inc.	14 wk. in utero	14½ wk. in utero	1½	2½	9⅓	7½	6–7	6–7
Lateral inc.	16 wk. in utero	16½ wk. in utero	2½	3	11	13¼	7–8	7–8
Cuspid	17 wk. in utero	17 wk. in utero	9	9	9½	19⅔	10–12	9–12
1st molar	15 wk. in utero	15½ wk. in utero	6	5½	15⅔	16	9–11	9–11
2d molar	19 wk. in utero	18 wk. in utero	11	10	28	26½	10–12	10–12

	Permanent Dentition Calcification Begins		**Crown Completed**		**Eruption**		**Root Completed**	
Tooth	*Maxilla*	*Mandible*	*Maxilla (Yr.)*	*Mandible (Yr.)*	*Maxilla (Yr.)*	*Mandible (Yr.)*	*Maxilla (Yr.)*	*Mandible (Yr.)*
Central inc.	3–4 mo.	3–4 mo.	4½	3½	7–7½	6–6½	10–11	8½–10
Lateral inc.	10–12 mo.	3–4 mo.	5½	4–4½	8–8½	7¼–7¾	10–12	9½–10½
Cuspid	4–5 mo.	4–5 mo.	5½–6½	5½–6	11–11⅔	9¾–10¼	12½–15	12–13½
1st premolar	1½–1¾ yr.	1¾–2 yr.	6½–7½	6½–7	10–10⅓	10–10¾	12½–14½	12½–14
2d premolar	2–2¼ yr.	2¼–2½ yr.	7–8½	7–8	10¾–11¼	10¾–11½	14–15½	14½–15
1st molar	32 wk. in utero	32 wk. in utero	4–4½	3½–4	6–6⅓	6–6¼	9½–11½	10–11½
2d molar	2½–3 yr.	2½–3 yr.	7½–8	7–8	12¼–12¾	11¾–12	15–16½	15½–16½
3d molar	7–9 yr.	8–10 yr.	12–16	12–16	20½	20–20½	18–25	18–25

The use of dental age as an index of maturity has recently been challenged because of contradictory evidence concerning the relationship of dental age to skeletal age. Although several investigators have found a significant association between the two indices (e.g., Demisch and Wartmann 1956; Marshall 1976a; Sutow et al. 1954), others conclude that dental maturity and skeletal age are not closely related (Steel 1965; Lauterstein 1961). For example, Wagner et al. (1963) frequently found a lack of association in cases of endocrine disorder, and Lacey et al. (1973) concluded that the association between skeletal and dental development is not sufficiently close to warrant the use of dental age assessments when skeletal age assessments are available.

Hormones and Growth

Like other body processes, the processes of growth are regulated by the nervous and hormonal systems. These two systems, in combination, form a complex interrelated biological control system that regulates cell function. Hormones are chemical substances that are secreted directly into body fluids for transport to all parts of the body. Certain hormones, called trophic hormones, exert their control over specific cells of target organs and stimulate production of another hormone within these target organs. For example, thyroid stimulating hormone (TSH) stimulates the thyroid gland to produce thyroxine. Hormones such as growth hormones and those produced in

Figure 19.16 A simplified summary of the relationships between the neurological and endocrine systems. FSH = follicle stimulating hormone; TSH = thyroid stimulating hormone. (From A. J. Vander, J. H. Sherman, and D. S. Luciano, *Human Physiology,* 2nd Ed. Copyright 1975 by McGraw-Hill Book Company. Used with permission of McGraw-Hill Book Company.)

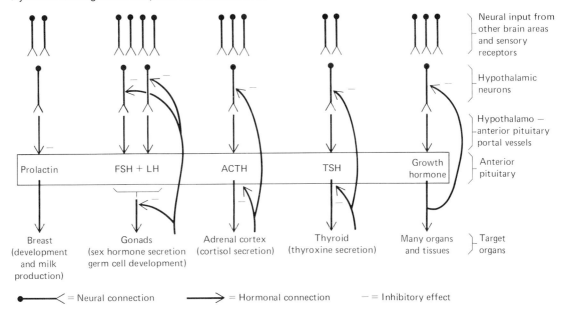

target organs are generally much less restricted in their activity than others, and affect many cells throughout the body.

The close integration between the nervous and the hormonal systems is evidenced by the control that the **hypothalamus** has over the anterior pituitary gland, an endocrine gland responsible for the secretion of six important hormones (Fig. 19.16). Figure 19.17 shows that the hypothalamus is strategically located directly above the pituitary gland and has direct contact with it through a unique capillary system that carries chemical messages from the hypothalamus directly to the pituitary cells. These neuro-hormonal messages are specific hypothalamic releasing factors (HRF), which cause the production and secretion of specific pituitary hormones. For example, a specific group of hypothalamic neurones produces a TSH releasing factor that acts on the anterior pituitary and causes the secretion of TSH. TSH, in turn, acts on the thyroid gland to cause the production of thyroid hormone.

The secretion of specific HRF is under partial control of (1) nervous impulses received by the hypothalamus from all parts of the body and (2) hormone levels in the blood, working via a negative feedback system. Figure 19.16 summarizes the interrelatedness of the neural and hormonal systems. Note that the circulating level of hormone from a specific target organ generally has an inhibitory effect on the production of a specific HRF. As the hormone level of the target organ decreases, an increased production of a specific HRF stimulates the anterior pituitary to increase production of the trophic hormone controlling the secretion of the hormone of the target organ. Specific hormone levels in the blood can also have a direct effect on the

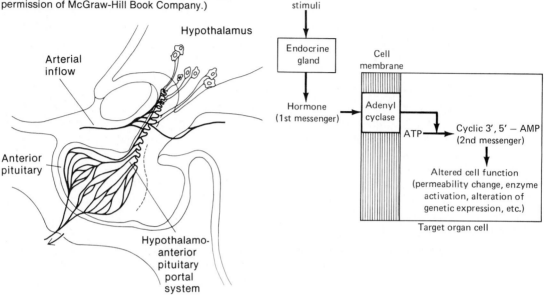

Figure 19.17 Relationship of the pituitary to the hypothalamic portion of the brain. Hypothalamic releasing factors are secreted into the capillary loops and are transported to the pituitary, where they stimulate specific cells to produce specific tropic hormones. (From A. J. Vander, J. H. Sherman, and D. S. Luciano, *Human Physiology,* 2nd Ed. Copyright © 1975 by McGraw-Hill Book Company. Used with permission of McGraw-Hill Book Company.)

Figure 19.18 The cyclic AMP (adenosine monophosphate) mechanism of hormone action. (From A. J. Vander, J. H. Sherman, and D. S. Luciano, *Human Physiology,* 2nd Ed. Copyright 1975 by McGraw-Hill Book Company. Used with permission of McGraw-Hill Book Company.)

anterior pituitary in terms of increasing or decreasing production of specific hormones.

The main regulatory function of hormones is to alter the rates at which specific cellular activities proceed. This function may be accomplished either by causing an alteration in the chemical reactions that occur within the cells, by altering the rate at which important substances are transported across cell membranes, or by activating some other important cellular process. Chemical reactions of a cell may be altered by promoting the increased synthesis of a particular protein (enzyme) responsible for the activation of a specific chemical reaction. Increased protein synthesis may be accomplished by stimulating the genetic apparatus within the cell nucleus to produce more of the messenger RNA responsible for the synthesis of the enzyme in question. Steroid hormones produced by the adrenal cortex and gonads are believed to function in this manner. Other hormones are believed to operate through a complex process involving the formation of a chemical substance called cyclic AMP [(adenosine monophosphate) (see Figure 19.18)]. Once formed, cyclic AMP is influential in initiating cellular activities such as activation of enzymes, alteration of cellular premeability, and stimulation of protein synthesis (Guyton 1976b).

While it is probable that all of the endocrine hormones influence growth processes in some way, those most important to human growth include growth hormone, thyroid hormone, insulin, and the **androgen** and **estrogen** hormones. Each is briefly discussed below.

Growth hormone. Also called somatotropic hormone or somatotropin, growth hormone is produced by the anterior pituitary gland. Unlike hormones that affect specific target organs and tissues, growth hormone has a stimulatory effect that is felt by nearly all growing tissues. Recent research has shown that the effect of growth hormone on tissues such as cartilage and bone is mediated by one or more factors called somatomedin(s) (Daughaday et al. 1972). The main effect on growth is in stimulating protein synthesis and increasing mitotic activity and cell division throughout the body. These effects are evident in the general enhancement of body weight and stature which follows the administration of this hormone to children who possess a deficiency.

The effects of growth hormone are particularly apparent on bone growth. Growth hormone, acting via somatomedin, increases protein synthesis and mitotic activity of the cartilage and bone cells within the epiphyseal plate and is responsible for the deposition of chondroitin sulfate and collagen necessary for bone growth (Guyton 1976b). Growth hormone does not influence bone maturation and, thus, does not affect the time of fusion of the epiphysis with the diaphysis of any long bone. However, excessive growth hormone prior to fusion of the long bones results in excessive linear growth and the abnormal condition called giantism. Excessive production of growth hormone after the epiphyses of long bones have fused results in a general thickening of those bones that have ceased linear growth and an abnormal enlargement of the vertebral elements and the membranous bones of the face and skull. The resulting condition is known as acromegaly. Dwarfism may also result from insufficient growth hormone production.

Thyroid hormone. Thyroid hormone (thyroxine) is secreted by the thyroid gland and functions to regulate the body's metabolic processes. Specifically, thyroid hormone influences the amount of energy available for normal body activities, including growth. Studies of subjects with a deficiency or absence of thyroid hormone have shown that it is important for (1) promoting general body growth and development, (2) promoting skeletal, dental, and sexual maturation, (3) promoting normal development of the brain, and (4) promoting a normal rate of metabolism (Lowrey 1973).

Although the basic mechanism by which these actions are accomplished is unknown, these effects are probably related, in part, to the positive effect that thyroid hormone has on the effectiveness of growth hormone. Without thyroid hormone, the effect of growth hormone on protein synthesis is insignificant. Stunted growth, mental retardation, abnormally slow metabolic rate, and severely retarded bone maturation are characteristic features of cretinism, a developmental disease resulting from thyroid hormone deficiency.

Insulin. Insulin is produced in the pancreas by the islets of Langerhans. It affects growth by promoting the diffusion of glucose into cells and by stimulating the synthesis of protein. A complex interrelationship between insulin and growth hormone has been demonstrated experimentally, and suggests that both insulin and growth hormone are necessary for either hormone to have its individual effect of promoting growth.

Androgens and estrogens. The general term androgen refers to several closely related sex hormones, of which testosterone is the primary one. The production of testosterone is controlled by the production of gonadotropic hormone by the pituitary, and it is secreted mainly in the testes by the interstitial cells of Leydig. The fetal development of male sexual organs is thought to be caused by the genetically controlled secretion of testosterone by the developing embryonic genital tissues (Guyton 1976b). An increase in the production of testosterone at puberty causes the development of sexual characteristics in the male and is involved with the fusion of the epiphyses of long bones. Small amounts of androgens, some of which are converted to testosterone, are secreted by the adrenal glands of both males and females.

Estrogen is a general term used to designate several closely related female sex hormones. Estrogens are mainly secreted by the ovary, although small amounts may be produced by the testes. Like testosterone, these hormones are under the control of the gonadotropic hormones of the pituitary. They are responsible for the development of female sexual characteristics and for epiphyseal closure of the long bones. Both estrogens and androgens act by initiating the transcription of RNA from DNA, thus causing increased synthesis of protein and altered cell function.

Growth at Adolescence

Adolescence is the time of developmental transition from childhood to adulthood. This period is marked by changes involving both behavior and physical and sexual development. Puberty is the term that refers more specifically to the period of sexual development that culminates in sexual maturity (Vander et al. 1975). The chronological timing of initiation, progression, and completion of the unique events associated with pubertal growth and development shows considerable variability among individuals and between the sexes. Genetic factors appear largely responsible for the variation in the age of onset of puberty (Kogut 1973). The events associated with puberty include an acceleration in the rate of linear growth and weight gain and the development of sexual characteristics. These changes in growth and development are the results of distinctive hormonal changes that occur during puberty.

Acceleration in the body's growth rate during puberty is frequently called the adolescent growth spurt (Fig 19.19 and 19.20). As Figure 19.19 illustrates, the typical growth spurt in height is marked by (1) a sharp acceleration in linear growth velocity that results in a rapid height increase, (2) the attainment of a peak height velocity (PHV), which is followed by (3) an immediate and sharp deceleration in growth velocity. Because frequent measurements can detect an individual's PHV, this event is a useful landmark in the growth process (Marshall 1976b). A study of English children showed that the PHV occurred between the ages of 10 and 14 in females and between 12 and 16 in males (Marshall and Tanner 1970). This reflects the substantial normal variability present in the timing of developmental events and indicates the approximate two-year difference between the sexes in the time of initiation of the growth spurt.

Females begin their adolescent growth spurt and reach their PHV earlier than males, and their maximum PHV is somewhat smaller than that of males. These two factors are primarily responsible for the differences in size between adult males and females. Males have a greater growth spurt and also benefit from a longer period of slow but steady growth prior to the growth spurt. Although the growth spurt begins about two years earlier in females than in males, other, less noticeable pubertal

Figure 19.19 Typical individual velocity curves for height in boys and girls. Note the beginning of the adolescent growth spurt and the point of peak height velocity (PHV). (Courtesy of J. M. Tanner, R. H. Whitehouse, and M. Takaishi, 1966, Standards from Birth to Maturity for Height, Weight, Height Velocity, and Weight Velocity; British Children, 1965. *Arch. Dis. Childh.* 41: 454–471.)

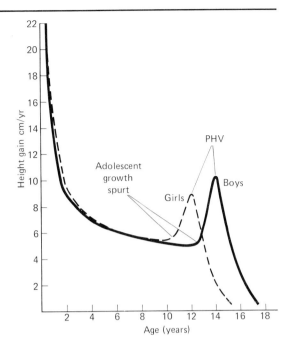

Figure 19.20 Typical individual velocity curves for weight in boys and girls. Note the beginning of the adolescent growth spurt. (Courtesy of J. M. Tanner, R. H. Whitehouse, and M. Takaishi, 1966, Standards from Birth to Maturity for Height, Weight, Height Velocity, and Weight Velocity; British Children, 1965. *Arch. Dis. Childh.* 41: 454–471.)

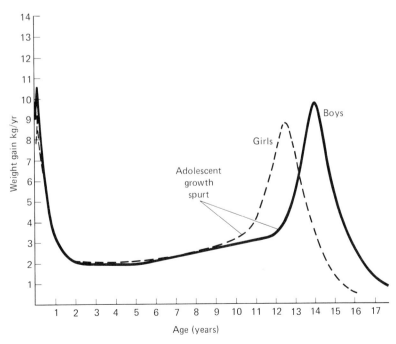

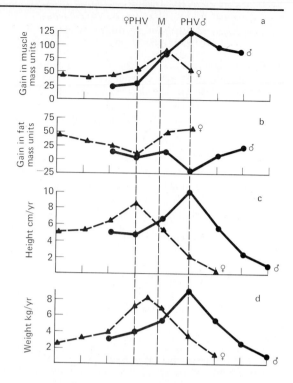

Figure 19.21 Mean changes in muscle mass, fat mass, height, and weight in relationship to age of menarche (M) and peak height velocity (PHV). (Adapted from H. V. Barnes, Physical Growth and Development during Puberty. *Med. Clin. North Amer.* 59: 1329–1335, 1975, by permission of the W. B. Saunders Co.)

changes begin in males only a few months after those of females. Mature development of sexual characteristics is reached at about the same age in both sexes (Marshall 1976b).

Changes in body composition are also noticeable at puberty. Figure 19.21 shows the dramatic increase in both muscle and fat, as well as how these relate in time to the adolescent increases in height and weight. Although muscle mass increases steadily in both sexes from the onset of puberty, this increase is more dramatic in males than in females and results in the greater strength of the male. Fatty tissue, while increasing in absolute amounts, shows a modest decrease in rate of accumulation in males during the three years prior to reaching PHV. Following the attainment of PHV, however, there is a marked increase in fat accumulation in the female and a more modest increase in the male. This difference in the rate of fat accumulation results in females having nearly twice as much body fat as males following completion of the maturational events (Barnes 1975). The amount of fat accumulation in the female may play an important role in the initiation and subsequent maintenance of regular menstrual cycles (see below under "Menarche").

Hormonal Influences

The acceleration of growth during puberty and the development of sexual characteristics are primarily controlled by the secretion of the gonadotropic and sex hormones. Gonadotropins are pituitary hormones which specifically stimulate and control the secretion of steroid sex hormones by the gonads. These include estrogen and progesterone in the female and testosterone in the male. Leutinizing hormone

(LH) and follicle stimulating hormone (FSH) are the names given to the gonadotropic hormones. Although these names are derived from their action in the female, they are also present in the male. LH in the male is sometimes referred to as interstitial cell stimulating hormone (ICSH) to indicate the testicular cell that is stimulated to produce testosterone.

Immediately prior to the adolescent growth spurt, the hypothalamus stimulates the anterior pituitary to begin producing gonadotropic hormones. These hormones act to stimulate the interstitial cells of the ovaries and testes to produce their respective sex hormones. What initiates the stimulation of the hypothalamus is an unanswered question. Some investigators hypothesize that maturational changes in the central nervous system, and particularly within the hypothalamus, result in a deceased responsiveness of the hypothalamus to the inhibitory effects of normally low circulating levels of sex hormones. This decreased responsiveness would result in the increased secretion of those hypothalamic releasing factors that control gonadotropic hormone production (Kulin 1974).

Although considerable variability exists in the timing of the onset of puberty and the development of sexual characteristics, the sequence of events is relatively invariable. Tables 19.5 and 19.6 outline the average time of appearance of sexual characteristics in American males and females. Note the wide range in the ages at which particular characteristics appear and develop. The onset of puberty in the male is marked by an increased production of gonadotropic hormone. This increase results in rapid growth of the testes, the first outwardly recognizable pubertal change. As the testes grow and mature, the greatly increased testosterone production is responsible for the subsequent appearance of the male sexual characteristics (see Table 19.5).

Standards for assessing and rating the development of sexual characteristics of both sexes may be found in Tanner (1962). Because each sexual characteristic shows an individual developmental rate, each must be assessed independently. There also appears to be independent control over the rate of sexual maturation as a whole, as well as the rate of skeletal or dental maturation (Marshall

Table 19.5 Average Time of Appearance of Sexual Characteristics in American Boys. (From G. H. Lowrey, *Growth and Development of Children*, 6th Ed. Copyright © 1973 by Year Book Medical Publishers, Inc., Chicago. Used by permission.)

Characteristic	Time of Appearance
Breasts	Some hypertrophy often assuming a firm nodularity, 12–14 years
	Disappearance of hypertrophy, 14–17 years
Testes and penis	Increase in size begins, 10–12 years
	Rapid growth, 12–15 years
Pubic hair	Initial appearance, 12–14 years
	Abundant and curly, 13–16 years
Axillary hair	Initial appearance, 13–16 years
Facial and body hair	Initial appearance, 15–17 years
Acne	Varies considerably, 14–18 years
Mature sperm	Average, about 14–16 years

Table 19.6 Average Time of Appearance of Sexual Characteristics in American Girls. (From G. H. Lowrey, *Growth and Development of Children,* 6th Ed. Copyright © 1973 by Year Book Medical Publishers, Inc., Chicago. Used by permission.)

Characteristic	Time of Appearance
Pelvis	Female contour evident in early childhood and becomes well-established by 8–10 years
Breasts	I. Preadolescent II. Bud stage: nipple and areola enlarged, small mound beneath, 9–11 years III. Nipple enlarged and areola forms mound above the surrounding skin of breast, pigmentation apparent, 12–13 years IV. Nipple projects but areola level with surrounding skin, glandular tissue palpable, histologic maturity, 14–17 years
Vagina	Some thin milky secretion often begins a year before menarche; glycogen content in cells and epithelial changes on smear, 11–12 years
Pubic hair	I. Initial appearance, 11–12 years II. Mainly labial, darker and coarser than body hair, 12–13 years III. Well-formed triangle, curly and dark, 13–14 years IV. Thick, spreads to thighs
Menarche	13 years
Axillary hair	Initial appearance, 12–14 years Increases in amount until early adulthood
Acne	Varies in severity and duration, usually precedes menarche

1974). Despite this independence, the development of sexual characteristics is more closely correlated with skeletal maturation than with chronological age. Females who are skeletally advanced at the time of adolescence also experience their first menstruation (menarche) earlier than those less advanced in terms of skeletal or dental maturation.

As previously noted, steroid hormones, including androgens and estrogens, affect growth by acting on the genetic apparatus within the cell and promoting protein synthesis. Although testosterone is primarily produced by the male testes, both males and females produce significant amounts of testosteronelike androgrens from their adrenal cortices. In females, the production of these adrenal androgens is primarily responsible for the female adolescent growth spurt. The heightened growth spurt and increased muscle mass in males are the results of the additional amount of androgens produced by the testes.

In addition to being responsible for the rapid increase in bone growth during the adolescent growth spurt, androgens in both sexes are ultimately responsible for obliteration of the epiphyseal plate and concomitant epiphysis-diaphysis fusion. Although further longitudinal long-bone growth is impossible, post-adolescent growth continues in other bones such as the vertebrae and in the craniofacial complex. Approximately 98% of growth in stature, however, is reached at about 17.5 years of age in males and 16 years in females (Harrison et al. 1977).

Figure 19.22 The relation of age of menarche to peak height velocity. Note that the time from peak height velocity to menarche is extended for later maturing girls in comparison to early maturing girls. (Courtesy of J. M. Tanner, *Growth at Adolescence.* 2nd Ed., 1962. By permission of Blackwell Scientific Publications, Ltd., Oxford.)

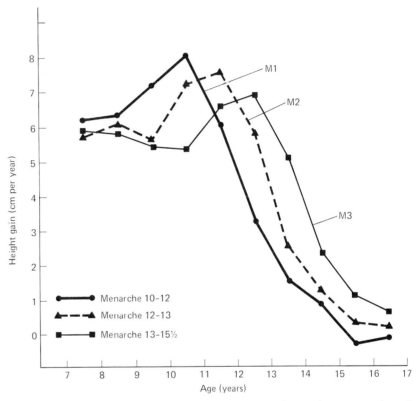

Because of the relationship of androgen secretion to bone growth and epiphyseal fusion, the time of onset of pubertal changes has a significant effect on stature. Individuals who initiate their adolescent growth spurt earlier than others will be taller than less advanced individuals throughout the time of the growth spurt. But because of the longer period of slow but steady growth prior to the growth spurt, slower maturing individuals will be taller when their growth spurt begins than early maturing individuals. Eventually, they catch up to the latter in adult stature. In general, late maturing individuals grow more slowly during their growth spurt than early maturing individuals, and they take longer to reach menarche after attainment of PHV (Fig. 19.22). Early and late maturers are of approximately equal height when growth has effectively ceased, but late maturers tend to be lighter and somewhat more linear as a result of their slower growth rate during the adolescent spurt (Frisch and Revelle 1970).

Estrogens play a similar role in the development of female sexual characteristics, as does testosterone in males. Prepubertal estrogen secretion in females is normally low. The change in hypothalamic responsiveness to these low circulating hormone levels signals the initiation of puberty. The result is an increased production of LH and FSH by the pituitary and an acceleration in the ovarian production of estrogens. Estrogens cause the appearance and development of female sexual characteristics (Table 19.6). Estrogen is also secreted in small amounts by the male adrenal gland and testes, and this hormone presumably is responsible for transient enlargement of the breasts (gynomastia) that occurs in pubescent males (Vander et al. 1975).

Menarche

Menarche refers to the first menstrual bleeding, an endocrine-controlled event that correlates well with skeletal maturation. Because menarche is a readily observable and memorable event, it is a particularly useful indicator of maturity. In the United States, the average age at menarche is 12.7 years (Zacharias et al. 1970). It generally occurs about one year after the PHV is reached, and shortly thereafter a maximal increase in weight is attained (Fig. 19.21). Much of this increase in weight is due to fat, which rapidly accumulates in females following the attainment of the PHV (Barnes 1975).

A recent hypothesis suggests that the onset and maintenance of regular menstrual cycles is dependent upon the maintenance of a minimal weight for height. This relationship apparently represents a critical amount of fat relative to total body weight (Frisch 1972, 1975; Frisch and McArthur 1974). On the average, menstrual cycles commence when the body reaches a relative fatness of 22 to 24% of total body weight. About 17% relative fatness was found to be the minimum level necessary for the onset of menstruation (Frisch and Revelle 1970, 1971). The attainment of this critical body weight may cause a change in the metabolic rate. This change would, in turn, reduce the sensitivity of the hypothalamus to circulating levels of gonadal and adrenal hormones. The resulting increased production of gonadotropic releasing factors by the hypothalamus would then stimulate the anterior pituitary to increase secretion of gonadotropic hormones. This increase, then, would result in a rise in estrogen secretion to a level sufficient to initiate menstruation (Frisch and Revelle 1969). Although some investigations have disagreed, in part, with this hypothesis and the proposed mechanisms (e.g., Cameron 1976; Billewicz et al. 1976), its inherent insights have stimulated research in this fascinating area of growth and development.

Growth and Biological Anthropology

Secular Trends

Studies of children and adults from the developed countries of North America, Europe, and Japan have demonstrated gradual increases in average body size measurements (Fig. 19.23) and maturation rates over the past century. The increase in maturation rates is particularly evident in a steady decline in the age of menarche over the last 100 years (Fig. 19.24). Such changes over time are referred to as secular trends.

Secular trends occur in both children and adults. At every age level, children in the United States today are taller on the average than children were a century or even a generation ago. Today's adults also attain their full stature several years earlier, on the average, than comparable adults of 100 years ago. In addition,

Figure 19.23 Secular trend in height of English boys measured in 1833, 1874, 1878, 1955, 1958. Note the difference between the mean stature of the two different classes measured in 1874. (Courtesy of J. M. Tanner, *Growth at Adolescence.* 2nd Ed., 1962. By permission of Blackwell Scientific Publications, Ltd., Oxford.)

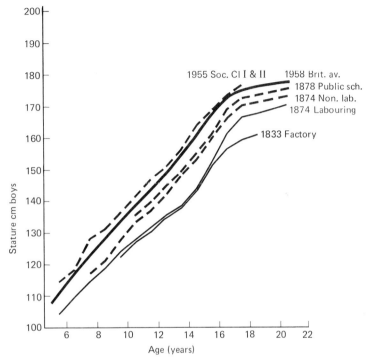

there appears to be a secular trend for increase in adult stature. This increase has been estimated at about one inch per generation (about 30 years), or about three inches over the last 100 years. However, several lines of evidence suggest that the secular trend in stature has ended, especially among the middle and upper socioeconomic groups.

The figures concerning the secular trend in the attainment of full adult stature correspond well with the dramatic and undisputed evidence for a secular decrease in the age at menarche. A similar and readily observable maturational event is not present in males, but males are clearly reaching maturity at an earlier age. In the United States and Europe, the present age at menarche occurs approximately three years earlier than it did a century ago. This represents an increase of approximately three to four months per decade.

Because menarche and the onset of sexual maturation begin the process of long-bone fusion, the decrease in the age of full adult stature attainment obviously associates well with the decrease in the age at menarche. However, the relationship between the developmental timetables of sexual maturity and stature increase has led some investigators to question the reality of a secular increase in maximum adult stature. For example, Brues (1977) suggests that at least some of this apparent increase over time may result from comparing less skeletally advanced individuals of decades

Figure 19.24 Secular trend in median age of menarche in Europe from 1840 to 1970. (Courtesy of P. B. Eveleth and J. M. Tanner, Worldwide Variation in Human Growth, 1976. By permission of Cambridge University Press, Cambridge.)

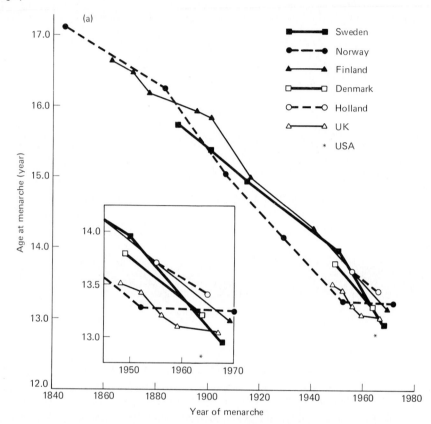

ago with today's individuals, who are more advanced in terms of reaching their maximum stature. Damon (1977), however, feels that the speed-up of growth, as indicated by earlier ages at menarche, is not a sufficient explanation for the increase in adult stature.

Most often, secular trends are thought to result from a combination of improved nutrition and health conditions. Both inadequate nutrition and chronic disease during the growth period may adversely affect individual growth and rate of maturation. Improvement in these factors, thus, would allow an individual to more closely approach the genetic growth potential. Other factors suggested as possible influences contributing to secular trends are the breakdown of genetic isolates, and the resulting effects of heterosis (Tanner 1968), and various undefined psychosocial influences within one's enviroment (Damon 1977).

The hypothesis by Frisch and Revelle, outlined above, can be related to these secular trends. The secular trend of decreased age at menarche may be explained in terms of more rapid growth in weight and an earlier achievement of critical body fat composition necessary to initiate menstruation. Improvements in nutrition and health would contribute to this more rapid growth. Obese children frequently experience an earlier menarche than their peers of normal weight. On the other hand, underweight children generally experience a delay in sexual maturation.

Because few studies of growth were undertaken prior to the 1800s, there is some question as to how long the secular trends referred to above have been continuing. If the rate of stature increase for the last 100 years is accepted as normal, and if similar increases had occurred over previous centuries, one might expect that individuals of 500 or 1,000 years ago would have been considerably smaller than people are today. However, skeletal evidence suggests that such is not the case. A detailed comparison of the mean maximum stature of United States males—a tall population by world standards—with stature estimates based on skeletal remains from a fifth to eighth century Medieval population from northern Europe and Britain shows that no significant increase has occurred during the past 1,200 to 1,500 years (Huber 1968). Similarly, studies that have evaluated the age at menarche in Classical and Medieval times have demonstrated no significant change from then to the present (Amundsen and Diers 1969, 1973). These findings at least suggest that the reported secular trends in maximum adult stature and age at menarche over the last 100 years reflect a return to levels that were established considerably earlier.

Population Variability

Population differences in growth are clearly evident in terms of differences in mean child and adult stature, weight, body proportions, and in overall rate of maturation. These growth differences among populations ultimately result from population differences in the average rate of cellular growth of the body as a whole and of its various components. Such differences in cellular growth rate stem, in turn, from differences in the genetic constitutions of individuals representing the different populations, as well as the complex interaction of these genotypes with their own particular environmental variables. Of great significance for variation in growth, both within and between populations, is the synergistic effect of inadequate nutrition and disease. In all populations where a dichotomy exists between upper and lower socioeconomic classes, the upper classes show enhanced growth. Presumably, this is due to better nutrition and health care of the child (Eveleth and Tanner 1976).

One of the more difficult goals of interpopulation growth studies is to determine the extent to which growth differences are due to genetic versus environmental factors. This has been attempted by comparing genetically similar populations that live under dissimilar environmental conditions, such as Frisancho's (1976) study of Peruvian Indians in high and low altitudes. Genetic and environmental effects on growth may also be partitioned by studies that compare genetically dissimilar populations or segments of populations within similar environmental conditions. An example of this approach (Amirhakimi 1974) has compared the growth of individuals within genetically dissimilar populations of similar socioeconomic, nutritional, and health backgrounds.

Comparisons of individuals in developed versus undeveloped countries frequently show considerable differences in stature and growth rate. But how much of this difference is genetic? Increasing evidence suggests that the short stature of representative individuals within some populations is mainly due to nutritional inadequacy instead of genetic differences in growth potential. Until at least 7 years of age, the growth of well-nourished children from undeveloped countries approximates the standards from normal growth in developed countries (Habicht et al. 1974). However, poorer children from undeveloped countries show normal growth for only the first six months, and during this time only if they are breast fed.

After about six months, the baby's growth is at a point where the mother's milk no longer provides an adequate quantity of calories and other nutrients to sustain normal growth. The second and third year of life may be a time of little or no weight gain, as the effects of inadequate nutrition, intestinal parasites, diarrhea, and various other diseases aggravate an already bad situation. The stunting caused by the interaction of nutritional inadequacy and disease may never be regained and will be reflected in the final adult stature (Farquharson 1976).

A major compilation and interpretation of world growth studies has recently been presented by Eveleth and Tanner (1976). They have attempted to minimize the environmental effects that poor nutrition and health conditions exert on growth by basing their comparisons on "well-to-do" populations or segments within populations. By comparing healthy and well-fed populations of Europeans, Africans (in Africa and America), and Asiatics (Chinese, Australians, Japanese, Amerindians, Eskimos, Pacific Island natives, Indomediterraneans of the Near East, Middle East, and India), they offer the following generalizations:

1. Asiatics are generally shorter than Europeans and Africans. This shortness results, at least in part, from an earlier adolescent growth spurt and subsequent earlier epiphyseal closure. Asiatics have considerably shorter legs relative to their trunks, a characteristic that begins during childhood and becomes more marked as completion of long-bone growth approaches. Arm length relative to trunk length is only slightly shorter among Asiatics as compared to Europeans.

2. African children, at all ages, who grow under good nutritional and health conditions are slightly taller and heavier than Europeans, a result of advanced maturational development that is evident from birth onward. Africans also have considerably longer arms and legs relative to trunk length than do Europeans, while Asiatics have the smallest limb-to-trunk ratio of all populations.

3. Populations are becoming more similar in growth characteristics because of improved conditions in nutrition and health care. However, within particular populations there are marked contrasts in growth between individuals from well-to-do families and those from poorer families. This points out the great influence of environmental factors on growth. Secular increases in height and weight and decrease in age at menarche reflect improved environmental conditions in the countries where such trends occur.

Summary

The growth of an organism from fertilization to adulthood involves an integration of the processes of cellular growth and cellular differentiation. Although these processes are ultimately controlled by genetic factors, they are also influenced significantly by the environment. Variation in human growth results from the complex interaction of these genetic and environmental factors. Studies have demonstrated that adverse environmental factors, including inadequate nutrition, disease, and harmful chemicals, have their greatest effect on growth when encountered during a critical period of rapid cell multiplication and differentiation. Such environmental disturbances may permanently affect growth processes or, if encountered during a less critical stage of growth, may only cause temporary growth retardation. An accelerated period of "catch-up" growth may follow.

The progress of growth in height, weight, and other size parameters can be illustrated through the use of growth curves. Such curves graphically portray the general pattern of an individual's growth and, when based upon accumulated standard data, may also be used for studying variability both within and between populations. Many investigations of growth are based upon an assessment of an individual's developmental maturity. Because chronological age is generally a poor indicator of maturity, such indices of maturity as skeletal age, dental age, and sexual age have been developed to more accurately assess maturational age.

The processes of growth are regulated through a complex integration of the nervous and hormonal systems. The hypothalamus and the anterior pituitary gland play an integral role in controlling the synthesis and secretion of numerous hormones. By acting on the genetic apparatus within cells and by altering the rates at which specific cellular activities proceed, these hormones stimulate and regulate growth processes. The hormonal control of growth is particularly evident during the period of adolescence, a time marked by a rapid acceleration in the rate of growth, changes in body composition, and the development of sexual characteristics and achievement of sexual maturity.

Growth investigators have utilized data collected over the last 100 years to document a gradual increase over time in average body size measurements and maturation rate. These secular trends are thought to result from a combination of improved nutrition and improved health conditions. Anthropologists are particularly interested in the considerable variability in growth among different populations. Although much of this variability is due to differences in nutrition and health conditions, comparisons of well-to-do Europeans, Africans, and Asians have also shown a significant genetic component in this variability.

Appendix 1
Basic Statistical Concepts and Methods

Introduction

When writing an introductory textbook, one finds inevitably that somebody has already said what needs to be said. It is difficult to improve on Abraham Kaplan's view of what statistics is and what it is not, and it seems especially appropriate to begin this appendix with his statement:

> But like every other kind of knowledge, statistical knowledge is not the product of spontaneous generation; it must have its parentage and nurture. Statistics is never in itself a source of knowledge. In these matters the mystique of quantity is especially widespread, as though a statistical formulation somehow provides its own content. The magic of numbers cannot produce cognitive rabbits out of truly empty hats. In common with all other branches of mathematics, statistics alone is but an instrument for transforming data, not for producing them. And when the data have been cast in statistical form, they are still data; they have not thereby been made into a scientific conclusion. The point to the statistical formulation and transformation is to enable us to extract all the information that the data contain, so that we can bring them to bear on the hypothesis for which they are data. (1964:220)

For a variety of reasons many individuals in a course in biological anthropology will rebel against learning the fundamentals of statistics. A common rationalization is that anthropology, defined as a social science in most quarters, has little need for statistical methods. This is a myth easily dispelled by a casual glance through social science journals, notably those dealing with demography and population analysis (a good place to start is with the review by Driver, 1965). Others will profess to have no mathematical ability. Certainly a thoroughgoing knowledge of the background of many statistical procedures presented here does require some mathematical sophistication. To understand how to apply the methods for the solution of certain problems, however, requires a mathematical ability not too far beyond that necessary for balancing your checkbook. If you can add, subtract, multiply, and divide, you should have little difficulty in repeating the methods outlined in this appendix.

At the risk of being anthropocentric, it may be suggested that the human brain is the most magnificent statistical machine (computer) available. It constantly receives, assimilates, and processes a variety of facts from the outside world. In a very short period of time, it produces a summary of this information upon which appropriate actions are based. Although we may have ample occasion for doubt, our brains usually make correct decisions when supplied with certain stimuli—we respond to sudden cooling by seeking appropriate devices for maintaining warmth. We may possess an innate sense of probability, as exemplified by the decision as to when to safely cross a street. We may also possess an innate feeling for variation. Nearly everyone recognizes the differences between various sorts of dogs and cats, both of which are often mentally categorized by size, coat color, hair length, disposition, and so forth. This is so obvious that it may not even deserve mention.

In everyday life, we depend upon these subjective observations and their associated generalizations. However, scientific endeavors demand quantification of such observations in order to express conclusions in mathematical probability levels. This involves statistics and biometry. For example, when the physical characteristics of one group of animals differ greatly from those of another group, it usually makes a considerable difference for classificatory purposes. But the meaning and magnitude of the difference can be determined only through the use of statistical methods. It cannot be determined by subjective opinion, which has no place in modern science.

As shown in previous chapters, biological anthropology is concerned with the origin and maintenance of human variation throughout the evolutionary history of the species. Such variation is most efficiently expressed in numerical form. This includes measurements of body dimensions and proportions, analyses of gene frequencies, and many other characteristics of populations. In every area of inquiry within the discipline, biological anthropologists are faced with the task of describing, analyzing, and interpreting these data. Of course, descriptions are often verbal expressions of a numerical idea (females are generally smaller than males), but a statement in this form provides nothing about the magnitude or meaning of the difference. Descriptions and measurements, by themselves, are nearly always of limited value without analysis, and as Howells has noted: "As soon as one goes beyond simple description . . . one is involved, consciously or unconsciously, in statistical ideas of variation and probability" (1969a:311).

Definitions of Data in Biological Anthropology

There are several terms that should be memorized for an understanding of biological data. We begin by adopting the definitions of Sokal and Rohlf for biometry as "the application of statistical methods to the solution of biological problems," and for statistics as "the scientific study of numerical data based on natural phenomena" (1969:2). The other necessary terms may be defined in the context of a hypothetical but realistic example.

Suppose you have returned from a study of a small (100 individuals) population inhabiting an island in the Pacific Ocean. Suppose also you have an idea that, in order to be tested, required you to determine the height, weight, and ABO blood group of as many of these islanders as possible, and that only 20 of the 100 people were available for study. Your records, then, contain the information given in Table A.1. These are *data* based on individual *observations* from the smallest sampling unit. In this case, the smallest sampling unit is each individual, and the

Table A.1 Height, Weight, and ABO Blood Type of Adults from a Hypothetical Island in the Pacific Ocean

Individual No.	Sex	Height (cm)	Weight (lbs.)	Blood Type
1	♂	168.9	146.5	A
2	♂	164.5	133.5	O
3	♂	164.6	142.5	A
4	♂	163.9	149.5	O
5	♂	169.8	152.5	O
6	♂	168.3	143.5	A
7	♂	169.9	145.5	B
8	♂	171.1	162.5	AB
9	♂	170.3	160.5	O
10	♂	171.8	154.5	B
11	♀	155.8	143.0	O
12	♀	154.3	153.0	O
13	♀	159.8	125.5	O
14	♀	153.3	132.5	A
15	♀	161.4	131.5	B
16	♀	165.5	152.0	A
17	♀	155.6	139.5	A
18	♀	156.6	145.5	O
19	♀	156.4	122.5	O
20	♀	152.8	124.5	AB

height, weight, or blood group of an individual is a single observation. The heights, weights, or blood groups on all 20 individuals represent the *sample,* defined as all of the observations taken according to a specific procedure.

Samples are drawn from *populations.* It is important to stress that the term "population" has two quite different meanings, depending upon its frame of reference. Biologically, a population is a community of individuals of a sexually reproducing species within which matings take place (Dobzhansky 1970). Considerably more attention was placed on this concept in Chapter 5. In statistics, a population is "the totality of individual observations about which inferences are to be made, existing anywhere in the world or at least within a definitely specified sampling area limited in space and time" (Sokal and Rohlf 1969:9). From what population has the hypothetical sample of Pacific Islanders been obtained? If one wishes to draw inferences applicable to all adult males and females, then the population consists of all living members of *Homo sapiens.* If the inferences relate only to the people living on a certain number of islands within a particular geographic area in the Pacific Ocean, then the adult males and females occupying this range comprise the population. If inferences apply only to the adults living on the island upon which the study was initiated, then the 100 individuals form the population.

Although all members of a population could conceivably be measured and observed, this rarely occurs in practice. The topic of ideal sample characteristics has therefore received much attention. Three characteristics of good samples are given below:

1. The sample should be free of bias. This means that variation in the sample should occur in approximately the same way and with about the same frequency as in the population. If the average height, weight, and relative blood group frequencies of the 100 Pacific Islanders are not reflected by the sample of 20, then the sample is somehow biased and inferences drawn from it are inaccurate. Unfortunately, sample bias cannot always be detected, much less controlled. This is especially true in anthropological studies where the data are often limited to observations of a handful of fossils from a few specific localities, or to observations of only the members of a population who are willing to cooperate with the observer. It is often impossible to choose a sample truly at random, even though random sampling is a necessary assumption for probabilistic inferences from sample to population.

2. The sample should be adequate, meaning that the range of variation in the population is reflected in the sample. This does not mean that the sample is identical to the population in all aspects but, instead, that observations in the sample are distributed in such a manner that reasonable inferences can be drawn about the population.

3. The sample should be biologically homogeneous, which means that all individuals upon whom observations are made should belong to the same breeding population. If one of the 20 individuals in the population of Pacific Islanders happened to be a shipwrecked sailor from Boston, then he should be excluded from the sample. At times, population homogeneity cannot be determined. In such cases, the sample can be used to indicate the degree of heterogeneity or homogeneity for some special purpose. Sampling has one very important limitation in this respect: it can never prove population homogeneity, but it often indicates population heterogeneity.

These definitions relate to the structure rather than the nature of biometric data. The term *variable* (or character) is used to denote the actual property measured by the observation. Thus height, weight, and blood type are three separate variables from each individual in Table A.1. In general, variables may be defined as features for which individuals in a sample differ. It follows that if a feature differs neither within nor among samples, then it is not a variable and is of no statistical interest. Skulls alone, if scored as either present or absent in living people, are not variables, because we all have a skull. Certain measurements of the skull are variables because they differ both within and between human populations. If a variable takes on a numerical value, it is usually termed a *variate*.

There are many different kinds of variables that can be conveniently categorized as follows (Sokal and Rohlf 1969):

1. Measurement variables
   a. Continuous variables
   b. Discontinuous (discrete) variables
2. Ranked variables
3. Attributes

Measurement variables are those which are expressed numerically. In biological anthropology, as in the biological sciences in general, it is most important to distinguish continuous from discontinuous variables.

Continuous variables can assume any value within two fixed points along a continuum. No matter how close together these two points may be, there is an infinite number of points in between that could be determined if the equipment and interest were sufficient. This is the primary distinguishing characteristic between continuous and discontinuous variables. As an example, consider your own weight. Whatever it may be represents a rounded-off estimate of a weight with an infinite number of decimal points. Examples of continuous variables commonly studied in biological anthropology include stature, weight, all measurements of body form, temperatures, skin pigmentation, bone and soft tissue densities, growth rates, and many others.

Discontinuous variables are those for which no intermediate values exist. A characteristic feature of humans, for example, is the possession of 24 presacral vertebrae—never 24.000001 or 23.999999. Discontinuous variables of interest include numbers of structures or objects of any sort, such as teeth, bones, and appendages. The important consideration in the determination of a continuous versus a discontinuous variable is the possibility of intermediate values.

Biological anthropologists occasionally study variables that cannot be measured, but are, rather, ranked according to a serial position. These are called ordinal or ranked variables. For example, one might want to code the rank order of the eruption of the deciduous (milk) teeth in children from diabetic mothers, without concern to the actual eruption times. The eruption order is a ranked variable.

Attributes, also called nominal variables, are variables expressed qualitatively rather than numerically. They are by nature discrete, such as male and female, or the presence or absence of a certain trait. Attributes are often expressed in terms of their population frequencies, such as the frequencies of certain blood groups.

Frequency Distributions

A frequency is the number of observations falling into a certain category, and a list or graph of these categories is called a frequency distribution. The first procedure undertaken in data analysis is often the construction of a frequency distribution for the variable in question. Suppose you wish to outline a frequency distribution on the male heights in Table A.1. These are plotted graphically (Fig. A.1a). In the following years you obtain more measurements and add these to the distribution (Fig. A.1b), until eventually your data include heights on several thousand people from a number of islands in the near vicinity (Figs. A.1c and A.1d). Note that the curve representing the frequency distribution of height assumes a more definite shape as the sample size increases. The symmetrical, bell-shaped curve given by the dotted line in Figure A.1d is called a normal frequency distribution, which will be discussed shortly.

Graphical representations of frequency distributions are of considerable interest to the biological anthropologist because they offer a rapid visual

Figure A.1 Sample size increases in height, from **a** to **d,** among hypothetical male Pacific Islanders.

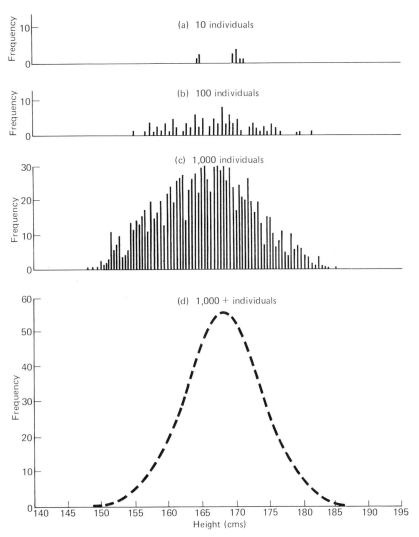

means of data inspection. In the present case, there is only one peak (unimodal). If females are added to the graph, the distribution will probably show two peaks (bimodal), indicating a sexual difference for height (Fig. A. 2). If there had been a bimodal distribution for height in one sex, on the other hand, then it might be possible that two genetically unrelated groups, one taller than the other, comprised the sample.

Figures A.1 and A.2 depict quantitative frequency distributions, because the variable is continuous. These are probably the most common types of distributions in biological anthropology, but qualitative distributions of attributes

Figure A.2 An example of a bimodal distribution for height among males and females from a hypothetical population.

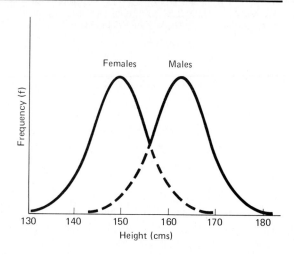

Figure A.3 Four different types of frequency distributions.

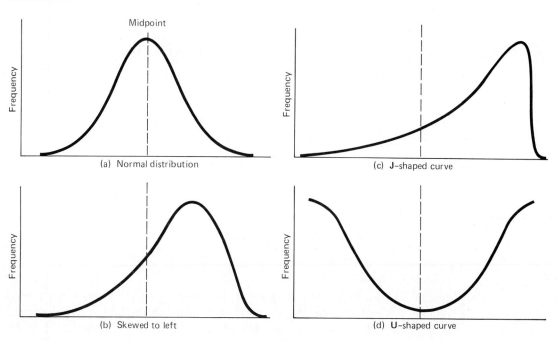

are also found. A frequency distribution of the blood group phenotypes in Table A.1 may be constructed by arranging, arbitrarily, the number of individuals in each class.

Blood Group Phenotype	Frequency (f)
O	9
A	6
B	3
AB	2

There are many different kinds of frequency distributions of anthropological variables, but most can be subsumed under a few general types (Simpson et al, 1960).

1. An approximation of the normal distribution, when the high point is at the midpoint and both tails of the curve slope away symmetrically (Fig. A.3a).

2. An approximation of the normal distribution, but where the peak is not at the midpoint and the tails slope away with moderate symmetry. This curve is usually termed moderately skewed. Distributions in which the right-hand tail slopes away more gradually than the left are said to be skewed to the right, or positively skewed, and those in which the left-hand tail slopes away more gradually than the right are skewed to the left, or negatively skewed. In positively skewed distributions, the class with the highest frequency (the peak) is to the left of the middle of the distribution, and the reverse holds for negatively skewed distributions (Fig. A.3b).

3. An exaggeration of (2) above, where the peak is either near or at the end of the distribution, with strong asymmetry. These are called J-shaped curves, and commonly represent the distributions of discontinuous variables (Fig. A.3c).

4. U-shaped curves, where the peaks arc at both ends, and the low point within the distribution. This is the least common type of distribution for data in biological anthropology (Fig. A.3d).

Descriptive Statistics

After the collection of observations and construction of their frequency distributions, data should be described numerically before attempting further analysis. This is done by descriptive statistics, which can be divided conveniently into (1) statistics of location (measures of central tendency) and (2) statistics of dispersion (variability). By statistics of location, one describes the position in a distribution where observations tend to cluster. Statistics of dispersion provide quantitative measures of the shape of the frequency distribution. To demonstrate the derivation of these statistics, we may utilize part of two actual samples of University of Wisconsin female students (R. H. Osborne, unpublished data) and Eskimo females from northwestern Alaska (Jamison 1972). For brevity, only two continuous variables will be considered—stature and sitting height. The data appear in Table A.2.

Table A.2 Stature and Sitting Height of Females from the University of Wisconsin and Northwestern Alaska

| University of Wisconsin Females | | Northwestern Alaskan Females | |
Stature	Sitting Height	Stature	Sitting Height
156.4 cm	83.0 cm	152.2 cm	79.8 cm
174.4	90.0	153.6	84.8
163.6	85.7	152.1	82.3
168.1	89.8	158.3	86.4
172.5	89.6	149.1	80.8
168.6	90.0	146.4	78.9
152.1	84.4	158.5	86.6
157.5	85.2	165.2	87.5
162.1	87.1	153.9	85.9
161.5	85.5	161.5	87.4
165.6	86.0	152.5	83.0
162.8	82.1	154.1	82.7
155.5	83.2	154.9	82.9
166.7	89.5	157.0	84.5
167.5	88.4	157.7	84.5
161.3	84.1	159.4	86.0
156.1	86.0	154.3	84.0
155.8	83.5	157.5	87.6
167.0	87.1	156.1	84.3
162.9	87.5	160.1	83.9

Simple Statistics of Location

The most widely used statistic of location is one with which most of you are familiar. This is the arithmetic mean $(\overline{X})$, often called the average. It is obtained by adding all observations in the sample and dividing the total by the number (n) of observations. Stated more efficiently with statistical symbols, the formula for the mean is

$$\overline{X} = \frac{\sum\limits_{i=1}^{n} X_i}{n}.$$

At first glance this formula may appear unduly complex for calculation of a quantity as simple as the mean, but it is actually quite simple. It also provides the opportunity, before discussing other statistics, to examine a few symbols that may be of future use.

Let any observation in a sample be denoted by X_i, where the subscript i refers to the ith observation in the sample. If you wished to refer to the third observation, then X_3 would be the proper notation. We have already learned that the sample size is given by n. Thus $n = 20$ for each of the Wisconsin and Eskimo samples. The entire array of observations may be indicated by

$$X_1, X_2, X_3 \ldots, X_n.$$

The capital Greek sigma, Σ, is a sign of operation, or an operator symbol. It specifies the procedure to be carried out on the items that follow. Sigma always indicates that the items must be summed, and it is usually referred to as the summation sign. Other operator symbols specify different functions. The capital Greek pi (Π), for example, indicates multiplication of the items following it.

To calculate the mean, then, the first step is the summation of all values of the items in the sample. In statistical shorthand, the numerator in the formula for the mean is

$$\sum_{i=1}^{n} X_i.$$

Put another way, this is $X_1 + X_2 + \ldots, X_n$. The subscript below and the superscript above sigma indicate, respectively, the first and last items to be summed. If for some reason the first five items in the sample were to be summed, the proper notation would be

$$\sum_{i=1}^{5} X_i.$$

If all items except the first one were to be summed, then

$$\sum_{i=2}^{n} X_i.$$

For simplicity in notation, these subscripts and superscripts are generally not used unless a particular case arises. It should be understood that in their absence all items are to be included in the calculation. Thus the abbreviated formula for the mean is

$$\overline{X} = \frac{\Sigma X}{n}.$$

The means for stature and sitting height for the Wisconsin and Eskimo samples are given in Table A.3. They represent the midpoints of the observations in the samples.

Another statistic of location is the median (M), which is far less important in biological anthropology than the mean. The sample median may be defined as the observation in the middle of a ranked array. In other words, when observations are ranked by magnitude, M has an equal number of items on both sides. It, therefore, divides the frequency distribution into two equal parts. If a sample consisted of

Table A.3 Means for Stature and Sitting Height of Females from the University of Wisconsin and Northwestern Alaska

	Wisconsin Females		Alaskan Females	
	Stature	*Sitting Height*	*Stature*	*Sitting Height*
n	20	20	20	20
ΣX	3258.0	1727.7	3114.4	1683.3
$\overline{X}$	162.9 cm	86.4 cm	155.7 cm	84.2 cm

Figure A.4 A comparison of the respective locations of the mean, median, and mode in the same frequency distribution.

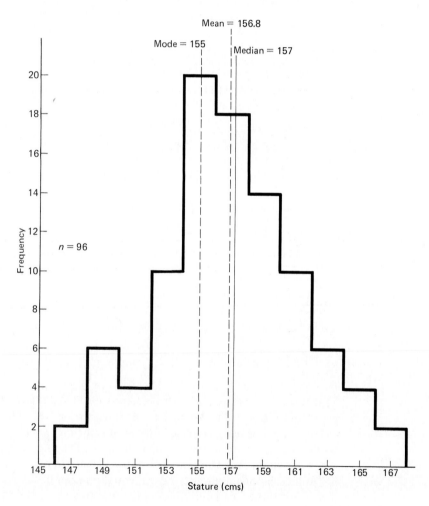

an odd number of observations, such as 23, 45, 56, 78, and 89, $M = 56$, since there are two observations on either side. When the sample number is even, however, as with the Wisconsin and Eskimo females, M is calculated as the midpoint between the $(n/2)$th and the $[(n/2) + 1]$th variate. Suppose you array the observations on stature in Alaskan females (Table A.2) from shortest to tallest:

146.4	153.6	156.1	158.5
149.1	153.9	157.0	159.4
152.1	154.1	157.5	160.1
152.2	154.3	157.7	161.5
152.5	154.9	158.3	165.2

Since the 10th and 11th observations are, respectively, 154.9 and 156.1, the midpoint between these two items, or M, = 155.5. Frequency distributions can be divided into any number of equal parts, and M is only one of a group of statistics serving this purpose. Others include quartiles (4 parts), deciles (10 parts), and percentiles (100 parts). Aside from the fact that the median is easier to calculate than the mean, the latter is a much more useful statistic of location. Medians do not lend themselves readily to comparative analysis, nor are they appropriate for important calculations in other statistical methods.

The third and final statistic of location considered here is the mode. Like the median, its applications in biological anthropology are limited. The mode is the most frequently occurring value in a distribution, and therefore is the peak of the distribution curve. As mentioned before, frequency distributions that have more than one peak are called bimodal (two peaks), or multimodal (more than two peaks). For comparative purposes, a frequency distribution showing the locations of the mean, median, and mode is given in Figure A.4.

Simple Statistics of Dispersion

Statistics of location are points about which the degree of clustering is calculated, but they produce no information about the nature of the frequency distribution. The nature or shape of frequency distributions, and therefore the inferences drawn from the observations in the distribution, may vary widely, even if their means and sample sizes are identical (Fig. A.5). We also need to know the length and height of the distribution curve, the slope of the tails away from the peak, and to what extent observations are concentrated in certain areas. Statistics of dispersion are used to gain this information.

The simplest dispersion statistic, which requires no calculation, is the observed range. The range represents the difference between the highest and lowest values of a variate, expressed in the same units as the variate. Most often it is expressed as the highest and lowest values, rather than the difference. The ranges for stature and sitting height on the Wisconsin and Alaskan females are

	Stature	**Sitting Height**
Wisconsin females	152.1–174.4	82.1–90.0
Alaskan females	146.4–165.2	78.9–87.6

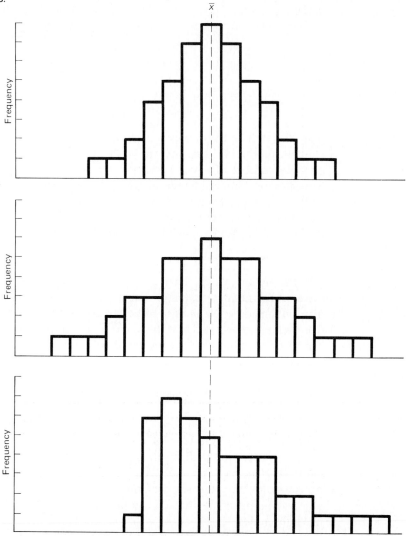

Figure A.5 Three examples of frequency distributions with the same sample sizes and means, but with different dispersions.

For at least two reasons, the range is an unsatisfactory measure of variability. First, it shows only where the distribution begins and ends, but indicates nothing about the shape of the curve. Second, it is clearly affected by an extreme value and may change considerably as new values are added to the distribution. For these reasons, it is probably the least informative of all measures of dispersion.

The standard deviation (s) and the variance (s^2), provide the most useful measures of dispersion of observations in a sample. The standard deviation takes into consideration all items in a distribution and weights each one according to its distance from the midpoint. For calculation of the standard deviation and the

Table A.4 Calculation of the Variance and Standard Deviation (Data from Milicer and Sczcotka 1966, on age at menarche in Warsaw girls)

X (age in years)	f	$d = X - \overline{X}$	d^2	fd^2
9.5	2	-3.63	13.18	26.36
10.0	5	-3.13	9.80	49.00
10.5	10	-2.63	6.92	69.20
11.0	25	-2.13	4.54	113.50
11.5	48	-1.63	2.67	128.16
12.0	92	-1.13	1.28	117.76
12.5	144	-0.63	0.40	57.60
13.0	195	-0.13	0.02	3.90
13.5	169	0.37	0.14	23.66
14.0	105	0.87	0.76	79.80
14.5	64	1.37	1.88	120.32
15.0	28	1.87	3.50	98.00
15.5	22	2.37	5.62	123.64
16.0	8	2.87	8.24	65.92
16.5	6	3.37	11.36	68.16
17.0	2	3.87	14.98	29.96
Totals	925			1174.94

$\overline{X} = 13.13$

$$\text{Variance } (s^2) = \frac{\Sigma fd^2}{n-1} = \frac{1174.94}{924} = 1.27 \text{ yrs.}$$

Standard deviation $(s) = \sqrt{1.27} = 1.13$ yrs.

variance, consider the data in Table A.4. Again, X indicates the observation, f is the frequency of each observation in the sample, and d represents the individual deviates from the mean $(X - \overline{X})$. By adding the squared values of the individual deviates (Σfd^2) and dividing this by $n - 1$, we obtain the sample variance, and extraction of the square root of the variance provides the standard deviation. Both of these measures are expressed in the original measurement units.

   Derivation of the variance and standard deviation in this way is both tedious and error prone, due to the effects of rounding. If a desk calculator is available, it is more efficient to calculate both quantities according to the following equations:

$$\text{variance} = s^2 = \frac{\Sigma X^2 - [(\Sigma X)^2/n]}{n-1}$$

$$\text{standard deviation} = s = \sqrt{\frac{\Sigma X^2 - [(\Sigma X)^2/n]}{n-1}}.$$

In these formulas, notice that $\Sigma X^2 = X^2_1 + X^2_2 + X^2_3 \ldots , X^2_n$, whereas $(\Sigma X)^2$ represents the square of the sum of all X's, i.e., the X's are added, and the total squared.

This is an important distinction, and care must be taken to ensure that these two figures are not reversed when entered into the equation. It is now an easy matter to calculate the sample variance and standard deviation for the Wisconsin and Alaska data, e.g., on stature in Wisconsin females.

$$s^2 = \frac{531,416.96 - (10,614,564/20)}{19} = 36.25; s = \sqrt{36.25} = 6.02 \text{ cms.}$$

To review the procedure verbally, only four basic steps are required to find the standard deviation: (1) sum all observations, square this sum to give $(\sum X)^2$, and divide by n; (2) square each observation and sum these, giving $\sum X^2$; (3) subtract quantity (1) from (2) and divide by $n - 1$ to give the variance; and (4) take the square root of the variance to obtain the standard deviation.

It was stated earlier that only part of two large data sets is given in Table A.2. If different subsamples had been chosen, their variance and standard deviation probably would differ slightly from those computed above. Thus the sample variance and standard deviation are estimates of the true population variance (σ^2) and standard deviation (σ). These quantities are calculated in the same manner, except that n replaces $n - 1$ in the denominator. Estimates of variance (s^2) as above, then, are said to be unbiased if done on large samples, because they tend to be a bit larger than the true population variance.

It is now possible to describe the samples in Table A.2 in terms of central tendency and dispersion. The most efficient way to do this is by setting up a table that lists the variables from each population, the sample sizes, means, and standard deviations (Table A.5).

You may have noted that these descriptive statistics are all absolute, i.e., in the same units as the observations and representing values of the variates located at certain points in the distribution. Given a set of observations on two unrelated samples, and knowing the mean and standard deviation of both, is it possible to compare the standard deviations directly to determine if the variability of the variate in one sample is greater than that of the other? The answer is generally no, especially if there is an appreciable difference in the two sample means.

For example, consider the problem in determining whether variability in human weight is greater than variability in the weight of tree shrews, specifically from the aspect of comparing the two standard deviations. Tree shrews, compared to humans, are tiny animals. An adult male tree shrew weighs, on average, about 175 g., or about 6 oz. A 150 lb. human male weighs about 320 times as much, and it is highly probable that the standard deviation in a human sample is much greater than the mean weight in a group of tree shrews. It follows that the absolute variation might be expected to be 320 times as great.

To compare the amount of variation in populations having drastically different means, the measure of absolute variation (the standard deviation) must be related to a measure of absolute size (the mean) to produce a measure of relative variability. The coefficient of variation (V) serves this purpose. The formula is

$$V = \frac{100(s)}{\overline{X}}.$$

Table A.5 Descriptive Statistics on Stature and Sitting Height of Females from the University of Wisconsin and Northwestern Alaska

	University of Wisconsin Females		Alaskan Females	
	Stature	*Sitting Height*	*Stature*	*Sitting Height*
n	20	20	20	20
$\overline{X}$	162.9 cm	86.4 cm	155.7 cm	84.2 cm
s^2	36.25	6.56	18.88	6.22
s	6.02	2.56	4.35	2.49

This expresses the standard deviation as a percentage of the mean. Unlike the standard deviation or the mean, the coefficient of variation is not a unit of measurement. It is a "pure" number, since the units of measurement in the numerator and denominator cancel each other in the ratio. In the Wisconsin and Alaskan samples, $V = 3.70$ and 2.79 respectively, for stature, and V is identical (2.96) for sitting height in both samples. The coefficients of variation indicate that, if the samples are presumed to be unbiased, adequate, and homogeneous, there is slightly greater variability in the Wisconsin sample for stature, but no difference between the two samples for variability in sitting height.

Probability and Probability Distributions

To understand genetic variation and the evolution of human populations requires knowledge of genetic transmission, which, in turn, is couched in terms of fundamental principles of probability. When the outcome of an event is uncertain, such as the sex or blood group of a prospective child or if the child will inherit a rare genetic disease, a variety of common terms is used to describe the situation. "The odds are," "the chance is," "in all likelihood," are everyday phrases that mean "the probability is," and an entire subdiscipline of mathematics has developed around this concept.

In biological anthropology, as in all other scientific disciplines, very little is known with certainty. As Hull states; "Probabilities are all that scientists ever have to go on, probabilities which sometimes are so high that they can be termed certainties" (1967:184). Those of you who develop a feeling for probability and a grasp of the fundamental principles will find the chapters in this book much more interesting.

Elementary Rules of Probability

Probability may be defined in the following manner: if an event can occur in m alternative ways, all of which are equally likely, and if a certain number n of these ways can be considered favorable, then the number n/m is the probability of success. Expressed numerically,

$$p(e_f) = \frac{n}{m}, \quad \text{or} \quad \frac{\Sigma e_f}{\Sigma e_i},$$

where $p(e_f)$ = the probability of the favorable event (e_f), $\sum e_f$ = the sum of the favorable outcomes, and $\sum e_i$ = all possible outcomes.

The probability that a single toss of a coin will land with the head showing is thus 1/2, or 50%, or as usually expressed, 0.50. The probability that a certain side of a cube will land face up is similarly 1/6, or 0.167. To determine the probability that an even number on the cube lands face up, the favorable outcomes (2, 4, and 6 = 3) are added, the result being 3/6 = 1/2 = 0.50. The probability of drawing a black bean out of a beanbag containing 30 black, 50 white, 40 brown, and 20 red beans is

$$p = \frac{30}{30 + 50 + 40 + 20} = \frac{30}{140} = 0.214.$$

Obviously, the probability of drawing a black bean increases when all of another color are removed, say the white beans.

$$p = \frac{30}{30 + 40 + 20} = \frac{30}{90} = 0.333.$$

The probability of drawing either a black or brown bean from this bag would likewise be

$$p = \frac{30 + 40}{30 + 40 + 20} = \frac{70}{90} = 0.778,$$

because there are two favorable outcomes possible.

There are two important extensions to the definition above:

1. Note that in none of the examples above does the probability exceed or equal 1. When an event is certain, $p = 1$; when it is certain not to happen, $p = 0$; in all other cases, p = some fraction between 1 and zero.

2. The probability of an event occurring is p; thus the probability of an event not occurring is $(1 - p)$, or q. Thus, $p + q = 1$.

We may now define two terms and three theorems (rules) that apply to problems dealing with *combined* probabilities.

Definition 1. *Mutually exclusive. Two or more events are called mutually exclusive if only one of them can occur in any given trial.*

Definition 2. *Independence. Two or more events are called independent if the occurrence or nonoccurrence of any one of them is unaffected by the occurrence or nonoccurrence of any other events.*

Theorem 1. *If p_1 is the probability that one event will occur, and p_2 the probability that a second event will occur, and if the two events are mutually exclusive, then the probability that either the first or the second event will occur is $p_1 + p_2$.* Thus the probability that a six or a seven will be drawn in a single drawing from a 52 card deck (in which there are 4 of each card type) is 4/52 + 4/52 = 0.154.

Theorem 2. *If p_1 is the probability that a first event will occur, and p_2 the probability that a second independent event will occur, then the probability that both will occur is the product of the two probabilities, i.e., p_1p_2.* The probability that a 7 may be drawn from a deck of playing cards is 4/52. If you replace this 7, the probability of drawing another 7 in succession is $(4/52)(4/52) = 1/169 = 0.006$, because the two events are independent of each other.

These basic rules apply not only to gambling, but also to various problems involving people. For example, suppose there are two children in each of a number of families. In what proportion of these families will the two children be of different sexes or of the same sex? Assume for the moment that the ratio of males to females at birth is equal. Letting M = male and F = female, and considering the birth order, four combinations are possible:

$$1MM : 1MF : 1FM : 1FF$$

If we disregard birth order and combine the families with one of each sex, then one-fourth of these families will have two males, two-fourths, a male and a female, and one-fourth, two females. Why? Since there is a one-half chance of a male being born on any trial, there is by the second theorem $(1/2)(1/2) = 1/4$ chance of either two males or two females being born on two independent trials. Since there are two different ways that a male and female may be born (either MF or FM), the probability will be $2 (1/2)(1/2) = 2/4$. Hence one-fourth of the families will, on average, have two males, two-fourths, a male and a female, and one-fourth, two females, and the ratio is $1 : 2 : 1$.

By the same rules, the chance that three males or three females will be born to one family is $1/2 \times 1/2 \times 1/2 = 1/8$. The chance that two males and one female, either FMM, MFM, or MMF, is $3 \times (1/2)^3 = 3/8$, and the same holds for families with two females and one male. The ratio now becomes $1/8 : 3/8 : 3/8 : 1/8$, or $1 : 3 : 3 : 1$. By the very same methods, the ratio in families with four children is $1 : 4 : 6 : 4 : 1$, and so on, for as many children as are assumed. These ratios are accurate, but rather cumbersome to calculate when large numbers are involved. An easier method is the binomial expansion.

Let the probability of event A (male) $= p$ and the probability of event B (female) $= q$. The expression for the binomial expansion is

$$(p + q)^n,$$

where n represents the number of events in the combination. In the previous examples the binomial is squared for two children:

$$(p + q)^2 = \begin{array}{r} p + q \\ \underline{p + q} \\ p^2 + pq \\ \underline{+ pq + q^2} \\ p^2 + 2pq + q^2 \end{array}$$

Ratio: $1 : 2 : 1$

cubed for three children:

$$(p + q)^3 = p^3 + 3p^2q + 3pq^2 + q^3$$

Ratio: $1 : 3 : 3 : 1$

and raised to the fourth power for four children:

$$(p + q)^4 = p^4 + 4p^3q + 6p^2q^2 + 4pq^3 + q^4$$

Ratio: $1 : 4 : 6 : 4 : 1$

Notice the coefficients (the numbers before the p's and q's) and the exponents (the powers to which the p's and q's are raised). The coefficients represent the number of ways an outcome may be obtained, and the exponents correspond to the numbers of events. For example, given the one-half probability of a child being one of the two sexes, what is the probability of two males and two females in a family of four children? This is given in the expansion of $(p + q)^4$ by $6p^2q^2$, or $6 (1/2)^2(1/2)^2 = 6/16$ $=0.375$. Similarly, the chance that the four children will be three males and one female or vice versa is, respectively, $4p^3q = 0.250$ and $4pq^3 = 0.250$. The chance that all children will be males is $p^4 = 0.0625$, and likewise for females. The total, or $0.375 + 2 (0.250) + 2 (0.0625) = 1$, since by definition $p + q = 1$.

The coefficients in a binomial expansion are more easily obtained by Pascal's triangle:

Power (n)

1						1		1		
2					1		2		1	
3				1		3		3		1
4			1		4		6		4		1
5		1		5		10		10		5		1
6	1		6		15		20		15		6		1

. . .

Note that the coefficients for any expansion of $(p + q)^n$ are obtained as the sum of the two numbers directly above it. The exponents are also regular:

$$(p + q)^6 = p^6 + 6p^5q + 15p^4q^2 + 20p^3q^3 + 15p^2q^4 + 6pq^5 + q^6.$$

The exponents of p begin with the power to which the binomial is raised and decrease to zero, and the reverse holds for the exponents of q.

Theorem 3. *If the probability of the occurrence of event $A = p$, and the probability of the occurrence of alternative event B (or the nonoccurrence of A) $= q$, then*

$$\frac{n!}{s! \, t!} p^s q^t$$

represents the probability that in n trials event A will occur s times and event B will occur t times. The exclamation point is a "factorial operator" and when used with a number indicates the product of all integers from 1 to n, i.e.,

$$X! = (X)(X - 1)(X - 2)(X - 3)\ldots, (1)$$

or, $4! = (4)(3)(2)(1) = 24$.

If a coin is tossed six times, what is the probability of tossing two heads and four tails in any order? Substituting $n = 6$, $s = 2$, and $t = 4$ into the formula above, and $1/2$ for both p and q (since there is an equal chance of one side of the coin landing face up), we obtain the probability

$$P = \frac{6!}{2!\,4!}(1/2)^2(1/2)^4$$

$$= \frac{(6)(5)(4)(3)(2)(1)}{(2)(1)(4)(3)(2)(1)}(1/4)(1/16) = 15(1/4)(1/16)$$

$$= 0.234.$$

Suppose you want to find the probability that two heterozygous parents will produce five children with a dominant and three with a recessive condition, in any order. Assume that there is a three-fourths chance for expression of the dominant and one-fourth chance for expression of the recessive. The probability, according to the third theorem, is

$$P = \frac{(8)(7)(6)(5)(4)(3)(2)(1)}{(5)(4)(3)(2)(1)(3)(2)(1)}(3/4)^5(1/4)^3 = 0.207.$$

The Binomial Distribution

These fundamental rules provide the groundwork for considering the binomial distribution, one of two very important probability distributions to be discussed. Return for a moment to coin tossing. It should now be obvious that one toss may be recorded as 0 or 1 head, two tosses as 0, 1, or 2 heads, etc. Since the probability of a head appearing after a single toss $= 0.50$, it should also be evident that 1,000 tosses of the coin will result in approximately 0.50 heads. The probabilities associated with the number of heads (or tails), given an indefinite number (n) of coins, may be derived according to the binomial theorem:

$$(p + q)^n = p^n + \frac{n}{1}p^{n-1}q + \frac{n(n - 1)}{2!}p^{n-2}q^2 + \frac{n(n - 1)(n - 2)}{3!}p^{n-3}q^3 \ldots, q^n.$$

The terms from Pascal's triangle are identical to those given by the binomial theorem, but both are tedious if the exponent n is high. Those algebraically inclined might wish to expand $(p + q)^{12}$, when $p = 1/2$, to determine for yourselves

Table A.6 Binomial Probabilities Associated with Obtaining Numbers of Heads When Tossing from One to Eight Coins

No. of Coins	Probability of Number of Heads								
	0	1	2	3	4	5	6	7	8
1	0.500	0.500							
2	0.250	0.500	0.250						
3	0.125	0.375	0.375	0.125					
4	0.063	0.250	0.375	0.250	0.063				
5	0.031	0.156	0.313	0.313	0.156	0.031			
6	0.016	0.094	0.234	0.312	0.234	0.094	0.016		
7	0.008	0.055	0.164	0.273	0.273	0.164	0.055	0.008	
8	0.004	0.033	0.109	0.221	0.273	0.221	0.109	0.033	0.004

Figure A.6 Histograms of binomial probability distributions, showing five of the eight sets of probabilities given in Table A.7.

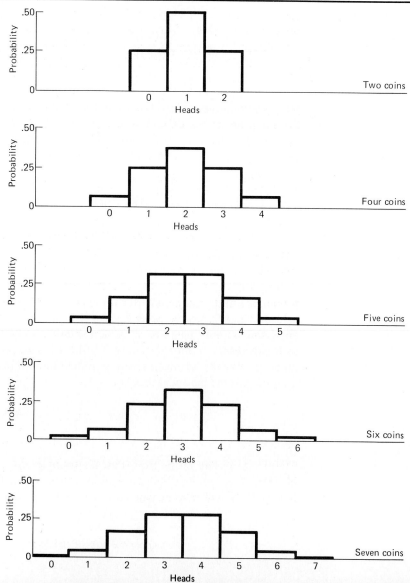

Table A.7 Frequencies of Various Sibship Sex Ratios in a Sample of 565 Sibships of Six Children (From Stern 1973)

Sibship Sex Ratio ♂ : ♀	Observed Numbers	Expected Sex Ratio Distribution	
		Probability	Numbers
6 : 0	11	p^6 = 0.01858	10.5
5 : 1	64	$6p^5q$ = 0.10514	59.4
4 : 2	129	$15p^4q^2$ = 0.24788	140.0
3 : 3	188	$20p^3q^3$ = 0.31170	176.1
2 : 4	130	$15p^2q^4$ = 0.22046	124.6
1 : 5	41	$6pq^5$ = 0.08317	47.0
0 : 6	2	q^6 = 0.01307	7.4
	565	1.00000	565.0

that these are two different ways of doing the same thing. The probabilities thus derived for eight coins and various numbers of heads appear in Table A.6, and these probability distributions are shown as histograms (plots of the probabilities against the numbers of heads) in Figure A.6. The histograms are binomial probability distributions, and are perfectly symmetrical in this example where p and q both $= 1/2$.

For application of the binomial probability distribution to a problem in biological anthropology, consider part of the extensive data set of Edwards and Fraccaro (1958, quoted in Stern 1973). They studied the sex distribution in sibships from a large number of Swedish ministers who lived at various times between 1585 and 1920. Our goal is to determine whether the number of sibships with various sex ratios actually observed agrees with that which is expected according to the binomial distribution. In other words, are the observed numbers of sibships with different sex ratios in agreement with the theoretical expectation that sibship sex ratio is determined by chance?

Table A.7 shows the sibship sex ratio in families with six children, the observed numbers of each sibship type, and the expected numbers of each. To find the expected numbers, Edwards and Fraccaro divided the total number of male births in their sample (13,400) by the total number of births (26,037) to give the proportion of males (p) = 0.51465. The proportion of females (q) $= 1 - p =$ 0.48535. By multiplying each probability by the number of sibships in this subset (565), the expected numbers for each sibship type are obtained. For sibships with two males and four females, for example, the expected number is

$$15(0.51465)^2(0.48535)^4(565) = 124.6.$$

Inspected visually, the observed and expected numbers are in fairly close agreement. You will probably be curious, however, about the existence of a method for determining if the difference is significant. Indeed there is one, and this example may serve as an initial exposure to one of the most important applications of statistics—the testing of hypotheses. These data will be used later to demonstrate one such statistical test.

The Normal Distribution

The binomial distribution is only one of several probability distributions applicable to discontinuous variables, whereas the normal frequency distribution describes the distribution of continuous variables. Without doubt, it is the most important theoretical probability distribution in statistics. The distribution for any continuous variable may be represented by a continuous curve (Fig. A.7a), where the relative concentration of variates along the X-axis for any given value of the variate is represented by the height of the curve.

To compare the expected and observed frequency distributions, we first arbitrarily divide both into class limits (given by the vertical lines in Figure A.7b). These class limits are arbitrary because all values of a variate are possible in a continuous distribution. The distribution may now be graphed as a histogram (Fig. A.7c). As long as the width of the class limits is identical, the frequency of each class can be determined from the ordinate scale. Expected frequencies may then be derived by calculating the proportions of the areas within the class limits.

The mathematical derivation of the normal frequency distribution is beyond the scope of this discussion, but those so inclined may wish to examine and

Figure A.7 Probability distribution of a continuous variable, represented as a curve, **a,** and a histogram, **c.** See text for explanation.

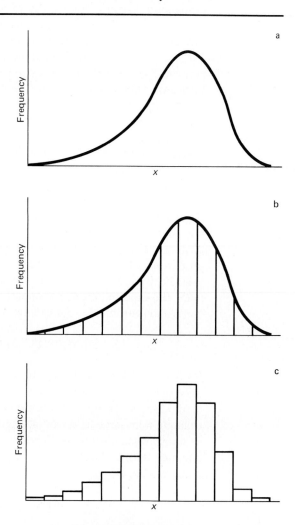

follow the proof by Feller (1957). For descriptive purposes, the intuitive approach of Sokal and Rohlf (1969) may be adopted. Consider the binomial distribution $(p + q)^n$, when n becomes indefinitely large. This is akin to the distribution of a characteristic that relies upon many factors for its expression. Assume that relative skin pigmentation is due to many different factors, each of which may be present or absent in any individual. When present, one factor contributes one unit of pigmentation. If absent, it contributes no unit. Assume also that each factor has an identical effect, and that each factor adds to that of every other: the presence of three of five factors in an individual gives a pigmentation intensity of three units. Finally, assume that each factor has an equal probability of being present, so that p_F (presence of the factor) $= 0.50$ and q_f (absence of the factor) $= 0.50$.

From previous statements, the binomial $(p_F + q_f)$ produces only two classes, one with a pigmentation intensity of one and the other with zero. Each has an expected frequency of 0.50. With two factors, or $(p_F + q_f)^2$, three classes occur:

Pigmentation classes	FF	Ff	ff
Expected frequency	0.25	0.50	0.25
Pigmentation intensity	2	1	0

The expansion may be carried out for as many factors as desired, and the number of classes increases with the number of factors. If five and then ten factors were assumed, the expected frequencies would be those in Table A.8. Furthermore, their associated histograms (Fig. A.8) approach the characteristic shape of the normal frequency distribution. As the number of factors increases toward infinity, the shape of the histogram becomes ever more close to a normal distribution.

Table A.8 Expansion of the Binomial $(p + q)^n$ When $n = 5$ and $n = 10$ (See text for explanation.)

	F	f	Pigmentation Intensity	Expected Frequency
Five factors	5	0	5	0.03125
	4	1	4	0.15625
	3	2	3	0.31250
	2	3	2	0.31250
	1	4	1	0.15625
	0	5	0	0.03125
Ten factors	10	0	10	0.001
	9	1	9	0.010
	8	2	8	0.044
	7	3	7	0.117
	6	4	6	0.205
	5	5	5	0.246
	4	6	4	0.205
	3	7	3	0.117
	2	8	2	0.044
	1	9	1	0.010
	0	10	0	0.001

Figure A.8 Histograms of the expected frequencies (see Table A.8) when a binomial is expanded to the 5th and 10th power.

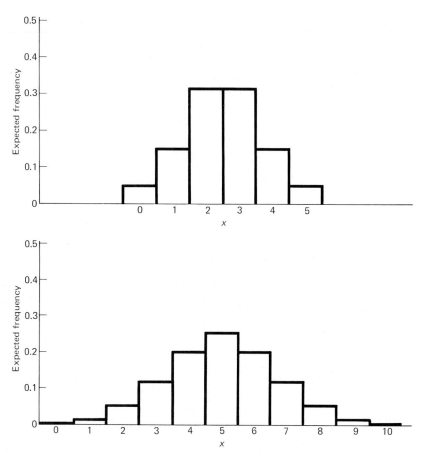

Because the population mean and standard deviation can assume an infinite number of values, an infinite number of normal curves are possible. Figure A.9, for example, illustrates three normal distributions resulting from changes in the mean and standard deviation. Curves A and B have the same means but different standard deviations—their locations on the X-axis are the same, but their shapes are different. Curves A and C have different means but identical standard deviations—their locations are different, but their shapes are the same. This supports what was stated previously about the mean and standard deviation. The former is solely a measure of location and has nothing to do with dispersion. The latter is solely a measure of dispersion and has nothing to do with location.

To illustrate one use of the normal probability distribution, suppose the value of a certain measurement in a distribution is one, two, or even three standard deviations from the mean. What does this mean in terms of probability? Without becoming involved with calculating parts of the area under the curve, the percentage of items lying within certain limits (see also Figure A.10) may be given directly.

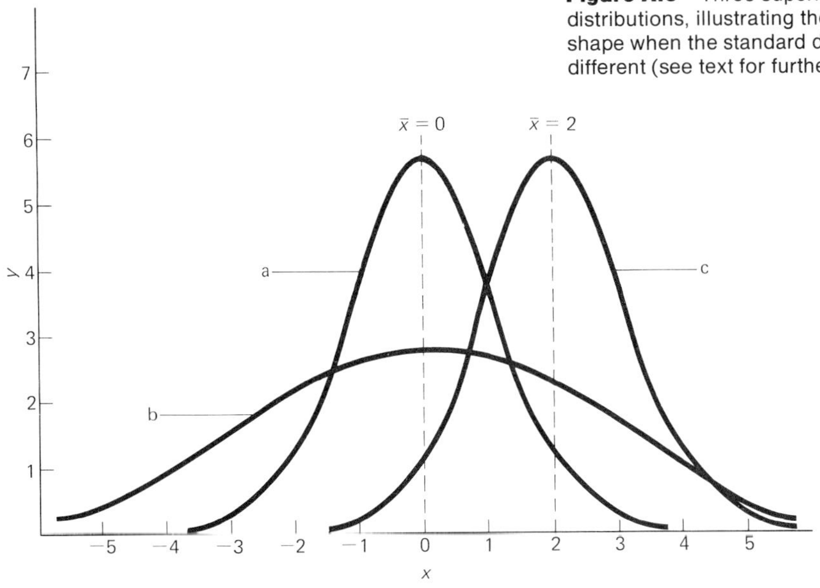

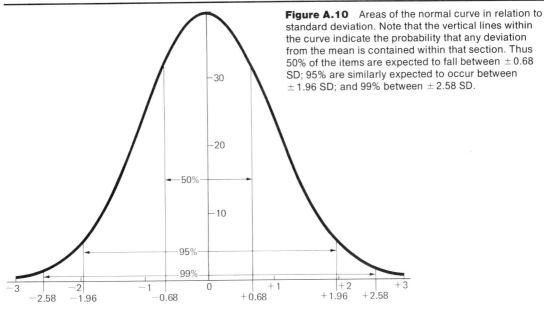

Figure A.9 Three superimposed normal distributions, illustrating the differences in location and shape when the standard deviations and means are different (see text for further explanation).

Figure A.10 Areas of the normal curve in relation to standard deviation. Note that the vertical lines within the curve indicate the probability that any deviation from the mean is contained within that section. Thus 50% of the items are expected to fall between ± 0.68 SD; 95% are similarly expected to occur between ± 1.96 SD; and 99% between ± 2.58 SD.

$\pm 0.674\sigma$ contains 0.50 of the items
$\pm 1.000\sigma$ contains 0.68 of the items
$\pm 1.960\sigma$ contains 0.95 of the items
$\pm 2.000\sigma$ contains 0.955 of the items
$\pm 2.576\sigma$ contains 0.99 of the items
$\pm 3.000\sigma$ contains 0.997 of the items
$\pm 4.000\sigma$ contains 0.9999 of the items

The proportion of the area under the curve that lies outside $\pm 3\sigma$ is very small (0.0027), and even less for $\pm 4\sigma(0.00006)$. This means, in turn, that the probability of a measurement being $\pm 3\sigma$ or 4σ from the mean is so small as to be virtually nonexistent.

The normal probability distribution may be applied to the data on stature and sitting height (Table A.2) on Wisconsin and Alaskan females. It was assumed that the distribution was normal, and we may now check this assumption. Recall (Table A.5) that the values for the standard deviation and the mean for Alaskan stature were 4.35 and 155.7 respectively. We may choose an arbitrary value above the mean but slightly less than the highest observed value, e.g., 163.0 cm, and determine the probability of obtaining an individual this tall or taller.

The difference between 163.0 cm and the mean is 7.3 cm. This difference must be standardized by converting it into a standard deviate. This is done by dividing the difference by the standard deviation, or $7.3/4.35 = 1.68$. Thus a value of 163.0 cm is a standard deviation of 1.68 above the mean. Under the assumption of normality, a value of 0.4535 for a standard deviation of 1.68 is found in Appendix 2, "Table of Areas under the Normal Curve." The area of the curve lying between the mean and a standard deviation point 1.68 above it is therefore 45.35%. Four point sixty-five percent of the area (4.65%) lies above a standard deviation of 1.68. This means that 465 individuals out of 10,000, or nearly 1 in every 20, is expected to be 163.0 cm tall or taller.

Bear in mind that this probability was calculated on only one tail of the distribution. To find the probability of an individual being either shorter or taller by a difference of 7.3 cm from the mean, or deviant by the same amount in both directions, the above probability must be doubled ($2 \times 0.0465 = 0.0930$). Does the sample, then, deviate from normality? As shown later, a probability level of 0.05 (1 in 20) is on the borderline of significance. There is no reason, therefore, to state that Jamison's (1972) sample is not distributed normally. As a matter of fact, only one individual above and one below a standard deviation of 1.68 from the mean occurs in our 20-individual subset from his sample.

When a frequency distribution appears to deviate from normality, however, the type and amount of departure can be measured. Curves that approach normality are often asymmetrical, with one tail sloping more gradually than the other. This is called skewness (S_k). In such a curve, the mode no longer coincides with the mean, as it does in a symmetrical curve. This is because, to repeat, the mean is always affected by outlying values, whereas the mode is not. At the beginning of this appendix, a brief reference was made to positively and negatively skewed distributions. In the former, the right-hand tail slopes more gradually than the left, and in the latter the reverse occurs. Thus in a right-skewed distribution the mean is greater than the median, the most extreme values are to the right of the mean, and the coefficient of skewness is positive. Similarly, the coefficient in a left-skewed distribution is negative (Fig. A.11). The coefficient of skewness is calculated by taking the difference between the mean and mode and dividing this quantity by the standard deviation:

$$S_k = \frac{\overline{X} - (\text{mode})}{s}.$$

Figure A.11 A left–skewed, **a,** and platykurtic, **b,** normal distribution.

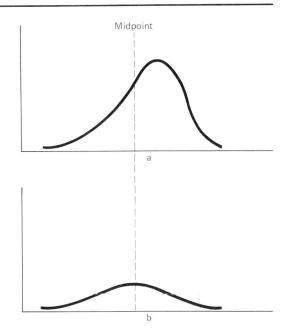

The value of the mode may be closely approximated by

$$3(\text{median}) - 2(\text{mean}).$$

For the Alaskan female stature, the median was given as 155.5 cm, the mean as 155.7 cm, and the standard deviation as 4.35 cm. The mode, as estimated by the above, is $3(155.5) - 2(155.7) = 155.1$. Substituting this in the equation for skewness we obtain

$$S_k = \frac{155.7 - 155.1}{4.35} = +0.14.$$

This moderate, positive skewness indicates that tall individuals in the sample are relatively more common than short ones.

Another departure from normality is kurtosis (K_s), which does not involve symmetry of the curve but, instead, represents the "peakedness" of the distribution (Fig. A.11). When the distribution is neither more peaked nor flatter than a normal curve, the coefficient of kurtosis is zero. When the distribution is more peaked or sharper (leptokurtic) than the normal curve, the value of K_s is positive. When the distribution is flatter (platykurtic) than the normal curve, the value of K_s is negative. The coefficient of kurtosis is given by the equation

$$K_s = \frac{\Sigma(X - \overline{X})^4}{ns^4} - 3.$$

Substituting the values for Alaskan female stature,

$$K_s = \frac{19817.12}{(20)(4.35)^4} - 3 = -0.09.$$

This indicates an almost negligible flattening of the distribution.

Statistical Tests

Until now, terms such as "highly improbable," "very unlikely," "in close agreement with," and "quite similar to," have been used to describe probabilities. It has been suggested that methods are available for determining the statistical significance of differences between data sets. An obvious difference, for example, exists between the means for stature and sitting height from Alaskan and Wisconsin females. An obvious difference exists between the expected and observed numbers of sex ratios in sibships from Table A.7. But are these differences great enough to warrant a search for cause? Or are they so slight as to be produced merely by chance? Visual inspection alone does not give a reliable answer to these questions, and the purpose of this section is to demonstrate a few simple tests that can.

Hypothesis Testing
Like other scientists, biological anthropologists have a specific problem in mind when they gather data, and they choose those observations and measurements that will contribute the most toward solution of the problem. The problem is usually couched in terms of a scientific hypothesis, and one of the most common uses of statistical methods is for hypothesis testing. Hypotheses can arise in many different ways. They may result from speculation or intuition, but more often from repeated observations of regularity in the occurrence of certain phenomena in identical subjects. Scientific investigations are often organized around a "working" hypothesis, which guides the investigator as to the most reasonable course of inquiry. This may lead to formulation of a "test" hypothesis, which relates to the final solution of the problem. Statistical testing determines whether a particular hypothesis is to be rejected, revised, or not rejected.

To reach an objective decision about a hypothesis, a series of procedural steps may be outlined similar to that of Siegel (1956) and others.

1. State the null hypothesis (H_0). Basically, H_0 is a hypothesis of no difference. It assumes no real difference between an observed and theoretical value in the population; it assumes that populations are the same unless a significant difference is demonstrated. Rejection of the null hypothesis may lead to a test of an alternative hypothesis (H_1). There are two kinds of errors in conjunction with nonrejection or rejection of H_0. If a true null hypothesis is rejected, a Type I error is committed. Acceptance of a false null hypothesis results in a Type II error. Obviously, acceptance of a true or rejection of a false H_0 are both correct decisions.

2. Specify the significance level. In other words, state the allowable amount of Type I error. Type I error (denoted by a) is also called the significance

level when expressed as a percentage. When $a = 0.05$ or 0.01, for example, the significance level is at 5% or 1% for a given trial. The choice of a probability level for rejection of H_0 is a matter of some subjectivity, but in nearly all biological work it has been set at 0.05 probability. Thus a hypothesis is rejected (meaning that the difference between the samples tested is statistically significant) if the probability is 0.05 or less. If it is 0.05 or greater, the hypothesis is generally not rejected. This, of course, neither proves nor disproves the hypothesis but, instead, expresses a degree of confidence in the results.

For mean stature in Alaskan and Wisconsin females, H_0 assumes that the two populations are the same for this variable. When we test H_0 (by a method to be discussed shortly), however, the probability of the distribution being the same and getting such different samples is unlikely—less than one time in a hundred. The null hypothesis is therefore rejected, and the difference between mean stature in the two samples is statistically significant.

Why has the 0.05 level, or one Type I error in 20 trials, become the standard as opposed to another level? After all, the 0.10 level still represents a fairly slim probability. I can give no convincing answer but, instead, offer a highly relevant quote from Simpson et al.:

> It not infrequently happens that an author, using the 5 per cent probability value as a criterion for rejection of a hypothesis, will reject one hypothesis under which the observations had a probability of 4 per cent while accepting another, the observations for which had a probability of 6 per cent, without disclosing these probability values. Having chosen the 5 per cent level for rejection, this procedure is perfectly correct logically, but abhorrent biologically. On such slender threads hang many theories! (1960:174)

3. Choose an appropriate statistical test and, based upon the data in the respective samples, compute the value and find the associated probability level. Complete descriptions of all available tests are not appropriate for this appendix, but many can be found in the elementary textbooks by Dixon and Massey (1969), Simpson et al. (1960), Siegel (1956), Snedecor and Cochran (1967), and Sokal and Rohlf (1969). A few tests are described below to illustrate how both discontinuous and continuous variables may be treated.

Comparisons of Sample Means

It was stated that the difference between Alaskan and Wisconsin female mean stature was significant at $p < 0.01$. This was determined by a well-known method called the "t-test." All that is needed for this test are the sample size, mean, and standard deviation for both samples.

	Mean	**n**	**s**
First sample	$\overline{X}_1$	n_1	s_1
Second sample	$\overline{X}_2$	n_2	s_2

The rather formidable-appearing but, nonetheless, simple expression

$$t = \frac{(\overline{X}_1 - \overline{X}_2)}{\sqrt{[((n_1 - 1)s^2_1 + (n_2 - 1)s^2_2)/(n_1 + n_2 - 2)](n_1 + n_2/n_1 n_2)}}$$

is the formula for the t-test, and the degrees of freedom are calculated as $n_1 + n_2 - 2$.

Degrees of freedom represent the number of independently variable classes, or, in other words, the number of items which are free to vary independently. To estimate variance from a sample of ten measurements, for example, the difference between the sample mean and each measurement would be obtained. The mean could remain the same even if nine of the ten measurements differed, but given the mean and these values, the tenth measurement would have a fixed value. Since this value is not free to vary, one degree of freedom is taken from the mean. If one deals with classes, as in the case of the Chi-square test (see "Analysis of Frequencies," below), then when the number of one class is set, the other is automatically determined. In general, degrees of freedom for statistical tests dealing with classes are determined as one less than the total number of classes. This is not an inviolable rule, however, and attention should be given to the formulas by which degrees of freedom are calculated for particular statistical tests.

To derive the value of t, let the Wisconsin females represent the first sample and Alaskan females the second. Substituting the respective values on stature in the equation, we obtain

$$t = \frac{(162.9 - 155.7)}{\sqrt{[((20 - 1)(36.25) + (20 - 1)(18.88))/(20 + 20 - 2)][(20 + 20)/(20)(20)]}}$$

$$= 4.337.$$

To find the probability associated with $t = 4.337$, turn to Appendix 3 ("Table for t-Test of Significance between Two Sample Means"). At the far left of the table is the column for degrees of freedom (d.f.) and at the top are probability values ranging from 0.9 to 0.01. The body of the table consists of columns of values under each probability level. The degrees of freedom for the present example are $20 + 20 - 2 = 38$. Since the column goes only to 30, we use ∞ (the symbol for infinity) because there are more than 30 d.f. in the present case.

Note that in all rows the values increase as the probabilities decrease. When $t = 2.228$ with 10 d.f., $p = 0.05$ and the difference is significant (recall the 5% level); when $t = 2.490$ with 25 d.f., the difference is significant at $p < 0.02$ but > 0.01; and in the present example where $t = 4.337$ with ∞ d.f., the difference is significant ($p < 0.01$) because 4.337 is much greater than 2.57582. The null hypothesis is therefore rejected.

You should bear in mind that the expression for the t-test just outlined assumes no significant difference in the variances of the two samples. Methods for determining equality of variances may be found, e.g., in Sokal and Rohlf (1969). Other forms of the t-test are used for certain problems. When sample sizes are equal, the equation is simplified, and degrees of freedom calculated as above.

$$t = \frac{(\bar{X}_1 - \bar{X}_2)}{\sqrt{(1/n)(s^2_1 + s^2_2)}}$$

When sample sizes are large but unequal, degrees of freedom are given by $2(n - 1)$ and the following equation is used:

$$t = \frac{(\overline{X}_1 - \overline{X}_2)}{\sqrt{(s^2_1/n_2) + (s^2_2/n_1)}}.$$

Another special case arises when an investigator wishes to compare a single specimen to a sample rather than one sample to another. Usually this is done to determine the probability that the specimen belongs to a particular biological population. The test involves another simplified version of the first equation given above. Since the single variate neither adds to the degrees of freedom (calculated therefore as $n_2 - 1$), nor does it usually contribute to the estimate of the within group variance, the formula becomes

$$t = \frac{\overline{X}_1 - \overline{X}_2}{s_2 \sqrt{(n_2 + 1)/n_2}}.$$

One limitation of the t-test is that it can be used only when two samples, or a specimen and a sample, are being compared. Biological anthropologists, however, often study characteristics affected by a number of factors that vary simultaneously. Hence a general test is needed which, in one operation, (1) tests the differences among several populations and (2) assigns the relative roles to the factors that affect the characteristic. Such a test is called the "analysis of variance." Although the concepts and mathematical ability for learning the method do not go too far beyond what has already been given, it is preferable here to describe the meaning of the technique rather than its formulation.

It was emphasized in earlier chapters that continuous variables are due to complex interactions between factors in the external environment and their interplay with equally complex factors interacting in the internal environment—the heredity of the individual. It is inconceivable that we could ever completely describe all interactions between environmental and genetic variables affecting, for example, human body weight. Every individual is genetically unique (barring identical twins), hence the interactions between environmental factors and their subsequent effect on body weight will vary slightly from one individual to the next. This is not to say that efforts to uncover the major factors and their relative importance in the determination of body weight are doomed from the start. To the contrary, these sorts of studies constitute a viable aspect of biological anthropology.

It is known that various environmental factors, such as nutrition, lead to considerable variation in body weight, while other external factors—perhaps available sunlight—have little or no appreciable effect. Through analysis of variance, it is possible to gain a probability statement of how much of the variation among observations is due to variation in the environmental variables that affect body weight. Nearly all good elementary textbooks on biometry devote considerable space to the method and its meaning, and the importance of mastering this statistic through outside reading and work cannot be overemphasized.

Analysis of Frequencies

The descriptions of statistical tests have thus far been limited to analysis of continuous variables. Methods like the t-test, however, are not applicable to discontinuous variables and attributes. Different techniques are used for analysis of discontinuous variables, although the questions and problems arising from the study of these variables often parallel those concerning continuous variables. We might wish to know the "goodness-of-fit" between an observed and hypothetical frequency distribution, as mentioned earlier in the discussion of the binomial distribution (Table A.7). We often want to determine the significance of the difference between attribute frequencies from two or more samples. We often need to determine association between two or more attributes. In various forms, a test statistic called Chi-square (χ^2) is utilized more widely than any other single measure to answer these sorts of questions.

When dealing with frequency data, such as gene frequencies of the various blood groups, the basic form of χ^2 is

$$\chi^2 = \sum \frac{(o - e)^2}{e},$$

where o = the observed and e = the expected numbers for certain classes in the sample. What is a class? If you happened to be studying the MN blood group system, for example, then each of the three possible blood types (M, MN, and N) would constitute a class. The above formula tells you to find the difference between o and e, square this difference and divide it by the expected number, and obtain χ^2 by summing all class values. The χ^2 distribution may be found in Appendix 4 ("Table of Chi-Square"). Similar to the t-distribution, the χ^2 distribution depends upon degrees of freedom. As χ^2 values in the body of the table increase for any numbers of degrees of freedom, the probabilities decrease. Thus the null hypothesis is usually rejected for comparisons when the χ^2 value has an associated probability level of 0.05 or less.

For a test of goodness-of-fit, review Table A.7, where the expected sex distribution of six-children sibships was obtained by the binomial theorem. Does the observed distribution fit the expected distribution, which represents the theoretical expectation that sex of the children is determined by chance? In Table A.9 the data necessary for the calculation are repeated, in addition to the calculated χ^2 value.

Table A.9 Observed and Expected Sibship Sex Ratios in a Sample of 565 Sibships of Six Children (From Stern 1973.)

Sibship Sex Ratio ♂ : ♀	Observed Numbers	Expected Numbers	$\frac{(o - e)^2}{e}$
6 : 0	11	10.5	0.024
5 : 1	64	59.4	0.356
4 : 2	129	140.0	0.864
3 : 3	188	176.1	0.804
2 : 4	130	124.6	0.234
1 : 5	41	47.0	0.766
0 : 6	2	7.4	3.941
	565	565.0	6.989

$\chi^2 = 6.989$, with 5 d.f., $P > 0.2$

For this example, the degrees of freedom are calculated as $a - 2 = 5$, where a refers to the total number of classes. To find the probability level corresponding to $\chi^2 = 6.989$, look in the "n" column in Appendix 4 under 5 degrees of freedom and follow the row to the right until you find 6.064 and 7.289. Since 6.989 falls between these two values, the probability is between 0.3 and 0.2, and the null hypothesis is not rejected. In other words, the difference between the expected and observed distributions of sex ratios in these sibships is not statistically significant.

You may have noticed in Table A.9 that the last class contributes the most (3.941) to the χ^2 value. Although the calculations are correct, expected numbers less than 5 are usually avoided by lumping classes at the end of the distribution when $o = 5$ or less for any class at either tail. For example, in the hypothetical distribution

o		e	
$\left.\begin{array}{c} 2 \\ 15 \end{array}\right\}$ 17		$\left.\begin{array}{c} 5 \\ 13 \end{array}\right\}$ 18	
21		22	
37		34	
19		20	
$\left.\begin{array}{c} 13 \\ 4 \end{array}\right\}$ 17		$\left.\begin{array}{c} 12 \\ 6 \end{array}\right\}$ 18	

the first two contiguous classes would be lumped and, correspondingly, the last two would also be lumped. The degrees of freedom are calculated after lumping, i.e., $a - 2 = 3$.

The χ^2 test and distribution are frequently used in a different manner to clarify problems concerning the relationships between two or more sets of observations. This is usually termed association (or, sometimes, lack of independence), which may be described as the relationship between two different sets of observations that occur together more often than can be due solely to chance. The simplest example of association involves two categories for each set of observations. A typical, but purely hypothetical, problem might involve the determination of the association between freckles and sex. Assume the categories of observations and their respective numbers are

a. girls with freckles ($n = 15$)
b. girls without freckles ($n = 20$)
c. boys with freckles ($n = 14$)
d. boys without freckles ($n = 35$)

Obviously, the percentage of girls with freckles is considerably higher than that of boys with freckles. However, does this represent an association significantly different from zero?

This may be tested by arranging the data in a contingency table (Table A.10), which is a set of cells giving the respective frequencies for each set of observations. The theoretical frequencies for each cell may be calculated from the marginal totals according to the following formulas:

Cell	Theoretical frequency
a	$A = \dfrac{(a + b)(a + c)}{n} = \dfrac{(35)(29)}{84} = 12.08$
b	$B = \dfrac{(a + b)(b + d)}{n} = \dfrac{(35)(55)}{84} = 22.92$
c	$C = \dfrac{(c + d)(a + c)}{n} = \dfrac{(49)(29)}{84} = 16.92$
d	$D = \dfrac{(c + d)(b + d)}{n} = \dfrac{(49)(55)}{84} = 32.08$

These theoretical numbers may be compared with the observed numbers in each cell by χ^2 to test for significance in the association

$$\chi^2 = \frac{(15 - 12.08)^2}{12.08} + \frac{(20 - 22.92)^2}{22.92} + \frac{(14 - 16.92)^2}{16.92} + \frac{(35 - 32.08)^2}{32.08}$$

$$= 1.847, \text{ with one d.f., } P > 0.1.$$

Notice that only a single degree of freedom was used for this example. For any contingency table, degrees of freedom are calculated as $(r - 1)(c - 1)$ where r = the number of rows, and c the number of columns in the table. For a 4×3 table, for example, the degrees of freedom would be $(4 - 1)(3 - 1) = 6$.

In most cases the only reason for deriving the expected frequencies is to calculate the value of χ^2. If the expected frequencies are needed only for this reason, they need not be derived, because χ^2 can be found by a simplified formula that uses the observed data directly.

$$\chi^2 = \frac{(ad - bc)^2 n}{(a + b)(c + d)(a + c)(b + d)}.$$

Table A.10 A Contingency Table of a Hypothetical Sample of the Numbers of Boys and Girls With and Without Freckles

	With Freckles	Without Freckles	Totals
Girls	a (15)	b (20)	$a + b$ (35)
Boys	c (14)	d (35)	$c + d$ (49)
Totals	$a + c$ (29)	$b + d$ (55)	n (84)

Substituting the observed values from Table A.10,

$$\chi^2 = \frac{[(15)(35) - (20)(14)]^2(84)}{(35)(49)(29)(55)} = 1.843.$$

The difference between the earlier value (1.847) and 1.843 is due to the the effects of rounding the expected frequencies in the former case. By either method, however, the associated probability is considerably higher than the 0.05 significance level. Although initial inspection of the data might lead to the hypothesis that the association between girls and freckles differs significantly from zero, the null hypothesis cannot be rejected on the basis of this sample. It must be stressed again that nothing has been proven either way by this test. To the extent that an apparent trend might exist, further analysis with increased sample sizes and additional samples from other populations would be especially illuminating.

Comments on Correlation and Regression

It has been shown how the association between two or more discontinuous variables can be determined, but it should be apparent that these methods are not suitable for similar problems dealing with continuous variables. How, then, can the nature of the relationship between two or more continuous variables be investigated? For example, is there a relationship between stature and weight in some particular population for either sex? Do tall males tend to be heavier than short males, and if so, is the relationship linear (straight line) or curved? In either case, is it possible to predict the increase in weight expected for a particular unit increase in stature? Indeed it is—by regression analysis.

But people are extremely diverse in their sizes and shapes, and it is not uncommon for a six-foot male to weigh less than a male six inches shorter from the same population. Of what value, then, is the prediction? Is there a way to generate a numerical term that reflects the intensity of the relationship between two covarying variables? Again there is—by correlation analysis.

These two aspects of problems dealing with relationships between two continuous variables—their functional relationship and the degree of their covariation—may appear to be closely interrelated, inasmuch as their mathematical relations are very close (Sokal and Rohlf 1969). However, an important point is that problems in correlation are not the same as those in regression. When one speaks of 100% correlation between two variables (which, incidentally, almost never occurs in anthropological data), one is stating that the two variables interact (covary) in the same manner all the time. Correlation coefficients, usually designated by r, may range from 1 to some fraction of 1, e.g., 0.95, which means that the intensity of association between the two variables is 95%. Coefficients may be zero, meaning that no association exists. They may also be negative, meaning that as the value of one variate increases, the value of the other decreases.

It has been stated that regression analysis may serve a predictive function. Given unit increases in the length of various long bones in individuals from known populations, their stature may be predicted (Trotter and Gleser 1958; Genovés

1966). Given age and certain anthropometric measurements of mothers in a Peruvian highland population, the percentage of offspring that will survive in tall versus short mothers can be predicted (Frisancho et al. 1973).

To derive a linear regression equation from the data in Table A.11, assume intuitively that some form of functional relationship exists between leg length and stature—as stature increases, leg length also increases. This can be shown graphically (Fig. A.12) by plotting the values of one variate against the other to produce a scatter diagram. Note that each dot represents the measurements of both stature and leg length in a single individual. Note also that by convention, X (in this case, stature) is the independent variable, and Y (leg length) the dependent variable. This means that the value of Y depends upon the value of X (which is free to vary), and that for any value of X, the corresponding value of Y may be predicted.

Because the dots in the scatter diagram tend to be arranged in a linear fashion from the lower left-hand corner to the upper right-hand corner, we suspect that the two variables possess a linear relationship. When this happens to be the case, then the following equation expresses this relationship:

$$Y = a_y + b_{yx}X.$$

The symbol a represents the Y-intercept, i.e., the value of variate Y when variate X = zero. The symbol b is the slope of the line, and is termed the regression coefficient. It possesses the subscript yx to denote the regression of variate Y on variate X. A brief examination of the equation indicates that, for any value of X, only the regression coefficient and the Y-intercept are required to obtain the corresponding value of Y.

Computation of a regression equation requires the quantities below:

n (sample size)
$\sum X$ (sum of the X variates)
$\sum X^2$ (sum of the squared X variates)
$\sum Y$ (sum of the Y variates)
$\sum Y^2$ (sum of the squared Y variates)
$\sum XY$ (sum of the products of the two variates)
$\overline{X}$ (mean of the X variates)
$\overline{Y}$ (mean of the Y variates)

Obtaining these quantities manually when n is fairly large is both prohibitively tedious and highly prone to arithmetic errors. With a desk calculator, on the other hand, they may be calculated rapidly and accurately. When these values have been derived, they are substituted into the equations below to give the regression coefficient and the Y-intercept, respectively.

$$b_{yx} = \frac{\sum XY - (\sum X \sum Y/n)}{\sum X^2 - [(\sum X)^2/n]}$$

$$a = \overline{Y} - b_{yx}\overline{X}$$

Table A.11 Measurements of Stature and Leg Length on 66 Adult Males from New York City (Data supplied by R. H. Osborne.)

Stature	Leg Length	Stature	Leg Length	Stature	Leg Length
156.0 cm	70.7 cm	171.3 cm	82.0 cm	177.7 cm	85.4 cm
159.0	75.2	171.4	79.8	178.7	86.4
160.9	75.4	171.4	81.3	178.8	85.1
163.7	76.3	171.6	82.4	179.1	87.2
164.2	81.0	171.7	81.3	179.3	86.5
164.7	75.5	171.9	81.7	179.4	82.7
166.0	78.5	173.1	79.9	179.7	87.8
166.3	75.6	173.2	80.4	179.8	86.3
167.0	80.7	173.2	81.2	180.2	87.6
167.5	78.0	173.2	83.4	180.3	86.4
167.8	83.2	173.2	84.5	180.7	85.6
167.9	77.7	173.6	82.8	181.0	87.4
168.3	79.5	174.1	82.6	181.6	91.0
168.5	79.4	174.3	81.0	182.8	90.2
168.5	79.7	174.4	84.2	183.0	87.7
169.0	82.2	174.4	86.2	183.0	92.0
169.3	81.8	174.9	82.9	183.4	89.2
169.4	81.6	175.6	83.7	185.4	90.3
169.5	81.8	176.4	83.2	185.4	90.6
170.5	80.2	176.5	83.9	186.9	91.4
170.6	83.9	177.3	82.9	188.5	89.7
171.2	81.8	177.4	87.2	199.3	97.2

Figure A.12 A scatter diagram of the data on leg lengths (Y-axis) and stature (X-axis) from Table A.11.

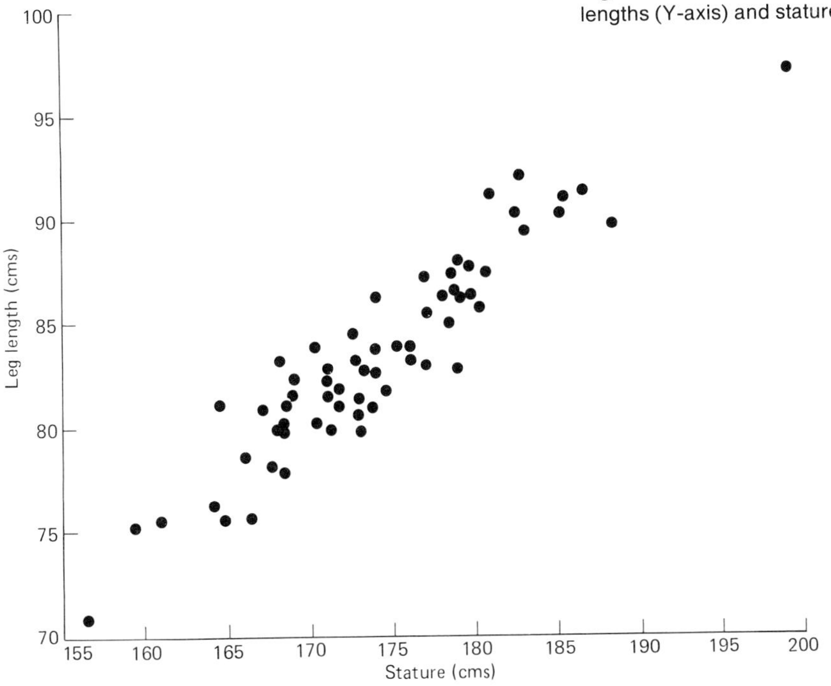

493

From the data in Table A.11

$$n = 66 \qquad \sum Y^2 = 460107.49$$
$$\sum X = 11503.9 \qquad \sum XY = 961146.31$$
$$\sum X^2 = 2008774.27 \qquad \overline{X} = 174.3015$$
$$\sum Y = 5501.9 \qquad \overline{Y} = 83.3621.$$

Substituting these into the formulas above, we obtain

$$b_{yx} = 0.5946$$
$$a = -20.2776.$$

And, substituting the values of the slope and Y-intercept into the regression equation $Y = a_y + b_{yx}X$,

$$Y = -20.2776 + 0.5946X.$$

A predicted value of Y for any given value of X may now be easily obtained. For example, if $X = 150.0$ cm, then $Y = -20.2776 + 0.5946\,(150.0) = 68.9$. Furthermore, a line can now be fitted to the scatter diagram in Figure A.12. Choose two arbitrary values for X (stature), e.g., 150.0 cm and 200.0 cm. Both of these values are outside the observed range of the values in Table A.11, but they need not be. Substituting 150.0 cm and 200.0 cm into the equation, $Y = -20.2776 + 0.5946\,X$, we obtain respectively 68.9 cm and 98.6 cm. To find the regression line, plot the values (when $X = 150.0$, $Y = 68.9$, and when $X = 200$, $Y = 98.6$) and draw a straight line between the two points. The line, incidentally, will pass through the point represented by $\overline{X}, \overline{Y}$ (Fig. A.13).

A regression line has been derived for leg length on stature from a sample of New York males. Given the stature of any male from this population, his leg length can be predicted with a high degree of accuracy. Without going into the derivation, suffice it to state that the correlation coefficient $r = 0.94$.

The reasons for performing a regression analysis can vary, but suppose the main purpose was to test the hypothesis that the relationship between leg length and stature in New York males was significantly different from that in Oregon males, and that this difference was somehow related functionally to a genetic or environmental variable. In other words, do New York males have shorter (or longer) legs, relative to stature, than Oregon males? By comparing the regression coefficients for the two samples, the significance of the difference can easily be determined (the method may be found in Simpson et al. 1960) and appropriate judgments made about the hypothesis.

Only the briefest introduction to regression analysis has been given here. The procedures for significance tests between coefficients, calculation of confidence intervals, estimation of values of X from Y, testing for curvilinear regression by orthogonal polynomials, and much more have been intentionally omitted. The main purpose has been to indicate a problem where regression analysis is applicable. It is a most valuable tool for the biological anthropologist, and those of you with an interest in data analysis are urged to pursue this topic further.

Figure A.13 The scatter diagram as presented in Figure A.12, with a regression line fitted according to the methods outlined in the text.

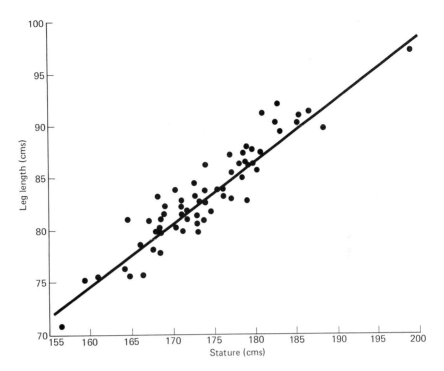

Appendix 2
Table of Areas Under the Normal Curve

Table of Areas Under the Normal Curve (From F. James Rohlf and Robert R. Sokal, *Statistical Tables,* W. H. Freeman and Co. Copyright © 1969.)

Standard Deviation Units	0	1	2	3	4	5	6	7	8	9	Standard Deviation Units
0.0	.0000	.0040	.0080	.0120	.0160	.0199	.0239	.0279	.0319	.0359	0.0
0.1	.0398	.0438	.0478	.0517	.0557	.0596	.0636	.0675	.0714	.0753	0.1
0.2	.0793	.0832	.0871	.0910	.0948	.0987	.1026	.1064	.1103	.1141	0.2
0.3	.1179	.1217	.1255	.1293	.1331	.1368	.1406	.1443	.1480	.1517	0.3
0.4	.1554	.1591	.1628	.1664	.1700	.1736	.1772	.1808	.1844	.1879	0.4
0.5	.1915	.1950	.1985	.2019	.2054	.2088	.2123	.2157	.2190	.2224	0.5
0.6	.2257	.2291	.2324	.2357	.2389	.2422	.2454	.2486	.2517	.2549	0.6
0.7	.2580	.2611	.2642	.2673	.2704	.2734	.2764	.2794	.2823	.2852	0.7
0.8	.2881	.2910	.2939	.2967	.2995	.3023	.3051	.3078	.3106	.3133	0.8
0.9	.3159	.3186	.3212	.3238	.3264	.3289	.3315	.3340	.3365	.3389	0.9
1.0	.3413	.3438	.3461	.3485	.3508	.3531	.3554	.3577	.3599	.3621	1.0
1.1	.3643	.3665	.3686	.3708	.3729	.3749	.3770	.3790	.3810	.3830	1.1
1.2	.3849	.3869	.3888	.3907	.3925	.3944	.3962	.3980	.3997	.4015	1.2
1.3	.4032	.4049	.4066	.4082	.4099	.4115	.4131	.4147	.4162	.4177	1.3
1.4	.4192	.4207	.4222	.4236	.4251	.4265	.4279	.4292	.4306	.4319	1.4
1.5	.4332	.4345	.4357	.4370	.4382	.4394	.4406	.4418	.4429	.4441	1.5
1.6	.4452	.4463	.4474	.4484	.4495	.4505	.4515	.4525	.4535	.4545	1.6
1.7	.4554	.4564	.4573	.4582	.4591	.4599	.4608	.4616	.4625	.4633	1.7
1.8	.4641	.4649	.4656	.4664	.4671	.4678	.4686	.4693	.4699	.4706	1.8
1.9	.4713	.4719	.4726	.4732	.4738	.4744	.4750	.4756	.4761	.4767	1.9
2.0	.4772	.4778	.4783	.4788	.4793	.4798	.4803	.4808	.4812	.4817	2.0
2.1	.4821	.4826	.4830	.4834	.4838	.4842	.4846	.4850	.4854	.4857	2.1
2.2	.4861	.4864	.4868	.4871	.4875	.4878	.4881	.4884	.4887	.4890	2.2
2.3	.4893	.4896	.4898	.4901	.4904	.4906	.4909	.4911	.4913	.4916	2.3
2.4	.4918	.4920	.4922	.4925	.4927	.4929	.4931	.4932	.4934	.4936	2.4
2.5	.4938	.4940	.4941	.4943	.4945	.4946	.4948	.4949	.4951	.4952	2.5
2.6	.4953	.4955	.4956	.4957	.4959	.4960	.4961	.4962	.4963	.4964	2.6
2.7	.4965	.4966	.4967	.4968	.4969	.4970	.4971	.4972	.4973	.4974	2.7
2.8	.4974	.4975	.4976	.4977	.4977	.4978	.4979	.4979	.4980	.4981	2.8
2.9	.4981	.4982	.4982	.4983	.4984	.4984	.4985	.4985	.4986	.4986	2.9

Standard Deviation Units	0	1	2	3	4	5	6	7	8	9	Standard Deviation Units
3.0	.4987	.4987	.4987	.4988	.4988	.4989	.4989	.4989	.4990	.4990	3.0
3.1	.4990	.4991	.4991	.4991	.4992	.4992	.4992	.4992	.4993	.4993	3.1
3.2	.4993	.4993	.4994	.4994	.4994	.4994	.4994	.4995	.4995	.4995	3.2
3.3	.4995	.4995	.4995	.4996	.4996	.4996	.4996	.4996	.4996	.4997	3.3
3.4	.4997	.4997	.4997	.4997	.4997	.4997	.4997	.4997	.4997	.4998	3.4
3.5	.499767										
3.6	.499869										
3.7	.499892										
3.8	.499928										
3.9	.499952										
4.0	.499968										
4.1	.499979										
4.2	.499987										
4.3	.499991										
4.4	.499995										
4.5	.499997										
4.6	.499998										
4.7	.499999										
4.8	.499999										
4.9	.500000										

Appendix 3
Table for *t*–Test of Significance Between Two Sample Means

Table for *t*-Test of Significance Between Two Sample Means (Reprinted with permission of Macmillan Publishing Co., Inc., from *Statistical Methods for Research Workers*, 14th Ed. by R. A. Fisher. Copyright © 1970, University of Adelaide.)

n	P = .9	.8	.7	.6	.5	.4
1	.158	.325	.510	.727	1.000	1.376
2	.142	.289	.445	.617	.816	1.061
3	.137	.277	.424	.584	.765	.978
4	.134	.271	.414	.569	.741	.941
5	.132	.267	.408	.559	.727	.920
6	.131	.265	.404	.553	.718	.906
7	.130	.263	.402	.549	.711	.896
8	.130	.262	.399	.546	.706	.889
9	.129	.261	.398	.543	.703	.883
10	.129	.260	.397	.542	.700	.879
11	.129	.260	.396	.540	.697	.876
12	.128	.259	.395	.539	.695	.873
13	.128	.259	.394	.538	.694	.870
14	.128	.258	.393	.537	.692	.868
15	.128	.258	.393	.536	.691	.866
16	.128	.258	.392	.535	.690	.865
17	.128	.257	.392	.534	.689	.863
18	.127	.257	.392	.534	.688	.862
19	.127	.257	.391	.533	.688	.861
20	.127	.257	.391	.533	.687	.860
21	.127	.257	.391	.532	.686	.859
22	.127	.256	.390	.532	.686	.858
23	.127	.256	.390	.532	.685	.858
24	.127	.256	.390	.531	.685	.857
25	.127	.256	.390	.531	.684	.856
26	.127	.256	.390	.531	.684	.856
27	.127	.256	.389	.531	.684	.855
28	.127	.256	.389	.530	.683	.855
29	.127	.256	.389	.530	.683	.854
30	.127	.256	.389	.530	.683	.854
∞	.12566	.25335	.38532	.52440	.67449	.84162

.3	.2	.1	.05	.02	.01
1.963	3.078	6.314	12.706	31.821	63.657
1.386	1.886	2.920	4.303	6.965	9.925
1.250	1.638	2.353	3.182	4.541	5.841
1.190	1.533	2.132	2.776	3.747	4.604
1.156	1.476	2.015	2.571	3.365	4.032
1.134	1.440	1.943	2.447	3.143	3.707
1.119	1.415	1.895	2.365	2.998	3.499
1.108	1.397	1.860	2.306	2.896	3.355
1.100	1.383	1.833	2.262	2.821	3.250
1.093	1.372	1.812	2.228	2.764	3.169
1.088	1.363	1.796	2.201	2.718	3.106
1.083	1.356	1.782	2.179	2.681	3.055
1.079	1.350	1.771	2.160	2.650	3.012
1.076	1.345	1.761	2.145	2.624	2.977
1.074	1.341	1.753	2.131	2.602	2.947
1.071	1.337	1.746	2.120	2.583	2.921
1.069	1.333	1.740	2.110	2.567	2.898
1.067	1.330	1.734	2.101	2.552	2.878
1.066	1.328	1.729	2.093	2.539	2.861
1.064	1.325	1.725	2.086	2.528	2.845
1.063	1.323	1.721	2.080	2.518	2.831
1.061	1.321	1.717	2.074	2.508	2.819
1.060	1.319	1.714	2.069	2.500	2.807
1.059	1.318	1.711	2.064	2.492	2.797
1.058	1.316	1.708	2.060	2.485	2.787
1.058	1.315	1.706	2.056	2.479	2.779
1.057	1.314	1.703	2.052	2.473	2.771
1.056	1.313	1.701	2.048	2.467	2.763
1.055	1.311	1.699	2.045	2.462	2.756
1.055	1.310	1.697	2.042	2.457	2.750
1.03643	1.28155	1.64485	1.95996	2.32634	2.57582

Appendix 4
Table of Chi–Square

Table of Chi-Square (Reprinted with permission of Macmillan Publishing Co., Inc., from *Statistical Methods for Research Workers,* 14th Ed. by R. A. Fisher. Copyright © 1970, University of Adelaide.)

n*	P = .99	.98	.95	.90	.80	.70
1	.000157	.000628	.00393	.0158	.0642	.148
2	.0201	.0404	.103	.211	.446	.713
3	.115	.185	.352	.584	1.005	1.424
4	.297	.429	.711	1.064	1.649	2.195
5	.554	.752	1.145	1.610	2.343	3.000
6	.872	1.134	1.635	2.204	3.070	3.828
7	1.239	1.564	2.167	2.833	3.822	4.671
8	1.646	2.032	2.733	3.490	4.594	5.527
9	2.088	2.532	3.325	4.168	5.380	6.393
10	2.558	3.059	3.940	4.865	6.179	7.267
11	3.053	3.609	4.575	5.578	6.989	8.148
12	3.571	4.178	5.226	6.304	7.807	9.034
13	4.107	4.765	5.892	7.042	8.634	9.926
14	4.660	5.368	6.571	7.790	9.467	10.821
15	5.229	5.985	7.261	8.547	10.307	11.721
16	5.812	6.614	7.962	9.312	11.152	12.624
17	6.408	7.255	8.672	10.085	12.002	13.531
18	7.015	7.906	9.390	10.865	12.857	14.440
19	7.633	8.567	10.117	11.651	13.716	15.352
20	8.260	9.237	10.851	12.443	14.578	16.266
21	8.897	9.915	11.591	13.240	15.445	17.182
22	9.542	10.600	12.338	14.041	16.314	18.101
23	10.196	11.293	13.091	14.848	17.187	19.021
24	10.856	11.992	13.848	15.659	18.062	19.943
25	11.524	12.697	14.611	16.473	18.940	20.867
26	12.198	13.409	15.379	17.292	19.820	21.792
27	12.879	14.125	16.151	18.114	20.703	22.719
28	13.565	14.847	16.928	18.939	21.588	23.647
29	14.256	15.574	17.708	19.768	22.475	24.577
30	14.953	16.306	18.493	20.599	23.364	25.508

n* = degrees of freedom.

.50	.30	.20	.10	.05	.02	.01
.455	1.074	1.642	2.706	3.841	5.412	6.635
1.386	2.408	3.219	4.605	5.991	7.824	9.210
2.366	3.665	4.642	6.251	7.815	9.837	11.345
3.357	4.878	5.989	7.779	9.488	11.668	13.277
4.351	6.064	7.289	9.236	11.070	13.388	15.086
5.348	7.231	8.558	10.645	12.592	15.033	16.812
6.346	8.383	9.803	12.017	14.067	16.622	18.475
7.344	9.524	11.030	13.362	15.507	18.168	20.090
8.343	10.656	12.242	14.684	16.919	19.679	21.666
9.342	11.781	13.442	15.987	18.307	21.161	23.209
10.341	12.899	14.631	17.275	19.675	22.618	24.725
11.340	14.011	15.812	18.549	21.026	24.054	26.217
12.340	15.119	16.985	19.812	22.362	25.472	27.688
13.339	16.222	18.151	21.064	23.685	26.873	29.141
14.339	17.322	19.311	22.307	24.996	28.259	30.578
15.338	18.418	20.465	23.542	26.296	29.633	32.000
16.338	19.511	21.615	24.769	27.587	30.995	33.409
17.338	20.601	22.760	25.989	28.869	32.346	34.805
18.338	21.689	23.900	27.204	30.144	33.687	36.191
19.337	22.775	25.038	28.412	31.410	35.020	37.566
20.337	23.858	26.171	29.615	32.671	36.343	38.932
21.337	24.939	27.301	30.813	33.924	37.659	40.289
22.337	26.018	28.429	32.007	35.172	38.968	41.638
23.337	27.096	29.553	33.196	36.415	40.270	42.980
24.337	28.172	30.675	34.382	37.652	41.566	44.314
25.336	29.246	31.795	35.563	38.885	42.856	45.642
26.336	30.319	32.912	36.741	40.113	44.140	46.963
27.336	31.391	34.027	37.916	41.337	45.419	48.278
28.336	32.461	35.139	39.087	42.557	46.693	49.588
29.336	33.530	36.250	40.256	43.773	47.962	50.892

Glossary

abduction
A type of movement whereby a structure such as an arm or leg is moved away from the median plane.

acclimatization
The functional compensation over a short time period as a response to environmental stimuli.

acetabulum
The socket formed by the ilium, ischium, and pubis into which the femoral head is received.

adduction
A type of movement whereby a structure such as an arm or leg is moved toward or beyond the median plane.

adenine
An organic base, one of the two purines found in the DNA and RNA molecules.

agglutination
An interaction between an antigen and antibody that leads to the clumping of red blood cells.

allele
An alternative expression of a gene.

Allen's rule
An ecogeographic rule stating that the relative size of exposed body appendages decreases as mean temperature decreases.

allopatric
Of the occurrence of two or more populations that occupy mutually exclusive geographic regions.

analogy
In comparative anatomy, refers to structural characteristics among different species that share a common function.

androgen
A general term referring to a class of several closely related sex hormones, mainly testosterone in males.

aneuploidy
A general term referring to the lack or multiplication of one or more chromosomes in the normal set. An inexact multiple of the haploid number.

antibody
A substance in the blood plasma that results from antigenic stimulation and reacts observably with the antigen responsible for its production.

antigen
Any substance that stimulates the formation of an antibody.

assortative mating
Mating that occurs on the basis of either similarity or dissimilarity in phenotypic characteristics.

autosome
Any chromosome other than the sex chromosomes.

balancing selection
A type of natural selection in which the heterozygote is at an advantage over both homozygotes.

Bergmann's rule
An ecogeographic rule stating that the body size of the subspecies within a homeothermic species will usually increase as the mean temperature of the habitat decreases.

bilophodont molars
Molars with enamel crests connecting each of the two front cusps and each of the two back cusps.

binominal nomenclature
The naming of a species with two Latin or latinized words.

biological species
A group of actually or potentially interbreeding natural populations that is reproductively isolated from other such groups.

bipedalism
A form of primate locomotion characteristic of the human species, involving standing, running, and walking on the hindlimbs.

brachiation
A mode of primate locomotion involving suspension of the body by the arms and hands.

carpals
The bones of the wrist.

cellular differentiation
In growth, the process whereby cells with the same genetic constitutions and initial functional potentials become specialized in terms of carrying out specific functions.

centriole
A small structure outside the cell nucleus that is involved with spindle formation during meiosis and mitosis.

centromere
That part of a chromosome that is associated with spindle fibers, important with respect to chromatid separation and chromosome movement to the poles after metaphase in mitosis and meiosis.

cerebellum
The posteroinferior part of the brain.

cerebral cortex
The outer surface of the cerebral hemispheres of the brain.

chiasma
The point of attachment between two

nonsister chromatids during the first meiotic prophase.

chromatid
One of the two structures comprising the duplicated chromosome arms before the centromere divides to form daughter chromosomes. After the centromere divides, each chromatid becomes a chromosome.

chromosome
A body composed of nucleoproteins within the nucleus that contains the DNA responsible for the storage of genetic information.

chromosome mutation
Any heritable change in the structure or number of chromosomes

chronometric dating
A class of dating methods that provides direct information on the actual age of the specimen under consideration.

cistron
The gene as a functional unit.

classification
In zoology, the ordering of organisms into groups according to their relationships to each other.

clavicle
The bone that forms the ventral part of the pectoral girdle.

cleavage
A process after fertilization during which the zygote undergoes rapid cellular division but with no increase in the size of the total cellular mass.

cline
A geographical character gradient.

coagulation
A general term referring to blood clotting.

codon
A sequence of three mRNA nucleotides that specifies a single amino acid.

consanguineous
Of mating between relatives.

coronal plane
Any imaginary vertical plane that bisects the body at right angles to a sagittal plane.

crepuscular
Of rhythm patterns that occur during dusk.

cytoplasm
The part of the cell that contains a number of small organelles and surrounds the nucleus.

cytosine
An organic base, one of the two pyrimidines found in the DNA and RNA molecules.

Darwinian fitness
The differential ability of certain genotypes to leave offspring.

deciduous dentition
The set of teeth that during development precedes the permanent teeth.

deficiency
A chromosomal mutation whereby a portion of the chromosome is lost.

deleterious
Harmful.

dendrochronology
Tree-ring dating.

dental formula
A shorthand method of expressing the number of teeth, by tooth type, in the mandible and maxilla.

deoxyribonucleic acid (DNA)
A polymeric molecule composed of different deoxyribonucleotides that stores genetic information.

diaphysis
The shaft of a long bone, separated from the ends of the bone during growth by a cartilaginous plate and having its own center of ossification.

diastema
A space between teeth, usually with reference to that which occurs between the maxillary canine and incisor.

diploid
Of chromosomes occurring in homologous pairs.

directional selection
A type of natural selection that favors phenotypes toward one end of a distribution and discriminates against phenotypes at the opposite end.

diversifying selection
A type of natural selection that favors both phenotypic extremes and acts against phenotypes around the mean.

dizygotic
Descriptive of twins produced by fertilization of two different ova by two different sperm.

dominance
A physiological or functional state in which an allele is expressed phenotypically in both the homozygote and heterozygote.

duplication
A chromosomal mutation whereby part of the chromosome occurs at least twice within the same chromosome.

ecological niche
All of the environmental factors relevant to the existence of a population or other group in a particular place.

electrophoresis
A biochemical technique involving the movement of charged particles in an applied electrical field.

electrophoretic mobility
A term referring to the distance that a protein will migrate under a given set of electrophoretic conditions.

encephalization
The evolutionary process whereby the higher centers of the brain increasingly dominate the functional activities of the lower centers.

endoplasmic reticulum
An organelle in the cytoplasm that contains enzymes and lipids, the latter being involved in energy storage.

enzyme
Any of a variety of biological catalysts that consists mostly of protein.

epiphysis
An end of a long bone, characterized by its own center of ossification, and separated from the shaft of the bone during growth by a cartilaginous plate.

epistasis
Interaction between genes at different loci such that the expression of one gene is prevented by another gene.

erector spinae
A group of intrinsic back muscles that extend the vertebral column and assist in the maintenance of trunk balance.

erythroblastosis fetalis
Hemolytic disease of the newborn as a result of maternal-fetal incompatibility, primarily in the Rh and ABO blood group systems.

erythrocyte
A red blood cell.

estrogen
A general class of several closely related female sex hormones.

eugenics
The discipline involved with the hereditary improvement of the human species.

euploidy
A general term denoting variation in the entire chromosome set. An exact multiple of the haploid number.

evolution
Change in gene frequencies through generation. Biological change through time.

expressivity
A term denoting variation in phenotypic expression of a particular genotype.

extension
A type of movement whereby the angle between two bones is increased.

external auditory meatus
The external opening of the ear.

femur
The largest and strongest bone of the skeleton. The bone of the upper leg.

fingerprinting
A biochemical technique combining electrophoresis and chromatography that separates the peptides in a protein.

flexion
A type of movement whereby the angle between two bones is decreased.

foramen
An opening in bone, serving primarily for the passage of blood vessels or nerves.

foramen magnum
The large opening at the base of the skull through which the spinal cord passes.

founder population
A population that contains only a small fraction of the genetic variation represented in the parental population.

frameshift mutation
Any mutation resulting from an addition or deletion of a deoxyribonucleotide that causes the nucleotide sequences to be read in a different register.

frontal
The most anterior bone of the cranial vault.

gametogenesis
The process during which gametes are formed.

gene
A segment of DNA recognized by a specific function. A unit of inheritance.

gene flow
Interpopulation exchange of genetic material.

gene mutation
A heritable change in the sequential order of base pairs in the DNA molecule.

genetic equilibrium
A state occurring in a population when it undergoes random mating and the gene frequencies remain constant from one generation to the next.

genotype
All of the genetic factors responsible for the genetic constitution of an individual.

geographic speciation
The acquisition of reproductive isolation by a population after a period of geographic separation from a related population.

gestation
The period of pregnancy.

glucose-6-phosphate dehydrogenase
An enzyme, the genetically controlled deficiency of which confers a relative resistance to malaria.

gluteal muscles
The large and powerful locomotory muscles located on the back of the hip.

golgi apparatus
An organelle in the cytoplasm that stores secretory products and may be involved in lysosome formation.

guanine
An organic base, one of the two purines found in the DNA and RNA molecules.

habituation
A very short-term stress response in sensory function and neural control.

haploid
Refers to organisms or cells with only one of each type of chromosome.

haplotype
A general term denoting the haploid genetic constitution of any complex locus, such as the Rh locus.

Hardy-Weinberg principle
The principle showing that the allele and genotype frequencies in a panmictic population will remain constant in the absence of the effect of any evolutionary force.

hemizygous
Refers to the heterogametic individual who has X-chromosomal genes but no homologous alleles on the Y-chromosome.

hemolysis
The rupture of the red blood cell, for any reason, and subsequent release of hemoglobin.

heterodont dentition
Within a dental complement, teeth that are morphologically and functionally differentiated.

heterogametic
The term used to denote an individual with two different types of sex chromosomes

heteroimmunization
The formation of an antibody by an antigen from an individual of a different species.

heterozygous
Denotes the presence of unlike alleles at homologous loci on a pair of chromosomes.

holandric inheritance
Inheritance controlled by genes on the Y-chromosome.

homodont dentition
Within a dental complement, teeth that are similar in shape and function.

homogametic
The term used to denote an individual with the same types of sex chromosomes.

homologous
With reference to chromosomes, those that contain identical gene loci.

homology
In comparative anatomy, refers to structures shared by different species as a result of a common ancestry.

homoplasy
In comparative anatomy, refers to structures among different species that are only visually similar.

homozygous
Denotes the presence of identical alleles at homologous loci on a pair of chromosomes.

horizontal plane
Any imaginary plane that bisects the body at right angles to both the sagittal and coronal planes.

humerus
The large bone of the upper arm.

hybridization
A cross between individuals from two distinct populations.

hyperplastic growth
Cellular growth that occurs through an increase in cell number.

hypothalamus
An important structure that regulates the activities of smooth muscle, cardiac muscle, and glands.

hypoxia
Oxygen deficiency in inspired air.

ilium
The expanded, curved, and fan-shaped bone located directly above the hip joint. The largest of the three bones of the *os coxae* that fuse together during development.

inbreeding
Mating between genetically related individuals.

incompatibility load
A genetic load that involves an unfavorable reaction between the genotypes of the mother and her fetus.

independent assortment
One of the two classic Mendelian Laws which showed that genes on different chromosomes segregate independently of each other during meiosis.

interstitial wear
A type of molar tooth wear that occurs between adjacent teeth rather than on their occlusal surfaces.

inversion
A chromosomal mutation whereby part of a chromosome breaks, inverts, and reattaches to the same chromosome.

ischium
One of the three bones of the *os coxae* that descends vertically from the hip joint.

isoagglutinogen
Any antigen that causes antibody formation in an individual of the same species.

isoimmunization
The formation of an antibody by an antigen from a member of the same species.

isolating mechanism
Any property of an individual of one species that prevents successful hybridization with an individual of another species.

karyotype
The cell's chromosomes. A graphic representation of chromosomes arranged by homologous pairs.

lactation
Milk secretion by a mammary gland. The period during which milk is produced.

lateral pterygoid
A masticatory muscle that, in conjunction with the opposite Lateral pterygoid, produces a grinding movement during chewing.

law of priority
A taxonomic rule stating that the old-est available name is the valid name of a taxon, provided there has been no transgression of the various articles in the *International Code of Zoological Nomenclature.*

leukocyte
A white blood cell.

linkage
The genetic association between certain genes located on the same chromosome.

locus
A chromosomal site occupied by a gene or one of its alleles.

lysosome
An organelle in the cytoplasm that is involved in the breakdown of complex molecules in a dying cell.

macroevolution
A general term sometimes used to designate evolutionary changes above the species level.

mandible
The lower jawbone.

masseter
A thick and powerful masticatory muscle that serves as a mandibular elevator.

maxilla
The large bone of the upper face that houses the upper teeth and takes part in the formation of the orbit, the hard palate, and the nasal fossa.

medial pterygoid
A masticatory muscle that elevates the mandible and produces a lateral motion of the jaw during chewing.

median plane
An imaginary plane that vertically bisects the body into two equal halves.

meiosis
The process of gametic cell division during which diploid precursor cells form haploid ova and sperm.

menarche
The first menstrual bleeding.

Mendelian population
A reproductive community of individuals sharing in a common gene pool.

metabolism
All of the chemical processes in the body involved with energy production and assimilation and synthesis of new materials.

metacarpals
The five slender bones of the hand between the wrist and fingers.

metopic suture
The cranial suture that separates the two halves of the frontal bone in fetuses and infants during the first two or three years of life.

microevolution
A general term sometimes used to designate evolutionary changes within a species.

migrational load
A genetic load, due to immigration of less favorable genotypes, that leads to a reduction in average population fitness.

missense substitution
A mutation in a codon that involves the substitution of one amino acid for another at the same position in the polypeptide.

mitochondria
Organelles in the cytoplasm that supply energy for protein synthesis.

mitosis
The process of cell division during which chromosomes are duplicated, leading to daughter cells that contain the identical chromosome content as the parent cell.

monophyletic
Having an evolutionary origin in only one lineage.

monozygotic
Descriptive of twins produced from a single ovum.

multidimensional species concept
A concept in which allopatric and allochronic populations are judged the same species if they have the capacity to interbreed.

multiple alleles
More than two different alleles that occur at the same locus.

mutational load
A genetic load, due to the accumulation of new, slightly deleterious mutations, that leads to a reduction in average population fitness.

natural selection
The differential change in relative frequency of genotypes due to differences in the ability of their phenotypes to obtain representation in the next generation.

negative assortative mating
Mating between individuals on the basis of phenotypic dissimilarity.

nocturnal
Of rhythm patterns that occur during the night.

nondimensional species concept
A concept in which sympatric and synchronic populations are judged as different species if they are reproductively isolated from each other.

nondisjunction
The failure of chromosomes to separate normally during cell division.

nonhomologous
With reference to chromosomes, those with different gene loci.

nonsense substitution
A mutation changing a codon specific for a particular amino acid into a chain-terminating codon.

norm of reaction
The range of developmental responses to all environments that can occur in a specific genotype.

nucleolus
A structure within the cell nucleus that may be involved with the synthesis of ribosomal RNA.

nucleotide
An organic molecule composed of phosphate, deoxyribose or ribose, and a purine or pyrimidine.

nucleus
The large structure inside the cell that contains the chromosomes.

occipital
The most posterior bone of the cranial vault.

occipital condyle
The surface at the base of the skull with which the first cervical vertebra articulates.

olfactory
Of the sense of smell.

oocyte
The female germ cell during meiosis. During the first meiotic division, the primary oocyte divides and gives rise to a secondary oocyte.

oogenesis
The process during which ova are produced.

oogonium
Primordial female germ cell that gives rise to an oocyte.

organelle
Any of several different kinds of small structures within the cytoplasm of a cell.

ossification
The process of bone formation.

ovulation
The formation and release of an unimpregnated ovum from the ovary.

ovum
The mature female gamete, or germ cell.

paleontological species concept
A lineage evolving separately from others and with its own unitary evolutionary role and tendencies.

panmixis
The process of random mating, or random combination of gametes.

parallelism
A trait similarity shared by different species, presumably as a result of similarities in selective factors as contrasted to commonness of ancestry.

parietal
The bone which, in combination with the opposite parietal, forms the sides and roof of the skull.

parthenogenesis
The development of an organism from an unfertilized ovum.

pectoral girdle
The structure, consisting of the clavicle and scapula, through which the arm is attached to the skeleton.

pedigree
A graphic representation of the individuals in a kindred according to their phenotypes and biological relationships.

penetrance
The frequency with which any particular genotype is phenotypically expressed.

petrosal bulla
Part of the temporal bone, on the lateral side of the skull, that contains the small auditory ossicles and other structures of the middle ear.

phalanges
The bones of the fingers and toes.

phenotype
An individual's characteristics resulting from the interaction between the genotype and the environment.

phenotypic plasticity
Nongenetic phenotypic variation, mostly as a result of environmental modification.

phylogenetic
Refers to the evolutionary development or descent of any taxonomic group.

physiological homeostasis
The maintenance of relative constancy in internal physiological processes.

pituitary gland
A small gland beneath the third ventricle of the brain that, among other functions, serves as the source of growth hormone.

plasma membrane
The membrane that encloses the cellular contents.

platelet
A highly modified white blood cell.

pleiotropic gene
A gene that produces more than a single phenotypic effect.

polygenic inheritance
Inheritance due to the action of more than two genes at different loci.

polymorphism
The occurrence together in the same locality of several discontinuous genes or phenotypes, the frequency of the rarest type being higher than that which can be maintained by recurrent mutation.

polypeptide
A chain of amino acids connected by peptide bonds.

polyphyletic
Having an evolutionary origin in two or more lineages.

polyploidy
Chromosomal changes in which the number of chromosome sets is more than the diploid complement.

polytypic
Refers to a taxonomic category that contains two or more immediately subordinate categories.

positive assortative mating
Mating between individuals on the basis of phenotypic similarity.

postorbital bar
A bony ring, occurring on the lateral side of each orbit, that offers some lateral protection for the eye.

proband
In a pedigree, the individual through whom the pedigree is constructed.

pronation
Hand movement whereby the radius is rotated diagonally across the ulna and the palm faces dorsally.

pubis
One of the three bones of the *os coxae* that curves anteriorly and medially from the hip joint.

quadrupedalism
A form of primate locomotion involving ground contact by all four limbs, divisible into ground-walking/running and knuckle-walking.

qualitative trait
Any phenotypic trait for which no intermediate values exist.

quantitative trait
Any phenotypic trait that can be measured and for which intermediate values exist.

recessiveness
A physiological or functional state in which an allele fails to be expressed in the heterozygote.

recombination
The reassortment and formation of new allelic combinations after meiotic segregation.

recombinational load
A genetic load due to the production of recombinants with lower fitnesses than the optimum genotype.

relative dating
A class of dating methods that describes the chronological position of a fossil as compared to another fossil or event.

reproductive isolation
A condition occurring when members of different populations either cannot or will not produce fully fertile and viable hybrids.

ribonucleic acid (RNA)
A polymeric molecule composed of several ribonucleotides and found in the cell nucleus and cytoplasm.

ribosome
An organelle in the cytoplasm that functions as a site of protein synthesis.

sagittal crest
A bony ridge at the top of the skull in the midline, characteristic of certain nonhuman primates.

sagittal plane
Any imaginary plane that bisects the body parallel to the median plane.

scapula
The large bone on the dorsal part of the thorax that in combination with the clavicle forms the pectoral girdle.

segregation
One of the two classical Mendelian Laws. The separation of allelic pairs during meiosis.

segregational load
A genetic load due to the production by heterozygous individuals of homozygous individuals less fit than the parents.

seminiferous tubules
Minute folded ducts, within the testes, that serve as the site for spermatogenesis.

sex-linkage
The genetic association between certain genes located on the sex chromosomes.

society
A group of individuals belonging to the same species and organized in a cooperative manner.

somatic cell
A cell of the body, as opposed to a gamete or germ cell.

speciation
The process of species multiplication. The acquisition of reproductive isolating mechanisms by a population.

sperm
The mature male gamete, or germ cell.

spermatid
In males, a haploid meiotic product that is the immediate precursor to the mature spermatozoon.

spermatocyte
The male germ cell during meiosis. A primary spermatocyte and secondary spermatocyte occur during the first and second meiotic divisions, respectively.

spermatogenesis
The process during which sperm are produced.

spermatogonium
Primordial male germ cell that gives rise to a spermatocyte.

spindle
A structure that occurs during nuclear division, responsible for chromosomal alignment and attraction to opposite poles.

stabilizing selection
A type of natural selection that tends to eliminate phenotypes that deviate from the population mean.

sternum
The elongated bone that forms the middle part of the ventral wall of the thorax.

subspecies
A formal taxonomic unit beneath the species level. An aggregate of local populations of a species inhabiting a geographic subdivision of the range of the species that differs taxonomically from other such aggregates.

supination
Hand movement whereby the radius and ulna are parallel and the palm faces ventrally.

sympatric
Of the occurrence of two or more populations within breeding range of each other.

systematics
The scientific study of the kinds and diversity of organisms and of any and all relationships among them.

tactile
Of the sense of touch.

taxon
A biological unit to which a formal name is attached.

taxonomy
The theoretical study of classification.

temporoparietalis
A muscle on the side of the skull that elevates the mandible during biting and chewing.

thrombocyte
A synonym for platelet, a highly modified white blood cell.

thymine
An organic base, one of the two pyrimidines found in the DNA and RNA molecules.

tibia
The largest of two bones forming the lower leg.

transcription
The process during which mRNA is formed from a DNA template.

translocation
A chromosomal mutation in which a part of one chromosome joins a non-homologous chromosome.

transposition
A chromosomal mutation similar to a translocation, except that the same chromosome breaks in three instead of two places.

transversospinalis muscles
The deepest group of muscles of the back that takes part in extension of the vertebral column and assists in the maintenance of trunk balance.

tuberosity
A raised eminence on bone, usually denoting an attachment area for tendons or ligaments.

tympanic ring
One of the structures of the petrosal bulla that serves for attachment of the tympanic membrane (eardrum).

typological species concept
A concept in which a species is defined on the basis of subjectively determined differences from other such groups.

uracil
An organic base, a pyrimidine found in RNA.

vasoconstriction
Constriction of the blood vessels.

vasodilation
Expansion of the blood vessels.

vibrissa
A tactile hair with a large bulbous root in direct association with a nerve.

viviparity
The process whereby the mother retains and nourishes the fertilized egg for a considerable period of time.

zona pellucida
A tough, transparent membrane that encloses the ovum.

zygomatic
A bone of the face, commonly called the cheekbone.

zygote
A fertilized ovum. The cell resulting from the union between the ovum and sperm.

Literature Cited

Akiyama, M., and R. W. G. Wyckoff
1970. The Total Amino Acid Content of Fossil Pecten Shells. *Proc. Nat. Acad. Sci.* 67:1097–1100.

Aldridge, A. O.
1951. The Meaning of Incest from Hutcheson to Gibbon. *Ethics* 61:309–313.

Allan, D.
1969. *Essentials of Human Embryology.* 2nd Ed. Oxford Univ. Press, New York.

Allen, G., D. Kirk, J. P. Scott, H. L. Shapiro, and B. Wallace
1961. Statement of the Eugenic Position. *Eugen. Quart.* 8:181–184.

Allison, A. C.
1954. Protection Afforded by Sickle-Cell Trait against Subtertian Malarial Infection. *Brit. Med. J.* 1:290–294.

———.
1958. The Genetical and Clinical Significance of the Haptoglobins. *Proc. Roy. Soc. Med.* 51:641–645.

———.
1964. Polymorphism and Natural Selection in Human Populations. *Cold Spring Harb. Symp. Quant. Biol.* 29:137–149.

Aloysia, M., A. G. Gelb, H. Fudenberg, J. Hamper, P. Tippett, and R. R. Race
1961. The Expected "Bombay" Groups Oh^A1 and Oh^A2. *Transfusion* 1:212–217.

Altmann, S. A., and J. Altmann
1970. Baboon Ecology. African Field Research. *Biblio. Primat.*, No. 12. S. Karger, Basel.

Amadon, D.
1949. The Seventy-Five Per Cent Rule for Subspecies. *Condor* 51:250–258.

Amirhakimi, G. H.
1974. Growth from Birth to Two Years of Rich Urban and Poor Rural Iranian Children Compared with Western Norms. *Ann. Hum. Biol.* 1:427–441.

Amundsen, D. W., and C. J. Diers
1969. The Age of Menarche in Classical Greece and Rome. *Hum. Biol.* 41:125–132.

———.
1973. The Age of Menarche in Medieval Europe. *Hum. Biol.* 45:363–369.

Andrews, C. P.
1971. *Ramapithecus wickeri* Mandible from Fort Ternan, Kenya. *Nature* 231:192–194.

Arambourg, C.
1954. L'hominien Fossile de Ternifine (Algerie). *C. R. Acad. Sci. Paris* 239:893–895.

Arambourg, C., and R. Hoffstetter
1954. Decouverte, en Afrique de Nord, de Restes Humains du Paleolithic Inferieur. *C. R. Acad. Sci. Paris* 239:72–74.

Auerbach, C., and B. J. Kilbey
1971. Mutation in Eukaryotes. *Ann. Rev. Genet.* 5:193–218.

Austin, D. M., and J. Ghesquiere
1976. Heat Tolerance of Bantu and Pygmoid Groups of the Zaire River Basin. *Hum. Biol.* 48:439–453.

Baker, J. R.
1974. *Race.* Oxford Univ. Press, New York.

Baker, P. T.
1958. Racial Differences in Heat Tolerance. *Am. J. Phys. Anthrop.* 16:287–305.

———.
1966. Ecological and Physiological Adaptation in Indigenous South Americans. In: *The Biology of Human Adaptability*, P. T. Baker and J. S. Weiner, eds. Clarendon Press, Oxford. pp. 275–303.

———.
1969. Human Adaptation to High Altitude. *Science* 163:1149–1156.

Baldwin, J. D.
1968. The Social Behavior of Adult Male Squirrel Monkeys (*Samiri sciureus*) in a Semi-Natural Environment. *Folia Primat.* 9:281–314.

Baldwin, L. A., and G. Telecki
1972. Field Research on Baboons, Drills, and Geladas: An Historical, Geographical, and Bibliographical Listing. *Primates* 13:427–432.

Balke, B.
1960. *The Effect of Physical Exercise on the Metabolic Potential, a Crucial Measure of Physical Fitness.* Colloquium on Exercise and Fitness. Univ. of Illinois College of Physical Education and the Athletic Institute. Champaign-Urbana, Ill.

Barnes, H. V.
1975. Physical Growth and Development during Puberty. *Med. Clin. North Amer.* 59:1305–1317.

Barnicot, N. A.
1977. Biological Variation in Modern Populations. In: *Human Biology. An Introduction to Human Evolution, Variation, Growth, and Ecology*, 2nd Ed. G. A. Harrison, J. S. Weiner, J. M. Tanner, and N. A. Barnicot, eds. Oxford Univ. Press, Oxford. pp. 179–298.

Bartalos, M., and T. A. Baramki
1967. *Medical Cytogenetics.* Williams and Wilkins, Baltimore.

Basmajian, J. V.
1976. *Primary Anatomy.* 7th Ed. Williams and Wilkins, Baltimore.

Bass, N. H., M. G. Netsky, and E. Young
1970. Effect of Neonatal Malnutrition on Developing Cerebrum. *Arch. Neuro.* 23:289–302.

Battle, H. I., N. F. Walker, and M. W. Thompson
1974. Mackinder's Hereditary Brachydactyly: Phenotypic, Radiological, Dermatoglyphic and Genetic Observations in an Ontario Family. *Ann. Hum. Genet.* 36:415–424.

Bayer, L. M., and N. Bayley
1976. *Growth Diagnosis.* 2nd Ed. Univ. of Chicago Press, Chicago.

Beall, C. M., P. T. Baker, T. S. Baker, and J. D. Haas
1977. The Effects of High Altitude on Adolescent Growth in Southern Peruvian Amerindians. *Hum. Biol.* 49:109–124.

Bearn, A.
1972. Wilson's Disease. In: *The Metabolic Basis of Inherited Disease,* 3rd Ed. J. B. Stanbury, J. B. Wyngaarden, and D. S. Fredrickson, eds. McGraw-Hill, New York. pp. 1033–1050.

Beck, G. J., and B. J. Van den Berg
1975. The Relationship of the Rate of Intrauterine Growth of Low-Birth-Weight Infants in Later Growth. *J. Pediat.* 86:504–511.

Beet, E. A.
1949. The Genetics of the Sickle-Cell Trait in a Bantu Tribe. *Ann. Eugen.* 14:279–284.

Behrman, S. J., J. Buettner-Janusch, R. Heglar, H. Gershowitz, and W. L. Tew
1960. ABO (H) Blood Incompatibility As a Cause of Infertility: A New Concept. *Am. J. Obstet. Gynec.* 79:847–855.

Beisel, W. R.
1975. Synergistic Effects of Maternal Malnutrition and Infection on the Infant. *Am. J. Dis. Child.* 129:571–574.

Benezech, M.
1973. *La Responsabilite Penale des Sujets Porteurs d'une Anomalie de Chromosome Y.* Editions Bergeret-71, Bordeaux, France.

Bennett, K. A.
1967. Craniostenosis: A Review of the Etiology and a Report of New Cases. *Am. J. Phys. Anthrop.* 27:1–9.

Bennett, K. A., R. H. Osborne, and R. J. Miller
1975. Biocultural Ecology. *Ann. Rev. Anthrop.* 4:163–181.

Benzer, S.
1962. The Fine Structure of a Gene. *Sci. Amer.* 206:70–84.

Berg, K., and A. G. Bearn
1968. Human Serum Protein Polymorphisms. *Ann. Rev. Genet.* 2:341–362.

Bernard, C.
1878–79. *Lecons sur les Phenomenes de la Vie Communs aux Animaux et aux Vegetaux.* Vols. 1 and 2. Librairie J.-B. Bailliere et Fils.

Bernstein, F.
1925. Zusammenfassende Betrachtungen uber die erblichen Blutstrukturen des Menschen. *Zeit. ind. Abstam.-Vererb.* 37:237–270.

———.
1930. Fortgesetzte Untersuchungen aus der Theorie der Blutgruppen. *Zeit. ind. Abstam.-Vereb.* 56:233–237.

Bertrand, M.
1969. The Behavioral Repertoire of the Stumptail Macaque. *Biblio. Primat.,* No. 11. S. Karger, Basel.

Beutler, E., M. Yeh, and V. F. Fairbanks
1962. The Normal Human Female As a Mosaic of X-Chromosome Activity: Studies Using the Gene for G-6-PD Deficiency As a Marker. *Proc. Nat. Acad. Sci.* 48:9–16.

Beveridge, W. I. B. (ed.)
1969. Using Primates in Medical Research. Part II. Recent Comparative Research. *Primates in Medicine,* Vol. 3, S. Karger, Basel.

Bhende, Y. M., C. K. Deshpande, H. M. Bhatia, R. Sanger, R. R. Race, W. T. J. Morgan, and W. M. Watkins
1952. A "New" Blood Group Character Related to the ABO System. *Lancet* 1:903–904.

Billewicz, W. Z., H. M. Fellowes, and C. A. Hytten
1976. Comments on the Critical Metabolic Mass and the Age of Menarche. *Ann. Hum. Biol.* 3:51–59.

Birch, H. G., C. Pineiro, E. Alcalde, T. Toca, and J. Cravioto
1971. Relation of Kwashiorkor in Early Childhood and Intelligence at School Age. *Pediat. Res.* 5:579–585.

Birdsell, J. B.
1975. *Human Evolution.* 2nd Ed. Rand McNally, Chicago.

Bishop, A.
1964. Use of the Hand in Lower Primates. In: *Evolutionary and Genetic Biology of Primates,* Vol. 2. J. Buettner-Janusch, ed. Academic Press, New York. pp. 133–225.

Bishop, W. W., and G. R. Chapman
1970. Early Pliocene Sediments and Fossils from the Northern Kenya Rift Valley. *Nature* 226:914–918.

Bishop, W. W., and J. A. Miller (eds.)
1972. *Calibration of Hominoid Evolution.* Scottish Academic Press, Edinburgh.

Bishop, W. W., J. A. Miller, and F. J. Fitch
1969. New Potassium-Argon Age Determination Relevant to the Miocene Fossil Mammal Sequence in East Africa. *Am. J. Sci.* 267:669–699.

Bjork, A.
1963. Variations in the Growth Pattern of the Human Mandible: Longitudinal Radiographic Study by the Implant Method. *J. Dent. Res.* 42:400–411.

———.
1964. Sutural Growth of the Upper Face Studied by the Implant Method. *Trans. Eur. Orthodont. Soc.* 49:49–65.

Black, D.
1931. On an Adolescent Skull of *Sinanthropus pekinensis* in Comparison with an Adult Skull of the Same Species and with Other Hominid Skulls, Recent and Fossil. *Palaeon. Sinica,* Series D., Vol. 7, Fasc. 2.

Blanc, A. C.
1958. Torre in Pietra, Saccopastore, Monte Circeo. On the Position of the Mousterian in the Pleistocene Sequence of the Rome Area. *Neanderthal Centenary,* Rome. pp. 167–174.

Blum, H. F.
1961. Does the Melanin Pigment of Human Skin Have Adaptive Value? *Quart. Rev. Biol.* 36:50–63.

1968. Vitamin D, Sunlight, and Natural Selection. *Science* 159:652–653.

Blumenbach, J. F.
1776. On the Natural Variety of Mankind. In: *This Is Race*, E. W. Count (1950), ed. Henry Schuman, New York. pp. 25–39.

Boas, F.
1892. The Growth of Children. *Science* 19:256–257; 281–282.

———.
1932. Studies in Growth. *Hum. Biol.* 4:307–350.

———.
1935. The Tempo of Growth of Fraternities. *Proc. Nat. Acad. Sci.* 21:413–418.

Boaz, N. T., and F. C. Howell
1977. A Gracile Hominid Cranium from Upper Member G of the Shungura Formation, Ethiopia. *Am. J. Phys. Anthrop.* 46:93–108.

Bodmer, W. F., and L. L. Cavalli-Sforza
1976. *Genetics, Evolution, and Man.* W. H. Freeman, San Francisco.

Bonner, J. T.
1962. *The Ideas of Biology.* Harper and Bros., New York.

Bordes, F.
1968. *The Old Stone Age.* McGraw-Hill, New York.

Bowles, G. T.
1932. *New Types of Old Americans at Harvard.* Harvard Univ. Press, Cambridge.

Boyd, W. C.
1939. Blood Groups. *Tab. Biologicae* 17:113–240.

———.
1950. *Genetics and the Races of Man.* Little, Brown and Co., Boston.

Brace, C. L.
1962. Cultural Factors in the Evolution of the Human Dentition. In: *Culture and the Evolution of Man*, M. F. Ashley Montagu, ed. Oxford Univ. Press, New York. pp. 343–354.

———.
1963. Structural Reduction in Evolution. *Am. Nat.* 97:39–49.

1964. The Fate of the "Classic" Neanderthals: A Consideration of Hominid Catastrophism. *Curr. Anthrop.* 5:3–43.

Brace, C. L. and A. Montagu
1977. *Human Evolution. An Introduction to Biological Anthropology.* 2nd Ed. Macmillan, New York.

Braidwood, R. J.
1975. *Prehistoric Men.* 8th Ed. Scott, Foresman and Co., Glenview, Ill.

Brain, C. K.
1958. The Transvaal Ape-Man-Bearing Cave Deposits. *Transvaal Mus. Mem.*, No. 11.

———.
1970. New Finds at the Swartkrans Australopithecine Site. *Nature* 225:1112–1119.

Brain, C. K., E. S. Vrba, and J. T. Robinson
1974. A New Hominid Innominate Bone from Swartkrans. *Ann. Transvaal Mus.* 29:55–63.

Brazier, M. A. B. (ed.)
1975. Growth and Development of the Brain. *Internat. Brain Res. Org. Monogr. Ser.*, Vol. 1. Raven Press, New York.

Brenner, W. E., D. A. Edelman, and C. H. Hendricks
1976. A Standard of Fetal Growth for the United States of America. *Am. J. Obstet. Gynecol.* 126:555–564.

Brock, D. J. H.
1972. Inborn Errors of Metabolism. In: *The Biochemical Genetics of Man*, D. J. H. Brock and O. Mayo, eds. Academic Press, New York. pp. 385–476.

Brody, J., M. G. Fitzgerald, and A. S. D. Spiers
1967. A Female Child with Five X Chromosomes. *J. Pediat.* 70:105–109.

Bronowski, J., and W. M. Long
1951. Statistical Methods in Anthropology. *Nature* 168:794.

Broom, R.
1936. A New Fossil Anthropoid Skull from South Africa. *Nature* 138:486–488.

1938. The Pleistocene Anthropoid Apes from South Africa. *Nature* 142:377–379.

———.
1943. An Ankle Bone of the Ape-Man, *Paranthropus robustus*. *Nature* 152:689–690.

———.
1949. Another New Type of Fossil Ape-Man. *Nature* 163:57.

———.
1950. The Genera and Species of the South African Fossil Ape-Man. *Am. J. Phys. Anthrop.* 8:1–14.

Broom, R., and J. T. Robinson
1949. A New Type of Fossil Man. *Nature* 164:322–323.

———.
1950. Man Contemporaneous with the Swartkrans Ape-Men. *Am. J. Phys. Anthrop.* 8:151–155.

Brose, D. S., and M. H. Wolpoff
1971. Early Upper Paleolithic Man and Late Middle Pleistocene Tools. *Am. Anthrop.* 73:1156–1194.

Brothwell, D. R.
1960. Upper Pleistocene Human Skull from Niah Cave, Sarawak. *Sarawak Mus. J.* 9:323–349.

Brothwell, D. R., and E. Higgs (eds.)
1970. *Science in Archaeology.* Praeger, New York.

Brothwell, D. R., and A. T. Sandison (eds.)
1967. *Diseases in Antiquity. A Survey of the Diseases, Injuries, and Surgery of Early Populations.* C. C. Thomas, Springfield, Ill.

Brown, A. W. A.
1967. Genetics of Insecticide Resistance in Insect Vectors. In: *Genetics of Insect Vectors of Disease*, J. W. Wright and R. Pal, eds. Elsevier, Amsterdam. pp. 505–552.

Brues, A.
1960. The Spearman and the Archer—An Essay on Selection in Body Build. *Am. Anthrop.* 61:457–469.

1963. Stochastic Tests of Selection in the ABO Blood Groups. *Am. J. Phys. Anthrop.* 21:287–299.

——. 1977. *People and Races.* Macmillan, New York.

Buettner-Janusch, J.
1973. *Physical Anthropology: A Perspective.* John Wiley and Sons, New York.

Buettner-Janusch, J. (ed.)
1962. The Relatives of Man: Modern Studies of the Relation of the Evolution of Nonhuman Primates to Human Evolution. *Ann. New York. Acad. Sci.* 102:181–514.

Butzer, K. W.
1974. Paleoecology of South African Australopithecines: Taung Revisited. *Curr. Anthrop.* 15:367–382.

Butzer, K. W., F. H. Brown, and D. L. Thurber
1969. Horizontal Sediments of the Lower Omo Valley: The Kibish Formation. *Quaternaria* 11:15–29.

Cachel, S.
1975. The Beginnings of the Catarrhini. In: *Primate Functional Morphology and Evolution,* R. H. Tuttle, ed. Mouton, The Hague. pp. 23–36.

Cameron, N.
1976. Weight and Skinfold Variation at Menarche and the Critical Body Weight Hypothesis. *Ann. Hum. Biol.* 3:279–282.

Campbell, B. G.
1965. The Nomenclature of the Hominidae, Including a Definitive List of Hominid Taxa. *Roy. Anthrop. Inst. Great Britain and Ireland,* Occ. Paper No. 22:1–33.

——. 1966. *Human Evolution. An Introduction to Man's Adaptations.* Aldine, Chicago.

——. 1973. A New Taxonomy of Fossil Man. *Yearbook Phys. Anthrop.* 17:194–201.

——. 1976. *Humankind Emerging.* Little, Brown and Co., Boston.

Campbell, B. G., and R. L. Bernor
1976. The Origin of the Hominidae: Africa or Asia? *J. Hum. Evol.* 5:441–454.

Cannon, W. B.
1932. *The Wisdom of the Body.* W. W. Norton, New York.

Cantarow, A., and B. Schepartz
1954. *Biochemistry.* W. B. Saunders, Philadelphia.

Carney, J., A. Hill, J. A. Miller, and A. Walker
1971. Late Australopithecine from Baringo District, Kenya. *Nature* 230:509–514.

Carpenter, C. R.
1934. A Field Study of the Behavior and Social Relations of Howling Monkeys. *Comp. Psychol. Monogr.* 10:1–168.

——. 1940. A Field Study in Siam of the Behavior and Social Relations of the Gibbon (*Hylobates lar*). *Comp. Psych. Monogr.* 16:1–212.

Carpenter, P. L.
1965. *Immunology and Serology.* 2nd Ed. W. B. Saunders, Philadelphia.

Carr, D. H.
1969. Chromosomal Abnormalities in Clinical Medicine. *Prog. Med. Genet.* 6:1–61.

Carr, D. H., M. L. Barr, and E. R. Plunkett
1961. An XXXX Sex Chromosome Complex in Two Mentally Defective Females. *Canad. Med. Assoc. J.* 84:131–137.

Carson, P. E., C. L. Flanagan, C. E. Ickes, and A. S. Alving
1956. Enzymatic Deficiency in Primaquine Sensitive Erythrocytes. *Science* 124:484–485.

Cartmill, M.
1970. The Orbits of Arboreal Mammals: A Reassessment of the Arboreal Theory of Primate Evolution. Ph.D. Dissertation, Univ. of Chicago.

——. 1972. Arboreal Adaptations and the Origin of the Order Primates. In: *The Functional and Evolutionary Biology of Primates,* R. Tuttle, ed. Aldine-Atherton, Chicago. pp. 97–122.

——. 1975. *Primate Origins.* Burgess, Minneapolis.

Caspersson, T., G. Gahrton, J. Lindsten, and L. Zech
1970. Identification of the Philadelphia Chromosome As a Number 22 by Quinacrine Mustard Fluorescence Analysis. *Exp. Cell Res.* 63:238–240.

Cavalli-Sforza, L. L., and W. F. Bodmer
1971. *The Genetics of Human Populations.* W. H. Freeman, San Francisco.

Chance, M. R. A.
1961. The Nature and Special Features of the Instinctive Social Bond of Primates. In: *Social Life of Early Man,* S. L. Washburn, ed. *Viking Fund Publ. in Anthrop.* No. 31, Wenner-Gren Foundation for Anthropological Research, Inc., New York. pp. 17–33.

Charles-Dominique, P., and R. D. Martin
1972. *Behavior and Ecology of Nocturnal Prosimians.* Paul Parey, Berlin.

Chautard-Freire-Maia, E. A.
1974. Linkage Relationships between 22 Autosomal Markers. *Ann. Hum. Genet.* 38:191–198.

Cheek, D. B. (ed.)
1975. *Fetal and Postnatal Cellular Growth: Hormones and Nutrition.* John Wiley and Sons, New York.

Childe, V. G.
1951. *Man Makes Himself.* Mentor Books, New York.

Chung, C. S., and N. E. Morton
1961. Selection at the ABO Locus. *Am. J. Hum. Genet.* 13:9–27.

Churchill, J. A., J. W. Neff, and D. F. Caldwell
1966. Birth Weight and Intelligence. *Obstet. Gynecol.* 28:425–429.

Ciochon, R. L., and R. S. Corruccini
1976. Shoulder Joint of Sterkfontein Australopithecus. *S. Afr. J. Sci.* 72:80–82.

Clark, C. C., and A. Veis
1972. High Molecular Weight α Chains in Acid-Soluble Collagen and Their Role in Fibrillogenesis. *Biochem.* 11:494–502.

Clark, J. D.
1975. African Origins of Man the Toolmaker. In: *Human Origins. Louis Leakey and the East African Evidence,* G. Ll. Isaac and E. R. McCown, eds.

W. A. Benjamin, Menlo Park, Calif. pp. 1–53.

Clarke, R. J., and F. C. Howell
1972. Affinities of the Swartkrans 847 Hominid Cranium. *Am. J. Phys. Anthrop.* 37:319–335.

Coale, A. J.
1974. The History of the Human Populations. *Sci. Amer.* 231:41–51.

Cockburn, T. A.
1971. Infectious Diseases in Ancient Populations. *Curr. Anthrop.* 12:45–62.

Cohen, B. H.
1970a. ABO and Rh Incompatibility. I. Fetal and Neonatal Mortality with ABO and Rh Incompatibility: Some New Interpretations. *Am. J. Hum. Genet.* 22:412–440.

———.
1970b. ABO and Rh Incompatibility. II. Is There a Dual Interaction in Combined ABO and Rh Incompatibility? *Am. J. Hum. Genet.* 22:441–452.

Coleman, W.
1964. *Georges Cuvier, Zoologist. A Study in the History of Evolution Theory.* Harvard Univ. Press, Cambridge.

———.
1971. *Biology in the Nineteenth Century: Problems of Form, Function, and Transformation:* John Wiley and Sons, New York.

Collins, E. T.
1921. Changes in the Visual Organs Correlated with the Adoption of Arboreal Life and with the Assumption of the Erect Posture. *Trans. Ophthalm. Soc. U.K.* 41:10–90.

Comas, J.
1969. *Historia Sumaria de la Asociacion Americana de Antropologos Fisicos (1928–1968).* Instituto Nacional de Antropologia e Historia, Mexico, D. F.

Commemoration of the Publication of Gregor Mendel's Pioneer Experiments in Genetics. *Proc. Am. Phil. Soc.* 109:189–248. 1965.

Conroy, G. C.
1972. Problems in the Interpretation of *Ramapithecus:* With Special Reference to Anterior Tooth Reduction. *Am. J. Phys. Anthrop.* 37:41–48.

———.
1976. Primate Postcranial Remains from the Oligocene of Egypt. *Contrib. Primat.* 8. S. Karger, Basel.

Conroy, G. C., and D. Pilbeam
1975. *Ramapithecus:* A Review of Its Hominid Status. In: *Paleoanthropology, Morphology, and Paleoecology,* R. Tuttle, ed. Mouton, The Hague. pp. 59–86.

Cooke, H. B. S.
1963. Pleistocene Mammal Faunas of Africa, with Particular Reference to Southern Africa. In: *African Ecology and Human Evolution,* F. C. Howell and F. Bourliere, eds. *Viking Fund Publ. in Anthrop.* No. 36, Wenner-Gren Foundation for Anthropological Research, Inc., New York. pp. 65–116.

Cooley, W. W., and P. R. Lohnes
1971. *Multivariate Data Analysis.* John Wiley and Sons, New York.

Coon, C. S.
1962. *The Origin of Races.* A. A. Knopf, New York.

———.
1965. *The Living Races of Man.* A. A. Knopf, New York.

Coon, C. S., S. M. Garn, and J. B. Birdsell
1950. *Races. A Study of the Problems of Race Formation in Man.* C. C. Thomas, Springfield, Ill.

Correns, C.
1900. G. Mendels Regel uber das Verhalten der Nachkommenschaft der Rassenbastarde. *Deutsch. Bot. Ges. Ber.* 18:158–168.

Cott, H. B.
1940. *Adaptive Coloration in Animals.* Methuen, London.

Crawford, M. H., and P. L. Workman (eds.)
1973. *Methods and Theories of Anthropological Genetics.* Univ. of New Mexico Press, Albuquerque.

Crick, F. H. C.
1962. The Genetic Code. *Sci. Amer.,* Oct. Reprinted in: *The Molecular Basis of Life. An Introduction to Molecular Biology,* Intro. by R. H. Haynes and P. C. Hanawalt. W. H. Freeman, San Francisco, 1968. pp. 198–205.

———.
1966. The Genetic Code: III. *Sci. Amer.,* Oct. Reprinted in *The Molecular Basis of Life. An Introduction to Molecular Biology,* Intro. by R. H. Haynes and P. C. Hanawalt. W. H. Freeman, San Francisco, 1968. pp. 217–223.

Cronin, J. E., and V. M. Sarich
1975. Molecular Systematics of the New World Monkeys. *J. Hum. Evol.* 4:357–375.

Crook, J. H., and J. S. Gartlan
1966. Evolution of Primate Societies. *Nature* 210:1200–1203.

Crow, J. F.
1972. Darwinian and Non-Darwinian Evolution. In: *Darwinian, Neo-Darwinian, and Non-Darwinian Evolution,* L. M. Le Cam, J. Neyman, and E. L. Scott, eds. *Proc. Sixth Berkeley Symp. Math. Stat. Prob.* 5:1–22.

Crow, J. F., and J. Felsenstein
1968. The Effect of Assortative Mating on the Genetic Composition of a Population. *Eugen. Quart.* 15:85–97.

Crow, J. F., and M. Kimura
1970. *An Introduction to Population Genetics Theory.* Harper and Row, New York.

Damon, A.
1977. *Human Biology and Ecology.* W. W. Norton, New York.

Dart, R. A.
1925. *Australopithecus africanus:* The Man-Ape of South Africa. *Nature* 115:195–199.

———.
1948. The Makapansgat Proto-Human *Australopithecus prometheus.* *Am. J. Phys. Anthrop.* 6:259–284.

———.
1956. The Relationship of Brain Size and Brain Pattern to Human Status. *S. Afr. J. Med. Sci.* 21:23–45.

———.
1962. The Makapansgat Pink Breccia Australopithecine Skull. *Am. J. Phys. Anthrop.* 20:119–126.

Darwin, C.
1859. *On the Origin of Species.* A Facsimile of the First Edition, Intro. by E. Mayr. Harvard Univ. Press, Cambridge, 1964.

Darwin, C., and A. Wallace
1859. On the Tendency of Species to Form Varieties; And on the Perpetuation of Varieties and Species by Natural Means of Selection. *J. Proc. Linnaean Soc. (Zoology)* III:45–62.

Daughaday, W. H., K. Hall, M. S. Raben, W. D. Salmon, Jr., J. L. Van den Brande, and J. J. Van Wyk
1972. Somatomedin: Proposed Designation for Sulfation Factor. *Nature* 235:107.

Davenport, C. B.
1913. *Heredity of Skin Color in Negro-White Crosses.* Carnegie Inst., Washington, D. C., Publ. No. 188. pp. 1–106.

Davidson, R. G., H. M. Nitowski, and B. Childs
1963. Demonstration of Two Populations of Cells in the Human Female Heterozygous for Glucose-6-Phosphate Dehydrogenase Variants. *Proc. Nat. Acad. Sci.* 50:481–485.

Davies, A.
1932. A Re-Survey of the Morphology of the Nose in Relation to Climate. *J. Roy. Anthrop. Inst.* 62:337–359.

Davis, R. L., S. M. Hargen, F. M. Yeomans, and B. F. Chow
1973. Long-Term Effects of Alterations of Maternal Diet in Mice. *Nut. Rpts. Internat.* 7:463–473.

Day, M. H.
1965. *Guide to Fossil Man. A Handbook of Human Paleontology.* World Publ. Co., Cleveland.

———.
1971. Postcranial Remains of *Homo Erectus* from Bed IV, Olduvai Gorge, Tanzania. *Nature* 232:383–387.

———.
1976a. Hominid Postcranial Material from Bed I, Olduvai Gorge. In: *Human Origins. Louis Leakey and the East African Evidence,* G. Ll. Isaac and E. R. McCown, eds. W. A. Benjamin, Menlo Park, Calif. pp. 362–374.

———.
1976b. Hominid Postcranial Remains from the East Rudolf Succession. A Review. In: *Earliest Man and Environments in the Lake Rudolf Basin. Stratigraphy, Paleoecology, and Evolution,* Y. Coppens, F. C. Howell,

G. Ll. Isaac, and R. E. F. Leakey, eds. Univ. of Chicago Press, Chicago. pp. 507–521.

Day, M. H., R. E. F. Leakey, A. C. Walker, and B. A. Wood
1975. New Hominids from East Rudolf, Kenya, I. *Am. J. Phys. Anthrop.* 42:461–476.

———.
1976. New Hominids from East Turkana, Kenya. *Am. J. Phys. Anthrop.* 45:369–436.

Day, M. H., and T. I. Molleson
1973. The Trinil Femora. In: *Human Evolution,* M. H. Day, ed. Taylor and Francis, London. pp. 127–154.

Day, M. H., and J. R. Napier
1964. Hominid Fossils from Bed I, Olduvai Gorge, Tanganyika: Fossil Foot Bones. *Nature* 201:969–970.

Day, M. H., and B. A. Wood
1968. Functional Affinities of the Olduvai Hominid 8 Talus. *Man* 3:440–455.

de Beer, Sir Gavin
1963. *Charles Darwin: Evolution by Natural Selection.* Thomas Nelson and Sons, London.

DeLong, M. R.
1974. Motor Functions of the Basal Ganglia: Single Unit Activity during Movement. In: *The Neurosciences Third Study Program,* F. O. Schmitt and F. G. Worden, eds. The MIT Press, Cambridge, Mass. pp. 319–325.

Delson, E.
1975a. Evolutionary History of the Cercopithecidae. *Contrib. Primat.* 5:167–217.

———.
1975b. Paleoecology and Zoogeography of the Old World Monkeys. In: *Primate Functional Morphology and Evolution,* R. Tuttle, ed. Mouton, The Hague. pp. 37–68.

de Lumley, H.
1975. Cultural Evolution in France in Its Paleoecological Setting during the Middle Pleistocene. In: *After the Australopithecines,* K. W. Butzer and G. Ll. Isaac, eds. Mouton, The Hague. pp. 745–808.

de Lumley, H., and M.-A. de Lumley
1971. Decouverte de Restes Humains Anteneandertaliens Dates du Debut

du Riss a la Caune de l'Arago (Tautavel, Pyrenees-Orientales). *C. R. Acad. Sci. Paris* 272:1739–1742.

———.
1974. Pre-Neanderthal Human Remains from Arago Cave in Southeastern France. *Yearbook Phys. Anthrop.* 17:162–168.

de Lumley, H., H. S. Gagniere, and R. Pascal
1963. Decouverte d'Outils Prehistoriques d'Age Villafranchien dans la Grotte du Vallonnet (Roquebrune-Cap-Martin, Alpes-Maritimes). *C. R. Acad. Sci. Paris* 256:4261–4262.

Demisch, A., and P. Wartmann
1956. Calcification of the Mandibular Third Molar and Its Relation to Skeletal and Chronological Age in Children. *Child Dev.* 27:459–473.

Denson, K. W. E.
1972. Coagulation Disorders. In: *The Biochemical Genetics of Man,* D. J. H. Brock and O. Mayo, eds. Academic Press, New York. pp. 603–638.

Dern, R. J., I. M. Weinstein, G. V. Leroy, D. W. Talmage, and A. S. Alving
1954. The Hemolytic Effect of Primaquine. I. The Localization of the Drug-Induced Hemolytic Defect in Primaquine-Sensitive Individuals. *J. Lab. Clin. Med.* 43:303–309.

DeVore, I.
1963. A Comparison of the Ecology and Behavior of Monkeys and Apes. In: *Classification and Human Evolution,* S. L. Washburn, ed. *Viking Fund Publ. in Anthropology* No. 37, Wenner-Gren Foundation for Anthropological Research, Inc., New York. pp. 301–319.

DeVore, I., and K. R. L. Hall
1965. Baboon Ecology. In: *Primate Behavior. Field Studies of Monkeys and Apes,* I. DeVore, ed. Holt, Rinehart and Winston, New York. pp. 20–52.

DeVore, I., and S. L. Washburn
1963. Baboon Ecology and Human Evolution. In: *African Ecology and Human Evolution,* F. C. Howell and F. Bourliere, eds. *Viking Fund Publ. in Anthropology* No. 36, Wenner-Gren Foundation for Anthropological Research, Inc., New York. pp. 335–367.

de Vries, H.
1900. Sur la loi de Disjonction des Hybrides. *C. R. Acad. Sci. Paris* 130:845–847.

DiCagno, L., and P. Franceschini
1968. Feeblemindedness and XXXX Karyotype. *J. Ment. Def. Res.* 12:226–236.

Dillon, L. S.
1978. *Evolution. Concepts and Consequences.* 2nd Ed. C. V. Mosby, St. Louis.

Dixon, W. J., and F. J. Massey, Jr.
1969. *Introduction to Statistical Analysis.* McGraw-Hill, New York.

Dobbing, J.
1968. Vulnerable Periods in Developing Brain. In: *Applied Neurochemistry,* A. N. Davison and J. Dobbing, eds. F. A. Davis, Philadelphia. pp. 287–316.

Dobzhansky, T.
1950. The Genetic Nature of Differences among Men. In: *Evolutionary Thought in America,* S. Persons, ed. Yale Univ. Press, New Haven. pp. 86–155.

———.
1951. *Genetics and the Origin of Species.* 3rd Ed., Revised. Columbia Univ. Press, New York.

———.
1962. *Mankind Evolving.* Yale Univ. Press, New Haven.

———.
1963. Possibility That *Homo Sapiens* Evolved Independently 5 Times Is Vanishingly Small. *Curr. Anthrop.* 4:360–367.

———.
1965. Mendelism, Darwinism, and Evolutionism. *Proc. Am. Phil. Soc.* 109:205–215.

———.
1968. Adaptedness and Fitness. In: *Population Biology and Evolution,* R. C. Lewontin, ed. Syracuse Univ. Press, Syracuse. pp. 109–121.

———.
1970. *Genetics of the Evolutionary Process.* Columbia Univ. Press, New York

Dorland's Illustrated Medical Dictionary. 24th Ed., 1965. W. B. Saunders, Philadelphia.

Dreizen, S., C. N. Spirakis, and R. E. Stone
1967. A Comparison of Skeletal Growth and Maturation in Undernourished and Well-Nourished Girls before and after Menarche. *J. Pediat.* 70:256–263.

Driver, H.
1965. Survey of Numerical Classification in Anthropology. In: *The Use of Computers in Anthropology,* D. Hymes, ed. Mouton, The Hague. pp. 302–344.

Dronamraju, K. R.
1960. Hypertrichosis of the Pinna of the Human Ear, Y-Linked Pedigrees. *J. Genet.* 57:230–243.

Dubois, E.
1894. *Pithecanthropus Erectus, eine Menschenahnliche Ubergangsform aus Java.* Batavia.

Dubos, R.
1965. *Man Adapting.* Yale Univ. Press, New Haven.

Dunbar, C. O., and J. Rodgers
1957. *Principles of Stratigraphy.* John Wiley and Sons, New York.

DuPraw, E. J.
1972. Stages in Chromosome Evolution: The Chromatid Twins and How They Grew. In: *Evolution of Genetic Systems,* H. H. Smith, ed. Gordon and Breach, New York. pp. 230–249.

Dyke, B., and J. MacCluer (eds.)
1974. *Computer Simulation in Human Population Studies.* Academic Press, New York.

Eagen, C. J.
1963. Introduction and Terminology: Habituation and Peripheral Tissue Adaptations. *Fed. Proc.* 22:930–932.

Eckland, B.
1968. Theories of Mate Selection. *Eugen. Quart.* 15:71–84.

Edwards, A. W. F., and M. Fraccaro
1958. The Sex Distribution in the Offspring of 5477 Swedish Ministers of Religion 1585–1920. *Hereditas* 44:447–450.

Edwards, J. G.
1954. A New Approach to Infraspecific Categories. *Syst. Zoo.* 3:1–20.

Ehrlich, P. R., and A. H. Ehrlich
1970. *Population, Resources, Environment. Issues in Human Ecology.* W. H. Freeman, San Francisco.

Ehrlich, P. R., and R. W. Holm
1964. A Biological View of Race. In: *The Concept of Race,* A. Montagu, ed. The Free Press, New York. pp. 153–179.

Eiseley, L.
1961. *Darwin's Century. Evolution and the Men Who Discovered It.* Doubleday and Co., Garden City, N.Y.

Eisenberg, J. F.
1973. Mammalian Social Systems: Are Primate Social Systems Unique? *Symp. IVth Internat. Congr. Primat.,* Vol. 1: *Precultural Primate Behavior.* Karger, Basel. pp. 232–249.

Eisenberg, J. F., N. A. Muckenhirn, and R. Rudran
1972. The Relation between Ecology and Social Structure in Primates. *Science* 176:863–874.

El-Hefnawi, H., S. M. Smith, and L. S. Penrose
1965. Xeroderma Pigmentosum—Its Inheritance and Relationships to the ABO Blood-Group System. *Ann. Hum. Genet.* 28:273–290.

Ellefson, J. O.
1968. Territorial Behavior in the Common White-Handed Gibbon, *Hylobates lar* Linn. In: *Primates. Studies in Adaptation and Variability,* P. C. Jay, ed. Holt, Rinehart and Winston, New York. pp. 180–199.

Elsner, R. W., J. D. Nelms, and L. Irving
1960. Circulation of Heat to the Hands of Arctic Indians. *J. Appl. Physiol.* 15:662–666.

Emlen, J. M.
1973. *Ecology: An Evolutionary Approach.* Addison-Wesley, Reading, Mass.

Ennouchi, E.
1962a. Un Crane d'Homme Ancien au Jebel Irhoud (Maroc). *C. R. Acad. Sci. Paris* 254:4330–4332.

———.
1962b. Un Neandertalien: L'Homme de Jebel Irhoud (Maroc). *L'Anthrop.* 66:279–299.

1963. Les Neandertaliens de Jebel Irhoud (Maroc). *C. R. Acad. Sci. Paris*
256:2459–2460.

Erikson, G. E.
1963. Braciation in New World Monkeys and Anthropoid Apes. *Symp.
Zoo. Soc., London* 10:135–164.

Eveleth, P. B., and J. M. Tanner
1976. *Worldwide Variation in Human
Growth.* Cambridge Univ. Press, Cambridge.

Evernden, J. F., and G. H. Curtis
1965. The Potassium-Argon Dating of
late Cenozoic Rocks in East Africa
and Italy. *Curr. Anthrop.* 6:343–385.

Fabia, J.
1969. Illegitimacy and Down's Syndrome. *Nature* 221:1157–1158.

Falconer, D. S.
1960. *Introduction to Quantitative Genetics.* Ronald Press, New York.

Farquharson, S. M.
1976. Growth Patterns and Nutrition
in Nepali Children. *Arch. Dis. Child.*
51:3–12.

**Feldman, M. W., M. Nabholz, and
W. F. Bodmer**
1969. Evolution of the Rh Polymorphism: A Model for the Interaction of
Incompatibility, Reproductive Compensation, and Heterozygote Advantage. *Am. J. Hum. Genet.* 21:171–193.

Feller, W.
1957. *An Introduction to Probability
Theory and Its Applications.* Vol. I,
2nd Ed. John Wiley and Sons, New
York.

Fenner, F.
1953. Host-Parasite Relationships in
Myxomatosis of the Australian Wild
Rabbit. *Cold Spring Harb. Symp.
Quant. Biol.* 18:291–294.

―――.
1965. Myxoma Virus and *Oryctolagus
cuniculus.* In: *The Genetics of Colon-
izing Species,* H. G. Baker and G. L.
Stebbins, eds. Academic Press, New
York. pp. 485–501.

**Field, C. M. B., N. A. J. Carson, D. C.
Cusworth, C. E. Dent, and D. W. Neill**
1962. Homocystinuria. A New Disorder of Metabolism. (Abstract).
Tenth Internat. Congr. Ped: 274. Lis-
bon, Portugal.

Fisher, R. A.
1930. The Genetical Theory of Natural Selection. Clarendon Press, Oxford. Revised Ed., 1958, Dover Press,
New York.

―――.
1935. The Detection of Linkage with
"Dominant" Abnormalities. *Ann.
Eugen.* 6:187–201.

―――.
1950. Gene Frequencies in a Cline
Determined by Selection and Diffusion. *Biometrics* 6:353–361.

Fitzhardinge, P. M., and E. M. Steven
1972. The Small-for-Date Infants. I.
Later Growth Patterns. *Pediatrics*
49:671–681.

Folk, G. E., Jr.
1966. *Introduction to Environmental
Physiology.* Lea and Febiger, Philadelphia.

Forbes, G. B.
1977. Nutrition and Growth. *J. Pediat.*
91:40–42.

Ford, E. B.
1940. Polymorphism and Taxonomy.
In: *The New Systematics,* J. S. Huxley, ed. Oxford Univ. Press, London.
pp. 493–513.

―――.
1964. *Ecological Genetics.* Methuen,
London.

Fraser, G. R.
1972. Unsolved Mendelian Diseases.
In: *The Biochemical Genetics of Man,*
D. J. H. Brock and O. Mayo, eds.
Academic Press, New York. pp.
639–652.

Frisancho, A. R.
1970. Developmental Responses to
High Altitude Hypoxia. *Am. J. Phys.
Anthrop.* 32:401–407.

―――.
1976. Growth and Morphology at
High Altitude. In: *Man in the Andes,*
P. Baker and M. Little, eds. Dowden,
Hutchinson and Ross, Stroudsburg
Pa. pp. 180–207.

Frisancho, A. R., and P. T. Baker
1970. Altitude and Growth: A Study
of the Patterns of Physical Growth of
a High Altitude Peruvian Quechua
Population. *Am. J. Phys. Anthrop.*
32:279–292.

**Frisancho, A. R., J. Sanchez, D.
Pallardel, and L. Yanez**
1973a. Adaptive Significance of Small
Body Size under Poor Socio-
Economic Conditions in Southern
Peru. *Am. J. Phys. Anthrop.*
39:255–261.

**Frisancho, A. R., T. Velasquez, and J.
Sanchez**
1973b. Influence of Developmental
Adaptation on Lung Function at High
Altitude. *Hum. Biol.* 45:583–594.

Frisch, R. E.
1972. Critical Weight at Menarche,
Initiation of the Adolescent Growth
Spurt and Control of Puberty. In:
Control of Onset of Puberty, M. M.
Grumbach, G. D. Grave, and F. E.
Mayer, eds. John Wiley and Sons,
New York. pp. 403–423.

―――.
1975. Critical Weights, A Critical
Body Composition, Menarche, and
the Maintenance of Menstrual Cycles.
In: *Biosocial Interrelations in Popula-
tion Adaptation,* E. S. Watts, F. E.
Johnston, and G. W. Lasker, eds.
Mouton, The Hague. pp. 319–352.

Frisch, R. E., and J. W. McArthur
1974. Menstrual Cycles: Fatness As a
Determinant of Minimum Weight for
Height Necessary for Their Maintenance or Onset. *Science* 185:949–951.

Frisch, R. E., and R. Revelle
1970. Height and Weight at Menarche
and a Hypothesis of Critical Body
Weights and Adolescent Events. *Science* 169:397–399.

―――.
1971. The Height and Weight of Girls
and Boys at the Time of Initiation of
the Adolescent Growth Spurt in
Height and Weight and the Relationship to Menarche. *Hum. Biol.*
43:140–159.

Gans, C.
1974. *Biomechanics. An Approach to
Vertebrate Biology.* J. B. Lippincott,
Philadelphia.

Garn, S. M.
1971. *Human Races.* 3rd Ed. C. C.
Thomas, Springfield, Ill.

Garn, S. M., D. C. Clark, and K. E. Guire
1973. Level of Fatness and Size Attainment. *Am. J. Phys. Anthrop.* 40:447–449.

Garn, S. M., C. G. Rohmann, and F. N. Silverman
1967. Radiographic Standards for Postnatal Ossification and Tooth Calcification. *Med. Radiogr. Photogr.* 43:45–66.

Garnham, P. C. C.
1966. *Malaria Parasites and Other Haemosporidia.* Blackwell, Oxford.

Garrow, J. S., and M. C. Pike
1967. The Long-Term Prognosis of Severe Infantile Malnutrition. *Lancet* 1:1–4.

Gazin, C. L.
1958. A Review of the Middle and Upper Eocene Primates of North America. *Smith. Misc. Coll.* 136:1–112.

The Genetic Code.
Cold Spring Harb. Symp. Quant. Biol. 31 (1966).

Genoves, S.
1966. *La Proporcionalidad entre los Huesos Largos y su Relacion con la Estatura en Restos Mesoamericanos.* Instituto de Investigaciones Historicas, Serie Antropologica No. 19. Universidad Nacional Autonoma de Mexico, Mexico, D. F.

Gerritsen, T., J. G. Vaughn, and H. A. Waisman
1962. The Identification of Homocystine in the Urine. *Biochem. Biophys. Res. Commun.* 9:492–496.

Ghiselin, M. T.
1969. *The Triumph of the Darwinian Method.* Univ. of California Press, Berkeley.

Giblett, E. R.
1969. *Genetic Markers in Human Blood.* Blackwell, Oxford.

Giese, A. C.
1962. *Cell Physiology.* W. B. Saunders, Philadelphia.

Giesel, J. T.
1974. *The Biology and Adaptability of Natural Populations.* C. V. Mosby, St. Louis.

Giles, E., and O. Elliot
1963. Sex Determination by Discriminant Function Analysis of Crania. *Am. J. Phys. Anthrop.* 21:53–68.

Gillispie, C. C.
1959. Lamarck and Darwin in the History of Science. In: *Forerunners of Darwin: 1745–1859,* B. Glass, O. Temkin, and W. L. Straus, Jr., eds. Johns Hopkins Press, Baltimore. pp. 265–291.

Gilmour, J. S. L.
1940. Taxonomy and Philosophy. In: *The New Systematics,* J. Huxley, ed. Oxford Univ. Press, London. pp. 461–474.

Glass, B.
1950. The Action of Selection on the Principal Rh Alleles. *Am. J. Hum. Genet.* 2:269–278.

———.
1954. Genetic Changes in Human Populations, Especially Those Due to Gene Flow and Genetic Drift. *Adv. Genet.* 6:95–139.

———.
1959. Heredity and Variation in the Eighteenth Century Concept of the Species. In: *Forerunners of Darwin: 1745–1859,* B. Glass, O. Temkin, and W. L. Straus, Jr., eds. Johns Hopkins Press, Baltimore. pp. 144–172.

Glass, B., and C. C. Li
1953. The Dynamics of Racial Intermixture—An Analysis Based on the American Negro. *Am. J. Hum. Genet.* 5:1–20.

Glass, B., M. S. Sacks, E. F. Jahn, and C. Hess
1952. Genetic Drift in a Religious Isolate: An Analysis of the Causes of Variation in Blood Group and Other Gene Frequencies in a Small Population. *Am. Nat.* 86:145–160.

Glass, B., O. Temkin, and W. L. Straus, Jr. (eds.)
1959. *Forerunners of Darwin: 1745–1859.* Johns Hopkins Press, Baltimore.

Glick, C. E.
1970. Interracial Marriage and Admixture in Hawaii. *Soc. Biol.* 17:278–291.

Glick, P. C.
1970. Intermarriage among Ethnic Groups in the United States. *Soc. Biol.* 17:292–298.

Glimcher, M. J., and E. P. Katz
1965. The Organization of Collagen in Bone: The Role of Noncovalent Bonds in the Relative Insolubility of Bone Collagen. *J. Ultrastruct. Res.* 12:705–729.

Goldberg, M. B., A. L. Scully, I. L. Solomon, and H. L. Steinbach
1968. Gonadal Dysgenesis in Phenotypic Female Subjects. A Review of Eighty-Seven Cases, with Cytogenetic Studies in Fifty-Three. *Am. J. Med.* 45:529–543.

Goldsby, R. A.
1977. *Race and Races.* 2nd Ed. Macmillan, New York.

Goldschmidt, R.
1940. *The Material Basis of Evolution.* Yale Univ. Press, New Haven.

Goodman, M., J. Barnabas, and G. W. Moore
1973. Man, the Conservative and Revolutionary Mammal: Molecular Findings. *Yearbook of Phys. Anthrop.* 17:71–97.

Graham, G. G., A. Cordano, R. M. Blizzard, and D. B. Cheek
1969. Infantile Malnutrition: Changes in Body Composition during Rehabilitation. *Pediat. Res.* 3:579–589.

Greene, J. C.
1959. *The Death of Adam. Evolution and Its Impact on Western Thought.* Iowa State Univ. Press, Ames, Iowa.

Gregory, W. K.
1920. On the Structure and Relations of *Notharctus,* an American Eocene Primate. *Mem. Amer. Mus. Nat. Hist.* 3:49–243.

Greulich, W. W., and S. I. Pyle
1959. *Radiographic Atlas of Skeletal Development of the Hand and Wrist.* 2nd Ed. Stanford Univ. Press, Palo Alto, Calif.

Groves, C. P.
1971. Distribution and Place of Origin of the Gorilla. *Man* 6:44–51.

Gruenwald, P., H. Funakawa, S. Mitani, T. Nishimura, and S. Takeuchi
1967. Influence of Environmental Factors on Fetal Growth in Man. *Lancet* 1:1026–1028.

Grundmann, E.
1966. *General Cytology. An Introduction to Functional Morphology of the Cell.* Williams and Wilkins, Baltimore.

Gunther, M., and L. S. Penrose
1935. The Genetics of Epiloia. *J. Genet.* 31:413–430.

Gurdon, J. B.
1968. Transplanted Nuclei and Cell Differentiation. *Sci. Amer.* 219:24–36.

Guyton, A. C.
1976a. *Textbook of Medical Physiology.* 5th Ed. W. B. Saunders, Philadelphia.

———.
1976b. *Basic Human Physiology: Normal Function and Mechanism of Disease.* 2nd Ed. W. B. Saunders, Philadelphia.

Gwei-Djen, L., and J. Needham
1967. Records of Diseases in Ancient China. In: *Diseases in Antiquity,* D. Brothwell and A. T. Sandison, eds. C. C. Thomas, Springfield, Ill. pp. 222–237.

Habicht, J. P., R. Martorell, C. Yarbrough, R. M. Malina, and R. E. Klein
1974. Height and Weight Standards for Preschool Children. *Lancet* 1:611–614.

Haldane, J. B. S.
1934. Methods for the Detection of Autosomal Linkage in Man. *Ann. Eugen.* 6:26–65.

———.
1946. The Cumulants of the Distribution of Fisher's "u_{11}" and "u_{31}" Scores Used in the Detection and Estimation of Linkage in Man. *Ann. Eugen.* 13:122–134.

———.
1948. The Theory of a Cline. *J. Genet.* 48:277–284.

———.
1949. Disease and Evolution. *La Ricer. Sci.* 19, Suppl. 1:3–10.

Hall, K. R. L.
1965a. Behavior and Ecology of the Wild Patas Monkey, *Erythrocebus Patas,* in Uganda. *J. Zoo.* 148:15–87.

———.
1965b. Experiment and Quantification in the Study of Baboon Behavior in Its Natural Habitat. In: *The Baboon in Medical Research,* H. Vagtborg, ed. Univ. of Texas Press, Austin. pp. 29–42.

Hall, K. R. L., and I. DeVore
1965. Baboon Social Behavior. In: *Primate Behavior. Field Studies of Monkeys and Apes,* I. DeVore, ed. Holt, Rinehart and Winston, New York. pp. 53–110.

Hall, K. R. L., and B. Mayer
1967. Social Interactions in a Group of Captive Patas Monkeys (*Erythrocebus Patas*). *Folia Primat.* 5:213–236.

Hamilton, W. J., J. D. Boyd, and H. W. Mossman
1964. *Human Embryology.* Williams and Wilkins, Baltimore.

Hampton, J. K., S. H. Hampton, and B. T. Landwehr
1966. Observations on a Successful Breeding Colony of the Marmoset, *Oedipomidas Oedipus. Folia Primat.* 4:265–287.

Hanna, J. M.
1970. Responses of Native and Migrant Desert Residents to Arid Heat. *Am. J. Phys. Anthrop.* 32:187–196.

Hanna, J. M., and P. T. Baker
1974. Comparative Heat Tolerance of Shipibo Indians and Peruvian *Mestizos. Hum. Biol.* 46:69–80.

Hanna, J. M., and R. M. Smith
1975. Responses of Hawaiian-Born Japanese and Caucasians to a Standardized Cold Exposure. *Hum. Biol.* 47:427–440.

Hardy, G. H.
1908. Mendelian Proportions in a Mixed Population. *Science* 28:49–50.

Harris, H.
1975. *The Principles of Human Biochemical Genetics.* 2nd Ed. Elsevier, New York.

Harrison, G. A., and A. J. Boyce (eds.)
1972. *The Structure of Human Populations.* Clarendon Press, Oxford.

Harrison, G. A., and J. J. T. Owen
1964. Studies on the Inheritance of Human Skin Color. *Ann. Hum. Genet.* 28:27–37.

Harrison, G. A., J. S. Weiner, J. M. Tanner, and N. A. Barnicot
1964. *Human Biology. An Introduction to Human Evolution, Variation, and Growth.* Oxford Univ. Press, New York. 2nd Ed. 1977.

Hausfater, G.
1975. Dominance and Reproduction in Baboons (*Papio Cynocephalus*). A Quantitative Analysis. *Contrib. Primat.* 7. S. Karger, Basel.

Hecht, F., and J. P. Macfarlane
1969. Mosaicism in Turner's Syndrome Reflects the Lethality of XO. *Lancet* 2:1197–1198.

Hemmer, H.
1972. Notes sur la Position Phyletique de l'Homme de Petralona. *L'Anthrop.* 76:155–162.

Hempel, C. G.
1965. Fundamentals of Taxonomy. In: *Aspects of Scientific Explanation and Other Essays in the Philosophy of Science,* C. G. Hempel, ed. The Free Press, New York. pp. 137–154.

Heywood, V. H., and J. McNeill (eds.)
1964. *Phenetic and Phylogenetic Classification.* The Systematics Association, Publ. No. 6, London.

Hiernaux, J.
1968. *La Diversite Humanie en Afrique Subsaharienne. Recherches Biologiques.* Editions de l'Institut de Sociologie de l'Universite Libre de Bruxelles, Brussels, Belgium.

Hiernaux, J., and A. Froment
1976. The Correlations between Anthropobiological and Climatic Variables in Sub-Saharan Africa: Revised Estimates. *Hum. Biol.* 48:757–767.

Higgs, E. S.
1961. Some Pleistocene Faunas of the Mediterranean Coastal Areas. *Proc. Prehist. Soc.* 27:144–154.

Hill, W. C. O.
1972. *Evolutionary Biology of the Primates.* Academic Press, New York.

Hirszfeld, L., and H. Hirszfeld
1918–1919. Essai d'Application des Methodes Serologiques au Probleme des Races. *Anthropologie* 29:505–537.

1919. Serological Differences between the Blood of Different Races. The Results of Researches on the Macedonian Front. *Lancet* ii:675–679.

Ho, Tong-Yun
1967. The Amino Acids of Bone and Dentine Collagens in Pleistocene Mammals. *Biochem. Biophys. Acta.* 133:568–573.

Hoerr, N. L., S. I. Pyle, and C. C. Francis
1962. *Radiographic Atlas of Skeletal Development of the Foot and Ankle, A Standard of Reference.* C. C. Thomas, Springfield, Ill.

Hofer, H. O., and J. A. Wilson
1967. An Endocranial Cast of an Early Oligocene Primate. *Folia Primat.* 5:148–152.

Hole, F., and R. F. Heizer
1969. *An Introduction to Prehistoric Archeology.* 2nd Ed. Holt, Rinehart and Winston, New York.

Holloway, R. L.
1966. Cranial Capacity, Neural Reorganization, and Hominid Evolution: A Search for More Suitable Parameters. *Am. Anthrop.* 68:103–121.

1968. The Evolution of the Primate Brain: Some Aspects of Quantitative Relations. *Brain Research* 7:121–172.

1973a. Endocranial Volumes of Early African Hominids, and the Role of the Brain in Human Mosaic Evolution. *J. Hum. Evol.* 2:449–459.

1973b. New Endocranial Values for the East African Early Hominids. *Nature* 243:97–99.

1975. *The Role of Human Social Behavior in the Evolution of the Brain.* Am. Mus. Nat. Hist., New York.

Holmberg, C. G., and C. B. Laurell
1945. Studies on the Capacity of Serum to Bind Iron. A Contribution to Our Knowledge of the Regulation Mechanism of Serum Iron. *Acta Physiol. Scand.* 10:307–319.

Holzinger, K.
1929. The Relative Effect of Nature and Nurture Influences on Twin Differences. *J. Educ. Psychol.* 20:241–248.

Hook, E. B.
1973. Behavioral Implications of the Human XYY Genotype. *Science* 179:139–150.

Hooton, E. A.
1930. *The Indians of Pecos Pueblo.* Yale Univ. Press, New Haven.

Howell, F. C.
1952. Pleistocene Glacial Ecology and the Evolution of "Classic Neandertal" Man. *Southwest J. Anthrop.* 8:377–410.

1955. The Age of the Australopithecines of Southern Africa. *Am. J. Phys. Anthrop.* 13:635–662.

1957. The Evolutionary Significance of Variation and Varieties of "Neanderthal" Man. *Quart. Rev. Biol.* 32:330–347.

1965. *Early Man.* Time-Life Books, New York.

1966. Observations on the Earlier Phases of the European Lower Paleolithic. *Am. Anthrop.* 68:88–201.

1969a. Remains of Hominidae from Pliocene/Pleistocene Formations in the Lower Omo Basin, Ethiopia. *Nature* 223:1234–1239.

1969b. Forward. In: *Man and Culture in the Late Pleistocene. A Case Study,* by R. G. Klein, Chandler Publ. Co., San Francisco. pp. xxi–xxvi.

1976. Overview of the Pliocene and Earlier Pleistocene of the Lower Omo Basin, Southern Ethiopia. In: *Human Origins. Louis Leakey and the East African Evidence,* G. Ll. Isaac and E. R. McCown, eds. W. A. Benjamin, Menlo Park, Calif. pp. 227–268.

Howell, F. C., K. W. Butzer, and E. Aguirre
1963. Noticia Preliminar Sobre el Emplazamiento Acheulense de Torralba (Soria). *Excavaciones Arqueologicas en España* 10:1–38. Servicio Nacional de Excavaciones Arqueologicas, Madrid.

Howell, F. C., and Y. Coppens
1976. An Overview of Hominidae from the Omo Succession, Ethiopia. In: *Earliest Man and Environments in the Lake Rudolf Basin. Stratigraphy, Paleoecology, and Evolution,* Y. Coppens, F. C. Howell, G. Ll. Isaac, and R. E. F. Leakey, eds. Univ. of Chicago Press, Chicago. pp. 522–532.

Howells, W. W.
1969a. The Use of Multivariate Techniques in the Study of Skeletal Populations. *Am. J. Phys. Anthrop.* 31:311–314.

1969b. Criteria for Selection of Osteometric Dimensions. *Am. J. Phys. Anthrop.* 30:451–457.

1972. Physical Anthropology. *Yearbook of Phys. Anthrop.* 16:141.

1973a. Cranial Variation in Man. A Study by Multivariate Analysis of Patterns of Difference among Recent Human Populations. *Papers Peabody Mus. Arch. Ethn.* 67. Harvard Univ. Press, Cambridge.

1973b. *Evolution of the Genus Homo.* Addison-Wesley, Reading, Mass.

1973c. *The Pacific Islanders.* C. Scribner's Sons, New York.

1974. Neanderthals: Names, Hypotheses, and Scientific Method. *Am. Anthrop.* 76:24–38.

Hrdlicka, A.
1927. The Neanderthal Phase of Man. *J. Roy. Anthrop. Inst.* 57:249–273.

Hseuh, A. M., M. Simonson, M. J. Kellum, and B. F. Chow
1973. Perinatal Undernutrition and the Metabolic and Behavioral Development of the Offspring. *Nut. Rpts. Internat.* 7:437–445.

Huber, N.
1968. The Problem of Stature Increase: Looking from the Past to the Present. In: *The Skeletal Biology of*

Earlier Human Populations, D. R. Brothwell, ed. Pergamon Press, Oxford. pp. 67–102.

Hughes, A. R., and P. V. Tobias
1977. A Fossil Skull Probably of the Genus *Homo* from Sterkfontein, Transvaal. *Nature* 265:310–312.

Hull, D. L.
1965. The Effect of Essentialism on Taxonomy. *Brit. J. Phil. Sci.* 15:314–326; 16:1–18.

———.
1967. Certainty and Circularity in Evolutionary Taxonomy. *Evolution* 21:174–189.

———.
1970. Contemporary Systematic Philosophies. *Ann. Rev. Ecol. Syst.* 1:19–54.

Hulmes, D. J. S., A. Miller, D. A. D. Parry, K. A. Piez, and J. Woodhead-Galloway
1973. Analysis of the Primary Structure of Collagen for the Origin of Molecular Packing. *J. Mol. Biol.* 79:137–148.

Hulse, F. S.
1957. Linguistic Barriers to Gene-Flow. The Blood Groups of the Yakima, Okanagon, and Swinomish Indians. *Am. J. Phys. Anthrop.* 15:235–246.

Hunt, E.
1972. Physical Anthropology. *Yearbook of Phys. Anthrop.* 16:141–144.

Huxley, J. S.
1938. Clines: An Auxiliary Taxonomic Principle. *Nature* 142:219–220.

———.
1943. *Evolution. The Modern Synthesis.* Harper and Bros., New York.

Iampietro, P. R., R. F. Goldman, E. R. Buskirk, and D. E. Bass
1959. Responses of Negro and White Males to Cold. *J. Appl. Physiol.* 14:798–800.

Ingram, V. M.
1957. Gene Mutations in Human Haemoglobin: The Chemical Difference between Normal and Sickle Cell Haemoglobins. *Nature* 180:326–328.

———.
1959. Abnormal Human Haemoglobins. III. The Chemical Difference between Normal and Sickle Cell Haemoglobins. *Biochim. Biophys. Acta* 36:402–411.

Irvine, W.
1955. *Apes, Angels, and Victorians. The Story of Darwin, Huxley and Evolution.* McGraw-Hill, New York.

Itani, J.
1963. Paternal Care in the Wild Japanese Monkey, *Macaca Fuscata.* In: *Primate Social Behavior,* C. H. Southwick, ed. Van Nostrand, Princeton, N.J. pp. 91–97.

Itano, H. A., and J. V. Neel
1950. A New Inherited Abnormality of Human Haemoglobin. *Proc. Nat. Acad. Sci.* 36:613–617.

Ito, M.
1974. The Control Mechanisms of Cerebellar Motor Systems. In: *The Neurosciences Third Study Program,* F. O. Schmitt and F. G. Worden, eds. The MIT Press, Cambridge, Mass. pp. 293–303.

Jacob, T.
1972. The Absolute Date of the Djetis Beds at Modjokerto. *Antiquity* 46:148.

Jamison, P.
1972. The Eskimos of Northwestern Alaska: Their Univariate and Multivariate Anthropometric Variation. Ph.D. Dissertation, University of Wisconsin-Madison.

Jay, P.
1963. The Indian Langur Monkey (*Presbytis entellus*). In: *Primate Social Behavior,* C. H. Southwick, ed. Van Nostrand, Princeton, N.J. pp. 114–123.

———.
1968. Primate Field Studies and Human Evolution. In: *Primates. Studies in Adaptation and Variability,* P. C. Jay, ed. Holt, Rinehart and Winston, New York. pp. 487–503.

Jenkins, F. A., Jr.
1971. Limbs, Posture, and Locomotion in the Virginia Opossum (*Didelphis marsupialis*) and in Other Non-Cursorial Mammals. *J. Zoo., London* 165:303–315.

Jennings, H. S.
1916. The Numerical Results of Diverse Systems of Breeding. *Genetics* 1:53–89.

Jensen, A. R.
1969. How Much Can We Boost I.Q. and Scholastic Achievement? *Harvard Educ. Rev.* 39:1–123.

Johanson, D. C., and Y. Coppens
1976. A Preliminary Anatomical Diagnosis of the First Plio/Pleistocene Hominid Discoveries in the Central Afar, Ethiopia. *Am. J. Phys. Anthrop.* 45:217–234.

Johnson, L. C.
1966. Discussion. The Principles of Structural Analysis. In: *Human Paleopathology,* S. Jarcho, ed. Yale Univ. Press, New Haven. pp. 68–81.

Johnston, F. E.
1973. *Microevolution of Human Populations.* Prentice-Hall, Englewood Cliffs, N.J.

Jolly, A.
1972. *The Evolution of Primate Behavior.* Macmillan, New York.

Jolly, C. J.
1970. The Seed-Eaters: A New Model of Hominid Differentiation Based on a Baboon Analogy. *Man* 5:5–26.

Jolly, C. J., and F. Plog
1976. *Physical Anthropology and Archeology.* A. A. Knopf, New York.

Jones, F. Wood
1916. *Arboreal Man.* E. Arnold, London.

Jones, W. H. S.
1967. The Prevalence of Malaria in Ancient Greece. In: *Diseases in Antiquity,* D. Brothwell and A. T. Sandison, eds. C. C. Thomas, Springfield, Ill. pp. 170–176.

Kaplan, A.
1964. *The Conduct of Inquiry. Methodology for Behavioral Science.* Chandler, San Francisco.

Karn, M. N., and L. S. Penrose
1951. Birth Weight and Gestation Time in Relation to Maternal Age, Parity, and Infant Survival. *Ann. Eugen.* 16:147–164.

Kaufmann, I. C., and L. A. Rosenblum
1967. The Reaction to Separation in Infant Monkeys: Anaclitic Depression and Conservation-Withdrawal. *Psychosomat. Med.* 24:648–675.

Kaufmann, J. H.
1966. Behavior of Infant Rhesus Monkeys and Their Mothers in a Free-Ranging Band. *Zoologica* 51:17–28.

Keiding, J.
1967. Persistence of Resistant Populations after the Relaxation of the Selection Pressure. *World Rev. Pest Control* 6:115–130.

Keith, A.
1949. *A New Theory of Human Evolution.* Philosophical Library, New York.

Kennedy, K. A. R.
1972. Physical Anthropology. *Yearbook Phys. Anthrop.* 16:156–157.

———.
1975. *Neanderthal Man.* Burgess, Minneapolis.

Kettlewell, H. B. D.
1961. The Phenomenon of Industrial Melanism in the *Lepidoptera. Ann. Rev. Entom.* 6:245–262.

———.
1965. Insect Survival and Selection for Pattern. *Science* 148:1290–1296.

Keyfitz, N.
1966. How Many People Have Lived on the Earth? *Demography* 3:581–582.

Keyfitz, N., and W. Flieger
1971. *Population. Facts and Methods of Demography.* W. H. Freeman, San Francisco.

Khatri, A. P.
1975. The Early Fossil Hominids and Related Apes of the Siwalik Foothills of the Himalayas: Recent Discoveries and New Interpretations. In: *Paleoanthropology, Morphology, and Paleoecology,* R. Tuttle, ed. Mouton, The Hague. pp. 31–58.

Kimura, M.
1968. Evolution Rate at the Molecular Level. *Nature* 217:624–626.

Kimura, M., and T. Ohta
1971. Protein Polymorphism As a Phase of Molecular Evolution. *Nature* 229:467–469.

King, J. L.
1972. The Role of Mutation in Evolution. In: *Darwinian, Neo-Darwinian, and Non-Darwinian Evolution,* L. M. LeCam, J. Neyman, and E. L. Scott, eds. *Proc. Sixth Berkeley Symp. Math. Stat. Prob.* 5:69–100.

King, J. L., and T. H. Jukes
1969. Non-Darwinian Evolution. *Science* 164:788–798.

Klissouras, V.
1971. Heritability of Adaptive Variation. *J. Appl. Physiol.* 31:338–344.

Koertvelyessy, T.
1972. Relationships between the Frontal Sinus and Climatic Conditions: A Skeletal Approach To Cold Adaptation. *Am. J. Phys. Anthrop.* 37:161–172.

Kogut, M. D.
1973. Growth and Development in Adolescence. *Pediat. Clin. N. Amer.* 20:789–806.

Kohne, D. E., J. A. Chiscon, and B. H. Hoyer
1972. Evolution of Mammalian DNA. In: *Darwinian, Neo-Darwinian, and Non-Darwinian Evolution,* L. M. LeCam, J. Neyman, and E. L. Scott, eds. *Proc. Sixth Berkeley Symp. Math. Stat. Prob.* 5:193–209.

Kornhuber, H. H.
1974. Cerebral Cortex, Cerebellum, and Basal Ganglia: An Introduction to Their Motor Functions. In: *The Neurosciences Third Study Program,* F. O. Schmitt and F. G. Worden, eds. The MIT Press, Cambridge, Mass. pp. 267–280.

Kosower, N. S., and E. M. Kosower
1970. Molecular Basis for Selective Advantage of Glucose-6-Phosphate-Dehydrogenase-Deficient Individuals Exposed to Malaria. *Lancet* 2:1343–1345.

Kretzoi, M., and L. Vertes
1965. Upper Biharian (Intermindel) Pebble-Industry Occupation Site in Western Hungary. *Curr. Anthrop.* 6:74–87.

Krog, J., M. Alvik, and K. Lund-Larsen
1969. Investigations of the Circulatory Effects of Submersion of the Hand in Ice Water in the Finnish Lapps, the "Skolts." *Fed. Proc.* 28:1135–1137.

Krog, J., B. Folkow, R. H. Fox, and K. Lange Andersen
1960. Hand Circulation in the Cold of Lapps and North Norwegian Fishermen. *J. Appl. Physiol.* 15:654–658.

Krukoff, S.
1970. L'Occipital de la Chaise (Suard), Caracteres Metriques, Distances de Forme et de Format. *C. R. Acad. Sci. Paris* 270:42–45.

Kulin, H. E.
1974. The Physiology of Adolescence in Man. *Hum. Biol.* 46:133–144.

Kummer, H.
1967. Tripartite Relations in Hamadryas Baboons. In: *Social Communication among Primates,* S. A. Altmann, ed. Univ. of Chicago Press, Chicago. pp. 63–72.

———.
1971. *Primate Societies. Group Techniques of Ecological Adaptation.* Aldine, Chicago.

Lacey, K. A., J. M. Parkin, and G. H. Steel
1973. Relationship between Bone Age and Dental Development. *Lancet* 2:736–737.

Lambert, S. W., W. Wiegand, and W. M. Ivins, Jr.
1952. *Three Vesalian Essays to Accompany the Icones Anatomicae of 1934.* Macmillan, New York.

Landsteiner, K.
1900. Zur Kenntnis der Antifermentativen, Lytischen und Agglutinierenden Wirkungen des Blutserums und der Lymphe. *Zbl. Bakt.* 27:357–362.

———.
1901. Uber Agglutinationserscheinungen Normalen Menschlichen Blutes. *Wien. Klin. Wschr.* 14:1132–1134.

Landsteiner, K., and P. Levine
1927. A New Agglutinable Factor Differentiating Individual Human Bloods. *Proc. Soc. Exp. Biol. N.Y.* 24:600–602.

Landsteiner, K., and A. S. Wiener
1940. An Agglutinable Factor in Human Blood Recognized by Immune Sera for Rhesus Blood. *Proc. Soc. Exp. Biol. Med.* 43:223.

———.
1941. Studies on an Agglutinogen (Rh) in Human Blood Reacting with Anti-Rhesus Sera and with Human Isoantibodies. *J. Exp. Med.* 74:309–320.

Laron, Z., and I. H. Hochman
1971. Small Testes in Prepubertal Boys with Klinefelter's Syndrome. *J. Clin. Endo. Metabl.* 32:671–672.

Lasker, G. W.
1972. The Future of Physical Anthropology. *Yearbook Phys. Anthrop.* 16:146–148.

———.
1976. *Physical Anthropology.* 2nd Ed. Holt, Rinehart and Winston, New York.

Lauterstein, A. M.
1961. A Cross-Sectional Study in Dental Development and Skeletal Age. *J. Am. Dent. Assoc.* 62:161–167.

Leakey, L. S. B.
1959. A New Fossil Skull from Olduvai. *Nature* 184:491–493.

———.
1961. New Finds at Olduvai Gorge. *Nature* 189:649–650.

———.
1970. *The Stone Age Races of Kenya.* 2nd Ed. Oxford Univ. Press, London.

———.
1972. *Homo sapiens* in the Middle Pleistocene and the Evidence of *Homo sapiens'* Evolution. In: *The Origin of Homo sapiens,* F. Bordes, ed. UNESCO, Paris. pp. 25–29.

Leakey, L. S. B., and M. D. Leakey
1964. Recent Discoveries of Fossil Hominids in Tanganyika: At Olduvai and Near Lake Natron. *Nature* 202:5–7.

Leakey, L. S. B., P. V. Tobias, and J. R. Napier
1964. A New Species of the Genus *Homo* from the Olduvai Gorge. *Nature* 202:7–9.

Leakey, M. D.
1971. Discovery of Postcranial Remains of *Homo erectus* and Associated Artefacts in Bed IV at Olduvai Gorge, Tanzania. *Nature* 232:380–383.

———.
1975. Cultural Patterns in the Olduvai Sequence. In: *After the Australopithecines,* K. W. Butzer and G. L1. Isaac, eds. Mouton, The Hague. pp. 477–493.

———.
1976. A Summary and Discussion of the Archaeological Evidence from Bed I and Bed II, Olduvai Gorge, Tanzania. In: *Human Origins. Louis Leakey and the East African Evidence,* G. L1. Isaac and E. R. McCown, eds. W. A. Benjamin, Menlo Park, Calif. pp. 431–459.

Leakey, M. D., R. J. Clarke, and L. S. B. Leakey
1971. New Hominid Skull from Bed I, Olduvai Gorge, Tanzania. *Nature* 232:308–312.

Leakey, R. E. F.
1970. Fauna and Artifacts from a New Plio-Pleistocene Locality Near Lake Rudolf in Kenya. *Nature* 226:223–224.

———.
1971. Further Evidence of Lower Pleistocene Hominids from East Rudolf, North Kenya. *Nature* 231:241–245.

———.
1972. Further Evidence of Lower Pleistocene Hominids from East Rudolf, North Kenya, 1971. *Nature* 237:264–269.

———.
1973a. Australopithecines and Hominines: A Summary on the Evidence from the Early Pleistocene of Eastern Africa. *Symp. Zool. Soc. London.* 33:53–69.

———.
1973b. Evidence for an Advanced Plio-Pleistocene Hominid from East Rudolf, Kenya. *Nature* 242:447–450.

———.
1974. Further Evidence of Lower Pleistocene Hominids from East Rudolf, North Kenya, 1973. *Nature* 248:653–656.

———.
1976. New Hominid Fossils from the Koobi Fora Formation in Northern Kenya. *Nature* 261:574–576.

Leakey, R. E. F., K. W. Butzer, and M. H. Day
1969. Early *Homo sapiens* Remains from the Omo River Region of South-West Ethiopia. *Nature* 222:1132–1138.

Leakey, R. E. F., and G. Isaac
1976. East Rudolf: An Introduction to the Abundance of New Evidence. In: *Human Origins. Louis Leakey and the East African Evidence,* G. L1. Isaac and E. R. McCown, eds. W. A. Benjamin, Menlo Park, Calif. pp. 306–332.

Leakey, R. E. F., and A. C. Walker
1976. *Australopithecus, Homo erectus,* and the Single Species Hypothesis. *Nature* 261:572–574.

LeCam, L. M., J. Neyman, and E. L. Scott (eds.)
1972. Darwinian, Neo-Darwinian, and Non-Darwinian Evolution. *Proc. Sixth Berkeley Symp. Math. Stat. Prob.* 5. Univ. of Calif. Press, Berkeley.

Lechtig, A., H. Delgado, R. Lasky, C. Yarbrough, R. Klein, J. Habicht, and M. Behar
1976. Maternal Nutrition and Fetal Growth in Developing Countries. *Am. J. Dis. Child.* 129:553–561.

Le Gros Clark, W. E.
1947. Observations on the Anatomy of the Fossil Australopithecinae. *J. Anat. Lond.* 81:300–333.

———.
1959. *The Antecedents of Man. An Introduction to the Evolution of the Primates.* Edinburgh Univ. Press, Edinburgh.

———.
1964a. *The Fossil Evidence for Human Evolution.* Revised Ed. Univ. of Chicago Press, Chicago.

———.
1964b. The Endocranial Cast of the Swanscombe Bones. In: *The Swanscombe Skull. A Survey of Research on a Pleistocene Site,* C. D. Ovey, ed. *Roy. Anthrop. Inst., Occ. Paper* No. 20. pp. 139–144.

———.
1967. *Man-Apes or Ape-Men? The Story of Discoveries in Africa.* Holt, Rinehart and Winston, New York.

Lehninger, A. L.
1975. *Biochemistry. The Molecular Basis of Cell Structure and Function.* 2nd Ed. Worth Publ., New York.

Lemli, L., and D. W. Smith
1963. The XO Snydrome. A Study of the Differentiated Phenotype in 25 Patients. *J. Pediat.* 63:577–588.

Lerner, I. M.
1950. *Population Genetics and Animal Improvement.* Cambridge Univ. Press, Cambridge.

————.
1954. *Genetic Homeostasis.* Oliver and Boyd, Edinburgh.

————.
1968. *Heredity, Evolution, and Society.* W. H. Freeman, San Francisco.

Levin, B. R.
1967. The Effect of Reproductive Compensation on the Long Term Maintenance of the Rh Polymorphism: The Rh Crossroad Revisited. *Am. J. Hum. Genet.* 19:288–302.

Levine, P., E. Robinson, M. Celano, O. Briggs, and L. Falkinburg
1955. Gene Interaction Resulting in Suppression of Blood Group Substance B. *Blood* 10:1100–1108.

Levins, R.
1968. *Evolution in Changing Environments. Some Theoretical Explorations.* Princeton Univ. Press, Princeton, N.J.

Levitan, M., and A. Montagu
1971. *Textbook of Human Genetics.* Oxford Univ. Press, New York.

Lewontin, R. C.
1957. The Adaptations of Populations to Varying Environments. *Cold Spring Harbor Symp. Quant. Biol.* 22:395–408.

————.
1974. *The Genetic Basis of Evolutionary Change.* Columbia Univ. Press, New York.

Lewontin, R., D. Kirk, and J. F. Crow
1968. Selective Mating, Assortative Mating, and Inbreeding: Definitions and Implications. *Eugen. Quart.* 15:141–143.

Li, C. C.
1955. *Population Genetics.* Univ. of Chicago Press, Chicago.

————.
1970. Human Genetic Adaptation. In: *Essays in Evolution and Genetics in Honor of Theodosius Dobzhansky*, M. K. Hecht and W. C. Steere, eds. Appleton-Century-Crofts, New York. pp. 545–577.

————.
1976. *First Course in Population Genetics.* Boxwood Press, Pacific Grove, Calif.

Li, Wen-Hsiung, and M. Nei
1972. Total Number of Individuals Affected by a Single Deleterious Mutation in a Finite Population. *Am. J. Hum. Genet.* 24:667–679.

Little, M. A., R. B. Thomas, R. B. Mazess, and P. T. Baker
1971. Population Differences and Developmental Changes in Extremity Temperature Responses to Cold among Andean Indians. *Hum. Biol.* 43:70–91.

Littlejohn, M. J.
1969. The Systematic Significance of Isolating Mechanisms. In: *Systematic Biology. Proceedings of an International Conference.* Nat. Acad. Sci. Publ. 1692, Washington, D.C. pp. 459–493.

Livingstone, F. B.
1958. Anthropological Implications of Sickle Cell Gene Distribution in West Africa. *Am. Anthrop.* 60:533–562.

————.
1964a. On the Nonexistence of Human Races. In: *The Concept of Race*, A. Montagu, ed. The Free Press, New York. pp. 46–60.

————.
1964b. The Distribution of the Abnormal Hemoglobin Genes and Their Significance for Human Evolution. *Evol.* 18:685–699.

————.
1969. Gene Frequency Clines of the β Hemoglobin Locus in Various Human Populations and Their Simulation by Models Involving Differential Selection. *Hum. Biol.* 41:223–236.

————.
1971. Malaria and Human Polymorphisms. *Ann. Rev. Genet.* 5:33–64.

————.
1973. Data on the Abnormal Hemoglobins and Glucose-6-Phosphate Dehydrogenase Deficiency in Human Populations. 1967–1973. *Tech. Rpts. No. 3, Cont. Hum. Biol. No. 1*, Museum of Anthropology, Univ. of Michigan, Ann Arbor.

————.
1976. Hemoglobin History in West Africa. *Hum. Biol.* 48:487–500.

Loizos, C.
1969. Play Behavior in Higher Primates: A Review. In: *Primate Ethology*, D. Morris, ed., Doubleday, Garden City, N.Y. pp. 226–282.

Loomis, W. F.
1967. Skin-Pigment Regulation of Vitamin-D Synthesis in Man. *Science* 157:501–506.

Lovejoy, A. O.
1936. *The Great Chain of Being.* Harper and Row, New York.

Lovejoy, C. O.
1974. The Gait of Australopithecines. *Yearbook Phys. Anthrop.* 17:147–161.

Lowrey, G. H.
1973. *Growth and Development of Children.* 6th Ed. Year Book Medical Publ., Chicago.

Luzzatto, L., E. S. Nwachuku-Jarrett, and S. Reddy
1970. Increased Sickling of Parasitized Erythrocytes as Mechanism of Resistance against Malaria in the Sickle-Cell Trait. *Lancet* 1:319–322.

Luzzatto, L., E. A. Usanga, and S. Reddy
1969. Glucose-6-Phosphate Dehydrogenase Deficient Red Cells: Resistance to Infection by Malarial Parasites. *Science* 164:839–842.

MacArthur, R. H.
1972. *Geographical Ecology. Patterns in the Distribution of Species.* Harper and Row, New York.

MacArthur, R. H., and E. O. Wilson
1967. The Theory of Island Biogeography. *Monogr. in Pop. Biol.*, No. 1. Princeton Univ. Press, Princeton, N.J.

MacKinnon, J.
1974. The Behavior and Ecology of Wild Orang-Utans (*Pongo pygmaeus*). *Animal Behavior* 22:3–74.

MacRoberts, M. H.
1970. The Social Organization of Barbary Apes (*Macaca sylvana*) on Gibraltar. *Am. J. Phys. Anthrop.* 33:83–100.

Mann, A., and E. Trinkaus
1974. Neandertal and Neandertal-Like Fossils from the Upper Pleistocene. *Yearbook Phys. Anthrop.* 17:169–193.

Margulis, L.
1974. Five-Kingdom Classification and the Origin and Evolution of Cells. In: *Evolutionary Biology*, Vol. 7, T. Dobzhansky, M. K. Hecht, and W. C. Steere, eds. Plenum Press, New York. pp. 45–78.

Marshall, I. D.
1958. Studies in the Epidemiology of Infectious Myxomatosis of Rabbits. V. Changes in the Innate Resistance of Australian Wild Rabbits Exposed to Myxomatosis. *J. Hyg.* 56:288–302.

Marshall, W. A.
1974. Interrelationships of Skeletal Maturation, Sexual Development, and Somatic Growth in Man. *Ann. Hum. Biol.* 1:29–40.

_____.
1976a. Growth before Puberty—Catch-up Growth. In: *Early Nutrition and Later Development*, A. W. Wilkinson, ed. Year Book Medical Publishers, Chicago. pp. 124–133.

_____.
1976b. Adolescent Development. In: *Early Nutrition and Later Development*, A. W. Wilkinson, ed. Year Book Medical Publishers, Chicago. pp. 190–197.

Marshall, W. A., and J. M. Tanner
1970. Variations in the Pattern of Pubertal Changes in Boys. *Arch. Dis. Child.* 45:13–23.

Martin, A. O., T. W. Kurczynski, and A. G. Steinberg
1973. Familial Studies of Medical and Anthropometric Variables in a Human Isolate. *Am. J. Hum. Genet.* 25:581–593.

Martin, R. D.
1975. Strategies of Reproduction. *Nat. Hist.* 84:48–57.

Martin, R. D., G. A. Doyle, and A. C. Walker (eds.)
1974. *Prosimian Biology*. Duckworth, London.

Martyn, J. E., and P. V. Tobias
1967. Pleistocene Deposits and New Fossil Localities in Kenya. *Nature* 215:476–480.

Mason, W. A.
1965. The Social Development of Monkeys and Apes. In: *Primate Behavior. Field Studies of Monkeys and Apes*, I. DeVore, ed. Holt, Rinehart and Winston, New York. pp. 175–196.

_____.
1968. Use of Space by Callicebus Groups. In: *Primates: Studies in Adaptation and Variability*, P. C. Jay, ed. Holt, Rinehart and Winston, New York. pp. 200–216.

Mata, L. J., J. J. Urrutia, R. A. Kronmal, and C. Joplin
1975. Survival and Physical Growth in Infancy and Early Childhood. *Am. J. Dis. Child.* 129:561–566.

Mather, K.
1964. *Human Diversity. The Nature and Significance of Differences among Men.* The Free Press, New York.

Matsunaga, E., and S. Itoh
1958. Blood Groups and Fertility in a Japanese Population, with Special Reference to Intra-Uterine Selection Due to Maternal-Foetal Incompatibility. *Ann. Hum. Genet.* 22:111–131.

Matter, P., and H. W. Miller
1972. The Amino Acid Composition of Some Cretaceous Fossils. *Comp. Biochem. Physiol.* 43B:55–66.

Mayo, O.
1975. Fundamental and Population Genetics. In: *Textbook of Human Genetics*, G. Fraser and O. Mayo, eds. Blackwell, Oxford. pp. 3–65.

Mayr, E.
1940. Speciation Phenomena in Birds. *Am. Nat.* 74:249–278.

_____.
1942. *Systematics and the Origin of Species*. Columbia Univ. Press, New York.

_____.
1944. On the Concepts and Terminology of Vertical Subspecies and Species. *Nat. Res. Council Bull.* 2:11–16.

_____.
1950. Taxonomic Categories in Fossil Hominids. *Cold Spring Harbor Symp. Quant. Biol.* 15:109–118.

_____.
1954. Notes on Nomenclature and Classification. *Syst. Zoo.* 3:86–89.

_____.
1956. Geographical Character Gradients and Climatic Adaptation. *Evolution* 10:105–108.

_____.
1957. Species Concepts and Definitions. In: *The Species Problem*, E. Mayr, ed. *Am. Assoc. Adv. Sci.*, Publ. No. 50. pp. 1–22.

_____.
1959a. Agassiz, Darwin, and Evolution. *Harvard Libr. Bull.* 13:165–194.

_____.
1959b. Darwin and the Evolutionary Theory in Biology. In: *Evolution and Anthropology: A Centennial Appraisal. Anthrop. Soc. Washington,* Washington, D.C. pp. 1–10.

_____.
1963. *Animal Species and Evolution.* Harvard Univ. Press, Cambridge.

_____.
1965. Numerical Phenetics and Taxonomic Theory. *Syst. Zoo.* 14:73–97.

_____.
1969. *Principles of Systematic Zoology.* McGraw-Hill, New York.

Mazess, R. B.
1968. The Oxygen Cost of Breathing in Man: Effects of Altitude, Training, and Race. *Am. J. Phys. Anthrop.* 29:365–375.

_____.
1970. Cardiorespiratory Characteristics and Adaptation to High Altitudes. *Am. J. Phys. Anthrop.* 32:267–278.

_____.
1975a. Human Adaptation to High Altitude. In: *Physiological Anthropology*, A. Damon, ed. Oxford Univ. Press, New York. pp. 167–209.

_____.
1975b. Biological Adaptation: Aptitudes and Acclimatization. In: *Biosocial Interrelations in Population Adaptation*, E. S. Watts, F. E. Johnston, and G. W. Lasker, eds. Mouton, The Hague. pp. 9–18.

McConnell, D.
1962. Dating of Fossil Bones by the Fluorine Method. *Science* 136:241–244.

McCown, T. D., and A. Keith
1939. *The Stone Age of Mount Carmel. Vol. 2: The Fossil Human Remains from the Levalloiso-Mousterian.* Clarendon Press, Oxford.

McCutcheon, F. H.
1964. Organ Systems in Adaptation: The Respiratory System. In: *Handbook of Physiology, Vol. 4. Adaptation to the Environment*, D. B. Dill, E. F. Adolph, and C. G. Wilbur, eds. Am. Physiol. Soc., Washington, D.C. pp. 167–191.

McKern, T. W.
1972. Physical Anthropology. *Yearbook Phys. Anthrop.* 16:144–145.

McKusick, V. A.
1969. *Human Genetics.* 2nd Ed. Prentice-Hall, Englewood Cliffs, N.J.

———.
1971. *Mendelian Inheritance in Man. Catalogs of Autosomal Dominant, Autosomal Recessive and X-Linked Phenotypes.* 3rd Ed. Johns Hopkins Press, Baltimore. 4th Ed., 1974.

McKusick, V. A., and G. A. Chase
1973. Human Genetics. *Ann. Rev. Genet.* 7:435–473.

McLean, F. C., and M. Urist
1968. *Bone. Fundamentals of the Physiology of Skeletal Tissue.* 3rd Ed. Univ. of Chicago Press, Chicago.

Medvedev, Z. A.
1969. *The Rise and Fall of T. D. Lysenko.* Columbia Univ. Press, New York.

Meldrum, B. S., and C. D. Marsden (eds.)
1975. *Advances in Neurology, Vol. 10. Primate Models of Neurological Disorders.* Raven Press, New York.

Mendel, G.
1866. Versuche uber Pflanzenhybriden. *Verh. Naturforsch. Verein. in Brunn* 4:3–47.

Mettler, L. E., and T. G. Gregg
1969. *Population Genetics and Evolution.* Prentice-Hall, Englewood Cliffs, N.J.

Meyer, M. B., and G. W. Comstock
1972. Maternal Cigarette Smoking and Perinatal Mortality. *Am. J. Epidemiol.* 96:1–10.

Michael, H. N., and E. K. Ralph (eds.)
1971. *Dating Techniques for the Archeologist.* MIT Press, Cambridge, Mass.

Michels, J. W.
1972. *Dating Methods in Archaeology.* Seminar Press, New York.

Mikkelsen, M., and J. Stene
1972. The Effect of Maternal Age on the Incidence of Down's Syndrome. *Humangenetik* 16:141–146.

Milicer, H., and F. Szczotka
1966. Age at Menarche in Warsaw Girls in 1965. *Hum. Biol.* 38:199–203.

Miller, D. S., and A. Wise
1976. The Energetics of "Catch-up" Growth. *Nutr. Metabl.* 20:125–134.

Miller, E. C., and J. A. Miller
1971. The Mutagenicity of Chemical Carcinogens: Correlations, Problems, and Interpretations. In: *Chemical Mutagens. Principles and Methods for Their Detection. Vol. 1*, A. Hollaender, ed. Plenum Press, New York. pp. 83–119.

Miller, E. J.
1973. A Review of Biochemical Studies on the Genetically Distinct Collagens of the Skeletal System. *Clin. Orthop.* 92:260–280.

Miller, M. J., J. V. Neel, and F. B. Livingstone
1956. Distribution of Parasites in the Red Cells of Sickle-Cell Trait Carriers Infected with *Plasmodium falciparum. Trans. Roy. Soc. Trop. Med. Hyg.* 50:294–296.

Milner, B.
1974. Hemispheric Specialization: Scope and Limits. In: *The Neurosciences Third Study Program*, F. O. Schmitt and F. G. Worden, eds. The MIT Press, Cambridge, Mass. pp. 75–89.

Mitchell, G., and E. M. Brandt
1972. Parental Behavior in Primates. In: *Primate Socialization*, F. E. Poirier, ed. Random House, New York. pp. 173–206.

Mohr, J.
1951. Estimation of Linkage between the Lutheran and the Lewis Blood Groups. *Acta Path. Microbiol. Scand.* 29:339–344.

Montagna, W., and W. P. McNulty (eds.)
1973. Nonhuman Primates and Human Diseases. *Proc. 4th Internat. Cong. Primatol.*, Vol. 4, S. Karger, Basel.

Montagu, A.
1962. The Concept of Race. *Am. Anthrop.* 64:919–928.

Moody, P. A.
1975. *Genetics of Man.* 2nd Ed. W. W. Norton, New York.

Morrison, D. F.
1967. *Multivariate Statistical Methods.* McGraw-Hill, New York.

Morton, N. E.
1955. Sequential Tests for the Detection of Linkage. *Am. J. Hum. Genet.* 7:277–318.

———.
1957. Further Scoring Types in Sequential Linkage Tests, with a Critical Review of Autosomal and Partial Sex Linkage in Man. *Am. J. Hum. Genet.* 9:55–75.

Morton, N. E. (ed.)
1973. Genetic Structure of Populations. *Pop. Genet. Monogr.*, Vol. 3. Univ. Press of Hawaii, Honolulu.

Morton, N. E., J. F. Crow, and H. J. Muller
1956. An Estimate of the Mutational Damage in Man from Data on Consanguineous Marriages. *Proc. Nat. Acad. Sci.* 42:855–863.

Morton, N. E., and D. C. Rao
1978. Quantitative Inheritance in Man. *Yearbook Phys. Anthrop.* 21:12–41.

Motulsky, A. G.
1960. Metabolic Polymorphisms and the Role of Infectious Diseases in Human Evolution. *Hum. Biol.* 32:28–62.

———.
1965. Theoretical and Clinical Problems of Glucose-6-Phosphate Dehydrogenase Deficiency. Its Occurrence in Africans and Its Combination with Hemoglobinopathy. In: *Abnormal Hemoglobins in Africa*, J. H. P. Jonxis, ed. F. A. Davis, Philadelphia. pp. 143–196a.

Motulsky, A. G., G. R. Fraser, and J. Felsenstein
1971. Public Health and Long-Term Genetic Implications of Intrauterine Diagnosis and Selective Abortion. *Birth Defects: Original Article Series* 7:22–32.

Motulsky, A. G., A. Yoshida, and G. Stamatoyannopoulos
1971. Variants of Glucose-6-Phosphate Dehydrogenase. *Ann. N. Y. Acad. Sci.* 179:636–643.

Mourant, A. E., A. C. Kopec, and K. Domaniewska-Sobczak
1958. *The ABO Blood Groups. Comprehensive Tables and Maps of World Distribution.* Blackwell, Oxford.

———.
1976. *The Distribution of the Human Blood Groups and Other Polymorphisms.* Oxford Univ. Press, London.

Moyers, R. E., and W. M. Krogman (eds.)
1971. *Cranio-Facial Growth in Man. Proceedings of a Conference on Genetics, Bone Biology, and Analysis of Growth Data.* Pergamon Press, Oxford.

Moynihan, M.
1964. Some Behavior Patterns of Platyrrhine Monkeys: The Night Monkey (*Aotus trivirgatus*). *Smith Misc. Coll.* 146, No. 5.

Muller, H. J.
1950. Our Load of Mutations. *Am. J. Hum. Genet.* 2:111–176.

Murayama, M.
1966. Molecular Mechanism of Red Cell "Sickling." *Science* 153:145–149.

Naeye, R. L., W. Blanc, and C. Paul
1973. Effects of Maternal Nutrition on the Human Fetus. *Pediatrics* 52:494–503.

Nagel, R., and O. Soto
1964. Haptoglobin Types in Native Chileans: A Hybrid Population. *Am. J. Phys. Anthrop.* 22:335–338.

Naismith, D. J.
1975. The Dietary Aetiology of Accelerated Growth in Infancy. *Postgrad. Med. J.* 51 (suppl. 3):38–41.

Napier, J. R.
1961. Prehensility and Opposability in the Hands of Primates. *Symp. Zoo. Soc. London* 5:115–132.

———.
1962. Fossil Hand Bones from Olduvai Gorge. *Nature* 196:409–411.

———.
1963. Brachiation and Brachiators. *Symp. Zoo. Soc. London* 10:183–195.

———.
1965. Comment on "New Discoveries in Tanganyika: Their Bearing on Hominid Evolution," by P. V. Tobias. *Curr. Anthrop.* 6:402–403.

Napier, J. R., and P. Davis
1959. The Forelimb Skeleton and Associated Remains of *Proconsul africanus. Fossil Mammals of Africa, Brit. Mus. (Nat. Hist.)* 16:1–69.

Napier, J. R., and P. H. Napier
1967. *A Handbook of Living Primates.* Academic Press, New York.

Napier, J. R., and A. C. Walker
1967. Vertical Clinging and Leaping: A Newly Recognized Category of Locomotor Behavior among Primates. *Folia Primat.* 6:180–203.

Neel, J. V.
1949. The Inheritance of Sickle Cell Anemia. *Science* 110:64–66.

———.
1958. The Study of Natural Selection in Primitive and Civilized Human Populations. *Hum. Biol.* 30:43–72.

———.
1970. Lessons from a "Primitive" People. *Science* 170:815–822.

Neel, J. V., T. Arends, G. Brewer, N. Chagnon, H. Gershowitz, M. Layrisse, Z. Layrisse, J. MacCluer, E. Migliazza, W. Oliver, F. Salzano, R. Spielman, R. Ward, and L. Weitkamp
1972. Studies on the Yanomama Indians. *Human Genetics: Proc. 4th Internat. Cong. Hum. Genet.* Excerpta Medica, Amsterdam. pp. 96–111.

Neel, J. V., F. M. Salzano, P. C. Junqueira, F. Keiter, and D. Maybury-Lewis
1964. Studies on the Xavante Indians of the Brazilian Mato Grosso. *Am. J. Hum. Genet.* 16:52–140.

Nei, M., and Y. Imaizumi
1966. Genetic Structure of Human Populations. *Heredity* 21:183–190.

Neumann, G. K.
1952. Archaeology and Race in the American Indian. In: *Archaeology of Eastern United States,* J. B. Griffen, ed. Univ. of Chicago Press, Chicago. pp. 13–34.

Newberne, P. M., and B. M. Gebhardt
1973. Pre- and Postnatal Malnutrition and Responses to Infection. *Nut. Rpts. Internat.* 7:407–420.

Newcombe, H. B.
1965. The Study of Mutation and Selection in Human Populations. *Eugen. Rev.* 57:109–125.

Newman, H. H., F. N. Freeman, and K. J. Holzinger
1937. *Twins: A Study of Heredity and Environment.* Univ. of Chicago Press, Chicago.

Newman, M. T.
1963. Geographic and Microgeographic Races. *Curr. Anthrop.* 4:189–207.

Newman, R. W.
1967. A Comparison of Negro and White Responses in a 5° C Water Bath (Abstract). *Am. J. Phys. Anthrop.* 27:249.

———.
1975. Human Adaptation to Heat. In: *Physiological Anthropology,* A. Damon, ed. Oxford Univ. Press, New York. pp. 80–92.

Newman, R. W., and E. H. Munro
1955. The Relation of Climate and Body Shape in U. S. Males. *Am. J. Phys. Anthrop.* 13:1–18.

Nirenberg, M. W.
1963. The Genetic Code: II. *Sci. Amer.,* March. Reprinted in: *The Molecular Basis of Life. An Introduction to Molecular Biology,* Intro by R. H. Haynes and P. C. Hanawalt. W. H. Freeman, San Francisco, 1968. pp. 206–216.

Noback, C. R., and N. Moskowitz
1962. Structural and Functional Correlates of "Encephalization" in the Primate Brain. *Ann. New York Acad. Sci.* 102:210–218.

North, A. F., S. Mazumdar, and V. M. Logrillo
1977. Birth Weight, Gestational Age, and Perinatal Deaths in 5,471 Infants of Diabetic Mothers. *J. Pediat.* 90:444–447.

Oakley, K. P.
1961. On Man's Use of Fire, with Comments on Tool-Making and Hunting. In: *Social Life of Early Man*, S. L. Washburn, ed. *Viking Fund Publ. in Anthrop.*, No. 31, Wenner-Gren Foundation for Anthropological Research, Inc., New York. pp. 176–193.

———.
1964. *Frameworks for Dating Fossil Man.* Aldine, Chicago.

Ogilvie, D. M., and R. H. Stinson
1966. Temperature Selection in *Peromyscus* and Laboratory Mice, *Mus musculus. J. Mammal.* 47:655–660.

Ohno, S.
1972. So Much "Junk" in Our Genome. In: *Evolution of Genetic Systems*, H. H. Smith, ed. Gordon and Breach, New York. pp. 366–370.

O'Riordan, M. L., J. A. Robinson, K. E. Buckton, and H. J. Evans
1971. Distinguishing between the Chromosomes Involved in Down's Syndrome (Trisomy 21) and Chronic Myeloid Leukaemia (Ph[1]) by Fluorescence. *Nature* 230:167–168.

Osborn, H. F.
1908. New Fossil Mammals from the Fayum Oligocene of Egypt. *Amer. Mus. Nat. Hist.* 24:265–272.

Osborne, R. H.
1971. The History and Nature of Race Classification. In: *The Biological and Social Meaning of Race*, R. H. Osborne, ed. W. H. Freeman, San Francisco. pp. 159–170.

Osborne, R. H., and F. V. DeGeorge
1959. *Genetic Basis of Morphological Variation. An Evaluation and Application of the Twin Study Method.* Harvard Univ. Press, Cambridge.

Osborne, R. H., G. A. Harrison, W. W. Howells, and R. Singer
1971. Graduate Training in Physical Anthropology: Report of the AAPA Study Committee. *Am. J. Phys. Anthrop.* 34:279–306.

Osofsky, H. J.
1975. Relationship between Nutrition during Pregnancy and Subsequent Infant and Child Development. *Obstet. Gynecol. Surv.* 30:227–241.

Ott, J.
1974. Estimation of the Recombination Fraction in Human Pedigrees: Efficient Computation of the Likelihood for Human Linkage Studies. *Am. J. Hum. Genet.* 26:588–597.

Ott, J., H. G. Schrott, J. L. Goldstein, W. R. Hazzard, F. H. Allen, Jr., C. T. Falk, and A. G. Motulsky
1974. Linkage Studies in a Large Kindred with Familial Hypercholesterolemia. *Am. J. Hum. Genet.* 26:598–603.

Otten, C. M.
1967. On Pestilence, Diet, Natural Selection, and the Distribution of Microbial and Human Blood Group Antigens and Antibodies. *Curr. Anthrop.* 8:209–226.

Overbeek, J. Th. B., and J. Lijklema
1959. Electric Potentials in Colloidal Systems. In: *Electrophoresis. Theory, Methods, and Applications*, M. Bier, ed. Academic Press, New York. pp. 1–33.

Ovey, C. D. (ed.)
1964. The Swanscombe Skull. A Survey of Research on a Pleistocene Site. *Roy. Anthrop. Inst., Occ. Paper* No. 20.

Oxnard, C. E.
1968a. A Note on the Fragmentary Sterkfontein Scapula. *Am. J. Phys. Anthrop.* 28:213–218.

———.
1968b. A Note on the Olduvai Clavicular Fragment. *Am. J. Phys. Anthrop.* 29:429–431.

———.
1969. Evolution of the Human Shoulder: Some Possible Pathways. *Am. J. Phys. Anthrop.* 30:319–331.

———.
1972. Functional Morphology of Primates: Some Mathematical and Physical Methods. In: *The Functional and Evolutionary Biology of Primates*, R. Tuttle, ed. Aldine-Atherton, Chicago. pp. 305–306.

Partridge, T. C.
1973. Geomorphological Dating of Cave Openings at Makapansgat, Sterkfontein, Swartkrans, and Taung. *Nature* 246:75–79.

Patterson, B., A. K. Behrensmeyer, and W. D. Sill
1970. Geology and Fauna of a New Pliocene Locality in North-Western Kenya. *Nature* 226:918–921.

Patterson, B., and W. W. Howells
1967. Hominid Humeral Fragment from Early Pleistocene of Northwestern Kenya. *Science* 156:64–66.

Pauling, L., H. A. Itano, S. J. Singer, and I. C. Wells
1949. Sickle-Cell Anemia. A. Molecular Disease. *Science* 110:543–548.

Pawson, I. G.
1977. Growth Characteristics of Populations of Tibetan Origin in Nepal. *Am. J. Phys. Anthrop.* 47:473–482.

Penrose, L. S.
1953. The General Purpose Sib-Pair Linkage Test. *Ann. Eugen.* 18:120–124.

Penrose, L. S., and G. F. Smith
1966. *Down's Anomaly.* J. A. Churchill, London.

Pfeiffer, R. A.
1967. Inborn Autosomal Disorders: The Phenotype of Autosomal Aberrations. *Proc. Third Internat. Cong. Hum. Genet.*, J. F. Crow and J. V. Neel, eds. Johns Hopkins, Baltimore. pp. 103–121.

Pianka, E. R.
1974. *Evolutionary Ecology.* Harper and Row, New York.

Picken, L. E. R.
1960. *Organization of Cells and Other Organisms.* Oxford Univ. Press, Oxford.

Pilbeam, D.
1972. *The Ascent of Man. An Introduction to Human Evolution.* Macmillan, New York.

———.
1975. Middle Pleistocene Hominids. In: *After the Australopithecines*, K. W. Butzer and G. L1. Isaac, eds. Mouton, The Hague. pp. 809–856.

Pilbeam, D., and S. J. Gould
1974. Size and Scaling in Human Evolution. *Science* 186:892–901.

Pimentel, R. A.
1959. Mendelian Infraspecific Divergence Levels and Their Analysis. *Syst. Zoo.* 8:134–159.

Piveteau, J.
1967. Un Parietal Humain de la Grotte de Lazaret (Alpes-Maritimes). *Ann. Paleont.* 53:165–199.

―――.
1970. Les Grottes de la Chaise (Charente): Paleontologie Humaine I. L'Homme de l'Abri Suard. *Ann. Paleont. (Vertebres)* 56:175–225.

Polyak, S.
1957. *The Vertebrate Visual System.* Univ. of Chicago Press, Chicago.

Post, P. W., F. Daniels, Jr., and R. T. Binford, Jr.
1975. Cold Injury and the Evolution of "White" Skin. *Hum. Biol.* 47:65–80.

Praeder, A., J. M. Tanner, and G. A. von Harnack
1963. Catch-up Growth Following Illness or Starvation. *J. Pediat.* 62:646–659.

Pratt, V.
1972. Numerical Taxonomy—A Critique. *J. Theoret. Biol.* 36:581–592.

Pyle, S. I., and N. L. Hoerr
1969. *A Radiographic Standard of Reference for the Growing Knee.* C. C. Thomas, Springfield, Ill.

Pyle, S. I., A. M. Waterhouse, and W. W. Greulich
1971. *A Radiographic Standard of Reference for the Growing Hand and Wrist.* Year Book Medical Publ., Chicago.

Race, R. R., and R. Sanger
1950. *Blood Groups in Man.* 1st Ed. Blackwell, Oxford. 6th Ed., 1975.

Radinsky, L. B.
1967. The Oldest Primate Endocast. *Am. J. Phys. Anthrop.* 27:385–388.

Ramachandran, G. N.
1967. Structure of Collagen at the Molecular Level. In: *Treatise on Collagen. Vol. 1, Chemistry of Collagen,* G. N. Ramachandran, ed. Academic Press, New York. pp. 103–183.

Rapley, S., E. B. Robson, H. Harris, and S. M. Smith
1968. Data on the Incidence, Segregation and Linkage Relations of the Adenylate Kinase (AK) Polymorphism. *Ann. Hum. Genet.* 31:237–242.

Read, M. S.
1975. Behavioral Correlates of Malnutrition. In: *Growth and Development of the Brain,* M. A. B. Brazier, ed. Raven Press, New York. pp. 335–354.

Reed, T. E.
1968. Research on Blood Groups and Selection from the Child Health and Development Studies, Oakland, California. III. Couple Mating Type and Reproductive Performance. *Am. J. Hum. Genet.* 20:129–150.

―――.
1971. Does Reproductive Compensation Exist? An Analysis of Rh Data. *Am. J. Hum. Genet.* 23:215–224.

Reid, R. M.
1973. Inbreeding in Human Populations. In: *Methods and Theories of Anthropological Genetics,* M. H. Crawford and P. L. Workman, eds. Univ. of New Mexico Press, Albuquerque. pp. 83–116.

Renwick, J. H.
1969. Progress in Mapping Human Autosomes. *Brit. Med. Bull.* 25:65–73.

―――.
1971. The Mapping of Human Chromosomes. *Ann. Rev. Genet.* 5:81–120.

Renwick, J. H., S. E. Bundey, M. A. Ferguson-Smith, and M. M. Izatt
1971. Confirmation of Linkage of the Loci for Myotonic Dystrophy and ABH Secretion. *J. Med. Genet.* 8:407–416.

Renwick, J. H., and S. D. Lawler
1955. Genetical Linkage between the ABO and Nail-Patella Loci. *Ann. Hum. Genet.* 19:312–331.

―――.
1963. Probable Linkage between a Congenital Cataract Locus and the Duffy Blood Group Locus. *Ann. Hum. Genet.* 27:67–84.

Riopelle, A. J., P. A. Hale, and E. S. Watts
1976. Protein Deprivation in Primates: VII. Determinants of Size and Skeletal Maturity at Birth in Rhesus Monkeys. *Hum. Biol.* 48:203–222.

Rivers, C.
1974. Genetic Engineering Portends a Grave New World. In: *Genetic and Reproductive Engineering,* D. S. English, ed. MSS Information Corporation, New York. pp. 83–88.

Roberts, D. F.
1978. *Climate and Human Variability.* 2nd Ed. Cummings Publ. Co., Menlo Park, Calif.

Robinson, J. T.
1954. The Genera and Species of the Australopithecinae. *Am. J. Phys. Anthrop.* 12:181–200.

―――.
1956. The Dentition of the Australopithecinae. *Transvaal Mus. Mem.,* No. 9.

―――.
1961. The Australopithecines and Their Bearing on the Origin of Man and of Stone Tool Making. *S. Afr. J. Sci.* 57:3–13.

―――.
1962. The Origin and Adaptive Radiation of the Australopithecines. In: *Evolution and Hominisation,* G. Kurth, ed. Gustav Fischer, Stuttgart. pp. 120–140.

―――.
1967. Variation and the Taxonomy of the Early Hominids. In: *Evolutionary Biology, Vol. 1,* T. Dobzhansky, M. K. Hecht, and W. C. Steere, eds. Appleton-Century-Crofts, New York. pp. 69–100.

―――.
1972. *Early Hominid Posture and Locomotion.* Univ. of Chicago Press, Chicago.

Robinson, J. T., and R. J. Mason
1957. Occurrence of Stone Artefacts with *Australopithecus* at Sterkfontein. *Nature* 180:521–524.

―――.
1962. Australopithecines and Artefacts at Sterkfontein. *S. Afr. Arch. Bull.* 17:87–125.

Robinson, S., D. B. Dill, J. W. Wilson, and M. Nielsen
1941. Adaptations of White Men and Negroes to Prolonged Work in Humid Heat. *Am. J. Trop. Med.* 21:261–287.

Robson, E. B., I. Sutherland, and H. Harris
1966. Evidence for Linkage between the Transferrin Locus (Tf) and the Serum Cholinesterase Locus (E$_1$) in Man. *Ann. Hum. Genet.* 29:325–336.

Roche, A. F., G. H. Davila, B. A. Pasternack, and M. J. Walton
1970. Some Factors Influencing the Replicability of Assessments of Skeletal Maturity (Greulich and Pyle). *Am. J. Roentg.* 109:299–306.

Romer, A. S.
1962. *The Vertebrate Body. Shorter Version.* 3rd Ed. W. B. Saunders, Philadelphia.

Rowell, T. E.
1969. Long-Term Changes in a Population of Ugandan Baboons. *Folia Primat.* 11:241–254.

Russell, B.
1945. *A History of Western Philosophy.* Simon and Schuster, New York.

Russell, D. E.
1964. Les Mammiferes Paleocenes d'Europe. *Mem. Mus. Nat. d'Hist. Nat. (Paris)* 13:1–324.

Russell, P. F.
1955. *Man's Mastery of Malaria.* Oxford Univ. Press, London.

Sade, D. S.
1972. A Longitudinal Study of Social Behavior of Rhesus Monkeys. In: *The Functional and Evolutionary Biology of Primates,* R. Tuttle, ed. Aldine-Atherton, Chicago. pp. 378–398.

Saldahna, P. H.
1968. Race Admixture in Chile. *Curr. Anthrop.* 9:455–458.

Sandstead, H. H.
1973. Clinical Manifestations of Certain Vitamin Deficiencies. In: *Modern Nutrition in Health and Disease. Dietotherapy,* 5th Ed. R. S. Goodhart and M. E. Shils, eds. Lea and Febiger, Philadelphia. pp. 593–603.

Sank, D.
1963. Genetic Aspects of Early Total Deafness. In: *Family and Mental Health Problems in a Deaf Population,* J. D. Rainer, K. Z. Altschuler, and F. J. Kallman, eds. New York State Psychiatric Institute, Dept. of Medical Genetics, New York. pp. 28–81.

Sank, D., and F. J. Kallman
1963. The Role of Heredity in Early Total Deafness. *Volta Rev.* 65:461–470.

Sargent, F., and K. P. Weinman
1966. Physiological Individuality. *Ann. N.Y. Acad. Sci.* 134:696–719.

Sarich, V. M.
1970. Primate Systematics with Special Reference to Old World Monkeys: A Protein Perspective. In: *Old World Monkeys,* J. R. Napier and P. H. Napier, eds. Academic Press, New York. pp. 175–226.

Sartono, S.
1971. Observations on a New Skull of *Pithecanthropus erectus (Pithecanthropus VIII)* from Sangiran, Central Java. *Proc. Koninkl. Nederl. Akad. Wetensch.,* Ser. B, 74:185–194.

Schade, A. L., and L. Caroline
1946. An Iron-Binding Component in Human Blood Plasma. *Science* 104:340–341.

Schaller, G. B.
1963. *The Mountain Gorilla. Ecology and Behavior.* Univ. of Chicago Press, Chicago.

Schiff, F., and W. C. Boyd
1942. *Blood Grouping Technic.* Interscience, New York.

Schlosser, M.
1911. Beitrage zur Kenntnis der Oligozanen Landsaugetiere aus dem Fayum (Agypten). *Beit. zur Pal. und Geol. Osterreich-Ungarns und Orients* 24:51–167.

Schull, W. J.
1972. Genetic Implications of Population Breeding Structure. In: *The Structure of Human Populations,* G. A. Harrison and A. J. Boyce, eds. Clarendon Press, Oxford. pp. 146–164.

Schull, W. J., T. Furusho, M. Yamamoto, H. Nagano, and I. Komatsu
1970. The Effect of Parental Consanguinity and Inbreeding in Hirado, Japan. IV. Fertility and Reproductive Compensation. *Humangenetik* 9:294–315.

Schull, W. J., and J. V. Neel
1965. *The Effects of Inbreeding on Japanese Children.* Harper and Row, New York.

Schultz, A. H.
1968. The Recent Hominoid Primates. In: *Perspectives on Human Evolution, Vol. 1,* S. L. Washburn and P. C. Jay, eds. Holt, Rinehart and Winston, New York. pp. 122–195.

———.
1971. The Rise of Primatology in the Twentieth Century. In: *Taxonomy, Anatomy, Reproduction,* J. Biegert and W. Leutenegger, eds. *Proc. 3rd Internat. Cong. Primatol.,* Vol. 1. S. Karger, Basel. pp. 2–15.

Scrimshaw, N. S., and M. Behar
1965. Malnutrition in Underdeveloped Countries. *New Eng. J. Med.* 272:137–144.

Sergi, S.
1944. Craniometria e Craniografia del Primo Paleantropo di Saccopastore. *Richer. Morf.* 20–21:1–59.

Sergovich, F., C. Uilenberg, and J. Pozsonyi
1971. The 49, XXXXX Chromosome Constitution: Similarities to the 49, XXXXY Condition. *J. Pediat.* 78:285–290.

Sergovich, F., G. H. Valentine, A. T. L. Chen, R. A. H. Kinch, and M. S. Stout
1969. Chromosome Aberrations in 2,159 Consecutive Newborn Babies. *New Eng. J. Med.* 280:851–855.

Serjeant, G. R., and M. T. Ashcroft
1973. Delayed Skeletal Maturation in Sickle Cell Anemia in Jamaica. *Johns Hopkins Med. J.* 132:95–102.

Service, E. R.
1971. *Primitive Social Organization. An Evolutionary Perspective.* 2nd Ed. Random House, New York.

Sever, L. E.
1969. ABO Hemolytic Disease of the Newborn As a Selection Mechanism at the ABO Locus. *Am. J. Phys. Anthrop.* 31:177–186.

Shea, B. T.
1977. Eskimo Craniofacial Morphology, Cold Stress and the Maxillary Sinus. *Am. J. Phys. Anthrop.* 47:289–300.

Sheagren, J. N., J. E. Tobie, L. M. Fox, and S. M. Wolff
1970. Reticuloendothelial System Phagocytic Function in Naturally Acquired Human Malaria. *J. Lab. Clin. Med.* 75:481–487.

Sibley, C. G.
1954. The Contribution of Avian Taxonomy. *Syst. Zoo.* 3:105–110.

Siegel, S.
1956. *Nonparametric Statistics for the Behavioral Sciences.* McGraw-Hill, New York.

Simonds, P. E.
1965. The Bonnet Macaque in South India. In: *Primate Behavior. Field Studies of Monkeys and Apes,* I. DeVore, ed. Holt, Rinehart and Winston, New York. pp. 175–196.

Simons, E. L.
1961. Notes on Eocene Tarsioids and a Revision of Some Necrolemurinae. *Bull. Brit. Mus. (Nat. Hist.) Geol.* 5:45–69.

―――.
1962. Two New Primate Species from the African Oligocene. *Postilla* 64:1–12.

―――.
1963. A Critical Reappraisal of Tertiary Primates. In: *Evolutionary and Genetic Biology of Primates, Vol. 1,* J. Buettner-Janusch, ed. Academic Press, New York. pp. 65–129.

―――.
1965a. New Fossil Apes from Egypt and the Initial Differentiation of Hominoidea. *Nature* 205:135–139.

―――.
1965b. The Hunt for Darwin's Third Ape. *Med. Opinion Rev.,* Nov.:74–81.

―――.
1972. *Primate Evolution. An Introduction to Man's Place in Nature.* Macmillan, New York.

―――.
1974. *Parapithecus grangeri* (Parapithecidae, Old World Higher Primates): New Species from the Oligocene of Egypt and the Initial Differentiation of Cercopithecoidea. *Postilla* 166:1–12.

―――.
1977. Ramapithecus. *Sci. Amer.* 235:28–35.

Simons, E. L., and D. R. Pilbeam
1965. Preliminary Revision of the Dryopithecinae (Pongidae, Anthropoidea). *Folia Primat.* 3:81–152.

―――.
1971. A Gorilla-Sized Ape from the Miocene of India. *Science* 173:23–27.

―――.
1972. Hominoid Paleoprimatology. In: *The Functional and Evolutionary Biology of Primates,* R. Tuttle, ed. Aldine-Atherton, Chicago. pp. 36–62.

Simpson, G. G.
1945. The Principles of Classification and a Classification of Mammals. *Bull. Am. Mus. Nat. Hist.* 85:1–350.

―――.
1953. *The Major Features of Evolution.* Columbia Univ. Press, New York.

―――.
1961. *Principles of Animal Taxonomy.* Columbia Univ. Press, New York.

―――.
1963. The Meaning of Taxonomic Statements. In: *Classification and Human Evolution,* S. L. Washburn, ed. *Viking Fund Publ. in Anthrop.* No. 37, Wenner-Gren Foundation for Anthropological Research, Inc., New York. pp. 1–31.

―――.
1964. *This View of Life. The World of an Evolutionist.* Harcourt, Brace, and World, New York.

Simpson, G. G., A. Roe, and R. C. Lewontin
1960. *Quantitative Zoology.* Revised Ed. Harcourt, Brace, New York.

Smith, C. A. B.
1953. The Detection of Linkage in Human Genetics. *J. Roy. Stat. Soc.* B15:153–192.

Smith. G. E.
1924. *The Evolution of Man.* Oxford Univ. Press, London.

Smith, H. H. (ed.)
1972. *Evolution of Genetic Systems.* Gordon and Breach, New York.

Snedecor, G. W., and W. G. Cochran
1967. *Statistical Methods.* Iowa State Univ. Press. Ames, Iowa.

Socha, W., M. Bilinska, Z. Kaczera, E. Pajdak, and D. Stankiewicz
1969. *Escherichia coli* and ABO Blood Group. *Folia Biol.* 17:259–269.

Sokal, R. R.
1962. Typology and Empiricism in Taxonomy. *J. Theoret. Biol.* 3:230–267.

Sokal, R. R., and J. H. Camin
1966. The Two Taxonomies: Areas of Agreement and Conflict. *Syst. Zoo.* 14:176–195.

Sokal, R. R., and T. J. Crovello
1970. The Biological Species Concept: A Critical Evaluation. *Am. Nat.* 104:127–153.

Sokal, R. R., and F. J. Rohlf
1969. *Biometry. The Principles and Practice of Statistics in Biological Research.* W. H. Freeman, San Francisco.

Sokal, R. R., and P. H. A. Sneath
1963. *Principles of Numerical Taxonomy.* W. H. Freeman, San Francisco.

Solecki, R. S.
1971. *Shanidar: The First Flower People.* A. A. Knopf, New York.

Solomon, M. E.
1969. *Population Dynamics.* St. Martin's Press, New York.

Solow, B.
1966. The Pattern of Craniofacial Associations. A Morphological and Methodological Correlation and Factor Analysis Study on Young Male Adults. *Acta Odont. Scand.* 24:1–174.

Spuhler, J. N.
1967. Behavior and Mating Patterns in Human Populations. In: *Genetic Diversity and Human Behavior,* J. N. Spuhler, ed. *Viking Fund Publ. in Anthrop.* No. 45, Wenner-Gren Foundation for Anthropological Research, Inc., New York. pp. 241–268.

―――.
1968. Assortative Mating with Respect to Physical Characteristics. *Eugen. Quart.* 15:128–140.

Stanbury, J. B., J. B. Wyngaarden, and D. S. Fredrickson (eds.)
1972. *The Metabolic Basis of Inherited Disease.* 3rd Ed. McGraw-Hill, New York.

Stebbins, G. L.
1971. *Processes of Organic Evolution.* 2nd Ed. Prentice-Hall, Englewood Cliffs, N. J.

Stedman, T. L.
1972. *Medical Dictionary.* 22nd Ed. Williams and Wilkins, Baltimore.

Steegmann, A. T., Jr.
1967. Frostbite of the Human Face As a Selective Force. *Hum. Biol.* 39:131–144.

_____.
1972a. How to Avoid Extinction and Find Happiness. *Yearbook Phys. Anthrop.* 16:154–156.

_____.
1972b. Cold Response, Body Form, and Craniofacial Shape in Two Racial Groups of Hawaii. *Am. J. Phys. Anthrop.* 37:193–221.

_____.
1975. Human Adaptation to Cold. In: *Physiological Anthropology,* A. Damon, ed. Oxford Univ. Press, New York. pp. 130–166.

Steel, G. H.
1965. The Relation between Dental Maturation and Physiological Maturity. *Dent. Pract.* 16:23–34.

Stehlin, H. G.
1916. Die Saugetiere des Schweizerischen Eocaens. Kritischer Katalog der Materialien, Teil VII, Halfte II. *Abh. Schweiz. Pal. Ges.* 41:1297–1552.

Steinberg, A. G.
1965. Evidence for a Mutation or Crossing-Over at the Rh Locus. *Vox Sanguin.* 10:721–724.

_____.
1969. Globulin Polymorphisms in Man. *Ann. Rev. Genet.* 3:25–52.

Steinberg, A. G., H. K. Bleibtreu, T. W. Kurczynski, A. O. Martin, and E. M. Kurczynski
1967. Genetic Studies on an Inbred Isolate. In: *Proceedings of the Third Internat. Cong. Hum. Genet.*, J. F. Crow and J. V. Neel, eds. Johns Hopkins Press, Baltimore. pp. 267–289.

Stellar, E.
1960. The Marmoset As a Laboratory Animal: Maintenance, General Observations of Behavior, and Simple Learning. *J. Comp. Physiol. Psych.* 53:1–10.

Stephan, H.
1972. Evolution of Primate Brains: A Comparative Anatomical Investigation. In: *The Functional and Evolutionary Biology of Primates,* R. Tuttle, ed. Aldine-Atherton, Chicago. pp. 155–174.

Stern, C.
1970. Model Estimates of the Number of Gene Pairs Involved in Pigmentation Variability of the Negro-Americans. *Hum. Hered.* 20:165–168.

_____.
1973. *Principles of Human Genetics.* 3rd Ed. W. H. Freeman, San Francisco.

Stern, C., W. R. Centerwall, and S. Sarkar
1964. New Data on the Problem of Y-Linkage of Hairy Pinnae. *Am. J. Hum. Genet.* 16:455–471.

Stern, J. T., Jr.
1970. The Meaning of "Adaptation" and Its Relation to the Phenomenon of Natural Selection. In: *Evolutionary Biology, Vol. 4,* T. Dobzhansky, M. K. Hecht, and W. C. Steere, eds. Appleton-Century-Crofts, New York. pp. 39–66.

Stevenson, A. C., and C. B. Kerb
1967. On the Distributions of Frequencies of Mutation to Genes Determining Harmful Traits in Man. *Mutat. Res.* 4:339–352.

Stini, W. A.
1975. *Ecology and Human Adaptation.* Wm. C. Brown, Dubuque, Iowa.

Strickberger, M.
1976. *Genetics.* 2nd Ed. Macmillan, New York.

Struhsaker, T. T.
1967. Social Structure among Vervet Monkeys (*Cercopithecus aethiops*). *Behavior* 29:83–121.

Strydom, N. B., and C. H. Wyndham
1963. Natural State of Heat Acclimatization in Different Ethnic Groups. *Fed. Proc.* 22:801–808.

Sturtevant, A. H.
1965. *A History of Genetics.* Harper and Row, New York.

Sutow, W. W., T. Terasaki, and K. Ohwada
1954. Comparison of Skeletal Maturation with Dental Status in Japanese Children. *Pediatrics* 14:327–333.

Sutton, H. E.
1962. *Genes, Enzymes, and Inherited Diseases.* Holt, Rinehart and Winston, New York.

Sylvester-Bradley, P. C. (ed.)
1956. *The Species Concept in Palaeontology.* The Systematics Association, Publ. No. 2. London.

Szalay, F. S.
1968. The Beginnings of Primates. *Evolution* 22:19–36.

_____.
1972. Paleobiology of the Earliest Primates: In: *The Functional and Evolutionary Biology of Primates,* R. Tuttle, ed. Aldine-Atherton, Chicago. pp. 3–35.

Szeinberg, A.
1963. G6PD Deficiency among Jews—Genetic and Anthropological Considerations. In: *The Genetics of Migrant and Isolate Populations,* E. Goldschmidt, ed. Williams and Wilkins, New York. pp. 69–72.

Szeinberg, A., C. Sheba, and A. Adam
1958. Enzymatic Abnormality in Erythrocytes of a Population Sensitive to *Vicia faba* or Drug Induced Haemolytic Anaemia. *Nature* 181:1256.

Szent-Gyorgi, A.
1940. Vitamins. In: *The Cell and Protoplasm,* F. R. Moulton, ed. *Am. Assoc. Adv. Sci.*, Publ. No. 14. Washington, D.C. pp. 159–165.

Takahashi, E.
1966. Growth and Environmental Factors in Japan. *Hum. Biol.* 38:112–130.

Tanner, J. M.
1962. *Growth at Adolescence.* 2nd Ed. Blackwell, Oxford.

_____.
1968. Earlier Maturation in Man. *Sci. Am.* 218:21–27.

Tanner, J. M., R. H. Whitehouse, and M. J. R. Healy
1962. *A New System for Estimating Skeletal Maturity from the Hand and Wrist, with Standards Derived from a Study of 2,600 Healthy British Children.* International Children's Center, Paris.

**Tanner, J. M., R. H. Whitehouse,
W. A. Marshall, M. J. R. Healy, and
H. Goldstein**
1975. *Assessment of Skeletal Maturity
and Prediction of Adult Height (TW2
Method)*. Academic Press, New York.

Tattersall, I.
1975. *The Evolutionary Significance of
Ramapithecus*. Burgess, Minneapolis.

Tattersall, I., and J. H. Schwartz
1974. Craniodental Morphology and
the Systematics of the Malagasy
Lemurs (Primates, Prosimii). *Anthrop.
Papers Am. Mus. Nat. Hist.*
52:139–192.

Telecki, G.
1973. *The Predatory Behavior of Wild
Chimpanzees*. Bucknell Univ. Press,
Lewisburg, Pa.

Thiessen, D. D.
1972. *Gene Organization and Behavior*. Random House, New York.

Thoday, J. M.
1953. Components of Fitness. *Symp.
Soc. Exp. Biol.* 7:96–113.

Thoma, A.
1965. La Definition des Neandertaliens et la Position des Hommes Fos-
siles de Palenstine. *L'Anthrop.*
69:519–534.

_____.
1966. L'Occipital de l'Homme Minde-
lian de Vertesszöllös. *L'Anthrop.*
70:495–534.

_____.
1972a. Cranial Capacity, Taxonomical
and Phylogenetical Status of Vertesszöllös Man. *J. Hum. Evol.*
1:511–512.

_____.
1972b. On Vertesszöllös Man. *Nature*
236:464–465.

Thomas, R. B.
1975. The Ecology of Work. In: *Physiological Anthropology*, A. Damon, ed.
Oxford Univ. Press, New York. pp.
59–79.

Thomson, A., and L. H. D. Buxton
1923. Man's Nasal Index in Relation
to Certain Climatic Conditions. *J.
Roy. Anthrop. Inst.* 53:92–122.

Tjio, J. H., and A. Levan
1956. The Chromosome Number of
Man. *Hereditas* 42:1–6.

Tobias, P. V.
1962. Early Members of the Genus
Homo in Africa. In: *Evolution and
Hominisation*, G. Kurth, ed. Gustav
Fischer Verlag, Stuttgart. pp. 191–204.

_____.
1964. Comment on "The Fate of the
'Classic' Neanderthals: A Consideration of Hominid Catastrophism," by
C. L. Brace. *Curr. Anthrop.* 5:30–31.

_____.
1967. Olduvai Gorge. Vol. 2. The Cranium and Maxillary Dentition of *Australopithecus (Zinjanthropus) boisei*.
Cambridge Univ. Press, Cambridge.

_____.
1971. *The Brain in Hominid Evolution*.
Columbia Univ. Press, New York.

_____.
1973. Implications of the New Age
Estimates of Early South African
Hominids. *Nature* 246:79–83.

_____.
1976. African Hominids: Dating and
Phylogeny. In: *Human Origins. Louis
Leakey and the East African Evidence*,
G. Ll. Isaac and E. R. McCown, eds.
W. A. Benjamin, Menlo Park, Calif.
pp. 376–422.

Tobias, P. V., and A. R. Hughes
1969. The New Witwatersrand University Excavation at Sterkfontein. *S.
Afr. Arch. Bull.* 24:158–169.

**Tobias, P. V., and G. H. R. von Koen-
igswald**
1964. A Comparison between the Olduvai Hominines and Those of Java
and Some Implications for Hominid
Phylogeny. *Nature* 204:515–518.

Towe, K. M., and A. Urbanek
1972. Collagen-Like Structures in Ordovician Graptolite Periderm. *Nature*
237:443–445.

Trager, W.
1941. Studies on Conditions Affecting
the Survival *In Vitro* of a Malarial
Parasite (*Plasmodium lophurae*). *J.
Exper. Med.* 74:441–462.

Trinkaus, E.
1973. A Reconsideration of the Fontechevade Fossils. *Am. J. Phys.
Anthrop.* 39:25–36.

Trivers, R. L.
1972. Parental Investment and Sexual
Selection. In: *Sexual Selection and the
Descent of Man*, B. G. Campbell, ed.
Aldine, Chicago. pp. 136–179.

Trotter, M., and G. C. Gleser
1958. A Re-Evaluation of Estimation
of Stature Based on Measurements of
Stature Taken during Life and of
Long Bones after Death. *Am. J. Phys.
Anthrop.* 16:79–123.

Turner, M. R.
1973. Protein Deficiency, Reproduction, and Hormonal Factors in
Growth. *Nut. Rpts. Internat.*
7:289–296.

Tuttle, R. (ed.)
1972. *The Functional and Evolutionary
Biology of Primates*. Aldine-Atherton,
Chicago.

**Tuttle, R., J. V. Basmajian, E. Re-
genos, and G. Shine**
1972. Electromyography of Knuckle-
Walking: Results of Four Experiments on the Forearm of *Pan gorilla*.
Am. J. Phys. Anthrop. 37:255–265.

Uhlendorf, B. W., and S. H. Mudd
1968. Cystathionine Synthetase in Tissue Culture Derived from Human
Skin: Enzyme Defect in Homocystinuria. *Science* 160:1007–1009.

Ulmer, F. A.
1957. Breeding of Orangutans. *Zoolo-
gischi Garten* 23:57–65.

U. N. Publication
1968. *The Concept of a Stable Population. Application to the Study of Populations of Countries with Incomplete
Demographic Statistics*. U.N. Population Studies No. 39, ST/SOA/Series
A/39. New York.

Vallois, H. V.
1949. The Fontechevade Fossil Men.
Am. J. Phys. Anthrop. 7:339–360.

_____.
1958. The Origin of *Homo Sapiens*.
In: *Ideas on Human Evolution. Selected Essays, 1949–1961*, W. Howells
ed. (1962), Harvard Univ. Press, Cambridge. pp. 473–499.

Vallois, H. V., and B. Vandermeersch
1972. Le Crane Mousterien de Qafzeh
(*Homo* VI): Etude Anthropologique.
L'Anthrop. 76:71–96.

Vander, A. J., J. H. Sherman, and D. S. Luciano
1975. *Human Physiology*. 2nd Ed. McGraw-Hill, New York.

Vandermeersch, B.
1966. Nouvelle Decouvertes de Reste Humains dans les Couches Levalloiso-Mousteriennes de Gisement de Qafzeh (Israel). *C. R. Acad. Sci. Paris* 262:1434–1436.

———.
1969. Les Nouveaux Squelettes Mousteriens Decouvertes a Qafzeh (Israel). *C. R. Acad. Sci. Paris* 268:2562–2565.

———.
1970. Une Sepulture Mousterienne avec Offrandes Decouvertes dans la Grotte de Qafzeh. *C. R. Acad. Sci. Paris* 270:298–301.

van Lawick-Goodall, J.
1969 Mother-Offspring Relationships in Free-Ranging Chimpanzees. In: *Primate Ethology*, D. Morris, ed. Doubleday, Garden City, New York. pp. 365–436.

Van Valen, L., and R. E. Sloan
1965. The Earliest Primates. *Science* 150:743–745.

Villee, C. A., and V. G. Dethier
1971. *Biological Principles and Processes*. W. B. Saunders, Philadelphia.

Vogel, F.
1965. Blood Groups and Natural Selection. *Proc. 10th Cong. Int. Soc. Blood Transf.*, Stockholm, 1964:268–279.

———.
1970. ABO Blood Groups and Disease. *Am. J. Hum. Genet.* 22:464–475.

Vogel, F., and M. R. Chakravartti
1966. ABO Blood Groups and Smallpox in a Rural Population of West Bengal and Bihar (India). *Humangenetik* 3:166–180.

von Bonin, G.
1963. *The Evolution of the Human Brain*. Univ. of Chicago Press, Chicago.

Vondra, C. F., and B. E. Bowen
1976. Plio-Pleistocene Deposits and Environments, East Rudolf, Kenya. In: *Earliest Man and Environments in the Lake Rudolf Basin. Stratigraphy, Paleoecology, and Evolution*, Y. Coppens, F. C. Howell, G. Ll. Isaac, and R. E. F. Leakey, eds. Univ. of Chicago Press, Chicago. pp. 79–93.

von Dungern, E., and L. Hirschfeld
1910. Ueber Vererbung Gruppenspezifischer Strukturen des Blutes. II. *Zeit. Immun.* 6:284–292.

von Koenigswald, G. H. R.
1937. Ein Unterkieferfragment des *Pithecanthropus* aus dem Trinilschichten Mitteljavas. *Proc. Konikl. Akad. Wetensch. Amsterdam* 40:883–893.

———.
1938. Ein Neuer Pithecanthropusschadel. *Proc. Konikl. Akad. Wetensch. Amsterdam* 41:185–192.

von Koenigswald, G. H. R., and A. K. Ghosh
1973. Stone Implements from the Trinil Beds of Sangiran, Central Java. *Proc. Nonikl. Nederl. Akad Wetensch.*, Series B, 76:1–34.

von Tschermak, E.
1900. Uber Kunstliche Kreuzung bei Pisum Sativum. *Deutsch Bot. Ges. Ber.* 18:232–239.

Wagner, R., M. M. Cohen, and E. E. Hunt, Jr.
1963. Dental Development in Idiopathic Sexual Precocity, Congenital Adrenocortical Hyperplasia, and Adrenogenic Virilism. *J. Pediat.* 63:566–576.

Wagner, W. H., Jr.
1969. The Construction of a Classification. In: *Systematic Biology. Proceedings of an International Conference*. Nat. Acad. Sci. Publ. 1692, Washington, D.C. pp. 67–103.

Walker, A.
1976. Remains Attributable to *Australopithecus* in the East Rudolf Succession. In: *Earliest Man and Environments in the Lake Rudolf Basin. Stratigraphy, Paleoecology, and Evolution*, Y. Coppens, F. C. Howell, G. Ll. Isaac, and R. E. F. Leakey, eds. Univ. of Chicago Press, Chicago. pp. 484–489.

Walker, A., and P. Andrews
1973. Reconstruction of the Dental Arcades of *Ramapithecus wickeri*. *Nature* 244:313–314.

Wallace, B.
1970. *Genetic Load. Its Biological and Conceptual Aspects*. Prentice-Hall, Englewood Cliffs, N.J.

Walls, G. L.
1963. *The Vertebrate Eye and Its Adaptive Radiation*. Haffner Publ. Co., New York.

Washburn, S. L., and C. S. Lancaster
1968. The Evolution of Hunting. In: *Man the Hunter*, R. B. Lee and I. DeVore, eds. Aldine, Chicago. pp. 293–303.

Waterlow, J. C., A. A. Hill, and D. W. Spady
1976. Energy Costs and Protein Requirements for Catch-up Growth in Children. In: *Early Nutrition and Later Development*, A. W. Wilkinson, ed. Year Book Medical Publishers, Chicago. pp. 175–189.

Watson, J. D.
1976. *Molecular Biology of the Gene*. 3rd Ed. W. A. Benjamin, Menlo Park.

Watson, J. D., and F. H. C. Crick
1953. Molecular Structure of Nucleic Acids. A Structure for Deoxyribose Nucleic Acid. *Nature* 171:737–738.

Weidenreich, F.
1928. Entwicklungs—und Rassetypen des *Homo primigenius*. *Natur u. Mus.* 58:1–13, 51–62.

———.
1936a. The Mandibles of *Sinanthropus pekinensis*: A Comparative Study. *Palaeon. Sinica*, Series D, Vol. 7, Fasc. 3.

———.
1936b. Observations on the Form and Proportions of the Endocranial Casts of *Sinanthropus pekinensis*, Other Hominids and the Great Apes: A Comparative Study of Brain Size. *Palaeon. Sinica*, Series D., Vol. 7, Fasc. 4.

———.
1938. The Ramification of the Middle Meningeal Artery in Fossil Hominids and Its Bearing upon Phylogenetic Problems. *Palaeon. Sinica*, New Series D, No. 3, Whole Series No. 110.

————. 1941. The Extremity Bones of *Sinanthropus pekinensis. Palaeon. Sinica,* New Series D, No. 5, Whole Series No. 116.

————. 1943a. The Skull of *Sinanthropus pekinensis:* A Comparative Study on a Primitive Hominid Skull. *Palaeon. Sinica,* New Series D, No. 10, Whole Series No. 127.

————. 1943b. The "Neanderthal Man" and the Ancestors of *Homo sapiens. Am. Anthrop.* 42:375–383.

————. 1946. *Apes, Giants, and Man.* Univ. of Chicago Press, Chicago.

————. 1947. Facts and Speculations Concerning the Origin of *Homo sapiens. Am. Anthrop.* 49:187–203.

Weinberg, W.
1908. Uber den Nachweis der Vererbung beim Menschen. *Jhares. Verein f. vaterl. Naturk. Wurttem.* 64:368–382.

Weiner, J. S.
1954. Nose Shape and Climate. *Am. J. Phys. Anthrop.* 12:615–618.

Weiner, J. S., and B. G. Campbell
1964. The Taxonomic Status of the Swanscombe Skull. In: *The Swanscombe Skull. A Survey of Research on a Pleistocene Site,* C. D. Ovey, ed. *Roy. Anthrop. Inst., Occ. Paper,* No. 20. pp. 175–209.

Weitkamp, L. R., D. L. Rucknagel, and H. Gershowitz
1966. Genetic Linkage between Structural Loci for Albumin and Group Specific Component (Gc.) *Am. J. Hum. Genet.* 18:559–571.

Wentworth, E. N., and B. L. Remick
1916. Some Breeding Properties of the Generalized Mendelian Population. *Genetics* 1:608–616.

Wessels, N. K.
1977. *Tissue Interactions and Development.* W. A. Benjamin, Reading, Mass.

White, J. M.
1972. Haemoglobin Variation. In: *The Biochemical Genetics of Man,* D. J. H. Brock and O. Mayo, eds. Academic Press, London. pp. 477–541.

White, M. J. D.
1973. *Animal Cytology and Evolution.* 3rd Ed. Cambridge Univ. Press, Cambridge.

Whittaker, R. H.
1969. New Concepts of Kingdoms of Organisms. *Science* 163:150–160.

Wiener, A. S.
1961. *Advances in Blood Grouping.* Grune and Stratton, New York.

————. 1966. The Blood Groups. Three Fundamental Problems—Serology, Genetics, and Nomenclature. *Blood* 27:110–125.

Wiener, A. S., and I. B. Wexler
1958. *Heredity of the Blood Groups.* Grune and Stratton, New York.

Wiesenfeld, S. L.
1967. Sickle-Cell Trait in Human Biological and Cultural Evolution. *Science* 157:1134–1140.

Wilson, D. R.
1972. Tail Reduction in *Macaca.* In: *The Functional and Evolutionary Biology of Primates,* R. Tuttle, ed. Aldine-Atherton, Chicago, pp. 241–261.

Wilson, E. O.
1975. *Sociobiology. The New Synthesis.* Belknap Press, Harvard Univ. Press, Cambridge.

Wilson, E. O., and W. H. Bossert
1971. *A Primer of Population Biology.* Sinauer Associates, Stamford, Conn.

Wilson, E. O., and W. L. Brown
1953. The Subspecies Concept and Its Taxonomic Application. *Syst. Zoo.* 2:97–111.

Wilson, J. A.
1966. A New Primate from the Earliest Oligocene, West Texas: Preliminary Report. *Folia Primat.* 4:227–248.

Wilson, R. S.
1976. Concordance in Physical Growth for Monozygotic and Dizygotic Twins. *Ann. Hum. Biol.* 3:1–10

Winick, M., J. Basel, and P. Rosso
1972. Nutrition and Cell Growth. In: *Nutrition and Development,* M. Winick, ed. John Wiley and Sons, New York. pp. 49–98.

Winick, M., and A. Noble
1966. Cellular Response in Rats during Malnutrition at Various Ages. *J. Nutr.* 89:300–306.

Wolfers, D., and H. Wolfers
1974. *Vasectomy and Vasectomania.* Mayflower Books, Frogmore, St. Albans.

Wolin, L. R., and L. C. Massopust, Jr.
1970. Morphology of the Primate Retina. In: *Advances in Primatology—Vol. 1. The Primate Brain,* C. R. Noback and W. Montagna, eds. Appleton-Century-Crofts, New York. pp. 1–27.

Wolpoff, M. H.
1971a. Interstitial Wear. *Am. J. Phys. Anthrop.* 34:205–228.

————. 1971b. Is Vertesszöllös II an Occipital of European *Homo erectus? Nature* 232:567–568.

Woo, J.-K.
1965. Preliminary Report on a Skull of *Sinanthropus lantianensis* of Lantian, Shensi. *Scientia Sinica* 14:1032–1035.

Wood, A. E.
1962. The Early Tertiary Rodents of the Family Paramyidae. *Trans. Amer. Phil. Soc.* 52:1–261.

Wood, B.
1976. Remains Attributable to *Homo* in the East Rudolf Succession. In: *Earliest Man and Environments in the Lake Rudolf Basin. Stratigraphy, Paleoecology, and Evolution,* Y. Coppens, F. C. Howell, G. L1. Isaac, and R. E. F. Leakey, eds. Univ. of Chicago Press, Chicago. pp. 490–506.

Wood, C. S.
1975. New Evidence for a Late Introduction of Malaria into the New World. *Curr. Anthrop.* 16:93–104.

Woolf, C. M., and F. C. Dukepoo
1969. Hopi Indians, Inbreeding, and Albinism. *Science* 164:30–37.

Workman, P. L.
1973. Genetic Analyses of Hybrid Populations. In: *Methods and Theories of Anthropological Genetics,* M. H. Crawford and P. L. Workman, eds. Univ. of New Mexico Press, Albuquerque. pp. 117–150.

Wright, S.
1922. Coefficients of Inbreeding and Relationship. *Am. Nat.* 56:330–338.

———.
1931. Evolution in Mendelian Populations. *Genetics* 16:97–159.

———.
1932. The Roles of Mutation, Inbreeding, Crossbreeding, and Selection in Evolution. *Proc. 6th Internat. Cong. Genet.* 1:356–366.

———.
1938. Size of Population and Breeding Structure in Relation to Evolution. *Science* 87:430–431.

———.
1955. Classification of the Factors of Evolution. In: *Population Genetics: The Nature and Causes of Genetic Variability in Populations. Cold Spring Harb. Symp. Quant. Biol.* 20:16–24D.

———.
1969. *Evolution and the Genetics of Populations. Vol. 2. The Theory of Gene Frequencies.* Univ. of Chicago Press, Chicago.

Wyckoff, R. W., W. F. McCaughey, and A. R. Doberenz
1964. The Amino Acid Composition of Proteins from Pleistocene Bones. *Biochim. Biophys. Acta.* 93:374–377.

Wyndham, C. H.
1966. South African Ethnic Adaptation to Temperature and Exercise. In: *The Biology of Human Adaptability,* P. T. Baker and J. S. Weiner, eds. Clarendon Press, Oxford. pp. 210–245.

Wyndham, C. H., N. B. Strydom, J. F. Morrison, C. G. Williams, G. A. Bredell, M. J. von Rahden, L. O. Holdsworth, C. H. van Graan, A. J. van Rensburg, and A. Munro
1964. Heat Reactions of Caucasians and Bantu in South Africa. *J. Appl. Physiol.* 19:598–606.

Yamada, Y., and S. Neriishi
1971. Penta X (49, XXXXX) Chromosome Constitution: A Case Report. *Jap. J. Hum. Genet.* 16:15–21.

Yamakawa, J..
1975. Muscle Strength of Female Adults. In: *Physiological Adaptability and Nutritional Status of Japanese. B. Growth, Work Capacity and Nutrition of Japanese,* K. Asahina and R. Shigiya, eds. *Jap. Comm. Internat. Biol. Prog.* 4:74–76. Univ. of Tokyo Press, Tokyo.

Yamamoto, M., A. Endo, and G. Watanabe
1973. Maternal Age Dependence of Chromosome Anomalies. *Nature New Biol.* 241:141–142.

Yanase, T.
1966. A Study of Isolated Populations. *Jap. J. Hum. Genet.* 11:125–161.

Yanofsky, C..
1967. Gene Structure and Protein Structure. *Sci. Amer.* 216:80–94.

Yoshiba, K.
1968. Local and Intergroup Variability in Ecology and Social Behavior of Common Indian Langurs. In: *Primates. Studies in Adaptation and Variability,* P. C. Jay, ed. Holt, Rinehart and Winston, New York. pp. 217–242.

Yoshida, A.
1967. A Single Amino Acid Substitution (Asparagine to Aspartic Acid) between Normal (B+) and the Common Negro Variant (A+) of Human Glucose-6-Phosphate Dehydrogenase. *Proc. Natl. Acad. Sci.* 57:835–840.

———.
1973. Hemolytic Anemia and G6PD Deficiency. *Science* 179:532–537.

Yoshida, A., E. Beutler, and A. G. Motulsky
1971. Human Glucose-6-Phosphate Dehydrogenase Variants. *Bull. World Health Org.* 45:243–253.

Young, J. Z.
1957. *The Life of Mammals.* Oxford Univ. Press, Oxford.

Zacharias, L., R. J. Wurtman, and M. Schatzoff
1970. Sexual Maturation in Contemporary American Girls. *Am. J. Obstet. Gynecol.* 108:833–846.

Zuckerman, S.
1932. *The Social Life of Monkeys and Apes.* Kegan Paul, London.

Author Index

Page numbers for references to Literature Cited are in italics.

Subject Index

Ehringsdorf, 335
Electroosmosis, 54–55
Electrophoresis, 53–57
Encephalization, 195
Endoplasmic reticulum, 18
Environmental physiology, 6–7
Epiloia, 116
Epiphysis, 435
Epistasis, 399
Erect bipedalism, 190
Erector spinae, 230–32
Erythroblastosis fetalis, 144
Erythrocebus, locomotion of, 190
Erythrocyte, definition of, 76
Erythropoietin, function of, 48, 414
Estrogen, 442–44, 446–47
Eugenics, 145–47
    moral implications of, 145–46
    negative, definition of, 145
    positive, definition of, 145
Euphenics, 147
Euploidy, 32
Eutheria, 164
Evolution
    as a belief system, 1
    components of, 151
    concept of, 94
    processes of, 105–106
        classification of, 105–106
        effects of, 106
Expressivity, 65
Extension, definition of, 223
External auditory meatus, 228

Favism, 393
Fayum, 272–78
Femur, 241
Ferungulata, 164–65
Fibrinogen, function of, 48
Fingerprinting, 57
Flexion, definition of, 223
Fluorine dating, 255
Fontechevade, 335–50
Foot, 242–43
    functions of, 242–43
    structure of, 242
Foraging strategies, primate, 204–206
Foramen magnum, 228
Fossils, classification of, 9–10
Founder effect, 129–30
Frequencies, analysis of, 487–91
Frequency distribution, 460–63
    normal, 460
Fungi, 163

Galago, 180
Gamete, 19
Gametogenesis, 19
Gastrulation, 420
Gene
    action, 63–65

definition of, 36
flow, 125–27
    definition of, 125
    static model of, 126–27
frequency, changes by natural
    selection, 120–24
mutation, 51–61
    causes of, 61
    detection of, 51
Generic name, in taxonomy, 160
Genetic
    background, 65
    code, 42, 45, 46
    counseling, 146
    drift, 106, 127–30
        effects of, 128–30
    engineering, 147–48
    equilibrium, 102–105
        definition of, 102
        departure from, 105
    linkage, 65–69
    load, 137–44
        definition of, 143–44
        and sickle-cell anemia, 143
        types of, 144–45
    markers, 369–96
        geographic variation in, 370–96
Genotype
    definition, 36
    frequency, calculation of, 96
    relationship with phenotype,
        398–400
Gestation, 430
Gigantopithecus, 282–83
    body size of, 282
    evolutionary relationships of,
        282–83
    teeth of, 282
Glires, 164
Glucose-6-phosphate dehydrogenase
    (G6PD), 74–75, 356–57,
    391, 393
    deficiency, 392–93
        effects of, 392
        and malarial association, 393
        and parasite resistance of red
            cells, 393
    function of, 391
    genetics of, 74–75, 392
    variation of, 356–57, 391–93
Gluteal muscles, 243–44
Gluteus maximus, functions of,
    243–44
Gluteus medius, functions of, 244
Golgi apparatus, 18
Gonadotropin, 446
Gorilla, 188–90, 212–14
    dominance interactions of, 212–13
    geographical range of, 212
    grooming behavior of, 214
    group composition of, 212
    intergroup contact of, 213
    locomotion of, 190

sexual behavior of, 213
skeleton of, 188–89
Group, social, definition of, 200
Growth, 421–54
    at adolescence, 444–50
    catch-up, 424
    cellular, 421–22
    critical period hypothesis of, 422–23
    effects of overnutrition on, 424
    genetics of, 422
    at high altitude, 416
    hormonal influences on, 440–44
    hyperplastic, 421
    hypertrophic, 421
    influencing factors, 432
    longitudinal, 435–37
    population variability in, 453–54
    postnatal, 430–31, 433–34
    prenatal, 429–31
    secular trends in, 450–53
    sex organ development during, 434
    skeletal, 435–39
    stages of, 425–26
Growth curve, 426–29
    cumulative, 426–29
    incremental, 426–29
Growth hormone, effects of, 443
Growth spurt, adolescent, 444–46
Guanine, 41

Habituation, definition of, 403
Hapalemur, 180
Haplotype, in the Rh system, 382–83
Haptoglobin, function of, 48
Hardy-Weinberg principle, 99–105
    applications of, 103–105
    underlying assumptions of, 102–103
    uses of, 102
Heat, dissipation of, 403
Heat exposure, physiological responses
    to, 404–405
Heat loss, prevention of, 403
Heat tolerance, population variation
    in, 405–406
Hemizygosity, 73
Hemoglobin, 47–49, 53–58, 388–89
    amino acid sequences of, 49, 58
    changes of, at high altitude, 415
    function of, 47
    molecular structure of, 57, 388
    molecular weight of, 48
    mutations in, 53
    oxygen transport by, 388
    sickle-cell, 56–58, 389
        distribution of, 389
        maintenance of frequencies of,
            389
        and normal hemoglobin, 64
        tertiary structure of, 50
Hemolysis, 74
Hemolytic disease of newborn, 144
Hemophilia, classic, 74

Mackinder's brachydactyly, 70–72
  inheritance of, 70–72
  symptoms of, 70
Macroevolution, definition of, 150
Macula lutea, in prosimians, 181
Makapansgat, 300
Malaria, 118, 386–87
  history of occurrence of, 386
  mortality caused by, 386–87
Mammalia, 164
Mammals, definitive features of,
      174–75
Mandrillus, locomotion of, 190
Markers, genetic, 83
Masseter, 226–28
Maturity, indices of, 435–40
Mauer, 330
Medial pterygoid, 226–28
Median, in statistics, 465–67
Median plane, 219
Meiosis, 25–28
Menarche, 450
Mendelian populations, 93
  definition of, 93
  mating between, 93
Mental retardation, and sex
      chromosome abnormalities,
      33–35
Metabolic block, 59, 61
Metabolism, 59–61
  definition of, 59
  inborn errors of, 59–61
Metanthropus, 152
Metaphase, in mitosis, 25
Metatheria, 164
Microevolution, definition of, 150
Migration, 125–27
  effects of, 125–26
Migrational load, 144–45
  increase in, 145
Missense substitution, 52
Mitochondria, 18
Mitosis, 23–25
MN blood group system, 64, 96
  allele frequencies in, 96
  genotypes of, 64
Mobility, electrophoretic, 55–56
Mode, in statistics, 467
Molar, 193, 279
  bilophodont, 193, 279
  Y-5 cusp pattern, 279
Monera, 163
Mongoloid, 348
Montmaurin, 333
Mousterian industry, 341
Mughharet es-Skhul, 335–37, 350
Mughharet et-Tabun, 336–37
Multiple alleles, systems of, 68, 75–81
Muscles, 219–49
  back, functions of, 230–33
  neck, 229
  types of, 223

Mutation, 106, 111–13
  effects of, 112
  as an evolutionary process, 113
  fixation of, 112–13
  frameshift, 53
  frequency of, 112
  randomness of, 112
Mutational load, 144–46
  increase in, 145
Mutica, 164
Myxomatosis, 387

Nannopithex, 267
Natural selection, 106–20
  balancing, 116
  concept of, 114
  and C. R. Darwin, 113
  Darwin's view of, 1
  definition of, 113
  directional, examples and effects of,
      118–19
  diversifying, 120
    definition of, 120
    results of, 120
  stabilizing, 115–16, 145
    effects of, 116
    and human birth weights, 116
    relaxation of, 145
Neandertal, 337–52
  anatomical description of, 337
  belief systems of, 341–42
  definition of, 337–39
  diet of, 341
  and *Homo erectus,* 332
  hybridization with Cro-Magnon,
      351–52
  Progressive, 351
  replacement of, by Cro-Magnon,
      351–52
  skin pigmentation of, 340–41
  tools of, 341
  transition of, 347–52
  Western European, 337–40, 351
    age of, 337
    facial skeleton of, 339–40
Neandertal Phase Hypothesis, 347–50
Necrolemur, skull of, 267
Neo-Lamarckian School, 397
Neontology, 153
Nitrogen dating, 255
Nomenclature, 159–60
  anthropological, 160
  binominal, 160
  definition of, 159
Nondisjunction, 33
Nonsense substitution, 52
Norm of reaction, 109, 399
Normal distribution, in statistics,
      478–84, 480–82

Notharctus, 180, 264
Nucleolus, 23
Nucleotide, 41
Nucleus, 16–18
  and cytoplasm, 18
Null hypothesis, 484–85
Nycticebus, 181

Occipital condyle, 229
Olduvai Gorge, 306–12
Oligopithecus, 275–78
  dental formula of, 276
Omo Valley, 312–13
One-gene-one-enzyme hypothesis, 399
Oocyte, 26
  primary, 26
  secondary, 26
Oogenesis, 19
Oogonia, 26
Organelle, 16
Ossification, 430–35
Ovarian follicle, 21–22
Ovulation, 22
Ovum, 15, 21
  dimensions of, 21
  weight of, 15

Palaeanthropus europaeus, 152
Paleontology, 153
Pan, locomotion of, 190
Pantotheria, 164
Papio, locomotion of, 190
Paranthropus crassidens, 292
Paranthropus robustus, 292
Parapithecus, 273–74, 277
Parental investment, 203
Pascal's Triangle, 474
Pectoral girdle, 230–37
Pectoralis major, 237
Pedigree analysis, 69–70
Pelvis, 237–48
  bones of, 237–43
  muscles of, 243–48
  structure of, 237, 239
Penetrance, 51, 65
Peninj, 316
Peromyscus, thermal preference of,
      398
Petralona, 330–31
Petrosal bulla, 265–66
Phalanges, numbers of, in humans,
      237
Phenotype
  definition of, 36, 398
  determination of, 108
Phenotypic
  plasticity, 109
    and malnutrition, 368–69
  variance, components of, 87–88
Phenylalanine, metabolic pathway of,
      59–61